THINKING ABOUT LAW

What calls for thinking about law? What does it mean to think about? What is aboutness? Could it be that law, in its essence, has not yet been thought about? In exploring these questions, this book closely reads Heidegger's thought, especially his later poetical writings. Heidegger's transformation of the very notion and process of thinking has destabilising implications for the formation of any theory of law, however critical this theory may be. The transformation of thinking also affects the notions of ethics and morality, and the manner in which law relates to them. Interpretations of Heidegger's unique understanding of notions such as 'essence', 'thinking', 'language', 'truth' and 'nearness' come together to indicate the otherness of the essence of law from what is referred to as the 'legal'.

If the essence of law has not yet been thought about, what generates deafness to the call for such thinking, thereby entrenching a refuge for legalism? The ambit of the legal is traced to Levinasian ethics, especially to his notion of otherness, despite such a notion being apparently highly critical of the totality of the legal. In entrenching the legal, it is argued that Levinas's notion of otherness does not reflect thinking that is otherwise than ontology but rather radicalises and maintains a derivative ontology. A call for thinking about law is then connected to Heideggerian ontologically based otherness upon which ethical reflection, that the essence of law protects, is grounded.

Thinking about Law

In Silence with Heidegger

Oren Ben-Dor

·HART·
PUBLISHING

OXFORD AND PORTLAND, OREGON
2007

Published in North America (US and Canada) by
Hart Publishing
c/o International Specialized Book Services
920 NE 58th Avenue, Suite 300
Portland, OR 97213-3786
USA
Tel: +1 503 287 3093 or toll-free: (1) 800 944 6190
Fax: +1 503 280 8832
E-mail: orders@isbs.com
Website: www.isbs.com

© Oren Ben-Dor 2007

Reprinted 2008

Hart Publishing, 16C Worcester Place, Oxford, OX1 2JW
Telephone: +44 (0)1865 517530 Fax: +44 (0) 1865 510710
E-mail: mail@hartpub.co.uk
Website: http//:www.hartpub.co.uk

British Library Cataloguing in Publication Data

Data Available

ISBN-13: 978-1-84113-354-6 (paperback)

Typeset by Forewords, Oxford
Printed and bound in Great Britain by
Biddles Ltd, King's Lynn, Norfolk

To Keren, Amos, Neriya and Noam

לזכר אבי, מאיר בן-דור ,היקר באדם

תהא נשמתו צרורה בצרור החיים

Acknowledgements

My greatest debt is to Ariella Atzmon, who, after a fateful encounter in the Round Reading Room of the old British Library, set me off on an exploration of Heidegger's thought. Always keeping me puzzled on the way to deeper and more unmediated understandings, she opened Heidegger's world for me. I thank her for countless paths that we have carved whilst walking and talking on the streets of London. I thank her also for reading the whole manuscript and for her criticism, encouragement and support all through the creative process of this book. I had many enlightening discussions with Andrew Halpin, who read earlier drafts of chapter three as well as the near-final drafts of other chapters and, as always, offered illuminating comments. Dennis McManus read an earlier version of chapter three. Stephen Mulhall provided some critical comments in relation to the same chapter, especially with regard to Levinas. His comments inspired the shaping of the path of this book more then he, or I, could have realised at the time. Numerous discussions with Sotirios Santatzoglou over many years both inspired and clarified important issues. Nick Gaskell and Andrew Rutherford as Heads of School have always backed up my journey. Thanks for my sister, Sidi Ben-Dor, for bringing EA Poe's *The Man of the Crowd* to my attention. I am grateful to my publisher, Richard Hart, for his open-mindedness and undiminished faith over the years. I thank Mel Hamil of Hart Publishing for seeing the publication process through. I am full of admiration for Jo Morton for her patient and highly sympathetic copy-editing. My thanks extend to *Volumes* bookshop in Romsey, Hampshire, for providing a friendly atmosphere and coffee, both of which are highly conducive to thinking.

It is to my beloved Keren and our Amos, Neriya and Noam that I dedicate this book. I also dedicate it to the memory of my dear father Meir Ben-Dor.

PAUL CELAN

Language Mesh (1959)

Eye's roundness between the bars.

Vibratile monad eyelid
propels itself upward,
releases a glance.

Iris, swimmer, dreamless and dreary:
the sky, heart-grey, must be near.

Athwart, in the iron holder,
the smoking splinter.
By its sense of light
you divine the soul.

(If I were like you. If you were like me.
Did we not stand
Under *one* trade wind?
We are strangers.)

The flagstones. On them,
close to each other, the two
heart-grey puddles:
two
mouthful of silence.[1]

---

[1] P Celan, *Poems of Paul Celan*, M Hamburger (trans) (Anvil Press Poetry, 1995). 'Sprachgitter' Augenrund zwischen den stäben//Flimmertier Lid/rudert nach oben,/gibt einen Blick frei.//Iris, schwimmerin, traumloss und trüb:/der Himmel, herzgrau, mus nah sein.//Schräg, in der eisernen Tülle,/der blakende Span./Am Lichtsinn/errätst du die Seele.//(Wär ich wie du. Wärst du wie ich./Standen wir nicht/unter *einem* Passat?/Wir sind Fremde.)//Die Fliesen. Darauf,/dicht beieinander,/die beiden/hertzgrauen Lachen:/zwei/ Mundvoll Schweigen.

Preface

Although Martin Heidegger has been silent on ethics never has he been silent about being ethical. Indeed his silence on ethics was his ethical stand. Thinking ethically is arguably the only thing he did in his oeuvre. His ethical voice was, rather, by and large silenced by assimilating it into simplistic notions of silence that are themselves embedded in the coordinates and hegemony of ethics. It is his tragic observation that 'most thought-provoking is that we are still not thinking although the state of the world is becoming constantly more thought provoking'. The very attentiveness and response to what is conceived as actuality involves looking away from what is actual in actuality.

Our world is highly legalised. The world which shapes human involvements and reflections is dominated by the legal. The dominance of being and thinking with and through law indicates deeper notions that condition human horizons of self-interpretation. Although law has always been around, never has being and thinking with and through law been so prominent and so entrenched. So entrenched is law that people obtain freedom under it only at the unnoticed cost of being already legal in their being and thinking. Law guarantees them freedom but the thinking behind their freedom already assures their serfdom. Conditions and procedures are seemingly very well established for mutual understanding and contestation. Our age is seemingly one of free doubt, an age that even challenges narratives of progress. However, never has understanding and freedom been so far away from humans. Never have humans been distanced from their essence in freedom. Rousseau's dictum that Man was born free and everywhere he is in chains could not be more relevant to today's world, surpassing anything Rousseau himself could have possibly envisaged.

Any capacity to withstand the mystery of actuality has been meticulously expelled by the legal. So much so that any reflective voice about the origin of the legal would no longer seem to be a problem. For humans, to be conditioned under the hegemony of the legal means that they can no longer bear, let alone have the desire for, reflecting about being and thinking with and through law. At most, they can resist this or that objectification by law, but even in so resisting they are already in the legal, anticipating new paths for law in the legal. The lawyer is part of each and every human, even the most morally critical of humans. That thinking which conditions the legal controls even critical reflections about otherness and difference.

Being, and with it actuality, has lost its audience. The legal has denial at its roots, the effects of which are still to come upon us. But, the actual in actuality cannot be legalised. Actuality speaks in one way or another, and there is little that humans, with their laws, can do about it. The hegemony of legalised responses to actuality is itself part of the very actuality of the actual that ought to be listened to, but is not. Is there law that could protect us from the grip the legal has on our being and thinking? If so, how could we account for such law otherwise than in terms of the legal?

What is the unsaid in being and thinking with and through law? Are there people who are not yet been silenced by the legal? But equally, what would be the silence that makes the silenced actuality gather closer to humans? It is timely to make audible the silence around the legal.

Humans have become arrogant in relation to Being by entrenching the legal. Here lies their tragic nature: that by suppressing their essential capacity to be perturbed by actuality, humans have themselves become the provocateurs of violence. Human thus serve as agents of the message that violence calls upon them to heed. The more peaceable and egalitarian the constitutional representations, the more suffocated listening to actuality is, the more violent means the call from actuality assumes. The more ordered the façade of law and order, the more legal being and thinking is internalised, the deafer and more violent participants in the legal become towards actuality.

Even in the context of such alarming deafness to it, the call of actuality is fatefully calm. Actuality is always itself. It speaks even when its voice is suffocated, even when it has a small and marginalised audience. Actuality speaks through occurrences in the course of which humans do convey its word. They may not be in control, or even aware of their involvement as missionaries of the actuality of the actual that speaks them and to them.

Eruptions of violence are an ethical call upon humans to think the very thinking that conditions them. In those eruptions of violence both those who perish or are maimed and those who administer violence are participating in an ethical pursuit that is antecedent to their immediate motives and justifications. In the theatre of Being everybody is always already guilty. Being calls for understanding not justifications. Also, the 'clock-time' of occurrences of violence is not primordial for grasping the Saying of the violence.

Recent eruptions of violence are an ethical call on a grand scale. On 9/11 thousands of people died as the buildings were hit and collapsed. Great symbols of free society have been destroyed. For once, amidst their indolence and legal chatter about freedom, humans were made silent by naked brutality and transgression. Being was speaking; humans were silent. These spectacular violent occurrences have met the intense violence of silencing. For a flicker of a moment, perhaps, there was an opening to actuality, there was an indication, a hint. Actuality brought *all* people together in an essential sense through this explosive call for thinking. That event, like any other great events, exposed human vulnerability and has revealed a secret: that violence is a call for thinking actuality that comes from a place nearer to those perished than all those critical egalitarian constitutions that they democratically established to protect themselves from harming, and being harmed by, one another.

But we just need to look at the response of those agents of the legal who claim that the world was changed on that date. The response could not be more legalistic, calculative and representational: first, the facts: how many were killed? What was the weakness of human control – that control that was not working as perfectly as it should have? Second, the ethico-legal responses: the axis of evil. Humanity responded by asserting more vigorously the need to resurrect value-based thinking. Humanity is poised to legally control violence by violence. The more spectacular the facts and value transgressions are, the more intense and urgent becomes that craving to reassert thinking with values. More laws and regulations are needed than ever before, more security measures against evil, more representations of the rights of society to be protected from that evil nature of the axis. Even the internal soul-searching is marked by the legal: instead of resorting to violence and representations of evil, we need, perhaps, to find that oppressed 'Other' whose values have not yet been conceptualised and contained.

People feel that they discharge their responsibility by canvassing the balance between security measures against terror and freedom under the law. But, can we not hear the chronicle foretold towards more violence? Everybody sings the song of deafness, saying the right things, exploring that right balance of representations as a way of 'doing something about'. Surely there must be sinister fate unfolding from such pervasive lack of contemplation? Surely then, Being can never educate its guardians – but, as we can see, they are guardians all the same.

Deafness to Being – to the actuality from which Being speaks to its legalised audience – is itself waiting for the call of Being. Will any waiting and the violence that characterises it wake humans up? Would it make them more attentive? This book tries to investigate philosophically the entrenchment of the legal. As such, it is an attempt to merely indicate at what is awaited. It does not pretend that we can bypass waiting. In terms of 'current affairs' and common-sense practicality, this book is a non-starter, but, a non starter it must be; otherwise it would not be about waiting.

Southampton, July 2007

Contents

Abbreviations

HEIDEGGER'S WORKS

ANAX 'The Anaximander Fragment'
BDT 'Building, Dwelling, Thinking'
BT *Being and Time*
BPP *The Basic Problems of Phenomenology*
EHP *Elucidations of Hölderlin's Poetry*
EPTT 'The End of Philosophy and the Task of Thinking'
ER *The Essence of Reasons*
ET 'On the Essence of Truth'
IM *Introduction to Metaphysics*
LH 'Letter on Humanism'
OWA 'The Origin of the Work of Art'
OWL 'The Way to Language'
PID 'The Principle of Identity'
PMD 'Poetically Man Dwells ...'
QCT 'The Question Concerning Technology'
TT 'The Thing'
WCT *What is Called Thinking?*
WM 'What is Metaphysics?'

LEVINAS'S WORKS

DR 'Diachrony and Representation'
EE *Existence and Existents*
EI *Ethics and Infinity: Conversations with Philippe Nemo*
FC 'Freedom and Command'
IOF 'Is Ontology Fundamental?'
LP 'Language and Proximity'
OB *Otherwise than Being or Beyond Essence*
TI *Totality and Infinity: An Essay on Exteriority*
TO *Time and the Other*

OTHER WORKS

VM J Derrida, 'Violence and Metaphysics: An Essay on the Thought of Emmanuel Levinas'

NOTES ON THE USE OF ITALICS, PARENTHESES AND THE CHOICE OF LANGUAGE IN QUOTATIONS

1. In quotations only, italics or round parentheses are original. Square parentheses indicate my clarification or a necessary completion of sentences.

2. In quotes from American editions, the English adheres to the American source (eg 'neighbor' rather than 'neighbour', as well as '–ize' instead of '–ise' endings).

1

Introduction

In his *Courts on Trial* Jerome Frank argues that it is very difficult, if not impossible, to establish what he calls the facts of the case.[1] This book has been conceived as fact-sceptical. Scepticism of facts, though, still retains a craving for the right facts. Because of such a craving Frank could not do justice to the depth of his own insight. Frank's notion was that of the indeterminacy of facts rather than the inauthenticity of the very notion of a fact, as norms, rules and principles are built upon the authenticity of reality that is based on facts. The authenticity of rule-based language will be questioned if the authenticity of facts is questioned. The depth of Frank's insight perhaps reveals a space, rather than amounting to any scepticism, indeterminacy or polemics. It is this space towards which this book attempts to indicate.

This book explores the thought of the German philosopher Martin Heidegger, with particular reference to the connection between fundamental ontology, ethics and law. It interprets Heidegger in relation to all three. This book is about how ethics and law feature in Heidegger's thought about the essence of truth, Man and language. What a person writes is how this person is. This, of course, holds for Heidegger the person, the thinker, but it also holds for any future explorer of Heidegger's *oeuvre*. In this introduction I would like to share with the reader of this book the path that made me ready to listen to Heidegger's Saying.

In this chapter I would like to comment on the ways of thinking about law that this book is trying to depart from. In this sense, it is about what the book is not about. This chapter links to chapter three, where I elaborate upon what it means to think about law. That chapter, though, has the benefit of an initial engagement with Heidegger's thought offered in chapter two.

My cursory engagement with Heidegger's thought started some years ago when I was in the process of finishing a book about the utilitarian Jeremy Bentham. Bentham and Heidegger – one could not think of a

---

[1] J Frank, *Courts on Trial: Myth And Reality in American Justice* (New York, Atheneum Press, 1966) ch 3.

deeper dissonance between the calculative and the contemplative. Bentham – a person of definitions and measurements who wanted to perfect knowledge – was haunted in my thought by Heidegger – a person who is poetic and mysterious and for whom knowledge was essentially impoverished. I did entertain a reconstruction of Bentham, but deep inside, in reading Heidegger, I was already revisiting and exploring a deep-seated worry that I had always had with regard to law. This worry had to do not only with law's imperfection but with questioning its essential authenticity in relation to what is actual.

It is difficult to remember when the intuition that guides this book and that attracted me to Heidegger took hold of me so intently. Articulation of beginnings is often already an amputation of some antecedent continuum into which particular intuitions are thrown and which thinking constantly attempts to commemorate. The intuition that already thinks and understands haunts, dormant, without words yet capable of hearing, waiting for thought to respond further to it.

I have always been bothered by something which has to do with the very world and language that characterises the practice of law. Even when I abandoned my vocational inclinations and started to analyse law more conceptually, attempting to articulate its nature and purpose, this bothersome feeling did not go away and persisted alongside those analytical efforts. Law seemed valuable enough, and thus to some extent necessary. However, the more I studied, reconstructed and taught theories of and about law, ranging from debates between legal positivism and natural law, law and interpretation, Marxist critique of law, critical legal studies, and critical constitutionalism, the more bothersome this feeling about law became. I read about theories of justice as justifications for law from Hobbes to Habermas and largely have shared, even came to admire, the informed debate and its profound conclusions. The constant transformation of liberal thought as a result of forceful criticisms directed against it fascinated me. Still, the worry continued to lurk. Being informed of these theories just served to highlight it.

One thing that bothered me with law was the language used in legal materials. On the one hand, it was all about precise definitions of both rights and duties or about the morally consistent interpretation of them. On the other hand, in almost every doctrine I came across, the notion of 'reasonableness' was pervasive. Reasonableness was used either as a containing metaphor for renegotiating moral criticisms and disagreements, or as an invisible gate for a dominant moral perspective. This duality of definition and reasonableness, as well as the ambivalence within the notion of reasonableness, was quite unique to the language used in the practice of law. The sign 'reasonable' seems to signify a justificatory metaphor no one can really dissolve. Yet, it is still used and the emptiness of its signification was still significant, somehow, to the practice of law.

To be sure, 'the reasonable', reasonableness, pervades legal doctrine. It can be used as a part of the reassuring, softening phrase 'to *explore* the reasonable'. Such a phrase has a critical edge because, as exploratory, it responds to the surplus of immorality that critical effort brings to light. The word 'explore' signifies the capacity for transgression of any objectification and totality. At the same time, the reasonable was used as a stabiliser/tranquilliser by seeking consensus between different moral perspectives – indeed, one way in which the reasonable is used in some non-comprehensive strands of contemporary liberal thought.[2] Reasonableness seems to combine contestation and containment in a way that can serve the equilibrium of insurgency and stability needed for the practical sustenance of a critical democracy. Exploration of the reasonable could somehow hold water and provide equality of stake to different moral perspectives thereby accommodating the constant challenge of otherness understood as a non-expellable surplus of difference. Embarking upon an 'exploration of the reasonable' could be used to supplement and to soften moral dilemma by launching a problem-solving ethos without being seen as giving up political conflict. Exploration of the reasonable could thus involve a handing over of the reality of probability and the probability of reality to a thorough process of risk assessment by scientists and other experts.

Being and thinking with and thinking through law focuses on actions and their harm, or likely harm to some rights. It belongs to the practice and language of law to talk about values from which rights and duties stem. The ethics that encapsulates the morality that law enforces yields a practice of argument about the meaning and priorities of values, rights and duties. The practice of law is all about the justification of such meanings and priorities, whether values of indirect moral content, namely such values as stability, finality, etc, or (and often in combination with) values of more direct morality, namely the embodiment of a given ideology or criticism of a given ideology. Thus, the 'facts of the case', however contestable themselves, are already questioned within, and dependent upon, the horizon of norms and actions, and therefore the horizon of truth, that the language of values, norms and actions presupposes. What can be said about facts can also be said as to risk assessment processes.

The term 'reasonable', unless mentioned with great irony, is entirely absent from poetry and from poetic thinking that characterises art. It is not used in all those efforts that aim to open up thinking to authentic clearing of actuality. Actuality of the actual is never reasonable, only distorted by it. Actuality of the actual cannot be tamed by a representational agreement on the reasonable and, as such, although may relate to it, cannot be reduced to the actuality of the reasonable. The 'suchness' of

---

[2] J Rawls, *Political Liberalism* (New York, Columbia University Press, 1993).

actuality is always itself. Similarly the language of values, rights, duties, actions and facts is used in art only as point of departure to unveil a much more subtle, personal and, above all, enigmatic world. From my very first exposure to legal materials and arguments I was, in short, struck by the difference between the very language used in the law and in art. They seemed to be totally different realms of reflection. I was constantly bothered by the effect of objectifying thinking that distances itself from the very actuality it attempts to think about. The tension between moral challenge and re-containment that characterises the exploration of the reasonable did not abate my concern about objectification and distancing. The stakes that propelled such concern seem to be not the negotiated nature of actuality but rather the very nature of it.

The reply could simply be that law is not art and this is why law and art use language so differently. However, the way in which critical moral, constitutional and legal scholarship has evolved seemed not to accept such simplistic explanation and went on to show that art could provide many insights that can then be incorporated into legal doctrines, revising those doctrines and even calling for the creation of new ones.

In observing the various manifestations of this interaction between art and law I felt somehow bemused, not to say baffled, that art was put to the service of the exploration of the reasonable. It looked odd to conscript aesthetic insights to the service of ethical challenge while this ethical challenge has already anticipated the possibility of conceptualisation within the horizon of the exploration of the reasonable. At any rate, I felt that there was something deeply distorting in this relationship between art and critical legal scholarship.

The mysterious and turbulent nature of human relationships begged the question of whether the very language used in the law – the moral language of values, rights and duties – went a long way to cover up the actuality of these relationships. Still, would it not be more appropriate to claim that there are two aspects to explain the actuality of human beings?

Surely, from the point of view of *justifying* law, law seemed authentic enough as a well-reasoned social practice. The fact that every human association has laws provided enough intuition to verify the irreducible, and hence, authentic, nature of that social practice. Yet, however much I justified law according to some purpose, the inauthenticity of the enterprise loomed large. That which governs human relations seemed to continue unabated beneath the façade of representations of jural relations.

The objectified and depersonalised language of law and the morality it enforces, that of individuals' values, rights and duties, is pervasive today. Rights and duties are personalised in the sense of being possessed by an individual in a particular situation from which an interpretative coherence/distinction is made in relation to more general/analogous situations. However, there still seems to be something about the very language of rights and duties which remains abstract from the actuality of the person who possesses, or who owes, rights. In other words, it does not matter whether the bearer of a right is a person or a group, or whether the subject matter of the right is a concrete situation or an abstract value, there is something which remains at a distance from what is irreplaceably intimate in human relationships. There seems to be something in the kind of language of rights itself which retains this objectifying nature. Moreover, critical legal scholarship seems to retain that abstractness of the language of rights and duties, the objectivity of which it seemingly abandons. This retention manifests in the ability of such scholarship in fact to translate its insights, to export them, from a horizon which is seemingly 'beyond law' into that horizon of rights and duties thereby nourishing and improving the latter.

Let me dwell on this point. The ubiquity of the language of rights and duties seems to reassure the authenticity of law. The readiness with which people submit their actuality to the language of definition, calculations and methodologies has always puzzled me. Again, even critical legal thought that took on board political struggles thereby incorporating into legal doctrine protection of marginalised groups conducts its effort only in order to return to the womb, namely to the language of rights and duties. Even such critical efforts did not quiet my intuition that a great secret is being covered up, perhaps most sophisticatedly, by these efforts. Critical *legal* scholars' criticism of law was precisely made what bothered me even more acutely. Such scholarship seemed to be capable of being both against law – that is against the objectification involved in law – but at the same still anticipating legal language. Such anticipation of transcending legal language in order to revise or refine law's content effectuated their success in retranslating their critical insights into legal doctrines. Going 'out' was merely a way of staying in, albeit 'critically'. Again, critical legal scholarship is critical of something that law does and hence seems to draw its insight from beyond the law while at the same time anticipating the possibility of the incorporation of those insights back into the law.

To label this process of transcending law in anticipation of incorporation and re-containment in the law as an *aporia* of law is not convincing. There seems to be something at the root of being with and thinking with and through law that critical legal scholarship does not manage to transcend. Such scholarship retains a certain notion of the 'valuable' which law enforces. This scholarship still connects to the ethical discourse of values, rights and duties. What is the ground for this retained connection?

In order to pursue critically 'legal' interpretation whilst retaining the legal, critical legal scholarship has shown that there was no need to view law and, say, art or poetry as different activities. They could be seen as complimentary: an insight from one realm can be translated into, and indeed transform, the other. Actuality between human beings was indeed richer than what law could capture, but then, this 'limit' of law was merely a suspension of law, not really overcoming it by a different kind of thinking. The suspense could be filled in by what is seemingly another activity. Various practices, seemingly different from law, could show not only the amorphous ground of law but also be used as unexpected sources of its critical powers.

The transcendence/retaining of the legal by critical legal scholarship meant that my doubt remained, despite the long way this scholarship went to alleviate it. Perhaps exploring anarchy, overcoming law, would be the answer. What does it mean to overcome law? Could there be a human association without law? Was that the question I had to pursue in order to explore my persistent doubt about law? My response to that doubt regarding the inauthenticity of law could be to embark upon a possible account of human society without law.

The obvious reason to have law is that without it people would harm one another. It was thus entrusted to law to enforce the morality that articulates such harm, thereby averting it. The discussion of what harm is to be averted by law is hotly debated amongst legal theorists. Some legal theorists identify legal obligation with moral obligation. The authority of law comes from it being a species of moral obligation that articulates a conception of harm. The harm averted, that which humans cannot avert by being left to their own devices, is moral harm, that is harming people physically or harming their fundamental interests in some way. Some other legal theorists believe that although law *enforces* such morality, the authority of law comes rather from some indirect harm that can result from the indeterminacy of moral views or from the perversity of moral disagreement. According to these theorists, we need to distinguish legal and moral obligations. Legal obligations are valid regardless of the moral evaluation of their content. This validity, which can be ascertained by a simple social test of recognition, is justified as authoritative for reasons of averting the indirect harm, such as lack of coordination, that would arise from the persistence of moral disagreement. The adherence to such indirect harm has the effect of maintaining legal order in an environment of moral criticism of the law thereby enabling and legitimising such criticism. Such an indirect moral evaluation does not run the risk of accepting the morality that law enforces because it is validated by a simply social test.[3] Some other theorists still see legal obligation as a species of moral obligation but distinguish the 'morality' of the obligation as morality which is unique to the law itself, for example, arguing for moral consistency, in a complex practice of argument with moral principles.[4]

---

[3] HLA Hart, *The Concept of Law* (Oxford, Clarendon Press, 1961) pp 203–7; J Dickson, *Evaluation and Legal Theory* (Oxford, Hart Publishing, 2001) ch 3.
[4] For example, R Dworkin, *Law's Empire* (Cambridge, MA, Fontana Press, 1986); L Fuller, *The Morality of Law* (New Haven and London, Yale University Press, 1965).

I will not go into these issues now. The point I want to illustrate is that in all of these theories the principle is maintained that we need law because leaving people to their own devices will result in harm. To the extent that people can avert the harm by themselves – they can generate moral obligations themselves – they do not need law.

However, whether humans can self-govern or not, as well as how much faith we should place in their nature, did not really touch upon my worry. I could ask the same bothersome question regarding authenticity whether people were governed by political institutions or by themselves. I have no doubt that at a certain stage of social development 'educated' people could internalise fundamental harms that law comes to avert but the extent to which that is the case did not impinge on my worry at all. Private ethics merely internalise that impersonal nature of law into people's psyche, thereby retaining all the sources of my worries. My worry seems to be otherwise than merely a polemic against law in defence of anarchy or, indeed, a reflection upon the extent of the internalisation of law.

II

So instead of just saying that people are harmful and justifying the aversion of harm through law, I thought of exploring an alternative to that line of reasoning by asking why people are harmful. This seemed promising enough as it involved the questioning of and tackling the reality of and between humans not through the distancing objectified justification of obligations. Instead of taking harm to cherished values at face value thereby generating moral justification for rights and obligations I wanted to explore a different approach to morality, one that involves the exploration of the forces leading a person to be harmful and to overcome those forces. An effort to overcome those forces could not be reduced either to law or to internalised obligations. True, internalised obligations could be the *result* of such an internal process but they would result from a process very different from the imposition of obligations. Further, I was not sure that a process of internal enlightenment, although it may result in something which, to an external observer, may look like an internal obligation, would have to go through the representational ideas of obligations in the mind at all. 'Being otherwise than one is', more according to one's true and eternal essence, could well result in not being harmful without the notion of obligation going into the process at all. This line of ethical effort was more a question of 'how' or 'in what manner' people are, so that they become harmful or not harmful. Instead of being protected by law, thereby assuming harm to be averted as a fact of life, I wanted to focus on a process of internal enlightenment that involves becoming a good person. This effort seems to be to tackle a reality that can go on even under the best system of laws.

Approaching the authenticity of involvement and its relation to the harmful nature of human beings is very different from merely striving towards the internalisation of externally imposed obligations. The ethics involved in the former conceives the mere internalisation of obligations as highly insufficient and still external, so that it has no hope of confronting what causes people to be hateful and harmful. People will be caught in their mental gaps that make them prone to hate under the best system obligation, external or internal. If the causes of involvement are not contemplated properly and overcome, the harm, although seemingly curbed by the obligation, will inevitably erupt from some unexpected direction again. Representation of harm in the shape of obligations could operate merely to cause the harm to ferment at its origin and erupt from another place and direction. I think that a façade of obligations, however educationally successful, will not bear upon the internal causes that make a person passively succumb to what it is that makes this person harmful. The 'how' of a person that causes this person to be harmful will come from a place and be of such intensity that an obligation, however internalised, could not stand a chance of withstanding.

So, thinking otherwise than with and through law, as an ethical effort, is something which seemed to be the right avenue to pursue. Internal enlightenment was a different and more primordial effort to that of morality of obligations and law. This brought me to Buddhism and to Spinoza. The body of Buddhist teaching, the *Dharma*, aimed at internal enlightenment, compassion and alleviation from one's own and others' suffering, does not seem to focus at all on legal obligation. Yet, also in the western philosophical tradition, a tradition within which this book is written, Spinoza's *Ethics*[5] is a prime example of an ethical philosophy that does not go through the morality of law. The means by which it brings about moral conversion was very unique, beyond representations of obligations.[6] Spinoza's approach to ethics was that of internal questioning that leads to the evaluation of ideas that manifest themselves as the causes of the various emotions. Spinoza's approach does not provide moral principles of justice nor does he defend a particular formulation of a master imperative. Instead, he focuses on the quality of people's involvement in the world. This is not the occasion to dwell on Spinoza but I would attempt to distil briefly the point that is important for the present introduction. In *Ethics* Spinoza does not speak about values, rights and duties according to some represented harm to be averted through prescription by moral or legal authority. Instead of good and evil, he talks rather about passivity and activity. Although there is an overlap here, his

---

[5] B Spinoza, 'Ethics', in *The Collected Works of Spinoza* (E Curley ed and trans) (Princeton, Princeton University Press, 1985).

[6] For an interesting discussion, see S Hampshire, *Two Theories of Morality* (Oxford, Oxford University Press, 1977).

approach to moral conversion and arriving at that which is unconditionally good is unique. The passive involvement of a person occurs when that person is under the spell of negative emotions, that is, under the spell of the ideas that give rise to these negative emotions. All these emotions and the ideas that bring them about can be traced to the emotion of hatred and the idea that brings hatred about. Spinoza systematically shows that an active involvement, that is an involvement that comes from the person's essence of self-preservation, that is, persistence according to his own nature, occurs when that person is involved *solely* through love. To be involved solely through love is to contemplate the only idea that brings only love – the idea of God. What Spinoza calls 'love of God' is not conditioned by any finite intellect that is entangled in endless chains of cause and effect that nearly always harbour some trace, and hence a manifestation, of ideas and the emotion of hatred. As God is in every existing thing and as everything has a godly nature, the godly essence can be intuitively grasped by an active intellect. To this intuitive knowledge of things in their essence, Spinoza referred to grasping things as species of eternity.

For Spinoza, humans are necessarily always both active and passive. The ethical effort relates to the emendation of the intellect, so that a person could, as quickly as possible, grasp the only sure and unconditionally adequate idea, namely that of God, and experience a moment of unconditional joy – beatitude. Once that happens it will be immeasurably easier for a person to be able to be more and more active in the face of his or her passions, that is passive emotions.

In reading Spinoza's *Ethics* and essays I thought that I found an adequate response to what bothered me about law and the kind of morality that law enforces. Spinoza argues that we must take Man as we find him, or as he is, rather than try to idealise him according to some ideal including prescriptions resulting from such an ideal. We must response to the 'isness' of Man rather than prescribe how Man ought to be according to some ideal. To take humans as they are is to acknowledge that they are both passive and active and, further, that they will at most times make attempts to preserve their passivity. However, any joy that stems from the preservation of passivity will always be tainted. Activity is much more vulnerable than passivity. To become more active is a kind of effort that will fill humans with intense joy, stemming from an unconditional unification with God. As God is never passive, humans' godly essence is in their capacity for being more and more active. Essential humanity is having the potential intellect, and with it the impetus for an effort to become more active and to experience the joy of the unification with God. An active person encounters things as they are, that is, as they would be seen in their particularity from a godly perspective of infinite intellect, although, of course, passive involvement and the endless chains of causation are also in the infinite intellect of God. Finite intellect can not comprehend passive involvements in their entirety. Being active is thus the only *confident* way of being unified with nature as a whole, connecting the universal and the particular in their eternal essence. The active person would not be harmful and would reflect love on every hateful act or thought towards him or her because such an act or thought would be, metaphorically speaking, like a gift that is not wanted. A person is good to the extent that he is active.

This focus on quality of involvement has some implications, all of which find echoes in this book, albeit in a radically modified way. Perhaps the most radical of these modifications is that the ethical, and even the valuable, is no longer conceived in a way which is subject to human control, in particular the notion and human craving for some *improvement* of involvement. Still, there are other echoes of Spinoza's thought: First, there is an echo in this book of the idea that the passivity of a person will not be tackled by any rehearsal of moral principles. Passivity connotes a gap within, or rather, the Achilles heel of a person, and a person can, and will, be caught in the gap regardless of the legal façade of representations and the internalisation of values, rights and duty. A duty, an *ought*, can never cater for the gap in the *is*. Thus we can easily envisage a world that is highly legalised and egalitarian, but which, under the surface, is full of hatred. What law protects is an objectified subject made up of representations, but not the real person, who remains passive and harmful. Such hatred cannot be tackled ethically by defining the actions of which it is the cause. What the law protects does not even perturb that from which Man has to be protected – from his own passivity. Also education to tackle that hatred would have to involve something other than value talk. In short, and this is an insight as to the effort which is required by ethics, values, rights and duties will have very little effect on the actuality of the actual of people. Furthermore, concentrated effort on values, rights and duties will give the sort of gratification which educates people to look at the representation of their actions rather than the quality of their involvement, the latter being much more difficult task as it would involve their own very being.

The second echo from Spinoza, albeit one which undergoes a radical change, is that of humility before forces over which Man cannot be the source of control. There is the recognition in Spinoza that a person can only become active, that is, acting from his or her own being, when he or she lets go in humble unification with God. Only by quieting those ideas that give rise to passive emotions, what Spinoza calls 'passions', can a person stand in the sun of God, in the eternal ubiquity of the divine. Only by contemplating the idea of God, slowing down and grasping things as they really are, only by overcoming those fast-moving self-centred causal connections that hopelessly and endlessly confuse the intellect, can a person overcome passivity with activity. So activity is achieved by letting go of ego-based 'activity'. The more ego-based active a person is, the more passive he or she in fact is and thus the less attentive he or she is to other humans and non-humans as the beings they are. Unconditional joy is achieved only by contemplating the idea of God, through the love of God and through experiencing the calmness and attentiveness that connect to things as they are.

III

Upon further reflection, though, the very effort of focusing on Man as he is – and this book will explore this question in great detail – does not seem to advance matters. Both the justification for law and together with it my intuitive worry about law remain intertwined. As the former gets sharper and more focused, the latter grows in intensity and anxiety.

As long as Man is passive other people need immediate protection from the consequences of this passivity. Such protection is very different from internal enlightenment, and absolutely necessary. As long as Man is harmful, to the extent that he does not change and is prone also to being manipulated by other passive people, and even more, to the extent that he is not capable of changing, there must be value, rights and duties talk. This 'as long as' now features not the same simple complementarity between public and private as obligation-based ethics, but is rather one falling between the triumph of activity and protection from the harm that occurs from prevailing passivity. Ethical enquiry has place for both an external 'ought' of values, rights and duties, and hence an ethics which is enforced by law, and another ethics which is about passivity and activity – about internal enlightenment. Crucially, both types of ethics are equally authentic and primordial. The thing that these ethics have in common is precisely the need to take Man as he is, namely as both active and passive. There seems to be a justification for two types of 'oughts'. Spinoza himself recognises that in his political writings. One ethics is based on a given harmful state of the 'is' and protects people from the harm that ensues from that state. This is the 'ought' of values, rights and duties. The other ethics which encapsulates an 'ought' that is directed internally attempts to combat directly the prevailing passivity that partly characterises the 'is' of Man with the result that a person could become less harmful. Each of these two ethical efforts can yield its own contemplation and complexities. However, they are both, by all means, and equally, essential.

To sum up, an ethics that is based on internal enlightenment and thus an ethics that tries to contemplate the quality of involvement that makes a person passive and thus harmful, would turn the question of 'What is Man?' or, 'What does it mean to be human?' into a question of '*How* is a human being involved in the world?'. But this question of the 'how' relates to how a human forms ideas about identity, that is, of 'who' he or she is, because the question 'Am I passive or active?' is related to the question 'Who am I?', or more precisely, 'Who am I, in the sense of what is that which conditions my involvement?'. Such a critical question goes to the very depth of personhood and the meaning, indeed possibility of, subjectivity, and with it, to the deepest desire that operates upon a person, whether hidden or out in the open. An interaction with such questions requires overcoming fetters by letting go of something. We can refer to this as 'internal enlightenment ethics'.

The question of 'how' human beings are, as an alternative to the representational ethics of law, can have its own dangers of domination and depersonalisation. As Foucault has so forcefully shown, power, exercised as an infinitely differentiating normalising rationality, uses the question of 'how' as a way of capturing people in an infinite economy of normalisation. The question of the 'how', in other words, could be as dominating and objectifying as representations of values.[7] There is, of course, much in Spinoza to overcome Foucault's critique of an ethics of the 'how' about the suffocating and ubiquitous domination by power that is exercised through normalising human sciences in complicity with a proliferation of objectifying representation-based thinking.

For the other type of ethics, a justification-based ethics – that of values, to 'take humans as you find them' would not be an intriguing mystery although, of course, it could contain its own questions and complexities. Humans carry out actions that are harmful to some fundamental interests of their fellow human beings. Such an 'external' observation would suffice to trigger this type of ethics. These fundamental interests might be physical securities, but they could also relate to abstract values, for example freedom of choice/reflection upon the adequacy of choice or some fundamental interests in equality. This justification-based approach to ethics also takes very seriously how human beings are. They *are* harmful. It is the fact that they are harmful, because their actions, or omissions, harm others, that constitutes the basis for such ethics. The only way of offering protection is not to wait until enlightenment is attained, to a greater or lesser degree, but rather to issue a duty, if necessary enforced by law, to ban the harmful conduct. Let us call this ethics 'external justification-based'.

If we look upon the relationship between these two types of ethics – internal enlightenment ethics and external justification-based ethics – we can see that not only are they complementary but also interdependent. The ethics that aims at internal enlightenment claims that a person is always

---

[7] See, for example, M Foucault, *Discipline and Punish: The Birth of the Prison* (A. Sheridan, trans), (London, Penguin, 1977).

partly conditioned and partly active. It maintains that we are never free to choose, because we are already determined by causes that are beyond our control. When we feel that we are free, we merely feign, as what is our innermost own being is for the most part hidden from us. To feel free simply means not to contemplate deeply enough the causes that condition us. However, when we contemplate things as they are, when we are active, when we do what is *necessary*, as for example when we contemplate the idea of God, we are free and hence responsible for our involvement, being response-able both to our passivity and to things as they are. I can be responsible only to the extent I overcome actively my own internal passivity. As long as, and to the extent that, I am dominated by passions, that is passive, I am unfree and it does not matter *what* I do. Freedom of choice is merely feigning that by changing what I do I may be somehow better off, as if my primordial freedom depends on the activity I do.

The notion that 'this activity was imposed on me' needs to be contemplated upon in this regard. From the point of view of internal enlightenment ethics, the passive person will find himself as passive in whatever he or she chooses to do and ends up doing. To put it shortly, problems can come to us when we do not have what we want and when we do have what we want. The extent to which the notion of 'talent' is not itself conditioned by certain causes that not only channel the preference of a person but also condemn this person in advance to do something half- or whole-heartedly is unclear. The active person may have also talents for many more activities. To be responsible for one's own life, then, occurs only at moments of activity. The responsible person is a person that responds to the ethical challenge that will continue to haunt him or her. To put it in terms of harm, what harms such a person and prevents him or her from being responsible is his or her passivity and enslavement to various delusions, including the delusion of his or her own whole self, and hence a constant state of oppression by the passions. That which challenges a person to response is the mystery of his or her own being.

For justification-based ethics, responsibility is conceived very differently. The question that it asks is the following: 'What are the conditions under which I could, in retrospect, say that *indeed I* have been responsible for my own life that is, that my life were entirely conditioned by my own passivity or activity?'. The criteria of success of justification-based ethics are precisely in creating the conditions for a moment whereby a person could say that his or her life has been tainted by his or her own passivity (and for that matter, being harmful to others because of this passivity). The target of such justification-based ethics is to create conditions for the other ethics to operate but, crucially, *only* for the other ethics to operate – that is without external fetters that harm such operation. To what degree such internally based ethics succeeds is a very interesting question but it is still dependent for its *exclusive* operation upon harm prevented by justification-based ethics. Justification-based ethics claims that I can be harmed, in a way that will either not enable me to evaluate my involvement *as being mine*, or if it does so enable me, it will do so in a way which will hinder me from acting upon my internal insights. So, if I suffer an injustice because, say, I am racially different, or because I am a member of this or that group, I will be harmed in such a way that will hamper me from being responsible to my own life. If I suffer racial discrimination it will be beside the point for me to look back at my life and accuse myself of my passivity. Again looking back, such discrimination can either prevent me from fighting my own internal battles or from acting upon the insights of such battles I have fought. The morality and law against discrimination will restore the exclusivity of internal fetters in determining the responsibility for my own life.

It would not do to view the internal succumbing to racial discrimination as an internal fetter and to use that move against justification-based ethics. There are conditions required even for the overcoming of self-stereotyping. Again only in conditions of justice can a person say, looking back on his or her life, that expectations of self-overcoming were not too strong. Further, looking back at my life, even if I overcome my inferiority complex, I would still look at failings in life and would attribute those failings to the enormous effort I have to exert to overcome self-stereotyping. This last argument can also apply to arguments that, to some extent, something in me created and prolonged the discrimination against me.

The point is thus made that some factors are external to my own dealing with my personal causation, that harm me in such a way that I am not responsible for my life. The point is, of course, extended to words or deeds by me that harm other people in not allowing them to be responsible for their lives. It is, then, precisely because some causes harm me, making the quality of my personal involvement not a genuine reason for my success or failure that responsibility has a greater reach than responsibility which is based on personal causation and authenticity of any kind.

The recognition of an external and impersonal realm of harm which hampers people from being genuinely responsible for their lives, then, and which therefore justifies seemingly impersonal talk about values, rights and duties that avert such harm, can raise questions such as: 'How can I harm others by pursuing my own authenticity?'. For example, asserting that political authority should be justified according to what furthers my authenticity by outlawing any activity which is considered inauthentic will harm all those who are different from me in such a way that they will no longer be able to be responsible for their own lives. So, perhaps the whole point of justice is, first, to provide conditions for responsibility for one's own life and, secondly, to make sure that the pursuance of responsibility does not harm others.

Both kinds of ethics, then, are important for one another, and are not reducible to one another. The two realms of reflection about responsibility, namely internal responsibility and as a justification for external and seemingly impersonal conditions for internal responsibility, should be kept conceptually distinct, even if those obligations that enable conditions for responsibility for a person's own life are internalised by fellow people. People could internalise the notion of harm to conditions for responsibility – and that is perhaps a very deep tenet of moral education. To have conditions for responsibility is a perhaps one of the deepest human interests, a due that is owed to humans, as humans, and as such, it is the basis for good, and justice which is based on values, rights and duties.

Understood thus, it is responsibility that both justifies and limits law. It is the aspect from which constitutional standards are considered. It is the aspect from which every action can be evaluated to be compatible with this deepest human interest – or, basic human right. Even the standards themselves are subject to self-reflection and evolution in the light of asking whether a set of standards caters enough for conditions of responsibility. Conditions of responsibility are both enabled by law and protect humans from abusive law.

This conclusion of compatibility and the interdependence between the two ethics would go a long way to calm any worry that law *by its nature* does not take humans as they are. Indeed, Spinoza perfectly reconciled his masterpiece – the *Ethics* – with a *proto* super-liberal political treatise in which he called for a political society to be organised so that the 'freedom to philosophise' would be the supreme principle. He regarded this principle as a very important condition for the realisation of the ethical work that he elaborated upon in *Ethics,* given that people are not, by and large, enlightened.

IV

I would like to concentrate on the phrase 'freedom to philosophise' for a moment because this phrase indicates the open-textured relationship between the two kinds of ethics and the two different views of responsibilities that they entail. As a result of internal enlightenment, people may well come to contest the ideological basis of the ethics that provides objective conditions for responsibility. I do not think that this is necessarily fatal to either the distinction, the compatibility or the interdependence of the two ethics. Let me briefly explore this point. The very vital human interests that consist of interpretation of clusters, as well as priorities, of values – the make-up of ideologies – can be seen as contingent and contestable. Any critical interpreter of ideologies, and the relationship between them, an interpreter who seemingly provides *the* conditions for responsibility, is already conditioned by an ideology which again could be contested. Thus conditions for responsibilities can be interpreted very differently for the liberal and the libertarian. Marxists have shown that the justification of the morality of conditions is just a superstructure of economic oppression and domination, and so called for bringing about the withering away of oppressive ideology.

The important feature to observe here is that it is internal enlightenment that brings about a destabilisation of the representation of conditions for responsibility. Ideological indeterminacy can be brought about by a process of inner freedom that has been oppressed and dominated under a symbolic order that constitutes part of the identity of the person, a symbolic order that gives rise to hegemony and universalistic pretensions of an ideology. The process of particularising the 'how humans being are in the world' – that 'how' of involvement – is antecedent and thus yields new values that are applicable to oppressed groups and individual identity. These new values cast new light upon the very interpretation of values, priorities of values, and, if necessary, the replacement of values. The whole basis of rights in terms of definition and distribution thereby changes as a result of a process of internal enlightenment.

The politics of difference starts by destabilising and contesting the subject's identification within a symbolic order. This identification results in the monological view of subjectivity. Such subjectivity, in turn effectuates an oppressive moral psychology which manifests as uncritically accepted representations of values, rights and duties. Critically, then, the identity of the subject, for the politics of difference, remains heterogeneous or 'not yet conceptualised'. The positive lever of such politics is awakened only by the oppressed and well-concealed, not-yet-conceptualised groups and with them subjects' identities. These are oppressed and dominated by the uncritical homogeneous subjectivity that is perpetuated within the totalising commerce of derivative mirroring of identification without any attentiveness to the challenge of genuine alterity.

Dialectics of insurgency in the name of the not-yet-represented Other and re-containment in a newly distributed representation of rights and duties is said to characterise critical ethical, political, and with it, legal thinking. Critical thought is about the not-yet-conceptualised Other which is always already not-yet-conceptualised, and hence, effectuates heterogeneous own-subjectivity. Such politics of difference, then, inaugurates the deconstruction of the received interpretation of legal materials, listening to what oppressive symbols such interpretations cling to, for example gender-dominated symbols, finding within them the expelled voice of the Other, the stranger, the marginalised group, the weak, all of which are barred from entering the hegemonic discourse of rights and duties. Politics of difference, then, re-conceptualises disadvantage in a way that goes to the very symbolic root of identity rather than merely as distributive privation under depersonalised representations of an 'individual' or uncritically accepted groups.[8] This is not to say that the politics of difference does not have distributive implications but just that the logic of distribution is already derivative of a subdued oppression and domination which itself stems from lack of contestation of identity.

The moral indeterminacy of thinking in terms of representations of harm, then, constitutes only the point of departure for the politics of difference. Indeterminacy that pervades how values originate and are interpreted and prioritised is already a result of such indeterminacy that infects the very constitution of subjectivity. Representational indeterminacy is based not only upon the incommensurability of different ideologies but also upon the essential contestability of subjectivity. The slogan 'The Personal is Political' sees subjectivity as 'not-yet-conceptualised within the game of identification'. From this, it follows that the origination, interpretation and prioritisation of values also occurs only as 'not yet conceptualised'. Critical thinking that traverses difference focuses on the contestability of identity for which it needs an absolute Other. Critical thinking thus focuses on that which is symbolically expelled by dominant ideology which harbours hegemonic conceptualisation of subjectivity.

Heterogeneous subjectivity as an opening for difference is very different from inter-subjectivity, dialogue and the problem-solving (and problem-smothering, for that matter) ethos that inter-subjectivity brings with it. Although the notion of inter-subjectivity is still critical in allowing for contestation, it still has the ethos of finding possibilities to construct some consensus which, while irreducible to each subject, is nevertheless reasonable to all subjects involved in communication. Although inter-subjectivity transcends metaphysics and the notion of the 'subject', it still focuses on the positivity of consensus rather than the positivity of difference. Inter-subjective consensus, based on the reasonable, can itself become the source of domination and oppression.

The surplus of difference, of heterogeneity, must have as its impetus irreducible alterity, which in turn constitutes the critical lever by virtue of which inter-subjective consensus can be constantly criticised. To put it another way, if inter-subjectivity constitutes a method of negotiating and renegotiating a consensual perspective, then inter-subjectivity becomes a super container. As such a container is anticipated even in the renegotiation stage, namely the stage of problem-solving, the 'inter' is still conceived as 'self-questioning-towards-a-new-common-denominator' and will not yet listen to difference.

Having said that, being inter-subjective *proper*, as Levinas has shown, could be possible only while genuine alterity is being faced. Understood as

[8] See IM Young, *Justice and the Politics of Difference* (Princeton, Princeton University Press, 1990).

genuine alterity, the inter-subjective opens up a critical and aporetic space between the ethical and political leading to a constant dynamics of insurgency and necessary discursive re-containment. The anticipation in such a movement is not towards consensus but towards the impossibility of containment. Interpreted thus, the notion of inter-subjectivity bears upon the tension between the challenge of alterity on the one hand, and the anticipation of both the necessity and the insufficiency of re-containment on the other.

The politics of difference, then, treats people as ends by challenging the heterogeneity of their subjectivity through genuine alterity – that is, by challenging constant domination and oppression of subjectivity by uncritically accepted identification. The politics of difference operates on an identity-identification horizon which relates the question of 'What is a human being?' to the question of identity, namely to that of 'Who am I?'. IM Young gives an account of how the abstract value of equality undergoes a change that makes it include not only a distributive aspect but also an aspect of oppression and domination. This challenge to the abstract understanding of the value of equality can then lead to a different critical role that equality can serve in bringing about critical thinking in both general and the most particular of situations.

The emergence of heterogeneous subjectivity as well as group differentiation from the constant ethical challenge of genuine alterity leads to values, rights and duties that cater to protect those groups and subjects who, for the time being, self-interpret their belonging and their group in a certain novel fashion. Genuine alterity of heterogeneous subjectivity and group differentiation propels the categorical ethical challenge, although always complimentary to the rhetoric of value-justification whereby the enclosed derivative identities as 'individuals' are protected by the uncritically accepted conception of harm by virtue of which rights and duties are interpreted as justifying and limiting law. The politics of difference sees heterogeneous subjectivity as a categorical challenge to any representation that is characterised by external observation by which values originate, and are interpreted and prioritised. The politics of difference, as the political implication of primordial ethics that preconditions any thinking upon goodness, is personal in that it opens up the endless game of self-interpretation in which identity and identification constantly play hide-and-seek with one another.

The ethical contestation offered by the politics of difference, which gets its confidence from innermost personal shouldering of the unceasing burden of alterity, provides for an *aporia*. It shows that a received and de-politicised ethical doctrine that provides conditions for responsibility is either not abstract enough (and hence can never be particular enough) or too abstract, and hence an effective vacuum to be filled up by totalising representations and thematisations.

So Spinoza's 'freedom to *philosophise*' can be seen as the *proto*-basic premise of *critical* constitutionalism and as the basic ethical premise of the politics of difference, namely that moral change must be freely allowed to occur from the very constitution of subjectivity. Moral change occurs from the very process of the ethics of internal enlightenment, from the moment during which people can see themselves as they are, as potential 'Others', as genuinely 'different'. Different values and/or different interpretation and prioritisation of values will be needed in order to provide these persons with the conditions of responsibility for their lives and the riddle of identity into which they are thrown.

The ethics of internal enlightenment that is now firmly embedded in the contestation of identity is itself a supreme value which should be the basis for the justification and limitation of law. Because the protection of freedom to philosophise enshrines the contestation of justification-based ethics, it changes the critical basis of such ethics. Such ethics becomes aporetic in that it cannot be reduced to any conventional self-interpretation. We are back to this wonderful expression 'exploration of the reasonable'. So, justification-based ethics must, and indeed, in order to provide conditions for responsibility, has, become a non-comprehensive conception of constitutionalism. Such a non-comprehensive justification ethics would have to invent terms that would allow it to re-contain newly established, different group and subject identities.

The main point here, though, is that the distinction, and interdependence, between the two kind of ethics holds sway even with the recognition of the non-comprehensive necessity of the external conditions for responsibility and the open-textured nature of internal enlightenment. The non-comprehensiveness that characterises the two ethics bears a paradoxical relationship between ethics and politics. Ethics *is* political in so far as it is capable of producing a particular and different voice that is silenced or marginalised. As a politics of surplus, ethics transcends the current political discourse of rights and duties. However, the political as the language of rights and duties also re-contains and anticipates the ability to accommodate the insights from ethics. The notion of 'exploration of the reasonable', again, seems to cater for both. The 'reasonable' is an empty signifier, the emptiness of which is constantly re-emphasised by the use of 'exploration'. The open texture of both being responsible for one's own life and providing conditions for such responsibility becomes coexistent and reinforcing within the exploration of the reasonable. That horizon of reasonableness which is to be explored, namely that horizon to which the subject ought to be able to respond in order to be responsible, would always lie ahead in the not-yet-conceptualised surplus of subjectivity. The reasonable ought to be capable of rejuvenating the contestability of the identity of the group within which this subject constitutes and contests herself.

Spinoza was indeed able to contain both types of ethics. His political philosophy enabled his first philosophy to operate. There is also contemporary complementarity between the politics of difference, which allow for heterogeneous subjectivity and morally pluralistic non-comprehensive liberal theories (which cannot be reduced to 'liberalism') such as that of Rawls' 'political liberalism', Isaiah Berlin's liberalism, and the political philosophy of Joseph Raz.[9] At the time of writing about Bentham and the potential of utilitarianism, I saw in utilitarianism a candid philosophy, which could take seriously the critical ethical question of 'What does it mean to be a human being?'. This it could do by catering for the 'howness' of human beings, namely the emotional basis for the formation of their identity and, with it, their interest (ethics of internal enlightenment). Utilitarianism could also cater for the indeterminacy that stemmed from the multiplicity and incommensurability of perspectives that pervaded such a conflict-ridden terrain as the discussion about harm according to which law could be limited and justified.[10]

The preceding discussion shows that law is authentic enough. It is authentic because as long as some conditions of responsibility are accepted uncritically, law provides a basis for moral criticism and contestation. Furthermore, law has been shown to be authentic in that it survives any uncritically accepted interpretation of the morality it enforces. Some anticipation of legality was moving the alterity that characterises the tension between internal and external talk about responsibility. Law's authenticity must not be confused with the inauthenticity of the horizon of uncritical ideological totality that characterises legal practice for the most time. The survival in law of the complementarity between two types of ethics within the occurrence of a still more original ethics of alterity that in turn propels the politics of difference shows how authentic law actually is. The origin of my worry about the authenticity of law could surely be considered as resolved and be put to rest.

However, this was not to be the case. Disturbingly, my worry about the authenticity of law became all the more tangible the more calming, sophisticated and critical became that explanation of the unshakeable authenticity of law through the politics of difference. The journey to the origin of the worry had to continue, but the grounds that it broke had to go yet deeper to a place where the politics of difference, and with it critical legal scholarship, had not yet visited. I felt that with the politics of difference and the ethics that propels it there was very little room for further elucidation and expression. Something about the politics of

---

[9] See J Rawls, *Political Liberalism*, n 2 above; J Raz, *The Morality of Freedom* (Oxford, Oxford University Press, 1986); CJ Galipeau, *Isaiah Berlin's Liberalism* (Oxford, Clarendon Press, 1994); J Gray, *Isaiah Berlin* (London, HarperCollins, 1995).

[10] O Ben-Dor, *Constitutional Limits and the Public Sphere* (Oxford, Hart Publishing, 1999).

difference, something that has not yet been expressed or is inexpressible, has to be the root of my intensely felt worry at this point of the journey. The deconstruction would have to be between something expressible as the politics of difference and something which is inexpressible and all the more primordial at that. This book tries to near this inexpressible without degenerating it into expression.

V

It is telling how close the right-based deontological ethical accounts which start by tackling the question of what is right in its own nature are to utilitarian-based theories which start by tackling that question from the formation of actual interests and preferences. Both, if pursued broadly, could cater for the paradoxical and open-textured relationship between ethics and politics. By facing up to the indeterminacy of calculation or the idle surplus of abstractness of the post-metaphysical deontology, both theories could yield critical, inter-subjective relationships in ethics and thus a politics of difference or, surplus.

Why 'telling'? This book attempts to show that the politics of difference itself, whether arrived by indeterminacy of calculation or by representation of 'rightness', presumed a certain notion of alterity. This notion of alterity conditions this paradox between ethics and politics, which leads to insurgency and re-containment. The politics of difference both transcends the language of representation that characterises values, rights, duties, the very fabric of the language of law while, paradoxically, at the same time, it re-contains its insights in so transcending the law. Thinking with and through law, what I refer to in the book as the 'legal', is perpetuated by this very paradox. Also the notion of 'democracy' can be self-preserving critically only within this horizon.

It is not by chance that both utilitarianism and post-metaphysics can find solace in such a paradox. I shall claim that this paradoxical relationship between ethics and politics and, with it, the notion of 'exploring the reasonable' constitutes a huge euphemism. It still conceals something, something that is not reducible to any politics of 'an Other' and with it to the politics of difference.

In questioning this euphemistic nature of the politics of difference, and with it the limit of being and thinking with the legal, there is no escape but to question thinking itself. That surplus that is covered up in this euphemism must be otherwise than the surplus that is established through the aporatic complementary relationship between ethics and politics.

At this point the mind is totally disorientated. It seems that there is an attempt here to make something out of nothing. Yet, if there is a whole world that is being concealed at *this* stage of critical reflection about responsibility, it is that 'to take human beings as they are' has a meaning not yet attended to. The surplus that still continues to bother has to do with whether the radicalisation of truth and otherness that is effectuated in this aporatic complementary relationship between ethics and politics is itself authentic or whether it is only a hint at some authentic occurrence which has already been given to it.

For that attempt to uncover the surplus that still bothers, a journey has to be taken to question the relationship between ontology and ethics and with it the 'howness' of the very primordial alterity that characterises ethics. This inquiry takes me on the journey of closely reading the corpus of Heidegger and Emmanuel Levinas. In a close reading of their *oeuvre*, we may catch a glimmer of a mystery which is not reducible or assimilable to the politics of difference. It is in this mystery that my worry about being and thinking with law, and using the language that law uses, finds at least its original locus, if not a solution. This mystery does not operate to overcome law; indeed, it is not polemic about law. However, it explains law in a way that not even the most sophisticated critical theory and critical accounts of constitutionalism are able to do. This mystery cannot be reduced to any complementarity that is based on scheme, structure or critical purpose. It cannot be reduced to any exploration of reason-ableness. It cannot even be reduced to any critical account of democracy.

A note is appropriate here about legal positivism. Indirect values that provide justification of law regardless of its moral content, such as stability, finality and the values associated with procedure, are most exten-sively used the more fundamental the moral disagreement is. The most critical constitutionalism, the politics of difference, is the very basis for legal positivism because of the silence of legal positivists on direct moral justification as a basis for authority of law. Yet, that which is left undeter-mined by legal positivists is still the world of value according to which they conceptualise conflict and disagreement. Legal positivists, by providing for indirect values, are still annexed to thinking with values, rights and duties, however indeterminate this thinking happens to be. The very paradigm of thinking about difference and alterity is itself presumed to be true by legal positivists.

Let us look at the aporatic complementarity between the ethics of internal enlightenment and external justification ethics. How is this complementarity possible? Truth about alterity is essentially in the 'not yet', and this 'not yet' could concern that which is regarded as the 'truth' of oppression and domination. Somehow, and the whole purpose of this book is to explain this 'somehow', this complementarity between the two ethics is not yet an authentic *aporia*. It is a hint of a more primordial *aporia* that, on the one hand, makes it possible, yet, on the other hand, is nearly completely covered up by it, silenced by it. There is still, in this pseudo *aporia*, the notion that the politics of difference reinstates a lurking assumption about truth, language, Man, although this *aporia* pretends to surpass these presumptions. The success of this cover-up is why this complementarity, with its paradox, is so widely accepted and ubiquitous. Critical political and legal theorists do not feel the need to question because they are made to believe they already do question the received notion of truth and the received notion of what it means to be a human being – a human subject.

That thinking that gives rise to the *pseudo* paradox of the relationship between ethics and politics still leads to a model. It still gives us some craving for an opening scheme within which our ethical efforts and their relationship to politics make sense. The thinking which has already anticipated a model, that has already been idle in its readiness for it, has not yet questioned itself *qua* thinking. Something mysterious about thinking, about Man, has been forgotten and distorted. Thinking about thinking cannot be assimilated into the complementarity, however dynamic, between responsibility that comes from internal enlightenment and value-laden ethics of conditions for responsibility.

To be a human being, and therefore to take Man as he is, consists in a unique way of being responsible. Indeed. What is it 'to be responsible for one's own life'? What is that 'own-ness' to which humans respond? Is this own-ness primordiality, thought about and responded to as long as humans are not oppressed and dominated as not-yet-conceptualised Others? According to such a response to the question, I am responsible for my own life, to my innermost own, only if I did not suffer external fetters as a not-yet-conceptualised Other. Equally, I am responsible for my own life only in so far as whatever I achieved was not achieved by the harming of an Other, with the result that the fruits of my life were achieved through moral 'stealing'.

Answering all these questions by defending a complementarity between ethics and politics still does not answer the question posed, to repeat: 'what is that own-ness to which humans respond'? Does the 'how' of that to which humans respond before all else as their own-ness, the 'how' of that own-ness that also calls for response on the part of humans, obey either representation about harm, or any story that humans tell themselves about their success or failure? Does alterity of an Other to which the subject responds, and from which we can build the modality of critical political and legal thought, advance us at all towards grasping the problem or does it merely hint, by way of what is left unsaid, as to that which calls for response? By hinting at that own-ness which both responds and is responded to before all else, has not the alterity of an Other already taken us further away from grasping that own-ness? Can, then, but for being a hint, critical complementarity between ethics and politics – which focuses on alterity of an 'Other', come anywhere near to the actuality of responsibility? How should we account for the relationship between the hint and that at which it hints? What sort of complementarity characterises the relationship between the hint and the hinted? Is it significant that by asking these questions there seems to be nothing according to which they make sense? This book attempt to listen to the hint. Finally, perhaps the actuality of responsibility can be grasped, but to what extent and how can this grasp be accommodated, as a saying articulated, by any ethics which could be made critically complementary to politics?

The ambit of this book, then, goes to the very relationship between ontology and ethics, and with it their relationship to the notion of otherness. In order to fathom my non-expellable worry with law, I needed to meditate about these issues. That to which humans are called for to give a *human* response and attentiveness makes humans' hearing and seeing unique and mysterious. Resisting a reduction of this mystery in critical ethical accounts of 'an Other' banishes this mystery to silence. This book aims to turn this silence into faintly audible Saying without reducing it to something which can be said in traditional discourses of ethics, namely the ethics of values, rights and duties and with it the ethics of the reasonable.

This mystery of responsibility, as coupled to the mystery of what it means to be a human being (or the mystery of taking Man as he is) needs saying without being said. Indeed, such saying is otherness itself. It is the inability to say the mystery but merely to indicate towards it, which makes it so primordial. It is the silence of its temporal saying which makes it so calm and eternal.

Let me borrow here, at least in tone, from Spinoza: while I was sure about the capability of articulating the paradox of critical ethical theory, its euphemistic nature held sway despite my success. The price of overcoming or at least the successful exposure of this euphemism means that I may not succeed in articulating it.[11]

In reading Heidegger I came to feel that there is something euphemistic in truth, inevitably so, a euphemism that is transported to the very essence of ethics. This euphemism cannot be shaken off but instead needs to be engaged with in humbleness and embraced. That such an engagement and embrace cannot be assimilated into what critical scholarship has to offer it does not imply the demise of critical ethical, political and legal scholarship. It demands thinking about it without reducing the abyss of the mystery into legitimising and comforting paradoxes.

Yet, the complimentarity of the two ethics' address of responsibility has another corollary. This corollary resorts to the language of conflict and to the greyer area of 'risk assessment'. Risk assessment is associated with being responsible. The perversity of 'risk analysis', judgements about the prediction of probabilities, has two main functions, both to do with

---

[11] B Spinoza, 'The Emendation of the Intellect', in *The Collected Works of Spinoza* (E Curley, ed and trans) (Princeton, Princeton University Press, 1985) pp 7–45, at p 8.

collaboration between a deep belief in representational reality and calculation. Given a clear representation of a norm, risk assessment can determine the likelihood of harm according to this norm. In this sense, risk assessment is preceded and conditioned by the norm. In this sense, being a norm belongs to an ethical category that is not dependent on the empirical likelihood of events. In other words, the likelihood of events to make this or that norm relevant in governing a situation as against other norms is distinct from the existence and relative weight of these norms. Yet, secondly and contrary to this view, the very moral status of a norm can be said to originate in risk assessment of harm. In this sense an assessment of risk is a preceding justification for the norm, so much so that the very existence of the norm, not only its weight, can be risk-dependent. However, that risk which precedes the norm can itself be preceded by another different norm so we can see the interdependence between these views. The relationship between risk and norms is dependent on the argument regarding the nature of morally theory, namely whether you derive moral premises from likely consequences or whether moral premises are independent of consequences in a way which constitutes their *moral* priority.

In both senses, however, the uses of risk assessment are plenty. Risk assessment is needed in order to dissolve the metaphors of the abstract norms, such as 'what is reasonable', because the metaphor refers to some process of determining the weight to be allocated to competing moral claims. In this sense the risk becomes the way to dissolve reconciling metaphors. In so doing, risk-thinking assumes enormous importance. Not only can risk assessment be used to determine what weight can be given to a norm, if any at all, but a representation of likelihood of risk can determine the very representation of the norm, in other words, alter that representation. Self-interpretation of norms and their respective modification through risk-assessment has an enormous potential in bridging problem 'construction' and problem 'solving'. Risk can lead to the construction of a genuine problem that is not solvable or, in other words, to the conclusion that there is no form of representation of norms that will approximate enough to risk-representations.

What becomes apparent from these very brief thoughts is that both norms and risks are dependent on thinking which is governed by the notion of correctness of representation. They both belong to the same way of thinking – representation-based thinking – thinking that believes in norms and in facts. They belong at the same horizon of truth.

In this introduction, I would like only to ask: could it be that despite the all-encompassing dealing with risk assessment as a category of prudent thinking and its potential and importance, no one has yet been risky? What *is* risk? What is primordial risk? Is primordial risk is to be obsessed with representation of the risky/non-risky or is it to face the inexpressible and that which cannot be predicted? Can the inexpressible be degraded to a mere decision under conditions of ignorance/uncertainty, which can find expression in some precautionary formula of prediction?

VI

Zygmunt Bauman correctly identifies the challenge that faces ethics and the challenge that faces the relationship between ethics and politics as located in a deep level of debate between ontology and ethics. Whilst developing and applying Levinas's insights, Bauman does not go into the debate between Heidegger and Levinas. Bauman takes for granted Levinas's argument of distinguishing an ethical reflection that occurs within the ontological horizon of 'Being-with' [*Mitsein*] – a central notion of Heidegger's argument about what it means to be a human being – and, on the other hand, 'Being-for-the-Other', which Levinas regards as the primordial ethical relation. Bauman identifies the ontological 'Being-with 'as thinking with and through law, rights, principles, rules, codes, a characteristic of being and thinking with law. A proper ethics, namely that of genuine alterity, is highly critical of many aspects of this ontological dominance and the ethics that derives from it. Being so critical, only the ethics of genuine alterity can think critically about law.[12]

The challenge of the ethics of alterity is very central to critical political and legal scholarship. Derrida portrays it in 'Violence and Metaphysics' by asking 'Are we Jewish or are we Greeks?', namely, are we Greek, by focusing the domain of ontology and meditation upon Being as a first philosophy, or are we Jewish, that is focusing upon the endless responsibility for the Other as that first philosophy?[13]

Bauman resolves this controversy all too hastily. Contemporary critical political philosophy seems to adopt almost without question, either explicitly or by implication, the answer that, as far as primordial ethics is concerned, we are all Jewish – we are all post-modern in the Levinasian sense of unceasing challenging alterity. The hermeneutic cycle of the Western, Greek-based philosophical tradition, culminating with Heidegger who, in the name of fundamental ontology, comes to question this tradition, is still seen as being within the reach of that tradition.

It seems to be acknowledged by many that the price Heidegger had to pay for criticising both the derivative ontology of the philosophical tradition and the ethics of humanism that such tradition advocates is that he had very little to say about ethics, about goodness. The atmosphere of

---

[12] Z Bauman, *Postmodern Ethics* (London/Oxford, Blackwell, 1993) chs 3, 4, esp pp 69–81.

[13] J Derrida, 'Violence and Metaphysics', in *Writing the Difference* [1967] (London, Routledge, 1978) pp 97–192, at p 192.

Heideggarian philosophy is said to have no ethics to speak of, and that is why Levinas urges us to move away from the climate of that philosophy. Heidegger's membership of the Nazi party and his subsequent persistent silence on the atrocities committed in the name of National Socialism confirmed for Levinas, and for many others, the poverty of ethical commitment in Heidegger. Levinas, who had not set foot on German soil after the Second World War, was hardly surprised that Heidegger could, in the name of the resurrection of the voice of Being, support, or at least seemingly be deaf to, the dreadful actions that had been carried out in the name of authenticity of the German *Volkgeist* and its ancient affinity, according to Heidegger, with the early Greeks.

It is not easy, if at all possible, indeed to see how Heidegger's philosophy can be situated within the accepted boundary of ethical reflection. Levinas, on the other hand, although also criticising the philosophical tradition, including its view of the ethical, for being ontology-dominated, is easier to connect to that tradition simply because he tries to capture the origin of goodness in alterity of the Other. Thus, although Levinas's thought portrays the ethics of alterity as a first philosophy and in this sense goes beyond the tradition including traditional ethics, his account of primordial ethics can connect to that tradition. This connection is achieved by installing in that tradition the moment of alterity as a constant impetus for ethical challenge to the very ethical thinking of that tradition.

So, why is it that critical scholars just uncritically accept that Heidegger had no ethics which could ground their effort? Further, why do they adopt Levinas so readily? The answer lies, I think, in that Levinas's grounds the ethical justification for difference, difference that goes much beyond mere problem-solving, contestation and renegotiations. Levinas radicalises alterity in such a way that strikes an intuitive cord with many critical scholars, providing the explanatory force for what they are doing. Alterity that attends to the 'Other', broadly understood as the dominated and oppressed, in systematising, thematising, and hence totalising the ethics of Being-with, is the only categorial ethical force that moves critical thinking beyond such totality. This 'Other' can be oppressed by the ethics of rights and duties that is enforced by law. From a psychoanalytic point of view this 'Other' can be oppressed by thinking that does not transcend the symbolic order within which subjectivity is constituted for the most part. Any critical insight, then, even if it was to regain some significance in ethics and law, which it transcends, must be assimilated to such alterity. Such insight must be translated into Levinasian transcendence or alterity. It is this alterity which is both the gate for transcendence of any ethical discourse and the gate for coming back to a modified discourse.

This is not a book about Lacan, but searching for critical political and legal insights from Lacan already implicitly anticipates that the only possibility for them to regain ethical and legal significance is by an ethical account that both transgresses law and retains it. Part of this book is to argue that Levinas does just that.

Our age is Levinas's age as far as ethical political and legal critical scholarship is concerned. In a recent book and an article, D Manderson hails Levinas as providing ethics that *inspires* law. It is Levinas, Manderson argues, who provides the basic ethical challenge posed to law, a challenge that critically deploys care for one's neighbour as the basis for a radical notion of responsibility. Drawing on many examples from substantive law, especially the law of tort, Manderson shows just how central Levinasian ethics is to the founding moment of law. As a founding moment of law and obligation, Levinasian ethics is able to maintain that force that preserves the law despite being also the ground for critical of the inherent totalisation of legalism.[14]

Levinasian ethics is the new natural law – natural law whose radical alterity enacts the *aporia* of law by both acknowledging the necessary limit of ethics that is enforced by law and at the same time retaining some lifeline for developing the law. The Levinasian 'ethics of ethics' as Derrida calls it, constantly criticises and changes its content to accommodate the insight of the ethical radicalisation. In entrenching the 'naturalness' of law as *aporia*, Levinas enacts the transcendent nature of goodness into the nature of humans and society. This kind of natural law can subsume the ethical ground for many critical schools of thought, whether neo-Hegellian, neo-Marxist or analytical. This Levinasian natural law, although it is highly legalistic, as I will show, is no longer a code or set of principles. It transcends principled thought; it is the basis for the scholarship, legal and political, of difference that is now provided with a master framework within which to situate and to ethically focus its effort.

There is a connection between four questions: 'Who is being oppressed and dominated?'; and, in turn: ''Who needs protection?'; 'Who am I?' and 'What is it to be a human being?'. The dominated and oppressed Other that causes the subject to think and be otherwise than he or she is, but at the same time regaining subjectivity in the process. can create a thread that connects all these common questions. Levinas shows that these questions cannot be answered ethically within the ontology-dominated tradition – a tradition within which the ethics that law enforces is preserved.

By connecting these four questions not only does Levinas establish a very deep critical platform – one that challenges the ontology-dominated philosophical tradition. His notion of alterity addresses responsibility, ethics and justice, while meeting the intuitive worry people have over

---

[14] D Manderson, 'Proximity: The Law of Ethics and the Ethics of Law' (2005) 28(3) *University of New South Wales Law Journal* 696–719 at 705. See also D Manderson, *Proximity, Levinas and the Soul of Law: Tort, Ethics and the Soul* (Montréal, McGill University Press, 2006) especially ch 7.

authenticity. This is why he can exert such a decisive influence on so many types of critical scholarship.

In an impressively comprehensive survey of critical jurisprudence and the notion of rights, C Douzinas discusses a broad sweep of critical legal scholarship, one that includes J Lacan, P Legendre, E Bloch, A Honneth and E Laclau, to name but a few. These critical theories attempt to overcome both positivism and the objectivism of the legal subject. With many hints throughout the book and explicitly at the end, Douzinas aligns these schools of thought to Levinas's ethics, and quite rightly so. Levinas does not come out as just another name among the list of critical thinkers. Douzinas shows forcefully how Levinasian ethical relations of radical alterity lurk within all those theories that criticise both the positivism and objectivism that reign in Jurisprudence making the subject politically indifferent and dull. As we shall see, to make politics ethical and to makes ethics political was, after all, at the heart of Levinas's preoccupations. Quite surprisingly, though, given the enormous influence that Heidegger exerts over Levinas, as well as over many of the schools of thought that Douzinas's critical exposition does cover, there is alarmingly brief, though dismissive, engagement over just a few pages.[15] Levinas himself did not banish a dialogue with Heidegger in such a manner.

This book entirely shares Manderson's and Douzinas's characterisation of Levinasian ethics as central to critical legal scholarship. However, this book attempts to *diagnose* this Levinasian dominance as a given ethical problem that faces Man. As a problem, Levinasian dominance is an ethical call for thinking that this book attempts to awaken. In other words, this book attempts to destabilise this Levinasian dominance. It also attempts to reinstate the centrality of the Levinas/Heidegger debate into the debate about critical legal scholarship. The intention, then, is to provoke various strands of legal scholarship to expose their Levinasian ground and to subject the master of ethics to ethical reflection.

So, in facing Levinas and examining my residual worry, the nature of the worry has changed. The politics of difference that took Levinas's voice into actual political struggles made a lot of sense. Side by side with the worry itself which, as I have noted, went into the realm of the inexpressible, there was an additional worry now that I would not be able to simply say that Levinas was inauthentic. The notion of alterity to which Levinas gave such detailed thought is deep and subtle. And yet it seemed to do away with an even deeper mystery – the mystery of alterity itself.

Facing Levinas's account as well as the perversity of it had to claim that his view still does not do justice to his own insight about alterity and alterity's primordial relationship with ethics. Because Levinas's account both transcends and retains what is expressible in ethics I felt that perhaps

---

[15] C Douzinas, *The End of Human Rights* (Oxford, Hart Publishing, 2000).

what had to be said in order to express the worry now must remain inexpressible within the Levinasian horizon. In other words, could it be that the ethics of alterity operates already within an irreducible otherness of primordial ethics, one that could not even be reduced to Levinas's account? Could it be that the nature of alterity, perhaps one that precedes and conditions the Levinasian alterity, one which is prior to Levinas, and with it to all critical political and legal scholarship, could be grasped and engaged with in silence?

Silence *seems* to characterise the way Heidegger responded to the atrocities of his own time. Silence as non-engagement pervades many critical scholars when they come to deal with Heidegger. No doubt Heidegger's so-called silence and the scholarly silence about Heidegger are connected. We ask: cannot this scholarly silence about Heidegger be explained in the light of the perversity of Levinas? Can we not hear the call that comes from the Levinasian sheltering coordinates?

Either to 'defend' Heidegger or to 'criticise' him can have its merits. However, could it be that neither of those engagements really understand either his omission or the scholarly omission to engage with his contribution to critical ethical thought?

This book involves a close reading of Heidegger and Levinas's work. Only by such close reading can I attempt to encounter the residual worry that Levinas's account exacerbates. Only by such close reading of both Heidegger and Levinas can I expose the surplus that speaks from within Levinas's conception of alterity, a surplus that pervades critical scholarship silencing the deeper mystery of alterity. Only through such a close reading can I de-emphasise, magnify and amplify Heidegger's silent ethical saying.

This book is about law. In order to think about law we have to think not only about the language that law uses but also about how this language is preserved in the critical scholarship that purports to transcend not merely the content of law but precisely such language. To think about law, then, is to think about how something that characterises law is retained in that *aporia* of law that critical legal scholars assume. I would like to show how dominant Levinas came to be, so much so that Heidegger's insights about poetic language, Being, ethics, Man and Truth, are twisted and distorted in order to enable the Levinasian conception of alterity to reign supreme over ethical scholarship. And over humans. Heidegger's silence is itself already captive within a discourse that bends Heidegger's arm.

Heidegger approaches the question of 'what does it mean to be a human being?' in a very unique way. It not only takes humans as it finds them but articulates without succumbing to alluring temptation, to that craving of 'oughtness to do good to fellow humans'. Heidegger adheres to that humbleness that humans are unique precisely because they are thrown into their world which both precedes them and is hidden from them, constantly other to them. The only 'oughtness' that he demands of humans is that they are attentive to the murmuring call that comes from that 'throwness', attentiveness, which though audible, is not quite possible within language. This attentiveness is to otherness that is internal to language itself. That humans are always already thrown into language has implications not only for ethics but for thinking about law in a way that cannot be reduced to 'the *aporia*' of law, namely thinking that both transgresses and retains the law.

Radicalisation of democracy survives the Levinasian complementarity between ethics and politics. However, precisely because that own-ness to which humans respond in being responsible is a mystery, democracy, however critical, can only be a distortion of that mystery. Any talk about, and craving for, democracy, as if by the radicalisation of alterity of an 'Other', democracy can be understood as some deepest equality of stake, conceals the mystery. Talk about democracy does not yet confront the mystery of responsibility and the constant inequality that nourishes that mystery.

A binary-based thought would immediately be that to overcome democracy – widely understood as the politics of difference – is to be prone to the danger of oppressive freedom, the kind which forces to be free in a way more primordial than protects radical difference. Such freedom characterises the most oppressive regimes such as National Socialism. The danger is there for sure. I cannot help recalling I. Berlin's caution against the notion of positive freedom, namely that freedom that constantly responds to the question of 'Who am I?', thus being grounded on self-determination and identity. Again, positive freedom promises something higher than any ongoing maintained and contestable diversity under the law – what Berlin referred to as negative liberty that responds to the question of 'How much am I governed?'.

It is worth pointing out here that the identity politics of heterogeneous subjectivity, although it has elements of positive freedom, is still, as the politics of difference of the Other, within the horizon of negative liberty.

We have to take seriously Heidegger's subscription to National Socialism and silence about the Nazi atrocities. Engaging with Heidegger's subscription to National Socialism and his silence have also a lot to do with the kind of thought that Levinas pursued with such subtlety. Not only do I doubt whether Heidegger has ever been silent but I have a serious doubt as to whether the discourse about his silence which is conducted explicitly or implicitly in a Levinasian climate, has not done a great deal to silence his ethical voice.

For the purpose of this introduction, it is perhaps sufficient to indicate that Berlin's caution against positive freedom is very true both in terms of what he cautions from but, also because his caution points towards the mystery of freedom and responsibility.

We can read Berlin's caution against positive freedom as a pointer towards the mystery of freedom rather merely as a warning against the danger of the suppression of diversity. If we do that we could thereby keep open the option that talking about diversity, and democracy, that is giving priority to negative liberty, can also be a very effective oppression of the mysterious actuality of humans.

What is the mystery of positive freedom? Once positive freedom is given priority, once humans seriously open up to the question of 'Who am I?', there are two ways that the response to this question can go. The first, which echoes Berlin, is that by letting human beings be according to their mysterious essence, positive freedom encapsulates the emptiness of that essence and with it the imaginary and oppressive identification – Fascism – that fills up this emptiness. In such identification, as Lacoe-Labarth has shown,[16] because everybody is identified with everybody else in the '*Volk*'s whole', everybody is barred from questioning his or her respective role. In such circumstances, everybody is compelled to perfect his or her current contribution to the effort to overcome the corruption of the *Volk* by earthly ideological contestations. However, secondly, positive freedom can harbour the only painful liberation that stems from attentiveness to, and identification with, that which conditions actuality and which surpasses representational ideas and reflection. In this respect, only positive freedom can connect to the mostly suppressed actuality of human being, thus unfolding the way for contemplative thought and being at one with the actuality of the actual. This interpretation of positive freedom,then, can resonate with some forms of Buddhist thought as well as with anything like National Socialism.

In both responses to the question of positive freedom, violence is involved. Even in the latter, violence to the word by the word is involved as the only path of the inaccessible mysterious essence of humans.

So positive freedom, as the most primordial ground to walk on ethically, is very dangerous. Still, the dangerousness, to recall Berlin, is with the potential abuse of the notion and not with the notion itself. We must not subordinate the notion of positive freedom to a negative one just because of its dangerousness. Confronting the mystery, while inherently difficult and unpleasant, is not dangerous. Moreover, only in confronting the mystery can we be confident of taking Man as he most primordially is.

So, it may be that National Socialism, despite being beyond any ideological analysis, still falls short of characterising the mystery of the *Volk* – falling short into the trap of a political programme into which also Heidegger might have fallen. What is again important to hint at here is that it is silence, irreducible silence and complementarity which involves

---

[16] P Lacoue-Labarth, *Heidegger, Art and Politics* (Oxford, Blackwell, 1990), chs 8, 9.

the unsaid of a primordial Saying, that characterises the overcoming of the hegemony of negative liberty-based thought.

VII

Heidegger has been, by and large, expelled and banished from the world of ethics and responsibility. Perhaps the most challenging claim that has been raised against any notion of ethics in Heidegger is that it cannot account for genuine alterity. In this book I connect three claims. First, I account for an ontological difference between the Being of law and what I refer to as the legal. Secondly, however, in order to do full justice to such claim, in order to appreciate the ambit of that legal, I have to leave the law aspect of the ontological difference and engage intensively in another aspect of that difference, namely the area between the ontological and the ethical. This relationship between the ontological and the ethical is then linked to a debate about the origin of alterity. I argue that Levinas's notion of alterity, if it exists at all, is derivative and, thus, within the horizon of the legal (despite Levinas's claim of advocating an ethics that is 'other' to that ethics which is enforced by law). My third claim is that it is in Heidegger that the call of alterity opens up that unfolding which generates originary response by human to their own-ness, a call to which overcomes the legal. The call of alterity constitutes an aspect of the essence of law which protects humans from the dominance of the legal.

Overall the book attempt to present what it conceives as the only way in which thinking reflectively about law is possible. All the three moves attempt to reinstate Heidegger as perhaps the *only* ethical philosopher, or rather, the only philosopher who is ethical by touching the origin of otherness and the ethical, and with it, the origin of law. To be ethical in the conventional sense of ethics, a sense that embodies the most extensive horizon of the legal, is to be in denial. This denial is itself a part of the ethical unfolding towards which Heidegger indicated.

Heidegger, contrary to the common view, was never actually silent about ethics or about ethical atrocities. That he did not condemn these atrocities, his contemplative silence about them, is the only way he could convey the saying of the ethical in these atrocities. The only way of overcoming the denial of the derivatively ethical was to resort to this contemplative silence. In his silence, Heidegger was first and foremost ethically responsible, responsible, holding the mirror to that way of thinking, the entrenchment of which is seemingly ethical but in fact one that is fateful to breed violence. Heidegger's mirroring was itself possible by being other to Levinas' 'ethics of ethics' and the legal.

The book has three parts. Part A consists of chapters two to four. It introduces Heidegger and delineates the questioning of this book. This Part culminates in chapter four, which constitutes a key saying of the book as far as Heideggerian thinking about law is concerned. In more detail, Chapter two gives my own initial introduction to Heidegger's thought. It will be noticed that I have relied mainly, though not exclusively, on Heidegger's later, largely poetic works. The so-called 'proper' philosophers, including Levinas for that matter, highly regarded Heidegger's *Being and Time* but usually dismiss his later work as incoherent, wordy and elliptical. The earlier Heidegger, many philosophers would say, is still a philosopher and writes as a philosopher. The later works, with their etymological journeys, cannot be considered as serious works in philosophy.

Most scholars try to reduce Heidegger's insights into some chronology, that is the 'early Heidegger' – the philosopher of *Being and Time* – and the 'later Heidegger' " – the poet, the mysterious. Scholars who defend a later Heidegger do so by attempting to articulate important changes in his thought about the relationship of humans to Being and about the relationship of humans to language. The reasons I introduce Heidegger in the main through his later works are threefold: the first is that I believe that Heidegger's thought is better approached by moving from the later works to the earlier. Approaching his work in this way can do the utmost justice to his whole ethos against chronology, namely that the future is already lurking in the unsaid of the past. Secondly, and in relation to the first point, it is my contention that the best grasp of *Being and Time* is to see, in the best of Heideggerian fashion, the 'unsaid' of it in the light of the 'said'. Heidegger the author was constantly 'on the way' displacing his own work by its own unsaid. As a result, engagement with the later poetic works contributes to a greater understanding of *Being and Time*, an understanding that Heidegger himself could not have had when he wrote it but also an understanding that future interpreters cannot have by treating Heidegger chronologically. As Heidegger remarks in 'What is Called Thinking?', every serious thinker has only one thought. In that lecture he also implied that the philosophical tradition had only one thought, one that simply could not have been asked from within the tradition. Heidegger's 'one thought', and the connection of that thought to the one thought of the tradition that is encapsulated in it, must be approached, I think, by reading Heidegger backwards.

The final reason for emphasising the later essays is that they are meant to hold the mirror to philosophers and to alienate them. If the later essays do that they have conveyed a deep point about philosophy. These lectures of great beauty are very engaging and are very courteous and sympathetic to the reader. At the same time, however, Heidegger never gives in to correctness. The Saying in these lectures is never reduced to concepts, to representation, but constitutes an etymological journey in which the questioning never ceases, thereby keeping the reader's sense of insight and ambiguity. These essays have coherence without correctness – coherence that plays hide-and-seek – a secret that both shares with, and protects itself from, the reader/listener. In these essays Heidegger philosophises while, to quote from his 'Letter on Humanism': '[letting] the habitual opening of philosophy fall away'.[17] That *Being and Time* meant to do the same and had the potential to do the same can be appreciate only by engaging with these later words.

Chapter three elaborates on what it means to think reflectively about law and, as such, constitutes a meditation on how Heideggerian reflection relates to theorising law. Chapters two and three are introductions to chapter four, which is where the multi-dimensional saying of this book truly begins to take shape. Chapter four reads Heidegger with reference to his notion of 'essence' and investigates the relationship between what I term the 'legal' and the essence of law. This investigation reinforces my point of departure, namely that to think about the Being of law, about its essence, cannot be reduced to making sense of, and also finding an ethical way of improving, the practice of being and thinking with and through law. This investigation of the relationship between the essence of law and the legal does not involve a radical change of meaning of the word 'law'. As a deconstructive move, it shows that the legal and the essence of law are connected through the theme of protection from harm.

Chapters five, six and seven in Part B open up the second deconstructive move in the book by undertaking a close reading of the ethical and political thought of Levinas. In order to explore the ambit of the legal as explained in chapter four, I resort to the debate around the relationship between ethics and ontology. The deconstruction here is of the notion that, with Levinas, ethics implies alterity. But the claim is that the radicalisation of alterity by Levinas in fact does not yet give an original account *of* alterity, or more accurately, an account of the origin of the thinking that responds to the otherness of the other. This shortcoming makes Levinas's ethics of alterity seem like a conclusion without a premise. Lack of original alterity results in Levinas being the last and more sophisticated preserver of what I termed 'legal' in chapter four. Levinas does not yet, cannot, engage with the first claim of the book – that any argument from the 'legal' is a distortion of the essence of law.

Finally, the reading of Levinas is constantly interrupted by Heideggerian responses that already hint at the argument to come in chapters eight and nine in Part C. In these chapters my own interpretation of Heidegger's notion of Being-with, and his later notion of dwelling and language, is interpreted so as to constitute an argument about Heidegger's ethics that is grounded in the mystery of otherness. Such an ethics connects both the essence of law and the essence of the ethical, both of which are grounded in the otherness of the other.

With the connection between the two deconstructive moves of the book

[17] *LH*, p 246.

– the first of which concerns the relationship of the legal to the essence of law and the second of which concerns the relationship between ethics of the 'other' to ethics which connects to the origin of the 'otherness of the other' – Heidegger's silence can be seen in a different light.

Heidegger's thought about law has already been interpreted, in his lifetime by Erik Wolf, Werner Maihofer and Erich Fechner, and, in recent years, by Finnish scholars, most notably P Minkkinnen and J Tontti, who wrote in English,, and A Hirvonen in Finnish.[18] These recent scholars have cast important light on the primordiality of fundamental ontology to thinking about law. Tontti attempts to interpret law as a 'regional' ontology and as such to distinguish the thinking about the Being of law from thinking-Being. However, both Minkinnen's account, which is largely based on Wolf's work and Hirvonen's (whose work I know of only indirectly by reading English summaries of it) attempt to conceive the question of the law's Being as an integral component to the question of Being. Like Minkkinnen and Hirvonen my own way of thinking developed in this book is based on a close encounter with Heidegger's writings and as such is another attempt at establishing such a connection.

Yet, in interpreting Heidegger's thought in my own way, without any mediation, relying heavily, though not exclusively, on his later reflection, I located the issue of thinking about law quite differently to them. I came to an interpretation which does not attempt to establish the juridical happening of metaphysics or to view law in a way which precedes its mundane occurrence. Nor does my interpretation connect to epistemology except through the notion of distantial distortion that occurs in ontic thinking of epistemology.

The interpretation here links thinking about law to the debate on the origin of ethical thinking and, with it, to the origin of otherness. This link between legalism and the origin of ethics and otherness means that the transcendence involved in thinking about law has much more at stake than either mundane practice or even legal theory. Heideggerian thinking about law has to contemplate what pretends to be the most radical transcendence of legalism – Levinasian ethics. My close reading of Heidegger's later works thus magnifies into the depth, or nearness, and connectivity that exists within Heidegger's notion of the order of Being between Heidegger's reflections on law and the ethical nature of his thought. Thinking about law is shown to belong to the same order of Being that also encompasses one of the central debates in twentieth century continental philosophy, namely *whether ethics is primordial to ontology or somehow an aspect, or attribute, of ontology*. A debate on the origin of ethics and otherness can

[18] P Minkkinnen, *Thinking Without Desire: A First Philosophy of Law* (Oxford, Hart Publishing, 1999); J Tontti, *Right and Prejudice: A Prolegomena to a Hermeneutical Philosophy of Law* (Aldershot, Ashgate, 2004) and A Hirvonen, *Oikeuden Kaynti. Antigonen laki Ja oikea oikeus* (Helsinki, Loki-Kirjat, 2000).

show just how transcendent, rather than mundane, legalism can, and has, become. Such a debate shows that thinking about the well-concealed legalised transcendence, rather than anything mundane, is arguably the deepest challenge facing thinking about law.

What readers of this book can expect is not merely a substantive change, that is another theory, or even a philosophy, of law. Along its meditative path, my reading of Heidegger is meant to bring about change in the very process of thinking that in turn, I believe, can generate a transformation of thinking about law. *The transcendence in the book involves transformation of thinking.* It does not aim at stating a new societal vision of law. In transforming thinking, my reading aims to cast new light in which the unlearnt thinking and all the efforts that have been carried out under its spell, may be seen for what they are – assurances for the perpetuation of the legal. I go to quite a great length to constantly distinguish my transcendence from any radical transcendence that radicalises thinking without ever transforming it. Critical legal studies, although radicalising thinking about law in order to overcome both positivism and objectivity, is an example. It is the human capability of undergoing such a transformation of a manner of thinking in general, and thinking about link between ethics, morality and law in particular, that this book attempts to awaken.

VIII

Finally, two points. First, the style of the text. The chapters are written in numerical paragraphs. Writing in this way fits my way of thinking and has enabled me to be more dialogistic, associative, even disruptive with the text when appropriate. Also, there are many little insights and questions about both Heidegger's and Levinas's texts that are linked to the main argument of the book. Sometimes these insights, or questions, already anticipate something to come. Writing in a paragraph form enabled me to put down my associations and comments as and when I read and reread what I wrote. So the paragraphs are situated somewhat between turning the book into a mere collection of remarks and a continuous prose.

Secondly, a note about the use of Hebrew. A brief explanation is needed of the way the Hebrew language works to extract latent significance. In Hebrew the alphabet has no vowels. Instead, it has some additional signs which give consonants different sounds. Also, the letters that are regarded as vowels in English are created in Hebrew by the letter 'A' together with a vowel-equivalent sign. The letter 'A' on its own is a consonant like all others.

In Hebrew each word has a root which consists of three root consonants. There are various ways in which any of the three consonants that constitute this root can be combined with vowel signs in order to produce a word. Employing different vowels can assemble different words that originate from the same root. Further, the root consonants can be inflected into different structures that give them a different sense.

Let me give a couple of examples. Let us take the three consonants A, D and M. With these three consonants the following words can be assembled: ADAMA (which means soil, earth); ADAM (a human being in general); ADOM/ODEM (the colour red); DAM (blood). That which connects these words together is always partly revealed, partly concealed in an endless hermeneutic game. The mystery of significance is in-built into the world of the language. The language is alive in that words can be played with to reveal the unsaid of a saying from within the idleness of what is articulated, or expressed as a 'said'.

As to the verbal form, let us take the consonants B, Y, and T. They can form the noun BAYIT (a house, but also home as in *Heimat* in German). As a verb they can form LEHITBAYET, which has a double meaning. It means to become tame/homely/civilised (also as the inflected adjective form of MEBUYAT). It also means to have a beacon, a direction, in this sense implying an unsaid signification of the potentially taming effect of coming home. Any word is mysteriously linked to another by the very grammar of the language.

In this way Hebrew has its own particular way of being alive and speaking a never diminishing unsaid. By constantly producing hidden connections and inflections of verbs which derive from the same root Hebrew can be used to lighten the dark points in conventional speech. This is the Hebrew way of wrinkling signification in a way that strictly logical talk cannot possibly convey.

In Hebrew, then, the hidden significance of a saying can assume many levels. It can appear as a double meaning of a single word. Secondly, it can appear as variations of words which are conventionally very closely associated and which share the same root, for example the words KADIMA (forward) and KEDEM (the early, the earlier), which share the root K, D, M. Finally, the hidden significance can lurk beneath what are seemingly entirely different words between which there is a hidden connection, and the example of A, D, M given above is one of those. It is in this last manifestation of hidden significance that enormous poetic potential is encapsulated. Connections made between different words which share the same root do force the user of the language to be attentive to its potential for connections in signification and its capacity to covey the world of particular moments. Furthermore, with certain inflections of different words which share the same root it is quite often possible to get one word which bears the double meaning of those original different words that were inflected. The word LEHAAMIR (to raise up and up) and the word AMIRA (saying) share the same root A, M, R. Yet, with inflection, the word AMIR can mean both 'the high' and 'that which is capable of carrying a saying'). So the language is actually capable of creating new words which will enable rich deployment of all three aspects to bring about the hidden signification. All of these possibilities have been used throughout the book, most extensively in chapters four and nine.

Heidegger's etymological journeys in his later work can be very effectively supplemented by examples from the manner that Hebrew speaks. I will leave it as an open question whether it is appropriate to call all the potentialities of the Hebrew language 'etymological' as the answer is not crucial for uncovering hidden signification. What is important is that poetic potential of the Hebrew language that lends itself perfectly to Heidegger's own way to language. In fact, we know that Heidegger learnt Hebrew, although it is not clear how proficient he was or, indeed how much he was influenced by Hebrew. As far as I know he has never made any reference to Hebrew.[19]

[19] H Ott, *Martin Heidegger: A Political Life* (London, HarperCollins, 1993).

PART A

2

Heidegger's Saying

1.

From now on, we will call 'most thought-provoking' what remains to be thought about always, because it is at the beginning, before all else. What is most thought provoking? How does it show itself in our thought-provoking time? *Most thought provoking is that we are still not thinking* – not even yet, although the state of the world is becoming constantly more thought-provoking.[1]

The last sentence keeps appearing during the series of lectures that Heidegger gave in Frieburg during 1951–52 under the title of 'What is Called Thinking?'. Heidegger's concern was thinking in general. The next chapter's argument is that Heidegger's own exploration opens a horizon on the very understanding of the question of what it is to think reflectively about law. In this chapter I would like to wander and wonder through the main tenets of Heidegger's thought about thinking so that the reader can become familiar with Heidegger's main moves. An initial grasp of what bothers Heidegger is needed for the question of thinking to show itself properly. Some of the tenets explored here will be revisited in much more detail in the chapters that follow. The flowers in Heidegger's garden are varied and rich in colour, varied as well as being seductive in the secrets held within their petals so this short overview attempts merely to unlock a door to this garden.

2.

Heidegger's question 'What is called thinking?' relates to anything that is to be thought *about*. How should the 'aboutness' of a thing be approached? Can that very aboutness become the main focus of inquiry? I am thinking about a chair, about a friend, about law, about liberty. Surely what is important is the object of thought – chair, friend/friendship, law, liberty – and not that 'aboutness'. Reflecting on aboutness opens up a new horizon for reflection on the way entities are – on their Being. Yet, focusing on the Being of beings – on Being as such – as the foreground of aboutness seems to be a non-starter:

[1] WCT, p 4.

Can something like [B]eing be imagined? If we try to do this, doesn't our head start to swim? Indeed, at first we are baffled and find ourselves clutching at thin air. A being – that is something, a table, a chair, a tree, the sky, a body, some words, an action. A being, yes, indeed – but [B]eing? It looks like nothing.[2]

3.   In order to understand how 'aboutness' can itself become an issue for thinking, we need to explore what Heidegger calls the *Seinfrage*, or 'the question of Being', sometimes put as the question concerning the 'Being of beings'. That 'aboutness' does not seem significant is precisely what makes it very significant and thought-provoking for Heidegger. It is precisely because the question of Being has been largely forgotten by the Western philosophical tradition that 'aboutness' as such seems a non-question, a non-event, nothing.

4.   This paragraph is the gist of what will be untangled in this chapter: *thinking for Heidegger is thinking-Being. Heidegger's thought perturbs and awakens the question of Being, bringing it into language and reflection and thereby radicalises the notion of language and understanding. But 'thinking-Being' does not mean that thinking somehow controls Being. Thinking is rather indebted to Being. Thinking as appropriated by Being is a process that makes its focused concern the contemplation of, responding to, Being. Thinking is always already thinking-after [Nachdenken] moments of encounter with, and clearing of, the being of Being, as given in the Being of beings.*

5.   Heidegger claims to awaken the question of Being that was lying dormant all through the Western philosophical tradition from the Plato to Nietzsche. In asking the question of Being, Heidegger aims to recover pre-metaphysical thought. Metaphysics, he claims, has been at the heart of that tradition. In Nietzsche Heidegger sees the last metaphysical thinker and in Nietzsche's thought the very expression of the twilight of metaphysics by metaphysics.

6.   The birth of metaphysical thinking occurs with the inauguration of the idea of 'truth'. In non-metaphysical thinking, as it was for the pre-Socratics, 'truth' [*alētheia*] connoted 'un-concealment', disclosedness, clearing, revealing. For the philosophical tradition, 'truth' has become 'correctness' [*Richtigkeit*]. Correctness entails correspondence between ideas and beings.[3] Heidegger, then, tries to trace an ancient notion of truth in the sense of unconcealment which is smothered in metaphysical thinking but nevertheless lurks there primordially. The shift from unconcealment to correctness had a

[2] *BPP*, p 13.
[3] *ET*, pp 116–23.

profound effect upon how beings are thought about, as well as about what is 'reason' and 'to reason'. The flourishing and sanctification of logic; how language is approached; the nature of reality; how humans self-understand what it is to be human – the grounds of ethics – all these have changed as a result of abandoning and forgetting truth as unconcealment. The relationship between truth as unconcealment and as correctness is essentially mysterious. It harbours an ever-renewed mystery.

7.   By thinking back to pre-Socratic understanding of truth as unconcealment, Heidegger endeavours to excavate that very moment when the question of Being has been forgotten and buried. He also excavates the forgetfulness of the question of Being in the work of each and every philosopher that he reads, as well as constantly in his own *oeuvre*. Heidegger wishes to transcend, to overcome, the metaphysical tradition and recover an 'aboutness' which is more primordial than that which is offered by metaphysics. What is offered by metaphysics? In a very much later essay Heidegger has this comment to make:

Metaphysics thinks beings as beings in the manner of a representational thinking that gives grounds. ... What characterises metaphysical thinking, which seeks out the ground of beings, is the fact that metaphysical thinking, starting from what is present, represents it in its presence and thus exhibits it as grounded by its ground.[4]

Metaphysics has both the craving and the focus to represent the positive essence of things. The positivity of the ground of metaphysics resides in what things 'are as such'. Understood thus, the problem for philosophy becomes and persists as a question of the adequacy of this or that representation of beings' extantness. But could it be that the primordial ground of beings is that which desta-bilises their very grounds *as* beings? Could it be that in order to overcome metaphysics what is needed is to focus on thinking that precedes any being as an individual being but which is nevertheless given to any being as its 'beingness'?

8.   Heidegger first approaches the overcoming of metaphysics, overcoming truth as correctness, through the transformation of philosophical reflection concerning Man's relation to Being. Alongside the transformation of Man's relation to Being, a second transformation takes place, namely that of what has become known as the subject/object relationship, or Man's relation to beings. Relating to beings in a subject/object manner results in the debate

[4] *EPTT*, p 432.

between, and reconciliation of, on the one hand, realism, which emphasises the object of thought, and, on the other hand, idealism, which emphasises the subject of thought. Truth as correctness aims to explain how representational ideas in the mind relate to things outside the mind. What results from the realism/idealism debate is perpetuating the forgetfulness of Being, by replacing one 'correct' representation with another. To overcome that forgetfulness, nothing less than the radicalisation of both thinking with subject and object (thing) needs to be undertaken. What is thinking, then? What is a thing? How does the radicalisation of things and thought relate to the radicalisation of 'aboutness'?

9.   Authenticity [*Eigentlichkeit*] is a moment where thinking successfully resists the craving for metaphysics, for correctness. Authentic thinking comports itself towards unconcealment, overcoming the craving for the so-called 'cool' philosophical correctness through representations, definitions and calculations.

10.   Being of beings – that which is to be thought about, to be encoun-tered – resists the capturing of what is thought about as a mere object-for-thought in the world. Fundamental ontology for Heidegger must make a leap [*Sprung*] from the mode of thinking, as well as the methodology, which aims to articulate or express a 'world view' of beings:

> The thesis that world-view formation does not belong to the task of philoso-phy is valid, of course, only on the presupposition that philosophy does not relate in a positive manner to some being qua this or that particular being, that it does not posit a being. Can this presupposition that philosophy does not relate positively to beings, as the sciences do, be justified? What then is philosophy supposed to concern itself with if not with beings, with that which is, as well as with the whole of what is? What is not, is surely the nothing. Should philosophy, then, as absolute science, have the nothing as its theme? What can there be apart from nature, history, God, space, number? We say of each of these, even though in a different sense, that it is. We call it a being.[5]

11.   Being gets its positive sense precisely by being given in any being although never being reduced to a mere 'extant thing'. Being is given by uncovering the being's 'thingness', which is concealed if the inquiry is directed towards it as 'a being/beings'" or as 'a thing/things'. What Heidegger calls the 'ontological difference' is that point of reversal of space and directionality, and, in this sense, discontinuity, between an inquiry about beings and their Being. This

---

[5] *BPP*, p 10.

difference is not a mere distinction between beings but between two distinct, though, as we shall see, related, ways of thinking.

12. From the uncritically accepted 'world view' Being seems to be nothing in the sense of 'there is nothing there to think about'. Heidegger's idea, however, is precisely that Being *is* nothing. What does this mean? Heidegger explains:

> In relating to it, whether theoretically or practically, we are comporting ourselves toward a being. Beyond all these beings *there is nothing*. Perhaps there *is* no other being beyond what has been enumerated, but perhaps, as in the German idiom for 'there is', *es gibt* [literally, it gives], still something else *is given*. Even more. In the end something is given which *must* be given if we are to be able to make beings accessible to as beings and comport ourselves toward them, something which, to be sure, is not but which must be given if we are to experience and understand any beings at all. We are able to grasp beings as such, as beings, only if we understand something like [B]*eing*. ... We must be able to understand actuality *before* all experience of actual beings. ... We must understand [B]eing – being which may no longer itself be called a being, being, which does not occur as a being among other beings but which nevertheless must be given in fact is given in the understanding of [B]eing.[6]

13. Heidegger's inaugural lecture 'What is Metaphysics?', given in 1929, is a meditation on the nothing. What is it to think about the nothing, or as Heidegger calls it 'to hold out into the nothing'?[7] After all, thinking is always about something, is it not? The nothing 'is', always nearest to us, preceding any conception of it as mere negation of beings. Despite being nearest to us, it cannot be made into an object, a 'thing'. The experience of the nothing characterises openness to Being. Such experience is hinted at in moments of genuine boredom, but can only be fully experienced in moments of anxiety. Anxiety is distinguished from fear in having no object (indeed, a being) that generates it.[8] It comes from the nothing, from no particular being. Whilst anxiety persists, the feeling is that of being oppressed by something which is not an object. The individuation of beings, their coherence and representation, the comfort of knowing them, is sucked out of them, ebbing away, in anxiety. Any articulation of beings does not help to meet anxiety where it bites. Anxiety has a ring of mystery and abyss to it. In anxiety there is openness to the continuum of things which cannot be captured or anchored. In anxiety a connection occurs to that which is inexpressible but which is given to beings. The 'no-thing' becomes

---

[6] *Ibid*, pp 10–11.
[7] WM, pp 103, 108.
[8] *Ibid*, pp 100–101. See also *BT*, section 40, pp 228–35.

something. Anxiety makes possible an opening up to the insight that no articulated beginning and end convinces any longer. In anxious moments the need to disclose that which is nearest, the need to transcend individuation of beings becomes urgent and oppressive, accompanied by the torment of not having any representation to articulate it, no concepts, no generalisations, calculations or logical forks to shelter behind. So, anxiety involves a certain sense of grasping beneath the condition of total exposure. In anxiety, unlike in fear, the nothing is bound with beings as that which is given to them, their Being, but which cannot be related to an account of them *qua* beings. In anxiety, beings become enlightened in *shrinking*, they are revealed in their strangeness: 'Only when the strangeness of beings oppresses us does it arouse and evoke wonder'".[9]

14.   Only in openness to the nothing can beings *be* rather than continually 'exist as ...'. The nothing estranges 'beings'. In this sense of estrangement the nothing annihilates any sense of individual beings that for-the-most-part representational discourse accounts for, including negations, of those beings. The nothing is never diminished by thinking about 'beings' but merely concealed and distorted by such thinking. The nothing is that primordial 'not' which does not amount to a mere negation of beings, but is distorted in every act of negation. The nothing is far less brutal, being much nearer than negation.

15.   In being open towards the nothing, no less than the whole legitimacy of metaphysical thinking is at stake:

> The nothing does not remain the indeterminate opposite of beings but reveals itself as belonging to the Being of beings.... Assuming that the question of Being as such is the encompassing question of metaphysics, then the question of the nothing proves to be such that it embraces the whole of metaphysics. But the question of the nothing pervades the whole of metaphysics since at the same time it forces us to face the problem of the origin of negation, that is, ultimately, to face up to the decision concerning the legitimacy of the rule of 'logic' in metaphysics.[10]

Although Being is given to any being – hence it being referred to as 'Being of beings' – it is never any kind of a being and in that sense it is nothing. The nothing is neither the affirmation nor the negation/annihilation of beings. It consists in a whole dimension concealed in a conception of the essence of things as individual beings. Grasped thus, the Nothing/Being does not amount to any being but is given to any being as its Being. Being of a table (a being)

[9] *Ibid*, p 109.
[10] *Ibid*, p 108.

is given to the table but gets its nature in not being reduced to what is expressed as being 'a table'. The contextual usage, in which the name 'table' corresponds to a meaning of a being, does not yet capture the Being of the table. The sameness of Being and nothing points towards ontological difference which happens only when for-the-most-part-accepted ontology, that of beings, is not alluded to in such a way that transcends it. Thinking-Being responds to a 'towardness', a clearing of Being which is given to beings. *Ex nihilo nihil fit* (from nothing, nothing comes to be) goes together with the explanation of the ontological difference between beings and their Being, a sense that radicalises philosophy to challenge the whole metaphysical tradition.

16. R May points out a striking similarity between Heidegger's under-standing of the nothing, his understanding of the 'thingness' of things – that nothing that belongs to them as their Being – and the Buddhist notion of *emptiness*.[11] In Heidegger's lecture 'The Thing', Being-as-nothing has also been conceived as the *unconditioned thingness* of things which cannot in itself be a thing – a thing being conditioned. As we shall discuss in detail in chapter nine, Heidegger refers to the metaphor of a jug, whose emptiness does the containing.[12] An unconditioned emptiness is given to beings into which they are nearer to themselves than merely existing as extant beings, into which their actuality is interpreted.

17. What is it in the actuality, in anything actual in beings, the Being of beings (as distinguished from the study, generalising methodology – a worldview – of a being) which is most thought-provoking is the first question to be asked as far as thinking is concerned. But what is thought-provoking comes also to the Being of the thinking subject and destabilises the subject's innermost own subjectivity, comporting towards, as well as nearing, a moment of un-paraphraseable own-particularity. What Heidegger refers to as 'the ontological difference' happens when the nothing – that which is inexpressible, but hence which is nearest to beings – is grasped in a moment of insight, of clearing, an authentic instance of being-in-the-world. It is a moment in which the Being, as that Being-of-beings, is glimpsed at, fusing the 'thingness' of things and innermost-own Being. Being-there glimpses, in anxiety, at that which is given by Being to beings. Such a moment happens as own-Being, or the human *Dasein* (literally translated as 'being-there'), comports itself towards the world which is opened up by the nothing, towards that which is thought-provoking.

[11] R May, *Heidegger's Hidden Sources: East Asian Influence on his Work* (London, Routledge, 1996) pp 21–34.
[12] 'The Thing' [1950], in *Poetry, Language, Thought* (A Hofstadter, trans and ed), (New York, Harper Collins, 1975 and 2001) pp 163–80 at p 166.

18.   Being is, then, not a 'thing'. Nor is it identical with precisely determined actuality. The actuality of Being is a cyclical and
open-textured process. 'Open-textured' means here that the Beings of
beings cannot be reduced to lack of precise correspondence between
representational ideas and those beings. Openness persists between
beings and their Being and, as we shall see, involves some other kind
of ruthless preciseness.

19.   Thinking-Being is a response to what Heidegger calls the *presencing*
of the appeal of Being. Maintaining that sense of hearing that attends
to presencing is to guard Being thereby letting Being be.[13] The abyss
of the Nothing amounts to nothing only in metaphysical thinking
from which thinking-Being must distance itself. This distancing is
ontologically near to what Heidegger called the 'actuality of the
actual'.

20.   Metaphysical thinking about beings, then, conceals the question of
Being. However, it is only one side of the coin. Metaphysical thinking
has the effect of promoting thinking that is characterised by
technical, calculative, enframing relations of people to the extantness
of beings. In *The Question Concerning Technology*, Heidegger
maintains that the essence of technology, rooted in the ancient Greek
word *technē*, is *nothing technological*. The essence of technology, the
way *technē* unfolds as a 'way of bringing about' and with it a 'way of
knowing', is covered up by technical relations. *Technē* has been
understood to mean knowing in the broadest sense, which includes
the arts. It means opening up. As opening up, *technē* is revealing and
in this sense connects to the idea of truth as revealing [*alētheia*].

> [*Technē*] reveals whatever does not bring itself forth and does not yet lie here
> before us, whatever can look and turn out now one way and now another ...
> what is decisive in *technē* does not at all lie in making and manipulating, nor
> in the using of means, but rather in the revealing ... It is as revealing, and not
> as manufacturing, that *technē* is a bringing-forth. Thus the clue to what the
> word *technē* means and to how the Greeks defined it lead us into the same
> context that opened itself to us when we pursued the question of what
> instrumentality as such in truth might be. Technology is a mode of revealing.
> Technology comes to presence in the realm where revealing and
> unconcealment take place, where *alētheia*, truth happens.[14]

21.   Technical relations also reveal, but in a distorted, enframed, way.
Enframing [*Ge-stell*] challenges humans in such a way that orients
their involvement towards demands to extract and to store. Instru-

---

[13] Heidegger, 'A Letter to a Young Student', 18 June 1950, in *Poetry, Language, Thought*, n
12 above, pp 180–84.
[14] *QCT*, p 319.

mental utility is the hallmark of modern technology – maximum effectiveness and minimum expense. In the enframed mode of revealing, human beings are challenged by language as representation to establish coherence that suits them. Because enframing is concealed, modern technology seems merely to be applied science.[15]
And yet, despite the danger of enframing, in being enframed, humans are participating in their fate of saving *technē* as the essence of technology. The enframed mode of revealing is creating the danger within which lies the saving power of *technē*. Human beings as enframed is but a stage on the way of being destined to be saved from that very enframing. As such, humans are the safe-keepers of the essence of technology:

Because the essence of technology is nothing technological, essential reflection upon technology and decisive confrontation with it must happen in a realm that is, on the one hand, akin to the essence of technology and, on the other, fundamentally different from it.[16]

22. The relationship between Being and human *Dasein* (to recap, 'being-there') gives rise to the ontological difference. For the most part, when not anxious, in everyday mundane situations, *Dasein* finds itself among beings and also reflects upon itself as a being – an ego, an 'I', a subject. In moments of anxiety, though, beings, including the ego, shrink so that their Being which has been given to them can be glimpsed at. Ontological thinking which involves glimpsing at Being occurs, in a sense, 'outside' beings as the 'suchness' which is nearest to them – their Being.

23. *Dasein* is said to 'ek-sist' rather than merely to exist. It only is in-the-world when leaping outside self interpreting as a being. *Dasein* is never fully identified either with the Being of beings or with beings. *Dasein* constantly oscillates between beings and their Being. For *Dasein*, encountering Being is a moment of insight, a moment of clearing, although *Dasein* always already falls back into its being among other beings.

24. This 'outside', then, characterises *Dasein*, which 'is' only as 'ek-sistent'. The term 'outside' can mislead as it can hint at extant enclosed beings. The term 'near' is better, conveying the 'ek-sistential' characteristic of *Dasein*. Being-in-the-world is a moment of nearness, nearer than the nearness that is arrived at whilst thinking about beings. The primordial 'not' of the nothing means that both Being

[15] *Ibid*, p 328.
[16] *Ibid*, p 340.

and *Dasein* have to be understood 'ek-sistentially', rather than merely existentially as an 'ego' and an extant:

[The It] as the location of the truth of Being amid beings, gathers to itself and embraces ek-sistence in its existential, that is, ecstatic, essence. Because man as the one who ek-sists comes to stand in this relation that Being destines for itself, in that he ecstatically sustains it, that is, in care takes it upon himself, he at first fails to recognize the nearest and attaches himself to the next nearest. He even thinks that this is the nearest. But nearer than the nearest and at the same time for ordinary thinking farther than the farthest is nearness itself: the truth of Being.[17]

It is this relationship of exile which characterises both *Dasein* and that which *Dasein* is comported to in moments of anxiety – the Being of beings. The relationship between beings and their Being, including *Dasein*'s own-interpretative relationship to both beings and their Being, is characterised by an uneasy manifestation of desire to come home, which comes to be heard in the murmuring homelessness that lurks beneath the mundane.

25. The space and directionality of this 'outside', or nearness, characterises the relationship between *Dasein* and Being. The space and directionality are *Dasein*'s 'world'. The direction of this world is always from the 'further' and 'far', towards that which is nearest, the actuality of everything actual. The direction is, in other words, from being amongst beings and other egos, towards being connected to the Being of beings and other *Daseins*: 'For us "world" does not at all signify beings or any realm of beings but the openness to Being.'[18]

26. To the involvement of *Dasein* in its own 'ek-sistence', together with its connectedness to the Being of beings, Heidegger gives the term 'care' [*Sorge*]. Thinking-Being is being-there-in-the-word as care. This should not be understood as a moral, or paternalistic, care, but as the way anxious *Dasein* connects to the nothing. The 'ek-sistence' of *Dasein* is experienced as care.[19] Care is prompted by *Dasein*'s anxiety especially when contemplating its own innermost possibility of not-being, or its own innermost death – the contemplation of the ultimate unification of home and exile. It is the contemplation of innermost own death that makes *Dasein*'s own Being and with it, Being of being, an issue for *Dasein*. *Dasein*, then, is unique because its own Being is an issue for it. The vivid possibility of death, together with the inability to rationalise death merely as an 'physical end', creates fundamental anxiety in *Dasein*. Only because death

---

[17] *LH*, p 235.
[18] *Ibid*, p 252; *BT*, pp 91–122, 134–48.
[19] *BT*, pp 217–65, at 234, 252. A detailed discussion of care is given in *BT*, at pp 225–41.

speaks to *Dasein* as its innermost nothing can *Dasein be* as 'ek-sistent'. Care is generated as the ongoing anxious process of 'being-towards-death'.[20] The possibility of death for *Dasein* connects it, as care, to the nothing. As humans are essentially guardians of Being, *Dasein* is referred to as the *human Dasein*. The human *Dasein* is, first and foremost, mortal, and as such it has this constant anxious connectivity to the nothing.[21]

27. *Dasein* is authentic in a moment of openness to Being, in a moment in which the language of beings shrinks and the inexpressible – that which can never be captured by expressing – raises its voice. When *Dasein* understands itself through a possibility that is its innermost-own it comes upon an authentic moment. Here there is an absolutely crucial twist. This twist must be grasped in order to highlight how different Heidegger's thought is from Sartreian existentialism. For Heidegger, it is not the case that existence always precedes essence. For him 'ek-sistence' as essence precedes both existence and essence. The unparaphrasable particular moment in which *Dasein* has insight into the Being of beings is the only authentic moment in which *Dasein*'s innermost nothing has already spoken *Dasein*. Openness to the preceding and nearest voice of the nothing which comes from *Dasein*'s hidden nearest is the only instant to which *Dasein* can authentically respond, although always somehow unsatisfactorily. Authentic speaking of *Dasein* is always already a trailing response to the Saying of Being which always already ahead in its withdrawal. Being thus appropriates, claims, *Dasein* as anxiously attentive thereby sending it on Being's way by eliciting an authentic, though belated, response. That is the meaning of *Dasein*'s constantly being thrown in a way over which it has no control. *Dasein*'s 'ek-istence' ahead of itself means thinking-after and speaking-after in response to the call of the thinking and the saying of Being. *Dasein*'s 'ek-sistence' should be understood as being essentially a response to Being. Only by giving up the centrality of itself as a being can *Dasein* connect to its Being and with it, to the Being of beings. The 'suchness' of *Dasein* is only when it is attentive to the call of its no-thing. Attentiveness that brings about an authentic moment is a moment of resoluteness in the face of for-the-most-part inauthenticity including the inauthenticity of the idle response to events that concern, and distinctions between, beings.

28. The centrality of human *Dasein* should not be mistaken for humanism. To be a human being, to 'ek-sist' cannot be reduced to any representational quality that makes up humanism. Heidegger is

[21] *Ibid*, pp 279–311.
[21] Note Heidegger's reflection on the term 'mortal' in *TT*, at p 176.

at pains to overcome the conventional way of relating to the question of what it is to be human by isolating a characteristic of, a yardstick for, humanity by virtue of which the human is distinguished from the non-human. *Dasein* must not be understood as having some inherent characteristic by virtue of which it subjects Being through discursive concepts and theories. Overcoming any representational character-istic is not easy for Heidegger as such avoidance necessitates precisely an articulation of the unique characteristic of *Dasein*, namely, that its Being is an issue for it. To do that Heidegger needs to defend a certain poetic relationship between the language of *Dasein*, thereby making sure that 'Being as an issue for *Dasein*' can never be reduced to a representation but is rather characterised, as we shall see, constantly on the way to language. For now, it will suffice to say that the poetic language characterises the relationship between Being and *Dasein*. Poetic language characterises the care-structure of *Dasein*, which in turn transcends the representational language of humanism. Again, overcoming humanism becomes a bit clearer when grasping that the relationship between human *Dasein* and Being is such that it is not *Dasein* which speaks Being but is rather spoken by it. *Dasein speaks* only when it hears the murmur that has already spoken it. *Dasein*'s essence as a mortal human consists in the ability to listen to Being rather than to represent its own essence to itself in a way which leads to a humanistic discourse. The nothing always precedes *Dasein* and hence *Dasein* is authentically in an inexpressible thought. What characterises *Dasein*'s authentic involvement is openness to the Being of beings. *Dasein* is a sign, a pointer towards Being. *Dasein* is already thrown into a world that it cannot control but, as care, it has the uniqueness of Being open to this world, this 'game of stakes', as Heidegger referred to in his *Letter on Humanism*, pointing towards it.[22] This openness is the holding-out into the nothing. *Dasein* is thrown into a world in which Being has already spoken:

But if man is to find his way once again into the nearness of Being he must first learn to exist in the nameless ... Before he speaks man must first let him-self be claimed again by Being, taking the risk that under this claim he will seldom have much to say. Only thus will the pricelessness of its essence be once more bestowed upon the word, and upon man a home for dwelling in the truth of Being.[23]

As *Dasein* 'ek-sists' it is never a 'whole', it is never a subject, an ego. Subjectivity is merely the situation in which *Dasein* finds itself for the most part, among beings, the point where the ego's affirmative or

---

[22] *LH.*, p. 245.
[23] *Ibid*, p 223.

negative reflections and assertions do not suffice to approach that which is nearest. In an anxiety-laden sentence, Heidegger writes:

Being is farther than all beings and is yet nearer to man than every being, be it a rock, a beast, a work of art, a machine, be it angel or God. Being is the nearest.[24]

In *Letter on Humanism* Heidegger explains that the structure of *Dasein* is not prior to Being but is already thrown in Being, already claimed by it. In a moment of readiness it is snatched by Being but it is always left hanging. The main message of *Letter on Humanism* is that it is not as if *Dasein* is playing the flute to which Being dances. Being has always already projected itself. 'Being is It Itself'.[25] *Dasein*, as a respondent to a call is always already a projection onto Being. *Dasein* oscillates/hangs as care, anxiously moving further from, and nearing, engagement with Being's projection. The essence of human beings is that they 'ek-sist' in that they are, expressly or through concealment, attentive to, as standing out in the midst of, the moment that the Saying of Being shows itself. 'Ek-sistence' means that there is no representation by which the Being of human beings can be 'captured' in its relationship to Being. 'Ek-sistence' means homelessness and exile through which nearing home occurs. But the home which is neared is always already further on the way, hidden in the nearest of the near. There is only a 'way' upon which human beings are destined to reflectively realise that they are mere pointers towards what Heidegger constantly refers to as the 'sending' of Being, thus destined to stay hanging above the 'ek-sistential' abyss. 'Ek-sistence' is not a characteristic but an ongoing flicker, revealing and concealing the event of the Saying of Being. Humanism, then, by craving to frame out a characteristic of humans *falls short* of the uniqueness of human beings. It does not set human beings high enough, namely as listeners, pointers, respondents to Being.[26] Only so long as the clearing of Being appropriates does Being conveys itself to Man. *Dasein*'s essence is that it has a unique capacity to stand, so to speak, with aerials open towards Being. In listening and responding, in the delay between hearing the call of its Being and responding to it, the essence of 'ek-sistent' *Dasein* lies. *The* unique phrase – *Dasein* – is neither a subject nor an object but rather that which is in the 'there' of 'ek-sistence'. *Dasein* can 'be in the world' only as the 'whilst' of this '*ek-*' unfolds as a world for it. *Dasein* stands *there* in the unfolding and it needs to unfold with the

[24] *Ibid*, p 234.
[25] *Ibid*.
[26] *Ibid*, pp 234–5.

unfolding of Being, always desiring the mysterious and inexpressible nearest.[27] If one insists on keeping the word 'humanism' for finding the essence of Man in 'ek-sistence', then one also has to admit that what matters is not Man as such. As its primordiality can only be in its derivativeness, then, the word 'humanism' does not bite at anything. Only if we see that the essence of Man, where Man is at home, is where it lets itself be claimed by Being, can we awaken the proper deep reflection of what the *Seinfrage* truly demands of humans.

29. The sending/withdrawal of Being draws us in and thereby we become a pointer towards what withdraws – Man is a pointer, a sign. As creatures, the only creatures who can listen to Being and think-Being – for whom their own Being is an issue – human beings are guardians of Being, they are pointers towards the great mystery of Being. They are spoken by Being but have the capacity of leaping thinkingly into moments of insight concerning how Being is expressed through their own involvement in the world. Leaping thinkingly does not involve generalisations, perpetuating metaphysical thinking: 'Thinking does not overcome metaphysics by climbing still higher, surmounting it, transcending it somehow or other; thinking overcomes metaphysics by climbing back down into the nearness of the nearest.'[28]

30. *Dasein*'s relationship with Being is that of attentiveness to Being, pointing towards Being. In *The Principle of Identity*, Heidegger sees the relationship between *Dasein* and Being as *mutual* appropriation.[29] In *The Essence of Reasons*, Heidegger says: 'The happening of the projecting "throwing the world over being", in which the Being of *Dasein* arises, we call Being-in-the-world.' *Dasein* always transcends into a world of its own Being that has already been spoken by Being.[30] This point needs further elucidation: although *Dasein* is attentive to Being, it does not mean that there is a 'thing' – Being – which precedes it. Being can only be as *Dasein*'s essential transcendence into *Dasein*'s innermost being-in-the-world, that is the world of beings that constantly opens up as *Dasein*'s own world. We can say, then, that without *Dasein* understood essentially as transcendence, there is no impetus to Being. There is no Being of beings without there being *Dasein* whose Being is an issue for it. Being of beings is never independent of *Dasein*. By its anxious attentiveness and its response which is already too late for the nearest, *Dasein* is, metaphorically speaking, the oxygen of Being. Being needs the innermost-own anxious attentiveness in order to maintain its

---

[27] *LH*, p 252.
[28] *Ibid*, p 254.
[29] *PID*, p 34.
[30] *ER*, p 89.

murmur. The 'thingness' of things is never opened up into a world without the thinking of *Dasein* which already thinks its own Being in anxious attentiveness.

31. The moment, or rather the 'event', of Being speaking – this world that opens up towards the nearest – Heidegger maintains, is itself *temporal*. This temporality is both that of *Dasein* [*Zeitlichkeit*] and that of Being itself [*Temporalität*]. The 'now' is attended to by the 'now' of attentiveness of *Dasein* and followed by the 'now' of the response of *Dasein*. That space and directionality in which the Sending of Being reveals–conceals itself from anxious *Dasein*-as-care is temporal. Being unfolds in time. Heidegger grounds time in the ecstatic unity of past, present and future. The event of the primordial 'now' is not interpreted as clock-time, whereby time is seen as a sequence of 'nows'. In clock-time we 'take' time. When we use clock-time we have this notion of the 'now' as meaning 'that much time until ... so that I have time to ...'. This view of time as successive 'nows' does not properly encounter the 'now' as such. The now is not an extant thing – that is a punctuation, with a beginning and an end. The now is already in a temporal continuum. Both the 'now' of Being and that of *Dasein* are interlacing in a play of antecedent saying from the nearest and delayed response from a place farther than the nearest. The near/far relationship of mutual appropriation between *Dasein* and Being is temporal.

32. Something has already been unveiled to us and this is the reason we cannot go back to it merely by looking at a clock. The position of the hands of the clock only determines a derivative 'how much'. If the now is encountered properly, say in the proposition '*now* it is cold', it is a moment where retaining something from the past and projecting some expectation/projection for the future are fused in unity with the present. The 'now', if contemplated upon, already belongs to a primordial temporal structure. In the 'now-saying' the speaker is already transient in time.[31] Time is not sequential,and in its primordial history is not just a succession of 'events' or a 'chronicle', as Heidegger calls it.[32]

33. Metaphysics, which attempts to find grounds for beings as beings, relates to entities only as existing in time but is not yet alluding to the temporality from which the metaphysical project distances itself. And yet, the term *a priori* means 'from the earlier'. *A priori* is above all a temporal, not a metaphysical, representational, term.[33] KEDEM in Hebrew which means 'the earlier' is temporal in that it is connected

[31] *BPP*, pp 257-61.
[32] *QCT*, p 329.
[33] *BPP*, pp 324-5.

by root to KADIMA, which means forward towards the future. The *a priori*, metaphysics, is then already a part of a temporal conditioning and hovering, but one which cannot be explained through metaphysics itself. Metaphysics already contains the need to outstrip itself but it cannot have recourse to itself in doing that. Philosophy is running out of its own resources if it confronts its own ground. This is why philosophy must dissolve the difficulty of finding a representational way for *a priori*, whilst by doing so it robs itself of *a priority*. The philosophical moment is nearer than any metaphysical representation and encapsulated in the temporal delay between the Saying of Being and *Dasein*'s response in an authentic moment of being-in-the-world. The effect of falling into the trap of traditional philosophy is to distort this unique moment.

34. *Dasein*'s 'ek-sistence', as care, is structured temporally. Temporal unity is that of 'ek-stasis'. Past, future and present are involved 'ek-sistently' in one another. The projection of future possibility has already been 'thrown' from the past and they unite in a moment of an authentic present, which is always too late. *Dasein* hovers in time where past, present and future are entangled in ecstatic unity. Another way of putting it is that *Dasein* is [now] always already self-interpreting what it has been. The past for *Dasein* come back to *Dasein* in the present as *Dasein*'s innermost future possibility. The past is not just sequences of events that occur until the 'now', and from 'now' on the future is a free possibility. Thinking of the possibility for *Dasein* is always thinking *back*, reminiscing about that which has been calling upon *Dasein*. There is a continuum between the 'ek-stasis' of the temporality of *Dasein* [*Zeitlichkeit*] as it is open to Being and responds to it, and the way Being itself 'ek-statically' temporalises itself, [*Temporalität*] in speaking whilst *already* withdrawing. *Zeitlichkeit* is the ecstatic unity of the constitution of *Dasein*'s Being. In the unfolding of *Zeitlichkeit*, *Dasein* encounters the Being of beings and in self-interpreting its comportment towards Being it understands:

To be one's own peculiar ability to be, to take it over and keep oneself in the possibility,... to understand oneself in the being of one's own most peculiar ability-to-be, is the original existential concept of understanding.[34]

In projecting itself onto its innermost possibility *Dasein* understands. The old German translation of understanding, *vor-stehen*, means 'standing-before'. Being ecstatic as 'ek-sistent' means 'being ahead of

[34] *BPP*, p 276.

itself as being alongside'[35]. The moment of *Dasein*'s understanding, something in its own innermost historicity, is always already late as that for-the-sake-of which *Dasein* comports towards – Being – has already withdrawn. That which is revealed is also already concealing. *Zeitlichkeit*, then, is hovering in some more primordial structure, that of Being as such, which ecstatically temporalises itself, as *Temporalität*. A primordial notion of history is here in the making – that of revealing the 'already' of any teleological historical process.

35. The hermeneutic, or interpretative turn towards ontology occurs only as the craving for articulating individual beings is resisted and overcome. The temporal structure of being-in-the-world is a *hermeneutic* cycle where the human *Dasein* comports its innermost 'own-ness' towards the nothing/Being. Being comes to the human *Dasein*, provoking it towards the nothing (to recap, towards the no-being,towards the thingness of things, emptiness). The circularity of contemplating own Being, which attends to what is thought-provoking involves thinking. Approaching the world as a world of distinct expressible *beings* – what Heidegger saw as the world which is present-at-hand – conceals the space of their Being – a space of what Heidegger referred to as beings being ready-to-hand. The basic constitution of *Dasein* in its comportment towards the Being of beings is characterised by *functionality, handiness, in-order-to relation, howness*, rather than extantness. The dimension of functionality relates to extant beings and other *Daseins* as *equipment*.[36] In the whilst of the event that characterises being-in-the-world, *Dasein* is involved in the equipmental reality which is of *Dasein*'s world.[37] This world and the opening-up of readiness to hand starts always when entities are encountered in their *average everydayness*, rather than in the 'higher' realm of philosophical reflection.[38] But then, this average everydayness is only the start of the unfolding of temporal-based functionality and, with it, significance.[39] A whole world of temporal ecstatic unity of the nearness of entities, of involvement, opens up in the dimension of everydayness. Heidegger seeks to reverse direction from abstraction to the depth of the ordinary and the near. The lurking of the near in the far is a characteristic of the equipmental world, the world of the handy.[40] The nearest is always too near, and hence the world is constantly unfolding. The near–far relationship that characterises *Dasein*'s

35 *BT*, p 237. See *BPP*, pp 275–6 for Heidegger's elaboration on 'understanding'.
36 *Ibid*, pp 95–107.
37 *BPP*, pp 292–6.
38 *BT*, pp 36–8.
39 *BPP*, p 262.
40 *Ibid*, p 304.

openness to Being occurs in the dimension of the everyday. The mundane of the average everyday conceals that buried significant of nearness to the Being of beings, although this mundane everydayness belongs to the same worldly continuum. The everyday has great depth, constantly accommodating a secret. The everyday should not be confused with something obviously 'given' or with 'common sense'. It is rather a realm in which *Dasein* interprets its own innermost world.

36.   But the moment which opens up to what is coming to be thought about, a moment of an ontological difference, is also the event of a withdrawal of Being, so much so that the Being of beings remains hidden, always already 'ek-sisting'. The withdrawal of Being characterises the very moment when *Dasein* grasps ontological happening. 'Ek-sistent' also means that *Dasein* is never outside the hermeneutic circle of the near and the far. This is why Heidegger's Saying, much more primordially than metaphysics and transcendental phenomenology, is referred to as *hermeneutic* phenomenology. *Dasein*'s comportment towards the sending of Being cannot be overstepped by the craving to account for some transcendental positive essences of 'things'. The only reflective 'stoppage' that can authentically occur is in moments of insight which transcend the world of separate beings. It is the craving to produce transcendental essences that is only part of the way towards more primordial Sending of Being. Metaphysics is part of the 'way' in which *Dasein* is related to Being. Thinking about beings is always already in part of *Dasein*'s own comportment towards Being. There is never a panorama of Being, only moments of insight, of connectedness, when its withdrawal has already been triggered. Ontology, being the connectedness to the Being of beings, is fundamentally different from a worldview that craves for a coherent account of beings. Ontology follows a path which brings the unfolding *Dasein* nearer to the unfolding world of the Being of beings.

37.   *Dasein* is always in the hermeneutic cycle. This always-in-already implies that *Dasein* is essentially transcendent. *Dasein is* always where it is not yet, never as a whole ego. Dasein is *always-already* nearer than its extant determination as a subject. It does not step over towards being a whole ego. Being transcendent means that it is the stepping over as such. This transcendence is the equipmental context of *Dasein*'s own understanding as readiness-to-hand.[41]

38.   Thinking ontologically always involves in part contemplating what is being for-the-most-part – what Heidegger calls the *ontic*. The ontic is

---

[41] *BPP*, pp 298–9. See also *ER.*, pp 37–45, where Heidegger explains how the notion of transcendence means the overcoming of subject–object relationships.

always the only gateway to the ontological, a necessary one. The ontic is the first horizon on a path towards (or more accurately, backwards to) the horizon of own-nearest path that is on the way to what is ontological – the Being of beings. The ontological is always embedded, albeit in a distorted way, in the ontic. An ontic grasping of beings, or 'things', always involves a pre-genuine ontology, is implied in a 'worldview' philosophy where a subject aims at an account of beings as well as seeing itself as an 'I', a subject, amongst 'others'.

39. Ontological thinking is always hazed by the ontic but the ontic is what is most accessible to the subject, the subject being 'a being' among 'beings'. The word 'hazed' is used to convey that the ontological is in the ontic, but is inexpressible in ontic terms. Thought in ontic terms is not yet thinking. *Dasein*, as 'ek-sisting', is always split between the ontic and the ontological. The ontic is *both* farthest from *Dasein*'s innermost own, but is what is nearest to *Dasein*, for the most part, most accessible to it. The ontic is characterised by the subject who knows and theorises about himself and his knowledge of object and concepts. It is also characterised with idle commerce with other people – what Heidegger referred to as the drowning of *Dasein* in the 'they'. I shall discuss the 'they' extensively in chapter nine. The main point here is that thinking about epistemology is merely ontic. Rather than succumbing to the craving towards the generalised 'What is ...?' and 'how the subject knows what he knows', *Dasein* is provoked by the wonder of 'How is this and that there?'.[42] Being imprisoned in ontic thinking, generalising thinking, is always expressed through representational ideas, definitions, conceptual structures, a horizon of truth in which language is investigated through formal logic. But that which is given to the ontic, that which is concealed, unsaid by it, that which is nearest, absolutely positive no-thing (or, not being), is ontological. The contemplation by which the Being of beings is neared necessitates not merely immersion in the ontic but being thought-provoked by that which is hidden – that which is given to beings but which is more than their extant for-the-most-part familiarity. There is no ontological without the ontic, and *Dasein* is never fully in either. There is no nearing without immersion in the far. For any genuine ontological insight there has to be a response to the comportment towards Being whilst attentively engaging with the ontic rather than cyclically and inauthentically being imprisoned in the ontic.[43] That is why the

[42] *BPP*, p 304.
[43] On *Dasein* immersing itself in an everyday inauthentic hermeneutic temporal cycle, see *BT*, pp 403–8.

thought-provoking 'It' which comes from Being, from the 'thingness' of things, rather than from affirmation of the thing's stand-aloneness, must happen in order for a particular ontologically comported engagement with the ontic to occur:

> Being is projected upon something from which it becomes understandable, but in an*unobjective* way. It is understood as yet pre-conceptually, without a logos; we therefore call it *the pre-ontological understanding of [B]eing.* Pre-ontological understanding of [B]eing is a kind of understanding of [B]eing. It coincides so little with the ontical experience of beings that ontical experience necessarily presupposes a pre-ontological understanding of [B]eing as an essential condition ... The way [B]eing is given is fundamentally different from the way beings are given.[44]

40.   To think about is to near this pre-ontological resistance to the craving for objectifying *an* ontology. The pre-ontological is a necessary condition for the objectification of beings. In the same way, dealing with beings is necessary for the pre-ontological to be felt, to show itself. A distorting but necessary objectification is what we can refer to as the complementarity between the ontological and the ontic. *Dasein* is essentially thrown into this complementarity. Being open to such complementarity as its essence, *Dasein* is never fully wholly accessible to itself. Its nature is that it is always partly in the pre-ontological, both of itself and of the things it encounters. *Dasein* is never a whole ego but is necessarily in a complementary relationship between its inexpressible nearest and its self-representation as an ego as its own farthest.

41.   A thought-provoking moment is immersed in temporality. It involves memory and recollection which haunts present possibilities. Thinking is always thinking *back*. But thinking back is mysterious as the 'that' of the past conceals itself as it is neared:

> It is plain that the word [Memory] means something else than merely the psychologically demonstrable ability to retain a mental representation, an idea, of something which is past. Memory – from Latin *memor*, mindful – has in mind something that is in the mind, thought ... Memory is the gathering and convergence of thought upon what everywhere demands to be thought about first of all. Memory is the gathering of recollection, thinking back. It safely keeps and keeps concealed within it that to which at each given time thought must be given before all else, in everything that essentially is, everything that appeals to use as what has being and has been in being.[45]

---

[44] *BPP*, p 281. In *ER*, p 19, Heidegger commented in the context of discussing Leibniz's principle of sufficient reason: 'Predication, to become possible, must be able to establish itself in the sort of manifesting which does *not* have a *predicative* character.'
[45] *WCT*, p. 11.

42. Ontological thinking is always in the ontic but only alongside, too near. Listening to the call of the Being of beings starts with the necessary attentive immersion in the ontic. Being attentive is already an act of making ready – a contemplation which prepares for moments of readiness for thinking-Being. By being attentive to the call of the ontological in the ontic, we are at the gate, or foothills, of the place of readiness to the ontological Being of beings, the nothing which is given to beings. The Being of beings and the temporal structure that makes what is thought about as well as preparing readiness for connectedness to own-time, is itself an expression of Being through Thinking.

43. The Being of beings is only glimpsed as what is innermost 'own-ness'. But the 'I' is not a thing. The 'I' who sees is more of a 'nothing, thingness, emptiness' of the 'I-the–thing'/the subject-as-object. The innermost own traverses that innermostness only in fleetingly overcoming itself as a thing, as a being, as an 'I', as a thing created conditionally and relationally to other 'I''s' – themselves seen as things. *Dasein*'s openness to Being is disinterested in itself as 'I' but it thereby becomes most interested in its innermost 'own-ness'.

44. Thinking-Being does not consider 'things' by attempting to approach them from various perspectives in order to arrive at an essential or, as Husserl referred to it, an essential – *eidetic* – account of them. Further, thinking-Being does not assume a subject – a 'thinking transcendental ego' who is comported towards these *eidetic* essences. It is precisely those moments of transcendental egoism which are on the ontic level in which some agreement is sought to distil the essences as experienced by such a transcendental consciousness. As Being clears and withdraws from both the own and the thingness of things, both the own and the thingness cannot be essentialised into some positive extantness, whether an 'ego' or a 'thing'. What is 'own' thinking is understood as a pointer towards, an intimate comportment towards, the call of Being. The ontological difference means that the innermost own and the thingness of things is always understood through the 'not' or rather 'not yet' which lurks in the near. *Contra* transcendental phenomenology, the 'I' cannot be transcendental, to step aside from the way of Being of beings, thereby controlling it. The 'I' is rather an ontic wave in the sea of Being. Another way of saying this is that any consideration and essentialising of inauthentic 'identity' (an 'I', a 'thing') is still within the worldview of concepts and representation, at the level of beings, and as such does not connect to the nothing and to what is the innermost own.[46]

---

[46] D Carr argues that Husserl's transcendental ego, by which the empirical 'I' is bracketed in a phenomenological reduction, is a way of overcoming subjectivity. The gist of Carr's argument is

45.   Thinking is an inflection which is other in directionality to any transcendental thinking. Thinking-Being transcends the transcendental. The 'phenomenon', so to speak, is the Being of beings, the nothing. The phenomenon relates to the primordial moment of experiencing actuality rather than to the investigation of how 'things' are experienced from different angles by a transcendental ego. Thinking contemplates, momentarily arrests, Being, by clearing its withdrawal or, rather, catching it right there – after Being's being ahead of itself. Heidegger maintains that Being remains the only authentic direction and space of encounter for thought. The thinking by Being which calls for *Dasein*'s thinking is the very moment of provocation of thought. But when ontic thinking prevails, the provocation is already derivative: 'that we are still not thinking stems from the fact that the thing itself that must be thought about turns away from man, has turned away long ago.'[47]

46.   In asking 'What is called thinking?', Heidegger also asks 'What calls for thinking?'. That which is to be thought about, that which is thought-provoking, is not 'out there', possessed as an object-of-thought to be united with a subject of thought, but is calling upon thinking – *Dasein*'s innermost own involvement. The horizon of thoughts which comes towards *Dasein*'s innermost own involvement, is 'aboutness'. Such thoughts slow down, looking ever so more into the thinking *Dasein* own-time and Being. The direction of that thought is not towards positive essences but towards the mystery of the ever-changing: *Dasein* is never essentially constant, and only as being anchored in its own temporal transience is it being allowed by Being to be and, as Being calls, *Dasein* responds to the call in a way that is too late but still letting Being be.

47.   As that which is thought-provoking connects to own-thought-provoking-time, it involves waiting and readiness and, with it, attentiveness. Thinking involves 'being there' at the moment of readiness, capturing and responding to an event of Being being cleared as it

that Heidegger's criticism of transcendental phenomenology is misplaced by Heidegger as 'metaphysical' while in fact such a phenomenology was a critique of metaphysics and subjectivity: see *The Paradox of Subjectivity: The Self in the Transcendental Tradition* (Oxford, Oxford University Press, 1999). But does not the transcendental ego which overcomes metaphysics remain a metaphor? Could the metaphor of the transcendental ego be dissolved by transcendental phenomenology in a way which articulates a particular moment? If the way of dissolving the metaphor is to generate another ego then the problem to be overcome reconstitutes itself, indeed endlessly, without ever being dissolved into the everyday particularity. The endlessness of transcendental phenomenology is what may perpetuate a mode of the 'ontic' circle. The only way of dissolving the metaphor is to transcend the ego as a thing and to view the ego as the ontic involvement of *Dasein*, which remains the point of departure for ontological thinking.

[47] *WCT*, p 7.

withdraws, an event which is *Dasein*'s innermost own event as being-in-the-world:

> Whatever withdraws, refuses arrival. But – withdrawing is not nothing. Withdrawal is an event. In fact, what withdraws may even concern and claim man more essentially than anything present that strikes and touches him … in being struck by what is actual, man may be debarred precisely from what concerns and touches him – touches him in the surely mysterious way of escaping him by its withdrawal. The event of withdrawal could be what is most present in all our present, and so infinitely exceed the actuality of everything actual.[48]

48. For Heidegger, then, the 'aboutness' of thinking is not directed at generalising some universal essence, thereby distancing thought from the intimacy of the process of call and response. Generalising essence distances from that which is to be thought about in beings – the call of Being to think, the innermost own hearing, and the belated response from the not-yet own thinking-Being. It distances from the mutual appropriation that takes place between *Dasein* and Being.

49. It can be seen that the 'it' *of* aboutness is never extant, a mere communicative idea but a *flickering murmur*. The murmur gets its positive 'openings' as an 'it' that has already gone by and can be responded to only as belatedly not-yet-there. The ontological thinking of what is given to beings aims at articulating what is not being neared yet by the ontic. Thinking-Being brings something hidden to the open, that is the murmur of Being that clears while simultaneously withdrawing. Aboutness takes *Dasein* nearer to the 'event' of the murmuring Saying of Being.

50. What is the medium by which Being sends itself towards *Dasein*, concealing itself at the very instance of *Dasein*'s reflective unconcealment of it? For Heidegger, it is language. Language is the house of Being.[49] It is in language that *Dasein* is always already thrown. Being speaks language and by so doing it nears a place of dwelling for *Dasein*. The following account attempts to articulate Heidegger's Saying about language from two chapters of *On The Way to Language*: 'The Way to Language' and 'Language'.[50]

51. Being is not 'a thing' that stands beyond or outside language, but is itself the unfolding of language. Indeed, in his later writing Heidegger refrains from referring explicitly to either *Dasein* or Being, not because he necessarily abandoned thinking with them but because he

[48] *Ibid*, p 9.
[49] *LH*, p 217.
[50] 'The Way to Language' [1959], (DF Krell (trans)), in David Farrell Krell (ed), *Basic Writings: Martin Heidegger*, (London, Routledge, 1978, 1993), pp 397–426; and 'Language' [1950], in *Poetry Language, Thought*, n 12 above.

wants to speak with minimal possibility of ontic misunderstanding of his Saying, namely understanding *Dasein* and Being as beings.

52. The murmur of Being is a way along which language always already nearer the actuality of the actual than its, for the most part ontic, coherence. Language has an inherently slippery quality to it. Articulating in language is always already a late-response to, already on the way *to*, language that has already been spoken. The saying is always already concealing itself. Language has always already spoken and differed its saying. This differed saying lurks within the audible signification that responds to that saying. This way to language is the manner in which Being, and, with it, meaning, murmurs. Language thinks always ahead and calls for thinking. The hearing of this call as well as the understanding from the 'before' of this call always mismatches the thinking that is already oriented towards an audible response. The pinpointing of actuality by thinking, that 'got it', is always already not yet there. An infinitesimal way towards the nearest of the near is opened up by language. Being's thinking in language can only be expressed as an afterthought and that inevitable delay makes the saying of language inexpressible. Language as a call that shows its saying already as concealed, murmuring, puts an impossible burden on the response. This burden means that the response constantly signifies on the way *to* language. Why 'to'? Because as the saying of language is on the way, so the response must be constantly on the way *to* that saying. The response is thus on the way along which there are ceaseless attempts to impose that speaking silence on what the ontic response merely articulates within a grid that enables a 'said' to be made out. This may be referred to as the humbleness of the response that constantly lags behinds its hearing of the saying of language. *Dasein* in both hearing and responding attempts to appropriate Being in a way which commemorates the manner in which *Dasein* has already been appropriated by Being. *Dasein* as care is anxious because it can never express what it hears. It can never express the nearest of the near. Language that constantly imposes silence on itself in order to near its saying is the poetic murmur of the Saying.

53. Moments of anxiety open *Dasein* to the unfolding of the nothing as language. That the being of Being is in language but is also concealed for the most part by language tells us something very important about language. As the voice of the no-thing, language precedes the language of beings, but it can only approach this preceding moment of its saying from the ontic involvement in which it finds itself. Language is thus both ontic and ontological. Ontically, by making itself accessible and usable, language punctuates a silencing prison for itself. Only by silencing this ontic silencing can language impose

silence on itself that would enable it to respond to its fleeting saying. Being is being concealed in this prison. Within this prison, the prison of truth as correctness, language becomes dead, mere-idle chatter [*gerede*], inauthentic. In correctness as the prison of language, the house of Being remains concealed although it is never completely locked. The saying of language is nearly always already as a distorted not-yet-near-enough to the actuality of the actual. What has been shown is already on the way towards the near while response arrives – hence the murmur.

54. Very important for the arguments to come, the ontic can itself become a cycle of inauthenticity, a cycle of craving towards correctness. *Dasein* is, by and large, smothered by language in this way. Being locked in an inauthentic cycle, *Dasein* denies itself the openness to language, it denies letting *language* work to bring the truth of Being, *alēthiea*, into the language of correctness. The ontological difference is first and foremost, then, allowing for distinction between a language that shifts from one set of representations to another and language that embattles itself to say its saying.

55. But denial cannot hold Being up completely, and also *Dasein* cannot be held up completely. *Dasein*, as essentially holding up to the nothing, means letting language work out its own 'ek-sistence' and openness to the Being of beings.

56. We can see that the forgetfulness of philosophical generalisation is that it takes away any poetic involvement, any murmuring dynamics of near/far, the way of the actuality of the actual. Philosophy of correctness delegitimises the poetic working of language. It is the make-up of poetic language to lag behind the saying of language, but, unlike philosophy, the directionality of poetic language is towards the nearness of the saying. Indeed, poetic language can never rid itself completely from correctness but unlike philosophy it never sanctifies correctness-begotten cycles of reflections.

57. Only with the temporal move on the way towards the authentic murmur of language is Being awakened to inaugurate the event for the sake of which the being-in-the-world of *Dasein* is always 'ek-sistently' comported. Language is the house of Being as only in the 'whilst' of an event of language reinventing itself does Being speak and is responded to. To say the inexpressible, to make Being withdraw again, is happening in an ontological response where *Dasein* embarks on authentic talk [*rede*] moving on the way to language, allowing language to appropriate it towards the nearer, but never quite the nearest, to the showing of its Saying. Language, the word, precedes *Dasein* in that the saying of the hermeneutic cycle in which *Dasein* always already resides as being spoken, is always inexpressible. The tragic nature of humans is that what is 'theirs' is

always a mere hint from the fatefully inexpressible, a hint which is too near for a response.

58. What Heidegger calls, in *The Way to Language*, the 'Showing of the Saying' is an event [*Ereignis*] on the way of language along which it appropriates itself as the actuality of the actual – the inexpressible – touching the nothing that is given to beings. Language is always on its way, that is comported towards the inexpressible, already saying the inexpressible which calls up in a manner that opens up a world whose nearness is for most of the time far from *Dasein*. This is the special sense in which we have to grasp that Heidegger's phrase 'language speaks' [*der Sprache spricht*] (and *Dasein*'s openness to this speech by letting Being speak and responding to it) can yield authentic talk [*rede*]. Language's call, the call from Being, conveys that Being is not a 'thing', a container, a 'Being', but rather the unfolding of language in temporality. Language commits worldliness and 'thingness' into a middle, a 'between', which is preserved in what Heidegger called a *dif-ference*. The dif-ference is a moment in which language speaks the inexpressible. Dif-ference – that delay between call and response – brings thingness and the world together but also keeps them apart by not letting their meeting last. That moment of 'between' is both still but also fragile in that any utterance of it breaks it apart. Worldliness and 'thingness' meet at a moment of stillness (connoting both stillness as 'resting' and stillness in the sense of 'he is still doing this' – deferral of movement). In this stillness Being's motion is the fastest. The intimacy of worldliness and 'thingness' is unique. In calling worldliness and 'thingness' to the 'between', language speaks and in speaking it *peals* through that stillness. The stillness is a moment of motion. 'The speaking does not cease in what is spoken. Speaking is kept safe in what is spoken.'[51] Human beings' openness to Being – *Dasein*'s uniqueness – is in the ability, in anxiety, to speak towards language's speech – to hear language speaking and respond to language.

59. Heidegger, then, places human *Dasein* in the speaking of language not language in the speaking of human *Dasein*. Thinking must contemplate language simply as language and not attempt to construct a 'theory of language' or 'philosophy of language':

Still, to talk about language is presumably even worse than write about silence. We do not wish to assault language in order to force it into the grip of ideas already fixed beforehand. We do not wish to reduce the nature of language to a concept, so that this concept may provide a generally useful view of language that will lay to rest all further notions about it.[52]

[51] M Heidegger, 'Language', n 50 above, pp 187–208 (the quote is from pp 191–2).
[52] *Ibid*, p 188.

60. Language is constantly on the way to itself, tormented into saying the silent, but in saying the silent it already falls off the edge into always-belated audibility. Any metaphysics, transcendental essences, ego-based thinking, is too far from the actuality of Being and deafens *Dasein* to the saying of language. All these methodological reflections think of language that articulates beings and not as an abyss of the inexpressible near. To focus on positive beings is not yet on the way to language. A way to beings is not the way to language in which beings are melted into their Being. Being is not a thing but a temporal whilst of the abyss of the near. The saying of language is the primordial understanding of 'way' – we may now say the way of aboutness. For thinking-Being, thinking on the way to language is the only path, and only through that path can the temporality of human *Dasein* connect to its own manifestation in temporality pointing towards the Being of beings and as such towards Being itself. Being/Nothing, *Dasein*/temporality, ontic/ontological, language as the oscillation between prison-of-the-far /abyss-of-the-near, all are cycles with no beginning or beyond, as both the beginning and the beyond are themselves temporalised. Thinking which nears Being will not have even the craving of finding a common essence of a Being, or a generalised denominator, as in 'theory of Being'.

61. We should not mistake the fact that *Dasein* has the capacity to overcome idle chatter for making *Dasein* primordial to language. On the contrary, that capacity is that which makes *Dasein* unique in that it can let itself be claimed by language. Metaphysical explanations that quite often produce critical use of language by *Dasein* still see an ego which is outside language, an ego which can map the world and theorise the extantness of 'things' on this map. This critical talk is the most sophisticated concealment of the very essence of *Dasein* as a dweller in language.[53]

62. Thinking is to let *language* work, to transcend itself and by that to express that moment of emptiness which is given by the Being of beings. *Heidegger's message is that the primordial 'there is' [es gibt] is in that delay on the way, the delay which is always already not yet the saying. It is in this sense that the 'there is' is always empty.* *Dasein*'s 'ek-sistence' is to hold out to language.

63. The saying of language unfolds temporally. Human beings can experience Being's temporality in which their own past will have been in a unique moment of present insight and clearing.

64. Reason, to reason, is for Heidegger being attentive to the call of Being as expressed in the Being of beings. This call presumes

[53] *LH*, p 237.

readiness. To prepare for reason is to be open to thoughts coming towards, and stirring something in, our innermost 'thingness'.

65. What is before language then? Before language, as the speaking of the nothing, there has surely been existence but not Being. Being is born with language. The moment the inexpressible was born, Being gave its first breath.

66. A criticism of Heidegger that he provides a 'theory of Being' would, of course, be in a fairly banal sense true. However, Being is not 'some-thing' and its truth, truth-in-nothing, resides precisely in contemplating away any 'model' – including a model of Being – overcoming the craving for any generalising sense of a theory. Indeed, Being temporalises itself as language. It is better just to speak about Being rather than to construct a theory of Being – this, I believe, is Heidegger's main point. There is only a 'Saying' which unfolds Being, and this is the only sense in which it makes sense to say 'there is Being'. In the banal sense a 'theory of Being' would merely be an attempt to articulate Being by pointing towards a completely different direction and space of thinking than the way of theory. Such a 'theory of Being' would still presume thinking about Being as the constant attempt to generalise and essentialise ideas which would represent general theories. But theorising Being is not yet letting Being be. By making Being the subject of philosophy explicitly one thinks about a theory of Being. This is perhaps one of Heidegger's most significant philosophical insights – one which will be dwelt upon in this book. It is one of *the* tensions in Heidegger that, in painstakingly attempting to articulate Being, his philo-sophical reflections go beyond Being. Being is itself, rather than an object to be studied in philosophy. Thinking about Being in a gener-alising theoretical sense, a sense that Heidegger still clings to in *Being and Time*, and later, understandably, abandons, has the contradictory characteristic of distancing itself from that which is most thought-provoking, namely the Being of beings. Heidegger's thinking, although in a banal sense it says something general about thinking, does attempt to reverse the directionality of thinking thereby bringing it closer to the moment of Being's clearing and withdrawal. Indeed, as he was himself constantly on the way, his prose become more attentive and humble before language rather than embracing any theoretical pursuit.

67. Thinking-Being is, then, not something that we control, as in designing a model which is supposed to 'work', 'correspond' or have some larger coherence. Being has always some residual freedom from representation and logic, although this freedom can be brought into language whilst being immersed in imprisoning logical gymnastics. What is concealed in the saying of language is not amenable to any

logical fitness, that is to syllogisms about the relationality of one representation to another. Logic is first and foremost metaphysical and is about beings and representations. There is still a deep mystery that logic cannot fathom but which is given to all those representations from which logic draws its seemingly universal basis, as the litmus test for truth.

68. Thinking-Being involves contemplation as a result of moments of insights, a reflection on that 'how' within which Being conditions our subjectivity in the process of Being's own withdrawal. Being comes to us, poking us while always in the shadow. Thoughts come to us and are experienced in our own temporality, or as Heidegger puts it, in our own thought-provoking time. But the call of that which is thought-provoking does not give a general answer as its problem is not a general problem that needs a general answer.

69. Is thinking a polemic against the subject matter which is being thought about? For Heidegger, 'Any kind of polemics fails from the outset to assume the attitude of thinking. The opponent's role is not the thinking role'.[54] Thinking involves contemplative reflection but it does not involve an opposition. A polemic occurs only at the ontic level in that only at that level, in the process of acquiring their respective identification, can beings and concepts be conditioned and hence logically distinguished from one another to the degree that will enable opposition. Moments of actuality can be neared only as logic-ridden ontic thinking is outstripped. Both at the moment something is clearly illogical or it is clearly logical, it is, ontologically speaking, dead. One way of thinking about the 'nothing', about emptiness, about the 'It', is to think of it as that unconditional, non-punctual, continuous, which is given to the conditional. Reflection, although critical, is not tantamount to polemic opposition. The process of reflection arises alongside thinking. Familiarity and strangeness play a part in it rather than categorical opposition. Even that which is reflected upon has its mysterious 'not yet' to take it on the path of thinking. Crucially, the reasons for seeing something ontically is already a part of the ontological path – the unsaid lurking beneath it. The process of near and far, then, does not involve a polemic. Criticism cannot be attentive to this subtle process of near/far. Reflection arises alongside a process of clearing of Being as it takes place. Thinking does not involve an attempt to oppose but being continuously open to Being, maintaining the effort of letting the Being of beings be, rather than arresting them as beings. As the space of this openness is temporal, thinking is wondering by contemplating Being back so that, in a flash of clearing, the 'aboutness' of

[54] WCT, p 13.

what is thought about is being made strange – strangeness which generates a reflection is taking place. This is why I use the adverb 'reflectively' rather than 'critically'. Thinking is not a polemic but results in clearing something about a subject in a way which facilitates a reflection. Reflective thinking is not some pseudo-critical process within the 'same', something which will be familiar from *Being and Time* as 'making present' or from *The Basic Problems of Phenomenology* as 'inauthentic retaining'.[55]

> In contrast to a steady progress, where we move unawares from one thing to the next and everything remains alike, the leap takes us abruptly to where everything is different, so different that it strikes us as strange ... Though we may not founder in such a leap, what the leap takes us to will confound us.[56]
> ...we can learn thinking only if we radically unlearn what thinking has been traditionally. To do that, we must at the same time come to know it.[57]

70. The distinction between essences that are aspired to by the methodology of transcendental phenomenology and the repetition of the hermeneutic cycle of *Dasein* should be borne in mind. The notion of transcendental essence relates to something unconditional which expresses itself in any mode of existence of beings. Both Husserl and Heidegger try to respond to the problem of the prejudicial perspectives from which things are experienced by the ego. Husserl's reductive method strives to purify the prejudices that characterise positive sciences in order to arrive at a pure *eidetic* essence of things, as would be experienced by consciousness, a pure transcendental ego. What Husserl refers to as *intentionality* is the direct comportment of the experiencing of the impure ego towards the experiences of the transcendental ego. To transcend, for Husserl, is to approximate the transcendental positive essence of beings. Heidegger's response to the problem of prejudices is to stop seeing them as 'prejudices' (a word that assumes truth as correctness) but rather as ontic utterances which indicate something. His approach is to constantly listen to that saying indicated by these so-called prejudices. Heidegger's approach is to work with and from the prejudicial perspective of things towards that concealed 'thingness' that is given to them. Intentionality for Heidegger was not towards transcendental consciousness but towards a place that is always too near for consciousness. Thus, consciousness and *a fortiori* transcendental consciousness become for him *the* prejudice to overcome. *Dasein* 'ek-sistence' means that its innermost own indicates that it is nearer

55 *BPP*, p 287.
56 *WCT*, p 12.
57 *Ibid*, p 8.

than its consciousness. *Dasein* is intentional only because it is essentially temporal and thus nearer than any self-interpretation of its consciousness which merely 'persists in time'.[58] For Heidegger, both the sanctification of positive sciences and the constructivism of the transcendental ego take thinking away from the way *Dasein* can be involved in that world which unfolds as *its* world and *its* encounter with the Being of beings. Whereas both positive sciences and transcendental phenomenology crave for the establishment of a correct view of the world by investigating beings, Heidegger abandons any notion of purity and makes the process of revealing and concealing that which radicalises, both the notion of things, world and consciousness. For Heidegger, it is transcendental phenomenology's attempt to generalise essences which gets stuck in endless possibilities, thereby gradually distancing itself from that which is nearest and thought-provoking. Although transcendental phenomenology yearns to open up to the direct experiences by consciousness, by focusing on 'consciousness' and maintaining the belief in the extantness of things, it belies its very purpose. For Heidegger's insight is that in order to account for what makes experience possible, anxious encounters with the not-yet nearness of beings have to be comported to as their Being. For Heidegger the 'I' is a necessary point of departure for hermeneutic phenomenological reflection. *Qua* point of departure, the 'I' is furthest from what is its innermost own. There is no potential ego which philosophy must find the language to articulate. Intentionality for Heidegger is possible only on the basis of transcendence of beings into their Being.[59] Husserl strives towards thin and empty universal linguistic agreements – a transcendental standing point. Heidegger strives towards that 'nothing' which is given by language to beings but yet is also being distorted by language for the most part. Husserl tries to maintain the subject and object of thought by making both of them transcendental. Heidegger tries to show that attentiveness to Being overcomes both objectivity and subjectivity in a moment of nearness. *Heideggerian reflection not only thinks differently about beings so as to approximate some essence of theirs. Rather, to reflect is to think differently about thinking about beings. Heidegger, in his response to Husserl, thinks thinking.*

71. Although I shall comment on this more extensively in chapter four, 'essence' for Heidegger means not the essence of a being but the essential unfolding of the Being in beings, the essence of unconcealing the Being of beings. A moment of transcending distinctions is

[58] *BP*, p 268.
[59] *ER*, p 30.

essential both in worldliness and in this moment's irreplaceable particularity:

> To embrace a 'thing' or a 'person' in its essence means to love it, to favor it. Thought in a more original way such favoring [*mögen*] means to bestow essence as a gift. Such favoring is the proper essence of enabling, which not only can achieve this or that but also can let something essentially unfold in its provenance, that is, let it be. It is on the 'strength' of such enabling by favoring that something is properly able to be.[60]

72.   Thinking, though not polemical, is never one-sided. Heidegger reflects upon one-sidedness in the summary of his third lecture of the series 'What is Called Thinking?'.[61] Here Heidegger talks about science. Science is always located in history and may, being within a period, explore great many opinions, but it will not ask itself scientifically 'what history is'.

> By way of history, a man will never find out what history is; no more that a mathematician can show by way of mathematics – by means of his science, that is, and ultimately by mathematical formulae – what mathematics is. The essence of their sphere – history, art, poetry, language, nature, man, God – remains inaccessible to the sciences.[62]

Science does not think, but science merely *has views*. But this, Heidegger warns, does not amount to the arrogance of giving the impression that thinking is superior to science because thinking 'always knows essentially less than the sciences precisely as it operates where it could think the essence of history, art, nature, language – and yet is still not capable of it'. Sciences are fields of knowledge. But thinking is not knowledge, not even the craving for knowledge, because thinking is on the other side of knowledge. But the other side of knowledge is not something like an inaccessible room. This is why '... the other-side nonetheless always appears as well. The sciences' one-sidedness retains its own many-sidedness.'[63] What creates the 'oneness' of the side, as it were, is a process of concealment and levelling down. Here comes the passage that explains why one-sidedness is itself essential and is not a polemic. This is very important for the distinctions I will be pursuing in chapters three and four and therefore it is quoted in full:

---

[60] *LH*, p 220
[61] *WCT.* pp 32–4.
[62] *Ibid*, pp 32–3.
[63] *Ibid*.

We should fall victim to a disastrous self-deception if we were to take the view that a haughty contempt is all that is needed to let us escape from the imperceptible power of the uniformly one-sided view. On the contrary, the point is to discern what weird, unearthly things are here in the making. The one-sided view, which nowhere pays attention any longer to the essence of things, has puffed itself up into an all-sidedness which in turn is masked so as to look harmless and natural. But this all-sided view which deals in all and everything with equal uniformity and mindlessness, is only a preparation for what is really going on. For it is only on the plane of the one-sided uniform view that one-track thinking takes its start. It reduces everything to a univocity of concepts and specifications the precision of which not only corresponds to, but has the same essential origin as, the precision of technological process.[64]

73. Let me end this brief account of Heidegger's saying by reflecting upon the issue of critical theory and reflection. Heidegger account of thinking takes us away from the idea of a critical 'theory' because he twists the way 'ignorance' is to be understood. Ignorance is no longer the 'not yet known' that generates a response to the evident inadequacy of whichever cathedral of concepts have been previously erected. Ignorance is not the 'hole in knowledge'so as to prompt replacement/modification of one theory by another. The re-emergence of the question of Being means overcoming the call for merely a renewed opening for generalising theories.

74. Ignorance has more of the character of that inexpressible nearness and therefore of that which can never be known. The 'about' which is awakened shakes the very notion of truth upon which the axis of knowledge/ignorance lies. Ignorance as a gap in knowledge responds only to 'thinking about' the object of an idea that the truth of correctness perpetuates. As such the aboutness which is involved in it does not yet involve thinking about primordial 'aboutness'.

75. By carrying out this destabilisation of correctness and exposing a more primordial truth which is given to it, Heidegger in effect argues that the instant of correctness/ignorance is already too far from that moment that actuality calls for thinking. The process of ontic-ontology, the never-ending hide-and-seek relationship between beings and their Being as reflected in the relationship between *Dasein* and Being, necessitates a different way of being-in-language than the language of theory including the critical theory in which correctness is constantly revived through the negation of ignorance. It is that craving for the filling up of ignorance that supplies the never-ending cycle of conceptual punctuation. This cycle perpetuates the forgetfulness of the question of Being.

[64] *Ibid*, p 34.

76. *It is the filling up of ignorance with an ever-existing account of correctness, as if this account forms and informs the dynamics of critical reason, which is the characteristic of primordial ignorance.* As a reminder, Heidegger 'thinks thinking' and this is not mere intellectualisation. Thinking itself changes as it thinks. The fact that the expression ' to think thinking' is seen as a mere intellectualisation is exactly the symptom of why the 'nothing' cannot be properly understood in the metaphysical philosophical tradition.

77. Is theory in general undertaken only after facing *ignorance* coupled with an attempt at a fresh generalisation?[65] It is important to reflect upon it as Being's withdrawal is, as Heidegger says, not nothing. It is an event.[66] The word 'ignorance' is conventionally used in the sense of either 'not being well versed in a given area of information/ knowledge' or in the sense of 'a lack of knowledge because of not yet having a given experience'. But in the context of attending to that which cannot ever be known, ignorance can also be interpreted as having a negative connotation, namely some opaqueness which causes one to 'ignore' something, not to interact with something, and not to face up, but to cover up. Also, ignoring one's lack of knowledge can mean more than not having knowledge in the light of limited experience. It can be taken also to mean not listening attentively to what is more, even most, primordial, but inexpressible in one's experience. In this latter sense ignorance connotes a failure to listen to what calls for thinking, not just for an apparent gap or deficiency in knowledge.

78. 'Ignorance' is used to describe the realisation that certain ideas and the concepts that express them, as well as the theoretical generalisations and models that such concepts are assembled to, do not correspond any more to, as well as not being able to account for, various human experiences, as well as not-yet-known human experiences. But can any generalisation account for that which is actual in human experience? In this sense, then, ignorance means that theory runs out of words and meanings to account for a given experience. But despite running out of words it does not run out of the craving for the words which would 'map' and represent the new object-experience correctly. The notions of 'critical theory' and 'philosophy of language' are trapped in the ontic cycle of correctness. Notions like these never let language, and Being, speak. The very ongoing reflection in terms of facing ignorance with regard to a theory about how the world is, about the failure of a given generalisation, itself

---

[65] For a good discussion of the role of ignorance, see A Halpin, *Reasoning with Law* (Oxford, Hart Publishing, 2001), ch 1, especially pp 14–17.
[66] WCT, pp 8–9.

perpetuates ignorance, and in this sense is bound to be one-sided in the same manner that sciences are. Moving from one generalisation to another ignores what is most thought-provoking in subjectivity's own thinking time.

79. Thinking can be understood differently than facing the 'need to generalise in different ideas and concepts'. Such thinking involves an approach to experience that faces the inexpressible in that experience without conjecturing from this encounter the need for a theory. It is such thinking that grasps the actual without resorting to theory. Never does the dynamics of theory–ignorance–theory confront what is both real and too near. *The moment of thinking, and there are these moments which science does face, is not a theoretical moment but a poetic one – a moment of overcoming thinking which is imprisoned in ontic ignorance. As long as the prediction of science is made to either fit or not, science does not yet think.* Note again that Heidegger was not against, that is polemical, about science. The capacity to near the poetic 'there' which wrinkles the coordinates of knowledge/ignorance lurks within the ontic cycle of critical scientific thinking. To recap, there is no ontological without the ontic. The dynamics of theory–ignorance–theory does not grasp what it is to think. Such dynamics cannot listen to that which calls for thinking. Thinking is resisting the perpetuation of the forgetfulness involved in the need to generalise afresh. It is in facing up, in responding to the call rather than ignoring it, in making the effort which overcomes another construction of theory, that the sceptical position that belongs to the theory/ignorance dynamics can be overcome. Thinking does not ignore what is nearest. Thinking is not based on ignorance but confronts the opaqueness of the intimacy between what is thought-provoking and the subject's own thought-provoking time. Thinking is grasping and confronting what is ignored in the thinking time of the subject who sanctifies continually theorising within the dynamics of theory–ignorance–theory. Thinking is making the ignorance embedded in the sanctification of theory into an issue for thinking. Far from being ignorant, thinking, being attentive, connects and faces up that presence of the inexpressible in the way expression is for most of the time.

80. Reflection does assume imperfection of human experience. But, unlike using that imperfection to enshrine the need for theory which fills in the ignorance with representation, authentic thinking unconceals the murmur of Being that lies in the shadow, which can be easily mistaken for some hole in the 'map' of the world. The world, nature, is not a thing that precedes knowledge and is simply to be discovered by the dynamics of ignorance/theory.

81. Ignorance has already been primordially manifested in a way which

necessitates a different response from a response which is already conditioned, either negatively or positively by the craving for theory. Not to ignore this primordial manifestation requires different thinking. Such thinking would not imply maps and methodologies. To think, to be attentive to that call which comes from what is nearest, from what is constantly concealed in one's experience, is a very different process from facing the limitation of generalisation with the view of replacing it with another generalisation. Thinking makes the effort to overcome ignorance embedded in the dynamics of ignorance/theory. It is in the moment of ignorance that Man can grasp his being the shepherd, or guardian, of Being, thereby understanding that he does not speak Being but is spoken by it. If there is a role for ignorance it is not in just *being ignorant* but in *facing ignorance*.

82. But we must emphasis that facing ignorance merely as the craving for further theory is not yet facing it anxiously. To crave for theory is the ontic way of covering up this anxiety, not listening to the call that this anxiety generates. The gap of knowledge is not the same as the abyss of nearness that characterises anxiety.

83. What is unveiled in a non-conceptual and pre-ontological way in the ontic is not the same as theory-based ignorance. The inexpressible that is being brought into language is itself a moment of particularity which reveals an 'it' or a 'such'. *The inexpressible is not a mere postponement of conceptualisation.* The inexpressible is not like parts of the map which are 'missing', but rather the non-conceptualisable background to any conceptual map as that which can be unveiled only in a particular saying of language. The perpetuation of metaphysical thinking expressed as an ignorance/knowledge axis never nears the actuality of the actual, however refined and nuanced the concepts such metaphysics generates. Metaphysics takes thinking away from any explanation of *Dasein*'s actual involvement of nearing.

3

What is Called Thinking Reflectively about Law?

> To reside in what is readily available is intrinsically not to let the concealing of what is concealed hold sway. Certainly, among readily familiar things there are also some that are puzzling, unexplained, undecided, questionable. But these self-certain questions are merely transitional, intermediate points in our movement within the readily familiar and thus not essential.
>
> Heidegger, *On the Essence of Truth*, pp 131–2.

> Even if we ask this question [what is a thing?], we shall not overnight become better botanists, zoologists, historians, Jurists or physicians. But perhaps better or more cautiously put – certainly different teachers, different physicians and judges, although even then we can start to do nothing with this question in our professions.
>
> Heidegger, *What is a Thing?*, p 10.

1. Law is being pervasively practised. It governs all areas of life, even those that *it* decides shall be beyond its reach. But is law understood? What is it about law which is to be understood?

2. Is the inquiry into what makes up the sense according to which legal obligation is true or false, legally valid or invalid, justified or unjustified, that which is to be understood about law? Does that which is to be understood about law involve the articulation of law's *purpose*? Does thinking about law involve asking whether law is unique in such a way that it cannot be just a species of activity that is essentially other to it – politics, morality or psychoanalysis? Does the proper inquiry to be pursued in order to understand law ponder the possibility and plausibility of proper differentiation of legal phenomena from all other social phenomena? More subtly, is separation of law, morality and politics compatible with law nevertheless being a unique aspect of morality and politics? If law is such a unique aspect of morality and politics, could we nevertheless conceive a justification for thinking about it as separate from morality and politics? These are all very interesting inquiries, ones that have led to rich debates among lawyers and jurists. Responses to these questions can have a profound impact on the practice of law.

3.   Yet, what is the original sense that makes possible the conception of law as a practice? What is a practice?

4.   Even from this initial reflection it can be sensed that there are many questions to be asked about law. It is such multiplicity which makes law such an interesting and inherently contestable social phenomenon. But have not such inquiries, in different ways perhaps, assumed an 'already' which is more primordial, an 'already' which will take us to the nature of thinking as such, to the nature of language as such, to the nature of Man as such, to the nature of truth? Have we even come close to primordial engagement with the first question, namely what is it about law which is to be understood and thought about? Could it be that in asking all those interesting questions about law and, *a fortiori*, in sensibly responding to any of them, we have already got very far away from that which has to be thought about in law? Despite all such interesting inquiries, has a question about law been asked yet? Does not the viability of such a question depend on some sense of who does the asking? How does the question about the person who asks relate to the question of what it is to ask a question? If it does so depend, asking what does it mean to think about law entails a transformation not only of that which is thought about, law, but also of the understanding of the nature of inquiry and inquirer. To put it another way, the 'howness' in the world of an inquirer would determine the nature of questioning and with it what the inquirer sees as a viable inquiry.

5.   So, in order to ask a question about law, we need to reflect upon asking questions. What is a question? What is the moment when a question occurs? From where do we get the *confidence* that a genuine question is being asked? What is the origin of our feeling that in asking a question about law we in fact, already deep inside, do not expect an answer?

6.   Has the very thinking about law been made into a problem yet? To explain law in a way which make common sense, or to criticise it as anarchists do, does not necessarily make thinking about law a problem.

7.   It may well be that the *Seinfrage* of law – the question of the Being of law – has not yet been asked. In this chapter I am raising the difficulty of what 'a question about' might mean with implication to the difficulty of asking a question about law. A part of such undertaking is to articulate what a question about law does *not* mean. The first question is conceived as the question about Being – *Seinfrage*. In asking *about* law, then, a first question is the question concerning the Being of law.

8.   What is being pursued here is a meditation upon the question of what it means to think reflectively about law. This meditation consti-

tutes an exploration and delineation of a sense of 'aboutness' which characterises thinking *about* law. With the delineation of this sense of 'aboutness', I argue that a primordial contemplation and reflection can be generated about law, a contemplation which is not reducible to, and has ontological priority over, other ways in which law is being thought about or theorised upon.

9. The main challenge here is to point towards the uniqueness of ontological 'aboutness' in the case of law and to its connection to the 'aboutness' of truth, language and ethics. There are many difficulties in magnifying the 'isness' of law, as in stating 'there *is* law' and alluding to the depth of this statement. The first difficulty is that the perspective from which the articulation of 'aboutness' occurs requires us to go deeper and nearer than the average *everyday* sense of the lawyer, or the jurist, or people more generally. Having said that, the everydayness of law is always the starting point for ontological thinking. The difficulty is that transcending the average everyday sense of law may well alienate those people who participate in the average everydayness of the law. Such everydayness, being a yardstick for the plausibility of their thinking about law, including the defence of a theory of law, may well hinder such very thinking. The understanding of 'people of the law', those who quite often 'just get on with the law' and who are involved with and through law on a daily basis, however critically, precisely by already knowing what they do, cannot yet engage with the question of the Being of law.

10. And yet, it is this average everydayness and its *potential* for resisting a grand theory of law which comes to explain their practice for them, which is extremely important for our investigation, in fact constitutes a gate for asking a question about the Being of law. For without magnification of that which average everydayness distorts, whether with or without theory of law, there is no way of nearing the actuality of the actual in law.

11. Even those who engage in critical legal scholarship, those, for example, who expose the ideological dependency or some other contingency of a specific content of the law may not yet give us a clue as to that 'aboutness' that we are after. Yet, again, it is their work which is vital to shed light on the 'aboutness' of the thinking about law.

12. We need to overcome the mundane everydayness of law in order to let the Being of law be thought about. However, it is the depth of everydayness that constitutes the world for original 'aboutness'. The most difficult thing to do is to let in the nearest call as that aboutness which is thought-provoking. The manner in which the nearest is distorted by all those who participate in the mundane everydayness of law, however critically, is perhaps not yet attentive to 'aboutness'.

The sense of *aboutness* that I would like to articulate comes about after a call for *Dasein* who is involved with the law to attend to, and to look at, the mirror. The call comes from any legal involvement – even a lawyer who cross-examines a witness. The call to mirror comes from nearing the 'it' of any lawyer's activity. It comes from the always nearer 'it' of theories of law and those who theorise law, including the most critical legal theorists. That which is most thought-provoking in law calls from nearer to the 'it' of those who seek the protection of the law. What is to be thought about in law would be nearer than all those involvements with the law of theorists and actual day-to-day actors.

13.   To think reflectively about law requires us to attend to the Being of law. What is understood today by the 'law' and 'legal' embodies in it the Being of law while at the same time distorting that Being. To see law for what it is, odd as it may seem, requires us to work from a different kind of 'within', a 'within' which needs to be nearer to the mundane involvements. This 'within' is otherwise than being with and through law in mundane everydayness. If law is being thought about, then, if the everydayness of law is dwelled upon, then the prevailing everyday and mundane 'legal' is bound to reveal some primordial strangeness, even incomprehensibility.

14.   The hiding of law's Being may be mistaken for a deliberate obscurity that hides a 'nothing to say'. Such a predicted reaction by common sense theoreticians of law would hardly be surprising, but would be revealing all the same. It is this seemingly 'nothing to say' which conceals the saying we are after.

15.   The claim that the Being of law is distorted by any theorising of law may lose potential audiences with the effect that the claim would make no imprint on their reflections. Alternatively, such a claim may be seen as involving a contradiction, as it seems both to preserve something about law whilst at the same time overcoming something else. Estranged audiences, if still willing to listen, may simply not see anything new in such a claim, thereby refusing to open up to a glimmer of a new field of inquiry. Although some estrangement is inevitable, perhaps even necessary, if such estrangement is to lead to reflection, to a moment of a genuine being at one with the Being of law, it must not be total. The need is to show something about law that is still *intimately* familiar, despite being somewhat alienated from the 'how' of the mundane. Moreover, it is precisely in grasping that there is no 'new' beginning offered here, but rather an encounter with, and reflecting upon, being with and through law, that the uniqueness of the argument can become more visible. The challenge here is to generate a conviction on the part of the reader that thinking about law in the sense to be departed from already harbours

some 'aboutness' which comes from nearness of the actuality of law. The reader will grasp that from firm reticence to the opening to legal theory, as embedded in a deeper resistance to the temptation of traditional philosophical reflection, some listening is already being carried out, transforming nothing into a murmur. With such resistance there comes some vision that, with legal theory, effort has already been given up in the most sophisticated of fashions. In a sense the urge 'to just get on with the law' is more open to the nearness of actuality that it may well distort than any grand justification of this 'getting on' through theorising law.

16. *There is no generic connection between making justificatory statements while getting on with the law and an explicit or implicit theorisation of it. Understanding that would set us on the way to unconceal the 'aboutness' forgotten by theory.*

17. To many legal philosophers the predicament of 'aboutness' that I try to open up here would not seem special as, after all, they would see themselves as engaging in thinking about law. However, despite the flourishing arena of thinking about law, in jurisprudence, in political and social theory, in critical legal scholarship, I would still argue that the 'aboutness' that conditions all these various ways of thinking about law takes thinking away from that which is most thought-provoking about law.

18. The Being of law does not connote correspondence between an 'idea of law' and a 'thing'" that is law. Similarly, the Being of law is not a thing. The Being of law is the unfolding of the essence of law. As such unfolding, law is itself rather than any theory of it. Being and thinking with law, which indeed is made possible by the 'thingness' of law, is temporal and, as such, historical. Any projection for the future requires us to go *back*, to think back. We need to think back to the origin of law. Origin here does not mean chronological beginnings – the first time there was law. By origin I mean the primordial saying of law which is before all other sayings and which lurks in all such sayings, not as a common denominator between them but as the actuality of the actual of them all.

19. It is always the grasping of some sameness that pushes reflection further and enables us to look further. But such sameness seems to be hard to come by with thinking about law, which is, after all, a complex phenomenon. Any look at a book on jurisprudence would reveal the wealth of different frameworks within which law is being theorised: constitutional, liberal, Marxist, sociological jurisprudence, regulatory and risk frameworks, critical legal scholarship, psychoanalysis, critical race theory, and it goes on. At least initially, it seems that there are distinct frameworks to theorise law. It seems that in each framework there are many competing theories. For example,

natural law versus legal positivism seems to belong to the constitutional framework of theorising. But what constitutes a framework is,
of course, interpretative and contestable. An initial description that
distinguishes frameworks for theorising is often shown to be
misleading and simplistic. Frameworks of theorising do overlap and
the boundaries between them are constantly hotly renegotiated. Even
the difference between two takes on a framework, for example a
Marxist and a liberal take on the constitutional framework, can be
contested and cannot be simply essentialised. It is possible, though, at
any given time, to list various tenuous conclusions about each
framework as a verification of 'the framework' and, further, to claim
that this list represents some 'reality of law' which is somehow
beyond interpretation. But, of course, this freezing of interpretation
is suspect, potentially reactionary, and can hardly be convincing.
Critical theorisation of law – where its complexity as a social
phenomenon really comes to the fore – lies in this contestability of
the very self-description and exclusivity of frameworks within which
law is being theorised. The ability to surprise with a new connection
that destabilises the uncritically accepted way in which a framework
self-interprets (always in relation to other frameworks) is the
hallmark of critical scholarship.

20. Is there any room, then, to call for sameness in all theorisation about
law including that of critical theory? Further, would not such a call
for sameness smack of a reactionary tendency? This book sets out to
explore this question.

21. Can we see some sameness in all of this complexity? How would
such sameness be accounted for, given the variety of frameworks in
which law is being theorised? It is the very nature of the never-ending
complexity which is part of the game of stakes involved in
thinking-Being. A certain view of complexity may itself reduce a
further complexity in which it plays an important part. We must ask:
is this picture of complexity and interpretation we have just outlined
an adequate characterisation of complexity? Does the complexity of
the phenomenon come from the multiplicity of frameworks, the
existence of which conditions and constrains various interpreters?
Does primordial complexity come from ongoing contestations of the
boundary between theoretical frameworks? I will claim in this book
that the complexity of law has not yet been touched upon by both
the multiplicity and contestability of frameworks within which law is
being theorised. Yet, I would claim that I am not simply offering
another theoretical framework as the very issue of theory becomes an
issue in my exploration of the 'aboutness' of 'thinking about law'. It
is in making theory itself an issue that I claim that the 'aboutness' of
'thinking about law' has not yet been attended to. There is arguably

something that is hidden in the very thinking with frameworks and methodologies, which is not affected even by critical contestations of self-interpretation of theoretical frameworks. This something concerns the very essence of interpretation, subjectivity, language, truth. Can, then, the very multiplicity of frameworks within which law is being theorised become possible only within an already interpretative activity which is itself conditioned by a certain way of being and thinking? Might we need to grasp something about all of these frameworks and methodologies, thereby interpreting our natures as interpreters, which will then, and only then, allow us to make some distinctions that concern all of these frameworks, thereby opening up a world for more primordial complexity in thinking about law? Might not a world that has been there all along open up? Can this picture of the multiplicity of overlapping frameworks be merely a little window towards a different complexity, a complexity that indicates a site nearer to the actuality of law? Is there not one-sidedness persisting that involves the very kind of thinking through methodologies and multiplicity of frameworks, however critically? Could there be some common matrix (rather than denominator) that puts all theoretical frameworks on the same interpretative horizon – a common matrix that relates to the way Man, language, history and truth are? Might it not be that the exposition of a historicity of language would point us towards ontological reflection that would in turn grasp law in its Being?

22. To argue that some one-sidedness, some sameness, which makes frameworks that theorise law possible might be well be unattended to within these frameworks is not to argue for a yet more abstract positive transcendental essence of some thing. Nor is it just to construct yet another framework on the same horizon of truth. These frameworks are themselves manifestations of a philosophical tradition within the historicity, or temporality of Being – historicity towards which humans and their laws are but silenced pointers. Methodologies and theoretical generalisations/constructions about law would already be too far for glimpsing at that nearest 'aboutness' regarding law. Yet, it is this distance that hints at that which is nearest. The Being of beings, the Being of law lurks in its ontic determinations. The near lurks in the far and for-the-most-part near. In all of these frameworks, then, this nearness is hinted at in a different manner but we can set forth to grasp that being and thinking which is concealed in all the frameworks.

23. The epochal nature of the understanding of law reflects the epochal way in which human beings understand themselves as thinking beings. The mystery of the Being of law necessitates humans to describe their experiences in law in a certain way, theory, method-

ology. The very situation that humans look for to methodology for the thinking about law is part of the historicity which conditions them. Part of the human condition is not merely lack of experience and hence having gaps in knowledge, but is rather the essential falling into the distortion involved in thinking-Being.

24. What is it, then, to think reflectively about law? To think about law is to think about the prevalent notion of 'aboutness' in which the current multiplicity of ways of theorising law is captive. For that, the way to language, truth, Man, ethics has to be visited. So thinking about law must not look like another theory of law, but yet it is about such a theory. Further, and crucially, if thinking has to make sense to those participate in law, it does so to them at their own innermost being 'there', as *Daseins*, in their own moment of Being in the world.

25. Every questioning is itself shaped, and preceded by, thinking. Perhaps thinking itself is preceded by an encounter with some actuality which makes for the provocation of thought. But then, thinking must already be ready for the encounter with actuality, and hence thought has already been sparked before the encounter. Thinking comes to *Dasein* from a 'before'. There has been thinking that precedes the *Dasein* who thinks thinking. It is that thinking which makes for thought-provoking. What is that thinking about law that makes it thought-provoking to a *Dasein* who thinks thinking? What is it, which is *ours*, that shapes the encounter between law and our thinking? Could thus viewing the matter, namely that there is no thinking about law without thinking about our own thinking, reveal a distinct approach to thinking about law? Heidegger's approach to thinking generates a distinct way of understanding thinking about law.

26. In exploring how the Being of law thinks, unfolds and in turn calls for thinking about our thinking of the 'aboutness' with which we think about law, it is necessary to explain its departure from, though not abandonment of, other ways which purport to think about law. The question of what is called thinking reflectively about law must interact with at least two other questions. 'What is it to think *reflectively* about law?' seems to be different from the question of 'What is it to think about law?'. This last question depends on another question 'What is thinking about?'. The difference between the first two questions involves the use of the word 'reflectively'. Does thinking *reflectively* about law imply more than just thinking about law? What is the distinction between 'thinking about' and 'thinking reflectively about'? Does the reflection add something to the 'about' or does the 'about' already contain the reflection? If the former, is ethics implied in 'reflection about'? Should not then our question be:

'What does it mean to think *ethically* about law?'. Would this ethics connect 'reflection' and 'evaluation' of law? If so, does such an ethical reflection anticipate either a value-based justification of law or indeed a polemic against law? Would, then, ethics mean an evaluation of the purpose of law in relation to some other, more ulterior, ethical purpose which law effectuates and enforces? *If there was some ethical dimension to the reflection about law, what would that kind of ethics be? Would this ethics have to relate to the purpose of law? If so, how is the issue of purpose to be understood in a most original sense as far as law is concerned?*

27. We have already visited the connection between the second and third question, between thinking about law and the act of thinking, which also relates to the meaning of 'aboutness'. Let me reiterate it. Does the 'aboutness' in thinking about law involve an exploration of an idea of what is law, that is treating law as a thing which has some kind of essence expressible as its idea? We have just contemplated that perhaps the multiplicity of frameworks and methodologies speaks against such an essence. But can we not detect some univocity of the understanding of 'about' in all of those frameworks – univocity which makes *Dasein* forgets a primordial 'about' regardless of any future theorisation and contestation? Does not the very thinking which strives to methodology, even critical methodology, entrench inauthentic thinking? *Thinking about law and its relatedness to thinking in general may relate to the most sophisticated way in which this univocity is being concealed in all those frameworks and methodologies that theorise law.*

28. My point is that the amalgamations, the distinction, and self-contestation of frameworks in relation to one another may still occur on the level of ontic thinking. Ontic thinking exercises hegemony on the 'aboutness' of 'thinking about law'. I am not against thinking of law as 'the thing in this or that framework'; all I argue is that all of these frameworks in their different ways may still adopt metaphysical thinking and that the ethics of humanism and subjectivity still prevails in them over thinking the Being of law. This is the case however radically subjectivity is thought about in those theories. Having said that, this ontic hegemony may itself be part of the historicity of thinking the Being of law. Thinking *Dasein* is in the world only when the familiar is first learned before defamiliarising it.

29. The characterisation of 'aboutness' creates a continuum between the question and the sub-questions raised above, concerning 'thinking about', 'thinking about law', and 'thinking reflectively about law'. This continuum concerns a unique sense in which aboutness is to be captured, which in turn would mean a unique sense in which thinking reflectively about law can hint at us.

30. Could it be, then, that what is most thought-provoking about law is that, despite thinking that is done, with and through it, even allegedly *about* it through various critical 'theories of law', we are still not thinking about law? Does our thinking have a blind spot, *our* own innermost blind spot, because of which what always remains to be thought about law, because it is so elemental and before all else, remains hidden?

31. Those theories which describe themselves as *critical* because they 'connect' to society, expose the hidden generalised dominant and oppressive ideological premises that given social relationships nourish, exposing also their contradictions in more concrete situations. From the perspective of these theories, any ideal purpose of law is shown to be either too abstract so as not allowing social criticism, or, if such an ideal does produce a critical purpose, this purpose is no longer abstract enough but rather ideology-dependent, an ideology that the critical method is set to expose. These theories sometimes expose domination within the current body of law by resorting to the psychoanalytical and then translate their insights into legal language. In both ideal-based and critical theories, doctrinal and theoretical levels are connected. These theories think *about* law by still ontically thinking with and through it as the *thing* it is. They either explicitly generalise features of that 'thing' called law or criticise the specific content of the doctrines that this 'thing' encapsulates. Being critical, such theories indeed get their impetus by translating insights from that which is seemingly other to law (for example, psychoanalysis, economics) into the language of this 'thing' called law. Even when critical theories come to deconstruct the content of the law, even to the extent of attempting to see the functions of law as symbolic rather than merely instrumental and definitional, they still resort back to ontic methodology, language and conceptions of truth that embody metaphysics and subjectivity. Despite the deconstruction and symbolic displacement, and with it destabilisation and de-grounding of certain relations that make up the representation of a given legal doctrine, something is not being deconstructed, not yet. Even the most critical of theories deconstruct a given ontic content of law but they do not deconstruct the distortion that prevails between the Being of law and its ontic determinations. These critical theories do not yet think about the Being of law hidden in their critical accounts whose concealment is perpetuated by those very accounts. These theories, then, may perpetuate ontic thinking and hence forget the question of the Being of law. They may not, as yet, open up the ontic to the ontological, thereby trying to overcome the ontic being and thinking for-the-most-part with and through law.

32. So, we must still ask, do these critical theories, despite thinking critically about law, attend to what is most thought-provoking about law in the subject's own thinking time? Despite all those levels of thinking ontically about law it seems that we have not even started to think reflectively about law. We may even ask: does the concealment not become more and more sophisticated the more *critical* the theory becomes? Is critical theory of law a step in the direction of being attentive to the call of what there is to think about in law or does it constitute the most sophisticated velvety hush of this call by having the appearance of being critical? Do not critical theories of law, despite having all the resonance of true thinking, look away from reflective thought about law?

33. At this point surely confusion ensues. How can the Being of law – its 'it' and 'there' – be thought about not as a thing – law? We must contemplate this confusion and its signification for thinking about law.

34. In approaching the question of what it means to think reflectively about law there are two distinct, though not unrelated, ways of thinking about law. One is to think about law as a thing – as a being. There is an 'about' here which is ontic. A perpetuation of such ontic thinking keeps avoiding clearing the way to the Being of law. The perpetuation ensures the forgetfulness of the Being of law by not enabling an event from law's Being to clear in any particular ontic instantiation of law. Another way of thinking about law does also have 'aboutness' but this 'aboutness' involves constant encounter with the Being of law. This way nears the Being of law, trying to bring the 'it' of law into language without it ever becoming conceptualised idle chatter. We then must allow language to speak the Being of law, thereby concealing its 'it' as words hints at its nearness. This way does not attempt to articulate a theory, or a philosophy, of law, certainly not making philosophy 'legal'. This way rather attempts to see all such theories or philosophies as being a necessary part of the ontological reflection about the Being of law.

35. Thinking the 'thingness' of law is not yet captured by thinking the thing-law. Any thinking about the identity of law, any framework within which law is 'seen as ...' should only open up the gate for us, the gate to the temporality of thinking law's Being. Indeed, encountering what is hidden in all the theoretical frameworks, never a being, will lead us to the clearing to which the Being of law has already withdrawn. Thinking of law as a thing should merely prepare us to go back to the moment of clearing in which the Being of law has already withdrawn, determining the future of ontic thinking with and through law. In thinking about law we should not just generalise from legal practice in order to justifying a framework of that

present-at-hand 'thing' called law. Thinking about law is to near the handiness of law – that for-the-sake-of-which law provokes *Dasein*. Law's handiness is unfamiliar to any ontic articulation of expression of it in which *Dasein* finds itself for-the-most-part. Thinking about law should look at the various aspects through which law has been generalised as a thing and listen to the unsaid in all these aspects in order to connect to the unfolding of the ontological path from which the Being of law speaks.

36. The overcoming of thinking of law as a thing on the way to nearing law's 'thingness' is linked, in thinking-Being, to the overcoming of subject-based thinking. That overcoming includes overcoming the so-called heterogeneous subject. I mean here subjectivity and not merely legal subjectivity. Critical legal theories can find their critical space between the subject which is heterogeneous and the objectified legal subject. When *Dasein* encounters law in the mundane everyday it still reflects neither about law nor about itself as subject. Heterogeneous subjectivity is not a proper response to the mundane and is still within its horizon. It still does not let itself be claimed by that which is thought-provoking about law.

37. *Dasein*'s essential constitution that overcomes the subject–object relationship is ethical. It is through this ethical constitution that *Dasein* may effectuate resistance to the temptation of thinking about law as a thing, namely ontic thinking with and through law. Thinking-Being about law, as a part of thinking-Being about any 'thingness' of beings, must be encountered by readiness to listen to the call of own-comportment, own-pointing towards Being. Own-thingness as comported toward things' thingness – one's own confrontation with nothing/emptiness – brings about the transition from an ontic to ontic/ontological thinking about law.

38. For thinking about 'aboutness', indeed for the interaction with Heidegger's philosophy, there must already be readiness. *Dasein* who is ready to undertake a Heideggerian move with respect to beings, including law, must be ready to attend to its own 'there' first. The Being which is given to human-*Daseins*, their own being which is an issue for them, is the well from which the call about that which is most thought-provoking about law comes. Being calls before it is being thought about with regard to any being.

39. The language used in law and the language that is used to arrive at the idea of law are related within the horizon which perpetuates ontic thinking about law. Any justification made within the practice of law already implies the ontic thinking about it. The Being of law which withdraws is the Being which relates to the whole way of Being and metaphysical/representational thinking through language used in both practising and theorising about law.

40. How do the questions 'What is called thinking?' and 'What calls for thinking?' bear upon law? Let us put together a response in crude terms. Thinking about law is thinking about the Being of law, law being the Being of which is being thought about. What calls for thinking in law is that which makes law thought-provoking. What calls for thinking in law is that 'aboutness' of law, which withdraws, and, if *Daseins* are ready and, in turn, attentive, responds to that which is thought-provoking in law when it withdraws. In enpresencing, the Being of law is itself already the withdrawal of Being which is given to law. Thinking has to go back to memory in order to seize the possibility of the present. Thinking about law is thinking-back towards the event of withdrawal of the Being of law.

41. An exploration of what is ontic in law requires us to follow many paths. Each has its own story of concealment to tell. Each conceals the Being of law. This concealment is itself a way in which the Being of law has already spoken. What is concealed in different ways could be thought about only in attentiveness to the plurality of ontic instantiations. It should be emphasised that although an inclusive insight is sought, this inclusive insight is not a generalisation but only a pointer towards a moment of clearing. It is not a general theory that is sought in thinking-Being.

42. Theory of law implies that the Being of law somehow can be arrested in a theory. A critical theory of law would still be submerged in a transcendental phenomenological swamp. Theories of law assume that some methodology and model can achieve either some correctness as to the Being of law, or a model and methodology for the generation of critical theoretical lever for thinking about the Being of law.. Theorisation of law still has the tendency to present the Being of law as a positive thing. The ontology of theory is always derivative ontologically already possessing that craving for the study of positive beings/things. It craves for the understanding of things according to some positive correctness or adequacy of the idea of them. Arguably, even in transcendental phenomenology, *idea* and *ideatum* – that of which it is an idea – must correspond in their essence. The ontology of theory seeks correspondence between the thing and an idea which represents that positive essence of the thing. Thinking-Being always gets its impetus from what the thing is always already not yet, from the nearness which always opens up as being too near.

43. As the Being of law is itself an aspect of the sending of Being, human *Daseins* are spoken to by the Being of law. Being spoken to puts them on the path to overcome their thinking-subjectivity that craves to represent a theory of law in a way which they cannot control, through being and thinking with and through law as it is for the

most part. The way law is in its Being leads to that overcoming. Thinking reflectively about law is for *Dasein* to let itself be claimed by law, to be spoken to by it. Thinking about law only occurs when law has already thought *Dasein* and the thought came to that nearness of *Dasein*'s innermost own, which no representation can access.

44. Thinking-Being about law does not amount to a polemic against law. Openness to polemics belongs to that craving for theorising law and ought to be resisted. We should let the Being of law speak rather than smother it with a theory of law, including a polemic against law. A polemic only perpetuates ontic reflection.

45. If thinking that is valuable to the practice *of* law involves ethics, then this ethics is also ontic. If thinking about law has an ethical dimension and if the ontic thinking perpetuates certain ethics, then thinking about law, thinking its Being, responding to it, would also involve thinking ethically about the 'aboutness' of ethics. A large chunk of this book is devoted to this argument.

46. Ontic thinking about law perpetuates being and thinking with and through the law as justified by a theory of law. Such a theory supplies certain vocabulary for the justification in law. Such justification (and a polemic for that matter) relates to a value of law which, either explicitly or by implication, follows an ethical account of law's purpose. The historicity of the Being of law, as meshed with the historicity of *Dasein*, has reached a summit of forgetfulness with the emergence of critical legal scholarship. Such scholarship shows itself as the twilight of the theorisation of law. In critical legal scholarship the concealment of law's Being through critical theory is at its most intense. The 'legal' of this scholarship is not itself being thought about, although there may well be in this scholarship pretensions that seem to be utterly to the contrary. The call for Man to transcend ontic thinking about law is given up in critical legal scholarship most decisively, namely just before this call can gain any ground. The *Dasein* who is being urgently called upon is tranquillised by well-entrenched ontological pseudo-critical reflection.

47. Theorising law pretends to know a lot, whilst thinking about law can never express just how little it knows law.

48. Being reflective about law occurs when *Dasein* realises that being embedded in the practice of law is merely a junction for thinking. On the one hand, generalised features of law are represented on the basis of this practice that is taken to be some rich actuality. On the other hand, ontic/ontological oscillation to the Being of law is also being hinted at by the richness of that practice.

49. The Being of law is encountered by *Dasein*. The Being of law is also an aspect of that which is innermost essential to *Dasein*. The Being of

law and the Being of *Dasein* are meshed. The Being of law may withdraw again, thereby coming closer to being of an aspect of *Dasein*'s own comportment towards the nearness of Being of law.

50.   What does it mean to say that law is essential? Does not saying that law is essential amount to the proposing of some *purpose*? To equate that which is essential in law with the law's purpose takes *Dasein* thinking away from thinking about the Being of law. The 'aboutness' of purpose is not yet the 'aboutness' of Being. In an uncanny way, though, thinking along the signifying path of 'purpose' can still point towards the Being of law. The whole notion of 'purpose' has itself to become an issue which is related to the notion of truth and language. Only if we contemplated the 'purpose', that is what it is to think purposefully, could we see that assigning law this or that value does not yet think about the mystery of its call. Indeed, the conventional notion of purpose is the one with which we have to begin to listen to the call of law's Being. It is the thinking about the thinking that leads to the formation of value-based purpose that glimpses at the Being given to the various stated purposes of the law. Perpetuation of a discussion on law's purpose as related to some value of law smothers the light which can give us the clue, the murmur from the sending of law's Being. *Value-based purpose has to be transcended in thinking-Being and only then can we glimpse at what is given to purpose. To think about 'aboutness' is to think about the origin of purpose and that need not make us thinking purposefully.* Talking about purpose as value-based is like looking directly at a big light which blinds us from seeing the shimmering of the near. The craving for value-based purpose generates forgetfulness of Being and, as such, it is the privation of thought.

51.   To reiterate, thinking about law, like any thinking that comes from the origins of actuality, is not for the sake of a predetermined end, *telos*, value or purpose, but is rather linked to the question of 'What is purpose?'. The question of what purpose is has its own historicity and its own revelations and concealments. By trying to grasp *what* is being sought, Being is already being harassed to withdraw. This holds sway also for purpose.

52.   Being thoughtful about law relates to being thoughtful about the Being of law. Thinking about law must first be attentive to that being and thinking that ontic for-the-most-part with law conditions. The relationship between law and its Being understands the relationship between the ontic manifestations of law and its Being.

53.   To ask a question about the Being *of law* is antecedent to asking *what law is*. These questions are different but by not means are they unrelated ontologically. The two questions are related on the near/far dynamics from the actuality of *Dasein* and its comportment towards

law. The first is about that which is essential in law, and the second is about law as 'thing', however critical it may be and however multiple the frameworks that attempt to answer it. The craving for an answer to the question of 'whatness' means already forgetting the world that opens up by asking about the 'aboutness' of the Being of law.

54. Does the Being of law express a certain kind of genealogy of law? If the Being of law is itself historical in that it has its own historicity, would it not be more appropriate to think about a given concealment of the Being-of-law, a concealment that has to be thought *back?*

55. Ontic thinking with and through law, however critically, may conceal certain epochal motionlessness in the temporal path of the Being of law. We can imagine an epoch when the Being of law, though still concealed, will be faced more readily and frequently. It may be yet to come as a possibility of 'thinking about' that has been forgotten. A dominant ontic 'aboutness' conceals and suppresses notions of thinking that have been calling for a long time. Such suppression takes thinking away from hearing, as well as from responding to, the voice of the Being of law. Ontic thinking with and through law, for example, may conceal an uncritically accepted belief in a thinking individual, or subject, who is subjected to the law who also gets some freedom under the law. It may conceal some dominance of thinking by using terms like 'society' of individuals. Thinking about law, then, is to think back to the point where the Being of law withdrew from direct encounter with *Dasein* and started to murmur more indirectly from the gaps that have remained by entrenched forgetfulness.

56. Thinking about law is thinking back to the withdrawal of the Being of law. Being neither thinking about value-based purpose nor a polemic against law, thinking will hold *Dasein* to the essence of law. Thinking about, reflecting upon, law, entails laying bare the one-sidedness embodied in ontic being and thinking with and through law. Being *reflective* entails the constant, and as I shall argue, ethical, laying bare of the one-sidedness of a *particular* manner of ontic involvement with law. That ethical effort entails not only what we would call 'legal' practice but also justification of this legal practice through theory of value or purpose of that legal practice.

57. The ontological in law always only murmurs. Murmuring occurs because, on the one hand, ontically being and thinking with and through law does resonate with the Being of law in a manner that is audible for *Dasein*. On the other hand, the ontic 'with and through law', in so resonating, is a temporal occurrence in the traversing of which the Being of law unfolds in a way which is strange and not reducible to any ontic 'aboutness'.

58. One-sidedness occurs in the entrenchment and perpetuation of ontic thinking. One-sidedness is challenged by the call of Being which is immersed in an ontic illusion of multiplicity. This challenge involves revealing/concealing, going near and far alongside the persistence of maintaining ontic differentiations. Letting thinking be open to the ontological difference of law is not to be one-sided.

59. In thinking about one-sidedeness of ontic thinking about law, the factors that stem from such thinking being embedded in the Western philosophical tradition, namely the core ideas about language, Man, essence, truth, ethics, must be touched upon. The strangeness of 'aboutness', here the strangeness of the 'aboutness' that comes from the thinking about the Being of law, comes from challenging all those aspects which hitherto constitute the horizon of 'aboutness'.

60. The contemplative attempt here is to reveal the nature of one-sidedness that is involved in thinking about law and to show it to be other than merely the ontic contingency of the conventional way of theorising about law. To put it differently, what is at stake here is to make being and thinking about law, however critical, contingent upon the forgetfulness fostered by the philosophical tradition.

61. In the same sense of one-sidedness which argues that science cannot think because it is not connected to the question of 'What is science?' that is asked in relation to the essence of fundamental issues such as history and language, we could also say that law does not think. In its ontic reflection upon itself it does not yet think its Being which is related to issues of language, history, truth and Man. *Having views* as a part of ontic thinking with and through law, however many of these views are puffed up together in order to represent superficial multi-sidedness, is still one-sided, and is still not thinking about law. Merely *having views* about the ontic with and through law, which may include various 'theories of law', constitutes a deceptive cathedral that takes *Dasein* further from the call for thinking about law. Law does not yet think if we grasp thinking in terms of unification of the Being of that which is to be thought about – law – with the Being of *Dasein*, the historicity of this unification, and the language that comes to a *Dasein* in signifying this unification. For attending this unification, thinking must have its concern with those things which remain inexpressible, or worse, silenced, by one-sided ontic thinking with and through law. It must be reiterated that, as thinking is not a polemic, it does not want to annihilate thinking with and through law. Thinking opens a window for *Dasein* to respond, a window from which to look at the one-sidedness which is embedded in ontic thinking with and through law, which, when

entrenched, further conceals that one-sidedness and obstructs the
path for the call upon *Dasein* for thinking the Being of law.

62.   If thinking about law meant a polemic against law, it would mean
that we could assume some kind of a beginning, a universal totalising
position, an initial missed junction, in which Man took the wrong
turn by embracing law. Recovering this junction would supposedly
reconstruct a great choice that Man faces between law and no law
and we would have to imagine what it would be like without law.
Doing that would glance over the positive role law has in our process
of learning and unlearning *Dasein*'s own Being or, in short,
own-Being. The call for thinking about law is not about yearning to
have no law but rather about learning the Being of law. But to learn
the Being of law we must first immerse ourselves in those factors that
entrench ontic being and thinking with and through law. *There can
be no thinking-Being about law without listening to the unsaid of
law's ontic determinations.* We need to lay bare, uncover and unmask
the moment of withdrawal of law's Being in order for us to unlearn
and endeavour occasionally to overcome the various concealments of
that very moment. In this process we need to learn how thinking
about law, which is expressed in its many theories, itself has been
traditionally, as an aspect of what thinking has been traditionally.

To learn means to make everything we do answer to whatever essentials
address themselves to us at a given time. Depending on the kind of essentials,
depending on the realm from which they address us, the answer and with it
the kind of learning differs.[1]

63.   If thinking reflectively about law was a polemic, we would have to
imagine a world without law, a world that would have no possibility
of constantly unlearning ontic being and thinking with and through
law by thinking law's Being. A polemic would take away all that
which law expresses essentially, which is a part of the historicity of
Being. A polemic would make thinking as vacuous as much as it
would be ignorant and utopic. Ontic determination of law is a part
of *Dasein*'s world and as such it is essential to *Dasein*. We must,
then, engage in contemplating that which is essential in ontic determination of law for thinking law's Being. Only then can we leap into
that unlearning that will enable us to be attentive to the call of the
Being of law.

64.   Thinking reflectively about law does not compare a state of 'law'
with a state of 'no law'. Nor do I attempt to engage in a thesis of a
value-based purpose of some extent to which law can be justified.

[1] *WCT*, p 14.

Nor do I wish to attempt to portray law as an instrument of oppression in the context of some *telos*-based historical dialectics or the use of such dialectics to revive some mode of natural law. That there is law as long as there are people is significant, and we must neither annihilate law nor condition it. We must contemplate both how ontic thinking about law and the significance attached to law have become so pervasive as well as how questions about law's primordial significance, that is about the Being of law, have become so deeply forgotten.

65. In asking what is it to think reflectively about law, then, there is a crucial difference between, on the one hand, the necessary falling into theorisation about law – which is a part of the ontological/ontic process – and, on the other hand, the thoughtless process of critical thinking that replaces one theory of law with another. These may look similar but they could not be further apart. The first characterises thinking, while the second characterises the entrenchment of forgetfulness. As we shall see, with Levinas, one of the most misleading modes of forgetfulness of the Being of law is to be highly critical of the mundane being and thinking with and through law by providing for ethical thought which is other to thinking with law. This mode of forgetfulness also claims to be highly critical of theories of law. Indeed, such a mode has many Heideggerian echoes. It will become all the more difficult, but *crucially important*, to differentiate between the 'aboutness' of such a mode of forgetfulness of the Being of law and the 'aboutness' that comes as the murmuring of the Being of law, albeit including this mode of forgetfulenes in such murmuring.

66. 'Aboutness' is itself historical. All ontic thinking with and through law perpetuates the forgetfulness of its Being, *inter alia*, by constant replacement of theories of law. This perpetuation of the ontic is itself a part of the historicity which prepares the way for the thinking. Even the process of the entrenchment of forgetfulness of thinking the Being of law is fated within the historicity of the Being of law.

67. In thinking-Being, *Dasein* learns the ways law has been thought about, in different frameworks and is thereby necessarily made ready to unlearn that ontic dominance that lies at the heart of all those frameworks and methodologies. Such is the process of historicity of thought reflecting upon its very essence. In still not touching the 'suchness' of law by all these frameworks, *Dasein* is already properly made ready to become anxious, to become ever more oppressed by the Being of law, to be oppressed by this feeling that something in the very nature of its cravings keeps preventing it from being near to the actuality of law. Only in such anxiety is *Dasein* in the position to

think the thinking about law, as Heidegger would put it. Only then is *Dasein* at the foothills of thinking about law.

68. Thinking about law is to think-back, to recollect, to connect to the memory of that prudence of jurisprudence, in order to see that which jurisprudence makes us forget. The effort of thinking, including thinking back, reveals that jurisprudence, being prudent, does not go onto the path of thinking about law ontologically. Thinking is not prudent but dangerous.² What calls for thinking about law is precisely to recollect what is prudent about law and to show that this prudent 'aboutness' turns us away from thinking the 'aboutness' that comes to *Dasein* who is involved with the law as a call from the Being of law.

69. Thinking, Heidegger maintains, occurs in our 'thought-provoking time'. The Being of law termporalises [*Temporalität*] *Dasein*'s own temporality when involved with the law [*Zeitlichkeit*] as care. Thinking about law is thinking about the historicity of its Being and it entails a different reflection from that in which other historical reflections are embodied. For example, HLA Hart's so-called historical description of a 'pre-legal' society with primary rules of obligation is formed in the context of already established predominant craving to establish a theory of law.³ Anything that occurred prior to the realisation of that theory is thus called 'pre-legal'. The theory justifies the *quasi* history. The same can be said for accounts that declare certain a 'pre-legal' situation as the 'state of nature'. The same can be said for the kind of history that was conducted by Sir Henry Maine and his famous account of the transition from Status to Contract.⁴

70. The state of nature may already contain a relationship to law which is more primordial than the enlightenment idea of law in a political society. The contrast between the 'barbaric', or unfree, state of nature to that of law and order under which security and liberty can flourish is already embedded in philosophical assumptions about subjectivity, truth, language, ethics, freedom and, of course, law. Again it is a philosophical tradition that craves to conceptualise nature as a 'thing', crafting a civilised world that precedes and conditions the history it tells. Dealing with the law in social relations that are 'raw' may reveal a more direct ethical participation of the ontic/ontological process, between being attentive to the Being of law through its ontic manifestations. It is the conceptualisation of

² WCT, p 31.
³ HLA Hart, *The Concept of Law* (Oxford, Clarendon Press, 1961) pp. 89–96.
⁴ H Maine, *Ancient Law: Its Connection with the Early History of Society and Its Relation to Modern Ideas* (Oxford, Oxford University Press, 1931).

'nature' as a being which is there to be conceptualised by the philosopher that gives birth to the forgetfulness of the Being of law in masquerading this forgetfulness through teleological histories and theories. A proper historicity of the Being of law would relate to tracing the moment where the question of the Being of law has been forgotten in order to grasp the historicity of that Being. A proper historical investigation would search for a more primordial temporality of law. Thinking the Being of law should take us back to that which sets the philosophical tradition in motion and thus involves the very thinking back of that tradition. Only in this thinking back could we talk about a primordial historicity that comes from the saying of the actuality of the actual in law.

71. Both thinking about law and ontic thinking with and through it carry with them the ambiguity that exists between the Being of law and law as it is encountered for-the-most-part. To think 'with' is to have an idea of how to use something as a tool – to have an idea of doing something with it. When *Dasein* thinks *with* law it uses law as a tool, a useful tool – it *does* something with law. It does something with law's concepts and with its materials. To think 'through' can mean 'to see happenings from a given perspective' as opposed to 'other perspectives'. To think through law, however critically, is to look *already* upon the world, from the perspective of assuming the 'whatness' of law. But, hidden in this ontic with and through lurks a nearer 'with' and a nearer 'through'. In the ontic thinking with and through law there is the inexpressible which has already been responded to unthinkingly.

72. How primordially, then, can we go in listening to that which is choking thought about law? What is being choked when lawyers raise their voice? The expression 'with and through' law also denotes that, primordially, the Being of law has already spoken on its way and its voice is being pronounced by lawyers, however critical of law the theoretical justification implied in their arguments. To think about law is to reflect upon this nearer 'with and through'.

73. The Being of law which is most thought-provoking is the actuality of the actual which is given in any ontic manifestations of thinking about law. The Being of law strikes *Dasein* as strange by making its inexpressible and non-commonsensical voice felt to be the most real.

74. But, a commentator may persist, is it not the case that thinking 'about' must articulate theories, or theories of law, respectively? Does not the argument here simply present a new theory of law? Is the exploration undertaken here candid? Of course, attempting to articulate what it means to think about law is part of a saying about the world. But thinking about law as thinking the Being of law would have a certain occurrence which is primordial to any theory of law

which is represented even by an idea/ideas of such a theory. The saying encapsulated in thinking the Being of law would be nearer to actuality than any representational idea about law. This saying itself, then, must never become a mere said so it does not become a representation. Thinking about law must occur without law becoming a thing said. Thinking about the Being of law is an aspect of thinking-Being and, as such, is intimately connected to thinking about language and truth, as well as about the origin of ethics. Grasping language and truth should make it more conspicuous why the saying about what it means to think about law is not a theory. Thinking about law is not a 'theory of' but about the 'suchness' of an unfolding of a primordial saying. Reflecting upon that 'suchness' of saying, thinking the Being of law relates, in a manner primordial to the representation in theory, to the 'how' of language and truth as well as to the ethical question of what it is to be a human being. A saying that there is a certain being and thinking that characterises a being, law, is already an idle saying and its entrenchment unethical.

75.   Thinking about law is an attempt at thinking law not from the point of theoretical ignorance about law but in *Dasein* asking what law does to its own 'thingness', or, how its own innermost 'thingness' causes it to think with and through law. As such, *Dasein* may become attentive to interact with that which speaks it in the name of the law in a manner that is not mediated by a theory. Thinking the Being of law involves also the question of how its own 'thingness' has come to the point where it reduces the saying of the inexpressible in law to mere 'ignorance of the practice of law' and is content with that reduction. Thinking-Being would also ask how it comes about that *Dasein* is content with the dialectic of theory of/ignorance about law. If a new theory of law is a response to ignorance followed by a fresh attempt to find common terms to make new generalisations about law plausible then the question of ignorance that relates to the inexpressible in law has not yet been faced. The danger of responding to ignorance by filling it with theory, with a theory of law in particular, perpetuates exactly the forgetfulness of what it is we are ignorant of.

76.   To think about is a temporal uncovering and revealing. It anticipates a recollection that uncovers an event in which the Being of law has withdrawn. In thinking about law, the path of law's Being, where it will have been, is approached and there will be a moment of clearing. To think about law is first to grasp what is concealed through received theories of law. It is further to grasp what is concealed by the *Dasein* who craves for theorising about law, about *Dasein*'s approach to truth, language, about its care for its own worldliness as well as for the worldliness of things. Further still, to think about law

is to think about the audience of *Dasein*s who receive without reflection not merely theories of law but the very usefulness of such theories. All theories of law are metaphysical in that, even when they spring from ignorance, they still accept the idea of the representational truth of schemes which adopt an assemblage of concepts and propositions which, apart and together, hold the truth of the 'It' of law. Such theories will produce representations of law, which, together and apart, will be expressive of the essence of law as distinguished from other social phenomena.

77. To think about law is to experience a moment of 'clearing' of the Being of law. But how does the Being of law send law on the way so as to make it thought-provoking? What is that in law which calls for thinking about it? As Heidegger would ask: 'What is called thinking about law and what calls for thinking about law?' Does not the call for thinking about law come from something in the thinker's own involvement? Does thinking about law come from the reflection of the thinker upon the concealment brought about by subjugation of the self as a thinking subject? Thinking about law, like all thinking, must come to *Dasein* even before *Dasein* considers itself a subject, even a transcendental one. *Dasein* must be ready to hear the call for thinking and to respond to it. Thought is embedded in readiness and so *must* involves *Dasein* in waiting. Speaking authentically about law cannot be rushed through calculative, intermediate conditions. The moment of thinking is that where the Being of law and the Being of *Dasein* can meet so as to generate a question about how what is thought-provoking in law shows itself in *Dasein*'s own thought-provoking time. Thinking about law characterises an 'ek-sistential' event in *Dasein*'s being-in-the-world and so detailed contemplation of such an event is part and parcel of thinking about law.

78. Human *Dasein*s have to think about both human law and how human law relates to that law which comports human beings, mortals, in the way they are essentially. In other words, in thinking about law, in thinking the Being of law, we must contemplate the 'thingness' of humans, thingness that humans cannot help but obey. How are human beings most essentially? A potential and complex reflection is involved here: human beings are essentially guardians of Being and to that extent they are also guarded by Being as its guardians. The statement seems illogical, as it indicates that human *Dasein* and Being both protect and are protected by one another. This seemingly illogical reflection is at the nub of the chapters that follow and is the source of why any theory of law would always be too far removed from the way human beings are spoken by law's Being. How can humans be provoked to think about the Being of law, law which is made for them and in a certain sense by them?

How is the Being of humans provoked by the Being of law? How does such primordial provocation relate to the ontic alluring provocation so as to make humans seek *value* and purpose in law which is made by them for them? *How does thinking about law, law which is thought about for the sake of human beings as they are in essence, connect to the thinking back to the Being of Dasein?*

79. Some theories about law see the existence and persistence of law quite apart from the existence of *Dasein*. This is true of social systems theory, whose account of law attempts to set law quite apart from human *Dasein*, perhaps generating its own system's *Dasein*. Such view of law as a social system, or sub-system, does not embark upon conventional methods of evaluation, direct or indirect, of law. Reasoning within law is explained not through the relationship of cause and effect, namely as law being open to outside influences, but rather through the way epistemic closure is perturbed by other systems. Law, being a closed social system, is held to be both ontologically and epistemically distinct from human *Dasein*.[5] I will not attempt a detailed discussion of this in this book but would merely ask whether the very 'machine' that is built by such an account is not itself a product of the human *Dasein* who still clings to the metaphysical craving for correctness. Is this not merely a new representational whole that leaves thinking-Being and thinking about *Dasein* outside its inquiry? The human *Dasein*s who theorise themselves away as 'psychic systems', by erecting system theory are still the very source of thinking that produce that conceptual cathedral. Further, is not the claim that captures the 'isness' of systems still clinging to phenomenology – that is to the ontic thought of beings rather than their Being, thinking that 'punctuates' actuality in a new way? A new punctuation is still punctuation and at the level of thinking there is nothing ontologically radical. The change from ontology of subject and state to ontology of systems is idle from the point of view of thinking.

80. Thinking reflectively about law is not the same as saying that law is capable of critical self-evaluation. Doctrinal ideas and concepts change, some might say, that they progressively evolve. As far as for-the-most-part ontic being and thinking about law is concerned, arguments with and through law involve a lot of creativity and imagination. But, to repeat, all theories of law, whether positivist, constructivist or critical, are still univocal in the way they conceive being and thinking with and through law. They do not yet think the Being of law. Their creative linguistic activity is not yet attentive to what is thought-provoking in language as far as our

---

[5] N Luhmann, *A Sociological Theory of Law* (London, Routledge, 1985).

thought-provoking time is concerned. The univocity that underlies their diversity occurs at the level of the notion of thinking that they presume. This univocity stems from the fact that 'theory of ...' does not yet think about 'aboutness'. *Is conceptualising and re-conceptualising value-oriented thinking involve Dasein's innermost own openness to the speech of language? Crucially, has the thinking of such conceptualisation yet been attentive to the language of law – to its saying?* Thinking about law has to involve thinking about those features of language that must remain silent however critical the use of ideas and concepts with and through law. To put it differently, the language that thinks with and through a theory of law is not yet attentive to the language of law. As far as law is concerned, theorising about it *is not yet language. A language that changes because of ignorance has already ceased being language.* It is merely a conceptual analysis or generalisation about the appropriateness of usage of terms. It does not matter, then, how critical the methodology is. Thinking about law has to lay bare what it is that brings forth *Dasein* in own Being/thinking to find such use of ideas and concepts useful. *Thinking about law has to ask what Dasein finds thought-provoking in such use of ideas and concepts and what is thought-provoking about Dasein finding such a use of ideas and concepts thought-provoking.* We must allow for the truism that the content of law changes as images of society change. But we have to attend to that notion of truth and grasp of language which remains unchanged in all that critical change. *We must start to grasp and fathom the ambit of the violence that is done to language with the most critical of theories.* Despite a conceptual change, indeed despite even change in a theory of law, there is no interaction thinking about the Being of law which is persistently concealed and forgotten. If a change has taken place in respect to the Being of law in this climate of multiplicity of theories, it has been manifested in the intensification of silencing *entrenchment* and *ubiquity* of forgetfulness of the Being of law. To ask the question of the Being of law shows that nothing changes despite the change and multiplicity in theories of law. We must emphasis yet again that *thinking about law is not about law's content but about law's Being.* Thinking reflectively about the Being of law hints that there is something which cannot be assimilated into mere critical thinking with and through law even if it can be admitted that the latter is 'about' law to such extent that it is critical of law. The 'aboutness' of thinking is what is nearest to *Dasein*, and from which for-the-most-part thinking is the farthest. Thinking takes *Dasein* nearer to the actuality of the actual of law, never craving to distance itself from actuality so that it can forgetfully generate a new kind of 'critical' question about law. The craving for distancing is a characteristic of the entrenchment of forgetting.

81. The forgetfulness of the question of the Being of law in conceiving critical theory about law as the most original and primordial 'about' is itself concealed. This concealment makes critical theory of law the most sophisticated forgetfulness, as it nearly robs *Dasein* from its attentiveness to Being. Critical theory wears the mask of content-debunker in a way that grabs *Dasein* in such a manner that it can, by and large, repress, or rather silence, *Dasein*'s anxiety, hence violently attempting to take away the need to think about that theoretical 'with and through' that dominates it.

82. Thinking about law, thinking the Being of law, cannot involve re-description of law because *Dasein* will find himself once again, in every new description, perpetuating the forgetting in a new manner. The leap from one-sidedness is a leap where *Dasein* lets itself be snatched by the language in which the Being of law speaks. By being snatched, *Dasein* lets the Being of law be. The relationship between law and its Being are not the same as the relationship between one ontic determination of law and another.

83. That we are still not thinking about law by for-the-most-part thinking with and through it, however critically, is itself a part of the practice of law and will somehow show in this practice.

84. That forgetfulness of the Being of law that is entrenched by the proliferation of theories of law is itself a manifestation of Saying of the Being of law.

85. How has ontic thinking about law become so dominant? How has it become that poetic insights have been put to the service of ontic being and thought with and through law? Thinking about law is to deconstruct the one-sidedness of the ontic, not to perpetuate that ontic thinking by pretending to be critical.

ABOUTNESS AND ALTERITY IN THINKING ABOUT LAW

86. The anxious burden of asking the question of 'aboutness', and the indication given of a world that is constantly avoided by perpetuating theoretical thinking about law, may well give rise to the idea that there must be, within the everydayness in which *Dasein* finds itself, something which is distinct from law and hence 'other' to it. In other words, law and what is seemingly its other are felt, on ontic reflection, to be distinct. This distinction between law and its other has many ramifications. According to this image of distinction, the thing that 'law' expresses is distinct from another 'thing' or 'being' – a 'practice' which is other to it. Thinking about law, then, would

mean thinking also about that which is other to it. So under this image we have the conviction that law is distinct from something other as part of there being a multiplicity of things in the world which in turn manifest themselves as different practices the justification of which grounds reasoning within them. This image makes a distinction between being involved in law and being involved in its other. Clearing the various theoretical frameworks in which law is captured as a thing distinguishes it from the theoretical frameworks that account for its other.

87. That alterity between law and its other is felt after an attentive immersion in the ontic. Perhaps in some forms this alterity makes itself felt even prior to such attentive immersion. But can the other of law, on reflection, be distinct? Ontic analysis would give us a strong feeling of such distinction, but have we really thought yet about the very thinking that grounds such a distinction? It could be that the other of law is not really distinct but is nevertheless being felt seemingly as 'other' precisely because of the anxious burden that comes from the Being of law. The feeling of that which is other to law that highlights the perpetuation of ontic reflection about law, including its discursive and practical differentiations, originates by from the Being of law which is nearer to *Dasein* than any ontic determinations. It is because of the lack that comes from the fact that, despite the exhaustion of ontic being and thinking with and through law, despite extensive theorising of law, the voice of law's Being does not yet speak in such instances. To put it more accurately, the lack does speak, but as *both unsaid and inexpressible*. Something bothers the mundane everyday involvement of *Dasein* with law in an instant of care. *Dasein*'s *being-in-the-world* is oppressed by the Being of law despite ontically engaging with the law in the everyday, and despite theorising upon law in this or that manner in a way that can differentiate law and its other.

88. There is an intimate connection between *Dasein*'s own oppression by its own nothingness and its ability to feel the oppression by the saying of the Being of law in its mundane everyday involvement with the law.

89. The otherness to law, then, is not a thing which is different from law. Otherness to law comes from the inexpressible nearness of the saying of the Being of law. It is otherness to ontic thinking about law. Thinking about the otherness of law involves a different 'aboutness' from the ontic 'aboutness'. Otherness to law is not otherness in the sense of being a practice which is completely distinguished from law but rather it is a saying of the Being of law as hazed by the ontic. Such haze manifests itself for-the-most-part as that which is a 'thing' other to law, and it is the haze that conceals more primordial

otherness. Ontic otherness to law is in fact a distorted saying that comes from the Being of law. To put it another way, thinking-Being about law may reveal that ontic distinctions are not genuine. Thinking-Being may indicate the primordial insight that many similarities can be found between the Being of law and the Being of its other.

90. The seeming otherness to law, an otherness whose distortion comes as the voice of law's Being, must be thought back either prior to the birth of philosophical tradition or, indeed, sideways to where pre-metaphysical thought or elements of such thought – that is a more direct connectedness to Being – have been preserved today in what may seem to be, ontically, other to law.

91. Entrenched thinking about law which is critical of law, in the name of activity that is other to it, or prior to it, for example, ethics that precedes law and is therefore more primordial and 'other' to it, may well be highly ontic and misleading in that it does its utmost not to let the Being of law speak.

92. Any distinction made by *Dasein* between law and its other is itself a little wave in the sea of Being from which the Being of law raises its voice. The other is that inexpressible which oppresses *Dasein* whilst *Dasein* attempts to utter through law, justify through law, theorise law and distinguish law from its other. The murmur of the Being of law may well have the for-the-most-part appearance as critical of law by claiming that there is an other to law – an alternative to law with which human relationship can be approached. One example of such an 'other to law', one that will be canvassed in detail, is the Levinasian internal process of ongoing ethical contestation of identity through facing that which is absolute 'Other'. In Levinas, 'other to law' and the 'ethics of an absolute Other' join forces. I will try to show why such otherness to law is both non-genuine and insincere, and thus not a primordial 'aboutness' in thinking about law. In fact, I shall argue that what is 'other to law' here is in fact highly legalistic, the ultimate refuge of legalism. At this stage, this is just an illustration that 'other' to law is not, although it does seem to hint at, the primordial otherness of the Being of law.

93. Ethical thinking shows itself as involving the saying from absolute alterity, one which the law cannot allude to, can be said to be other to law. Similarly, poetry can be seen as 'other to law'. As an other to law, poetry is nevertheless being used by critical legal scholars to then enhance law's self-criticism. But what I have argued is that that which is other to law, ethics which is based on alterity, indeed on poetic language, may well be nothing other than an indication towards the Being of law, one that already comes as a call from the

Being of law. The Being of law would be, on this view, a manifestation of poetic language.

94. There is an undecidability here that is internal to the phrase 'otherness to law' which will have to be explored. Once this undecidability is grasped, the Being of law, may no longer be conceived as ontically distinguished from the Being of something else.

95. We need to grasp the voice of that which is seemingly other to law and to discuss its relationship with law so that we can listen to the otherness of law's Being. This otherness will be that which the thing-law expressed by law for-the-most-part, as distinguished from law's other, does not yet reach. 'Does not reach' not in the sense of a distinction but in the sense of nearing. We need to examine the *relationship* of ontic alterity between law and its other so as to bring into the open the essential nature of the thing-law and with it the essential inauthenticity of its being for-the-most-part. Such an exploration is necessary in order to prepare the ground for asking a truly ontological question about the Being of law.

96. What is the relationship between law and what is seemingly its 'other', an 'other' which is nothing but an indication towards the murmur of the Being of law? The very thinking in terms of tenuous alterity – between law and its other– is a mark of the perpetuation of ontic thinking. But the murmur of otherness to this very ontic thinking is thought-provoking and thus indeed invites thought. The feeling that there is something other-to-law, then, is the most immediate, albeit misleading, expression of this invitation for thought. Again, to give poetry as an example, poetry may seem very other to law but, essentially speaking, poetry is involved in the very Being of law. Poetic thought is thinking the Being of law, not merely a source of insights that could then be accommodated into a radically new content. Poetic thought as the saying of the Being of law is essentially distorted in its paraphrase into legal content.

97. Thinking reflectively about law that allows us nearer to the Being of law does not confuse the study of law or even legal science with law's Being. The mask of otherness that the Being of law wears is not experienced as influencing, or as overlapping with, the for-the-most-part ontic being and thinking with and through law. Nor is the Being of law experienced as a call for a fully operable, workable, *alternative* to for-the-most-part ontic being and thinking with and through law. The Being of law can be neared only by listening to what appears as other to law. The otherness of law's Being is not an otherness of distinction but rather that of a distortion made up of temporal, and with it, linguistic, *distance*. A translation from the Being of law into the for-the-most-part being and thinking with law necessarily occurs when the insights which are arrived at as a result

of ontological reflection are expressed and presented as insights in a manner which has already fallen into the world of truth, the language of subjectivity that belong to the ontic for-the-most-part being and thinking with and through law. This process of translation and expression characterises the necessary 'falling' of *Dasein* into ontic thinking. Translation of the ontological into the ontic, then, characterises the very relationship between ontic thinking about law and thinking its Being. In extreme forgetfulness of the question of the Being of law, constant paraphrasing buries the possibility of the bringing this relationship into the open for reflection. This is because every insight is already articulated in a way which silences this relationship of nearness between the ontic and the ontological while still paying lip service to the originality of the insight. Silencing the rift that characterises the ontological difference of law in that way creates an apparently convincing continuum and harmony of thinking or common ground between the Being of law and for-the-most-part thinking about it. Convincing, because one-sidedness is entrenched in superficial open-mindedness. The forgotten distortion of the translation between the ontic/ontological and the ontic/ontic does not occur by 'fitting' something with something else. The translation has occured already before any *difference* between the two can surface. The way in which the Being of law is connected to language, truth, history, and subjectivity is translated before it is allowed to authentically distort. Such one-sidedness and any translation which effectuates it may sound open-minded *and* reassuring in that it always implies some perspective from which successful assimilation of the inexpressible can be made. However, such translation which entrenches the ontic constitutes the most sophisticated concealment of the Being of law, making it harder, in the sense of seeming unnecessary for *Dasein*, for it to be neared and perturbed. Thinking reflectively about law must involve also thinking about, and detecting echoes of, this kind of translation. It also involves getting to the root of such translation, which in this book, will take us to the debate on the nature of ethics and otherness.

98. Let us take an example of such translation. Critical insights that are legally relevant and important can be enriched by opening legal discourse to psychoanalysis. Insight from psychoanalysis can lead to radical critique of all too abstract and generalising legal provisions, as well as oppressive objectification of the legal subject. Psychoanalytic insights can lead to the destabilisation of symbolic order that dominates the unconscious subjectivity whose legal thinking is abound with impoverished conscious and oppressive representations. Poetic language is thus being made a tool and as such co-operates with the law, so that its insight can be re-contained in a new articu-

lation and distribution of legal rights and duties. The critical thinking which is thus generated about law, by the use of poetic language, is at the same time highly critical of law and the generic objectification of legal subjectivity. Poetic language can be hailed both as the other to law and one that enriches critical legal development. Such a view purports to show how law can be deployed, critically, in order to give effect to insights that were arrived at by poetic involvement. Such a process of critical translation of poetic language into legal language is seen to be a part of critical legal scholarship and enables the expansion of the critical role of law, making it draw upon aesthetic insights to the point of contesting the ambit of law's own critical powers. Looking at aesthetics and giving effect to its insight in law is being moral in a way which a merely instrumental look at law cannot be.

99. But that idea of translating aesthetic insights – even the way of being moral by making subjectivity more heterogeneous by these insights – into an expression of law's for-the-most-part being and thinking has already been consumed by *this very thinking that is generic to thinking for-the-most-part* before translation took place. That thinking conditions thinking about law for-the-most-part. The craving for, and the possibility of, the anticipation of, re-containment has occurred before the aesthetic insights were drawn. The seeker of the insight is nothing other than inauthentic *Dasein*, just like the practitioner of law, and even more so, the theoretician of law. For-the-most-part being and thinking with and through law has been there before the seeking. Certain conceptions of thinking, reason and truth predominate the process of translation before it even starts. So, I ask,: is fighting unconscious oppression and domination through for-the-most-part being and thinking with and through law an authentic critical move? *How can an involvement of care which connotes constant oscillation of nearness between the ontic and the ontological be translated into an already hegemonic and inauthentic hermeneutic cycle?* Is care not violently suffocated in a velvety way if poetic insights are already conditioned by ontic anticipation? Ontic anticipation which conditions poetic insights is, then, a sophisticated manifestation of carelessness. Being critical of law whilst in fact perpetuating ontic being and thinking with and through it is careless. This carelessness, though, is already being cared for, as it is itself anticipation of careful attention and contemplation by that which was carelessly treated. The cycle of care has no outside.

100. A reflection which is seen as the other to law while in fact perpetu-ating law's ontic manifestations is part and parcel of that ontic manifestation. Primordial otherness to ontic thinking, which is otherwise to both ontic reductionist amputations of poetic insights

and to ontic thinking with law, as we shall see, does harbour actual unification between poetic language and the Being of law. As will be discussed in the next chapter, law's Being is poetry, and as such, it shows itself as care.

101. Let us look closely at this discussion about otherness between law and another activity. It might be claimed that law is imperfect, not merely in its imperfect content in relation to this or that value, or in relation to critical theory as based on the reinterpretation of ideology. This imperfection of law is rather in that law cannot address all actual and potential ways in which human beings are related. Such a claim maintains its force even if the range of application of the law is growing to cover many areas that it has not hitherto covered. Such an imperfectability thesis seems to put law 'in its place' and, in that, it claims that, however expansive law might be, it is still generically imperfect because it addresses human relationships from its own perspective while not attending to and confronting other perspectives. The imperfectability thesis claims in fact that, within its domain, law and the morality it enforces can be a unique process. To advance this seemingly humble claim that law is imperfect includes a crude ontological argument about the severance of law and the morality it enforces from other approaches to human relationships. This crude severance legitimises the forgetfulness of thinking reflectively about the nature of the severance, about the nature of the otherness, about otherness. We have to dwell on the question of the way in which law is imperfect. What is thought-provoking in a statement of such imperfectability?

102. Further, it needs to be considered if and how the imperfectability thesis is merely a response to a polemic which is advanced against law. The response is that 'of course, law does not do that, it cannot do everything'. But thinking reflectively about law, it must be remembered, is not a polemic but a clearing of the ontic so that we can brought to the foothills of thinking ontologically about the Being of law. Being attentive to the call of Being, as expressed distortedly in the way law is for-the-most-part, may well show that it is a reduction to take the imperfectability thesis too simply. We cannot be confident whether imperfectability encompasses the Being of law or only its ontic manifestations. Can there be such a segregation of 'nature of activity' or 'purpose' as far as the Being of law is concerned, so that this activity can be said to be imperfect? Further, what would 'perfect' mean as far as the Being of beings, in this case that of law, is considered? Could it be perfect in the sense of being an essential aspect of the manner human *Dasein* is primordially?

103. To claim that law is not all-inclusive would seemingly have to acknowledge that human relationships can be approached from

many *alternative* dimensions, for example, psychoanalysis, which emphasises the poetic, symbolic and imaginary way that human beings are. On this basis it will be a matter of course that 'law is not psychoanalysis' or anything else, simply because 'law is law' and not something else. It will be bursting into an open door to advance the *critical* claim that law does not do what psychoanalysis does, because it is not meant to be psychoanalysis and in this sense it is imperfect. A fair critical thinking about law would criticise law 'in its own playground' and according to what it purports to do. Alterity between law and its other, on such a view, is a matter of course implying such alternatives.

104. How does the issue of 'alternative approaches' feature in thinking about the Being of law? Let us continue our discussion of psycho-analysis and law. Psychoanalysis and law are seemingly 'alternatives' ways of approaching human beings. *But, is it really the case that the Being of law is so exclusive that it can be distinguished so clearly from the Being of another activity? Does the distinction between activities correspond to the relationship of alterity between the Being of law and of its others?*

105. The translation thesis comes to the fore here. Translating psychoanalytical insights into, to make them useful in, law, can be said to be critical about law. This practice of translating poetic symbolic insights has widely influenced critical ideas in legal and political theory. For example, some feminists' contribution to critical legal theory was to show law's self-criticism not to include symbolic unconscious oppression of the feminine. Such moves do draw a lot from psychoanalysis but they do not turn law into psychoanalysis. In other words, the translation thesis holds that psychoanalysis is still an approach to human relationships that is *alternative* to law, but still law is not exclusive to psychoanalysis and open to its insights and influences.

106. Here lies the problem: on the one hand, law is not psychoanalysis. However, on the other hand, law would not seem to be so exclusive to psychoanalysis in the sense that 'to criticise law on its own terms' would be to contest these very 'terms' thereby resorting to insights from psychoanalysis for such contestation. Despite its apparent uniqueness, law's self-interpretation would have to involve a constant contestation of its overlapping boundary with the other activity. In short, it seems that law and psychoanalysis are alternatives in that each has its own unique way to conceptualise human relationships. At the same time, though, both may have some common matrix that would serve for mutual contestation of each, a contestation that could then be translated into critical view of each. We can already see, even on this initial reflection, that to criticise law 'in its own

playground' by hailing its exclusivity, and thus imperfectability, would seem far too simplistic.

107. So to admit influence between law and psychoanalysis in that law can turn psychological insights within its own being does admit some common matrix, and hence translatability, between them but it does not make them identical. Although it will be felt that psychoanalysis is an 'other' to law, the origin of this otherness are not clear.

108. What is the origin of such otherness? Relationships of alterity may hint that something in psychoanalysis, the manner in which it approaches the human, being more poetic, may not be so translatable and could only be carried out at the expense of authenticity of the translation. The uniqueness of the psychoanalytical approach is that which makes it seem 'other' to law. The alterity of poetic grasp of the human condition seems to originate in an approach to truth, to language, which is 'other' than the approach taken by law. So in seeking the origin of otherness between psychoanalysis and law, we should ask: can the poetic approach to truth and language be translatable to the approach which is presumed by law? Moreover, and crucially, is this the only way of viewing the matter? I shall claim the problematic origin of the otherness between law and psychoanalysis hints in fact at ontological similarity between them.

109. Let me explore this last point. Would it be the right approach to essentialise law to a given approach to truth and psychoanalysis to another, defending their otherness in this way? Could not translation between them be possible because both are already instantiated ontically within the dominance of a 'correctness' approach to truth and language, and it is such an approach which distorts their *common* Being? Could we not identify events where *both* psychoanalysis and law have essential common poetic origins? Could it be that the inauthenticity of translation between the two, and our gut feeling of otherness between them, is in fact the necessary ontic mode that hints at the otherness of their original common ontological ground? Could such ontic otherness hint at deeper otherness between, on the one hand, the Being of both and, on the other hand, the ontic determination of both as the otherness that we seek in thinking-Being? Could it be the case that the translation which is done in critical legal studies between psychoanalysis and law in fact still effectuates some economy between the ontic manifestation of both? Locating the non-translatability between psychoanalysis and law in the fact that such translation is being done for the most part, would mean to contemplate their difference as an aspect of the ontological difference and not some ontic commerce.

110. Could it be that the commerce and translation between activities occur on a apparent common matrix that both distorts and hints at

their common Being? Again, the fact that the haze that persists between that intuition that sees something 'other' in poetry is coupled to the critical practice of translation between them hints that, ontologically speaking, distinction of activity is not the distinction we seek. The distinction that we seek is between the poetic approach to truth and language which characterises the Being of both psychoanalysis and law and the distorted manifestations of that Being in ontic instantiations of both.

111. What is crucial for this book is to get to the essential difference between activities, like psychoanalysis, that are seemingly different to law as a preparation for the question which has both an ethical and an ontological dimension. This question is: 'What could *really* be learned, from the fact that psychological insights have actually been "translated" into legal ones, seemingly even very successfully?'. If we are really pursuing the 'alternative approach' argument we have to find that which makes psychoanalysis and law *real* alternatives and then look again at the implication of the translation between them.

112. It should become clearer now that the distinction we seek is not a mere distinction in activity but a distinction between beings and their Being. This distinction murmurs and can be easily misled by being maintained by ontically dominated *Dasein* to be a distinction between activities.

113. Primordial otherness has already spoken and its locus is not between psychoanalysis and law but between both of their instantiations as activities and their Being . In their Being, in their essence, psychoanalysis and law may not have a relationship of alterity. The Being of law and the Being of psychoanalysis may not be as distinct, separate or different as it seems. In their Being, law and psychoanalysis may not be so straightforwardly distinguished from one another. Psychoanalysis and law may be like different strands of a rope but still woven together to form the same rope. The strands of the rope, if seen individually, are distinct and other to one another, while the primordial otherness is between each strand and the togetherness of the strands that make the rope.

114. From the perspective of thinking-Being, then, despite the conventional distinction between psychoanalysis and law, in their Being they are not distinct *simpliciter*. In their essence, activities are not merely alternatives but are connected as a weave. In the sense of the essence-as-weave, law and psychoanalysis are together.

115. So we need to modify the translation thesis. Translation should work with both of them being part of the same 'rope' and not as distinct beings. The Being of law and psychoanalysis may belong together and in this sense 'translate' but only in the same sense that the essences of technology, history, Man and language 'translate' from

one to the other. I shall say much more about essence in the next chapter. The distinction between mere activities is still ontic and does not entail ontological togetherness. A distinction between activities is ontic and hence originally *arbitrary*. The ontological difference nears the Being of beings but is never about different beings and activities. If this is correct, it is not good to assert mere alternatives to, and in turn, the mere imperfection of, law, by fiat. Another way of saying it is that Being speaks *inter alia* through the Being of law, as well as through the Being of ontically other activities. It is, then, not original enough to say that we have to criticise law in its own playground. The Being of law, on the way of the sending of Being, unfolds together with the Being of other beings. They may unfold into a world together, in unity. Being transcends particular identifications, *qua* beings/practices/activities.

116. An important reiteration needs to be heeded at this point. We have made the initial contemplation that there might well be a relationship of alterity between law and its Being. Thinking about primordial otherness to law, we have located otherness in the ontological difference, namely between thinking about the being 'law' and thinking-Being of law. Thinking about the Being of law would be an aspect of thinking-Being. When I speak about otherness between law and its Being, I mean at the same time otherness between thinking with and through law and thinking-Being.

117. But further reflections ensue. Are law and its Being completely separate, or are they somehow complementary as between first and second bests, mutually facilitating and supportive. If so, could their relationship result in a 'middle' ethos, some comfortable (or even uncomfortable) togetherness of law and its Being? However, if the relationship between them in some sense gives rise to *harm*, to *Dasein* and with it, to thinking-Being, then there will be a reflective call for some act of overcoming that harm.

118. If the relationship between law and its Being gave rise to harm, it would be a peculiar sort of harm. It is the conventional way of looking at law to claim that its essential justification is in enforcing the aversion of some harm. We may be thinking, further, that law and its Being may harm one another while no law could protect that which is harmed.

119. What is thought-provoking in harm between both law and its Being, encompasses *Dasein*'s own being. The harm resulting from the coexistence of law and its Being is that human beings would be hindered from being ready to grasp the power of self-overcoming, the call of which is essential to their own nature. The distortion that is not allowed to clear in the relationship between law and its Being may colonise and perpetuate a distorted relationship of *Dasein* to its

own essence. Ethically, then, thinking *reflectively* about law can awaken a particular expression of a call to overcome inauthentic own-ness.

120. Harm between law and its Being may stem from the very thinking of them as coexistent. If this kind of harm is to be grasped it would mean that law may never be a mere condition or a framework for the realisation of its Being. The immersion in the former cannot directly further the unconcealment of the latter. Note, it is not said that in the ontic realm, the realm of purpose, for example, law could not be talked about as having the purpose of educating *Dasein*. It is just that harm can occur despite the success of this or that purpose, harm which hides underneath the celebration of success. Let us consider some of the parameters by which success can be celebrated. Let us consider some inauthentic relationships, and therefore potentially harmful ones, between law and its Being.

121. Complementarity between law and its Being can be seen as enabling one another to be, even to grow and to flourish. To enable can mean 'to provide a condition for being and flourishing'. In being a condition for being and flourishing 'enabling' can be understood as providing a framework without which the other could not possibly be and flourish. In another sense of condition for being and flourishing, 'enabling' means to guide or to enlighten, to educate. In this sense, law provides the mindfulness towards an involvement in its Being, and vice versa. In this sense, a condition opens gates, relieves internal fetters, focuses the mind.

122. Another sense of 'complementarity' is understood as doing something as long as the other cannot be done without it. Here, complementarity would entail monologic thinking of mutual purpose between law and its Being. According to this complementarity thesis, law and thinking-Being are simply different means of doing the same thing and in that they complement one another. For example, an expression of the complementarity thesis is that if, in thinking-Being, *Dasein*s do what law does on their own, then law to that extent becomes needless. The limit of legal intervention is tied here to human capacities to think morally on their own, to have a private ethics. Thinking about the Being of law here would mean the psychological internalisation of some moral code. Again, there is no real alterity here between law and its Being as both are conscripted to advance moral thought in terms of rights and obligations. The other to law here, its Being, is not really different but simply a different means to do what the law does, some private ethics arrived at in an exchange of sympathies and the internalisation of obligations that would otherwise would be determined by law. But the complementarity of law and sympathy is very different from alterity

between law and its Being. It involves the cultivation of some 'private' capacity to administer the kind of ethics that law also represents and effectuates.

123. But, thirdly, does complementarity in the sense of 'as long as something cannot be done without it' need to be within the monological rather than alterity? It may be claimed that, until some state of man is achieved in relation to that which is originally other to law, thinking-Being, we have to think *to some extent* with and through law or vice versa. This is complementarity of law not with regard to the internalisation of what law does but with its other – with thinking-Being. This view has already fallen into the trap of understanding 'thinking-Being' as an ontically different activity. This would mean that there is ontic parity between law and thinking-Being, and it would face a lot of same kind of objections which were raised above regarding the thesis of viewing law and its other as alternatives, or as translatable to one another. The thesis that 'as long as people are in a given state we complement their own deficient thinking-Being by thinking with and through law' needs to be reflected upon. There is a need to go to the very nature of alterity between them to show that such a thesis could not be advanced. The implication of this way of accounting to the thesis of complementarity between law and its Being would be to regard one of them as 'best' and the other as a 'second best'. This would mean that some quality of involvement by law can, to some agreeable extent, be replaced by its other. This would mean that thinking reflectively about law is turning into some kind of process of *modus vivendi* between it and its other. It would have to be reflected whether such *modus vivendi* is not *itself* the 'in-between' which constitutes the harmful relationship or the complementarity between law and its other.

124. If the relationship between law and its other is that of harm it would mean that, despite the distinction between law and its other, namely its Being, there would have to be some common preoccupation upon which any contemplation of harm to one another could be meaningful. Part of the understanding of this harm should reveal what this common preoccupation is. Both law and its other would involve different ways of addressing problems which may be shown to be to some extent similar, although the way these problems are conceived may be very different in the case of law and in the case of its other. For example, in thinking about morality, law and its other – its Being – may both be preoccupied with morality. However, the manner in which each approaches morality may be so different as to clear some alterity that is prevalent within morality itself. If what distinguishes law and its other is nothing but different approaches to

truth and language, that distinction, embodied in the ontological difference, may well correspond to such a distinction that exists within ethics and morality. We may then need to stop thinking too simplistically about moral harm that law enforces. Harm could be discussed as the consequence of the relationality between two very different view of ethics that characterise the ontological difference, namely between ontic manifestations of ethics and the Being of ethics. The proposition that the law enforces some harm would leap into a completely different perspective. The rest of this book very much contemplates the relationship between law and its Being, on the one hand, and ethics and its Being.

FINAL REFLECTIONS

125. It is possible, even desirable, to think reflectively about law, using the idea of nature. This term has been used extensively in thinking about law before, especially in ideas like 'natural law' or 'human nature'. The inauguration along the lines of a 'thing-nature' marks an enormous significance to thinking about law, in particular the relationship between natural law and divine law. The very question of what is nature, and how humans are in nature – being expressions of that nature – would have to relate to what the relationship is between law and its Being. The conception of nature as a 'thing' within which humans exist as the beings that they 'are' has given rise, in many ways to a characteristic of Man that led to metaphysical humanism. According to this metaphysical humanism, the natural characteristic of Man is to harm one another, and so some values are conceived, which are interpreted and prioritised, thereby providing for a universal natural code of law that averts that natural harm that humans inflict on one another. The construction of harm is part of the craving to construct 'nature' and 'Man in nature' correctly. We shall see that there is much in this statement on the connection between nature, Man in nature, and natural law. But once we stop thinking about nature as a thing and start thinking-Being, including thinking the Being of law, we shall open up this connection for deconstruction. Once we do not capture nature as a thing, because the ontological difference is grasped, approaches to truth and language and indeed 'nature', are radicalised to such an extent that talk, however critical, about natural law and the nature of Man, would not yet do justice to such radicalisation. Any connection between representational values to the nature of Man would essentially mischaracterise such radicalisation. Such is the radicalisation of 'aboutness'. To overcome nature as a thing which is expressible

through representational ideas would involve sending Man – the way Man is in the law of nature, as well as the way humans are in ethical relation to one another, the way they are protected in natural law – on the way to language as the unconcealment of Being.

4

The Essence of Law

Every epoch of world history is an epoch of erring.

Heidegger, *Holzwege*, p 311

What do we have in mind when speaking of essence? Usually it is thought to be those features held in common by everything that is true. The essence is discovered in the generic and universal concept, which represents the one feature that holds indifferently for many things. This indifferent essence (essentiality in the sense of *essentia*) is, however, only the inessential essence. What does the essential of something consist in? Presumably it lies in what the entity *is* in truth. The true essential nature of a thing is determined by way of its true being, by way of the truth of the given being. But we are now seeking not the truth of essential nature but the essential nature of truth. There thus appears a curious tangle. Is it only a curiosity or even merely the empty sophistry of a conceptual game, or is it – an abyss?

Heidegger, 'The Origin of the Work of Art', [p. 49]

1.   The essence of law is not legal. This statement must strike the reader as strange. Surely there is something of the essence of law in every-thing that is named 'legal'. The statement does not make common sense. Yet, thinking primordially about law is forgotten in common-sense thinking about law, including the most critical thinking within this horizon of the 'common'. Critical thinking within the 'common' does not yet think *about* law. To introduce primordial strangeness into ontic thinking with and through law, as well as to appreciate how what is essential in law is embedded in the ontic thinking, we need to slow down a lot and dwell in the strange. The essence of law is not legal. How are we to approach 'essence'; the 'the essence of law'; the 'not'; the 'legal'?

2.   What did Heidegger mean by the word 'essence' [*Wesen*]? His point of departure was the signification of essence in transcendental phenomenology as being:

Seeing and, in analysis, interpreting in an unprejudiced way and rendering accessible and holding fast on to suchlike as an intentional structure of mak-ing something, and forming one's concepts to measure regarding what is thus got hold of and seen – this is the sober sense of the much chatted about so-called phenomenological intuition of Essence.[1]

Transcendental phenomenology regards essence as that idea which corresponds to a being – to that which makes a thing the thing it is. The methodology of phenomenological reduction, or *epoché*, aims to describe the manner in which this essence is experienced by a transcendental ego. This ego is supposedly more universal and reliable than the Cartesian ego that has to take on all the prejudices of positive sciences as it goes about reflecting upon things. For phenomenology, there is transcendental, present-at-hand, 'thingness' of things, and the method is to grasp this universal thingness reliably. This universal thingness is essence for phenomenology, an essence which can be constructed by a transcendental ego. The methodology of the phenomenal reduction approaches a purer way in which thingness – the thing itself – is experienced by consciousness. The transcendental method claims to overcome psychological ego's prejudices by exposing the way the transcendental ego, or transcendental subjectivity, has intentionality towards a transcendental thing or object of thought. The response of this method to the prejudices of the positive sciences results in abstractions about the 'true' nature, or essence, of 'beings'. Transcendental phenomenology provide us with a methodological way towards essences of things. Such methodology enters a metaphysical infinite process of distilling these essences and so, in the process of so distilling, this method finds itself caught in constantly attempting to release itself from its own prejudices, yearning to find the language to describe the thing as it *really* is – in its essence. The ontology presumed by transcendental phenomenology is still a present-at-hand ontology – that of positive 'essence'. Its methodology still adheres to the notion of truth as 'correctness' and 'correspondence between idea and beings', which it still shares with the positive science that it aims to criticise. Language is still approached as signifying the positivity of beings. *Eventually* (if this moment ever comes) the transcendental phenomenological method attempts to grasp the universal *eidetic* essences.

---

[1] M Heidegger, *Die Grandprobleme der Phänomenologie, Gesamtausgabe,* vol 24 (Frankfurt, Vittorio Klostermann, 1975) p 161, quoted and translated by A Grieder, 'What did Heidegger mean by "Essence"?', reprinted in C Macann (ed), *Martin Heidegger: Critical Assessments* (London, Routledge, 1992) pp 183–212, at p 186. The translation in *BPP*, p 114 is: 'To see something like such an intentional structure of production and interpret it in one's analysis without prepossession, to make it accessible and keep hold of it and adapt one's concept-formation to what is thus heed fast and seen – this is the sober sense of the much ventilated so-called phenomenological *Wesensschau*.'

3.   For Heidegger, *essence* is bestowed by the thinking-Being of a being. Essence is bestowed as a result of being embraced by Being. *Essence* means that which 'enables' and which

> not only can achieve this or that but also can let something essentially unfold in its provenance, that is, let it be. It is on the 'strength' of such enabling by favoring that something is properly able to be. This enabling is what is properly 'possible' [*das 'Mög-liche'*], whose essence resides in favoring.[2]

> Heidegger explains that he does not contrast the 'potential' essence with 'actual' existence', as metaphysical thinking about 'beings' or 'things' does. The 'possible' does not mean a mere number of possibilities or the essence as the 'potential' of existence. The essence as the 'possible' is never reduced to an essential thing but rather that which is given to beings – that which lets beings be. The essence is the unfolding possibility of the thingness of things. Essence is the thingness that is encapsulated in that readiness-to-hand towards which *Dasein* is comported as moments in which its Being is an issue for it. The essence of things is intimately connected to the essence of *Dasein*. Essence connects the 'there' of things and the 'there' of *Dasein*. Essence is nothing less than the quiet power of Being itself.[3]

4.   Along the way of his own thinking-Being, Heidegger mentions the word 'essence' a lot. He writes about the Essence of Truth, the Essence of Technology, the Essence of Reason, the Essence of Humans, the Essence of Art. This word 'essence' in all of these expressions keeps a close connectedness to thinking-Being. The word 'essence' conveys the sense in which Being needs the being-there, the *Da-sein* as the entity which can be claimed by Being, thus pointing towards it. The word 'essence' conveys one of the main insights of Heidegger: that *without Dasein there is no Being although this is precisely the feature that makes Dasein subservient to Being. Dasein* is both necessary and subservient to Being by being open to, and also bringing, Being's Saying or Speaking – which is always already lurking inexpressibly in its ontic engagements – into language.

5.   The understanding of 'essence', for Heidegger, connects this relationship between *Dasein* and Being. The very term 'understanding' connotes that relationship. Understanding, standing before [*vor-stehen*], characterises that relationship. To understand is already to be subservient to the call of Being before responding to it. Also, grasping essence means to grasp essence as the 'how' of Being and *Dasein* as standing-before one another. Essence connotes the

[2] *LH*, p 220.
[3] *Ibid.*

temporal site – the always-already-before that both *Dasein* and Being meet.

6.   The phrase 'essence of ...' reveals an aspect of the way Being lets beings be in the whilst of its Saying, Sending and fateful temporality. All essences are already given in the mundane everydayness of *Dasein*. All essences are immersed in the mundane everyday and point towards the depth of the nearness of the everyday. Essences are given to beings. But the way they are given to beings is, for the most part, distorted, and authentic temporal engagement with them, the very moment of disclosure, has already withdrawn and left only a trace of itself. Essences are both primordial and fragile within the overwhelmingness of the mundane everyday. They are concealed in the ontic, that is in for-the-most-part being and thinking.

7.   In *A Question concerning Technology* Heidegger maintains that the essence of technology is *nothing* technological. In stating 'The essence of law is not legal', I use the term 'not' instead of 'nothing' because I feel that it conveys three senses that best capture Heidegger's subtle meaning of 'not' in this key phrase. First, the 'not' can be understood as 'not like the conventional way in which the term in question [here 'technology'] is used'. So this first sense connotes an etymological opening towards the primordial and ancient understanding of a term, one which has not totally disappeared but has been suppressed and highly distorted. The second sense of the 'not' is temporal: it captures the concealed 'not yet' within the mundane everyday and, as such, a distorted manner by which essence appears, and is expressed, in the everyday. But, thirdly, the 'not' conveys the very sense of the primordial nothing with which the notion of essence is associated. For Heidegger, essence does not mean focusing on what things are. Essence rather conveys the nearness of the worldliness of things which connotes thinking about them *not* as things/beings.

8.   The 'not' in the phrase 'the essence of technology is not technological' is not a term of negation. It does not say that there is something 'technological' which is completely distinct or totally 'other' than the 'essence of technology'. A negation would immediately throw thinking into representation, definitions and logic. What is conveyed by the 'not' is rather that the relationship between essence and its ontic occurrence is characterised by a 'not' which is both a distortion and a temporal deferral as 'not yet'. This double sense of 'not yet' is manifested as that engagement with the ontological which itself is always 'already' withdrawn upon the event of engagement. The essence is given by Being to beings and is the way Being is distorted in any craving for accounts or methods or theories of beings. In thinking the essential we need both to expose the distortion and to

think *back*. The ontological difference manifests itself in the distortion between thinking about beings and thinking about their Being. The ontological difference manifests itself also in the distortion between the 'quiet power of the possible' of essences and the essence of things as that which is transcendental. The latter is merely an endless search for representation of the common denominator between the different experience of beings by consciousness. Essence for Heidegger is not the transcendental manifestations of what are merely accidental properties of a being – a thing.

9. Essence is itself the essential unfolding of Being in beings. This is the way *Conatus essendi* should be grasped from Heideggerian perspective. Putting it verbally, as Heidegger often does, the persistence of essence in beings' 'essencies'. This verbal expression was Heidegger's way of not turning essence, and indeed Being, into a mere representation of a thing. Heidegger coined a verbal term for essences – essencing [*Wesung*] – to stress the dynamic unfolding of the 'howness' of essences as manifested distortingly in the 'whatness' of beings.

10. All this is very general and needs much more magnification. To recap, we want to grasp the essence of law and magnify the sense in which this essence is not legal. The understanding of essence itself will help us a lot to understand what is the 'not' in 'not legal'. To fully grasp what characterises the distorted relationship between essence and its ontic occurrence it is necessary to read Heidegger's lecture *On the Essence of Truth* in which he contemplates at length his understanding of 'essence'. This reading will be supplemented by Heidegger's insights about essence in *The Origin of the Work of Art*.

11. In *On the Essence of Truth* the 'not', both as distortion and as deferred 'not yet', touches also the meaning of essence itself, as it were, the notion of 'essence of essence'. Heidegger was preoccupied in this lecture not only with the 'essence of truth', but also with the 'truth of essence'.[4] The grasping of the truth of essence is linked to the grasping of the essence of truth. When we try to understand the essence of law we are inevitably linked to the question of what is the origin of the truth of law, what is primordial in law – its Being. Further, we are after the question of how truth itself is seen by law whilst law is being thought about for-the-most part. We could then try to grasp the 'not' between the essence of law and law-for-the-most-part, as encapsulated in the statement that 'the essence of law is not legal'.

12. The contemplation of the essence of truth is central to Heidegger's attempt to think-back the whole Western metaphysical philosophical

---

[4] *ET*, pp 135–8.

tradition. At first sight, the question of 'essence' seems to lead to a superfluous general philosophical quest that takes the mind away from thinking anything actual: 'with this question concerning essence do we not soar too high into the void of generality that deprives all thinking of breath?'.[5] Whilst acknowledging the seriousness of such a criticism against the seeking of essences, Heidegger maintains that it is highly unsatisfactory just to attack generalisations and to take refuge in 'common sense', the so-called actual truth, for it would still beg the question of what truth is, as such. To reiterate, it is clear that we are not after essence as a generalised distilled 'extract' or 'common denominator' by which different understandings of a term are interlinked in order to communicate some 'thing-essence'.

13.   Truth in Western thinking lies in *Correctness* [*Richtigkeit*]. Correctness assumes without question a *correspondence* between a statement and an object, a thing. But the question remains as to what makes this correspondence correspond. What conditions the relatedness between the statement and the thing? This relatedness depends upon the nature of the comportment of people towards beings. But there is some open region, the unfolding space of which is a way, a comportment towards which has been already indicated while speaking about beings as they are.[6] There is a pre-given comportment prior to the statement that corresponds to a thing which allows the speaking of that thing to be contemplated as 'the thing it is'. This pre-existing comportment towards an open region is the proper 'site' to look for an origin of the essence of truth. Truth as the origin of correctness is not originated by the correspondence between representational propositions thought about by a subject and objects. Truth as origin is 'disclosure of beings through which an openness essentially unfolds [*west*].[7]

14.   In *Being and Time* Heidegger maintains that *Dasein* is both in truth and in untruth.[8] That is another way of saying that *Dasein* essentially 'ek-sists'. Truth here is referred to by Heidegger as *uncovering* – 'Being true as Being-uncovering'.[9] We can read the phrase 'Being-uncovering' as having a double sense. It can be read as *Dasein* uncovering Being in its 'ek-sistence', but also, and relatedly, (as unsaid at this stage of *Being and Time*) an antecedent uncovering by

[5] *Ibid*, p 115.
[6] *Ibid*, p 122.
[7] *Ibid*, p 127. Grieder acknowledges Heidegger's notion of essence as a *be-wegen*, or 'making way'. As making way, essence is not understood verbally. An essence essences: Grieder, 'What did Heidegger mean by "Essence?"', above n 1, at pp 200–201.
[8] *BT*, p 265. Heidegger discusses truth at length: *ibid*, pp 256–73.
[9] *Ibid*, p 261.

Being of itself for *Dasein*. For its own Being to be an issue for it is for *Dasein* to uncover Being, but it uncovers Being that has already left a trace of its own uncovering for *Dasein*. *Dasein is* in truth as long as it is being uncovered as uncovering. *Dasein* is always already ahead of itself in being thrown into its own innermost world – in this sense *Dasein* is in the truth. But the way *Dasein* is also always already late (by being ahead of itself) means that it falls into the ontic. If, as a reader of Heidegger, I incorporate Heidegger's later vocabulary of nearness into that of *Being and Time* we can say that *Dasein*'s 'throwness' is always nearer to the event of truth than its ontic fall. In the language of the later reflection which shifts attention from *Dasein* to Being that *Dasein* is comported to, we can say that *Dasein* is in truth when the inexpressible Saying of Being calls *Dasein* as *Dasein*'s nearest although *Dasein*'s response must be a necessary fall into untruth. Truth/untruth characterises truth as uncovering. This reading of *Dasein*'s 'ek-sistence' in uncovering echoes as the unsaid of *Being and Time* precisely the call/response that characterises the mutual appropriation of *Dasein* and Being. But the fact that truth conceals itself as it reveals is also concealed. The fact that truth's nature is truth/untruth is itself concealed in what Heidegger referred to as double concealment. In 'The Origin of the Work of Art' Heidegger had this to say:

The nature of truth, that is, of unconcealedness, is dominated throughout by a denial. Yet this denial is not a defect or a fault, as though truth were an unalloyed unconcealedness that has rid itself of everything concealed. If truth could accomplish this, it would no longer be itself. *This denial, in the form of a double concealment, belongs to the nature of truth as unconcealedness.* Truth, in its nature, is un-truth.[10]

15. Let us see how these themes are developed in *On the Essence of Truth* and in relation to the discussion of 'essence'. Part of over-coming the notion of truth as correctness and understanding the origin of truth as correspondence between ideas and things/beings is to understand the essence of truth as residing in the between of 'already' and 'not yet', between revealing and concealing. Being both in truth and in untruth seems illogical. In order to grasp this, two things need to be elaborated upon. The first is that the notion of correctness, although being overcome, is part of the unfolding of the essence of truth. Second, the essence of both truth and untruth are two sides of the same coin. One implies the other.

16. The essence of truth is antecedent to the immediate representation

---

[10] *OWA*, p 53.

and calculative familiarity with beings. When familiarity with beings becomes boundless, openness to Being, openness to what Heidegger referred to 'beings as a whole' is completely covered up and forgotten.[11] 'Beings as a whole' means that the suchness of any 'being' is never isolated so it can be represented as a whole being. The suchness of beings is already a part of a web of relations that constitutes a referential totality or a world. This world is never readily available for *Dasein*. It is too near for *Dasein*. Comportment towards beings as a whole is kept concealed whilst familiarity with 'beings' predominates. Indeed, from the point of view of familiarity with beings *qua* beings, the open region of beings as a whole seems indeterminate and incalculable.

17. Truth, as the correctness within the immediately familiar, is furthest from the essence of truth. Mere knowledge, as well as seeking for models that lead to the advancement of knowledge, is indicative of what Heidegger calls the 'non-essence' of truth. *Dasein*'s 'ek-sistence' means that Being always precedes *Dasein*, or to put it differently, *Dasein* is always already comported towards that which precedes it as its innermost own – as its nearest – and so untruth cannot be just a matter of Man's will or negligence. The untrue is a part of the hermeneutic temporal cycle within which truth as unconcealment [*alethēia*] reveals itself in its withdrawal. Truth and untruth in their *essence* are not irrelevant to one other.[12] There is a role for the non-essence of truth or untruth to reveal the grasp of the essence of truth. It should be stressed that the untrue here does not mean incorrectness but rather something that belongs to the very process of revealing and concealing that which is nearest. The non-essence is the essence of truth.[13] The comportment towards beings as a whole conceals as it reveals.

18. Concealment preserves unconcealment. 'Considered with respect to truth as disclosedness, concealment is then undisclosedness and accordingly the untruth that is most proper to the essence of truth.'[14] Truth in its conventional sense – correctness – prevents the disclosedness of untruth proper, unconcealment so essential to the *mystery* of Being of beings.

19. The mystery of essence is characterised by primordial concealment of the 'it' which is itself concealed in the ontic said. Untruth proper, the non-essence of truth, is the mystery. Understood not merely as indeterminacy or privation of knowledge but as unconcealment of

---

[11] *ET*, p 129.
[12] *Ibid*, pp 127–32.
[13] *Ibid*.
[14] *Ibid*, p 130.

the near, the mystery is part of the essence of truth. This is what Heidegger calls pre-essential essence which never becomes irrelevant to truth.[15] The process of unconcealment of the Being of beings conceals itself in revealing and, mysteriously, conceals this concealment. The 'it' gets its essence only as being essentially and mysteriously deferred. The relation of any being to 'beings as a whole' is mysterious. 'Ek-sistence' refers to *Dasein*'s anxious comportment towards the mystery. *Alethēia* is essentially already too far (untruth proper) in its unconcealment of the near. The openness towards the open region which precedes, and is given to, correctness is characterised as the openness towards the near as *alethēia*. Truth in essence relates not to what is but towards what is mysteriously and necessarily 'not yet'. But in any given epoch the mystery is being forgotten and so, for the most part:

man clings to what is readily available and controllable even where ultimate matters are concerned. And if he sets out to extend, change, newly assimilate, or secure the openedness of the beings pertaining to the most various domains of his activity and interest, then he still takes his directives from the sphere of readily available intentions and needs.[16]

20. Heidegger conceives any movement within the readily available as not authentically essential, namely as not confronting that which is always mysteriously too near. Even though such an inauthentic movement reveals disagreements, indeterminacies, ignorance, puzzles and undecided matters, the engagement is still not essential. All these clashes, although they may well present themselves as fundamental, still do not confront the mystery, untruth proper, the proper concealment that occurs in unconcealment of the open region of beings as a whole. An essential movement *preserves* the mystery without forgetting it, without moving too far from it. Forgetfulness of concealment, of untruth proper, is characterised by a particular presence nourished by subject-based thinking, representations and planning. The presence, and the necessity, of this forgetfulness of the world that is opened up by beings as a whole is itself a distortion of Being, it is the 'not':

From [the latest needs and aims] man then takes his standards, forgetting being as a whole. He persists in them and continually supplies himself with new standards, yet without considering either the ground for taking up standards or the essence of what gives the standard. ... He is all the more

---

[15] *Ibid*, pp 130–31.
[16] *Ibid*, p 131.

mistaken the more exclusively he takes himself, as subject, to be the standard for all beings.[17]

21.   Such a presence of what is unessential to truth *as not confronting untruth proper* Heidegger calls error, or errancy. This error is one component of distortion or the 'not' when we say that an 'essence is "not"'. The distortion of essences in the ontic involves both untruth proper and error.

22.   As we have seen, to the essence of truth as *alethēia*, belongs untruth proper or concealment. The mystery is the essence of truth and so the essence of truth is in the 'not' of things that comes from their relationship to beings as a whole, a relationship which unfolds towards the near, concealing its unfolding. Truth essentially unfolds as already untruth. That is the ontological difference.

23.   We must take care to distinguish untruth proper as essential to *alethēia* from error, as well as to appreciate the relationship between them. Untruth proper is part of the nature of truth. Error, although related to the essence of truth, is what characterises the historicity of *Dasein* because *Dasein*'s existence in truth is that of 'ek-sistence'. *Dasein*'s 'ek-sistence' means that *Dasein* essentially errs: 'As insistent, man turns towards the most readily available beings. But he insists only by being already ek-sistent, since, after all, he takes beings as his standard.'[18] So, if the essence of truth is understood as *alethēia* and belongs to the 'ek-sistential' *Dasein*, error must be configured into the ontological difference. In its comportment towards the near, *Dasein* already, and essentially, falls back to an ontic relationship with beings. I mentioned that error is also historical. The perpetuation of the forgetfulness of the mystery also belongs to the historical hermeneutic cycle of Being's unconcealment/concealment. The forgetfulness of Being and, with it, truth as *alethēia,* is also an epoch of, a phase in, the cycle of the Sending of Being: 'The insistent turning toward what is readily available and the ek-sistent turning away from the mystery belong together.'[19]

24.   A complex picture emerges of the mystery of the essence of truth and the epochal forgetfulness of this mystery. There is the essential 'non-essence' of truth as the concealment which is essential to truth, that is, part of the characteristic of the essence of truth. As a part of concealing the oneness of the essence of truth and its non-essence Heidegger accounts for the more temporal or history-oriented forgetfulness of Being. During each epoch in the history of Being, *Dasein*'s

[17] *Ibid*, p 132.
[18] *Ibid*, pp 132-3.
[19] *Ibid*, p 133.

bathing unthinkingly in its existence for-the-most-part is being deaf to its essential 'ek-sistence'. Error, as the forgetfulness of the mystery of that essential oneness of the essence and non-essence of truth, is thus still within the essence of truth being unessential or, rather, not yet attentive to that which is essential.

25. Errancy, although not yet essential to truth, is part of *Dasein*'s hermeneutic cycle of 'ek-sistence'. Errancy is not just a mishap but is part of the constitution of *Dasein* as its fateful 'ek-sisting' towards Being. The mis-take is constantly made and is essential to *Dasein*. Errancy is what Heidegger calls the 'counter-essence' of truth. Being a part of the constitution of *Dasein*, counter-essence is also essential for the concealment of the mysterious question of questions to hold sway. To err and to perpetuate the counter-essence of truth is the very make-up of *Dasein* and *in this sense* it is essential (essential means here 'always relevant') to both *Dasein* and to the historicity of truth.

26. Within the domain of the readily available present-at-hand, error is manifested as incorrectness, and this can show itself as mis-judgement, error of calculation, incompleteness of description, or emphasising one aspect in giving an account of a being at the expense of another. Error, which is a part of the constitution of *Dasein*, does not yet-relate to such present-at-hand one-sidedness.

27. Error is historical and is a part of the cyclical temporality, that is, the historicity of Being and *Dasein*. Being open to one-sidedness *as such* is antecedent to simply exposing the arbitrariness of this or that representational account. Letting Being be involves being open to, and thus free towards, the non-essence which is a part of the essence of truth. Being open to one-sidedness means that error itself is the window to the essence of truth – as a turning of *Dasein* towards overcoming truth as correctness and with it the conception of truth prevailing in Western philosophy:

But, as leading astray, errancy at the same time contributes to the possibility that man is capable of drawing up from his ek-sistence – the possibility that, by experiencing errancy itself and by not mistaking the mystery of Da-sein, he *not* let himself be led astray.[20]

28. Can we see in this last quote a seed of ethics and a seed of some necessary protection of *Dasein* in its 'ek-sistence'?

29. Thinking about law is to think about the concealment of the essence of law, of the untruth proper. Thinking about law is thinking about the error that involves seeing law as a thing rather than grasping how law is connected to the mystery of the relationship of the essence of

[20] *Ibid*, p 134.

law to all other essences. Thinking about law is thinking about how the Being of law unconceals itself within the mystery of beings as a whole.

30. Bearing in mind the distinction and relationship between the essence of truth (truth/untruth proper) and error (historicity of 'ek-sistential' *Dasein* that falls into counter-essential thinking) we need to clarify a point here. Errancy, as always part of, always relevant to, the essence of truth, has degrees of intensity of forgetfulness. There are epochs in which being-in-errancy is by and large attentive to the call of the mystery, so permitting the ontic/ontological interaction to be more readily confronted. There are epochs, however, when the forgetfulness is by and large entrenched, the error becomes the hegemonic, calculative, way of thinking about both the truth of essence and the essence of truth. In such epochs, except for small number of attentive *Dasein*s who keep nearing the mystery, ultimate correctness is equated with the divine. Further, correctness becomes the root of considering difference. The point to be made here is that both of these characterisations of error are part and parcel of the way the essence of truth unfolds. In the next three chapters the extent of error and the sophistication it has assumed will be dealt with.

31. By *essentially* experiencing errancy, *Dasein* preserves its essence, its openness to Being, and does not let itself go astray. The error makes for a little glimmer of a window towards unconcealing that which is self-concealed nearest to *Dasein*. Errancy oppresses Man in anxiety. Anxiety is the experience of errancy as that call of something forgotten. Anxiety is the emotion in which the mystery shows itself as a call. The 'not' of errancy and, more primordially, of the non-essence of truth (untruth proper which is part of the essence of truth), brings up the connection between authenticity and inauthenticity as one of *distortion*. The mystery keeps impressing itself upon *Dasein* distortingly as some inexpressible otherness and strangeness. Authenticity as the being-in-the-whilst-of the call of Being already involves concealment.

32. Errancy, then, is a necessary part of the process of what it is to be human *Dasein*, namely a creature whose Being is an issue for it, and because of that it can retain some openness, some capacity for oppression by the essence of truth (which includes untruth proper). Errancy is necessary in the sense of being an essential part of the relationship of appropriation between human *Dasein* and Being. It is necessary in being fateful and inevitable in the sense of leaping towards the temporality of Being which precedes it, revealing and concealing itself.

33. Even the signification of *Dasein*'s birth and death is revealed and concealed in a world that goes beyond *Dasein*'s life in clock-time.

Conceiving *Dasein*'s life in clock-time is part of the errancy and is precisely what leaves *Dasein* always hanging over the abyss.

34. *Essential error is an epochal manifestation of the distortion that characterises the essence of truth.* The essence of truth, including its essential non-essence, keeps *Dasein* oppressed in errancy. Errancy is the manifestation of the primordial essence of truth – what Heidegger called the rule of the 'mystery in errancy'.[21] *This mystery points at perhaps the most original signification and manifestation of a 'problem'.* Concealment occurs because the openness to Being is already on its way to errancy. This mystery connotes the 'withdrawal of Being' – that insights of the inexpressible occur from time to time, always too late and always distortingly expressed.

35. Errancy belongs to the way essences are. Essences *are* in a distortion-begotten way because errancy holds sway essentially. The 'not' belongs to essence *qua* essence or we can say that the 'not' is the essence of essence. To repeat, unconcealment is never of a being but of its Being – of the being's openness to 'beings as a whole'. Essence is the 'is-as-not', not as a confirmation of both a thing and the idea that represent that thing, that is a correspondence between *idea* and *ideatum* (that of which it is the idea). Because of this rule of the mystery in errancy, the *Seinfrage*, the question of the Being of beings, is necessarily and inherently a misleading question, and the essence of truth understood through the rule of the mystery of errancy explains how *Dasein* comports itself towards such a question. 'In the concept of essence philosophy thinks Being.'[22]

36. Let me sum up the relationship between the non-essence of truth (which is a part of truth) and error (which is a part of the 'ek-sistential' historical process in which Man essentially dwells). The truth of essence involves a 'not' of distortion. This distortion consists of the characteristic of truth as its own essential concealment, and error. Error is counter-essence because in *Richtigkeit* Man does not yet grasp the essence of truth and the truth of essence – namely the unification of essence and non-essence of truth.

37. Heidegger sums up his lecture by maintaining that the essence of truth and the truth of essence are intertwined. In a note to the lecture he says that *the essence of truth is the truth of essence*.[23] The essence of truth moves on the way from abstract generalisations which are tied to the idea of truth as correctness, *back* to truth as an 'ek-sistent' letting be, which is the grounding of truth as concealment and

[21] *Ibid*, p 135.
[22] *Ibid*, p 137.
[23] *Ibid*.

errancy. The truth of essence involves the mystery of errancy as distortion.

38. Understood as *alethēia*, truth as correctness is part of the essence of truth. Indeed, it is its non-essence. Understood as *alethēia* the essential interlacing of the essence and non-essence of truth is more primordial than correctness and must also be distinguished from scepticism and indeterminacy, which are but extreme affirmations of the hegemony of correctness. As the mysterious nearest of the near, *alethēia* is the furthest from scepticism and indeterminacy. All sceptics are very near the metaphysicians and very far from actuality.

39. Untruth proper is the concealment of beings as a whole as it reveals. *Richtigkeit* is a part of the process of *alethēia* in which the non-essence of truth is part of the essence of truth. Truth *is* the mystery of the near. Actuality of the actual, the primordial 'is', conceals its own concealing in revealing. The 'is' is essentially and mysteriously 'not'. It can never 'be' or crave to 'be' fully itself.

40. Grasping the essence of truth as *alethēia* has important implications for difference. It has important implications for ethics and for thinking about law. We can pose the main question here: is difference to be sought in terms of multiplicity or in terms of distance? To this question the rest of the book is dedicated.

41. Essence is on the way to the near and, as such, is a verb. The essencing of essence involves a distortion in which truth is considered. Essence does not involve some extracted 'whatness' or 'reality', and truth is not mere knowledge. Essence is a process in which a characteristic of Being as a whole – a process that can murmur only thorough immersion in ontic distortion. As such, any essence has a foothold in primordial unconcealment-whilst-concealing (including concealment of what is concealed – the mystery) as manifested in the historical process of necessary errancy. Primordially, the truth of essence is in its being a characteristic of Being itself and likewise any 'essence of ...' would be an aspect of Being. As such, any essence always appears distortingly for the immediately available, for-the-most-part, thinking.

42. It is with this in mind that we should approach Heidegger's remark in 'The Origin of the Work of Art' about the primordiality of truth as unconcealment:

But it is not we who presuppose the unconcealedness of beings; rather, the unconcealedness of beings (Being) puts us into such a condition of being that in our representation we always remain installed within and in attendance upon unconcealedness. Not only must that in *conformity* with which a cognition orders itself be already in some way unconcealed. The entire *realm* in which this 'conforming to something' goes on must already occur as a whole in the unconcealed; and this holds equally of that *for* which the conformity of a proposition to fact becomes manifest.[24]

43. What is a distortion? 'A being appears, but it presents itself as other than it is.'[25] Any distortion has both truth and untruth in it. A distortion that relates a well-known and available standard is the most superficial. A distortion which is within the horizon of representation is also already too far from actuality. A primordial distortion, which stems directly from the ontological difference, has in it something which is deeply truthful but which is 'there'.

44. *Distortion persists between ontic thinking that is within the horizon of correctness and an ontological event of call/response that is within the horizon of distance and authenticity. In the whilst 'between' correctness and distance, that is in the distortion which is already the necessary opening for the near, there persists complementarity between ontic and ontological – between nearest and more distanced articulations and expressions.*

45. Distortion without the possibility of a 'correcting standard' to help is the most difficult to get a hold of – that is the basis for anxiety. What is distorted is both very important as the actuality of the real thing, being inexpressible. As Heidegger teaches, the mystery is that concealment of what is concealed. It is not 'a being' which is mysterious but that nearest Being of a being – the Being of beings.

46. The mystery is constantly *other* to ontic thinking. It is antecedent to than any otherness that ontic thinking can generate. Any thinking about the potential ontic otherness is already subject to the rule of the mystery in errancy and as such it is already part of the ever-haunting mystery. What does it mean? It means that the mystery 'ek-sists' as a continuous space which is too near for the punctual ontic, whether actual or potential. Although the world of the mystery is larger than, and in turn other than, ontic thought, it includes the distorting ontic error. *The error is between confusing the otherness between continuum of the nearest and the punctual ontic to ontic otherness.* The mystery 'ek-sists'. Although consisting of the complementarity between the continuous and the punctual, the mystery manages to capture the nearest as that which is antecedent to any thinking that points towards the punctuating horizon of distinctions and separations. The mystery keeps overflowing any distinctions between sameness and separation. Its truth has a continuous quality to it, a 'there' before any punctuation. Error and distortion stem from the constant hide-and-seek between the

[24] *OWA*, pp 50–51.
[25] *Ibid*, p 52.

continuous and the punctual. Error does not simply connote the not-yet-conceptual otherness but the otherness *to* any chain of punctualising thinking which is always the nearest and which is distorted in the next-nearest to the nearest. Truth cannot be replaced by groundlessness. Truth is grounded in the mystery. The paraphrasing of the otherness that the mystery harbours into the otherness of potential ontic interruptions and separations is itself an 'it' which indicates that the mystery has concealed its concealment. Such paraphrasing is already an indication of error. From an ontological perspective such paraphrasing is reactionary to the mystery.

47. 'Essence of ...'has this primordial distortion that stems from the mystery of the continuous nearest. On the one hand there is aberration of it in the for-the-most-part thinking. On the other hand, something of it is present in such thinking so much so that it even *seems* to be an 'application' of that essence. Essence cannot be reduced to a thing. Rather, it always remains a verb that characterises the way along which Being conceals itself in unconcealment. An essence always involves this distortion which entails neither 'yes' nor 'no', neither same nor other. The essence calls as the continuous mysterious unfolding whose otherness, its persistent 'not', lies in the whilst of the event of the murmuring of its continuous nature. The errancy which holds the distortion occurs in philosophy's attempt to enact the mystery of essence into 'this' or 'that'. Both in concealing and in error, the truth of essence takes *Dasein* back, following the hints of the distortion to its origin.

48. The distortion of essence is nothing less that the distortion of Being itself and is the manner in which the ontological difference shows itself. The distortion of the essence of a being has its own non-essence in it, or its own primordial concealment, but this concealment of the distortion is also a *necessary* occurrence in the way *Dasein* is open to the Being of beings. Confronting the being as a being leads necessarily to error, or to the counter-essence. The 'not' of the ontological difference, then, is a distortion that keeps the question of Being both alive and necessarily misleading. In this necessity the error is itself a part of the hermeneutic cycle of Being and as such is occurs as a part of the hermeneutic actuality of the actual – it is true.

49. *How* is essence distorted in the ontic? How does errancy hold sway? The 'not' between essence and its ontic occurrence speaks distortingly as the 'not' which is otherwise than negation and that of an 'other to ...' – as the 'not' which distinguishes an ontic essence of one thing from another ontic essence of another thing. The authentic otherness which is enlivened, again distortingly, by errancy, occurs as

a murmur between the otherness that stems from one-sidedness of perpetuating ontic thinking and the otherness of oscillating between the ontic and the ontological. Such distortion bothers *Dasein* and requires listening and responding to the essence's authentic call that distinguishes itself as the genuine otherness of being lost in ontic, discursive, relational identifications.

50. Essences, for Heidegger, as given by Being to beings are essential aspects of Being itself. They all dwell in the house of Being within which language speaks. Essences are aspects of Being. This does not mean that we now have established a being called 'Being'. Rather the essence of Being, as the nothing, speaks through the 'not' of all other essences. 'Hearing' the distortion – an engagement with the 'not' that persists between essences and their ontic occurrence – brings out the distortion as a shimmer of light. This hearing is the first step of thinking-Being. Listening to the essence as it spoken by language allows the 'not' to speak authentically, that is, listening exposes the distortion of one-sidedness in for-the-most-part ontic thinking. In thinking-Being, essences are aspects of what Heidegger called the stillness. Any 'essence of ...' is an aspect of 'been-hood', as in having been [*Gewesenheit*].[26] The unfolding of essence is temporal and confronting it involves thinking back to an event in the course of 'having been'. An engagement with the unconcealing and deferring from which language speaks means overcoming the continuous ontic *postponement* of the primordial question of Being although, of course, the mystery means that deferral is effectuated by the very engagement with the question of Being. An ontic postponement is characterised by a replacement of one ontic relationship with another. Deferral is the temporal withdrawal of Being as a part of the near/far relationship of unconcealment-in-concealing. There is a relationship of 'not', then, between, on the one hand, essences which are different manifestations of letting be and, on the other hand, thinking which characterises essence as an essential extant 'thing' or 'a being'. A perpetuation of the ontic is the forgetfulness of the 'quiet power' of the distortion that belongs to essencing of essence. An attempt to arrive at a transcendental essence is a perpetuation of ontic thinking and so perpetuation of this forgetfulness – hence one-sidedness. The distortion in which the essence is given in the ontic is forgotten in the perpetuation of such one-sided thinking.

51. In all of his essays Heidegger spoke about essences. The essence of truth, the essence of humans, the essence of technology, of reason, of history, of language. Indeed, to recap, in *What is Called Thinking?*, Heidegger, in the context of explaining one-sided thinking, refers to

---

[26] *BT*, p 373, and fn 4.

the understanding of science being connected to understanding many other essences. There is a sense, then, that Heidegger envisages some order, order-of-Being, primordial order which is characterised by a 'not' that characterises each of its essences and which conveys different aspects of Being and thinking-Being. All essences hold sway in concealment and errancy, and *Dasein* comports towards them in 'ek-sistence'. All essences belong together as aspects of Being which speaks through re-concealment and the opening to errancy. What is essential to essences is that they are necessarily being distorted but inconspicuously in those points of nearness, those points of unsaid 'in-betweens', within the codification and punctuation of ontic being and thinking.

52. This 'order' of essences is not a 'model' or a 'system' or a 'structure'. The way essences are intertwined in the order of Being is what Heidegger referred to as 'fugal' connection. Heidegger referred to his own philosophy as not forming a philosophical system but rather being fugal. The order of Being is fugal in that it has many aspects, all spoken by language to hint at the mystery. Although short of being a 'system', essences are aspects which make for a systematic order. By this I do not mean systematic in the sense of a model with some input and predictable output, but rather in the sense of inter-connection which points at the same question: 'The "systematic place" of a problem is the substantial interconnections that mark out the direction and range of our questioning.'[27] The order of Being comes about as a result of essences which are connected fugally, that is, they are all different elements that are combined to produce one order, the order of Being. 'One' is meant here not as a numerical but as an all-encompassing essence in the depth of the temporality of its nearness.

53. Within the order of Being essences are interwoven and as such are not simply distinguished from one another. Their otherness is not an otherness of distinction. Within the order of Being there is no distinction. All thought of the essences converges towards a single thought – of thinking-Being. For example, the essence of technology, *technē*, is interwoven with the essence of language as 'speaking Being', and the essence of language is interwoven with the essence of reason. In all of the essences, primordial concealment and errancy hold sway.

54. The essence of law is not legal. If law is to be thought about ontologically, namely in its Being, its essence must keep its 'not' in

---

[27] Quoted from *Vom Wesen der menschlichen Freiheit. Einleitung in die Philosophie* [Lectures of 1930] (*Heidegger's Collected Works*, vol 31) (Frankfurt, Klostermann, 1975) p 201. Quoted in M Inwood, *A Heidegger Dictionary* (Oxford, Blackwell, 1999) at p 205.

for-the-most-part-thinking with and through law. The 'aboutness' of 'thinking about law' incorporates the 'not' in the sense of a distortion. This distortion, to recap, consists of what is concealed in such for-the-most-part-thinking about law, but also a double concealment, the concealment of what is concealed – the mystery of law. The essence of law, is, like any other essence, a fugal aspect of Being. The mystery of law is an aspect of the mystery of Being.

55. We have to find the 'howness' of law as an aspect of Being. By 'howness' we mean to relate the 'howness' of law as a thing to the more primordial 'howness' of the manner in which the essence of law is woven with all other essences as a part of the fugal order of Being.[28]

56. But surely there will be an objection here. What does all this have to do with the 'real' law that is so familiar to lawyers and indeed, for that matter, jurists, such as codes, statutes, case-law? What does it have to do with legal reasoning or precedents? What does it have to do with experts' risk calculation? How is it relevant to the real law, to what is going on in courts, in Parliaments, in various bureaucracies? Can what we have said so far ever be about what J. Austin called 'law properly so called', which is to be sharply contrasted with using law as a metaphor such as in 'the law of physics'? This talk about the essence of law seems to be too far-fetched, goes the objection.

57. The short and preliminary response to such 'common-sense' objection is that precisely what is being sought in an effort to think the primordial 'aboutness' of thinking about law is in order to know 'what is going on' in courts and in Parliament. We are after the actuality of the actual in law. However, this may not satisfy the objector. Although the objector may feel the cover-up effectuated by 'common sense', he or she can still maintain the second-best argument, saying: 'What is going in courts and in Parliament is a *response*, a quite sensible, even if not ideal response, to the forecasted chaos by unveiling what is really going on. Would it not be sensible to strive to remain in controlled concealment of "what is going in Parliaments and courts" even as far as critical thinking about statutes and case-law is concerned?'. Again, the provisional response is that

---

[28] It is misleading in my view to attempt to view the Being of law as a mere ontological horizon and not as an aspect of the fugal order of Being. There is a lurking echo here of viewing law as a thing, a specific 'object' and with it already perpetuating ontic tendencies. What is the 'of' in 'horizon of ...'? Arguably, seeing any ontological horizon has already been given the ontic errancy of derivative ontology. This error leads again to an investigation of the ontic essence of the legal and not of law. This so-called ontological horizon is a point of departure of my efforts here. The question that has to be asked about the 'aboutness' of thinking about law is not yet asked there. See J Tontti, *Right and Prejudice: Prolegomena to a Hermeneutical Philosophy of Law* (Aldershot, Ashgate, 2004) especially pp 85–99.

this objection is precisely the kind of craving that leads to forgetting the question of the Being of law. Striving for a secure second-best is already a part of the way *Dasein* comports in error to the fateful Saying of Being. But, as much as error is necessary, Man's attempt to gain control of what he does not control is a petty one. What is primordial will assert itself from the nearest. The essence of law must speak with or without Man's forgetfulness of it. Humans' petty attempt to control that essence through concealing representations is itself temporal in the way that the mystery in errancy holds sway. With every seemingly successful attempt at human control, the deeper the errancy, the more perfect the representational structure that conceals the event of errancy. The tighter the representational structure the stronger the power of Being becomes and the more intense the anxiety that haunts *Dasein*.

58. Here is another relationship between fear and anxiety. As law becomes more sophisticated in 'mapping' humans actions as well as in re-containing new insights through new definitions of new actions, facts, norms or risks, fear will be reduced, but anxiety will intensify because the question of Being will become even more forgotten in the concealment. The more perfect the error, the more deaf people become to potential insights that come from the essence of law, the more intense will be the anxiety. People become inattentive to the thoughtlessness of their theoretical attempts. As the 'common-sense' theory of the practice of law opens its arms and embraces the whole of being and thinking, anxiety will be at its highest.

59. We must be careful here not to blend, on the one hand, insecurity that is averted by law when some object of fear is defined and, on the other hand, the lessening of security by the intensification of anxiety which is caused by grasping that inexpressible forces are being unleashed, forces which are not reducible to the language used in legal practice.

60. The wheel of Being of law goes round and round, and distortion is the force that rotates it.

61. The rule of the mystery-in-errancy has to hold sway in the case of for-the-most-part thinking about law. The essence of law is distorted in such thinking. 'Legal' here conveys any involvement in for-the-most-part thinking with and through law, from the craving to establish and modify legal doctrines, to constitutional thinking with and through law, and to theories of law, however critical these theories may be. All these are the 'legal'. We shall see in the next three chapters just how sophisticated the error of forgetting the essence of law in the legal can become. In all of these ontic instances, the essence of law is distorted; namely, it holds sway in concealment

and errancy. All of these kinds of thinking have not yet thought about law.

62. The essence law is an aspect of the order of Being. It is tied to all other essences. That 'the essence of law is not legal' means that its happening is more primordial than the 'legal'. The 'not' of the essence of law is an aspect of the 'not' of the order of Being it is tied to. The essence of law belongs to the 'not' of the essences of language, Man and history. The essence of law is distorted as an aspect historical part of Being itself. The 'legal' is a distortion that is also part and parcel of the Sending of Being and as such it is connected to the way language, history and Man are distorted in being thought about for-the-most-part.

63. To recapitulate: the essence of law is not legal. First, the essence of law is distorted in its ontic occurrence – the 'legal' in all its manifestations. Let us stress the interdependence or even necessity between the legal and the essence of law. There is no ontological reflection – nearness – without immersion in the ontic – the far. The concealment and the errancy of the legal are the 'not' that holds *Dasein* in some manner that has not been unconcealed yet, in 'ek-sistence' towards the Sending of Being. This is not to say that the legal is related to the essence of law in a dialectical process of progression towards some ultimate reality of the realisation of the essence. The legal is necessary for holding the mystery and so it must persist in order to hold *Dasein* in anxiety towards its own innermost being-in-the-world – its primordial comportment towards Being. Being with and through the legal, in whatever fashion, makes *Dasein* anxious. It is anxious because it is 'not' through the perpetuation and anticipation of anything legal. It is such anxiety that makes *Dasein* listen to the call of the Being of law and respond by thinking that Being. What is distorted in the legal – what is unsaid but inexpressible in the legal – is important for *Dasein*. *Dasein* must immerse itself attentively in what is legal to find that 'not' – the non-essence of the truth of the essence of law. In order to do so *Dasein* must engage with the 'not' of all the other essences which constitute the order of Being. So we should not negate the legal but rather find what is being distorted in being with and through it and how it is being distorted in relation to all other essences. We need to think through the essence of law in the order of Being. The exploration we conduct must attempt to expose the essence of the concealment and errancy. As such it will take us, in due course, seemingly away from, but actually nearer to, what is the actuality of the actual of law.

64. That the essence of law is not legal means that it is nearer to actuality than the legal. It is nearer in that in order to think the essence of law, the engagement has to be made with the truth of the legal, the way

language speaks in choosing to articulate concepts deployed by the legal, the way history is viewed in the legal and how Man sees himself in the legal. Thinking about law, that is, thinking about the distortion of the essence of law in the 'legal', pertains not to law but to the notions of truth, language, history and Man that the legal nourishes distortingly. Thinking about the essence of law means thinking about the whole of metaphysical tradition, including the fateful occurrence of this tradition in the history of Being, because the essence of law is part of the order of Being which sends and speaks this very tradition. This is why the Being of law is not 'distinct' from the Being of any other activity, as the 'not' would reside in the ontic–ontological oscillation in which the essence of any other activity distorts its essence. The fugal meaning of the order of Being means that activities are not distinguished *in essence*. All activities, for example, morality, psychology, law and, of course, language, have their essential occurrence in distortion. To put it another way, it is the consequences of the essence of law as being primordially distorted in the legal that make this essence indistinguishable from the essence of any other activity.

65.   The essence of law is manifested distortingly in all manifestations of the legal. It *has* to do a lot with judicial decision, with litigation, with legislation, with constitutions, with legal theories however critical, with regulations which are based on risk assessment. All these point towards certain approaches to truth, language, Man and history, the unsaid of which has to be thought about together with thinking about the essence of law. All these embody the rule of the mystery in errancy and in this sense they are true. The errancy is the fact that the more we try to generalise from the practice of law – and, even further, the more we feel that we touch the complexity of law as based on its practice– the further away we move from the essence of law, the more we forget the distortion, we forget the mystery.

66.   To summarise: in doing more with the legal we get further away from what law is about primordially. This getting far away, however, is part of the way that we have to go – the way which already thinks us back regardless of our ontic forgetfulness and deep error. Our errancy is dangerous but it also brings with it the saving power. Thus, even in deep errancy, humans are fated as the guardians of Being. Any ontological investigation of the legal has to be undertaken with a view to the 'not', with a view to trying to echo the inevitable murmuring that lurks in the near – the mystery in errancy.

67.   The means of being attentive to essences is to listen to the simple saying of language, saying that by its nature remains unsaid in what is said. The mystery murmurs, never becomes a thing, a being, a 'said'. Like many other invocations of early Greek words used by

Heidegger to connote the primordial signification of essences, the essence of law lies in the early Greek word *dikē*. The word appears in Plato's *Republic* and is usually spoken about in connection with morality and law. Heidegger sees in Socrates, Plato and Aristotle the dawn of Western metaphysical philosophical tradition and with it the forgetfulness of the question of Being. He wants to trace back the meaning of those words to the Pre-Socratics in order to establish that signification of them which can embrace a constant direct engagement with the mystery, with Being, with the fugal order of Being. For Heidegger it was the Pre-Socratics who dwelt in the house of Being by experiencing Being through the way they used language. The mystery was more readily engaged with by the Pre-Socratics. For Heidegger, to think the present, current problems which are thought-provoking, in the stillness of the twilight of philosophy, is to listen to the Sending of Being in the way it has been concealed in the whole philosophical tradition. Listening to the unsaid of Plato, in the Myth of the Cave, for example, would be to dwell at the site where thinking-Being makes its significant and fateful march into forgetfulness. The same would, of course, be true of the present age where that tradition retains its stronghold. Amidst the quietness of this stronghold, the echoes of Being's call with the fateful battle it brings in its wake, must be made audible.

68. This is the way that Heidegger approached the essence of law – *dikē*. I intend to follow closely Heidegger's work on *dikē* as that which conveys the essence of law. I will interpret *dikē* in the light of Heidegger's view of essences relating my interpretation of *dikē* to what I have called the 'legal'.

69. In order to think 'about' law, the aboutness must encompass the 'legal' so that the relationship of the 'not', of the distortion between essences and their ontic occurrences can be glimpsed. We have to see the birth of the forgetfulness of (rather than merely concealing) the mystery of law by the legal. The fate of entrenching the 'legal' occurred together with the birth of Subject and Truth. Ancient Greeks (and for that matter possibly all those cultures whose thinking was not tainted by the Western philosophical tradition), although also embodying the legal, experienced the mystery of Being, the mystery of the ontological difference, in a much more direct manner. The Pre-Socratics' relationship with time, language, Man and knowledge,was very different from, and primordial to, the Western tradition's thinking. Investigating the Pre-Socratics' world, as hinted at in their language in relation to law, opens a door to the mystery of law in a way that traditional thinking which is immersed in the legal cannot do.

70. The essence of law as related to the word *dikē* is discussed in the

main by Heidegger in three works: in his essay 'The Scope and Context of Plato's Meditation on the Relationship of Art and Truth'[29]; in his essay 'The Anaximander's Fragment' now published in the collection of *Early Greek Thinking*,[30] and most profoundly in his lecture 'The Limitation of Being' [1935] published in the collection *Introduction to Metaphysics*.[31]

71. What we get from all these three works is a primordial view of the essence of law and how it interacts with the essences of truth and technology within the order of Being. Most importantly, the essence of law is closely related to the essence of ethics, or the ethical, as discussed in chapters eight and nine. In these chapters I explore the fugal ethical relationship in the happening of the order of Being between the essence of law and the ethical essence of human beings as being relational to one another. The role of the essence of law, then, *must* be understood in relation to the essences of Man, technology and truth as they are all woven into one another in the fugal order of Being.

72. In *An Introduction to Metaphysics*, Heidegger discusses Parmenides' third dictum: 'Thinking and Being are the same'. This dictum is discussed by Heidegger in the context of the first chorus of Sophocles' *Antigona*, which starts by stating that Man is the strangest of the strange. Heidegger attempts first to regain the original truth of Parmenides' maxim and then to show how this truth is distorted in the Western philosophical tradition. The word 'original' here means something which is primordial in that: 'The original remains original only if it never loses the possibility of being what it is: origin as emergence (from the concealment of the essence).'[32]

73. Heidegger traces the relationship between Being in thinking to the words *deinon* and *deinotaton*. The latter refers to the essence of Man as being the 'strangest', the uncanniest, whose being is characterised by extreme limits and sudden abysses. This abyss-essence cannot be discerned through searching for attributes, characteristics and states, but it is only available through poetic insights.[33]

74. The word *deinon* encapsulates the never-ending abyss within which the essence of Man 'ek-sists'. One the one hand, *deinon* signifies the overpowering, the terrible, not in the petty sense of terrible but in the

---

[29] [1936–7], in *Nietzche (Vol 1: The Will to Power as Art)*, DF Krell (ed and trans) (New York, Harper Collins, 1991) pp 162–70.

[30] DF Krell and FA Capuzzi (trans) (London, Harper and Row, 1975) pp 13–58. This fragment is the last essay in Heidegger's untranslated book, *Holzwege* ('Woodpaths' – paths for collecting wood in the forest that do not have any beginning or destination), published in 1950.

[31] R Manheim (trans.) (Yale University Press, 1961).

[32] *IM*, p 145.

[33] *Ibid*, p 149.

sense of that which inaugurates panic and fear. It is so mighty that a person cannot escape from fearing it. The overpowering, however, is always too far and can never fully been fathomed: 'Where it irrupts it *can* hold its overpowering power in check. Yet, this does not make it more innocuous but *still* more terrible and remote.'[34] This notion of the terrible goes some way to explain the relationship between fear and the anxiety of the overpowering. Its primordial and ubiquitous nature can be feared in general but can be experienced only as anxiety. All human beings fear it *vis-à-vis* themselves. The remoteness also means that the overpowering can-not be seen, can never become an object but rather is 'collected, silent awe that vibrates with its own rhythm'.[35] In this sense of *deinon* it has the sense of terrible calmness that stems from its omni-present primordiality. It is everywhere as the very 'thereness' of the 'there'.

75. Second, *deinon* connotes the powerful, who is violent in using his power in his very being-there. Heidegger surmises that 'violence' here, again, is not understood in the conventional sense of 'disturbance of the peace'. It is the violence that is required to say the inexpressible. Let us listen to Hebrew: the word 'violence' is ALIMUT, to be violent, ALIM, which has the same root as the word ELEM, which means not being able to speak because of some shock force that silences. To be-there is to be violent in the face of what is silenced by the said — to hear the Saying of the overpowering that lurks within the immediately said. Not being able to speak, to be speechless, is to be oppressed and requires violence towards everything that does not let the oppression be manifested. The understanding of violence here is subtle and relates to intellectual and poetic violence towards the immediate – the violence of thinking-Being.

76. Man, as *deinotation,* as strange in *essence,* 'ek-sists'. Man is *deinon* because he is on the one hand exposed within the overpowering. His own Being is an issue for him. At the same time Man is *deinon* in that he is violent. The strangeness is 'the uncanny, as that which casts us out of the "homely" ie the customary, familiar, secure. The unhomely prevents Man from making himself at home and therein it is overpowering'. Man is the one who violently departs from the familiar.[36] Heidegger refers to the sentence in the chorus in *Antigona*:

---

[34] *Ibid.*
[35] *Ibid.*
[36] *Ibid,* pp 150–51.

> [Man] sets sail on the frothing water
> amid the south winds of winter
> tacking through the mountains
> and furious chasms of the waves.[37]

'Sea' is not understood as a geographical or geological area but rather as a metaphor of the 'unfolding of many depths and waves. Man sets sail into the unsettled deep'. The origin of Man is strangeness, and strangeness is at its most abundant at the 'beginning', the origin. It is not true to say that man 'progresses' from the primitive to the 'builder of cities'. The most sublime 'harbours the beginning', where there is maximum violent openness towards the overpowering in trying to master it. The beginning is also the point where the mystery of the overpowering holds sway. The mystery holds sway because the essence of Man is strangeness in that he is driven out of his essence, into the concealment of his essence, into his non-essence. The strangeness is the reason why Man could invent language and listen to the Saying in language. The strangeness of Man, then, is 'made' by the overpowering. In order to attend to the overpowering, Man needs to be violent:

The violent of poetic speech, of thinking projection, of building configuration, of the action that creates states is not a function of faculties that man has, but a taming and ordering of powers by virtue of which the essent opens up as such when man moves into it. The disclosure of the essent is the power that man must master in order to become himself amid the essent, ie in order to be historical. ... Only if we understand that the use of power in language, in understanding, in forming and building helps to create (ie always, to bring forth) the violent act of laying out paths into the environing power of the essent, only then shall we understand the strangeness, the uncanniness of all violence.[38]

The being-there of Man is strange because the very 'isness' of Man is in the issuelessness of death.

77.

> Clever indeed, mastering
> The ways of skill beyond all hope,
> He sometimes accomplishes evil,
> sometimes achieves brave deeds.
> He wends his way between the laws of the earth
> and the adjured justice of the gods.
> Rising high above his place,

[37] *Ibid*, p 146.
[38] *Ibid*, p 157.

> He who for the sake of adventure takes
> the nonessent for essent loses
> his place in the end. [39]

The final strophe of the chorus' poem in *Antigona* tells how the essence of Man – strangeness – is woven into the order of Being. *Deinon* has two meanings. The first relates to the *technē*, which means 'knowledge', not in the sense of generalised observation from data but rather in the sense of initial and persistent looking beyond what is given at any time. Knowledge is the ability to put into the work of art the being of any particular essent. The Pre-Socratics called the work of art *technē* in that

[A]rt is what most immediately brings [B]eing (ie the appearing that stands there in itself) to stand, stabilizes it in something present ... [The work of art] brings about [B]eing in an essent; it brings about the phenomenon in which the emerging power *physis* comes to shine. It is through the work of art as essent [B]eing that everything else that appears and is to be found is first confirmed and made accessible, explicable, and understandable as being or not being. ... [Knowledge] is the 'superior' realising opening and keeping open.[40]

In *technē* as knowledge, Heidegger saw the violent in which Man, as strange, manifests power against the overpowering, and ventures into the terrible in order to bring Being into the open. *Deinon* is the violent, and is manifested as *technē*.

78. But the word *deinon* as the overpowering points at Being as manifested in the idea of enjoining order [*Fug*] or, in Greek, *dikēo* or *dikē*. The word *dikē* has three senses, all interconnected: of order, of protection and of justice. Order, protection and justice are, as I shall argue, the threefold senses of the essence of law distorted in the ontic for-the-most-part being and thinking with and through law.

79. Heidegger discusses *dikē* as meaning the fugal order of Being. *Dikē* conveys enjoining order [*fügender, Fug*] and, as such, resembles the many meanings that the word *Fug* has in German. As order, *dikē* has many connotations. It is understood as sense of joining together and framework [*Fuge* and *Gefüge*]. *Dikē* is also understood as a decree, a direction that the overpowering imposes on its reign. Finally it is understood as the governing structure [*das fügende Gefüge*] which compels adaptation [*Einfügung*] and compliance [*Sichfügen*].[41] The picture that we have here is of an order that joins many parts of the

---

[39] *Ibid*, pp 147–8.
[40] *Ibid*, p 159.
[41] *Ibid*, p 160.

overpowering. As primordial order of the overpowering, it decrees a direction that compels adaptation and obedience. The strangeness of human being, its essence as 'ek-sistence', is within the order of Being, compelled by the overpowering that this order manifests. Being, as power, is based on original togetherness. The governing order [*Fügender Fug*] of the overpowering is *dikē*.

80.   Man as 'ek-sistent' strangeness is caught up in the confrontation between violence [*technē*] and the overpowering order [*dikē*]. The actuality of the actual of Man as *Dasein*, as strange, violently listens and open up to the dominant order. The overpowering order of Being tosses Man between order and mischief, structure and structure-lessness. In the violent battle with the overpowering order of Being, Man constantly wins and loses. *Dikē*, as the order of the over-powering, precedes *Dasein* which violently throws itself against it, trying to master its Saying, master the unsaid, the unthought, unseen, compelling the un-happened. As violent, *Dasein* risks dispersion, disorder, mischief.[42] Order and disorder are prevalent to the strangeness of *Dasein* which violently confronts *dikē*, the order of Being.

81.   *Dikē*, then, is not simply the order of the legal but rather the order of Being. This order, which involves all the essences, resembles a rope in which all the essences are woven together to constitute the rope to the point that it is difficult to conceive of each essence independently and difficult to conceive of the rope independently of them. *Dikē* is the fugal order, and all essences play an essential role in this order so as to bring about togetherness. *Dikē* is that against which *Dasein* in its essence violently struggles. So when Heidegger speaks of going against *dikē*, he has this double signification of confronting the order of Being. The first is the sense of 'ek-sisting' into the essence of the law of Being, the compelling order of Being. The second signification is that Man's essence is to go against *dikē*, into the ordinarily said, defined, oriented, representational, stable, legal. In this sense, his essence lures Man into the distorted, unrisky *dikē* – the order that reassures him and keeps him from living the violent aspect of his essence.

82.   As far as the first signification is concerned, we can echo here the notion of the non-essence which is *essential* and think about law on the same lines as the 'not' that applies to all essences. The second meaning relates to how errancy comes into the hermeneutic cycle of the essence of law – *dikē*. The 'legal' resorts to:

[42] *Ibid*, p. 161.

The evaluation of being-human as arrogance and presumption in the pejorative sense takes man out of his essential need as the in-cident. To judge in this way is to take man as something already-there, to put this something into an empty space, and appraise it according to some external table of values. But it is the same kind of misunderstanding to interpret the poet's words as a tacit rejection of being-human, a covert admonition to resign onself without violence, to seek undisturbed comfort.[43]

83. These double meanings of *dikē*, both as the primordial order of Being – a part of which Man violently *understands* – and as the mundane 'legal' into which Man falls are different aspects of that kind of relationship that persists between the essence of techology – *technē* – and mundane technical relations, or the relationship between the essence of man as ek-sistent' and as subject. The relationship of the 'not' represents the whole way in which the question of Being as a hermeneutic question of *Dasein* is distorted in the transcendental, metaphysical tradition and the inauthentic transcendence that it encapsulates.

84. Both the 'legal' and the manner *Dasein* is in the legal are themselves a part of the overpowering order of Being. It is in the conflict between overwhelming presence of *dikē* as the order of the overpowering and the distorted *dikē* that the violent and strange reality of humans persists in its essence. The essence of human beings is in the need for the conflict that comports *Dasein* into a scene of disclosure prepared for by Being itself.[44]

85. '*Dikē* is the overpowering order. *Technē* is the violence of knowledge. The reciprocal relation between them is the happening of strangeness.'[45] This relationship of strangeness, this primordial 'not' is the relationship between Being and thinking in the maxim of the Parmenides' fragment. But *dikē* is the fugal order of Being, in which the 'nots' of the essences of human beings as 'ek-sisting' *Daseins*, *alētheia* as the essence of truth, *technē* as the essence of technology and the essence of language are all interwoven. It is in this sense that Heidegger's remark that 'Every philosophy is systematic, but not every philosophy is a system'[46] should be understood.

86. But understanding *dikē* as the order of Being, as entailing strangeness, conflict and violence, means that this order itself involves raptures and is in the process of Being itself coming together and setting apart. Heraclitus reflects on *dikē* along similar lines: 'it is necessary to bear in mind setting-apart as essentially

---

[43] *Ibid*, p 164
[44] *Ibid*, p 163.
[45] *Ibid*, p 165.
[46] Quoted in M Inwood, *A Heidegger Dictionary*, above n 27, pp 204–5.

bringing-together and order as contending'.[47] There is no Being without 'ek-sistent' *Dasein*. Without *Dasein* as 'ek-sisting', Being cannot be thought about as the unfolding itself. The 'not', then, belongs to the way of Being, and this is the mystery of each and every essence that makes up the order of Being, the order of the 'not', the order of nearest of the near. Togetherness and apartness, strangeness, is the characteristic of Being itself.

87. Heidegger discusses *dikē* in his reflections on *The Anaximander Fragment* in the context of discussing the cosmology of the totality of things present. The word *adikon* is normally translated as injustice, *a-dikon*, namely that *dikē* is absent. *Dikē* is normally translated as 'right'. So, whenever *adikon* is present, all is not 'right' with things. Something is out of joint. What is present as such is out of joint. Being out of joint is how things are present: 'To presencing as such jointure must belong, thus creating the possibility of its being out of joint.'[48] The 'while' [or 'stillness'] really lingers [or is deferred] in the *between* of arrival and departure. The primordial, real, 'joining' occurs in the 'between'. Arrival is already in departure. The while which lingers is in essence partly a disjunction as a thing not right [*a-dikon*]. There is necessarily disjunction in lingering awhile. That which is on the way, lingering, still rebels and insists of 'winning for itself a while'. This insistence is the disjunction.[49] Anything which lingers awhile comes to present as disjoined all the while as a 'lack'. The jointure of lingering awhile is *given* 'with a view' to disjunction. The withdrawal and clearing is what belongs to every being and is given to it. The jointure which is given is order: *dikē*, or, better, 'order of the while'.[50] A-*dikia* is 'not-rightness' in the sense of dis-order. This is the sense in which injustice in things should be understood, namely as the disjunction of the persistence of that which lingers awhile. What lingers is continuous, like a flow, a flux. A proper image is that of a wave, which may, if looked upon, be seen as a thing-wave, but if looked upon carefully can be seen as part of the continuing motion of the sea. The wave and the sea join together and it is part of that which is given to the wave to be in the order which makes it both the 'yes' and the 'no' of the lingering continuous sea.

88. When beings linger in the while they have an inherent force that impels them to 'persist as things' which makes them inconsiderate towards 'others' as beings. The words 'inconsiderate' and 'considerate' do not mean a psychological state of human beings but

---

[47] *Ibid*, p 166.
[48] *Anax*, p 41.
[49] *Ibid*, p. 43.
[50] *Ibid*, pp 43 and 45.

connote something that relates to the togetherness of all beings. But despite the ontic nature of 'persistent things', the considerate togetherness of beings *in their Being* is the way they are in *dikē*.[51] This 'consideration' of togetherness in Being and 'care' [*reck* in German – the origin of the word 'reckless' in English] lead to a significance that runs through the whole cosmic 'order' in the fragment:

> *within the open expanse of unconcealment each lingering being becomes present to every other being.* The more unequivocally this relation emerges *... each one giving reck to the other, is the sole manner in which what lingers awhile in presence lingers at all ... granting order.*[52]

89. What I refer to as the 'legal' is that part of the order of Being which characterises beings striving for persistence as beings, including of course the subject of legal order. It is the order that governs individuals where definitions correspond to actions by individuals. The order of Being is the order of 'care', which is primordial togetherness. The disorder – *a-dikia* – carelessness or recklessness – is the world of individuals' beings – the legal.

90. We are reflecting upon *dikē* as the governing order of Being, the essence of law. It is in the context of the discussion of Parmenides' maxim and the chorus in *Antigona* that Heidegger's reflections on art and truth in Plato are to be approached. Quite superficially, *technē* connotes 'art' in its broad sense of 'the ability in the sense of being well-versed in something, of a thoroughgoing and therefore masterful *know-how*'. But, originally art, *technē*, means something deeper – something more akin to what Heidegger discussed as primordial violent knowledge in relation to Parmenides' maxim. In this sense, *techne* means 'care', that is:

> acquired capacity to carry something out which, as it were, has become second nature and basic to *Dasein*, ability as behavior that accomplishes something, then the Greek says *meletē, epimeleia*, carefulness of concern. Such carefulness is more than practiced diligence; it is the mastery of a composed resolute openness to beings; it is 'care'.[53]

Heidegger then adds another meaning of 'art' as *poiein* and *poiēsis* (the art of the word), or poetic bringing-forth.

---

51 *Ibid*, pp 46–7.
52 *Ibid*, p 47.
53 M Heidegger, 'The Scope and Context of Plato's Meditation on the Relationship of Art and Truth', [1936–7], above n 29, at p 164. The translator's note refers to the expressions in Plato's *Republic* of *he melete*, which is 'care for', 'sustained attention to action', and *epimeleia* which means 'care bestowed upon a thing, attention paid to it'.

91. How come, Heidegger asks, Plato came to consider *technē* and *poiēsis*? It is here that *dikē* comes to the fore. Again, as in *An Intro-duction to Metaphysics*, Heidegger maintains that we miss the primordial sense of *dikē* if we merely transpose it into justice in the moral and the legal realm. *Dikē* is understood as the 'law of the Being of beings' and is even equated to philosophy itself.

92. Here, Heidegger is after the *essential* understanding of the word *polis*. Knowledge of *dikē* is the deepest sense of *polis* and with it the primordial understanding of the philosopher-king. In Plato this primordial sense of *polis* becomes buried in a 'metaphysical' sense that *dikē* seems initially to have. The understanding of *polis* also comes about in the Parmenides' discussion. There, *polis* is under-stood as the

> [F]oundation and scene of man's being-there, the point at which all these paths [*poros*] meet... *Polis* is usually translated as city or city-state. This does not capture the full meaning. *Polis* means, rather, the place, the there, wherein and as which historical being-there is. The *Polis* is the historical place, there *in* which, *out* of which, and *for* which history happens.[54]

The political community in its essential sense is, once again distorted, into the orderly state or city-state. The political community is the site where all humans in their essence come to dwell in their strangeness. It is also their deepest *interest*: the word 'interest' being understood from the Latin '*intersvm*', which connotes 'to be in the company of', to be among, to be a member of a group. Polity, also a primordial notion of sociality, must bring people in their most original togeth-erness. For that we need to consider in depth the notion of being-with [*mitsein*] and its relationship to *Dasein*'s innermost being – a task which is attended to later in the book.

93. We can echo here again the deepest sense of Rousseau's 'general will', meaning such a *polis* in which people are free in that their innermost own as 'ek-sistent' and the political are fused. Because he was still thinking within the philosophical tradition, Rousseau could not allude to the depth of his insight and the ontological reflection that might have already conditioned this insight.

94. It seems an odd understanding of *polis* that Heidegger refers to here. Such a *polis* is a place where the actuality of the actual of all *Daseins* dwell. For now, we can sense that such *polis* is certainly not a collection of individuals who form a political community in order to further some value-based 'oughts' which will critically benefit them

[54] *IM*, p 152.

as individuals. Heidegger's *polis* is not a community, a simple totality, in the sense of collective consciousness. *It is community in the sense of distortion, the 'not' of any 'legal' and 'moral' community*. It is a community that bows before and obeys the order of Being by conceiving the essence of its humanity by immersing itself in the 'not' concealed in the legal. Of course, the *potential* right-wing conservative and even fascist politics echo from such a community, in which everybody is 'forced to be free'. Lacoue-Labarth has forcefully shown the power and danger of this extreme form of humanism, namely of the transcendent empty *mimesis* of such ontological identification in a polity.[55] Yet, authenticity is both liberating and dangerous. What Heidegger accounts for here is the most authentic community because it touches not how Man 'ought' to be but the deepest sense of how Man *is*. Abstraction of ought, any unity in some 'positive thing', takes us away from this *polis* by going away from the contestation of the nearest, the very contestation that haunts man as its 'isness'. This *polis* is not aimed at realisation in one scheme or another. The *polis* is rather the power that exists nearer to any pretentious scheme of representational 'oughts', including the transcendence of a given scheme with the anticipation of another. The *polis* is first and formost where man's deepest strangeness as *Dasein* dwells amongst other *Daseins*. The way Man is, first and foremost, cannot be changed because it is the 'it' itself of Man, beyond 'individual' control and any attempt to tame it in definitions and metaphysical language of values, although such language continues the necessary distortion. This is the 'not' that sophisticated political organisations coax Man, in necessary errancy, to distance himself from, thereby distancing man from his essence. The overpowering power of Being by which Man is oppressed and towards which he is violently comported is terrible precisely because of the reassuring quietness in which it cannot be tamed. The 'moral' and the 'legal' moved by the aim of 'doing something about it' without contemplation that whatever they regard the 'it' to mean will already be a part of Man's necessary falling into errancy. The most difficult thing to grasp here is that errancy is part of the 'isness' not some 'incorrectness' of it:

[Philosopher-ruler] does not mean that philosophy professors should conduct the affairs of state. It means that the basic modes of behavior that sustain and define the community must be grounded in *essential* knowledge, assuming of course that the community, as an order of [B]eing, grounds itself on its

55 P Lacoue-Labarth, *Heidegger, Art and Politics* (London, Blackwell, 1990) pp 77–99.

own basis, and that it does not with to adopt standards from any other order. [emphasis added][56]

95.　As the order of Being and as a part of this ontological significance looms large an ethical significance. The essence of law, *dikē*, has also the function to *protect*. The theme of protection is very familiar to the body of laws. This essence of protection shows itself, albeit distortingly, to *Dasein* in the legal. Protection is a very familiar purpose of law. It is a familiar feature of law to protect from harm. Aversion of harm justifies law and also marks the limitations of harmful lawmaking. Surely if there were not harm involved in human relationships, law would be futile.

96.　It sounds familiar to claim that protection is in law's essence. The essence of law is to protect. *Dikē* is the goddess that protects. Heidegger interprets the 30 opening verses of Parmenides' didactic poem about *dikē*, the goddess whose object is to protect that which most originally requires protection:

She guards the alternately closing and opening keys to the gates of day and night, ie to the paths of being (that discloses), of appearance (that *distorts*) and nothingness (that closes). This means that the essent discloses itself only insofar as the structure, *Fug*, of Being is guarded and preserved. Being as *dikē* is the key to the essent in its structure ... [B]oth the poetic and the philosophical discourse of [B]eing name, ie create and define, it with the same word, *dikē*. ... It has already been pointed out how in apprehension as ac-cepting, anticipation the essent as such is disclosed and so comes forth

[56] 'The Scope and Context of Plato's Meditation on the Relationship of Art and Truth', above n 29, p 166. The notion of *Polis* in *IM* is discussed incisively by M de Beistegui in *Heidegger and the Political: Dystopias* (London, Routledge, 1998) at pp 114–45. de Beistegui relates the understanding of *polis* as the strife between *technē* and *dikē* to a later interpretation by Heidegger of the same chorus in *Antigona* in 1942–43. de Beistegui claims that in *IM* Heidegger's interpretation of the chorus was still within the economy of a home, that is of an authentic abode for Man on earth. The centrality of the notion of a home thus retains metaphysical echoes. In his latter interpretation of the chorus Heidegger saw homelessness rather than home as essential to Man and so he gave freedom to original and creative violence (p 128). I could not hear any such taming metaphysical tendencies in *IM*, especially when read together with the notion of error that stems directly from Man's essence as 'ek-sistent'. The notion of 'ek-sistence' connotes essential homelessness. If the account in *IM* is read together with Heidegger's later argument that Man is the guardian of Being and as such dwells in language itself being essentially the House of Being, then the notion of a home become essential homelessness. The deconstruction of home is at the heart of Heidegger's oeuvre. Both his inaugural lecture – *WM* – and his lecture *ET* imply essential homelessness as the home of man. But importantly, the notion of homelessness embodies the notion of error that characterises both the manner in which Being shows itself, and the way *Dasein* comports towards Being. The ontological difference that embodies the ontic as error and essential non-essence of truth means that Heidegger never thought of polity as naïve homelessness and a pre-economical polity (p 145). Indeed, I would argue that Heidegger's own politics of national socialism was a particular manifestation of errancy that tamed the mystery of the homelessness-as-home.

from concealment. For the poet, the assault of *technē* against *dikē* is the happening whereby man ceases to be at home. In his exile from home, the home is first disclosed as such. Through the event of homelessness the whole of the assent is disclosed. In this disclosure unconcealment takes place. But this is nothing more than the happening of the unfamiliar.[57]

The essence of law is not legal. *Dikē* stands for both the Being of the essent as a whole (the order of Being), and the goddess who needs to protect that whole, protect the structure of Being of which the legal is a distorting, though essential, part.

97.   But we need to magnify further than that. What requires protection first, and before all else? What is primordial harm? What is the process of protection? To be protected is to be left unharmed. In this sense to protect is like a shield that defends from external forces. In order to defend against danger, there must be capacity to defend and this means being able to be attentive to the danger, that is being able to be attentive and to respond to the danger. This is the case for perceived danger, but also for the murmuring sound of danger. The capacity, then, is needed precisely when the danger is well disguised. Another sense of 'to protect' is to enable. It is to enable the protected to be – to let the protected be, to release any fetter that does not enable the protected to be. Yet another sense of protecting is also to be decent, to be just, to give what is due. For protection of what is due to be given, again there must be a capacity to connect to the actuality from which what is due arises. There is a strong connection between the notion of protection and the notion of being fair and just.

98.   What is due to be given back in justice immediately brings to mind representations, calculations, comparisons, allocations, values, rights and duties. To become 'due' means both to 'give back something that was taken', but it also means to become appropriate, even urgent, as in 'something is now due'. What is that due which calls for protection in an urgent manner? Could it be that the craving for immediately resorting to calculations and representations generates the need for protection against it? Could it be that the perversity of such a craving makes the need for protection all the more urgent?

99.   But it is only through the event of 'ek-sistence' that what is due can be evidenced and achieved, because only in grasping the actuality of the actual, only in realising the distortion of the legal in an instant of being-in-the-world can the murmur of the primordial 'due' be responded to.

[57] *IM*, pp 166–7.

100. In Hebrew the root H, G, N makes HAGANA (defence, protection) and HAGINUT (justness and fairness). We can connect the two senses of *dikē*, of justice and protection, by saying that to be just is to give a person his due. This would mean to protect this person both in the sense of shielding and in the sense of enabling. By giving humans their due not only do we protect them from thinking along the lines of not-yet-represented oppression and domination but we also enable them to comport humbly towards the call of Being, even if only for a while, with few of their own fetters that stop them from hearing and responding resolutely to that call. Humans are given their due only when they are protected from the fetters that most threaten their essence. Humans are just only when they are protected in their essence. Furthermore, only a human with a protected essence, thus being potentially attentive to the murmur of essences of language, truth, as his or her own essence, can be just to other humans and give them their due.

101. How should we account for the most needed and primordial protection? What is there in humans' essence, namely as being strangest of the strange, that is to be protected first and foremost? Bearing in mind that the essence of law is not legal, the 'not' must mean that what seems to be protected by the 'legal' – all of the instances of ontic thinking along harm of values that we see in all legal doctrines – is an error. This error belongs *beyond* the law as it is thought about for the most part, an error which relates to the very nature of 'thinking about', namely to language, history, truth and Man. This error is that very error that propels the call of the essence of law, the essence that protects. The legal protects human beings but the error essentially, and *truthfully*, holds sway in that it does not protect what it is most important to protect.

102. *The essence of 'ek-sistence' that characterises the relationship between being and thinking – between Dasein and Being – is that it cannot be protected by representations, methodologies, both actual and potential. The craving for those representations and methodologies, however understandable and rationalisable as second-best, is essentially impoverished. Such an essential craving for protection-in-errancy is already on the way to truth, as error.*

103. The 'mystery of errancy' of law which characterises the truthful call of its essence, as well as the event of responding to it by *Dasein*, is that in perfecting and entrenching the errancy the need for primordial protection becomes all the most urgent as it becomes less conspicuous.

104. The legal can become so pervasive and entrenched that it no longer merely harms *Dasein* – which is part of ontic–ontological oscillation – but also does harm in concealing the actuality of such

harm. The harm can become such that the very distortion of the essence of law in the legal (a distortion which makes law as thought about for the most part thought-provoking) is buried in ontic possibilities.

105. It is important to emphasise that, in essential terms, nothing changes in terms of the distorting relations between the essence of law and its ontic manifestation. The mystery in errancy does not change. What changes is the manner in which error, the going further away from the actual, manifests itself.

106. *The distortion of the essence of law as a fugal part of the order of Being protects* Dasein *in its 'ek-sistential' essence enabling it to be just, to give due. Giving due both to itself and other Daseins is preserved. However, that protection means that* Dasein *persists in its essence, namely being kept in the distorting error of the legal.*

107. Error can become intensely harmful. Indeed, it is becoming so. The need for protection, and hence injustice, becomes more and more sophisticatedly concealed, and thus urgent, as almost no one attends directly to the order of Being. The very need for protection and justice becomes systematically a non-issue with the ubiquitous and pervasive nature of the legal. As thinking-Being is forgotten and the forgetfulness itself is buried under the critical pretensions of self-overcoming of the legal, the need for protection that comes from Man's essence is at its most urgent. In the next chapters we shall explore just how concealed the need for protection has become.

108. What harm is involved in the distortion? The distortion of the essence of law in the 'legal' threatens that which is in need of utmost and own innermost protection. That oppressive threat of harm is necessary for occasioning the openness of ontological reflection. To that extent, the legal is a necessary part of thinking. However, *the harm becomes harmful when it consists not so much in the occurrence of the distortion as in the entrenchment and forgetfulness of the distortion. It would take much more intense anxiety to generate openness to the distortion by the legal.* To forget the distortion is to perpetuate an ontic interpretation of beings, including self-interpretation as an ego and individual, or simply logically distinguished 'such' or 'as such' thus enshrining this or that value that will then be protected by certain interpretation, prioritisation and distributions of rights and duties. It should be emphasised that it is not the content of such distribution which makes up the legal but the whole thinking that represents, but also which anticipates re-representation that constitutes the enshrining of the legal and with it the actual harmfulness of the harm. The harm occurs in persistently flattening the being of Being which is both terrible as the calm force that comes from the actuality of the actual, but also very vulnerable because of

that.[58] This harm, as we shall see in the next chapters, can face us as primordial ethics, an ethics which misleadingly seems to go beyond law, against law in the name of ethics. This pretence of what is beyond law but which is the supreme origin of the legal and legalised thinking is the very efficient tranquilliser of anxiety.

109. Ontological reflection is a precondition for the possibility of ontic occurrence, and, as we shall see, transcendent ontic recurrence, both of which include derivative ontology based on objectification and conceptualisation. The essence of law is given distortingly to the ontic as its 'not', and hence its unconcealment is essentially coupled to its concealment. Although the essence of law is lurking in any ontic manifestation of it, it could not be further than this manifestation. The essence of law is always at the farthest point from the legal, although it is nearer to the actuality that the legal conceals.

110. *Thinking about law must involve occurrences of all essences which are fugally connected to the essence of law as protecting the comportment of thinking towards the nearness of the order of Being. The truth that makes up the 'not' of all essences is already a fugal part of the truth of the essence of Being as the origin of essencing.*

111. Humans need the legal, they need to establish, or even to entrench, the order of calculation and representation, as it is from that error and even from denial that their 'in-order-to' can, with the help of friends, open their ear to the call that hints at the protecting, and thus saving, near. To think otherwise than with and through the legal, to respond to the call of the near, necessitates the erring of subject/actions of the legal

112. The harmfulness of the harm that accrues in entrenching the legal is slow to be averted by the protection of the essence of law. This is so because the voice of that essence is buried underneath ontic 'history of law', an approach to language, to truth. It is buried to such an extent that the call from amidst the error becomes completely overlooked and overheard. Both the essence of law and its non-essence are buried.

113. The forgetfulness of the distortion brought about by the legal comes about through the entrenchment of talk, especially through critical *legal* scholarship. Such talk craves for constitutional aversion of harm through the representation of rights and duties. The gist of this critical scholarship is to resort to different methods of grasping and representing that harm. The myth entertained by those who are dominated by the thinking that conditions the legal is that side by side with the prevention of certain actions in order to avert the represented harm people can be free.

[58] *ET*, p 129.

114. But freedom consists of attending, and responding, to the call of actuality of the actual. Free-floating freedom, freedom 'from', is an ontic illusion and an arrogant one at that. Freedom is letting be in a way which will be humble enough not to surrender to the myth of the far. Freedom consists of accepting the serfdom of attentiveness to the call of actuality of the actual to own-ness, as well as responding to that call. The call of the actuality of the actual murmurs from that very 'there' whose depth and richness, understanding (as standing-before) and in-sights, are conceptualised as 'harm' by the legal. The thinking with and through the legal protects subjectivity before attending to Being, thus vulgarly craving to preserve and represent harmful actions, or, by way of other means, sanctifying calculative thought and risk assessment.

115. Amidst the legal, the mystery, and with it the call of the essence of law, flickers from a place in which interacting humans are in their essence. Thinking about law comes from that place. What is interpreted by the legal as harm is already distanced from that place. But beneath such ontic interpretation is the necessarily distorting manner of the actuality of the actual. Grasped as a distorted hint from the near, the ontic is 'useful'. Usefulness is deployed here in the sense of readiness-to-hand, that is the capability of carrying a hint from the near. Nearing this hint is dwelling in the place in which a trace of the hint was left. The listening and responding to such hinting cannot be averted, but only distorted, by an objectifying scientific inquiry or the representation of any ethical and legal code which objectifies actions and consequences.

116. Ontological usefulness as hinting the 'howness' of each and every interacting human being hints at that which already fatefully conditions their interaction. A craving for conceptualising representations of harm is one manner of distancing, and thus erring, response to that which has already been hinted. In this sense, ontically represented harm calls for thinking. To recap, error should be grasped in terms of nearness not correctness: that actuality from which what is erroneously conceptualised as harm cannot be averted.

117. But, in this chapter, the harm, from which the essence of law protects, was understood in a different manner. The harm occurs as the transformation of nearness to correctness. The distorting ontic response by the legal to this mysterious occurrence of hinting–responding threatens harm, and if entrenched, becomes harmful, to that thinking that nears that occurrence. Thinking about law is thinking about this occurrence in the midst of the representational and the calculative, of which the legal is a prominent aspect.

118. The harm is not to let the distortion hold sway thus silencing the saving power, the call of *dikē*. Thus, the harm of law is epochal and

is itself fugally connected with other epochal harms that occur to other essences whose 'not' is not allowed to speak. The harm occurs because what is in greatest need of protection is left there buried in legal thinking. The forgetting is epochal and constitutes the limiting horizon of *Dasein*'s attentiveness to Being.

119. Having said all that, the essence of law holds sway regardless of the forgetfulness of Being. The awakening will have occurred despite the epochal forgetfulness because the epoch in which the legal holds sway is itself part of the turning of the wheel of Being. The 'legal' which epochally harms is part of the historicity of Being. Indeed, with forgetfulness – the more perfect the being and thinking that conditions the 'legal' becomes – the more entrenched is the error to the point when it is almost unnoticed. But, even though the call of the essence of law becomes muted, does this essence also become less powerful? Certainly not. On the contrary, it becomes much more powerful. That is part of the essence overpowering and terrible calmness. As the distortion of the essence of law through the legal becomes by and large forgotten, the reliance upon the legal is prone to be shaken ever more powerfully from the near more profoundly. The anxiety that exists in the wake of the perfection of the legal is at its highest. The anxiety intensifies, as there is a sense of being unprotected despite so much legalism, a sense which cannot be remedied by merely constructing more refined representation within the horizon of the legal. There is no legislation, case law, policy, risk assessment in which to take refuge so as to comfort the deep anxiety amidst the perfection of the thinking that gives rise to them. The thinking which conditions the legal becomes so colonising that it becomes entangled in a double bind. It can only seek protection by rethinking the legal, refining it, modify it, still always within it, a protection that the legal cannot supply. Such a call for something 'other than the legal', or for the 'extra-legal', results in what might be extra-legal but certainly not yet other than it but rather a further entrenchment of it. The epochal cycle is characterised as a process whereby the forgetfulness of the distortion cyclically leads to the strengthening of it. This cycle of transgression/entrenchment of the legal characterises an epoch in which forgetfulness is at its most entrenched manifestation. Protection is called for precisely when it seems least needed.

120. The power of the overpowering, of *dikē*, is never diminished but only distorted. The ontological difference always holds sway. There is no outside to it. There is no before or after the actuality of the actual. Epochal distortions of essences are distinguished by intensity of error. Both the necessary distorted human response to the actuality of the actual and the response by the order of Being are beyond human

control, although humans are the actors in this theatre of danger and saving power.

121. As we shall see, the call of Being which oppresses does not come from any 'other'. Individual beings do not stand as 'other' to one another *simpliciter* as far as the otherness of their Being is concerned. For the moment I only wish to make the point that, as the distortion is at its greatest, the essence of law, that which protects the *Dasein*'s comportment towards the order of Being – which is a fugal order of essences – speaks. It speaks by pointing intuition towards something which is 'other' than the legal. What is called for is a response to the distortion that persists between the 'essence of law' and the legal. The saving power is generated by the historical process of protecting the essential distancing and against the intensification and entrenchment of forgetting. The saving power is the protecting supreme power of *dikē*, the essence of law. *The essence of law protects the distortion, thereby protecting the whole order of Being on its aspects and essences.* The saving power of *dikē* is freeing in the sense of letting essences be.

122. What needs protection is *Dasein* in its essence as 'ek-sistence'. *Conatus essendi* would mean that kind of protection and perseverance. The way *Dasein* 'ek-sists' in the order of Being needs protection. *Dasein* must never be locked in its involvement, itsself-understanding as an individual 'human being', a subject, that is protected, although, of course, this is what the 'legal' does. This is not a normative statement but a statement of the protection which is part and parcel of how *Dasein* essentially *is*. The 'legal' attempts to protect human beings in their humanity. The essence of law protects the order of Being and *Dasein*'s 'ek-sistence' towards the innermost nearness that this order calls from. If humanity is deconstructed to connote that essential subservience to Being, so be it – indeed it should be emphasised once again that there is no Being without *Dasein*'s 'ek-sistence'. The essence of law protects that which requires primordial protection and this is not human beings but rather *Dasein*'s openness and holding to the nothing that the order of Being sends towards *Dasein*. Here, then, is another way of looking at the 'not' or the 'distortion' of the essence of law and the harm caused when its ontic occurrence, the 'legal', is entrenched and when that entrenchment is concealed. The more the legal is preoccupied with protecting human beings and the more entrenched such protection becomes in terms of approaches to truth, technology, language, history, and, of course, ethics, the more harm is caused to the essence of human *Dasein*, its ethical openness towards listening and responding to the truth of the unconcealment of Being. The entrenchment of the legal attempts to kill what is essential in human

Dasein. To involve a legal metaphor, such entrenchment is an attempted murder. The entrenchment of the legal hinders *Dasein* from thinking-Being although it cannot hinder Being thinking and speaking *Dasein.* Being speaks even that *Dasein* who is ontically imprisoned. The entrenchment of the normative, through the legal, including being constantly pulled back to language that captures humans as subjects who possess rights and obligations, harms *Dasein*'s openness towards the Sending of Being. The essence of human *Dasein* – as a pointer towards Being and through which Being speaks – comports *Dasein* in an opposite direction to the legal – towards nearness – and, of course, resists any dominance of the legal. If, then, there is some ontological 'ought', it would be not to protect human beings but to be the counter-power which calls for thinking and which protects against the protection of human beings as subjects. This counter-power protects humans in their essence, in their being essentially the shepherds of Being. In this protection there is also an element of letting humans be as they really are. The fetters are the humanity which is protected by the legal. As *dikē* protects human being it lets them into the saying of language, Being's house.

123. Between the 'legal' and the essence of law there dwells the 'not' which has its origin as the ontological difference, part of which entails the reversal of the relationship between human *Daseins* and Being, giving the latter primordiality. This reversal has the strict implication that between the essence of law and the 'legal' there is a complementarity of distortion but never that of a translation. There is no way for *Dasein* to assume centre stage by paraphrasing the 'not' of an essence into some ontic articulation and expression. Any attempt to essentialise law as an assemblage of things, practices, activities, is ontic. Any attempt to translate the essence of law into some matrix of the 'legal', even if *Dasein* goes seemingly 'beyond' the legal, would locate transcendence within the legal, anticipating re-accommodating the legal logic and language. On the contrary, the more refined the translation of the essence of law into the legal, the more seemingly near and evident are the attempts to perfect the legal and to make it accommodate more 'insights' within its domain, the more harm has already been caused which calls for protection. Such translations, and their disguise as ethical, critical and deconstruction-ist, are indeed the signs of a dawn of an epochal concealment.

124. A deconstruction *of* the legal would mean opening up a way out of its entrenchment, an authentic listening and responding to the call of *dikē,* that is for restoring that complementarity of distortion the makes up the impetus of *dikē.* An entrenchment of the legal already contains the fate of the saving of such complementarity.

125. It is *Dasein* that needs protection, not in its ontic existence as some humanists and transcendental phenomenologists would have it, but in its essential anxious 'ek-sistence', in its allowing itself to be claimed by Being. The protection must not be understood as protecting *Dasein* as a human ego but rather as protecting it in its letting go of its ego, letting go of its indulgence in humanism, of its abstract empathy to 'human beings' who are totally Others.

126. There is a connection between the Being of law and the law of Being. Being of law connotes essence of law, namely that which offers protection to the relationship between *Dasein* and the order of Being, thereby enabling the giving of what is due in just moments. But the essence of law, as protection and justice itself, belongs to the law of Being, to the order of Being, the order with which the essence of law is fugally connected to all other essences, guarding and protecting them.

127. There is a connection between the way the human *Dasein* and the Being of law are a part of the fugal order of Being. The way humans are essentially makes them fall back into errancy and ontic being and thinking within the domain of the legal. They avert harm to one another but the more they do so they substantiate the harm that is done to their own very essence. This ontic entrenchment connotes parallel epochal errancy in ethics, truth and language. *Dikē*, the essence of law, protects humans, so that the oscillation of complementarity between ontic and ontological is resorted by overcoming ontic *dominance*. This ontic dominance is part and parcel of the way the historicity of the essence of human beings unfolds.

128. We must not, then, see the essence of law in a divine or universal code of law. We must not associate the essence of law with a supreme form of legalism. Such a universal code is only an expression of the craving for relief offered by ontic dominance. At the same time, this craving for a universal code of law, towards the entrenchment and forgetfulness of the distortion between the essence of law and its ontic occurrences, is part of the actuality of the actual of law.

129. The essence of law, then, ensures that Being is always its own *conatus essendi* in protecting *Dasein*'s openness to the saying of language that is distorted in the ontic language of the legal. Such is the path along which the law of Being is protected by the Being of law, itself as a part of the fugal order of Being.

130. In order to think about law, then, we must not think about the legal. Two distorting 'aboutnesses' are being entangled in error, and it is about the manifestations of the actuality of this error that we are called upon to think. In order to unconceal an event of the *isness* of law we must focus on the 'not' rather than upon any-thing which 'is',

that is on any thing that can be generalised into a theory, practice or methodology.

131. Being is like a wheel that turns round and round. The Being of law protects its turning. In one sense, all occurrences belong to that turning. In another, this turning of the wheel of Being means that, in a sense, nothing really occurs. The hermeneutic cycle in which *Dasein* is helplessly embroiled holds sway regardless of whether errancy occurs as an ontic–ontological oscillation or as the idleness of an epoch of ontic dominance. Both are equally primordial in the unfolding of the historicity of Being.

132. The essence of law is not legal. The essence of law is in protecting the mystery, the concealment of what is concealed, that is the fugal order of Being. The protection is from concealing the entrenched forgetfulness of the mystery, already entrenched in the feeling of being 'ignorant of ...'. *Dasein* in its 'ek-sistence' as the essence of human beings is what is protected by the essence of law because it is only through this 'ek-sistence' that the Saying of Being can be brought to language by *Dasein* who listens and responds. Protecting the mystery is the task of the goddess *dikē*. *Dasein* has to be protected so that it can be both in truth and in untruth, as the process of *alētheia* unfolds. The essence of law *ought* to protect *Dasein* both from the legal and from the entrenchment of the legal.

133. To this essence that comes straight from Being, *Dasein* owes an absolute and unconditional obedience and authority. This authority from the nearest so any mediation of legitimacy, that is the ethics and morality of values, rights and duties, is already a distortion. The response of *Dasein* is that of obedience, for a being cannot resist its *conatus essendi*. The same holds for *Dasein* because the call that protects essential preservation comes from *Dasein*'s innermost essence.

134. To think about law means to acknowledge that law already thinks about people and all they can do is to respond to the hint of that primordial thought. This is the only sense in which people can authentically think about law. Any other way is merely ontic rethinking the legal although it is on the way to primordial thinking. Thinking about law never puts people before the law. That *Dasein* can be attentive to *dikē* constitutes thinking about law. But, again, that does not mean that *Dasein* precedes law. Thinking about law cannot occur as a subject who thinks about law as a thing. The essence of law comes to people as that which is most thought-provoking. Part of the conventionally cited saying regarding the rule of law is that one of the purposes of law is that people would be under the law rather than under men. Well, indeed. I would just slightly modify this and say that it would be better for people to be

under the law than under the entrenchment of being and thinking that results from man-made law. To be claimed by divine law is to think about law in its essence. This claiming occurs whether *Dasein* ethically grasps that essence or not.

135. Thinking about law anticipates the essence of law to speak. This anticipation is different from the anticipation and preservation of the legal that precedes any critical reflection upon a given form and content of the legal. But these two anticipations belong to the same historical process in the course of which the call for thinking about law perturbs *Dasein* in its essence.

136. Let us go back to connection between 'silencing' and 'violence'. The between where actuality of the actual of law occurs, happens in between the essence of law – *dikē* – and its ontic non-essence, the legal, which distorts it. The perpetuation and entrenchment of the ontic harms in that it imposes silence. This silence which is heavily embedded in entrenched forgetfulness of Being is imposed on *Dasein* by the legal. *This ontic silencing is not the silence that is necessarily involved in the struggle to say and preserve the inexpressible in belatedly responding to its saying.* The violence by the perpetuation of the legal imposes silences on the inherent violence of *technē* – the violence that is in the complementarity of strife with *dikē*. The subtle and invisible entrenchment of the legal by and large blocks the essential confrontation of *technē* – as violence – and *dikē* – as order, protection and justice – at least for the epoch when the legal predominates. Predomination of the legal is the origin of all terror and invites terror. Terror occurs when one-sidedness imposes silence on the possibility to be silent in the face of the strange. No terror that Man imposes can overcome the power of Being, of the iron protection of *dikē*. Indeed, it is from the perpetuation of being and thinking by Man, through the notion of Man, for the protection of Man, that *dikē* protects the essence of humans, the complementarity which is entailed in the very 'ek-sistence' of *Dasein*. But *Dasein* in its essence as 'ek-sistence' is a stranger to Man. Although Man is a necessary part of the structure of *Dasein* as care, the entrenchment of Man's ventures smothers *Dasein*, in setting *Dasein* to predominate Being. As a violent act of complementarity between *Dasein* and Being, *dikē* has to erupt in order to re-ignite the necessary complementarity that comes from *Dasein*'s essentially humble manner.

137. So much for the legal protection against terror. That which causes terror cannot protect from it. Terror occurs when the inexpressible is not allowed to be violently comported towards into the order of Being. Terror occurs when no protection is offered to *Dasein* but through the very legal that forgets *Dasein* in its inception. From the

point of view of justice, when *Dasein* is not allowed to get its
essential 'dues', terror occurs. The possibility of terror is getting all
the much stronger under the perfect democracy and the rule of law.
The more perfect are democracy and the rule of law the tighter is the
smothering of that which cannot be over powered as the strangeness
of Man. The more the legal tries to refine its mapping of human
actions and relationships through representations and definitions, the
more a framework is put in place for critical thought in this regard,
the more deaf humans to the actuality of the actual. Terror teaches
the calm protective power of *dikē* to all architects of the legal.

138. Only being and thinking which is protected by *dikē*, however
violently, can be just and decent. Only in an 'ek-sistent' moment, can
Dasein confront the actuality of the actual and understand the 'situation' so a due can be given to other *Dasein*s. But the 'due' itself is not
a thing, it is that place when the near contests subjectivity and so
becomes strange to any thinking in which a thing 'due' is owed to a
subject. The due itself speaks. The 'site' of justice is to touch the
unsaid, to face the inexpressible. As 'care' *Dasein* grasps the
temporal 'howness' of what happens and it can bring about justice.
Justice occurs in the give and take of the space where the ontic 'facts
of the case' are interpreted so as to unconceal the inexpressible in
them. The site of justice is the due that dwells in 'ek-sistence' rather
than in the calculative due to individuals. The moment Man stops his
primordial effort to near actuality by merely craving facts and
following on from that craving by 'deciding' the facts, by imposing a
language of 'norms' which designate an 'ought' or a 'reasonable
man', any talk about justice immediately becomes idle chatter. As I
shall claim in the next three chapters, even the radicalisation of the
'Other' in ethics tames the mystery of what is due to a person. The
essence of justice is not justness of values and *oughts* which
themselves team up with the legal.

139. Justice cannot be decided. Justice is essentially undecided. Not
undecided because a fact is not yet known, or because a value is not
yet interpreted in this or that way. To crave for facts and norms is
already comes from an entrenched anticipation of more facts and
norms. When the essence of truth becomes undecided, its essence
becomes one with its non-essence, justice becomes possible.
TZEDEK, TZEDEK TIRDOF in Hebrew is translated as 'Justice,
thou shalt chase Justice'. Justice has to be chased and can never be
caught. This can be interpreted in a simple way, namely that any set
of norms, or values, however refined, could not achieve justice.
Justice has to be chased into the refinement of construction and interpretation of particular and general norms or 'rights'. However,
justice can be seen as that 'not yet near enough the due of the

nearest'. This kind of chase would subject the very thinking behind any calculative, normative representational idea of justice to the chase as well. It would make the chase of justice such that justice constantly escapes into the inexpressible 'there', into the temporality of the situation rather than towards the erection of a conceptual façade of dues under which all sides remain indebted.

140. Heidegger's reading of Parmenides, Heraclitus, Anaximander and the chorus in Sophocles' *Antigona* casts light on an ontological reading of Antigona's dilemma. In the said of the text, the dilemma is presented as that between whether to be loyal and to obey the law of the state, that is human laws, when these conflict with the laws and justice of the gods. On a legal reading of the play – on a cursory understanding of Antigona's words, Antigona herself portrays her own predicament to herself, as that between certain divine commandments versus merely human law. But a more attentive listening to the play makes Antigona herself fall into the errancy of the legal by not following the origin of the very dilemma she portrays, namely between human laws and divine law. The predicament between divine law and human law must dwell on the question of the divine. By understanding the divine as that which decrees representational commandments, however abstract these commandments be, by legalising the divine, have we yet attended to the mystery of the divine and divine law? The dilemma between human law and divine law must be read in the light of the mysterious nature of Man as portrayed by the chorus in the play. The chorus hints that human understanding of the relationship between divine and human law must embody humans' necessary error of their own self-understanding in relation to the divine. Understanding the divine as the mystery of the Saying of Being, the order of which is a house of Being in which human *Dasein* dwells, radicalises both the notion of divine reason and the notion of 'nature', making it a dynamic mystery.[59] The radicalisation of Man's relationship to the divine and to divine reason and law radicalises as error any attempt to tame the mystery of the divine and human comportment to that mystery by some concealed divine ordinance of a natural code in which natural laws essentially reveal and participate. Between the divine law/natural law that stems from it and any code of natural law in which human laws participate the only unity can be that that of the complementarity that characterises the ontological difference. Antigona's characterisation of the dilemma is still human centred and

---

[59] Note Heidegger's discussion of nature in *BP*, at p 262: 'We know, of course, that the world is not an extant thing, not nature, but that which first makes possible the uncoveredness of nature.'

does not yet touch that human strangeness that connects the nature of humans and the divine. Aquinas's thought, and his inspiration, Aristotle, need some revising which I cannot undertake here.

141. The mysterious relationship between divine and human law reveals Antigona's dilemma to connote an ethical tension between a legal understanding of what it is to be human and an essential understanding of the same question. The genius of Sophocles is to conceal the origin of the dilemma through the hints of the chorus. The origin of Antigona's dilemma is hinted to us by the chorus, and comes deeply from the nearness of the situation that cannot be reached either by the law of the state or by any representation of natural code. Further, it is not touched yet by Antigona's representations to Ismeina of her predicament. Antigona is the embodiment of the arrogant human who thinks that they touch the essence of being human by simply subjecting state law to some higher values and code.

142. The origin of Antigona's dilemma, then, can be read as being between, on the one hand, the essential degradation by human law of the essence of humans as strange and, on the other hand, how divine law is intimately connected to what is it essentially strange in humans. In that to which Antigona's dilemma is a metaphor, the human *Dasein* and the divinities unite. Grasping the essence of law as the triad of the mysterious order of Being, the protection of that order, the justice that is effectuated by this protection, and its distorted relationship to the legal, can reveal the terrible, truly tragic, extent of Antigona's predicament. Antigona's tragedy is, that, being human, what is nearest to her was yet not grasped by her – she was too near to attend. Sophocles' saying is a warning against seeing the dilemma between human law and divine law within the coordinates of the legal. Any presentation of the dilemma as that between obeying the law of the state and a voice that comes from one's own conscience would not yet really touch the predicament although it would hint towards it. The essence of law, as guardian of the divine, divine law, makes Antigona's character really anxious even with her consciousness. Antigona's dilemma is between the legal and the essence of law. The dilemma of Antigona is whether or not to obey the 'legal' or whether to follow violently the essential comportment towards *dikē* – the essence of law as the order of Being itself. On this reading, Antigona is really a play about the tragedy of losing face in the hegemony of the legal in a way which is coupled to the impossibility of regaining such a face in front of the law of Being. The torment of Antigona is nothing but the anxiety of the oppression of the overpowering, an invitation to a horizon that the law of the state as well as a code of 'natural law' can take her away from. This

dilemma, hinted at by the chorus, questions her essence as a human being who lives in a society of 'individuals' and who has to obey that legal horizon with which society's laws are made and critically approached. This she has to do despite the more primordial, richer but inexpressible, strange essence inexpressibly in her and which she can approach only with her legally dominated mind. Antigona is the figure of a societal legalised world and as such she opens up to the harm of the legal and has at stake everything in order to get nearer to her essence. That is her tragic faith. Overcoming the promise of the legal is what *Antigona* is all about. It is that human beings have to attend violently and humbly to the overpowering, attending it alone. If we listen to the play we see that what murmurs there is first and foremost the dilemma of the human who is saturated with the legal in essential distortion of the human as 'ek-sistent' *Dasein*. Sophocles made Antigona relevant in a world that is nearly totally hegemonised by the legal, and as we shall see, the ethics that this legal enforces.

143. The word OMETS in Hebrew means 'courage' and it has the same root as the word 'LE-AMETS', which is the infinitive 'to adopt' or 'to embrace', as in the expression 'to embrace somebody to one's heart'. For Man to embrace his essence in strangeness is to obey the dictate of *dikē*. Only then can Man be truly right and just. This would be to embrace the law of the Gods. But this very embrace is to perpetuate the strife that is essentially between human law and divine law. It takes courage to be just, not according to an 'ought', to be silent in this realm of the ought of facts and norms, thereby being just in the sense of being open to what is 'there'. Antigona is about the courage of mortals to let their Being be and obeying their essence. This is the courage of Antigona for having this inexpressible insight, misapprehending it in errancy and following it courageously.

PART B

5

Ethics of the Other as the
Origin of the Legal

1. We now have to both fathom the ambit of the legal and to trace its origin. Origin here is understood as 'that from and by which something is what it is and as it is'.[1] In so doing we will better appreciate the reach of the distortion of the essence of law. The reach of the distortion of the legal can, and has, become very deceptive. So deceptive has it become that the notion that the essence of law is not legal can actually be used to harbour the legal and to entrench legalism. This well-disguised entrenchment effectuates the hegemony of the legal.

2. We must trace the origin of the legal and legalism in order to appreciate the critical impact of what has been said in the previous chapter. I trace such origin of the legal to the ethical philosophy of Emmanuel Levinas. It is in Levinas's ethics, and, according to him, in Judaic ethical thinking as preceding Greek ontology-based thinking – Abraham preceding Ulysses – that the origin of legalism can be located. I do not intend my exploration to constitute any scholarship about Jewish thinking but rather to be an exploration of the origin of the legal as stemming from the characteristics of a first philosophy.

3. It is the task of the next three chapters to argue why Levinasian *transcendence* is itself a manifestation of the legal and why this transcendence is a distortion of the essence of law. In arguing that the very transcendence of objectifying and totalising forms of legalism can itself be within the ambit of the legal we can better appreciate the epochal concealment of the essence of law. Once it is grasped that the legal can be manifested as transcendence it can be appreciated just how much legalism can constitute the suffocation of the call of the essence of law, of *dikē*. By completely replacing the distortion between the ontological and the ontic with a distortion that preserves the predominance of the legal, the call of *dikē* seems needless. The preservation of the *ambit* of the legal as Levinasian transcendence is the task of chapter seven.

---

[1] OWA, p 17.

4.   Chapters five and six argue for the *origin* of the legal in Levinas. That is why these chapters take us sideways from a discussion of law. Levinas's notion of ethics as radical alterity, as well as his notions of truth and language, all indicate that the legal may have as its origin a certain approach to ethics and morality. The origin of the preservation of the legal and the implication of this origin – the legal's disguised ambit – can be traced to a debate about the relationship between ethics and ontology and, with it, a debate about the very nature of ethics. *The very nature of ethics is at stake in debating the origin and ambit of the legal and is thus crucial for thinking about law.*

5.   Levinas claims that ethics as a first philosophy is complementary to Heidegger's notion of thinking-Being, albeit primordial and other to it. Nevertheless, the influence and echoes of Heidegger's radicalisation of truth from correctness to unconcealment, the truth in that which is essentially deferred, even Heidegger's notion of nearness, are echoed in the evolution of Levinas's thought. I shall claim, however, that Levinas's notion of otherness is derivative. The implication of that is that his notion of ethics and responsibility are also derivative. The other implication of their derivative nature is that they serve as the well-concealed origin of the legal.

6.   The debate about the relationship between ontology and ethics, between Levinas and Heidegger, is focused on the nature of otherness. It is in the nature of otherness and the kind of togetherness that otherness at itself hints that the origin of the legal can be traced. This debate about otherness in the next two chapters is carried out in the form of a close and comprehensive reading of Levinas's thought, which is woven with Heideggerian comments. Chapters eight and nine return to Heidegger and interpret the Heideggerian notion of ethics, otherness and togetherness that is also argued to be a part of the fugal order of Being together with the essence of law. Such ethics transcends Levinas's ethics, namely that ethics that also entrenches the legal-*as-transcendence*. Reading Heidegger's latest essays connects the notion of alterity and identity at the essence of ethics to the essence of law, showing all of them to be themselves dependent on the essence of language, truth and the nature of 'things'.

7.   Finally, Heideggerian ethics shows many of Levinasian insights about ethics, namely his notions of radical alterity and responsibility, to be hints rather than essential understanding of these terms. So we could say that Heidegger was here deconstructing Levinas, thus exposing the forgetfulness and entrenchment of the legal in Levinas's thought.

8.   I will follow Levinas's path along which he advances the argument that ethics is a first philosophy, prior to ontology. Levinas claims that ethical reflection is 'otherwise than' ontological reflection. Crucially,

he claims that ethical reflection is otherwise than *the notion of otherness* that is presumed in thinking-Being. In this chapter and chapter six, I contest this statement, arguing that Levinas's 'otherwise than otherness of ontology' is possible only as a derivative 'said'. The claim is that Levinas's otherness of an Other is a distorted response to more the primordial ethics of nearness that is encompassed in thinking-Being and which encompasses the origin of the very alterity that grounds Levinas's reflection. For ethics, the most primordial alterity is essentially a distortion between thinking nearness and thinking on the line of proximity to Other. As I shall argue, this distortion, the distortion of primordial alterity, retains the character of distance. Levinas, it is argued, takes us further away from the near. Only ontic–ontological hermeneutic engagement can attend to the unconcealment that characterises the truth of alterity.

9.   I am aware that in following Levinas a constant repetition is involved. The repetition of a point in different formulae and contexts is not only essential for grasping something better. A repetition can open up uncritically examined interpretations to new insights, which these interpretations repress and attempt to expel. Repetitions are a way of exposing and reiterate the unsaid of a text. In short, such a repetition has an ethical dimension, namely to make it possible to comment upon Levinas's text in a way which opens his interpretation of ontology to interpretation from Heidegger's point of view.

10. The philosophy of Emmanuel Levinas describes the prescriptive ethics of radical subjectivity. A sense of subjectivity for Levinas can only be felt while facing an infinite and asymmetrical debt to the Other, an Other which is not reduced to the otherness within thematisation and negotiation within which subjectivity represents itself to itself. Strictly speaking, Levinas attempts to salvage subjectivity by overcoming it. Subjectivity is understood as involving a radical desire that always possesses the 'I' under the gaze of the face, especially the eyes, of the Other, a desire that the need of 'I' cannot renounce, marginalise or assimilate. For Levinas, the subject ought to be despite itself. For Levinas an obligation for the Other is a condition for a transient though successful mirroring of the subject as exterior to his or her egoity: 'The most passive, unassumable, passivity, the subjectivity or the very subjection of the subject, is due to my being obsessed with responsibility for the oppressed who is other than myself.'[2] Levinas's notion of responsibility is radical in that in preceding the ego there is desire for responsibility, a desire that the ego cannot help but be haunted by. The condition of a free ego as central to responsibility is inverted so that responsibility

---

[2] *OB*, p 55.

precedes the ego. It weighs upon the ego thus prompting it towards transcendence in the process of which the subjectivity 'is'. The ego faces an anterior responsibility which is its own and no one else's, which is absolute, particular, inalienable, never-ending and not reciprocal, thus asymmetrical, towards the Other. Responsibility, always being own-responsibility, is radically asymmetrical with what the Other may or may not do. The ego-identification which is achieved by violently reducing, and thus repressing, the otherness of the Other, by attempting to kill him, remains lame and derivative. Here is the tension of subjectivity: the Other is both radically separated but at the same time remains the originator of the imperative by virtue of which the subject desires its endlessly deferred identity. Identity resides only in some 'not yet' that pervades the ego, exterior to that ego, and which can be activated only by responding absolutely to the Other. Identity can only arise in asymmetry between the self and the Other rather by an idle reciprocal dialectic between two people – self and other – which must assume a dominant totality of identification that conditions such derivative 'commerce'.

11. Levinas conceives ethics as a first philosophy. As such, ethics is more primordial than ontology but, importantly, it is irreducible to ontological reflection, however fundamental, including the derivative ethics that ontological reflection might yield.

12. What is key to the next two chapters is to established the different conceptions of otherness that that are implicit in Levinasian and Heideggerian transcendence. Both transcendences are *contra* transcendental phenomenology in seeing 'it' as movement of deferral, which transcends representation. This movement is indeed Levinas's greatest debt to Heidegger.

OVERCOMING THE DOMINANCE OF ONTOLOGY

13. At no stage of his thought does Levinas deny the central place ontology has for human thinking. However, part of the ethical challenge would be to overcome ontology-centred thought. The call for this overcoming and the justification for it form the deepest philosophical move on Levinas's part. It is the deepest move because it claims to also include Heidegger as perhaps the last of the great defenders of ontology in a philosophical tradition that has been dominated by ontological (Greek) thinking. In the same way as Heidegger saw in Nietzsche the last metaphysician, Levinas saw in Heidegger the last ontologician. An enormous tension follows, then, from such a claim by Levinas regarding the ontology-dominant tradition of western thought. The tension is immense because it was

Heidegger who claimed that he had completely broken apart from the ontic-based derivative ontology of the philosophical tradition. What is at stake in Levinas's work is the questioning of the primordiality of Heidegger's radical philosophical move. According to Levinas, this failure on Heidegger's part to account for genuine alterity made his *oeuvre* yet another stage in ontologically centred thinking. Further, Heidegger's support for National Socialism and the parallel apparent lack of ethics in his thought are, for Levinas, the implications of taking ontology to the extremes that Heidegger has taken it. The inability of ontology-centred thinking to discriminate in fundamental ethical questions can have the effect of nationalism and brutality. Ontology-based thought is indifferent to the way people are governed.[3]

14. Having said that, there is another possibility that looms large here, which is that Levinas, especially given his near-exclusive concentration on the Heidegger of *Being and Time*, did not fully appreciate the Heideggerian move. It is possible that Levinas was not reading Heidegger's 'un-thought', to use a Heideggerian term, in *Being and Time*. If this is the case, and Levinas failed to grasp Heidegger, his declarations of overcoming ontology in the name of ethics as a first philosophy may well be heavily misplaced. Not only misplaced, this failure can actually show Levinas's efforts to be, in fact, part and parcel of the very ontology Heidegger sought to overcome.

15. Levinas's ethical move is best described in the first pages of *Otherwise Than Being*:

> Transcendence is passing over to being's *other*, otherwise than being. Not *to be otherwise*, but *otherwise than being*. And not to not-be; passing over is not here equivalent to dying. ... The *otherwise than being* is stated in a saying that must also be unsaid in order to thus extract the *otherwise than being* from the said in which it already comes to signify but *being otherwise*.[4]

I shall argue that, despite considerable refinement and subtleties both in *Totality and Infinity* and, even more so, in *Otherwise than Being*, Levinas never does reflect adequately upon fundamental ontology, giving it the most charitable interpretation. He claims that the ethical order of transcendence is antecedent to ontology. He characterises ontology as talk without responsibility to the Other, without dwelling upon what 'otherness' means to fundamental ontology.

---

[3] See 'Emmanuel Levinas and Richard Kearney: A Dialogue with Emmanuel Levinas', in RA Cohen (ed), *Face to Face with Levinas* (Albany, State University of New York Press, 1986) pp 13–33.

[4] *OB*, pp 3, 7.

Ontology subordinates any Saying to an already preceding Said, and this subordination holds sway even with the most fundamental ontology, that of Heidegger, which characterises the ontological difference as the distinction between beings and their Being. In a more refined way, Levinas claims that ethical Saying also transcends any alterity, and with it any ethics, that ontological thinking can account for in terms of Saying that is hidden in the Said. The Saying of fundamental ontology – thinking-Being – cannot accommodate radical alterity and is therefore not yet ethical.

The order of Being will still be within the said in which the exception still does not inaugurate genuine transcendence: :

> ... the fact that the ex-ception shows itself and becomes truth in the *said* can not serve as a pretext to take as an absolute and apophantic variant of the saying, which is ancillary or angelic.[5]

Ontology is always within the logic of the said, and as such will be ethically uncritical and conservative, however innovative it might be about stating the exception to a given essence of entities. Ontology will be locked within the totality of the presence of the 'there is ...' and 'to be ...' and will not be able to open up towards genuine alterity.

16.   Levinas associated ontology with maintaining the reproduction of thematisation of beings in their essence. Even in transcending any representation of essences, ontological reflection persists within the co-ordinates of essence. Levinas associates ontology with the craving for articulating the essence of beings, as perpetuating being's *conatus essendi*. Ontology reduces and neutralises heterogeneity by striving to a panoramic view of beings in their Being. The primacy of ontology is the bedrock for the perpetuation of the same and totality. The 'bringing into light' of the Being of being entails the production of Being. Human *Dasein* is captured as subservient to the primacy of Being and thus to thinking-essencing. The Being of the existent dominated philosophical reflection. The hallmark of ontologically based thought – the intentionality of *Dasein* – is its manifestation towards Being and as such is itself conditioned by the Saying of Being.[6] For Levinas, ontology perpetuates thinking with themes, representations and totalities. Even if an ontology is overcome it merely serve to reproduce another ontology, that is another scheme of totality within which beings are related to one another in their essences.

---

[5] *Ibid*, p 6.
[6] *TI*, p 294.

17. Ethics, then, entails its own horizon, which happens in the face-to-face encounter with the Other. Ethics entails the possibility of being caressed, prior to perception, imagery and representation, by the face of the person who is totally other than me. Ethics radicalises exteriority in a way that ontological reflection cannot do. This radicalisation opens up true infinity prior to ontology that always produces infinity conditioned by its tendency to assimilate primordial alterity into sameness. A constant engagement with the absolute Other gives rise to an ethical challenge that is not reducible to, as well as not encapsulated within, the question of Being.

18. As early as in his essay *Is Ontology Fundamental?* Levinas understood the path of his thinking to involve ontological reflection as the point of departure. Levinas's contention is that the relationship to the Other cannot be characterised just by letting his or her being be, by understanding her Being. The relationship should be understood as a face-to-face encounter which is preconceptual. The relationship to the Other is ethical and not ontological because it involves speaking *to* the other and being *for* him or her rather than merely being *with* him or her. 'I have spoken [to the Other], that is, I have overlooked the universal being he incarnates in order to confine myself to the particular being he is.'[7] Ontology cannot account for responding to the address of the other as Other. Such address is involved in this face-to-face relationship. There is a dimension in which understanding of the other is fused with mere interlocution and commerce of identification with the other: the understanding that merely comporting oneself towards the being of the other person does not capture the preconceptual understanding that is coupled with addressing the other as Other. To face the other as Other is not the same as letting the other be in his Being. Language as an address to the Other is not the same as the ontological language of understanding. Some sociality precedes ontology. As part of articulating the irreducibility of the 'for/to the Other' into ontology, Levinas says: 'I cannot deny him partially, in violence, by grasping him in terms of being in general, and by possessing him'.[8]

19. We may ask, in this initial investigation of Levinas: what does this primordial distinction between ethics which is based on 'for/to the other' and that which is based on 'with the other' consist of? What is the characteristic of the depth of the mere 'being with the other' of ontology?

20. Levinas's account of subjectivity involves an infinite desire for the Other. Levinas views subjectivity as that which survives any account

---

[7] *IOF*, p 7.
[8] *Ibid*, p 9.

of the human *Dasein* in ontology. That is arguably the nature of the phenomenological reduction that Levinas carries out, bracketing the ontological 'prejudices' from subjectivity, but in doing so also transcending a Husserlian transcendental ego. Primordial not-yet subjectivity desires to overcome ontology. The disinterestedness of the subject is enabled only while facing exteriority or genuine alterity. Such an offering of one's own to the Other is summed up by Levinas in the ethical gesture of pronouncing 'here I am' – *me voici*. Identity is always a not-yet that is being caressed by what Levinas calls the *ipseity* of the self, its sense impressing only through exteriority.[9] It is exteriority, infinite alterity, which makes subjectivity heterogeneous. Subjectivity as ontologically egoistic is merely a constant satisfaction of an actively needful identification within the Same. Ethical subjectivity-in-alterity transcends the ego and as such it characterises primordial egoity:

Here the unicity of the ego first acquires a meaning – where it is no longer a question of the ego, but of me. The subject which is not an ego, but which I am, cannot be generalized, is not a subject in general; we have moved from the ego to me who am me and no one else.[10]

21.   What is the origin of the 'me'? What is the origin of subjectivity-in-alterity? What is the origin of the never-ending desire for such subjectivity? Levinas calls that origin the 'event of separation'.[11] The event of separation for Levinas marks the point where alterity overflows the Same, destabilises it, and breaks it from the totality logic of continuous representations. Representations, for Levinas, yield the temptation for idealism and are the domain of the absolute sovereignty of the subject who thinks within the Same and paraphrases any alterity into the logic of the Same. Representation is the

possibility for the other to be determined by the same without determining the same, without introducing alterity into it ...[I]t is always the same that determines the other. To be sure, representation is the seat of truth: the movement proper to truth consists in the thinker being determined by the object presented to him. But it determines him without touching him, without weighing on him – such that the thinker who submits to what is thought does so 'gracefully', as though the object, even in the surprises it has in store for cognition, had been anticipated by the subject.[12]

[9] *TI*, p 257.
[10] *OB*, pp 13–14.
[11] *TI*, p 122.
[12] *Ibid*, p 124.

Representation is the arrogance of subjectivity that involves distortion of the meaning of a 'pure present' by utilising the past in the represented object. Representation does not allow for passivity and constant refusal to be determined by totality. Alterity is thus not faced.

22. The holding on to exteriority, to alterity, the suspension of representation prior to any affirmation, is what Levinas refers to as 'enjoyment' [*jouissance*]. Only in enjoyment does the 'me' exist and is it experienced.[13] Only in transcending ontological experience can the 'me' be experienced. That moment of enjoyment is a moment that Levinas calls '*living from*', being *nourished* in self-constitution. Levinas characterised selfhood at that moment as *fecundity*. In *Time and the Other* and *Totality and Infinity* fecundity comes to signify the being apart and together, together and apart, that characterises the paternal relationship of the Other and the self. Fecundity refers to the self that transcends the Same and survives as the 'me'. The notion of fecundity comes to explain as parental the relationship of the self that transcends itself in ethical relations and still remains. The notion of fecundity is invoked because in a parental relationship my children are at the same time a part of and not part of myself. Sometimes you look at your child and you become that child yourself, meaning that there is a sublimated fatherhood speaking to you from the child.[14] The vocabulary of fecundity is later replaced in *Otherwise than Being* as the idea of 'substitution', on which I shall reflect more on in the next chapter.

23. Alterity necessitates revisiting the notion of time and temporality. Time for Levinas is diachronical. Time is not that of the Same, namely that of *Dasein*'s own. Only alterity can awaken time. Levinas provides a conception of time in both of his early works, *Time and the Other* and *Existence and Existents*. Levinas points out the connection between thinking-Being and loneliness. To ek-sist in time is to hover in one's own innermost temporality. Hovering in temporality means to be locked in one's own past, present and future. The present moment becomes a moment of fusion between reminiscence (past) and anticipation (future). Thinking-Being, then, involves *synchronous* temporality: 'The present is welded to the past, is entirely the heritage of that past: it renews nothing. It is always the same present or the same past that endures.'[15] All involvements are assimilated into this locked temporal perspective. Levinas maintains that the hovering of Being in time is *lonely*: 'Solitude is the very unity

---

[13] *Ibid*, p 127.
[14] See *TO*, pp 91–2; *TI*, pp 267–9.
[15] *TO*, p 48.

of the existent, the fact that there is something in existing starting from which existence occurs. The subject is alone because it is one.'[16] Alone means, 'being identical to itself'.[17] In a sense, then, the prison of the self is the coercion of self [*moi*] and ego [*soi*] into an ontological temporality where the self is alone. In being alone the self gets materiality and it is this materiality which prevents the self from own-nourishment and enjoyment.[18] In a later essay Levinas characterises the inclination of the self to thematise itself as the basis for intentionality of the '*I think*' and with it all phenomenology.[19] This includes the hermeneutic phenomenology of Heidegger despite the radicalisation of intentionality that it offers, namely intentionality towards Being, towards the Nothing rather than towards the positivity and essential features of experiencing beings advocated by transcendental phenomenology. Solitude also means that language is imprisoned in ego-based representations.[20] The imprisoned temporality, this loneliness, means that time *loses* any significance: 'solitude is the absence of time'.[21] Under the hegemony of ontological thinking, a solitary selfsame will precede any transcendent ethical reflection about being 'with others'. Time regains significance only when absolute alterity is confronted.

We can see what Levinas means by passivity here. In looking at the face of the Other which transcends any ego- imprisoned pseudo-active involvement and re-representation the passive person is unlike Ulysses who keeps coming back. Alterity is to let the other speak and pardon. There is the tension in Levinas that, although ontological time is 'my innermost' time, I can never be as a subject precisely when so ontologically imprisoned. Only in a disturbance, which comes about when alterity confronts me, can I 'be', in a different sense from the Being of a fundamental ontological reflection. It is the gist of Levinas that only exteriority yields originary subjectivity. The result of ontological synchronicity is the loss of what Levinas refers to as an 'instant', a moment of genuine present, whereby the subject loses its selfsame centre and becomes genuinely passive and disinterested. It is the Other which pardons the subject, and thereby gives rise to, or frees, subjectivity from its ontological prison.[22] The instant amounts to the 'appropriation of existence by the existent',[23] which suspends the flux of the

[17] *Ibid*, p 54.
[18] *Ibid*, p 55.
[19] TO, p 67.
[20] DR, pp 160–61.
[21] *Ibid*, pp 171–2.
[21] TO, p 57.
[22] EE, pp 94–7.
[23] *Ibid*, p 83.

ontological. The instant breaks away from the dialectic of time.²⁴ The moment of the instant is paradoxical because the locus of it is outside totality and its temporality, so it looks as if it comes from nowhere. A moment of present is a moment of encounter with alterity. A moment of future is characterised as a 'not yet' relationship of alterity and, as such, should be distinguished from the anticipation of *Dasein* of its own possibilities: 'The futuration of the future does not reach me as a to-come [*a-venir*], as the horizon of my anticipations of pro-tensions.'²⁵ Similarly, a past moment is something that is not in any way relating to that moment of present. It is something that has happened and gone by: 'Here we have, in the ethical anteriority of responsibility (for-the-other, in its priority over deliberation), a past irreducible to a hypothetical present that it once was.'²⁶ Levinas initiates a severance, an incision, of the temporal continuum that Heidegger associated with Being.²⁷

24.   *Dasein* is alone in encountering this temporality and the comportment of *Dasein* near to this temporality is 'being towards death'. For Heidegger, death is always *my own* death which I *anxiously* anticipate. The *fear* of death for Levinas stems from the awareness that I am always already not alone, always beyond my own ontological prison. It is in death that we are *not* alone. For both Levinas and Heidegger, death is central. For both, death is a metaphor for a genuine tremor of temporality. For Heidegger, the anxiety that accompanies the contemplation of death is a mark of the being-in-the-world of *Dasein*. For Levinas, death is a moment of primordial sociality of alterity. For Levinas, in death, consciousness stops ek-sisting for itself. Time is punctuated from an own-synchronous continuum into diachronical 'breaks' of moments of genuine presents. For Heidegger, in death, the punctuality that conditions subjectivity is lost in an oppressive moment of inexpressible temporal continuum which is nevertheless *Dasein*'s innermost own – hence the anxiety. The subject that is reborn after such letting be only distorts that moment of inexpressible encounter. Hence the strangeness of Heidegger's encounter. For Levinas, the encounter with the Other is not strange but rather involves feelings of realisation of a deep *ignorance* which is yet to be regained. For Heidegger, death is a relentless abyss which is not reducible to sameness and alterity, and *that is its otherness*. For Levinas, death is a clash between sameness

²⁴ *Ibid*, p 72.
²⁵ *DR*, p 173.
²⁶ *Ibid*, p 170.
²⁷ In *EE*, at p 71, Levinas writes: 'The present is an ignorance of history. In it the infinity of time or of eternity is interrupted and starts up again. The present is then a situation in being where there is not only being in general, but there is a being, a subject.'

and alterity. There is a feeling that Levinas's account of alterity and death is more in control of its 'objectives' than that of Heidegger, which keeps the mystery much more alive. It seems that the fear of death for Levinas also involves a birth. But death is not as mysterious in Levinas as it is in Heidegger, because, for Levinas, 'nothingness' is impossible in death. For Heidegger, death (the contemplation of which occurs in *Dasein*'s bodily life) is a moment of freedom, of the possibility of authentic involvement of *Dasein*. For Levinas, death implies that it is no longer possible for the self to bear the suffering of being imprisoned in its own self-same centre.[28]

25. For Levinas, then, time becomes meaningful *only* when I transcend my loneliness, when I open up a present instant to the Other. For Levinas, time connotes a succession of 'nows' but not in a trivial sense of clock-time. The succession of genuine presents comes together only by the absolute severance alterity effectuates with the past (thinking otherwise than through memory) and the future ('not yet' otherness which the present cannot anticipate). Time for Levinas is the constant transcendent of the temporality of the same in a present 'now', encapsulated in the gesture towards alterity: 'Here I am' [*me voici*] or in Hebrew *Hineni*.[29]

26. It is important at this stage to note the punctual nature of time in Levinas. For him, 'Time does not flow like a river.'[30] Although punctuation is infinite here in trying to escape self-centred totality-time, it is still punctual in nature. This will be important for my reading of *Totality and Infinity* to follow.

27. For Levinas, ontology, however fundamental, presents an anonymous, impersonal and ubiquitous presence, which he calls in his early works the 'there is' [*ill-y-a*].

For the Being which we become aware of when the world disappears is not a person or a thing, or the sum total of persons and things; it is the fact that one is, the fact that *there is*. Who or what is does not come into communication with its existence by virtue of a decision taken prior to the drama, before the curtain rises; it takes up this existence by existing already.[31]

28. Thinking the existence of the existent completely envelops the existent. Ontological thinking, which connects the existent with its

[28] TO, pp 68–73.
[29] An account of Levinas's early conception of time and death is given by RJS Manning, *Interpreting Otherwise than Heidegger: Emmanuel Levinas's Ethics as First Philosophy* (Pittsburgh, Duquesne University Press, 1993) pp 31–123.
[30] EE, p 71.
[31] *Ibid*, p 8. In *ibid*, p 52, Levinas characterises the 'there is' as the 'impersonal, anonymous, yet inextinguishable "consummation" of being, which murmurs in the depth of nothingness itself ... The *there is*, inasmuch as it resists a personal form, is "being in general"'.

existence (including for that matter *Dasein* and its innermost Being), overwhelms the subject so there is no escape from it. There is no sociality in the 'there is', and the subject is 'locked' by this prison of anonymity into a prison of the loneliness of its own perspective, its own temporality. Indolence and weariness come about as a result of the impossibility of a beginning that transcends sameness.[32] Weariness is a sign of the ego retreating into itself to its own innermost Being, thus forced to repeatedly 'let' the anonymity of Being nourish self-imprisonment within the same. Existence becomes like a shadow of the existent pursuing the ego.[33] In this it relates to time in that the ego is locked in a temporal prison, as all its futurity is conditioned by the mutually reinforcing anonymous 'there is' and the selfsame perspective.

From an ontological perspective, being an 'active' subject means to have the power of the agent 'to remain free from any bond with what remains present to it, of not being compromised by what happens to it, by its object or even its history, is just what knowing qua light and intention is'.[34] The subject being locked up in itself and its own innermost intentionality towards the world leads to a detachment from what actually occurs to the subject in its history. Loneliness terrifies the subject and the only escape would be to go to sleep, but even this sleep is no escape from the omnipresence of the 'there is' that awaits any waking up and so amounts to terrifying insomnia.[35]

The 'there is' oppresses even though that 'there is' is neither a being nor consciousness functioning. In the loneliness the 'I' is deprived of itself as it is 'submerged by the night, invaded, depersonalised, stifled by it'.[36] The lonely subject, being submerged in the 'there is' is in actuality deprived of the possibility of subjectivity, subjectivity which would be outside the clutch of both the lonely embeddedness in totality and being submerged in the anonymous 'there is'.

Subjectivity has to emerge in a unique form which would not fall pray to the loneliness of totality or anonymity of the ubiquity of the 'there is'. As long as thinking-Being dominates, any 'event' occurs within this prison. Ethical transcendence of that loneliness, love, is the only possibility 'against the anonymous *there is*, horror, trembling and vertigo, perturbation of the I that does not coincide with itself, the happiness of enjoyment affirms the I at home with

---

[32] *EE.* pp 12–13.
[33] *Ibid*, p 16.
[34] *Ibid*, p 43.
[35] *Ibid*, p 62.
[36] *Ibid*, p 53.

itself.' Levinas adds 'The veritable position of the I in time consists in interrupting time by punctuating it with beginnings.'[37]

It is the locus of my inquiry to meditate about the nature of these infinite beginnings and to ask whether the relationship that is to be thought about as 'mine' is between these beginnings and the continuous elements from which they spring. Levinas wishes to revive subjectivity and sociality in that very alterity which destabilises consciousness.

29.   Is the 'there is' really anonymous? Is it the continuous nature of the Nothing that makes the Nothing anonymous? Does Levinas do justice to the ontological difference as explained by Heidegger? Surely the important event for Heidegger is that interaction between the world of beings and their Being. We must not accept uncritically, as Levinas seems to do, that the 'there is' is akin to Heidegger's Being and that the ontological difference is just an advanced mode of the Same being imprisoned in the 'there is'. To be sure, at the time of writing *Existence and Existents* Levinas was familiar with Heidegger's *What is Metaphysics?* and the characterisation of the Nothing there. However, to be fair to Levinas, Heidegger's notion of *alētheia* was not fully developed in 1947, and *Letter on Humanism* had just been published. Still, we have to ask whether Levinas has captured the sense of the nothingness in interpreting it as the 'end and limit of being, as an ocean which beats up against it on all sides'. He distinguishes the 'there is' which is ubiquitous from the nothing that is that negation of being.[38] But has he captured Heidegger's notion of nothingness interpreted as a distortion arising out of a near/far relationship – between the unconditional and the punctual? Is the giving of Being to beings [*es gibt*] impersonal in the way that Levinas wanted to portray the 'there is'?

30.   The Other nears me as a 'face'. This face is not merely a face of another human being, another person – another figure that has perceptible eyes, ears, lips, etc. The face comes near and faces me but cannot be reduced to either perception or representation.[39] The face exceeds my powers and its gaze overflows any conceptualisation of myself. The face is the way in which the Other caresses the subject, exceeding the idea of the other in the subject. The face is all-powerful, but in a non-belligerent way. It 'speaks to me and thereby invites me to a relation incommensurate with a power exercised, be it enjoyment or knowledge'. The face pleads with me: 'do not kill me', 'you shall not commit murder'. The face does not

---

[37] *TI*, p 143.
[38] *EE*, p 60.
[39] *EI*, p 86.

oppose me by a greater force but by its infinite and ubiquitous transcendence. This epiphany of the face is ethical and transcends my 'consciousness of' which cannot fix and conceptualise it.[40] 'The face is exposed, menaced, as if inviting us to an act of violence. At the same time, the face is what forbids us to kill.'[41] The face comes about as the overflow of meaning and identity. The face-to-face first social relationship with the Other precedes any preceding context or theme. The face constantly questions, challenges, demands infinite responsibility. The face constantly generates a desire in me for alterity which is 'otherwise than', knowledge, context, coherence, theory. Ontological reflection does not provide shelter from the face. I am entirely powerless in the relationship of face-to-face with the Other. Derrida conceives the notion of the face as that which *sees*: 'not so much that which sees things – a theoretical relation – but that which exchanges its glance. The visage is a face only in the face-to-face. As Scheler said ..."I see not only the eyes of an other, I see also that he looks at me."'[42] The face is the primordial encounter that brings about thinking with goodness, values and obligations. The face-to-face encounter with the Other is the origin of obligation.[43]

31. The face is the opening of humanity which looks at me with all its destitution and poverty. It appeals to my power, but this appeal is actually also a powerful command that is addressed only to me, that puts me in its gaze.[44] The gaze comes from what Levinas refers to as the dimension of 'height'. The Other's inarticulable face approaches me from on high. But this 'high' is yet addressed to me privately and informally, with what Levinas refers to as 'the feminine'. The Other is not high, in the sense of a justified imperative from a high authority but is rather an intimate command or prohibition.

32. The face has this combination of being full of destitution and being all-pervasive and powerful in a non-violent way. The face, having all these qualities, keeps on impressing despite any effort to mute it and so it opens up the signification of infinity to me. Infinity means a non-exhaustible surplus of alterity that keeps overflowing my themes, concepts, history, consciousness. This infinity is all-powerful because it cannot be paraphrased into an existing web of concepts or themes, it cannot be swept under the carpet, it cannot be expelled.

33. Any representation of the Other, any attempt at thematising it, would amount to violence towards it. Violence is done to the Other by

---

[40] *TI*, pp 198–201.
[41] *EI*, p 86.
[42] *VM*, p 122.
[43] *TI*, p 201.
[44] *Ibid*, p 213.

attempting to assimilate, to reduce otherness into totality or the 'Same' – by attempting to be symmetrical to, and resonant with, the Other. Violence consists in, as Derrida puts it, the neutralisation of desire. We cannot reduce the desire for alterity to the satisfaction of 'need' for the Same. Violence would be the 'abstraction of seeing'.[45] Allowing for the ethical is to overcome violence to the Other by keeping responsibility for the Other asymmetrical, that is never reciprocal or equal to me. The infinity of the otherness of the other, of the ethical, is the never-ending surplus which, although enticing the violence of ontological reflection, cannot be destroyed by violence. Philosophy is inaugurated only when violence is overcome in an ethical moment. Any entrenchment of the Same would be mere theorisation/replacement of theories, but not philosophy. Philosophy is born with powerlessness in the face of alterity.

34.   The ethical relationship is characterised by Levinas as infinity. Infinity supposes an everlasting and continuous, never-ending responsibility for the Other. This responsibility is not something that one can thematise and so be conscious of it in the same way as a person is conscious of this or that obligation articulated in some rule or principle. The ethical relationship consists of infinite debt, whereby the self lives from the Other, whereby the self is nourished by the otherness of the Other. The self can only 'be' *after* an ethical moment of facing its own responsibility to the Other.

35.   Responsibility for the Other, as well as living for, and from, the Other, cannot be redeemed but burdens the subject relentlessly from the subject's innermost own. 'Me' involves facing the absolute Other. Only in transcending totality can I have an instant in which I can have a *trace* of who I am. Ethics occurs in facing genuine alterity, as contrasted with mirroring, which occurs by a representation of the idea of the other in me, that is through an encounter with an idle alterity. This 'who' is thus original and not assimilable to the question of 'what I am'. The identity-in-alterity is not reducible to identification of a 'who' within the 'what' of totality. Identity, and with it, freedom, becomes a difficult matter of responding to the origin of an ethical challenge. Difficult because identity comes not as a result of realising some already accepted 'commitment'.[46] Subjectivity attends to that which takes it away from ego-based homogeneity into the heterogeneity of alterity. I face my own deepest nudity in the face of the Other.

36.   My innermost desire is that for alterity, for the Other, and it is this desire which is the origin of 'ought'. The 'I am' occurs in the ethical

45 VM, p 123.
46 OB, pp 136–40.

encounter and leads to innermost enjoyment which, *because it engages with original 'ought'*, is better than any enjoyment from satisfaction of need within totality. The alterity of the Other, its exteriority, which appears only as a face, a temporal 'trace', comes not from 'history' or 'memory' but from a deeply desired ethical encounter.

37.   In *Time and the Other* Levinas seeks to account for existents (beings) as separate, rather than merely distinguished, from their existence (their Being). The ontological difference that Heidegger elaborates upon in *Being and Time* and *The Basic Problems of Phenomenology* creates a connection between beings (existents) and their Being (their existence) although Heidegger distinguishes between the two. The result of this peculiar combination of connection and distinction is what Levinas interprets to be Heidegger's notion of *throwness* [*Geworfenheit*] – the fact-of-being-thrown-in existence. Existence precedes existents. Existence is given to the existent but the latter can never master it so it is left abandoned. That distinction, though not separation, between existent and existence accounts for the strange independence of existence in Heidegger, which is independent of any existent: 'I would also gladly say that existing does not exist. It is the existent that exists. And [referring here to Heidegger's ontological difference] the fact of having recourse to what does not exist, in order to understand what does exist, hardly constitutes a revolution in philosophy.'[47]

Could we not, however, wonder, at this point whether Levinas does not caricaturise Heidegger here? Is it not the whole point of Heidegger's philosophy to differentiate between, on the one hand, the Being of beings, and, on the other hand, existents and existence, the latter still characterising the preoccupation with beings? Being, given as the 'not' of beings is very different and much more subtle than the wholly 'positive' notion of existence that Levinas tries to attach to existents under a Heideggerian banner. The notion of Being is positive only in the sense that beings are 'not yet' and as such cannot take refuge in their positive existence as the 'things they are'. 'Letting Being of being be' is not the same as 'grasping the existence of beings as the beings they are'. The former involves a radicalisation of the thingness of the thing, not yet neared by the latter formulation.

38.   Levinas referred to that in which the subject is most immediately involved as the 'elemental' or the 'elements'. Levinas said: 'Every relation or possession is situated within the non-possessable which envelops or contains without being able to be contained or enveloped.'[48] The elements are not transformable into things, with

[47] *TO*, pp 44–6.
[48] *TI*, p 131.

them 'nothing ends, nothing begins'. Man bathes in the elements, plunging into the continuous and the unconditioned. Bathing gives rise to primordial enjoyment, and Levinas uses an ontological metaphor to convey this enjoyment: 'as though we were in the bowels of being'.[49]

39. To enjoy bathing in the elements means to enjoy without utility, in 'being for', and 'living from', as he puts it 'in pure loss, gratuitously, without referring to anything else in pure expenditure'.[50] It is enjoyment that is based on deafness to the Other. This enjoyment nourishes in a way different from the satisfaction of need. This enjoyment is in somewhat naïve disinterestedness – the disinterested joy of play.[51] Enjoyment is to go back to this primordial living, bathing in the elements. Significantly for the argument to come, enjoyment in the elements for Levinas is prior even to any engagement with the Other, that is with exteriority and alterity. This sense of enjoyment would become in his later work something quite different, namely the sensation of transcending the Same by being open in responsibility to the Other.

40. The discussion of the elements has been interpreted as the initial ego-based way in which Man enjoys the world, breathing the air, swimming in water, a state of spontaneous egoism, something that is prior to all social relations.[52] I would like to look at Levinas's discussion of the elements in some detail, for it is of crucial importance to my argument to come to grips with his move from something continuous into the punctuability that characterises ethical relationships. I regard interpreting the elements as pre-social and egoistic existence as too simplistic, for the reason that something has to be given to people already in the state of being egoists. Something elementary must have already been given to them as separate egoistic beings.

41. Sensibility for Levinas means the surplus of desire for enjoyment that is otherwise than being involved with representations, thematisation, essences, with the content-based enjoyment which arises out of mere finite objects and concepts. There is already some sensibility that involves bathing in the elements. Levinas associates sensibility with enjoyment rather than with representations:[53] 'In sensibility itself and independently of all thought there is announced an insecurity which throws back in question this quasi-eternal immemoriality of the

---

[49] *Ibid*, p 132.
[50] *Ibid*, p 133.
[51] *Ibid*, p 134.
[52] AT Peperzak, *Beyond: The Philosophy of Emmanuel Levinas* (Evanston, Northwestern University Press, 1997) pp 9–10.
[53] *TI*, p 136.

element, which will disturb it as the other, and which it will appropriate by recollecting (*se recueillant*) in a dwelling.'[54]

42. It is at this point that Levinas starts to mix the punctuated and the
continuous, unconditioned, elements. The Other here equivocates
between something whose otherness is unconditioned and continuous
and, on the other hand, something which is already some-thing,
which is a completely Other to me, something which is already
punctuated and punctuating, something on the matrix of punctuation despite not yet being conceptualised or thematised. In this
quote, the interruption by this Other must be dwelled upon. We must
listen here not merely to the interrupting Other but rather to this
equivocation that characterises otherness from the elements. Here,
the first sense of otherness is still dominant, namely otherness of the
elemental, the pre-decoded unconditioned continuum but, as we shall
see shortly, this dominance is shifting dramatically towards the
second, more punctual, sense. This is a key shift because, as flux, the
desire, the hunger for the elemental is tantamount, I will claim, not
to pre-social egoity but to the ontological, which is given to the
otherness of the other as its Being (the Nothing). This would locate
the ethical as being in between the matrix of punctuation and
primordial continuity rather than exclusively within the second sense
where ethics is already a relationship on the punctuated horizon of
'for-the-Other'. Has the equivocation about the locus of otherness
been made into a problem? This problem becomes more apparent as
the argument of *Totality and Infinity* develops.

43. Levinas swiftly moves on to claim that the sufficiency of the 'I', in
enjoyment, resides in the insufficiency of the 'living from' which
characterises the relationship to the Other.[55] There is no further
mention of the elements, the spring of Being, which he briefly
discussed just a few pages earlier.

44. In order to go beyond representations, not replacing them with other
representations, Levinas needs to really create a rift, a difference,
between these two senses of otherness. But instead he forgets this
primordial moment of movement out of the unconditioned and
rather takes for granted the otherness of a totally not conceptualisable 'Other' which is already discussed within a matrix of
punctuation. Levinas, I will claim, locks his transcendence to operate
within what Heidegger referred to in *Being and Time* as the ontic
'present-at-hand', and from there on within an ontic and inauthentic
cycle, as discussed in *Being and Time*.

45. Sensibility, as the mode of enjoyment, survives all experience of

54 *Ibid*, p 137.
55 *Ibid*, p 143.

'consciousness of'. Yet, and this is the key in Levinas's statement, 'the sensible is not to be ascribed to the totality to which it is closed. Sensibility enacts the very separation of being – separated and independent'.[56] Sensibility, and the desire it encapsulates, already assumes, foresees, anticipates, the possibility of the separate. Sensibility assumes the primordial separation of the not conceptualised yet dominant 'me-in-relation-to-the-not-me', however merely caressing, dynamic, pre-conceptual, this relationship of separation might be. Indeed, Levinas claims that the 'I', the ego, is transcendable to the 'me', but it is transcendable into infinitude that itself primordially anticipates decoding and punctuation. Crucially, the punctuation itself is not seen as distortion or, to put it differently, the impossibility of the conceptualisation, and hence distortion is already on the horizon of punctuation. There is no genuine encounter with something that is prior to any difference, namely with the elemental that is continuous. In this sense, there occurs a violent severance from the elements, never to be attended to again in Levinas's thought. From that moment on, Levinas unreflectively assumes this severance. 'Difference' would mean infinite differentiation and deferral within the punctual, or, as I will call it, the panctu-able.

The moment of transcendence constitutes that severance from the elemental thereby constraining otherness by the economy of the Other. In other words, Levinas describes infinite responsibility but already conditions the infinite in an ethics of 'an Other'. The conception of the 'thing' that linked Levinas's conception of difference will taint his notions of proximity and substitution to come. His whole notion of difference as distance will be tainted by punctuation. The 'beyond' in Levinas, beyond need, beyond representation, beyond thematisation, beyond history, beyond consciousness and intentionality, the beyond of all aspects of punctuated totality is still impregnated with, and imprisoned within, a punctuable logic. The gentle, non-violent, feminine, velvet-toned, nature of Levinas's ethics of the Other is made possible only by a violent act of separation and imprisonment of futurity within the alterity of an Other. Levinas's move of erasing elemental otherness from any future ethical relationship which involves the otherness of the Other is a move that preserves the ontic. The destiny of Levinas's transcendence is already punctuated, although its content may seem to call for the radicalisation of any punctuated meaning. Levinas's transcendence prevents own attentiveness to Being. The tension, the distortion, between the continuous and the punctual is smothered in his transcendence. The separation from the elements precedes the

[56] *Ibid*, p 138.

separation from totality. There is a double movement here which consists of both the separation from the elements and the retention of a separated sphere as the new limit for enjoyment and transcendence of alterity.

46. In closely reading Levinas, this punctuable infinite comes across many times in *Totality and Infinity*. The originality of enjoyment is said to be 'unreflected', unconditioned,[57] but is that the case? Is not violent punctuability the only way to effectuate separation between existent and 'ek-sistence'?

47. Levinas describes original 'bathing' in the elements. The use of the term 'bathing' by Levinas gives the impression of a primal state, a prior unconditioned, pre-social state. But bathing in the elements is a necessarily unstable process, complementary to the social relation that is severed from the elements. But could we not see this situation as primordial bathing in the elements that can be enjoyed only by coming near and far from the unconditioned nature of bathing? There seems to be a whole other (ethical) dimension already severed by Levinas at this point: the elements ought to be engaged with, although never ought to near the reminiscence of bathing. For Heidegger, it will be remembered, human *Dasein*s are thrown into the world, into their conditioned state by the murmuring Saying of language. Language becomes the elements. Language is both that through which Man is severed from the elements, and the only path Man can dwell on in the space and directionality that constantly struggles to near the elements. It is through language that constant near/far engagement with the elemental can be experienced. It is this enjoyment [*jouissance*] which results from the flickers in which language desires silence that Levinas's separation in its violence silencing denies by enacting the sphere of transcendence as that of 'the Other'. Enjoyment of the Levinasian ethical transcendence as something primordial, however unreflected it might be, is for Levinas still tainted with both the separation from the elements and the retention of this separation.

48. Levinas is careful to distinguish between the enjoyment that comes with desire, with infinity and alterity, and 'the separation accomplished as enjoyment, that is, as interiority, [which] becomes a consciousness of objects'.[58] But is there no implied common matrix between the two kinds of enjoyments? Is there genuine alterity between them? Despite the transcendence of a given representational content, can we not sense similarity between the two kinds of enjoyment? Does not the logic of separation precede Levinas's

[57] *TI*, p 139.
[58] *Ibid*.

conception of the infinite so as to already be disposed to punctuate in the ethical encounter? In other words, does not transcendence in Levinas anticipate punctuation as its very unfolding?

49.   What are things for Levinas? The thingness of things goes beyond their form, content and identity.[59] But if this is the case, then surely this surpasses even the hidden logic of 'the Other', which still gives them some form.

50.   The notion of face that is used by Levinas to transcend 'consciousness of' is revealing. Although such a face, and the gaze of this face into my eyes, is pre-conscious, prior to consciousness, pre-conceptual, it is still on the horizon of extantness, or rather, a way of thinking of the thingness of this thing-face. From a Heideggerian perspective, this thinking is already not elemental, as it defines itself by a face and not by a continuous emptiness.

51.   The primordial temporality of the elements both transcends and conditions consciousness ontically. It is crucial, though, to understand that by consciousness I also include also Levinas's so-called pre-conscious time of alterity of the 'Other'. I will argue below that Levinas's account of the origin of ethical sociality, including the temporality within which such sociality is to be understood, is still within the co-ordinates of consciousness. The moment of present, coming from punctuating the elements seems, on my reading of Levinas, to be the result of a violent separation from the elements that is the origin of consciousness, that is the origin of erring. The anxiety of the continuous of the elements is tamed by consciousness. By this severance Levinas does not show how the otherness of the Other relates to the otherness of the elements, or to what I will call 'otherness of the nothing'. The otherness of the Other is a datum which is not dealt with by Levinas. The otherness of the Other is taken as ontic difference that is infinitely not-yet-conceptualised. But this rather non-mysterious process of ontic difference does not yet engage with the elements.

But it is the elements from which existents are thrown and from which they can *never* be fully separated that constitutes a mystery – the point where language speaks – the point when language as articulation meets language as silence. In Levinas, desire originates only within the realm of the otherness of the Other. However, Levinas ignores that such otherness is itself grounded in deeper temporality, elemental temporality which temporalises the 'how' of the very thinking the otherness of the Other. The Saying of the elements is always already ahead of the Saying from where the otherness of an

[59] *Ibid*, p 141.

Other happens. The continuous precedes, overflows any overflowing which is conditioned by the punctual.

52. I would call that potential which is encapsulated in such retention of the site of transcendence 'punctu-able'. Punctuability is the horizon of transcendence that does not confront the elements again, that does not confront the continuous and unconditioned, that does not confront, and no longer desires to confront, the distortion of the punctual.

53. In his later comment on Levinas, Derrida locates the ethical in the Levinasian texts within the latent invitation for the 'ingratitude' of deconstruction that is encapsulated in these texts. One must not read Levinas's ideas with gratitude and make sameness out of them. Reading of Levinas should be carried out by displacing Levinas's approach to his own main themes.[60] It is the undecidability that pervades the relationship between the othernesss of the elements and the otherness of the Other which I would argue marks the beginning of precisely such an ethical reading of Levinas. Levinas's ethical language is itself coerced into being language of the Other. From this point of severance from the elements onwards, the discussion is about totality and infinity. The discussion is about separation, nourishment and enjoyment as the face of the Other is being encountered. But there is no discussion about the 'how' of the face nor any reflection about the origin of the face. Such a process enables Levinas to present a fundamental 'ought', an original 'ought', as the form of infinite responsible transcendence. He is so enabled because there is already an anticipated re-subjectification of the subject that survives and precedes the transcendence, a potential 'me' to hold responsible the ontology-bound subject that is being submerged in totality. There is already that craving, for such a subject to re-emerge from such transcendence, and so the movement both overcomes subjectivity and retains a horizon of subjectivity. Forgetting that nearing innermost 'mine', the howness of the how, is not yet facing, not yet responding to, something punctuable but rather attending the moment of the continuous that has already gone. In Levinas, the anxious 'ought' of the inexpressible is hijacked into the fearful 'ought' of the high and infinite Other. The inexpressible 'ought' – which calls from the elements – is indeed beyond values, beyond representations, beyond thematisation, but it is also a call nearer actuality than that entrenchment of the ethics of an Other. The 'not yet' of facing the face of the Other is not yet facing that which faces.

54. The initial punctuation of the self–Other, the birth of the subject

---

[60] S Critchley, *The Ethics of Deconstruction: Derrida and Levinas* (Oxford, Blackwell, 1992) pp 107–20. This point is discussed in much more detail in the next chapter.

from the nearest, is being denied recollection by Levinas. In discussing the emergence of ethical thinking out of the elements, this primordial happening is turned into the subjectivity from on high, in fecundity. The dimension of 'height' comes to connote a command by the Other that cannot be overcome by the violence of paraphrasing it into the Same. It is again very significant for the argument to come that the origin of the actuality of the ethical is conceived as a commandment. Subjectivity is characterised by Levinas as intimate, gentle, feminine. 'This gentleness is not only a conformity of nature with the needs of the separated being, which from the first enjoys them and constitutes itself as separate, as I, in that enjoyment, but is a gentleness coming from an affection [*amitié*] for that I. The intimacy which familiarity already presupposes is an *intimacy with someone.*' The mixture of height and intimacy characterises the moment of separation of the 'I'/Other. The Other is only in his or her amorphous deferral so that he or she can generate the intimate recollection which ignites the 'I'-ness.[61] Levinas refers in the third person – *illeity* (from *Ill*) – to the unique interlocutor that emerges from the relationhship of fecundity.

55. Levinas indeed cautions that separation does not mean an isolated individual extracted from the elements.[62] He claims to keep the door open to the elements from which the very possibility of a 'me' was inaugurated and effectuated in a pure present of separation. Levinas regards separation as the ambiguity of distance, a suspension, some dwelling within a gaze. And then the primordiality of the elements to the 'I' is swiftly reversed: 'The elements remain at the disposal of the I – to take or to leave. Labor will henceforth draw things from the elements and thus *discover* the world.'[63] The talk is no longer about that which is continuous, which is primordially given, but rather *of* things, however intricate and ambiguous. Levinas here does give up the question concerning the thingness of things, or the Being of beings, and the distortion that prevails between beings and their Being.

56. Levinas claims that the 'uncertainty' of the elements is 'suspended' in separation.[64]

Possession masters, suspends, postpones the unforeseeable future of the element – its independence, its being. 'Unforeseeable future', not because it exceeds the reach of vision, but because, faceless and losing itself in nothingness, it is inscribed in the fathomless depth of the element, coming from an

[61] *TI*, p 155.
[62] *Ibid*, p 156.
[63] *Ibid*, pp 156–7.
[64] *Ibid*, pp 158–9.

opaque density without origin, the bad infinite or the indefinite, the *apeiron*.[65]

Why should we uncritically accept the relationship with the elements as something which should be overcome? Is there not forgetfulness of Being at this very point, forgetfulness that is masqueraded as something which is separated from Being as its 'other'? The very suspension and violent retention of the suspension of the elements precedes ethical relations, and conditions them.

57. The suspension of the elements is carried out by what Levinas called *Labour*. Labour is carried out by 'the hand': 'The hand delineates a world by drawing what it grasps from the element, delineating definite beings having form, that is, solids.'[66] 'The access to values, usage, manipulation and manufacture rest on possession, on the hand that takes, that acquires, that brings back home.[67]

58. Contemplation can occur only 'after the suspension of the chaotic and thus independent being of the element, and after the encounter of the Other who calls in question possession itself'.[68] It is noticeable that there are two 'afters' here. The first 'after' is after leaving the elements (from an ontological perspective, the inevitable going-far of the punctuable, the ontic). This is the violent move from contemplative continuous thinking into punctual thinking. Forgotten primordial violence requires overcoming such amputating violence of punctuability and is never to be encountered again. The second 'after' is after already violently retaining the segregated sphere, namely an after which signifies the already ethical reflection within the ethical realm when encountering the Other in transcendence of the Same. 'Same' and 'Other' are already the co-ordinates of transcendence that follow the uprooting of the continuous ground of things and keeping it at bay. Should we not make the first 'after', and with it the hegemony of the second 'after', the point of departure for contemplation, moreover, a point of departure for *ethical* contemplation?

59. Levinas characterises this move from the elements into a segregated realm of ethical relationships with the Other as being 'otherwise than Being' or 'otherwise than Ontology'. This 'otherness than Ontology' signifies a sincere claim by Levinas because he indeed ejects any possibility of fundamental ontological thinking from his reflections.

60. The violence of Levinas's move, that is the separation from, and retention-as-apart-from, the elements, stems from and indeed

[65] *Ibid.*
[66] *Ibid*, p 161.
[67] *Ibid*, p 162; compare Heidegger's contemplation of the hand in *WCT*, at p 16.
[68] *Ibid*, p 163.

reaffirms his ontic notion of time. Levinas's notion of diachrony means that time for Levinas is punctuated and entirely aligns itself to the logic of the 'not conceptualisable in the sense of the not yet conceptualised'. We can see in Levinas a particular conception of diachrony which is inexorably connected to a particular conception of deferral. To persist in time for Levinas means already to live from the Other, for the Other and to speak to the Other. The 'I' in relation to the 'non-I' occasions time most primordially for Levinas.[69] We must persist in asking whether the elements have not themselves got a temporal aspect. Are not the elements temporalised in such way within which subjectivity's time, even a time of subjectivity-as-transcendence, is born?

61. That realm which forgets this moment of severance effectuates the forgetfulness by opening a horizon of infinity-as-ontic deferral/differentiation. In forgetting, reflection does not seek to recover that moment of severance. It is such a separation that conditions the desire to transcend totality into infinity. The inability to think-back the moment of severance creates an insurmountable difficulty for ethics-of-the-Other as a first philosophy. Violence occurs in the imprisoning and entrenching of infinity in a punctuable horizon, while forgetting the very severance which ought to have been made into a first question, into a first event, *prior even to any first philosophy,* in a question which holds the mirror to the face of such philosophy. Levinas's philosophical 'saying', in order to have any actuality, must rescue subjectivity from ontology's neutrality. But by doing that the 'mine' of *Dasein,* that *mine* of listening to Being, is muted. The continuous within which the 'mine' occurs should not be just dubbed impersonal and neutral. It is Levinas's apparent re-personalisation that neutralises a moment of 'own-ness'.

62. The 'abyss of separation', as Levinas calls it[70], its 'otherwise', is still subject to overflow by the elements. To make the abyss, the oscillation of subjectivity, lost and regained in relation to the absolute Other, is derivative and not primordial. Although at the same place in the work Levinas emphasises that the relationship of alterity is not reducible to an objectified relationship of counterparts, his account, in terms of the kind of potential differentiation it perpetuates, has broadly all the echoes with such a relationship. Thinking is already subjected to a method and punctuability in the asymmetry with the Other. There is synchrony in the diachrony. Diachrony in the punctuable must be tainted.

[69] *Ibid,* p 166.
[70] *Ibid,* p 180.

63. We must doubt whether Levinas succeeds in separating existence and existents. The throwness of *Dasein*, as he said, connotes a distinction (between ontic and ontological) but it cannot entail separation. The relationship of near/far between the continuous and the punctual is subtler than separation of horizon and retention of transcendence within that horizon. *Dasein* is thrown into its own innermost temporality, its own world in a way that any account of existents only distorts but also any account of linear existence distorts. *Dasein*'s throwness is a hovering in time, nearing the elements with *no possibility of separation.*

64. The diachrony that Levinas articulates with regard to the immemorial past is also not genuine. The temporality within which the 'I'/Other relationship does recollect and reflect is already punctuated, not in the pattern of totality and thematised history but rather in recollecting a primordial desire to infinitely and ontically differentiate further and further. This reflection does not yet consider that such desire is already too conditioned to be the primordial desire. In Levinas, the desire for the Other is still within the realm of the *need* to punctuate. The absolute past, which is allegedly deeper than the throwness of *Dasein,* is the mark of forgetfulness of origin. Although there is diachrony in Levinas, the diachrony still obeys already the regular notion of time not as a flux and continuous, but as a punctuated succession of 'nows' – a succession of 'nows' which is well masqueraded in the vocabulary of 'caressing' and 'face-to-face'. The 'now' of the facing is the origin of all punctuation. Levinas does not dwell deeply enough on what precedes the 'now' of subjectivity, including the fecund subject, despite its futurity and past in alterity.

65. The question is: does thinking about law involve contemplating the distortion of the essence of law as encapsulated within the very transcendence of the ethics of an Other, or is it that the very 'ontological' thinking about law needs to be transcended by such ethics? *Are we not beginning to witness, with Levinas, the preparation for the perpetuation of the legal in the name of ethical reflection which is seemingly 'other'than the legal, separated even from the realm of the Being of law?* Cannot the entrenchment of the 'other' to the legal follow from that forgetfulness of some primordial distortion whose call can now be felt to begin to take a clear shape?

66. Levinas's fecund subject is marked by passivity 'prior to all passivity of the will' in facing the Other. The passivity stems from the command by the Other for the subject to look at itself through the eyes of the Other, thereby abandoning itself as a totality – as an 'active' source of will (including active and passive will). The primordiality of the passivity of fecundity means that the desire that

moves subjectivity into the heterogeneity of fecundity is something
that the subject can repress but not eliminate.

67.   *Fecundity* is, for Levinas, the temporal relationship within which
subjectivity-in-alterity occurs and persists. Fecundity is the very
temporality, the future in which subjectivity is empowered to foresee
itself through responsibility for the Other. Fecundity is both the
possibilities of myself and of the Other. Subjectivity is grasped at
points of a never-ending process of being together and apart, apart
and together. Subjectivity-in-fecundity is the very involvement of love
that effectuates the teachings of, and the feminine invitation by, the
primordial ethical relationship of alterity. Fecundity connotes the
caress of the 'I' by the Other – of interiority by exteriority. Fecundity
happens in facing the face of the Other. In fecundity all firm
thematised categories are diminished, giving rise to non-reducible
separation, which can only approximate as a caress. It is as this separation that the face of the Other gazes, thus occasioning fecundity.
The face is insurmountable and powerful in its destitute and non-
eliminable command. It is in fecundity that subjectivity *is* but only in
passivity and humble response to the caress of alterity. Fecundity is
continuity of subjectivity at the moment of discontinuity of the
ego-in-totality-and-same: 'Infinite being, that is, ever recommencing
being – which could not bypass subjectivity, for it could not recom-
mence without it – is produced in the guise of fecundity.' In
fecundity, desire goes beyond 'the simply renewal of the possible in
the inevitable senescence of the subject'.[71] Fecundity transcends
totality-based subjectivity: 'In the I being can be produced as
infinitely recommencing, that is, properly speaking, as infinite ...
Fecundity is part of the very drama of the I.'[72] Fecundity is the
horizon of diachrony, of infinity, that is inaugurated with
separation.[73]

68.   Subjectivity is central for Levinas, and it is understood as fecundity.
Understood as fecund, subjectivity is essential to the 'me'. Although
subjectivity transcends identity conceived as a perpetuation of identi-
fication-in-totality, subjectivity is still the bedrock for such thinking
of 'me' in anticipation of such re-identification. In a deep sense,
which will become more and more clear as this chapter and the next
progress, Levinas's ethical transcendence perpetuates the punctual
quality of that which it constantly transcends. The otherness argued
for by Levinas, and the occurrence of fecundity is still within the
ontic same. Levinas's notion of otherness still craves for distinctions

[71] *Ibid*, pp 267–9.
[72] *Ibid*, pp 272–3
[73] *Ibid*, p 301.

between beings and, as such, does not yet near the origin of the very alterity that he preaches so much. The 'I' of fecundity, which is momentarily grasped only in relation to the face of the Other, is a sphere of transcendence which colonises the possibility of the inner-most 'mine' in relation to the elements. It replaces a conditioned/unconditioned oscillation (that is, continuous/puntuated difference and deference) with transcendent-of-punctuation-but-punctu-able/punctuated logic. Such is the consequence of seeing subjectivity as fully supreme. The craving for subjectivity, even a fecund subjectivity, is not yet passive and, furthermore, as I shall argue, *it is not yet passive in relation to the otherness of other Daseins*. Self/Other, inside/outside are primordial encoders and decoders for Levinas, and the relationship between them constitutes two sides of the same coin. The desire for such exteriority of the Other is itself a distortion of the ethical – the 'not' within which subjectivity is understood ontically for the most part.

69. Levinas also attempts to overcome the depersonalisation of ontology, including fundamental ontology, by claiming that subjectivity is prior to ontology. It is important to see that if, for the sake of argument, Levinas does not manage to convince on the primordiality of subjectivity-in-alterity, if fundamental ontology is primordial, than any ethical potential that this ontology entails is primordial to Levinas's ethics that sees its origin in the alterity of 'an Other'.

70. If enjoyment of alterity does not result from separating a horizon which is other to being and nothingness but rather occurs as a distinction within such horizon then this is a good enough indication that the ethics of otherness does reside in the realm of Being. Enjoyment can result from a pure exercise of Being.[74] Alterity would then reside in that which conditions the very 'to be', namely in the 'who' that relates to the 'how', and not in the 'who' that is related to 'what', however separated from any implication of the verb 'to be' this 'what' might be.

71. For Levinas, the subject is separate only in alterity and thus the desire for subjectivity, the desire for transcendence is aporetic and asymmetrical. Aporetic, because the self-innermost desires to transcend itself as self. Only in facing that *aporia* is the self truly and deeply passive and only then can it be. Asymmetrical, because there is always a surplus over and above a mere reciprocal relationship that characterises the ontological world of merely 'being-with' [*mitsein*] others. This destabilising surplus that is not yet conceptualised places responsibility always first and foremost on the self, regardless of what the Other does or does not do. The self is never content in

---

[74] *Ibid*, p 144.

being separated. Thematisation and the satisfaction of need it produces only partly constitute subjectivity. Not-yet-conceptualised alterity perturbs the subject and disturbs its totality-based satisfaction: 'In the separated being the door to the outside must hence be at the same time open and closed.' The interiority shocks itself with the 'apparition of a heterogeneous element in the course of this descent into itself along the path of pleasure ...'[75]

72.   But what is the nature of the 'openness' to the Other? Is it not openness to exteriority already decodable in *seeking* 'that which is interior' and, with it, 'that which is not yet conceptualised exterior'? Could that kind of exteriority ever amount to primordial otherness?

73.   Levinas does employ ontological language when he argues that the moment of enjoyment is marked by a feeling of insecurity that does not come from the Other but 'somehow from nothingness' and relates to this nothingness as interaction with the elements. There is, then, in Levinas's words a 'margin of nothingness about the interior life'.[76] But this insecurity from, and anxiety of, the nothing, is left, either consciously or unconsciously, undeveloped.

74.   Levinas emphasises that he does not talk about a brutal separation by oppositions but rather about a feminine gesture characterised by grace and radiance. But how could punctuability, both in separation and retention, be graceful? Does not grace imply letting-flow in the continuous? The vertical, informal [*vous*] dimension of 'height' from which the Other speaks in this separation is softened by Levinas into the familiar, homely and welcoming voice of the feminine [*tu*]. With the feminine recollection can take place of a primordial 'home', recollection that caresses the soft ignition of severance from the elements.[77] But this hardly changes the punctuated character of the sphere of transcendence that he conceives as the arena for the ethical. Levinas introduces an embryo of a *method* into ethics by conditioning a punctu-able infinitely Other and as such his account is about beings and subjectivity, not about the Being of beings and *Dasein*'s innermost own, including that very otherness that enables *Dasein*'s innermost particularity. Levinas's account predisposes to relate to ethical infinite separations and differentiations within the ontic.

75.   The face-to-face occurrence, the encounter with the Other in fecundity is not conceptualisable in that it infinitely defers conceptualisation. The alterity *is* only as a not-yet-conceptualised surplus. As such, it is not capable of being reduced to theory, thematisation

[75] *Ibid*, pp 148–9.
[76] *Ibid*, p 150.
[77] *Ibid*, p 155.

and representation. But the very configuring of the 'beyond' as the 'I'-Other, subjectivity-in-alterity relationship directs thinking and tone towards punctuation. There is no other path but that which leads to further punctuation of this pre-configured desire. Is not desire for an Other a desire for punctuation? If so, *what is the desire that constitutes such a desire and does not such primordial desire amount to some primordial intentionality?*

76. Levinas's 'ought' is attentive to the Other rather than to Being. The reward is the good feeling that we do something for a totally marginalised Other. Do we not resemble divine holiness more if we think otherwise than through the totality of thinking-Being? Alas, the craving for this holy reward constitutes the very vulnerability of *Dasein* to succumb to punctuability and to forget Being. Punctuable transcendence is itself a mark of forgetfulness. The craving for this reward is nothing but the craving to tranquillise primordial 'ek-sistential' anxiety, and to softly but firmly shut the doors that such anxiety might open up. But, by adopting Levinas, the anxiety paradoxically becomes all the stronger. However, there might be a paradox here, a paradox which itself belongs to the historicity of Being. The more sophisticated the attempt to shut down this anxiety through the comfort of punctuability, the more such an attempt borrows from the spirit that moves such anxiety, and the more closely the effect of the fraud must be felt.

77. Levinasian ethical reflection oscillates between the punctuable 'beyond' and representations of the Other. Thus oscillating, it puts a very heavy load on the possibility of being attentive to the actuality of the actual which does not obey an imposed guidance or method, does not, at a moment of attentiveness, even embody the craving for such guidance to be imposed. Thinking back is not the impression of the Other which follows from the primordial beyond of the face-to-face encounter with the Other. The event of *Dasein* being thought about by Being and its response by the thinking-back of futurity does not encapsulate any future conceptualisation of the Other. Something has already been given to the Levinasian 'beyond'.

78. For Levinas, the primordial question is the question of the 'who', as it envisages a face. As such, it indeed precedes the question 'who-as-what', which is a question of knowledge and thematisation.[78] One can not fail to trace the Heideggerian echo in this move. Heidegger himself treats the *Seinfrage* as the question of the 'how' of beings (which assumes their temporal involvement in the world as care [*Sorge*]) to be distinguished from the 'what' question, which is a present-at-hand question. As we shall see in chapters eight and nine,

[78] *Ibid*, p 177.

the who-as-how question configures his notion of alterity. But do not the 'who' and the 'what' have still a mutually enforcing resonance, however thin, between them? Levinas's question of 'who' (and, with it, 'to whom (to whose face) do I speak?') expects a name, something to become a name, a future of naming even if it does not yet have a name. Has Levinas's notion of Otherness yet confronted namelessness? If not, could we not feel in Levinas a haughty arrogance beneath pretentious passivity? Naming is the horizon of 'how's possibility. 'Howness' always falls back into the potential of naming even though it is not nameable, or nameless. The question of 'how' is constantly rekindled by, and hovering in, the temporality of the inexpressible.

79.   The *not-yet conceptualised 'who?', in harbouring a thin and punctuable 'who-as-what' is not yet near the inexpressible 'who-as-how'. Concealing this not-yet-nearing is perhaps the most despicable form of human arrogance and can generate inexplicable hostility that comes from the near.*

80.   Language is still a tool for Levinas through which Man effectuates his subjectivity-in-alterity. The surplus of the Other in language overflows the language of totality – that surplus from which language speaks for Levinas – is for the sake of subjectivity as realised in alterity. Man is both transcended and retained as the central stage of ethical reflection. In Levinas the subject has not yet faced the event of silence, an encounter that is needed in order to unlearn its craving for being prior to language. Original 'own-ness' can be faced only in responding to the continuous inexpressible as the happening of language. Levinasian reflection, by establishing the punctuable horizon of a 'not yet conceptualised Other' is not yet on the way to language.

81.   By subordinating language to Man, despite his pretensions to overcome metaphysical humanism, Levinas is a sophisticated member of the group that perpetuates such ideas. Even if his theory can lead to good deeds, the price would be further sheltering from actuality and as such harmful. His humanism, the absolute alterity that disguises punctuability, is the perpetuation of the human capacity for arrogantly making language subservient to subjectivity. Humanism becomes punctuable alterity. As such, it is susceptible to the Heideggerian claim in *Letter on Humanism*, that his philosophy does not rank the essence of human beings, namely their capacity to be on the way to language, highly enough. Levinasian transcendence detaches humans from their innermost desire to attend to the saying of language.

82.   Levinas craves to salvage subjectivity from the so-called 'anonymous' ontology. In *Totality and Infinity*, Levinas sees ontology, and the transcendence that ontology enables, as the hallmark of

power, tyranny and domination of Being. In ontological reflection, every possibility is inverted into power and domination.[79] The transcendence is all about the subject mastering its own possibilities by participating in this power and domination of the existent. *Dasein* is understood as having no control over Being. This lack of control is its relationship to power. Even in Heidegger's 'On the Essence of Truth', where truth seems to be beyond the control and power of the transcending human, Levinas seems to find continuous submission to human being that is apprehended as power and domination.[80] For Levinas, then, the problem is 'the necessity of maintaining the I in the transcendence with which it hitherto seems incompatible. Is the subject only a subject of knowing and power? Does it not present itself as a subject in another sense?'[81]

83. Levinas characterises, rightly, the distinction between Being and the existent.[82] But then he goes on to characterise Being as one kind of 'object'-thought which is not itself a being but rather a third, neutral, term which unaffected by any relationship of alterity. This 'neutral' term, 'Being', is criticised for deadening the encounter with the Other, with alterity. Being objectifies alterity in such a way that all particular existents can find refuge from alterity in togetherness under its auspices. Being, claims Levinas, is a neutralising term, anonymous, which is different from beings, yet it is not nothing. He characterises Being as the 'light' from which existents become intelligible. Levinas moves quickly to state by fiat that ontology, as the theory of Being, reduces the Other to the same, that is to representation, and deadens the desire that can happen only when there is an opening for some relationship of exteriority. He names his ethics of the Other as being alert to the limit of what can be done with ontology. Ethical reflection calls for spontaneity that cannot occur within the egoistic spontaneity, the easy freedom, of the Same in ontology. Levinas presents ontology as dogmatism to be contrasted with the dynamism and genuine spontaneity of the ethics of alterity.

84. The way Levinas understands 'nothing' is as some void which stands in binary opposition to Being. He views the Nothing as that which negates Being, while fundamental ontology views Nothing *as* Being. Levinas's notion of the Nothing is a punctuating horizon of being/nothing, while for fundamental ontology the Nothing is that which is given to beings as their Being, that which is given to them not as punctuated beings. The Nothing of fundamental ontology is a

---

[79] Cf Derrida's point that power characterises the relationship between existents and, as such, power characterises ontic, rather than ontological, involvement: *VM*, p 171.

[80] *TI*, pp 275–6.

[81] *Ibid*.

[82] *Ibid*, pp 42–8.

continuous Saying, which speaks silently between the for-the-most-part punctuated derivative ontology of beings, and the worldliness of Being. Because it is Levinas we are commenting on, quite ironically, it is the Nothing as that which is given to beings as their Being, whose Nothingness is the primordial form of exteriority. The Nothing connotes the unattainable nearness of actuality as distinguished from the Other as not-yet-conceptualised actuality. Does not the alterity of an Other occur as a result of the grounding of *Dasein*, which is oppressed by the Nothing which precedes any 'Other', even that Other which is not-yet-conceptualised? Even the skin of the face of the Other, the non-thematisable, non representational Other is already being given that otherness which can not be expressed and is *inexpress-able* – No-thing. Being inexpress-able is not the same as that which is 'there' but is not yet properly expressed.

85.   In ontological thought, the relationship with someone who is an existent, Levinas claims, is subordinated to the question of the Being of the existent.[83] The notion of justice between existents is subordinated to the impersonal freedom that is encapsulated in fundamental ontology. In such a reflection, Levinas again situates the dwelling of his account in the ontic. The relationship with the Other human being is the seed of ethics. As Peperzak puts it, the gist of criticism Levinas advances against ontology-dominated reflection is that the horizon of Being only allows us to conceive the other as a particular mode of that horizon. To 'be with' [*mitsein*] the other, letting the other be as a particular mode of Being, in general necessarily involves loss of that very particularity. By contrast, the Other invites me to greet him in his separability and uniqueness. The face-to-face encounter of ethical Saying connotes this separability and exteriority to any intentionality and discourse.[84] But what exactly is that otherness that prevails in speaking 'to', and does such otherness not involve being 'with'? Why cannot speaking to an other, as Other, stem from genuine otherness that relates to the 'how' of that other in a way which does things to the 'how' of me? Does such process amount to sameness? Why? Even deeper, is the separability of the Other the aim of ethical reflection, or is the aim of ethical reflection the enigma of otherness in which sameness and separability are transcended? Should we not learn to think about otherness in a way that is more primordial to the otherness of an Other? Is not otherness thought about primordially in a way which is more amorphous than the punctuability of 'Others'? Has Heidegger's notion of 'with' been

[83] *Ibid*, p 45.
[84] A Peperzak, 'Phenomenology-Ontology-Metaphysics: Perspective on Husserl and Heidegger' (1983) 16 *Man and World* 113–27, at 124–5.

charitably fathomed by Levinas so that his own notions of otherness could be thought about? Derrida interprets Heidegger that *mitsein* can signify being together in language in which there is understanding 'but the ether in which dissonance can resonate'.[85] As he observes, such togetherness is more original than any ontic solidarity, team or companionship. Indeed, *mitsein* is human togetherness, the human togetherness in its essence, namely being immersed in the furthest ontic and the murmur of the nearest ontological, dwelling in language.

86. *Dasein* is, then, not obeying *Being*, but is already involved in a world of the Being of beings. Being-with is dwelling in this world *together*. Otherness that comes from Being is nearer to actuality than any ontic opposition of Otherness; for example, it is neither masculine nor feminine. It does not come from above or below. *The breath of Being is pure* and could not be reduced into punctuability. Nor should the purity of the continuous actuality of the actual be confused with any notion of sameness, although, of course, humans are the same in their essence. Levinas can only criticise the ontology to which his own punctuable account in fact belongs, namely an autocracy and as a philosophy of power and tyranny.[86] Levinas's insistence on an interpersonal, fecundal relationship with the Other is itself one aspect of the twilight of a philosophy that is dominated by the very ontology which is part of the philosophical 'world' the historicity of which Heidegger wishes to radicalise.

87. *But ontological thinking, by reflecting on the Being of the Other, by thinking the Being of the Other, does not preoccupy itself by seeing the Other as a being. In this sense, it is other than thinking in terms of a being – an Other. But, crucially, as we shall see, ethical thinking in terms of an 'Other' cannot precede ethical thinking that thinks the Being of an Other because the otherness upon which the former is grounded is impoverished and dependent upon the otherness of the latter. The punctual is indeed otherwise than the continuous but it originates in it all the same. As its own possibility, ontological thinking attempts to destabilise the dichotomy of 'separate otherness/togetherness', a destabilisation that leads to the very notion of otherness to feature as a surplus of the other as 'a different being'.*

88. Levinas's many misguided attributes to the supremacy of ontology can be summed up in this passage:

[Heidegger's] analyses do not start with the thing-object, to be sure, but they bear the mark of the great landscapes to which the things refer. Ontology

[85] *VM*, p 183.
[86] *TI*, pp 46–7.

becomes ontology of nature, impersonal fecundity, faceless generous mother, matrix of particular beings, inexhaustible matter for things.[87]

Sometimes Levinas conceives of ontology, Being, as designating sameness that totalises – a totality that homogenises genuine multiplicity. When he does that he does not account for *fundamental* ontology. In other places, though, he does conceive of ontology as thinking-Being which does not necessarily connote sameness but rather depersonalisation and anonymity. His notion of alterity attempts to overcome both totality and anonymity. I shall argue that it is his notion of otherness that does not overcome the derivative ontology that he presumes, namely that ontology Heidegger wanted to radicalise. Alternatively, he does not yet near the origin of the immermost personal. He does not yet near the radical personalisation that is entailed in the nothing, in the continuous.

89. Fundamental ontology can *never* be impersonal. By overcoming subjectivity in the 'whilst' of an ontological event neutrality is overcome. 'Letting Being be' is precisely the nearest way of being interested. Thinking-Being, responding to Being's call, is the only authentic way of being interested. Crucially, being ontologically interested by transcending the horizon of subjectivity is not the same, not even similar to, being disinterested from thinking-Being but remaining within the horizon of subjectivity within the ontic. To be disinterested subjectivity while retaining subjectivity as a part of the transcendence is the hallmark of the non-originary transcendence.

90. Levinas, as I have argued, struck out at the primacy of ontology not only by caricaturising ontology but also by projecting upon ontology the problem of his own philosophy – namely that it presumes that very derivative ontology. Infinity and alterity as he portrays them are, from the point of view of thinking-Being, precursors for totality, that is entrenchment of continued punctuation. From thinking-Being, Levinas's thinking must itself be 'on the way to language' although interprets itself as a 'beyond' and 'otherwise than thinking Being'. Ontologically, the 'otherwise' of Levinasian alterity is the furthest of the far.

91. The passivity that he repeats on many occasions in *Otherwise than Being*, a passivity more passive than any passivity of the will, is still a mere ontic passivity although it transcends the activity of the subject-as-an-ego-in-totality. The 'activity' of this passivity is its entrenchment of the detachment from thinking-Being, that is from letting Being be. This passivity is quite aggressive and conceals arrogance and not humbleness. Towards the attentiveness to Being

[87] *Ibid*, p 46.

Levinasian passivity is still active and violent – in a sense, the most violent. This utmost violence is also harmful because of the distance to which Levinas takes transcendence, thereby making fundamental ontology out of reach.

92. The notion of face already implies thinking-Being but at the same time it stifles such thinking.[88] It is indeed a desire for Man to stifle it. This is why Levinas's call for a departure from the climate of Heidegger's thinking is so appealing.[89] Levinas helps out human beings' most ferocious essential denials, *the denial that their subjectivity is a distortion of their essential 'ek-sistenc'e*. Indeed, thinking along Levinasian lines helps humans to forget that essential erring means that humans are in a *climate* of denial. By conscripting the notion of a primordial ethical Saying from infinite alterity and fecundity, Levinas plays to the hand of the vulnerability of *Dasein*, with the difficult escape, but all the more concealed at that, into the talk of ethical infinite responsibility and duty towards the Other, the craving for both transcending and retaining a value-based 'ought' [*sollen*].

93. Can we not feel the tension of the ontological difference precisely at this point of such a powerful forgetfulness of Being? Can we not feel the distortion between the idle speech [*Gerede*] of the face-to-face, and the authentic speech [*Rede*] of what is *Dasein's* innermost own, that is the un-paraphrasable attentiveness to the inexpressible Saying of Being? Can we not see that with Levinas the silence that is imposed on the possibility of an *ontological* ethical Saying is almost absolute, making an attentive audience to such a Saying highly unlikely? Could we not feel the intensity of oppression of ontological thinking which, coming from the depth of actuality, must realise itself only through violent eruptions as long as a Levinasian climate predominates?

DERRIDA'S CRITICISM OF LEVINAS

94. In 'Violence and Metaphysics' Derrida provides powerful criticisms of Levinas's take on ontology. These criticisms go to the nub of Levinas's claim that his account is otherwise than ontological. Levinas responds with what is arguably his finest book, *Otherwise than Being*, in which he states his case for overcoming the hegemony of ontology in Western thought, including the apex of this hegemony, Heidegger's fundamental ontology. Critchley claims that in the light

---

[88] *VM*, p 180.
[89] *EE*, p 4.

of the later writings of Levinas, in particular his writings on Derrida, the claims of 'Violence and Metaphysics' are in fact used by Levinas as a lever to deconstruct Derrida. In these writings, Levinas shows that Derrida's criticisms in 'Violence and Metaphysics' could be read not as a polemic against Levinas but as actually affirming the latent Levinasian ethical aspect of Derrida's own efforts.[90] The next chapter canvasses this view and argues that the initial separation that Levinas effectuated from ontology, including fundamental ontology – to wit, the separation from the notion of otherness within the horizon of thinking-Being – is not yet deconstructed, by his later subtle writings. The result is that even Levinas's sophisticated moves of his later writing cannot be argued to be an implicit Levinasian Saying which lurks beneath the ontological language used by Derrida in 'Violence and Metaphysics' to seemingly criticise Levinas. Indeed, Levinas's later writings can highlight better than ever the non-Levinasian nature of Derrida's comments in 'Violence and Metaphysics'. Indeed, these writings can show that only thinking-Being and the notion of otherness it encapsulates are both given to, and indeed otherwise than, Levinas's notion of otherness. To deconstruct Levinas, to be ethical *to* him would mean to displace the very notion of otherness, as we shall see from the dynamics of proximity to an infinite surplus of a non-yet conceptualised Other, into the dynamics of otherness that nears the continuous.

95. In my reflections upon Derrida and Levinas, which occupy the remainder of this chapter and the main argument of the next, I intend to claim that: (a) the depth of Derrida's criticisms was not met in 'Otherwise than Being'; and (b) that Derrida does not go far enough in following up the implications of his own criticisms of Levinas. The result is that some features of deconstruction have been understood as having, or more subtly, as *capable* of having, Levinasian thinking as both their ground and tone.

96. Derrida raises few arguments against Levinas in 'Violence and Metaphysics'. Focally, Derrida criticises Levinas for misunderstanding the Heideggerian move, namely the ontological difference. His first claim is that Being is not something which can have 'priority' over the existent as Levinas would have it. Being is something which is given to the existent and is the 'there' in the existent. Derrida has in mind the distinction between beings and their Being which is not paraphrasable to any *priority* of Being. There is not such a thing as existent and another thing 'Being of the existent' which has priority over it or which precedes it. As Being simply is, the Being of the existent is simply in the world. Of course, to recap,

---

[90] S Critchley, above n 60, chs 3, 4.

to study the existent as a being would be ontic and so would bathe thinking in the forgetfulness of Being. Derrida's point is rather that primordiality of Being is different from the 'priority' which Levinas has given it, namely as a higher order which takes priority over primordial ethical thinking. The term *priority* cannot belong to the language of fundamental ontology but belongs rather to the ontic realm where the relationship between two existents come to further some theoretical or practical argument.[91] Being which is given to the existent is very different from 'priority'.

97. Secondly, the neutrality with which Levinas conceives ontology is in fact a characteristic of the ontic thinking that fundamental ontology attempts to overcome. There is no sufficient principality or root in Heidegger's thought which could ground neutrality. Any neutrality would presume a first and foremost philosophy that would be above any connectedness to existents, indeed metaphysics, but this is precisely what Heidegger tries to overcome.[92]

98. Thirdly, Derrida criticises Levinas's misuse of the term 'ontology'. Ontology is not first philosophy, indeed it is not a philosophy at all. Ontology is what persists as the actuality of the actual, Being. The ontological difference makes fundamental ontology *foreign* to any first philosophy, to the very notion of first philosophy.

99. Fourthly, thinking-Being is not subjected to any human design and that means anthropology, ethics, psychoanalysis. Thinking-Being is attending to the way of Being and that is all there is to it.

100. The 'letting be' of Heidegger is prior to any 'letting be' which is associated with either the essence or existence of an existent as Other. Thinking-Being is a condition for the possibility of that which is given to the existent. Thinking-Being cannot dominate the existent.[93]

101. Derrida's main claim in 'Violence and Metaphysics' is that Levinas misunderstood the ontological difference. An articulation of Being, which lightens from the dark and which points to that which makes up the ontological difference, necessarily ends up as a metaphor which resembles beings as it involves partly the ontic. It is easy, then, to fall into the trap of assimilating thinking-Being to thinking-beings. Language speaks and hides Being in the very act of attempting to disclose it via ontic metaphors. The necessity to resort to metaphors, the necessary distortion of metaphors, is the voice of the 'has been' of Being. The ontological difference is the rekindling of Being as it withdraws in the very attempt, indeed the only avenue possible, at disclosing Being through ontic metaphors. Being remains hidden as it discloses.

---

[91] VM, pp 169–70.
[92] *Ibid*, p 171.
[93] *Ibid*, p 172.

102. Derrida claims that, for Levinas, both in 'Is Ontology Fundamental?'
and in *Totality and Infinity*, 'ontology' is understood as a *concept* of
Being. Being is misunderstood as a concept, as some-thing, albeit as
an absolutely undetermined and abstract anterior concept to which
every determined existent is submitted. But Being is not subjected to
difference like any other concept but involvement in it precedes any
being. As Being is entirely trans-categorical it must be given to any
existent as part of its being-in-the-world, for a being whose Being is
also 'there' in the world as an issue for it to be attentive to. The
primordiality is absolute and Being is needed in order to think about
any ethical relation to a 'same' and 'other'.[94] The origin of Levinas's
alterity is not the derivative ontology that Levinas transcends and
maintains but preserves in transcendence. Being is what is given to
beings, and these beings would include the Other and subjectivity of
Levinasian ethics. Levinas's ethical departure is ontologically
involved and subject to the same distortion of the essence of Being as
any other ontic occurrence: 'ethico-metaphysical transcendence
therefore presupposes ontological transcendence'.[95]

103. Levinas's transcendence is within the ontic, and by claiming an
ethical 'departure' from ontology it detracts reflection from showing
its ontic nature. That alone is enough to make it harmful, if harm is
understood as hampering the effort of thinking-Being:

> By refusing, in *Totality and Infinity*, to accord any dignity to the ontic–onto-
> logical difference, by seeing in it only a ruse of war, and by calling the
> intra-ontic movement of ethical transcendence (the movement respectful of
> one existent toward another) *metaphysics*, Levinas confirms Heidegger in his
> discourse: for does not the latter see in metaphysics (in metaphysical ontol-
> ogy) the forgetting of Being and the dissimulation of the ontic–ontological
> difference?[96]

104. For ontology, for thinking-Being, there is no outside and inside, no
interiority and exteriority. This is the crux of Derrida's criticisms:
Levinas views Being as a 'concept'. This leads him to claim that there
is irreducible neutralising act on the part of thinking-Being and that
ontic–ontological differentiation is a perpetuating hallmark of this
neutralisation. By viewing Being as a concept Levinas is capable of
enslaving it to some conceptual apparatus. But, as Derrida forcefully
claims, Heidegger never did attempt to conceptualise Being but
rather to show the distortion of the thingness of things in the ontic.
Being *is* nothing (no-thing) but is given to beings and, as such, it has

[94] *Ibid*, pp 176–7.
[95] *Ibid*, p 177.
[96] *Ibid*.

no 'outside' that can make it a point of departure to transcendence that is originated in the existent. Levinas pays lip service to the ontic–ontological oscillation without ever really accounting for its 'otherwise than' (to use Levinas's favourite phrase) being a concept.

105. Derrida says:

> Why does the phrase impose itself? Because if one does not uproot the silent origin from itself violently, if one decides not to speak, then the worst violence will silently cohabit the *idea* of peace? Peace is made only in a *certain silence,* which is determined and protected by the violence of speech.[97]

Derrida interprets Levinas as associating the ethical with a non-violent language, although such non-violent language can spring to life only after the face has provoked violence. Such non-violent language would have no verbs, no implied 'to be' or predication. Language, for Levinas, tries to clean itself up from Being and thinking-Being. The oscillation of violence/non violence that overtakes thinking-Being is one that forgets Being and as such does not let the 'about' of Being come to the surface. Derrida argues that Levinas gives us an ethics that transcends law by professing an occurrence without law, without violence. For Levinas, to think about law would rather be to confine law to the violent ethics of totality and contrast it with an ethics without law, a 'beyond', namely the pure non-violent language of the ethics of the Other. Derrida shows the poverty of that non-violent language, its inability to actually be violent, to open otherness up to violent desire.[98] And, indeed, it is quite violent at doing precisely that. It is thinking-Being which is the primordial transcendence, which can claim violence even towards the gentle, feminine, non-violent Other. Otherness and its violent/non-violent oscillation, passivity, ought to be understood in the context of thinking-Being and *not* as a 'non-violent' Other. It is the otherness of thinking-Being which makes possible the very distortion that Levinas wants to generate by the ethics of 'the Other'.

106. The Levinasian oscillation precisely continues the reliance on the legal by professing an 'other' to law which is in fact a preparation for its continuation. The falsity is that an 'ethics without law' is an ethics which in fact perpetuates the legal.

107. Derrida characterises the violence of thinking-Being as 'non-ethical'.[99] This needs dwelling upon because the context of this discussion is the attempt by Derrida to distinguish Heidegger's historicity from Levinas's diachronical a-historical ethics in *Totality and*

---

[97] *Ibid,* p 185.
[98] *Ibid.*
[99] *Ibid,* p 186.

Infinity. Derrida does *not* mean to affirm that ontology is not ethics. I interpret the expression 'non-ethical' as relating to 'non-Levinasian ethics'. True, Derrida does not develop any ontology-based otherness and ethics. But should we not see beneath Derrida's position the possibility that the ethical resides in that violence which involves language and which responds in silence to the murmuring Saying of Being? Originary violence, the effort and attendance that it requires, *is* ethics. It is primordial ethics. Ethics is violent, as any deconstruction must involve violence. Derrida's point is that Levinas's notion of infinity, and attached to it, the notion of 'infinite alterity', sucks the violence out of Being while at the same time accusing ontology of reducing difference. But the occurrence of difference, the rapture in language, in which the silence which dresses the Saying of Being is being articulated into language, is difference itself. The dynamics of alterity cannot be associated with either Levinas's lifeless infinity or the hegemonic and monologic ontology that silently grounds it. Within Levinas's coupling of lifelessness and hegemony, Being cannot speak. It is suffocated by the violent anaesthetic at the hand of the Other, the Other's rights, the orphan, the poor, the woman, or any other Other to be conscripted to the determined effort to silence the nearness of Being. Infinity, in its abstractness and detachment from the ontic–ontological oscillation, leaves us with the need for theory, for ontically hungry ignorance which anticipates such a new theory. Such infinity, quite unethically, fills us with the need to find a new object to perpetuate the ontic inauthentic cycles without ever nearing the ontological. As Derrida points out, infinity, for Heidegger, would relate to the game of disclosure and concealment of ontological moment amidst the for-the-most-part ontic.

108. The implication of Derrida's claim is that in order for deconstruction to cater for the ontological difference, it must not be conditioned by any craving for the mere relationship between existents even if those existents are not yet represented in language. This last claim is quite separate from the truth of *alētheia* itself – that there is no ontological without the ontic – that in order to face the ontological moment *Dasein* immerses itself in the ontic. Language speaks nearer than the ontic in an ontological event. That ambit of the ontic characterises the whole of Levinasian transcendence and that makes that transcendence a part of the historicity of Being.

109. The call of alterity and difference is not responded to by the craving and the perpetuation of the process of differentiation of one being from another. They come from the flickering location that occurs in the 'between' of the occurrence/the temporality of such differentiations and the ontological unconditioned and continuous character.

Difference of distinction between beings is not the same as difference between the punctual and continuous which is characterised by distance.

110. This difference of distance may be even more primordial to the difference between decidability and undecidability which arguably still persists on the horizon of the ontic. The indeterminacy of oppositions is not as primordial as the continuous although it disguises itself as a response to it.

111. Levinasian transcendence remains within the horizon of thinking that attempts to find the origin of the language of ethics. It does not yet attend to the ethics of language upon which it is grounded. Derrida says: 'By making the origin of language, meaning, and difference the relation to the infinitely other, Levinas is resigned to betraying his own intentions in his philosophical discourse.'[100]

112. How has it come about that Levinasian ethics has become so influential? How is it that people accept so readily the origin of ethical experience in the question of an Other? In other words, how has it come about that the Other accounts for the origin of that which is experienced as otherness?

113. Derrida's hesitancy to opens the gate to the possibility of the ethical being a part of the ontological difference means that he does not destabilise the relationship between ontology and ethics well enough. To do that would require him to defend the ontological difference *as* ethical encounter. This he does not do in 'Violence and Metaphysics'. This omission opens the interpretative possibility of putting Derrida and Levinas in the same boat, as if Derrida's own attempts to deconstruct Heidegger echo together with Levinas's attempt to overcome the hegemony of ontological reflection in the name of ethics.[101] As we shall see, Levinas certainly uses Derrida's hesitance to claim that the ethics of deconstruction is itself part and parcel of Levinasian ethics. Thus, Derrida's undecidability about the precise nature of the relationship between ethics and ontology is, to me, not yet ethical. Derrida's efforts encapsulate an omission that actually stifles thinking about this relationship.

114. By putting Derrida and Levinas in the same boat I do not mean that they are the same, but only claim that they may be, and have been, put on the same continuum to the extent that the ethics of decons-

---

[100] *Ibid*, p 189.
[101] S Critchley, above n 60, pp 76–88. Cf Bernasconi, who argues that ' Just as Heidegger sees the demand for an ethics as a destiny of Being, so for Levinas the demand would already be a manifestation of "the ethical relation"': 'Deconstruction and the Possibility of Ethics: Reiterating the "Letter on Humanism"', in R Bernasconi, *Heidegger in Question: The Art of Existing* (New Jersey, Humanity Press, 1993) pp 211–24 at pp 222–3. The next chapter engages deeply with this argument.

truction is Levinasian. For example, as explained by Critchley it is Levinas himself who attempts to deconstruct Derrida's criticism of him as deploying ontological language within which Levinas's ethical Saying lurks. It was such complementarity between Derrida and Levinas, presented as the interplay between ethical Saying and the ontological Said that could be the fruit of Derrida's omission to face the full implication of his comments in 'Violence and Metaphysics' on the derivative ontology of Levinas's ethics. The argument in 'Violence and Metaphysics' about the complementarity of fundamental ontology – that between thinking-Being and the ontic nature of Levinas's ethics – has been assimilated by Levinas as a complementarity between ethical and ontological reflection in which Levinasian ethics does the Saying.

115. Thus, Levinas successfully tames the critical impetus of 'Violence and Metaphysics'. Let me explain. Of course, there is complementarity between ontology and ethics. But the question is how the nature of such complementarity is affected by the complementarity between the ontic and ontological that characterises fundamental ontological reflection, complementarity that, according to 'Violence and Metaphysics', Levinas does not allude to. Derrida's omission of hinting at primordial *identification* between fundamental ontology and ethics as an implication of his argument about Levinas's derivative ontology means that *such identification is not yet even contemplated as a part of the complementarity between ethics and ontology.* Derrida's omission to draw the implications of his account to the very characterisation of the complementarity between ethics and ontology can be used to make such complementarity itself a matter for deconstruction – just another undecidable. But in this instance Derrida's omission is not even yet any hesitance, not even a 'perhaps', thus considerably limiting the range of the argument in 'Violence and Metaphysics'. This omission makes the implications of 'Violence and Metaphysics' idle with regard to ethics, an idleness that is used in Levinas's later reflections. As far as ethics is concerned, has Derrida fallen prey to Levinas, despite his recognition of the derivative ontological co-ordinates within which Levinas operates? (We can raise the question here, has Derrida fallen prey to the hegemony of legalism?) What is needed is to open up the question of the complementarity between ethics and ontology. *Is not the complementarity, in actuality, between, on the one hand, ethics as fundamental ontology and, on the other, ethical Saying that transcends derivative ontology? Does the Levinasian notion of complementarity between ethics and ontology not function as a part of a more primordial complementarity?* The next chapter goes deeper into this question.

116. Indeed, what is at stake in opening up the very characteristics of the complementarity between ethics and ontology to questioning, is the whole nature of the ethics of deconstruction. This impinges, of course, on how genuine is Derrida's own criticism of Heidegger, a topic that will be left for another occasion.

117. Had Heidegger interacted with Levinas's attempted radicalisation of ethics, he would have approached Levinas as a central and characteristic culmination of metaphysical thought, albeit as the twilight of such thought, characterised by violence of Being. He would have argued for the metaphysical disguise of Levinas's radicalisation of alterity in the name of Hebraic thinking of radical responsibility to the Other. That is why I think that Derrida's wearing the mask of deconstruction only for deconstructing Levinas ontologically and not continuing it to ethics, namely to the very complementarity that characterises otherness itself, is unethical. Furthermore, this hesitancy to take his ontological criticisms of Levinas into ethics continues to reverberate in his subsequent writings on Levinas.

118. This chapter ends with the feeling that Heidegger's arm was bent. It was bent for the purpose of assimilating it into Levinasian ethics and also by Derrida who pre-empted this bending by not looking more closely at the well he himself had been drinking from. *The silence of the origin of the otherness of the Other has not yet been neared.*

6

Otherwise than Being as Forgetfulness of Otherness

1. It is in *Otherwise than Being* that Levinas is at his best. In this book he no longer seems to simply criticise ontology, but rather to present a very subtle complementarity between ontology and ethics. The otherness encapsulated in Jewish thinking on responsibility is made complementary, primordial, and separate, to otherness and responsibility as encapsulated in the Greek thinking-Being. What makes the book so strange is that Levinas maintains deep sense of *separation* and exteriority to thinking-Being while at the same time defending a *complementarity* to it. This chapter challenges his enigmatic combination of complementarity and separation. Moreover, it is argued that Levinas's ontic trick is playing with fire that can burn humanity back to itself. The covering-up of brutality as a gentle enigma takes humans away both from the nearness of their essence, which always already dwells in the saying of language, *and* from the totality of metaphysics. The enormity of this double transcendence robs humans of the continuous near/representational far complementarity of the mystery of Being. But, tragically, if the enigma of Levinas is still within the unboundedness of Being, if the radicalisation of ontic thinking can take place only whilst thinking has already dwelled in the antecedent mystery of the ontological, the ontological will have to speak in circumstances where attentiveness has been hijacked and then, to quote Heidegger, 'only God can save us'. To overcome the combination of transcending metaphysics and maintaining the ontic notion of things may well prove the most serious, and bloody, challenge that faces humanity.

2. Levinas's distinction in *Otherwise than Being* between the ethical Saying of alterity and the ontological Said echoes Heidegger's distinction between authentic speech [*Rede*] and idle chatter [*Gerede*] respectively. This chapter dwells on the relationship between these two distinctions and the kind of complementarity that this relationship entails.

3. *Otherwise than Being* was dedicated to the relationship between ethics and thinking-Being. In it, Levinas, seemingly, abandons the

somewhat metaphysical language of absolute alterity and resorts to language full of twists, turns and contradictions that forces the reader to constantly displace conventional oppositions. The book's main aim is to show that thinking otherwise than thinking-Being entails a radical departure from thinking in terms of 'Being otherwise', the latter still a characteristic of ontological thinking.

4.   The problem that Levinas puts up for question in *Otherwise than Being* is whether subjectivity occurs on what he calls the 'hither side' of being/nothing. Is there a whole horizon which is neglected by ontology? Is there subjectivity whose temporality of occurrence, language, is otherwise than the subject that is reasoned, even reasoned away, in fundamental ontology? In ontology the question 'What?' dominates all other questions. Even the question 'Who?' gets lost in the 'What?'. But Levinas attempts to revive the question of subjectivity as a 'who' which signifies a dimension excluded from that of being and not-being.[1]

5.   By the time *Otherwise than Being* was published, Levinas would have studied Derrida's *Violence and Metaphysics* well. He had to make his argument more subtle, somehow doing more justice to Heidegger's thought yet without compromising his claim for ethics to be other than ontology. Levinas introduces the major theme of his book, the distinction between the [ethical] Saying and the [ontological] Said:

> The said, contesting the abdication of the saying that everywhere occurs in this said, thus maintains the diachrony in which, holding its breath, the spirit hears the echo of the *otherwise*. The hither side, the preliminary, which the pre-originary saying animates, refuses the present and manifestation, or lends itself to them only out of time. The unsayable saying lends itself to the said, to the ancillary indiscretion of the abusive language that divulges or profanes the unsayable. But it lets itself be reduced, without effacing the unsaying in the ambiguity or the enigma of the transcendent, in which the breathless spirit retains a fading echo.[2]

We can clearly see in this passage the Heideggerian move of establishing a necessary process of complementarity between that which is not primordial and that which is primordial but hidden. The other reminiscence of Heidegger is that what is primordial saying signifies as the unsaid of the said, which is both necessary for articulation and criticism but at the same time, reductionist at that. Many commentators see the almost impenetrable nature of *Otherwise than Being* as more than merely a change of style but rather as an attempt to

---

[1] *OB*, pp 26–31.
[2] *Ibid*, p 44.

abandon the philosophical language of *Totality and Infinity*. For example, Reed argues that infinity has been refined in *Otherwise than Being* as the infinite return of the ethical Saying to the ontological Said.[3] In the same way that there is no ontological without the immersion in the ontic, there is no ethical Saying that is not reduced in the ontological Said. From his early reflection of seeing ontology merely as sphere which should be overcome in absolute alterity, Levinas modifies his terminology to suggest a process of complementarity whereby ontology is a *necessary* reduction of ethics. One cannot be ethical without being involved in ontological reduction first. Further, ethical criticism would often be disguised in ontological language, the language of Being and 'to be'. Ontological language must be resorted to in order to reach the murmur of the unsayable Saying. The dynamic of *alētheia* is highly influential on Levinas, making his argument more subtle. The resonance with *alētheia*, namely the dynamism of complementarity, is configured by Levinas to account for the origin of responsibility to the Other rather than to account for attentiveness and response to the murmuring unconcealment of Being. Levinas's complementarity attempts to account for the otherness of the Other that propels radicalised *conatus* of responsible subject, rather that the otherness of the Other that propels the *conatus essendi* of thinking-Being.

6. For Levinas, the moment of temporal diachrony is that which characterises an incision between the self-perpetuating synchrony of the ontological Said and the ethical Saying. What happens, what happened 'then' and what will happen are not synchronous but are bracketed to connote moment of facing the Saying of the Other. Ethical Saying thus imposes silence on the synchronous silence of thinking-Being. Language becomes austere to connote the poverty of the way to language.

7. So it may be asked at this stage: where lies the diachrony that characterises primordial complementarity? The diachrony of ontology is the temporality of Being in which Being speaks its Saying in a murmur from the past which is presently captured by *Dasein* as a possibility, as anticipation. This diachrony is 'ek-static' in the difference between the continuous and punctual time in which *Dasein* inauthentically pursues ontic involvements. The mutual appropriation between *Dasein* and Being constitutes an event of nearing the actuality of the actual. This event constitutes temporal diachrony because a leap is made from merely distorting existing in time into primordial hovering in the historicity of the unbounded and the continuous. The

---

[3] CW Reed, 'Levinas' Question', in RA Cohen (ed), *Face to Face with Levinas* (Albany, State University of New York Press, 1986) pp 73–82, at p 76.

diachrony is an event of nearing the continuous, not of punctuating exteriority. Levinas indicates at diachronic punctuation with his notion of the 'trace',[4] namely the trace of the ethical Saying in the ontological Said. But we may ask whether the notion of otherness that thinking-Being encapsulates and that Levinas allegedly transcends is really synchronous. Has Levinas not confused the continuous nature of thinking-Being, that which gives it its primordiality to any punctuation, with a derivative notion of synchrony which would also be transcended by fundamental ontology?

8.   In *Otherwise than Being* Levinas conceives of negation as a hallmark of ontology, of totality and of essence. Infinite responsibility to the Other is otherwise than thinking-Being and otherwise than negation. But is it not an insight of fundamental ontology that the Nothing is not negation? Further, is the negation that Levinas's ethics transcends not a negation imprisoned within the present-at-hand?

9.   In *Otherwise than Being* Levinas continues to develop the fecund subject using not so much the notion of fecundity as the notions of sensibility, recurrence and substitution. The basic theme is that the subject has to lose itself in the Other, which amorphously has always been part and parcel of subjectivity, and then get itself back, in an infinite cycle of substitution. Only when I substitute myself for, that is give myself to, the Other, can I be the subject I am, and so I am ethically recurring. This infinite recurrence and substitution is given the term *illeity*, to connote the third person (*ill*) future perfect, a term used by Levinas to bring about the disinterestedness of the temporality of his ethics.

10.   The characterisation of proximity to the other as Other is achieved, somewhat paradoxically, only in facing a moment of radical separation. Proximity to the Other transcends subjectivity but is still within the horizon of subjectivity. Proximity means the unbridgeable distance of separation. Viewed ontologically, argues Levinas, proximity cannot account for that otherness that radicalises subjectivity. Ontologically, proximity will involve reducing distance in the sense of assimilating under the hegemony of essencing. For Levinas, ontology constantly acts as a 'limit or complement to the accomplishment of the adventure of essence, which consists in persisting in essence and unfolding immanence, in remaining an ego, in identity'.[5] In ontological reflection, proximity is conceived as a proximity to essence or, *conatus essendi*. Ontology, Levinas claims, empties the meaning from the distinction between subject and being. Subject *is* a

---

[4] *OB*, p 100.
[5] *Ibid*, p 16.

subject only as a being, as existent. Subject is reduced to the essence of being/nothing.

11. Levinas aims to reintroduce subjectivity that is not reducible to the subjectivity that is dominated by essence. Heidegger's aim of overcoming subjectivity is seen by Levinas as imprisoning the subject within the confines of essence. Heidegger saw subjectivity as derivative from *Dasein*. Heidegger saw subjectivity as a characteristic of metaphysics, namely a characteristic of an epoch, along the historicity of Being, within which the craving to represent the world by, and for, a subject dominates. Levinas, however, interprets Heidegger so as to claim that *Dasein* itself which overcomes subjectivity was in fact that very imprisoning of subjectivity in thinking along the lines of essence. He writes:

> subjectivity, consciousness, the ego presupposes Dasein, which belongs to essence as a mode in which essence manifests itself. But the manifestation of essence is what is essential in essence; experience and the subject having the experience constitute the very manner in which at a given 'époque' of essence, essence is accomplished, that is, is manifested.[6]

12. But does Levinas not misunderstand Heidegger here? Heidegger wants to overcome subjectivity as he saw subjectivity as synonymous with metaphysics or the craving for metaphysics. The presupposition of *Dasein* to the ego is attributed by Heidegger only to the ontic determinations of *Dasein* as subject. Hence, for Heidegger, for-the-most-part *Dasein* finds itself as subject. Levinas misuses Heidegger in so far as he blurs the acceptable claim that Being's essence speaks *Dasein* with the more derivative claim that the ontic notion of essence dominates subjectivity. Heidegger is *diagnosing* that the hegemony of thought with subjectivity pervades any attentiveness to the continuous manifestation of, and hence nearness to, Being's essence, and it is in this sense that he wants to overcome subjectivity. In short, essence, for Heidegger, transcends that notion of essence that dominates the ontic subject in the complementarity of the ontological difference.

13. But there seems to be a deeper misunderstanding here. This quote illustrates the point that the 'essence', that is the thinking within the horizon which Levinas wishes to overcome, is the very thinking that Heidegger wished to overcome, especially in his 'Letter on Humanism'. What Levinas refers to as 'essence' and which he claims does not allow for irreducible subjectivity is not the sense of essence that Heidegger calls to be awakened.

[6] *Ibid*, p 17.

14. The key misunderstanding of Levinas in this quote is manifested in his own phrase about *Dasein* – 'which belongs to *essence* [my italics] as a mode in which essence manifests itself'.7 Levinas represents Heidegger's position correctly but at the same time is seemingly unaware that there are two essences at play in his own interpretation of Heidegger. The term 'essence' which I have italicised is the essence of Being, presumed by the ontological difference and to which the second 'essence' of *Dasein* is either attentive or not in manifesting itself as essence. Subjectivity *is* derivative from these two essences. But the essence that Levinas claims colonises subjectivity does not even mention the ontological difference and the kind of 'mineness' that it brings with it.

15. Levinas's proposed radicalisation of subjectivity, then, can only already presume the derivative essence that subsumes what he sees as ontology-dominated subjectivity. This notion of derivative essence is precisely what Heidegger was constantly complaining about. Levinas writes: 'The *otherwise than being* which, to be sure, is understood in a being, differs absolutely from essence, has no *genus* in common with essence, and is said only in the breathlessness that pronounces the extra-ordinary word *beyond*.'8 But Levinas's conception of essence and with it, that of ontology, seems still to be derivative. The ontology and the essence that he assumes do not yet account for thinking-Being but echo more with transcendental phenomenology whereby the ego experiences existents in different ways that, if accounted for, can transcend prejudices and approximating, 'constructing' and 'reconstructing', infinitely assembling, their essence – as experienced by transcendental subjectivity. Levinas's view of essence is still viewing the thingness of the thing as an existent with an essence that dominates as the existence of this existent.

16. I want to caution against a possible misunderstanding of what I am saying here. It is certainly the case that Levinas departs from the transcendental ego, thereby establishing ethically responsible subjectivity-in-alterity. But his characterisation of ontology is not as significant, or fundamental, as it seems. The ontology he articulates still does not yet seem to attend to the truth of essence in fundamental ontology and the implication of this notion of essence to thingness of things including subjectivity. As Levinas does not yet displace the very notion of essence, the essence he transcends may still be within the horizon of ontic thinking.

17. The implication of being locked in an ontic cycle is that if Levinas wants subjectivity to transcend essence he must also presume an

7 *Ibid.*
8 *Ibid*, p 16.

ontic conception of that very essence that precedes his ethical transcendence. In his own way he indeed does just that. The essence of subjectivity is changed from ego-based subjectivity, which is locked in the logic of the Same, into a heterogeneous, but still ontic, conception of essence, which is proximate to the Other in infinite alterity. But, again it is important to see that this transcendence of the essence by radicalising subjectivity leaves the conception of essence totally intact. As we shall see, the heterogeneous subject that is arrived at 'otherwise than essence' radicalises ontic thinking only, and indeed in truth dresses this ontic transcendence up as deferral, which gives his transcendence a Heideggerian echo. The conception of essence is still not deconstructed because a deconstruction of the whole notion of subjectivity, including his radicalised one, would come with it. Subjectivity in alterity, indeed his notion of alterity, merely produces *ontic indeterminacy* of a derivative conception of essence. Levinas's conception of essence still involves residual 'things' or individual beings. *Overcoming sameness that is manifested along the lines of thinking with and through essence is not yet to displace the very notion of essence in the manner that thinking-Being does. In order to be genuine, overcoming essence must also overcome the displacement of essence by thinking-Being and that Levinas does not yet do.* It is very important to see that in this overcoming one preserves the craving, the epochal craving to preserve subjectivity and the metaphysics that it entails. Levinas overcomes mainly instances of this metaphysics, little 'essences', but he does not overcome the ontic thinking that gives rise to that essence. Levinas is subject to the very ontology that he criticises and wants to overcome. He makes ontology a thematic instance that calls for more primordial ethics, which itself presumes that very ontology: 'It is being which is understood in the – first or last – word, but the last saying goes *beyond* the being thematized and totalised.'[9]

18. Fundamental ontology is not beyond essence. It is not beyond anything. As such, it is itself. In fundamental ontology there is no beyond, only hide and seek with the nearest. In that it is much original (that is, coming to the origin of the actuality of the actual) than thinking 'beyond essence'.

19. Levinas does not deny the central stage, or the importance, of ontological thought. Although, then, Levinas wants to transcend ontology, including the thinking-Being of fundamental ontology, by an ethics of alterity which is complementary to, but otherwise than,

---

[9] *Ibid*, p 18. See also *ibid*, p 26, where Levinas claims that the subject arises earlier than Being and cognition. Here again he caricaturises Being by identifying it with cognition.

ontology, the opening pages of *Otherwise than Being* already cast doubt on his efforts.

20. Ontology, for Levinas, perpetuates the Said, by making language 'adverbial'. Being – to be – is a verb-begotten. It makes nouns verb-begotten. It is the verb-character of a Said-language within which Being resonates. In the Said, nouns are tainted by the verb 'to be'. Any alterity, potential Saying, is assimilated in advance into the Said and suppressed. The verb-character, the seed of ontological termporalisation and historiography, pervasively thematises every part of the language. In the Said things become themes, representations, agents of usefulness and function. Diachrony is 'synchronised into a time that is recallable, and becomes a theme.'[10]

21. But the ontology that Levinas presumes is the ontology of 'things'. Certainly, things exist in the Said in chronological time, history. The argument of Levinas whereby he connects the verb to a 'noun' shows that he is still talking about a derivative, rather than fundamental, ontology. The verb 'to be' may well be fundamental, and ontology does presume that the verb pervades and sneaks into language. But there is a sense of 'to be', a sense of 'how', which is given to any entity not in its existence but in its Being. The process of the unfolding of Being is that verbality of it. The 'to be' that Levinas talks about is ontic. Verbality as the process of unfolding is not the same as the verbality of 'to be' in the ontic sense. This 'to be' is always nearer, unconditioned and continuous, and realised as a distortion. To 'ek-sist' harbours otherness between two kinds of 'to be' and just to generalise hegemony of 'to be' in order to thematise both kinds does not do justice to that otherness. The primordial letting beings Being be – what is given to entities – is furthest from their ontic existence as thematised, historical beings. The synchronicity that Levinas seeks to transcend does not apply to fundamental ontology. This statement marks Levinas's misguided argument: 'Fundamental ontology itself, which denounces the confusion between Being and entities, speaks of Being as an identified entity. And the mutation is ambivalent; every nameable identity can turn into a verb.'[11] Primordial 'to be' is not 'implied' in nouns, it is given to nouns as their temporality of thingness. Does Levinas seriously think that he can entertain any projection of subjectivity in a primordial way to the continuous of 'to be'? This issue of the verbality of the unfolding is discussed in more depth below when I dwell on Levinas's conception of language.

[10] *OB*, pp 34–43.
[11] *Ibid*, pp 42–3.

22. Saying features prominently in Heidegger's later thought, where language that constantly re-speak itself is *Being-thinking* and is responded to by *Dasein thinking-Being*. What Levinas calls the 'Said' would be nothing but the ontic for-the-most-part account of the world. Unlike thinking which craves for subjectivity, the Nothing, the emptiness of Being accounts for an opening of an horizon which is not yet decoded thinking which craves subjectivity. Saying means a murmur of the continuous. What is 'mine' or 'innermost own', my own moment of Being-in-the-world, would be a moment when speech becomes inexpressible, nameless, subject-less, No-thing.

23. The other terms that Levinas uses in *Otherwise than Being* to account for subjectivity overcoming the Said and ontology are 'sensibility' and 'proximity'. Sensibility is primordial signification and is to be conceived as 'vulnerability and a responsibility in the proximity of the others, the one-for-the-other, that is, signification'.[12] To be sensible of something is to be more than being conscious of its being. Sensibility is more than an intuition that is said to be prior to a concept. To be sensible is not to merely be conscious of a representational idea. The conventional notion of sensibility again links it to representation of things only within a structure of totality. Sensibility, for Levinas, however, is the residue of subjectivity at the point where subjectivity is subsumed by doxic ontology and signification of systems: 'sight and hearing caress the visible and the audible'.[13] Levinas attempts to articulate a sense other than that of a subject within an ontological structure and synchronicity. Sense is not exhausted by the fact of something showing itself to consciousness as the thing it is. For Levinas, sense originally resides in the diachrony of proximity to the Other, in the proximate face-to-face with the Other.[14] In this connection, Levinas claims that even thinking-Being need not monopolise sensibility. For Levinas, the oscillation between the ontic and the ontological still yields to comprehension and knowing.[15] However fundamental the ontology it still does not change the kind of exteriority from within the Same:

Nothing is changed when one enlarges the notion of consciousness of ..., and describes it as an 'access to Being.' The exteriority that this way of speaking presupposes is already borrowed from thematization, consciousness of ... the self-sufficient correlation of the saying and the said.[16]

---

[12] *Ibid*, p 77.
[13] *Ibid*, p 80.
[14] *Ibid*, pp 61–8.
[15] *Ibid*, p 80.
[16] *Ibid*, p 68.

24. But *Dasein* as 'consciousness of ...' is already a distortion of the moment when Being becomes an issue for it in a moment of being-in-the-world, namely only when *Dasein* has been called upon by Being. Conscious understanding should not be confused with primordial attentive understanding to the Saying of Being. There is no continuum of consciousness in the ontological difference but rather a necessary distortion by consciousness. To that extent ontology does not borrow from any thematisation and correctness. Sensibility for Heidegger would come from emptiness which is not redeemed even if, especially if, *Dasein* ontically approximates a totally Other. To apply a Levinasian metaphor to fundamental ontology here, *a surplus of otherness survives the caress by the ontic Other*, and sensibility would come from the anxiety that ensues from such survival. Sensibility of the inexpressible survives sensibility that propels ontic transcendence. The primordial 'how' of the readiness-to-hand gives rise to a call which *Dasein* can sense and indeed a nearness which it can comport itself towards. But nearing the continuous could not be further away in terms of distance from the proximity that characterises ontic transcendence. We could say that nearness is given to ontic proximity and is always distorted by such proximity even if proximity is understood as resulting from radicalisation of alterity. The continuous always murmurs before any punctuability. The 'sense', and in turn 'sensibility', that survives ontology in Levinas cannot account for *fundamental* ontology. The only extent to which Levinas's account does 'survive' fundamental ontology, indeed the way in which Levinas is a part of the historicity of such ontology, is the sense of its entrenchment of the forgetfulness of Being.

25. The radicalisation of difference, the extremity of alterity which transcends the Same, is already to think in decodable terms, being 'decoded in disguise' even if it leads to questioning of existing conceptual punctuations. It is still ontic because it perpetuates the myth, the ultimate myth of the ontic, namely that of the possibility of a real distinction, a separation, a real outside. Within the ontic horizon of correctness, a separation between beings becomes the most operative actuality: with Levinas, ethical actuality. Thinking-Being, in speaking from nearer to subjectivity and in destabilising the very opposition of Same and Other, still conceives residual sensibility in the humbleness of the being-there.

26. That Levinas does not yet speak, does not yet think 'about' his notions, makes the absence of thinking-Being in his account all the more visible through the loudness of ontic denial. We can feel the tension between sensibility which is ontic towards a being and its

grounding in the more primordial ability to sense, or 'sense-ability' which comes from that which makes us ready to sense.

27.   As Smith argues, Levinas replaces the notion of absolute separation between people that characterises *Totality and Infinity* with the notion of infinite proximity.[17] Levinas understands proximity as somewhat paradoxical relations to the Other. Understanding what he means by proximity in *Otherwise than Being* is key to understanding what the ethical encounter of the face-to-face means. To be in contact with the Other for Levinas is to be caressed by the Other: 'A caress takes form in the contact without this signification turning into an experience of a caress. In the caress proximity remains a proximity and does not become an intention of something, although the caress could become an expressive gesture, a bearer of messages.'[18] To be caressed is to maintain the Other's alterity by maintaining separation from him. The separation occurs *as if* both subject and Other have always been others. The Other commands the subject as the subject's Other. But it is in the subject that the ethical command occurs. Hence the proximity. Such proximity is nothing but obsession that cannot be annulled by consciousness nor, one might add, by monopolising ontology. Such proximity is otherwise than ontology. The surplus of passivity of subjectivity resides in proximity to the Other that is irreducible to ontology. Responsibility to the Other in such proximity is boundless.[19] Proximity obtains only in alterity and hence its encapsulates a paradox of distance. Only with facing absolute exteriority to the Other is the subject proximate. Proximity is nudity, nudity of passivity before the Other. Subjectivity-in-proximity to the Other does paradoxically contest the boundary between the subject and the Other at the very moment of separation: 'The distance that is enlarged in the measure that proximity narrows ...'.[20]

28.   Levinas diverts attention from his preservation of the ontic in his further developments on fecundity – with the notions of enjoyment and substitution and recurrence.[21] Enjoyment for Levinas is that egoity which comes back to the subject in the process of facing the Other. Substitution for Levinas is the contestation during which the subject loses its conscious self in proximity to the other, goes into an exile within itself, only to regain itself in transcendence. Levinas calls what happens when the self loses itself, substitutes itself for the

[17] SG Smith, 'Reason as One for Another', in *Face to Face with Levinas*, above n 3, pp 53–71, at p 63.
[18] *LP*, p 118.
[19] *OB*, pp 86–9.
[20] *Ibid*, p 145.
[21] *Ibid*, pp 99–129.

Other while regaining its own self back, the 'recurrence' of subjectivity. The recurrence is the process of egoity which transcends the conscious ego. Recurrence is the process of 'not assumed, anarchical, subjectivity of a bottomless passivity'.[22] Recurrent subjectivity, Levinas argues, is beyond the essence of Being/Nothing. The 'responsibility for ...' (what Levinas called in *TI* 'living from ...') cannot be captured by thinking-Being.

29.   It is in his discussion of substitution and recurrence that Levinas takes reflection away from the ontic–ontological oscillation of fundamental ontology. The otherness which is faced in ontological thought, argues Levinas, is not passive enough, not proximate enough. However much otherness is radicalised in thinking-Being it cannot account for the otherness of the Other – cannot face the other as Other. All ontological reflection is still monopolised by consciousness and ego. Because ontology's 'well of transcendence' is nothingness and not otherness, ontological reflection cannot attend to the face and command of the Other as this attendance would be beyond ontology's 'seeing and hearing range'. To make the otherness of the Other an ethical issue that haunts the subject as face is not reducible to otherness that is subsumed by *Dasein* while having its own Being as an issue for it. Ontological thinking would obey the nothingness of consciousness before it could encounter any voice of the Other. Ontology cannot occasion substitution. Levinas uses the moment of substitution or proximity in a bold announcement 'here I am' for everybody and not for my consciousness. Substitution and recurrence is more than freedom of consciousness: 'Recurrence becomes identity in breaking up the limits of identity, breaking up the *principle* of being in me, the intolerable rest in itself characteristic of definition.'[23] Self cannot hide behind the occurrences and desires of my consciousness. In this process of substitution the self 'gnaws' at itself. In the ethical process of substitution there is a moment where the Other and the self are together and apart in a way which is otherwise than in ontology, where they always merely limit one another.

30.   In the following passages, the punctual alterity that Levinas invokes in order to explain the sensibility of the most particular of encounters with otherness is evident:

The other is in me and in the midst of my very identification. The ipseity has become at odds with itself in its return to itself. The self-accusation of remorse gnaws away at the closed and firm core of consciousness, opening it,

---

[22] *Ibid*, p 111.
[23] *Ibid*, p 114.

fissioning it. ... The recurrence in the subject is thus neither freedom of possession of self by self in reflection, nor the freedom of play where I take myself for this or that, traversing avatars under the carnival masks of history. It is a matter of an exigency coming from the other, beyond what is available in my powers, to open an unlimited 'deficit' in which the self spends itself without counting, freely. ... In substitution my being that belongs to me and not to another is undone, and it is through this substitution that I am not 'another', but me. ... The ipseity is then a privilege or an unjustifiable election that chooses me and not the ego. I am unique and chosen; the election is in the subjection. ... This transcendence separating itself from the consideration that conceptualizes it, the diachrony of subjectivity, is my entry into the proximity of the neighbour ... To say that the ego is a substitution is then not to state the universality of a principle, the quiddity of an ego, but, quite the contrary, it is to restore to the soul its egoity which supports no generalisation.[24]

Levinas uses substitution to connote the process whereby I substitute myself for the Other thereby regaining myself in my absolute singularity and nudity. It is in substitution that no one can substitute themselves for me. The process of substitution brings out what is inviolably mine, the incision that characterises the ethical origin of subjectivity which transcends any identification within the same. Transcendent subjectivity is otherwise than either Husserl's transcendental ego or its hermeneutic phenomenological other – the neutered, violent and tyrannical horizon of thinking-Being.

31. But cannot Levinas's arguments be applied not only to ontologically based ego, as he has done admirably, but also to subjectivity itself? What is the 'there' within which substitution takes place? What is the 'there' from which the Other can supposedly be identified/separated from the subject? Does responsibility to the Other not assume already some actuality that has been given to the situation in which consciousness could be overcome? Does not subjectivity-in-proximity and substitution still perpetuate subjectivity? Does the transcendence involved in substitution not perpetuate the looking upon the world, upon things in the world as beings, present-at-hand? What is the nature of the 'otherwise than being' in substitution? Is substitution not merely an ethics that involves self-reinterpretation within ontic logic?

32. I would argue that the transcendence of representation and the thematised self, the difficult freedom of infinite responsibility, is epistemologically dynamic – a dynamism fully exploited by Levinas to transcend the uncritically appraised self within the 'said' – but it is ontologically static. It does not ask a single ontological question.

---

[24] *Ibid*, pp 125, 127.

Levinasian subjectivity is passive and naked, but it does not yet attend to its own anxiety. It is a defence mechanism against anxiety. Real passivity and own-mirroring and with it real ethics occur only in anxiety. The moment of total ontic nudity may give the impression of the possibility of an exteriority; while at the same time it anticipates all the craving for the re-enactment of the kind of concepts that it left in the transcendence. The detached enormity of transcendence in Levinas leaves the subject totally dependent on the kind of ontic thinking that it has transcended. It educates the subject in this velvety violence to confine attentiveness within the punctual horizon. In the name of ethics, Levinas's thought can be critical of principled thought, law, while in fact leaving the subject at the very moment of transcendence with nothing but a craving for re-principlisation and re-legalisation. The emptiness of the Levinisian saying, its 'beyond' of separation, in fact ties the subject to ontic thinking. It does not allow him to interrogate language into the nearest but rather to keep producing language that criticises existing punctuated themes in language but which is in complete complicity regarding that which is to be preserved. The move from the language of absolute alterity in *Totality and Infinity* to complementarity between ethical Saying and the ontological Said in *Otherwise than Being* is subtle and impressive. However, it does not change the ontic horizon of that ethical Saying and, with it, of proximity, substitution, and recurrence.

33. Ontology, ethically, makes the subject confront the distortion of his subjectivity, not merely the hegemony within which this subjectivity is presently articulated. The call of Being from beneath the ontic is very fragile and is easily overcome by ontic desire.

34. Levinas's argument resonates with Heideggerian echoes when he claims that the supremacy of subjectivity in substitution and recurrence occurs after the subject has been chosen by the Good.[25] The subject is chosen by the Good, and this has a Heideggerian echo of the *Dasein* spoken by Being, by language. Again, however, to dissolve the metaphor of 'Good' that 'chooses', the subject reveals only ontically based thinking that perpetuates the infinity within which the subject is being chosen. The Good originates in punctuable absolute alterity, a pre-conceptual moment at which conceptual distinctions always have an overflowing, non-expellable trace of an Other.

35. Levinas is after the origin of values and, for him, responsibility for the Other is that origin: 'Responsibility is what first enables one to catch

---

[25] *Ibid*, p 122.

sight of and conceive of value.'[26] To be chosen by that origin and to renegotiate values that are already conceptualised and prioritised is still to speak the logic of values, to yearn for conceptualisation through values, to anticipate values. It is to assimilate the valuable into thinking with values.[27] The Good of alterity, which chooses the subject, occasions difference between itself and the subject. This difference between the Good and 'me' generates what Levinas called 'non-indifference'. Non-indifference can occur only in the midst of radical punctuation between the Good and 'me'.[28] But is not the light of the valuable denied though the entrenchment of the craving to let subjectivity be chosen by the Good of punctuation, thus being imprisoned in value-based anticipation?

Is to be 'called' as punctual as being 'chosen'?

36. There are many more occasions in *Otherwise than Being* in which Levinas attributes qualities to ontology which show that the ontology he speaks of is derivative, rather than fundamental. He presents the preoccupation of ontology as 'the exhibitions of being's essence in truth'[29] without problematising the notion of 'Being's essence in truth' as Heidegger has done. At the same place in the book Levinas sees ontology as concerning the system of grouping of entities (beings). He argues that 'The intelligibility of being is always high noon without shadows, where the subject intervenes without even projecting the silhouette of its own density'.[30] Still in the same place, he sees ontology as 'theoretical consciousness in its purity'. Further, his objections to 'committed subjectivity', which are based on the argument that 'commitment' must be grounded in a theme and in turn in ontology, show again the derivative nature of the ontology he criticises.[31]

37. Is the gentleness of Levinas's violence not alarming? If the epoch is such that *Dasein*s are predisposed to assimilate Heideggerian moves into Levinasian co-ordinates, can humans do something about it or is it a part of Being's fate, part of the twilight of its forgetfulness?

38. Levinas's passivity is not to be confused with humbleness before Being. His notion of proximity is not to be confused with nearness to Being. But, above all, his complementarity between ethical Saying and ontic Said is arguably not yet touching the complementarity between authentic and inauthentic speech within which it occurs. Perhaps Heidegger is seemingly transcended by Levinas, but at the

---

[26] *Ibid*, p 123.
[27] See *LH*, p 251.
[28] *OB*, pp 122–3.
[29] *Ibid*, p 132.
[30] *Ibid*, p 133.
[31] *Ibid*, pp 136–40.

same time the impression of the 'transcended Heidegger' that the reader gets is a Heidegger with a twisted arm.

SAYING, SAID, SCEPTICISM AND LANGUAGE

39.   Saying is the arena of signification, associated with the ethical, with subjectivity-in-alterity, with temporal diachrony, and connotes insurmountable and asymmetrical responsibility. The Said is associated with ontology, where there is no subject, and which is imprisoned in the same, in themes, concepts and representations. The essence of Being is said to thematise and to regenerate temporal synchronies. Ontology is characterised by Levinas as a game without responsibility. Ontology is conceived as a *game* of beings/nothingness.

40.   Complementarity for Levinas retains the ethical Saying as a non-expellable surplus in any theme and ethical conceptualisation. The Saying needs ontological language but at the moment it is expressed it is no longer ethical. There is a double bind here: Ontological language reduces the Saying into a Said, and it is necessary for such a reduction to take place. The 'otherwise than' in 'Otherwise than Being' does not mean that there is an opposition or polemics between ethical Saying and the ontological Said. Complementarity means here that the Saying hides within the Said so there is no access to it but through the reductionist and impersonal Said. Ethics haunts ontology, despite ontology's tendency to suppress ethics.

41.   Critchley has advanced the thesis that the constant challenge to overcome the ontological Said is the very ethical challenge of the *clôtural* reading embedded in deconstruction.[32] Deconstruction always attempts a rereading and rewriting of a text, by exposing its undecidability which is oppressed by the latent, presumed, binary oppositions which constitute the 'presence' of the voice in the text. *Clôtural* reading of a text is a double reading. It reads the text, in a very detailed and laboured, repetitive, way so as both to extract the conventional reading of it and to grasp the oppressed undecidable saying within it, thereby giving the text an ethical rereading and rewriting (rewriting as the hegemonic presence of the author is overcome in this process). A text becomes an invitation to reread and rewrite and so it speaks to the rereaders and rewriters in a way which is over and above the conventional 'presence' of speaking. Deconstruction, then, does not 'criticise' as wrong, the conventional reading,

---

[32] S Critchley, *The Ethics of Deconstruction: Derrida and Levinas* (Oxford, Blackwell, 1992).

but rather exposes the 'not yet' difference which is deferred in such reading. Deconstructive moves do not completely eliminate conventional interpretation but endlessly twist it, creating new paths and new possibilities for the text, without ever succumbing to some overarching coherence, or polemic, of previous readings. Deconstruction, then, involves both retention and twisting of saying in a way which preserves undecidability.

42. Levinas argues that criticisms of his account through ontological language, namely a language that constantly negates the 'what' of that text, will continue to be haunted by the ethical Saying. Levinas finds an analogy in scepticism that continues to haunt any of its refutations. The analogy persists between, on the one hand, the relationship between ethical Saying and the ontological Said, and the foretold unsuccessful refutation of scepticism on the other. The persistence of scepticism and its refutation *simpliciter* ('there is'/'there is not') is analogous to the cycle of ontologically based deconstruction. But there is, Levinas claims, an impetus in scepticism which goes beyond the analogy with ontological deconstructive cycles. This impetus is that the very sceptical claim can connote a different dimension which cannot be reduced to those ontological cycles of affirmation and refutation. The origin of scepticism is, then, not in some logical (and ontological) claims and refutations, but rather in an unexpellable ethical claim that is hidden in every reduction of that claim and, with it, a reduction of the impetus of scepticism to ontological language. Scepticism, then, resides in the surplus of ethics over ontology, namely as the original Saying that is primordial and otherwise than mere oscillation between one ontology and another.

43. Levinas's account of scepticism attempts to conceive of scepticism and its refutation in a more original way than philosophy conceives of it. Classical scepticism attempts to generate a general negation of all knowledge but this very attempt is thereby refuted by the logical argument that its 'said', namely that there is no knowledge, is contradictory, as it must also be false together with that which it criticises. As a philosophical thesis which is critical about philosophy, scepticism endlessly haunts its own inevitable refutation. From a philosophical point of view, both its refutation and revival are locked in a way which fails to explain, according to Levinas, the positive surplus of the sceptical argument and the fact that it always continue to haunt its refutation. In philosophy both the continuous affirmation and refutation of scepticism are perfectly complementary so that both scepticism and the philosophy that is refuted by it and yet refutes it neutralise one another. From philosophy's point of view, scepticism keeps returning but understanding this return philosophically is fundamentally *idle* because scepticism does not yet generate a

force of return which originates in a saying prior to the philosophical 'said'. Philosophy, although it is the medium in which scepticism and its refutation must be articulated, cannot have the resources to explain scepticism and its continuous return:

Philosophy is not separable from skepticism, which follows it like a shadow it drives off by refuting it again at once on its footsteps. Does not the last word belong to philosophy? Yes, in a certain sense, since for Western philosophy the saying is exhausted in things said. But skepticism in fact makes a difference, and puts an internal between saying and said. Skepticism is refutable, but it returns.[33]

Scepticism, then, must get its residual force of return not merely from its own 'saying about what is being said', or indeed from scepticism's own implicit and global said. Rather, scepticism's return comes from the irreducible exteriority of an ethical Saying which continues to haunt any philosophical thesis which merely exposes the saying-in-a-said as its correlative un-said. To put it another way, for Levinas, there must be a complementarity, which combines some surplus of saying over how this saying features in a said. One aspect of this complementarity, the ethical, is an original sceptical position, a surplus to any logical negation of logocentrism and comes from a diachronical temporal trace. The other aspect of the complementarity is an ontological scepticism which, viewed on its own, is idle and synchronous, endlessly oscillating between being and nothingness.

44. Grasping this complementarity, original scepticism is refuted by the necessary reduction of it into ontologically begotten scepticism. But it returns because 'skepticism, which traverses the rationality or logic of knowledge, is a refusal to synchronize the implicit affirmation contained in saying and the negation which this affirmation states in the said'.[34] To view deconstruction mainly ontologically, the use of logocentric language against that very language[35] is not yet doing justice to that original scepticism. So while scepticism has, in Western philosophy, been contested within the domain of philosophy, this contest is not yet sceptical, for the sceptical resides in the complementarity between the ontological Said and the ethical Saying which transcends it. Deconstruction must also involve a diachrony of the very ontological horizon within which its claim to transcend logocentrism lies. If viewed solely from ontology, deconstruction,

---

[33] *OB*, p 168.
[34] *Ibid*, p 167.
[35] E Levinas, 'Wholly Otherwise', (1973) (S Critchley, trans), in R Bernasconi and S Critchley (eds) *Re-reading Levinas* (Bloomington, Indiana University Press, 1991) pp 3–10, at p 5.

despite its contestation of logocentrism, is still logocentric.[36] But notice that scepticism finds its endless return *because* of the complementarity that exists between saying, which is *necessarily* reduced to a said. The necessary deployment of ontological language is the language through which deconstruction speaks. But the deep Saying, the original ethical relations that are exterior to that language, is the original mover of this deconstruction, so much so that every text is already under the gaze of scepticism over and above the ontological way in which the text has been deconstructed. Pure future that refuses synchronisation of being/nothingness awaits any text, and that will, of course, as we shall see, include Levinas's text.

45. We can say that the trace of the Saying in the Said, in a way which is not correlative with that which the Said says, is another formulation of what Levinas has referred to as 'face'. But is 'face' a face of another person or is it the 'how' of a person?

46. Some observations: First, to what extent does Levinas's view of scepticism capture Levinas's own argument about the characterisation of this deep Saying as the ethics of the Other? Notice that I ask a question of *extent*, as Levinas does accept, as we shall see, that his text should be subjected to deconstructive reading like any other text. My question is rather to what extent the deconstruction of Levinas's text will show that his view of deep ethical Saying does not do justice to a deep ethical Saying that precedes and conditions it. Is the notion of ethical Saying itself subject to the deconstruction of ethical Saying? In order to address this question and to 'do Levinas to Levinas', we shall have to reflect upon his conception of otherness and with it his idea of language. Second, Levinas's clinging to the notion of scepticism is somehow odd and perhaps does not sit very comfortably with the idea of complementarity. Why? Because scepticism of whatever persuasion, even the ethical persuasion that Levinas provides, must assume the possibility of a real distinction, and real distinction does not sit very well with true complementarity which involves both continuity and a distortion. What bothers me here is that Levinas preserves the separation of (rather as a distinction between, as he puts it in *Existence and Existents*) 'ethics' and 'ontology', while at the same time keeping them complementary. He keeps the notion of some absolute exteriority, which attaches

---

[36] For accounts of Levinas's scepticism see J De Greef, 'Skepticism and Reason', in *Face to Face with Levinas*, above n 3, pp 159–79; R Bernasconi, 'Skepticism in the Face of Philosophy', in *Re-reading Levinas*, above n 35, pp 149–61; S Critchley, *The Ethics of Deconstruction*, above n 32, pp 156–69, A Peperzak, *Beyond: The Philosophy of Emmanuel Levinas* (Evanston, Northwestern University Press, 1997), pp 148–53, and 'Presentation' in *Re-reading Levinas*, above n 35, pp 51–66; SG Smith, 'Reason as One for Another', in *Face to Face with Levinas*, above n 3, pp 53–71, at pp 59–66.

itself to ontological deconstruction. His notion of deep ethical Saying still adheres to total separation, from which a vocabulary of scepticism can be generated. Punctuability still lurks behind the deconstructive complementarity that characterises the relationship between the ethical Saying and the ontological Said, and this punctuability is a characteristic of the ethical Saying itself. We need, then, to dwell on how exactly the deferral of the Saying as that of an 'Other' at the heart of the ethical saying is to be conceived. Arguably, the vocabulary of scepticism does not fit deconstruction. Poetic language is other than both totalities and scepticism. In Levinas's view ontology seems to be a totality that skepticism can attach itself to it even as a deep ethical Saying. It might just be that the language of scepticism, like that of 'an Other', is ontic language, the language of correctness, and that in resorting to complementarity in *Otherwise than Being* Levinas assimilated the spirit of *alētheia* into that kind of language.

47. Critchley argues that Derrida, in his reading of Levinas, speaks in an ethical voice and what seems to be ontological criticism is in fact reducing a Levinasian ethical reading of Levinas's own text. This has the overall effect of affirming Levinas's distinction between Saying and Said. Critchley shows Levinas's point to be that each text is reductionist and thematising, however refined it might be, and as such it cannot fully articulate the Saying repressed in it. Critchley shows that Levinas is well aware that this argument also applies to his own writings, so much so that he anticipates the requirement to subject them to ethical challenge by awarding them the ingratitude of a deconstructive reading. Such a deconstructive reading of Levinas is undertaken by Derrida in his essay 'At This Very Moment In This Work Here I Am', in which he shows undecidability between the femininity of the Other and the male dominance of Levinas's account of *illeity*.[37] The requirement of a *clôtural* reading of a text, this time a text by Levinas, means that the text is handed over to the Other thus allowing the Other to 'drink'. '*Bois*' is used to connote the thirst of the Other that lurks within any text, and so the ethics of deconstruction would be to treat this text ethically, with ingratitude as perhaps the deepest manifestation of respect for that text. The ingratitude involves *both* interpretative transgression and appreciative retention. The deconstructionist lets the Other interrupt and thus ethically interpret the text. It is Levinas who articulates the ethical

---

[37] J Derrida, 'At This Very Moment In This Work Here I Am', in *Re-reading Levinas*, above n 35, pp 11–48; S Critchley, 'Bois: Derrida's Final Word on Levinas', in *ibid*, pp 162–89 (see also a modified version in S Critchley, *The Ethics of Deconstruction*, above n 32, pp 107–44).

horizon, which is otherwise than the ontological horizon, for such reading.

48. Critchley's argument is that Derrida affirms the link between decons-truction and Levinas by his ontological criticism of Levinas. The ontological criticisms of Levinas do not diminish the ethical challenge that Levinas posed to such an ontological re-reading. Re-readings of Levinas are themselves to be made subject to ethical deconstruction. The *ontological* way in which deconstructive readings of Levinas occur as a double reading is already part of the very attempt to overcome the 'reduction of the Saying by the Said' in Levinas. Levinas's texts are shown to contain the ethical Saying, as well as confirming the impossibility of reducing the ethical Saying to the ontological said.

49. Let us take Levinas at his own word and ask what is the deepest ingratitude with which we can read his text. Would not this ingrat-itude be a deconstruction of the very notion of his ethical Saying and its relationship with ontological reflection? Could we embark on such a deconstruction while retaining some of Levinas's insight about ethics, namely the notion of fundamental alterity?

50. At this point a dilemma that arises should be fully faced: I would call this dilemma the ontological difference versus the ethical difference dilemma. On the one side of the dilemma is the argument that Levinas misses the full implication of ontological difference and is locked in an ontic spiral. On the other side of the dilemma, Levinas claims that the ethical Saying is otherwise then the ontological difference, or otherwise than the ontological horizon altogether. According to the ontological difference side of the dilemma, both the ethical Saying and the ontological Said that this ethical Saying precedes and haunts are ontic and so do not account for the moment of unconcealment of Being in its withdrawal. Such an ontic cycle does not yet confront the otherness of *alētheia*. Levinas would have replied that the ontic–ontological difference is locked within the cycle of the question of Being. Although the ontological difference – the complementarity between ontic and ontological – confronts represen-tation and conceptualisation, the notion of otherness that it harbours is still within the horizon of the question of Being.

51. Let us look at the ontological approach to this dilemma. The ontological difference hints that ethics and fundamental ontology are tied together and so give rise to a complementarity between the ethical Saying of Being that comes from the continuous and the unconditioned, and the ontic Said which contains any ethical Saying of a punctuated nature. To put it another way, there is a connection between ethical Saying and the Saying of Being that lurks within Levinas's account of complementarity between Saying and Said.

Indeed, alterity can be at the heart of such connection between ethics and thinking-Being. From an ontological perspective, then, there is alterity which is tied up with the continuous nature of fundamental ontology in such a manner that the ethics that craves for conceptualisation of 'an Other' would necessarily be a distortion of it.

52. The very dilemma of the ethical difference versus the ontological difference must itself bear deconstruction. If ethics is seen as part and parcel of the ontological difference, the full argument from fundamental ontology would be that Being as the fugal order of manifestation has, as an aspect, the essence of ethics of alterity and, with it, the essence of the valuable. It could be made more difficult for Levinas to attach the sense of 'otherwise' between ontology and ethics as that sense may turn out to be a distorted conclusion of a more primordial dynamics.

53. The complementarity in the ontological difference between *rede* (ontological) and *gerede* (ontic) itself encapsulates complementarity between ethical Saying and ethical Said, the latter which includes Levinas's notion of 'Saying'. To put it differently, the Saying which is comported towards an Other, even this Other who comes as a surplus of a 'not-yet conceptualised Other', is already idle as it does not allude to that Saying from which otherness has already spoken.

54. So now the dilemma can be understood. It is noticeable that both sides of this dilemma conceive ethics as rooted in alterity. In order to think about this dilemma, therefore, we need to think about the origin of the otherness of the Other. What is the origin of otherness? The key question that we have to focus on in reading both Heidegger and Levinas is: *Has Levinas managed to explain alterity in a way which leads to complementarity described as the 'otherwise' of ethics from ontology?* This chapter begins this inquiry. I return to the origin of otherness in chapters eight and nine, this time from the perspective of fundamental ontology.

55. From fundamental ontology, the origin of otherness is distorted by the ethical Saying that disposes to punctuate 'an Other'. The 'not', the distortion and complementarity, between the essence of ethics and its ontic occurrence, encapsulates a relationship of *alētheia* between the otherness of the Other and the otherness of the Nothing. To put it succinctly, the otherness of the Other has its essence in the otherness of the Nothing. The otherness of the Other is always already given that which precedes the otherness of an Other in its otherness. The otherness of the Other always manifests as not-yet nearing the continuous Nothing. We could formulate the argument that Levinas does not account for the otherness of the Other because that otherness must already be embodied in an Other and not in that which is given to the Other essentially as its otherness. The otherness

of the Other is already an ontic distortion with the occurrence of which the origin of the otherness of the other is deferred. The Nothing is strange both to the 'I' and the Other but, as strange, speaks as the essence of the otherness of the Other.

56. So, does otherness consists of a being which is totally 'other to me', or does otherness refer to that which is prior to the very craving for the conceptualisation of the other as an Other, something which is given to the other as Other upon which it can be what it is 'in otherness to ...'?

57. Despite the centrality of alterity in Levinas's philosophy, there is, then, no dwelling on the origin of otherness in Levinas. Must we not dwell on *how* the other is in the world as Other, thus touching the otherness of amorphous mystery which is given to the other as otherness? Does not the otherness of the Other precede any otherness of ontic transcendence, the latter being already derived as distorted contemplation and manifestation? Should we not relate to the actuality of the actual of the other in order to understand its otherness? Can we not see that nothing but the origin of ethics is in question here?

58. We have to ask the question concerning the origin of otherness of the other in order to be ethical. But in turning this question into mere *difference between beings* we are not yet asking the question of otherness. The otherness of the Nothing, in which beings seem strange to *Dasein*, when *Dasein* dwells in strangeness, slowing down and allowing itself to be taken by strangeness, is the point where the question of the otherness of the Other ought to be asked. Otherness of the Other, then, is not another being, another human being, another group which is 'not yet conceptualised'. It is much more primordial and strange. The otherness of the Other is that strangeness that is inexpressible in the other *Dasein*s.

59. We thus retain Levinas's Saying in as much as the origin of ethics is in alterity and in being-for the Other. But our deconstruction of Levinas takes place by displacing being-for, that is by showing the 'not' that is essential between being for an Other and the 'being-for' as the origin of the otherness of the Other. Being for the Other signifies being for the origin of the otherness of the Other. As such, as we will see, being-for is a mystery. Being for the otherness of the Other signifies being for the sake of otherness. The otherness of the Other is already in a face, of the not-yet-represented face of the other. But face is merely the point of departure for asking the question of the otherness of the Other. Otherness calls us to think about and from the event of epiphany of the face of the Other.

60. Thus, in dwelling upon the relationship between, on the one hand, the otherness of beings that dwell together in the continuous near

and, on the other hand, the otherness of beings as 'not-yet-concep-tualised Others', we would pay our deconstructive ingratitude to Levinas. Only than can we respond ethically to Levinas's thought. The origin of otherness is that 'other' which is suppressed by Levinas's writings. It is this origin to which these writings stand in complementarity.

61. To be ethical, to be an 'other' as an ethical deconstructionist reader would be, then, is to destabilise the ontic otherness that is all too decidable in Levinas. In doing that we can show that Heidegger's thought was itself an ethical deconstruction of a derivative punctuable ontology which has alterity at its heart.

62. Arguably, then, to deflect Derrida's criticisms of Levinas both in 'Violence and Metaphysics' and in subsequent texts by showing the ingratitude towards Levinas of their Saying as confirming the primordiality of Levinasian ethics is a masterful move by the Levinas of *Otherwise than Being* and the 'Wholly Otherwise'. But the success of this move is assured only as long as otherness itself is not probed near enough to its actuality.

LANGUAGE FOR LEVINAS

63. How does Levinas understand language? The severance from the elements had implications for Levinas's view of language. The ethical Saying, the responsibility for the Other, ethically conditions the speaking of language. Language is the language of proximity to the Other. Facing is ethical only if it harbours openness to the Saying of language – Saying that signifies primordially as the exteriority of the not-yet-conceptualised 'I'/Other. The *aporia* of freedom, for Levinas, is to let oneself go in a language of infinite opposition and twists in order to effectuate the prior idea of proximity, substitution and recurrence. Such attentiveness is of a very different predisposition than attentiveness to the inexpressible. We may ask: is opening up to the Saying of language understood as a not-yet-conceptualised Other opening up yet to the murmuring of the Saying of language? To put it another way, in what sense is the language of proximity on the way to language?

64. For Levinas, ethical disposition to punctuate prevents us from attending to language simply as language. We cannot borrow a metaphor from Heidegger and say that language is the house of an Other. We can say, though, that a face of a not-yet-conceptualised Other looks at us from the house of language. For Levinas, however, language is derivative from the ethical relations of separation and can only signify following the severance of separation.

65. Levinas made some remarks in 'La Pensée de l'être et la question de l'autre'[38], discussed extensively by Critchley, concerning the distinction Husserl made in *Logical Investigations* between *expression* [*Ausdruck*] and *indication* [*Anseichen*]. Critchley's argument, on which I shall dwell slowly, reads the Levinas of *Otherwise than Being*[39] as pointing out that Derrida failed to see (or as he puts it, failed to intend) the surplus of the ethical over the ontological in the process of the radicalisation of Husserl's notion of 'indication' that Derrida himself had carried out in his ground-breaking commentary on Husserl in *Speech and Phenomena*.[40] The true origin of deconstruction can be both seen from an ontological perspective as transcending metaphysics of presence but, crucially, it carries together with the linguistic ontological event an ethical event that is reduced to this ontological event. According to Levinas, Derrida's account of the primacy of indication still resides in ontologically dominated reflection and does not yet bring to the open the ethical 'otherwise' that his ontological transcendence reduces but does not expel.

66. Reflecting on Levinas's ethical radicalisation of Husserl's indication is crucial for grasping the derivation of language from separation in Levinas. The ontological still contains an ethical Saying, yes, but I shall argue that it was not necessary for Derrida to adopt Levinas's ethical Saying to exhaust the potential radicalisation of indication. Indeed, it is necessary for deconstruction not to adopt the Levinasian conception of the radicalisation. Let us take the argument slowly.

67. For Husserl, 'indication' relates to the connections that are made prejudicially by every psychological ego as a result of which arbitrary, rather than essential, meaning is produced. Indications cannot generate meanings from how consciousness experiences things. For example, a blue mark in my notebook can indicate an importance reference for a thought I had about Levinas's view of language. As opposed to that arbitrary subjective association, the statement that the sum of the angles of a triangle is always 180° is a correct *expression* of an essential, objective, meaning. The transcendental phenomenological reduction consists of a constant attempt to 'bracket', that is to filter out, indications so that what is left is essential expression. The whole transcendental phenomenological project is about how intentionality transcends the way that the psychological ego experiences the world (indication) into the way a

---

[38] E Levinas, 'La pensée de l'être et la queston de l'autre', (1978) 369 *Critique* 187–97.

[39] The Levinas of *Totality and Infiinity* still sees ethical relations in terms of expression.

[40] S Critchley, *The Ethics of Deconstruction*, above n 32, pp 171–6, discussing Derrida's 'Speech and Phenomena', in DB Alison (trans), *Speech and Phenomena and other essays on Husserl's Theory of Signs* (Evanston, Northwestern University Press, 1973) pp 1–104.

transcendental ego experiences eidetic essences (expressions). Derrida threatens the phenomenological project by reinstating indication as a necessary supplement to any expression. Indication destabilises expression, either by pointing towards that which the expression does not express but which is vital, or by adding new complications. Indication consists of a surplus that points towards the disordered nature of actuality and so is primordial to expression. Derrida argues that expressions and indications are bonded, and indications are primordial because they are the forces that set the dynamism of meaning going. Indications are the surpluses that constantly defer meaning.

68.   Critchley explains that, according to Levinas, indicative *meaning* must be inferior in comparison with expression if understood only ontologically. From an ontological point of view, the arbitrariness of pure indication robs it of any additional value over expression in which thinking and being are less arbitrarily united. The originary value designated to the surplus of indicative meaning, value that disrupts expression, must then be grasped not as a surplus content of being that is still related to *what* is expressed (ontological surplus) but rather as exteriority that excludes all relations. The ethical value of indication must reside in something other than, and completely exterior to, the 'content of being'. Levinas's radicalisation of indication entails externality of all relations that make some sense in ontological talk. Levinas claims that properly radicalised indication says something other than that which is encapsulated in the ontologically begotten radicalisation of indication as a supplement to expression. Levinas's move is to account for a gap, a punctuation of exteriority, that characterises the moment of indication being manifested so much so that this move almost detaches indication from any possibility of being in language. With this move the ethical event as radicalised indication is explained as a moment of exteriority to language. This ethical moment is a moment not only of separation but also of detachment. It is such detachment that persists between the ethical and the ontological dimension of indication that enables Levinas's claim for ethics to be otherwise than even fundamental ontology. Any radicalisation of indicationthat is still captive of ontological thought or 'content of being' – even as a radical negation of such content – (and this is Levinas's implicit criticism of Derrida) does not yet explain the ethical indicative moment. Ethics hides even in the pure indication of fundamental ontology.

But how can such a moment of pure indication be conceived? Can exteriority be radicalised in such a manner? If yes, does not such a possibility of an outside assume an unbridgeable, irreducible gap, total otherness, a possibility of a real distinction? If a real distinction is possible in such ethical radicalisation of indication, such a beyond, is it not already a sign of punctuation? As punctuation, would not such a possibility, from the point of view of fundamental ontology, still force complementarity to 'content of being', 'content of being' still being understood as an inquiry about beings and, hence, ontic? This is the nub of the punctual nature of Levinas's radicalisation of indication: *it both detaches in order to radicalises exteriority but at the same time creates complementarity on the level of meaning to an ontic view of deconstruction that it calls misleadingly 'ontological'.*

69. Levinas does not really transcend fundamental ontology. He still caricaturises it. Fundamental ontology does not merely see radicalisation of indication on the level of the simple 'whatness' of beings. One cannot reduce fundamental ontology to the simple impoverishment of ontological horizon that stems from the non-correspondence and arbitrariness in indicative meaning between thinking and being. Fundamental ontology indicates rather towards the *distance* between thinking-Being and thinking beings.

70. We need to ask what a repetition of the ontological involves. What is otherness in such repetition? How is language as indication to be magnified to explain a mere repetition of ontology and otherness? Perhaps if we meditate upon indication we can see that the ethical moment of Levinas's transcendence is always already within fundamental ontology, namely being manifested as one mature instance of ontic fall?

71. What is indication? At what does indication indicate? Does Man indicate at Being in the same way as indicating, for example, at another human being or at a car? Man, by indicating, by pointing towards, is a pointer. In *What is Called Thinking?*, Heidegger had this to say:

What withdraws from us, draws us along by its very withdrawal, whether or not we become aware of it immediately, or at all. Once we are drawn into the withdrawal, we are drawing toward what draws, attracts us by its withdrawal. And once we, being so attracted, are drawing toward what draws us, our essential nature already bears the stamp of 'drawing toward'. As we are drawing toward what withdraws, we ourselves are pointers pointing toward it. We are who we are by pointing in that direction ... To say 'drawing toward' is to say 'pointing toward what withdraws'

To the extent that man *is* drawing that way, he *points* toward what withdraws. *As* he is pointing that way man *is* a pointer ... His essential nature lies in being such a pointer. Something which in itself, by its essential nature, is pointing, we call a sign. As he draws toward what withdraws, man is a sign. But since this sign points toward what draws *away*, it points, not so much at what draws away as into the withdrawal. The sign stays without interpretation.

In a draft to one of his hymns, Hölderlin writes:

'We are a sign that is not read'.

He continues with these two lines:

'We feel no pain, we almost have
Lost our tongue in foreign lands.'[41]

72. Man thus is an indicator. His essential nature is to indicate at that
which withdraws. What reveals itself to Man in its withdrawal is the
process of unconcealment or *alētheia*. The essence of Man is to
constantly battle through language, thus indicating, pointing
towards, that inexpressible mystery that withdraws away from him.
Man points towards actuality that is always too near to him, too
close. It is that process of concealment, with the constant regener-
ation of the riddle of actuality, that is indicated at. There is sociality
and otherness involved in this process on which I dwell in the last
chapters. The point here is, however, that there is no detachment, or
gaps, no distinctions or an 'outside' in this process. We, all human
beings, cannot help hovering in the mystery of pointing towards that
which withdraws in its unconcealment, something that conceals even
the concealment and hence remains a mystery. The mystery, the
boundary towards which Man points, is language. Man indicates
towards the almost impossibility of language responding to its own
Saying. Indication conveys the silence of wrestling with the impossibility of responding to language through language. Silence is
pointing. Crucially, pointing is not to create an ultimate punctuated
'gap' but towards the withdrawing nearness of the Saying of
language, to indicate pointing at the continuous while all the tools
you have are those of punctuation – that is why 'the sign stays
without interpretation'. Indicating indicates an understanding of that
which is nearer than interpretation. Man is, in essence, in a foreign
land, homeless.

73. How does the essence of Man being a pointer towards the mystery
relate to Levinas's radicalisation of indication otherwise than in
ontology and the content of being? For Heidegger, the ontological
difference, which Man is a part of in his essence and towards which
Man indicates, does not simply radicalise indication as pointing
towards an absolute exteriority. Primordial indicating could never
amount to any expression of positive essence, as essence exists in
absence. But crucially it would not merely amount to radical exteri-

[41] *WCT*, pp 9–10.

ority with positivity manifested as ontic absence, namely a 'not yet' totally other connection.

74. From a Heideggerian perspective there is indeed a continuum between Husserl, Derrida and Levinas. Husserl does not attend to indication which originally determines expression. But does Derrida not also have some methodology of exposing the contradictions and undecidability in expressions in the texts he analyses? *Derrida exposes the primordiality of indications, but does he 'indicate at ...' by doing that in the way poetic language does? Is not any methodology still within the horizon of expressions, within the horizon of correctness?* But Levinas, with the claim that the ontological language of deconstruction does not indicate the *absolute* exteriority, also conceives the moment of indication as punctuation and separation. In Husserl, Levinas, and arguably also Derrida, there is still a method, a process that Man can control – methodology, punctuation.

75. Absolute exteriority is the hallmark, perhaps the twilight, of correctness [*Richtigkeit*]. It amounts to an ontic radicalisation of indication carried out by the punctuation of absolute exteriority. The otherness of Heidegger stems from his otherness to any ontic deconstruction where he sees the directionality of language as leading the way. The otherness of language is in the boundary of *both* the expressible and the radical ontic indication. The otherness of language is in the sign itself, not in a signification that relies on 'other' beings. Proximity and substitution are hallmarks of radicalised indication which does not yet indicate.

76. In pointing, in indicating, a deconstruction of the very significance of 'indication' occurs that does not imply merely undecidability (itself arguably an ontic notion) but rather a poetic saying which murmurs straight to the heart of being-there-in-the-world. When moving from correctness to unconcealment the whole notion of the indicative potential of language changes. It no longer indicates at an absolute 'Other who is not-yet-conceptualised'. Ontologically, indication is not just 'content of Being', as Levinas puts it. It is rather unconcealment of the near in its strangeness that stems from the hint at the impossibility of absolute distinctions.

77. Llewelyn points out the problem that Heidegger has in the characterisation of Being, Time, Event and, we may now add, Pointing. Because the ontological difference is not about beings, Heidegger cannot turn Being into a being. This paradox forces him to 'verbalise' nouns, for example to say, 'the event eventises' [*das Eregnis ereignet*]. But this is just Heidegger attempting to put the inexpressible into language, to articulate the essential unfolding of the mystery in *alētheia*. *Alētheia* is not a process of 'to be or not to be', a process of

'being and non-being' but is the endless process of the 'how' of being, which is understood as distance between the punctual and the continuous. Indication indicates at the process that is given to beings, not at beings. Llewelyn explains that the Saying of the ontological difference is correlated and reducible to the horizon of the 'what' of the Said, a correlation and reduction that can be accounted for only by verbalised nouns.[42] The ethical Saying is outside that horizon. However, the resonse would be, while there is complementarity between Saying and Said in the ontological difference, this complementarity is characterised by a distortion and not a correlation, and this distortion relates to a nearer 'how' of the ontological Saying. The process of deconstructing the ontological difference, in pointing towards the near, never claims to detach itself completely from the process of unfolding actuality – that is the verbality.

78. By insisting on the separation of the ethical process from the ontological, although he claims to be clinging to some notion of complementarity with the ontological, Levinas creates an autonomous exterior horizon of Saying which is detached from the dynamics of *alētheia* thus allegedly transcending the verbality of language. I say '*claims to be* clinging' to some complementarity because it is actually impossible to overcome the distance between the ontic and the ontological, and what Levinas attempts is to deflect us away from this distance into the ontic complementarity which is *otherwise than ontology*. Again, I say 'attempts' because even this attempt is itself on the way of *alētheia*.

79. Levinas's attempt to establish an even deeper Saying than the Saying of the ontological difference is detachment dressed up as complementarity. Such detachment from the unfolding of nearness replaces that unfolding with a radical, punctual and paradoxical notion of proximity between beings. Levinas's language entrenches the ontic by his violent separation that retains 'separate beings'.

80. Levinas's view of language is in the twilight of the ontic and thus itself 'on the way to language'. This unfolding of language is at the heart of the claim that the otherness of the Other points towards the mystery in a way that Levinas does not overcome. Otherness must somehow imply a togetherness of dwelling in language, indicating at its saying. This otherness is very different from claiming that language could generate an ethical Saying from and towards a 'not-yet-conceptualised Other'.

---

[42] J Llewelyn, 'Levinas and Language', in S Critchley and R Bernasconi (eds) *The Cambridge Companion to Levinas* (Cambridge, Cambridge University Press, 2002) pp 119–38, at pp 125–7, 134. See also A Peperzak, *Beyond*,above n 36, pp 58–60.

81. Heidegger understood intentionality as pointing, indicating, and in doing that, signifying. Intentionality that is 'mine', that can come about in *overcoming subjectivity*, is the mystery. To claim that such 'mineness' is incompatible with original sociality[43] is still to play into the hand of the embedded ontic instinct of understanding sociality as something between subjects. Doing that is precisely to forget the origin of 'dwelling amongst' other *Dasein*s, detaching thought from such dwelling. *Would not such dwelling be the most original characterisation of the notion of nearness to another human Being?* 'Mineness', which dwells amongst all other 'mine's, in the silence of response to the call the Saying of Being, in pointing, is very different from the radical ontic alterity, proximity and substitution between subjects and the language of the 'not yet' that such radicalised ontic sociality generates. *Transcending intentionality, transcending pointing, reducing them to a mere radical 'not-yet-conceptualised Other' is unethical in being detached.* Intentionality that stems from language and not from an ego is intentionality that is antecedent to any proximity that seemingly overcomes intentionality.[44]

82. Peperzak argues that in addressing myself to the Other as the characterisation of the ethical relations, the Other is not an object of intentionality; in this sense it is more than intentional communication but still it is an address to somebody who is completely other than myself. Speaking to another, addressing an Other, is not capture by the language of Being. Also Heidegger's *being-with* does not yet account for the addressing nature of Saying, does not account for the ethical contact.[45] But if, for example, we think of a poem as a call or as a form of addressing, what in another humans does the poem address? It addresses not just 'another human being'. It address the very dynamics of the 'how' in which this human being dwells, it addresses his own innermost thing and this embodies, as we shall see in chapters eight and nine, the primordial origin of his otherness.

83. Should we, then, be surprised that Levinas denies that language is in essence poetry?[46] It is true that the 'human Other breaks into the House of Being like a thief'.[47] But what is that which is stolen? What

---

43 J Llewelyn, 'Levinas and Language', above n 42, p 123.

44 Levinas distinguishes proximity from intentionality in *LP*, p 125.

45 Peperzak, *Beyond*, above n 36, pp 60–66. Cf *IOF*, pp 4–7.

46 E Wyschogorod, 'From Ethics to Language: The imperative of the Other', (1993) 97 *Semiotica* 163–76 at 167. Wyschogorod characterises the address to the Other as interruption in time, a trace. The noun-verbs of Heidegger come to cover up what is actually synchronous time (*ibid*, p 168). But is not an address to the otherness of the Other in poetic language, the meeting of 'hows' in mystery, the very possibility of the ontically based diachrony presented as address to a 'not-yet-conceptualised Other?'

47 J Llewelyn, 'Levinas and Language', above n 42, p 124, referring to *Otherwise than Being*, p 13.

is stolen in order to be hidden and forgotten is original sociality of dwelling together, only to be represented distortingly as the ethics that everyone expects, with the potential of ethical language that everyone accepts. Indeed, Levinasian ethics can be accused of stealing and burying the insight, the secret, the mystery, which is nearest to humanity.

84. In *Language and Proximity* Levinas maintains that 'proximity is *by itself* a signification'.[48] Ethics is subjectivity 'that enters *into contact* with a singularity, excluding identification in the ideal, excluding thematization and representation – an absolute singularity, as such unrepresentable. This is the original language, the foundation of the other one.'[49] Language, as signifying from the Other, is original language that goes beyond consciousness, understanding, thematisation and representation. Crucially, the language of alterity goes beyond, is exterior to, any discourse which harbours some commerce of otherness, that is for some a way to essence which assimilates alterity, however faintly. Proximity means radical disinterestedness and with it non-indifference or, as Levinas puts it, a relationship which is completely non-allergic to the Other. In any assimilating discourse, such radical proximity and exteriority appear as a trace. What Levinas opens up for ethical Saying is the trace of the 'not-yet-conceptualised Other'. But does not the surplus of the 'not-yet-conceptualised' already encapsulate and anticipate radical reconceptualisation? Is there no relationship between radical punctuation and the craving for radical reconceptualisation here?

85. *The otherness that is implied in ethical proximity is not the otherness that is implied in ontological nearness.* Proximity signifies the trace of alterity of the face of the Other, the proximity achieved from a distance which is beyond the totalising act of interpretation, and so prior to understanding and rectitude. Proximity yields an ethical command which precedes any interpretation. In ontological nearness, however, the dimension of distance between beings, their radical alterity, is just a point of departure on the way to the continuous near, or 'howness', which is *Dasein*'s own. Distance between beings is already given an interpretation and is on the way to interpretation. Distance between beings is still distant from the continuous near and thus only pre-interpretative.

86. The relationship of alterity to nearness, as we shall see in chapters eight and nine, is very different from that of ontic proximity-in-alterity. Alterity that is embedded in nearness connotes an interpretative comportment of beings towards the continuous which has

[48] *LP*, p 116.
[49] *Ibid.*

no outside and in which they all mysteriously dwell. Proximity is intimacy with Otherness which claims alterity to punctuate not the continuous but beyond the domination of the continuous. *Proximity-as-alterity is a trace of detachment. Its distance is that of detachment from the continuous.* Proximity sees the continuous as violent. As far as language is concerned, the continuous sees the proximate as violent detachment from the word which is not yet violent to the word. In a certain sense, one that Levinas latches on to, no nearness can seemingly be as radical as proximity. Indeed, in ontic thinking this is certainly the case. But from an ontological perspective, proximity is not-yet-nearing the continuous, a continuous whose otherness and strangeness connote neither sameness/totality nor radical ontic alterity.

87. *Language is a mystery. The mystery conceals its concealment as it reveals. Could it be that the prime concealment effectuated by the mystery shows itself as the trace of proximity? Has proximity neared yet the otherness of the continuous nearest? Better, is not proximity-in-alterity always already the belated response to the call of the continuous near? Is not proximity itself on the way to language?*

88. In 'Language and Proximity' Levinas claims that the sign is 'not yet language': 'The trace in which a face is ordered is not reducible to a sign for the simple reason that a sign and its relationship with the signified are already thematized.'[50] But human beings as signs are never outside a sign. The sign as a pointer is a signification anterior to the signification that forgets (that is, signification colonised by representation and logic), anterior even to the hesitant signification that responds. The sign is capable of nearing the continuous without generating any 'outside' to it.

89. *Can we not see the ontic connection between the transcendence of punctuating proximity and the entrenchment of the ontic language of beings, namely that of representation? Is it not the case that detachment from language, precisely because of its arrogant detachment, retains humans in the prison of representation without them being aware of it? Is not the passivity of proximity the enemy of all humbleness? How could such arrogance of detachment, which is dressed up as passivity, not be an infinite source of resentment?*

90. In the section on 'Dwelling' in *Totality and Infinity*, Levinas, unlike Heidegger, represents his idea of language without allowing any space for his text to be written by language as it unfolds: 'The calling in question of the I, coextensive with the manifestation of the Other in the face, we call language.'[51] For Levinas, the site of dwelling is

---

[50] *Ibid*, p 124.
[51] *TI*, p 171.

that ethical surplus of infinite deferral, postponement of the not-yet of conceptualisation of the Other. Levinas *defines* language, and hence puts language on a way, rather than making language itself a way. Language is being put on the path of ontic alterity rather than on the path of self-unfolding. Does not proximity and its deep Saying imply a certain *kind* of language? More specifically, is not the separation that Levinas's transcendence radicalises a 'language of beings', ontic language, in a way that makes such transcendence look beyond language? Peperzak maintains that 'If language primarily is not an anonymous condition or source of Saying, but Saying itself, a signature is a gesture by which writers signal their responsibility for possible readers.'[52] But I have tried to emphasise the fact that, for Heidegger, there is no 'source' of Saying. *There is literally nothing beyond Saying.* Being is not a condition of Saying but it is the very unfolding of Saying, and the human *Dasein* unfolds as a pointer toward that Saying. If anything, it is Levinas who subjects language to a 'condition' that is a punctuating and detached notion of proximity and this is precisely what keeps his oeuvre in the ontic horizon. For Heidegger, humans dwell in language and language necessarily instantiates its own deferral. There is no outside to the hermeneutic cycle, no world which is anterior to it. Language for Heidegger is the impossible Saying of the nearest and inexpressible. Levinas makes language a tool, the medium of sensibility that responds to the face of a 'not-yet-conceptualised Other'.

91.   But it is important that the notion of deferral in Heidegger which stems from language is distorted by Levinas into an ontic deferral. The inexpressible continuous in language is paraphrased into a 'not-yet-conceptualised Other'. Both Levinas and Heidegger are beyond the notion of dialogue, communication, representation and totality. Both are in transcendence. But Levinas's radicalisation of the otherness of thinking-Being is possible only in caricaturising the notion of nearness, that is, presenting it ontically as totalising allergy.

92.   Llewelyn argues that Levinas provides an additional linguistic possession 'by others' to ontology, which clings to the linguistic possession 'with others'.[53] But I argue that detached punctuation of the proximity that is implied by the surplus possession 'by others' may well not yet be, or may still be, on the way to the 'with' of nearness. Being 'with others', sociality, as a pointer of fundamental ontology is different from any being 'with other beings' in the same, or totality, of a more derivative ontology or indeed from being possessed by others. both of which are still locked in an ontic cycle.

[52] Peperzak, *Beyond*, above n 36, p 69
[53] J Llewelyn, 'Levinas and Language', above n 42, p 123.

93. The mystery of the face in Levinas is not as mysterious as it seems. It is not so ambiguous or enigmatic, as Llewelyn puts it.[54] The mystery, if there is one, of Levinas's infinite transcendence feels forced because what can be mysterious in radical punctuation? Is not punctuation the enemy of mystery?

94. The peculiar thing in Levinas, the pretence, is that through detachment and punctuation language seems to radicalise itself, seems to impose upon itself the silence of punctuation, while in fact it is arrogantly pushed to encircle itself in deafness to its own continuous essence. Its openings, its movements, shut beings off from their Being, do not allow beings to experience their 'there' – the abyss – the temporal horizon of their Being.

95. Levinas tames the mystery of the continuous into some allergy that restrains otherness. That may be true. But the restraint of ontic otherness does not yield to sameness. Only in ontic thinking can it so simplistically yield. The vulnerable and valuable Saying of language is shattered into pieces with the reassurance of the decodable – with the coming home and the ontic desire to think and do good that Levinas's account nourishes.

96. Levinas gives us the most radical meaning of being a 'subject', namely to be subjugated to ontic thinking whereby the impossible transcendence of the 'beyond' of ontic transcendence leaves you hanging in the air, beyond language, beyond historicity, beyond the call of the actuality of the actual. To be a subject in its deepest ethical sense of proximity is to be detached. Otherness of an Other connotes punctuation and detachment: 'The Saying is not from the first held in the structure of subject–object, signifier–signified, saying–said correlation. A sign given to the other, it is sincerity or veracity, with which glory is glorified.'[55] The holy, in Levinas, is the language of the beyond. The holy would be tyrannical in as much as it throws the subject back into the ontic, entrenches the subject through radicalisation of the ontic, leading the subject into the endless exploration of that punctuation-begotten trace of the relationship with an 'Other'.

97. I have argued that deconstruction can occur, albeit in too limited a fashion, within the ontic cycle that Levinas perpetuates between the ethical Saying of proximity to an 'Other' and any saying that correlates with an ontological Said. Levinas is right to claim that the thrust of the ethics of deconstruction is indeed an ethical Saying that relates to otherness, one which is not reducible to the Said. But the 'Said' in this would include the ontically based ethical Saying that is

---

[54] *Ibid*, p 136.
[55] *OB*, p 148.

both detached and complementary, as a trace, to the [derivative] ontological Said. It is Levinas's 'ethical Saying' which should be deconstructed as ontic in relation to the otherness which is both prior to it as its origin – otherness which cannot be reduced to totality, allergy – and which is shrouded in mystery and strangeness. Such a deconstruction is the ingratitude with which Levinas ought to be read. The ethical, deconstructive challenge according to Levinas is to deconstruct ontically based otherness, exposing its origin in the continuous, thus displacing Levinas's main insights, about responsibility, about obligation.

98. Levinas is, of course, right in identifying otherness as the 'site' of ethics. He was also right in identifying obligations and responsibility to otherness as the central features of ethics. But, and this is crucial, he never faces the origin of otherness because he caricatures a distinction between otherness and nothingness. By speaking about responsibility for a being that is Other than any representation of that Other in me, he already does not ask the question concerning otherness. Punctuation and detachment do not yet face the mystery of otherness.

99. Levinas's notion of the trace of the Saying in the Said transcends the notion of correctness while retaining a horizon of correctness. Punctuated transcendence is under the dominance of correctness. That which is given to correctness as its continuous origin is not faced, and the notion of otherness in it is not attended to charitably by Levinas.

100. Could we not argue that it is Levinas who calls for alterity which is itself, from the point of view of ontology, within the ontic 'same' – that is the sameness of a derivative ontology? What is primordial otherness? What is the origin of the otherness of the Other? Does merely asking a question of the origin of otherness imply an interpretation that will assimilate otherness into totalising interpretation? Is not primordial otherness the 'not' that exists between Being and its ontic occurrences? Does not the perpetuation of ontic cycles, without attending to this 'not', pretending to be 'otherwise than that "not"', actually *forgets* the origin of alterity as dwelling together on the way to language? How does the otherness of face of the Other originate? How does facing the face of the Other manifest? Should we not magnify further that which Levinas designates as 'otherwise than being' for the sake of facing the origin of the otherness of Other? Is not the transcending of the mystery of otherness as nearness by subjecting language to the detachment and punctuation of proximity the best assurance of not facing that mystery? How does the mystery call upon us amidst such colossal denial?

RESPONSIBILITY

101. It is the notion of responsibility, for Levinas, that marks the point of departure from the totalising game of ontology. Responsibility of proximity to the Other is not the same as responsibility to the Other as a fellow-dweller in nearness to the actuality of the actual. For sure, to respond to Being is not the same as to respond to an ontic duty or to be capable of bearing such a duty. 'Response-ability' to the Other is complementary to the 'response-ability' to the otherness that comes about by dwelling in the continuous near, the nothing, but how is that complementarity to be conceived? We must ask: *How come we have such a craving for ontic responsibility? How come such a craving has not yet been called into question?* Is not an ability to respond to the origin of the otherness of the Other a categorical imperative which is antecedent to, and more original than, that imperative which calls for the approximation of 'an Other' as a being? Is it not precisely in tranquillising moral reflection into ontic transcendence that the categorical imperative is robbed of its sublime nature, of its universality? Is punctuation of an Other at the heart of responding to the call of the imperative?

102. The ethical 'beyond' originates in a trace of responsibility for the Other.[56] The face-to-face encounter with the Other is that encounter which is original and ubiquitous yet feminine and destitute, beyond my will, beyond any ego which thinks it, beyond interpretation and rectitude. But only ontic thinking can have the arrogance of claiming to go beyond interpretation. What Levinas calls passivity releases us from selfish assimilation of the Other and gives us the illusion of ethical growth, of transcendence, of being beyond ego-based thought. This Levinasian passivity is sanctimonious in its gentleness. It is not yet humble before actuality. To be humble is not the same as being passive. Are passive/active primordial characteristics of responsibility? Passive/active are themselves ontic oppositions which fit very well with the ontic notion of proximity and substitution.

103. Despite the 'beyond' of the Saying in relation to the Said there is a common matrix between the Saying and the Said. This common matrix is presented as complementarity of reduction. The Saying, despite its 'beyondness' is, reductively and distortingly of course, in the Said. Levinas says: 'In correlation with the said (in which saying runs the risk of being absorbed as soon as the said is formulated), the saying itself is indeed thematized, exposes in essence even what is on the *hither side of ontology*, and flows into the temporalisation of

[56] *OB*, p 100.

essence.'[57] The Said never exhausts the Saying. *The common matrix is the ontic thinking in which responsibility that is encapsulated in the ethical Saying is reduced in the Said.* The relationship between the Said and the Saying is indeed dynamic and *ontically* radical, but it is a dynamism which does not yet call for, nor does it yet respond to the call of, a different kind of approach to thinking, language and truth. The signification of the Saying as proximity can only call for a punctuable response, and it nourishes a closure of ontic, punctuable 'response-ability'.

104. Does not the language of values, rights and duties presume responsibility that is encapsulated in punctuable transcendence?

105. 'Proximity as a suppression of distance suppresses the distance of consciousness of ... involves, opens the distance of a diachrony without a common present ... This difference is my non-indifference to the other.'[58] But the distance of diachrony that is opened up by proximity still foresees 'an Other-in-relation-to-me' as a punctuable origin of responsibility.

106. Levinas questions ontology's supremacy by claiming that ontology does not yet discriminate what is the original goodness of the Good, and he asks: 'How could one understand the *conatus* of being in the goodness of the Good?'. The signification of goodness cannot be attended to by what Levinas refers to as 'ontological finality'.[59] But it is precisely in meditating upon goodness as the dimension of responsibility that the displacement of the opposition of ethics and ontology can take place. This is so because with fundamental ontology the Being of goodness also changes with such displacement. Fundamental ontology displaces the term 'good' to connote authentic 'ek-sistence' rather than any primordial moral obligation that is otherwise to the (derivative) ontology of existence. The Saying that responds to the question of 'What is my responsibility, obligation, duty to my Other, proximate, neighbour?' may not yet be responding to the first question of the Good.

107. The argument in this chapter may be subject to the criticism that it reduces everything for the sake of uniformity. Accounting for ethics in ontological terms can be successfully carried out, but only at the price of a distortion of what ethics is about. As Reed puts it, Levinas's question is not a 'how' and 'why' question as to 'why there is being rather than nothing', but rather a totally different question, 'Have I the right to be?', which is a justification question, a question of rights and duties.[60] According to this criticism, ethics is never

[57] *Ibid*, p 46.
[58] *Ibid*, p 89.
[59] *Ibid*, p 95.
[60] CW Reed, 'Levinas' Question', above n 3, pp 80–81.

reducible to ontology, and so I reduce plurality in philosophy to some logocentric account of what philosophy should be about. The criticism is that I am trying to coerce the ethical into the ontological where, in candour, it has no place. My provisional reply at this stage is that all I do is meditate upon the complementarity between ethics and ontology, namely that we have to overcome ontological philosophy in order to be ethical.

108. One of the insights that we must draw from this chapter is that what is presented in *Otherwise than Being* as a subtle complementarity between Saying and Said, a complementarity that encapsulates genuine and punctual exteriority, alterity and proximity, is not complementarity at all but a common ontic matrix. The alterity that it contains is not yet genuine alterity. Such genuine alterity would be a genuine complementarity of distortion between the punctual and the continuous.

109. *The otherness of the Other originates on the way to something which is given to another being. This being, as other, dwells in the otherness of the nothing – the otherness of the continuous near. Levinas's notion of otherness is still impoverished and does not yet near what was given to it – its origin in the mystery of otherness.*

110. Let us contemplatively conclude this chapter and prepare for what is to come. Levinas distinguishes punctual and detached proximity from continuous nearness. *Qua* transcendence, he also conceives the ethical Saying of otherness that is encapsulated in proximity as primordial, yet complementary, to otherness that is encapsulated in ontological Saying – in thinking-Being. Approximating the other as Other is 'otherwise than', viewing the other merely as a thinker of Being, that is as a responder to the call of Being. In other words, the ethical Saying of proximity connotes a primordial notion of other-ness that is complementary to the ethical Saying that stems from a merely ontological notion of otherness – an ontological Said. Both the ethics of proximity and nearness involve otherness but the otherness of nearness is always a reduction and distortion of proximity, involving the entwining of the same and the other on the way to essence, invoking interpretation and with it, totality.

111. For Levinas, the punctual is more primordial than the continuous. Diachrony is more primordial than synchrony. The radicality of silence that characterises the interval of punctuation is more primordial than the silence that is associated with the murmur of the continuous near. Detachment from the continuous characterises the punctual that is seemingly only complementary to the continuous.

112. The argument of this chapter is that Levinas takes ontic thinking to its ultimate conclusion by producing a *transcendence* that transcends any representation and thematisation while getting its ethical impetus

from the preservation of the ontic domain of reflection, namely punctuation and detachment. In terms of thinking, as well as the notion of truth, Levinas's diachronious trace is conditioned by ontic synchrony with the derivative ontology within which it lurks. This conditioning is being concealed as a transcendence of ontology. The argument then continues that such ontic transcendence is otherwise to thinking-Being, but the complementarity is such that the very transcendence is on the way to thinking-Being. Levinas confuses the relationship of near/far that persists between the ontic and the ontological, between the punctual and the continuous, with interpretation, totality and sameness. Otherness that for thinking-Being is the manifestation of the comportment towards essence, that is otherness that persists between the continuous and the punctual, is said not to be genuine. It is here, in the inability to bear the mystery; in reducing the mystery to a complementarity that harbours radical punctuation, in the violence of this inability to bear original manifestation of alterity by insisting that otherness is *opposed* to sameness, that we can find perhaps the best, and deepest, clue to the ontic logic that pervades the Levinasian transcendence.

113. Levinas's transcendence overcomes any totality and, as such, seems to be the most post-metaphysical transcendence. It claims that ontology is residually metaphysical. But the origin of Levinas's transcendence, at the punctuation of the same/other, despite the immediate impression of radicality and 'non-allergy' between different beings, does retain echoes of metaphysics. Of course, it is more radical than the metaphysics of transcendental phenomenology. However, by not being able to bear the otherness of the continuous near, by reducing the otherness of the continuous to sameness, by locating otherness in punctuation, thinking along an 'Other' is already distanced from otherness at the very moment of punctuation. The radical notion of proximity and non-indifference to the Other is not yet facing otherness. The metaphysics of 'the Other' is a victim of its own attempt to arrogantly claim the possibility of separation and exteriority. The somewhat tragic nature of Levinas is that by being the ultimate Other to metaphysics it retains metaphysics, or rather, it retains a horizon of punctuating the 'metaphysics of metaphysics'. It is important to see that the critical power of the metaphysics of the ultimate Other is both detached and oppressive in claiming the ability to hold the key to the outside. Being committed to such a radical exteriority, Levinas is committed to a critical horizon that replaces punctuation critically rather than humbly opening up and seeing nearer than punctual thought itself. Only an ultimate Other can advocate otherness as a meta-punctuation in the manner Levinas did. No human can punctuate radically enough.

114. It is Levinas, I argue, who, by his inability to bear the mystery of otherness, by his radicalisation of otherness to a degree of exteriority, entrenches an ontic totality, claiming that humans can undergo the epiphany of godly power that consists of separation and distinction. Levinas, passive and sanctimonious both in substance and tone, is in fact the entrencher of totality, holding humans hostage by taming their attentiveness to ontic co-ordinates. They drown in the arrogance of thinking that they transcend any essence of themselves in the name of otherness, while in fact becoming the guardians of ontic thinking that craves for not-yet-conceptualised separation. Human attentiveness to the continuous, their essence, is buried within the infinite abyss of punctuation. This burial is important for thinking about law. As the next chapter shows, Levinas transcends any law but maintains the legal. Levinas robs humans of their ability to think about their innermost essence in 'ek-sistence' and in doing so assures the dominance of the legal. But, as humans are sure to discover, Levinas's transcendence is itself a manifestation of humans' essential error as essentially 'ek-sistents'. Humans are always protected by the essence of law even in the midst of being tranquillised so as not to hear the call of Being.

115. The ethics of the mystery, indeed the mystery of otherness, calls upon us to think of otherness without immediately suffering the paralysing worry that by grasping the mysterious nature of it, we give it up. Levinas deflects humans away from the depth and the mystery and the otherness of the continuous by relegating any dwelling together in the continuous as tainted with totality. I use the strong verb 'deflect' to connote that what Levinas does, although itself a distortion of that mystery, also operates to conceal this distortion by presenting ontic transcendence as something which is otherwise than the whole dimension of ontological transcendence. Levinas seems to transcend the whole ontologically based tradition. The pervasive success of the infiltration of his thinking shows precisely why the mystery holds sway. Humans think that they have found, in the horizon of separation and punctuation, the Holy Grail of otherness. The mystery seems to be successfully concealing the fact that it conceals as it reveals. Indeed, it is difficult to come by radicalisation of responsibility that will be leading to such entrenchment of ontic logic of legalism and irresponsibility. Being can only speak violently amidst the hegemony of punctuable, and, as we shall see, legal, transcendence. Indeed, the preservation of the legal is evident in Levinas, as we shall see in the next chapter. The separation of ethics from thinking-Being has implications for the way complementarity is viewed between, on the one hand, separating external representations

of harm to actuality, and thinking the actuality of the actual of harm (or harm to the actuality of the actual), on the other.

116. I end this chapter by providing a few thoughts preluding the arguments to come in chapters eight and nine. This book about law is turning out to be a meditation on ethics and on otherness. But the meditation of otherness itself, as a meditation upon the origin of legalism, is dependent on interpreting the relationship between the continuous and the punctual. How are we to characterise the complementarity between them? We are now echoing the questions that we advanced at the end of chapter five. Levinas sees the ethical Saying as an incision where language stops to listen to its own cyclical Said. For Levinas, language signifies ethically only when punctuating itself, and thus stops interpreting its slippery, elusive, and totalising, cyclical signification. In Levinas, language does not murmur nearness but really subjugates itself to silence. Language imposes silence on itself in order to reach the silence of the ultimate punctuation. The face of the Other has as its gaze a master-punctuation which opens up the horizon of genuine punctuability not yet conceived. Levinas's silence consists in facing the totality of ontology thus going even beyond the surplus of otherness of any Saying of Being. Ethical saying thus signifies in the silence that arises out of the poverty of all significations dependent on the signifier/signified.

117. As at the end of chapter five, let us resort to Derrida, this time in the context of the continuous and the punctual. In 'At This Very Moment In This Work Here I Am', Derrida provides an account of the trace which supplements Levinas's.[61] The problem with Derrida's account is that it can be read as making Levinas's account dependent on the Heideggerian notion of the primordial continuous, while at the same time he seems to condone the notion of the trace that can be otherwise than, and separate from, thinking-Being. Derrida meditates deeply on the relationship between punctual and the continuous. Like Levinas, Derrida accounts for the trace of the ethical Saying as an interruption of language that at the same moment makes language possible. Derrida maintains that the interruptions themselves, rather than the interrelated 'saids' of language, constitute a series of erasures – what Derrida refers to as 'dia-synchrony'. An interruption, *qua* trace, involves two simultaneous moments. An interruption simultaneously triggers both a tearing apart of the coherence of woven knots of the 'saids' of language *and*

---

[61] J Derrida, 'At This Very Moment In This Work Here I Am', above n 37, pp 24–30, 36–40. An excellent summary of Derrida's account is given by K Ziarek, *Inflected Langage: Toward A Hermeneutic of Nearness: Heidegger, Levinas, Stevens, Celan* (Albany, State University of New York Press, 1994) pp 94–102.

an inevitable re-weaving into language. But the reconnection does not imply the simple restoration of language. The interruption, the tearing of the mesh of language, already displaces its gaps, already re-weaving new gaps/new interruptions. A continuous series is manifested not of positive knots but out of interruptions/gaps beneath the series of knots. This series constantly constitutes the surplus of tracing. The trace has a surplus over the said and can never be eliminated by returning into language. In such a serial movement of interruptions, the trace recreates its own birth and, crucially for the distinction from thinking-Being, always remain exterior. The trace traces, that is exceeds, its own inevitable manifestation as tracing. Its exteriority is its being [dis]located beyond displacing knots. To this extent, the trace always remains Other, exterior, to tracing. A trace is not a singular event but always on the way of tracing, or what Derrida refers to as 'letting-the-trace' [*l'entr'élacement*]. The seriality of tracing means that the trace remains a surplus to the economy of the sign and the 'letting' of it is otherwise than 'letting Being be'. The latter characterises already some contamination of that trace of exteriority to these series of interruptions. The letting-the-trace, then, constitutes a separation or, a 'dislocation without return' which is otherwise than a movement in the horizon of Being, or Saying, other than the Said. The continuity of letting Being be contaminates, and is always preceded by, the continuity of letting the Otherness of the trace manifest itself in the tracing.

118. It is difficult to say whether or not Derrida succeeds in providing an account of a continuous punctuating trace that claims the primordiality of the continuous Being. On the one hand it seems that the movement that Derrida describes is quite similar to the tracing of the near in the far that characterises thinking-Being. The 'Other' here would not be absolute but rather a movement of nearing. An undiminished surplus does not yet turn the trace into an 'Other'. On the other hand, Derrida seems to explain the possibility of Levinasian separation as a 'continuous of punctuation' that necessitaties a 'separate' Other, an exterior 'segment'. On this view, Derrida becomes complicit in seeing the interruption of language as a 'gap' in punctuation rather than an inexpressible continuous mystery of nearness. Derrida refers to '"contamination" between ontological récit and the Relation of responsibility for the Other'.[62] He also characterises the trace as the between the 'the' of the *beyond language* [my emphasis], and as the 'the of the economic immanence of language'.[63]

[62] J Derrida, 'At This Very Moment ...', above n 37, p 26.
[63] *Ibid*, p 38.

119. Making the gap in punctuation into a continuous series that constantly yields an 'Other' is still a punctuation. It is still committed to the separation of proximity rather than to the continuity of nearness. In this respect, Ziarek, who describes so carefully and thoughtfully the relationship between Derrida and Levinas in *Inflected Language*, does not yet ask the following Heideggerian questions: Is not the radical continuity of punctuation itself traced by a preceding saying of the mysterious continuous near? Does not the very notion of a 'series of ...', even that of gaps, presume ontic punctuation –cycles of birth and death, a *samsara*[64] of punctuation? Is a series of punctuation not itself a part of the error in which thinking inevitably distances itself from the unbounded? Finally, is not the poetic mysterious 'no outside' of unbounded nearness primordial to any vocabulary (even methodology) of series, interruptions, gaps, tears, incisions, exteriorities, beyonds, separations, even, arguably, contaminations, that characterise both Levinas's account and its Derridian enhancement? The gentleness of the complementarity of ontic deconstruction is not yet the calm radicality of the hermeneutics of nearness. The trace of the hermeneutics of nearness is nearer than any series of 'contact without contact, in proximity'.[65] The possibility of language as the hesitant 'perhaps'/'possible' of gapping and tearing that characterises Levinas and Derrida, is not yet the 'perhaps' and 'possible' of the Saying of nearing. Language traces from the nearest and that is its hermeneutic inside.

120. Continuous and punctual. Sameness and other. Silence. *The entrenchment of the legal is in viewing transcendent punctuability as primordial to the continuous.* However, this book is called '*In Silence with Heidegger*' because it claims that it is in attending to the continuous in the face of the punctual, and even more so, in the face of the entrenchment of the punctual, that thinking finds its silent moment of calling upon us to think and to respond. In such silence *all* punctuation is derivative – a movement in the unbounded. In such silence, all radicalisation of an 'Other' melts into the mysterious and ubiquitous wheel of Being. Silence responds to the call of the mystery. Silence finds its origin in the distance of the punctual from the continuous, that is, not yet in the gap of radical punctuated separation. The grasping of error in the silence of the continuous involves a momentary grasping of the necessary distortion that accrues to temporal unbounded 'ek-stasis' in attempting to make sense of it. Silence is then responsibility to the continuous and not to

---

[64] *Samsara* is the Buddhist notion of the cycle of birth and death, which is transcended by *Nirvana*.
[65] J Derrida., 'At This Very Moment ...', above n 37, p 29.

the punctual. Only a response to the continuous connotes a response to the mystery of otherness. Only such a response can be ethical.

121. Let us look broadly at punctuation. To punctuate is to create a beginning and an end. The craving to punctuate is the craving to create beginnings and ends. Punctuation seems to create the basis for *difference* between beings through the illusion of separation. Something ends; something begins. Punctuation, as the creation of beginnings and ends, is also an attempt to cut off a flow, approaching the flow with a knife. Separation creates an incision by cutting the flow into segments.

122. Punctuation can be seen as under the spell of totality. As such, the beginnings and ends differentiate themselves in relation to one another. The totality gives sense of this differentiation. That which gives sense to the differentiation is itself punctual and hence total. It has a beginning and end – hence the totality. Those who punctuate are negotiating and renegotiating their identity which persists as identification with the totality. They do not yet transcend totality.

123. It is in the way we characterise a primordial transcendence that we can have different views of the relationship between the continuous and the punctual. Levinas's transcendence sees the interpretation of the continuous as a mark of endless mutual negotiation of totality. The talk of totality that is similar to the continuous is itself a big punctuation. This big punctuation creates a punctuating opening to an 'outside'. The continuous is caricaturised as a totality and then constantly forgotten by creating a chain of infinite punctuations of totality and its transcendence. This punctuating and punctuable transcendence, by constantly reducing the continuous into totality and sameness creates a chain of infinite ontic differentiations – infinite punctuation. The reduction of the continuous into totality, however, is a mark of the calm oppression of the continuous that results in forcing a characteristic of simple essence which consists of beginning and end onto something which does not have a beginning and end. In this sense of reduction, the continuous is punctuated and is forgotten. *Any attempt to create complementarity between the punctuating of an outside and interpretation under totality does not attend any more to the unbounded continuous which is antecedent and given to any act of punctuation.* The persistence of infinite punctuation gains its persistence and potency from the gaps – the 'outsides' of totality.

124. The second way to view the relationship between the continuous and the punctual is to grasp that the continuous, being unbounded, cannot be reduced to totality – does not lose its unboundedness by its inevitable punctuation into totality. The continuous murmurs from within the most radical punctuation as something nearer to any

punctuation. Here, the punctuation does not force beginnings and ends. The call of the continuous never punctuates, never succumbs to the temptation. It is a flicker, a murmur, of the unbounded, from which every punctuation stems and into which everything returns. *The sea within which waves are distinguished is not viewed as a totality but the waves themselves are viewed as totality and the sea as unbounded.* Otherness is a mystery in that any punctuation still has its origin, essence, in the unbounded. Otherness to punctuation, not reducible to totality, is what characterises the mystery. Finite intellect punctuates. Such intellect cheats itself by thinking that it overcomes its finiteness by producing infinity of a yet more radical and ambitious punctuation. *Dasein's* grasp of its finiteness in the unbounded is not as arrogant as that.

125. The silence of the 'call of' and 'response to' the continuous murmurs from nearer than the derivative silence of punctuations. *The movement between the continuous and the punctual, revealing and concealing, is not itself a punctuation but a near/far movement.* Once essence is understood as the continuous unbounded, the very transcendence which reduces it to an allergy between beings – to a dominating totality of their self-interpretation – is grasped as a punctuation on its way to the near.

126. In this chapter I have claimed that Levinas's notion of otherness is not original but derivative. It cannot be otherwise than Being because it is in Being in a way which is not yet attentive to Being. Despite its radicality, it is still based on the punctuated notion of identity and difference founded on extantness. Difference of nearness is not the difference of proximity.

127. The legal and its entrenchment originate in the punctuation of the continuous. The punctuation that brings about the entrenchment of the legal comes to us as ethical transcendence. In transcending law by punctuation, the legal is entrenched. The entrenchment of the legal comes as a critical ethical challenge to being and thinking with and through law. But, as we shall argue, punctuation already anticipates punctuation. Because of that, anticipation punctuating transcendence is not yet ethical.

128. The essence of law, which calls us to thinking about the legal, is conceived as an aspect of the continuous.

7

Levinas's 'Ontic Logic': The Common Matrix between the Ethical, the Political and the Legal

1. The argument of chapters five and six was that the perpetuation of ontic thinking in the name of infinite responsibility which originates in punctuation creates a horizon of punctuability within which Levinasian transcendence operates. The implication of this punctuability is that there is a continuum, a common matrix, rather than a complementarity of distortion, between representation and representation-ability. Although representation is transcended, the nature of transcendence already anticipates the craving for further representation – a representation of a 'not-yet-conceptualised Other'. The ethics of the Other is representation-able and hence positively within the horizon of representation. The term 'representation-ability' must be distinguished from the ontic–ontological oscillation in which there is a genuine complementarity of distortion, indeed genuine alterity. Representations are a characteristic of the ontic. Between the ontic and the ontological there is an ethical effort which displaces the very horizon of ontic thinking. The ontological difference is a self-transformation of thinking, and this transformation constitutes the alterity that is involved in it. When language speaks it clears what is given to beings and surpasses one distortion only to fall back into another distortion. Between *Richtigkeit* and *alētheia* there is constant distortion. The attempt to articulate this distortion, to say the inexpressible, to force language to make an effort towards silence, is ethical.

2. Representation-ability is thus not the same as the relationship of near/far that characterises the ontic–ontological difference including the necessary fall into the 'far' which is for the most part 'near' to *Dasein*. As there is no possibility to attend to the Saying of Being from 'outside', thinking-nearness must start from the ontic and must always fall into it. In this sense, one could say that the ontic is anticipated in the ontological. But the distortion of the ontological in the ontic does not make the ontological representation-able.

3. To emphasise, the ethical attempt of near/far transcendence – the ontic–ontological oscillation – is not representation-able. The ontological is what it is beneath the ontic. There is no ontological without the ontic, but this does not mean that the complementarity between the ontological and the ontic is that the former always already anticipates the latter in the sense of 'anticipates' as 'being on the same horizon'. There is a genuine 'not' in the ontological difference. The distortion between thinking about beings and thinking their Being is a fundamental mutation within thinking itself. The ontological does not anticipate the ontic. Essentially the ontological stays inexpressible.

4. Representation-ability foresees, always already anticipates, representation. The word 'ability' here connotes both disposition and potential. As a critical platform, an ethical challenge is representation-able where there will be a disposition towards and anticipation of re-presenting in the same manner in which the transcendence originates, namely as a radical punctuation of a not-yet-conceptualised Other. Ontic radical transcendence that originates in punctuation retains the horizon of representation. In current representation there will always be privation, something that is not yet conceptualised, but not a distortion of the very thinking that is given to representation as its other. In ontic transcendence there is potential for representation in the challenge so that, despite remaining irreducible to any given representation, it would still contain all the necessary manner of thinking which will lead to a different representation. The way actuality is captured in the representation-able is already, in advance, the actuality of representation. In this sense, representation-able transcendence entrenches representations.

5. Being representation-able still means that a reflection can be pre-representation, but nevertheless be one which embodies the disposition and the positive potential to represent that characterises the non-conceptualised surplus. For pre-representational thinking to have a potential for representation, *Dasein* must be in an epoch that conditions its own critical reflection in a way which entrenches the ontic. In such an epoch, the ontological difference would be for *Dasein* to feel anxious in being ontically entrenched. In such an epoch the ontological difference would mean that *Dasein* would have to comport itself to asking the question regarding such entrenchment of the ontic. The ontological reflection is always nearer to the actual than the ontic. For *Dasein* to enter an epoch in which it becomes entrenched in the inauthentic hermeneutic cycle of ontic reflection, that is internalising the disposition to represent in a way which conditions any critical transcendence, the ontological effort to

displace this conditioned transcendence becomes very difficult and seemingly unnecessary. Disposition means that, for the most part, and in a seemingly obvious and unproblematic way, *Dasein* anticipates possibilities for itself in a way which is already conditioned by a kind of representational language. *Dasein*'s anticipation already dwells in punctuation and its vision is constrained by its relationship to an 'Other'. Even in the pre-representation stage of reflection, *Dasein* already looks for a way to punctuate the relationship to the Other, looking forward to the use of language that punctuates the Other, the language of segregation, marginalisation, as well as with the rights and duties language that is built into that horizon. The disposition to represent means that *Dasein*'s innermost ground is by and large silenced by a colonising ontic rationality.

6. Representation-ability characterises a punctuable account of transcendence. The characteristic of the epoch of representation-ability is, then, first the hegemony of the punctuable account of transcendence, and second, the silencing and de-legitimising of the primordial anxiety of *Dasein* – its 'ek-sistential' guilt and resolution. This guilt and resolution is substituted by fear and guilt towards an 'Other', with a sense of supreme duty which is beyond any given conceptualisation, yes, but is already embodying all the cravings for such conceptualisation. To point at an Other that resides in the gap of conceptualisation is to still remain in representation. The gap which is the totally 'other' to representation is the primordial source for re-representation. In genuine anxiety there is no face. A gaze of a face from the 'not' of the commerce of representations is not yet anxiety. Anxiety is such a burden that we should not be surprised that *Dasein* gives it up happily for a face of an Other. *Dasein* gives up its essence for what seems to be a very radical transcendence.

7. Note that by representation ability I do not mean something which is 'other' than the ontic–ontological reflection. Representation-ability is part and parcel of the complementarity that characterises ontic–ontological reflection. Representation-ability only extends the meaning of 'ontic' to include a radical transcendence. I only specify the historical situatedness of *Dasein* within such a reflection as being representation-able. By that I mean that the Saying of Being, its fate, is ontically manifested in an epoch in which the ontic is entrenched and reigns, and in which the call of Being become de-legitimised and weaker but more vivid and stronger all the same. The comfort of the entrenchment of the ontic reflection is always priced with a more tangible and intensive anxiety. The ontic gives rise to anxiety, and that is the way Being is in *Dasein*. But when the ontic is characterised in an epoch of ontic reassurance, namely that an ontic punctuable platform is the authentic route for critical exploration, this is when

anxiety becomes more debilitating as it is repressed. That which cannot be expressed, the inexpressible, becomes a much more intense manifestation of anxiety because of this enormous additional hindrance which prevents it from perturbing *Dasein*.

8.   From the ontic–ontological complementarity, representation-ability blocks the path to the free and open. Representation-ability already coerces the manner in which transcendence takes place and hence encloses representations away from the directionality of the effort towards the ontological, towards the continuous. An ontic ethical imperative which entrenches representation-ability is a kind of religion. It imprisons thinking in an ontic conception of the divine. The insight of letting Being be in an instance of freedom, an instance of getting nearer than the ontic, is prevented by a transcendence that goes beyond representation but which is disposed towards its own potential further representation. Such transcendence according to an ontic imperative takes thinking away from the actuality of the actual.

9.   In representation-ability the entrenchment of the ontic in both disposition and punctuability creates the illusion of *detached* transcendence. The entrenchment of the ontic, representation-ability is marked by a detaching reflection from any concrete dominance of interpretation, conceptualisation and thematisation. The radicalisation of alterity is the hallmark of the ontic imperative. The occurrence is not directed towards the nearest, the actual, but towards the 'beyond', a beyond which is then both in a common matrix with models, theory and methods (being representation-able) but at the same time detached from them all, being able truly to provide a phenomenological account of critical occurrence. Such 'beyond' is the perfect pretension for 'exploring', while the very exploration is heavily constrained by the anticipation of the representational nature of that which is to be found. The representation-able 'beyond' can appear to be vigorously against representation, thematisation, but in fact it encapsulates all disposition and potential for that which it condemns. As such, it is highly legalistic. If, then, there is a 'not' between representations and what transcends them, this 'not' is not alluded to by the 'about' of representation-able transcendence.

10. Thinking about law is to think thinking, namely to think that other that is strange to the ontic representation-able transcendence within which the legal is being entrenched.

11. What is the representation-ability in Levinas? Despite its radical 'beyond' there is a craving to anticipate the paraphrasing of some insights or clues into the representational language of values, rights and duties. This craving is to make the basis of responsibility already punctuable by capturing the nature of transcendence as being in

relation to an 'Other'. The conception of ethics as an infinite respon-sibility towards the Other already prepares the way for translation of that sensation into the legal representation of rights and duties that enforces some value-based ethics. Of course, the Other always surpasses representation of any kind in its ethical Saying. That is the nature of the beyond. So at the same time as displacing what Levinas regards as the ontological, impersonal language of law as the language of the *mitsein*, the ontological 'said' of being with, Levinas entrenches the legal and its representation-ability and, with it, the representational re-personification of the subject in the ethical. Being critical of law while in fact perpetuating the legal is *not being able to encounter the 'not' of the legal, to encounter the distortion of the essence of law in the legal.*

12.   Let us follow how representation-ability features in Levinas, both in *Totality and Infinity* and *Otherwise than Being*. In *Totality and Infinity* representation is discussed in relation to the ethical relations with the absolute Other, and in *Otherwise than Being* in relation to the relationship of the ethical Saying and the ontological Said.

13.   In *Totality and Infinity*, representation, for Levinas, amounts to a description by a self, of an 'other', but without facing the Other. Representation is articulation which is thematised under the imper-sonal control of totality, and as a result, under the control of consciousness that is constituted and persists, unchallenged, within that totality:

Intelligibility, the very occurrence of representation, is the possibility for the other to be determined by the same without determining the same, without introducing alterity into it; it is the free exercise of the same. It is the disap-pearance, within the same, of the I opposed to the non-I ... in [representation] the same is in relation with the other but in such a way that the other does not determine the same; it is always the same that determines the other. To be sure, representation is the seat of truth: the movement proper to truth consists in the thinker being determined by the object pre-sented to him. But it determines him without touching him, without weighing on him – such that the thinker who submits to what is thought does so 'gracefully', as though the object, even in the surprises it has in store for cognition, had been anticipated by the subject.[1]

14.   Here Levinas expresses very forcefully that ethical transcendence means to be passive, in the sense of letting go, allowing oneself to transcend the hegemony of representing consciousness, thus allowing the subject to be determined initially by the Other. Ethical *listening* to the Other is not the same as already *hearing* the Other through the

[1] *TI*, p 124.

consciousness of the Same. To be ethical is to let alterity 'weigh' on you. But the last sentence goes on and tells us something about how Levinas accounts for the persistence of subjectivity in this process. The 'grace' by which this process is articulated means that the subject does not annul itself in it, in what would amount to a vulgar description of the ethical experience. It belongs to the own projection, or anticipation, of the subject that the surprise brought about by the ethical encounter with the Other will be part and parcel of the post-encounter reconstitution of the subject. There is a movement of subject–Other–subject which goes on and on that has always been forecasted by the subject. The subject anticipates its temporary post-encounter reconstitution after alterity caresses. The subject anticipates surviving the transcendence of totality. The kind of conceptualisation which will accommodate such survival and which will support the reconstitution of a *good* subject is also anticipated. The surprise of alterity is conditioned by the anticipation of the kind of vocabulary that reconstitutes the subject and which continues to implement an infinite protection of the Other. This anticipation is what I regarded as the 'ability' which characterises the representation-ability of the non-representational ethical transcendence. The overflow of meaning, the surplus, that which representation attempts to expel, actually nourishes the anticipating subject. It nourishes the subject because that subject anticipates its reconstitution in the midst of the burden of total alterity. The anticipation for a decoded way of thinking makes the whole transcendence decodable, even if it is not yet expressed or conceptualised in any new articulation of the Other and his or her rights. Representation involves no passivity, says Levinas, and he is right. But the passivity of ethical transcendence is not passive either, it gives the illusion of a difficult passivity, but it is still within comforting active anticipation. The 'letting' involved here, then, is not authentic, as the enjoyment of an authentic letting involves no comfort of a horizon of decoding. Rather, authentic letting would follow the inevitable distorting fall into decoding. An involvement cannot be 'mine' if it already anticipates the reconstitution of subjectivity.

15. *A categorical imperative is pure, and it is pure of anticipation of subjectivity, punctuation and representation-ability. To treat the Other as an end is to attend to the origin of otherness rather than merely radicalise the ontic gap of otherness.* Only by encountering the continuous can the imperative become pure and with it become an essential universal moral law – a universal sublime grasp of the essence of law – nearer to any code or representation but also to ontic representation-able transcendence. Only then does the good converge with the morally right. But such an inexpressible

imperative, one that Kantian formulations only hint at, is shrouded by silence rather than by continued ignorance, which facilitates the thirst for continuous representation through representation-ability.

16. The enjoyment of being ethical is always an enjoyment which is linked, quite obsessively, with desire, which is nothing but the call of Being engendered in me as that which is inexpressible but nevertheless innermost mine. It is not enjoyment in anticipation of the entrenchment of the infinite perpetuation of the domain of representation which still clings to positive enjoyment – one which does not allow the enjoyment of the inexpressible to show up. The enjoyment encapsulated in the representation-able, which marks the infinite desire from ontic alterity to re-represent, to re-map the world as that which keeps producing infinite Others, is on a common matrix with the pleasure of need which characterises that very totality that it transcends. Desire for an Other is not yet primordial.

17. Levinas contrasts representation which reduces the world to an 'unconditioned instant of thought', with 'living from …', which is a moment of supportive nourishment, or *alimentation,* constitution by an overflow of own meaning. Alimentation is not something that is grasped after the event of representation but as overflow of meaning 'the conditioning is produced in the midst of the relation between representing and represented, constituting and constituted – a relation which we find first in every case of consciousness'.[2] Something is always more than the representation of a situation. It is alterity of the Other which is the aliment. The aliment is the very contestation of representations. But does not alimentation nourish precisely because it is still clinging to the matrix of representation by merely suspending it – contesting, yes, but at the same time maintaining the adequacy of the conception of truth upon which representation depends? For the overflow of meaning, the contestation of representation still allows language to crave correctness, an altogether 'Other' map of the world, whilst still clinging to 'mapping' conception of truth. The internal contestation, the alteration, the connections within a given map, occur only after an exposure to some 'Other' who is not yet allowed to be conceptualised within the totalising discourse. But when such alteration happens, a contestation of the very question of 'mapping' is also not allowed to happen, although I must emphasise, *something otherwise than mapping has already taken place – has already been given.*

18. Levinas's notion of multiplicity is ontic through and through and connotes the radical plurality of beings, never fully contained in any totality, and resists any attempt to so contain them. Subjectivity

---

[2] *Ibid*, p 128.

never finds congruence with the being in which it is produced. In multiplicity, subjectivity is still conceived as a surplus in the face of totality. The plurality that is maintained only in overcoming plurality-under-totality, implies war over that totality:

> In war beings refuse to belong to a totality, refuse community, refuse law; no frontier stops one being by another, nor defines them. They affirm themselves as transcending the totality, each identifying itself not by its place in the whole, but by its *self*.[3]

The very asymmetry, then, that does not allow I and not-I – the plurality of beings – to be contained in a total reflection, is binary in nature – it is a binary asymmetry. Asymmetry belongs to the same logic of symmetry and is very different from fluidity, from flux. There is a residual and embryonic method in Levinas's asymmetry, one that could constitute a limited substance for a procedure, one in which a new formulation of multiplicity is to be represented and contained. '[That which decides war] is the relation between beings exterior to totality, which hence are not in touch with one another.'[4] For Levinas, antagonism, war, all this dramatic language cannot be a language of actuality. The language of actuality is in the space between identity and difference, prior to correctness, using language to point to the 'there' resolutely, without the trumpets and drums of war. The language of actuality is not subjecting the play of signifiers to the iron rule of the I/not-I and its wars. *What the representation-able needs is a drama to produce the spectacle of detachment that is supposed to convince us that a genuine transcendence is taking place.*

19. The anticipation and the potential of language to remain within the logic of I/the Other is in evidence when Levinas focuses on asymmetry. The ontic, punctuated, binary nature of the transcendence could not be starker:

> Language does not take place *in front of* a correlation from which the I would derive its identity and the Other its alterity. The separation involved in language does not denote the presence of two beings in an ethereal space where union simply echoes separation. Separation is first the fact of a being that lives *somewhere*, from *something*, that is, that enjoys. The identity of the I comes to it from its egoism whose insular sufficiency is accomplished by enjoyment, and to which the face teaches the infinity from which this insular sufficiency is separated. *This egoism is indeed on the infinitude of the other, which can be accomplished only be being produced as the idea of infinity in*

---

[3] *Ibid*, p 222.
[4] *Ibid*, pp 220–23.

a separate being. The other does indeed invoke this separated being, but this invocation is not reducible to calling for a correlative. (my emphasis)[5]

20. The representation-able nature of the transcendence for the absolute Other does not change in the less metaphysical account of *Otherwise than Being*. In this work the relationship between the ethical Saying and the ontological Said is important in order to see the relationship between representation-ability and representation. In this work, to recap, Levinas refines the idea of metaphysical language of the absolute Other in the claim of the infinite ethical residue that survives its articulation through the ontological Said. What I understand as 'ability' characterises the relationship of a common matrix between the ethical Saying and the ontological Said. Thus understood, this relationship, as articulated by Levinas, does not yet grasp the ontological ethical Saying which is always the 'not' in relation to representation-ability and *a fortiori* in relation to the Said.

21. The 'legal' resides in this common ontic matrix between the ontic ethical Saying and the derivative ontico-ontological Said. The whole Levinasian distinction between Saying and Said perpetuates the legal in that way, despite the pretension for the ethical Saying to occur and reside outside the law (which it would regard as persisting within the 'ontological' Said).

22. To grasp the legal it is necessary to grasp that of which the legal is a distortion rather than to forget that distortion in a pseudo-, and still a *humanist*, distinction (despite its pretension to the contrary) between the ethical Saying and the ontological Said.

23. Indeed, the Saying that survives the Said is ethical. The Saying and the comportment towards that Saying constitutes the noblest, if not always the most pleasant, ethical effort. This ethics is the comportment towards the actual, towards the near. It is neither good nor bad because punctuable thinking with and through values does not mediate here between Saying and Said. Nor does it have an output that sorts things out, an output that ethically *improves*. Ethics is for its own sake, in the simplest manner of 'there', being free in a Saying from the shackles of both representation and representation-ability. The unconcealment of that which has already concealed itself is a moment where all ontic anticipations have been shattered valuably – a moment in which *all ontic ethics*, including its most forgetful variety, is grasped. This moment is grasped when, between ontic manifestations, there is a comportment towards the error, or distortion, of the 'there-itself' that these manifestations keep reinstating and in resistance to the smoothing of this ontic manifes-

---

[5] *Ibid*, pp 215–16.

tation in a common matrix of an ethical 'beyond'. This resistance is quiet and humble, wrestling the nothing as the 'is' of the withdrawal movement of Being, rather than taking thinking away into a comforting and self congratulating 'otherness of an Other'. However, this resistance is already a response to a primordial understanding of distortion of a call and so is valuable as it involves overcoming the most difficult of cravings, the craving for ontic perpetuation. The means of such resistance must be extreme in the face of ontic silencing. The relationship that seeks the origin of ethics is between the Saying of ontological ethics and the Said of the ontic pseudo-complementarity that seemingly establishes primordial ethics. Such transcendence allows for the distortion between the two to speak, rather than smothering it. Ontic ethics includes Levinas's own forgetfulness of Being in articulating a relationship between Saying and Said – between representation-able ontic ethical Saying and derivative representational ontology, which this Saying in actuality presumes. This derivative ontology characterises ontological reflection as based on knowledge, cognition and comprehension of Being, something that could not be more foreign to fundamental ontology. For thinking-Being is not some cognition of Being or knowledge of it. Nor does it signify a mere 'being otherwise'. Thinking in terms of 'ontology', 'Being' and 'being otherwise' still relates to the derivative conception of truth as correctness [*Richtigkeit*], which includes incorrectness. However, such thinking does not yet relate to the nearest relationship of unconcealment. The ethical representation-able Saying of Levinas does not yet confront the elusive simplicity of the actual.

24. But Levinas's attempt is itself a phase of forgetfulness of Being. Levinas's harmful denial of the distortion of actuality that has to be confronted marks a point of departure into a period of righteousness and terror, which are all a consequences of such entrenchment of the legal, precisely in its being seemingly 'otherwise' than law, an entrenchment which silences the call of Being which must, then, find its audience through violent means. Being's speaking is not directed against the 'innocent' but gets its energy from the inauthentic cycles that cripple humanity from facing the complementarity that characterises and confronts the essential distortion involved in Being concealing its unconcealment. From that point of view, all-encompassing and colossal atrocities, ontically classed as 'wrong', nevertheless hint at a call from an otherness more primordial than the call of all those commissars of ethics who condemn these 'actions' in the name of an 'Other' which faces in a manner otherwise to ontology. Atrocities are carried out as an address to people who cannot yet hear the Saying of Being.

THE IMPLICATION OF REPRESENTATION-ABILITY

25. The ontic is necessary for the ontological but is always a complementary error, a distortion. Levinas's ethical thesis poses the ethical
challenge as if it can never be captured by representational ideas. But
the beyond of Levinas's account makes the primordial encounter
already translatable into the re-allocation of rights of the oppressed
Other. The translatability from representation-able to actual representations colonises *Dasein* in such a way that it forgets the 'not' of
the necessary error between ontic and ontology. The oscillation
between the representation-able and the representational is in fact a
translation which challenges the content of the representational but
does not yet bite into the conditions and constitution of representation (and representation-ability) in the first place. To dwell on these
conditions is to confront the inexpressible, the 'not', the primordiality impossibility of translation between the ontic and the
ontological. The ontologically 'idle' translation from the representation-able to the representational lures *Dasein* away from that
which is to be looked at, that actuality which oppresses. This luring
is what makes Levinas able to be against law while at the same time
perpetuating the legal. Levinas does not allow us to grasp the Being
of law, that is to think about law.

26. Aboutness is to contemplate the nothing and must anticipate not
merely a transcendence of given representations, but a transcendence
of the very thinking with representation including with the representation-able which in effect preserves such thinking. Representation-
ability creates the impression of being other than representations,
other than law, other even than the legal, but in fact is the ultimate
preserver-in-disguise of them.

27. To caution again, we must not call the fundamentally ontological
representation-able, despite the fact that it anticipates representations on the level of its distorted ontic determination. Such
anticipation is rather an anticipation of ontological error. The
ontological difference is an altogether different complementarity
than that of the pseudo-complementarity of representation-ability
and the representational.

28. Error holds sway and is a part of the ontic–ontological process. The
'not' 'ek-sists' between thinking that is representational (including
the Levinasian climate of ethical transcendence, namely represen-
tation-able/punctuable/decodable) and the continuous flux of Being.

29. The 'not' of Levinas is not yet ethical.

30. The representation-ability of the ethical Saying already determines
the ontic horizon of ethics in advance so that new human experiences
of ignorance can be hijacked and paraphrased into this horizon and

be re-presented as a responsible response to that ignorance. What Levinas does is to create a dialectic whereby the ethical Saying is the representation-able basis for moral criticism of existing conceptual-isations of values, principles, rules, rights and duties. Levinas is a critical legal scholar *par excellence*, one who legitimises critical *legal* scholarship like no other. The legal subject is both transcended and anticipated.

31.   The notions of substitution, proximity and recurrence ensure the perpetuation of representation-ability and vice versa. It is in the symbolic oppression of the Other that the root of moral critical theory is to be found and new rights and duties of the Other can be justified and anticipated. The ontic continuum persists between the detachment of the Other, which is ontically unbearable although supplying the intuition with a feeling of an ultimate transcendence, and the not-yet thinking about the inability to bear that detachment, leading to filling up the gap with new rights and duties. This continuum persists between the is and the ought, between the ontological Said and the ethical Saying.

32.   In Levinas, the ontic continuum between representation-able and the representation does condition ethics. It does not yet allow the ethical 'how' to come through. This continuum is not attentive to the saying of the inexpressible which speaks despite Levinas's sophisticated attempt to silence it. Ontic hegemony does not allow that which is first and foremost 'mine' to speak. Such an opportunity for 'howness' to speak would dislocate, displace ethics in a manner which is more original than thinking with and through values, however critically. The Showing of the Saying when language speaks is not represen-tation-able Saying.

FROM REPRESENTATION-ABLE TO THE LEGAL – LEVINAS'S ACCOUNT OF THE THIRD PERSON.

33.   The perpetuation of the legal in Levinas could not be expressed in a stronger way than in his account of the relationship between ethics and politics – an account which he gave in both *Totality and Infinity* and *Otherwise than Being* as well as in various essays. Despite the radical asymmetry that characterises the relationship between ethics and politics in Levinas, the transcendental echoes of his ethics become audible here and assume the exploration of the relationship between alterity and reasonableness. It is in the way that ethics and politics intersect and interact that the relationship between ethical Saying and ontological Said, between ought and is, between moral imperative and the exploration of the reasonable, comes to the fore.

It is in this relationship that the ontic characteristic of Levinas's account, its derivative ontology and representation-ability, its punctuability and representation-ability, all meet together to perpetuate and entrench thinking *within* the legal, that is the being and thinking with and through law.

34. Levinas has always been aware of the considerable tension between the demands of ethics and politics, all the more so given the radical nature of his ethics. If ethics is based on radical exteriority, beyond totalisation, conceptualisation, thematisation and representation, then any reduction by way of commensurate comparisons will be unethical. The demand for alterity would be severely compromised in the cry, from the necessity of togetherness, for interpretation, allocation, generality and totality. The moment of preparing for a decision is not ethical. Any form of containing and re-containing alterity in the name of justice will be unjust to alterity. *Prima facie*, in justice, people's alterity will not get its due.

35. For Levinas, however, we cannot avoid this tension between ethics and politics. Furthermore, a tension is quite a healthy sign. Ethical moments thrive on tension, so we need to look closely at the nature of the tension between ethics and politics and ask whether this tension itself does not hold the key to that which is ethical in the relationship between ethics and politics. In other words, there are very good ethical reasons for encompassing the tension between ethics and politics from within ethics in a way which would not eliminate the tension but would rather champion it as the very ethical challenge that ethics poses to politics. And the mirror image is that the tension between ethics and politics can show the ethical nature of the political challenge to ethics. Finally, we can, before delving into Levinas's writing on the matter, appreciate that, from a Levinasian perspective, the tension is never to be resolved but rather to be kept alive and open. The very attempt to close the tension off, to contain it, would be already unethical, but that ethics should not be reconcilable with politics is a mark of an ethical dynamic relationship rather than bracketing a moment of closure as a proof of the unethical nature of politics. What is needed is stop to see tension as a problem to be sorted, but as a problem to be constantly recreated. From Levinas's point of view we ought to conceive the tension as the necessary continuation of the ethical challenge, echoing the very challenge that characterises the relationship between the ethical Saying and the ontological Said. We can dub this healthy tension between ethics and politics that binds them together in critical complementarity *the politics of alterity*.

36. In *Totality and Infinity*, Levinas writes that 'The face opens the primordial discourse whose first word is *obligation*[my emphasis],

which no 'interiority' permits avoiding'.[6] The notion of obligation, so intrinsic to the language of rights and duties, to the language of the legal, constitutes the raw material which allows Levinas later to move from the ethical Other, to the ethical 'right of the Other', to the 'right of the all others as Others'. The whole dynamics of surplus between ethics and politics is based on the notion of obligation. The notion of responsibility for the Other, as I have argued in the previous chapter, presumes an ontic logic of otherness. This ontic logic connects responsibility to the notion of obligation. Obligations are connected to the notion of 'an Other' the responsibility towards whom is representation-able. The connection of surplus between ethics and politics for Levinas is ontic through and through. Both his ethics and politics anticipate represented obligation: 'What obligation does the Other impose on me?' (ethics); 'What obligation ought I justify in being imposed upon both me and the Other'? (politics).

37. In addition to 'obligation', the other key term for Levinas is 'value'. Levinas's ethics approach the origin of the valuable in terms of values, although, of course, what values and how they are prioritised infinitely defers generalisations. Evaluations through values is another cementing factor through which ethics is connected to politics. Values can justify obligations imposed upon institutions to intervene in people's lives and impose obligations upon those people. Some values impose limitations upon political institutions and prevent institutions from encroaching upon people's private ethical challenges.

38. In discussing the relationship between ethics and politics Levinas is interested in the origin of values, both ethical and political. The ethical challenge – that of relating to an 'Other'– for Levinas encapsulates ethical and political relations. Values are generated through continuous ethical engagement with an Other and as such they generate rights and obligations. That would be a *private* and very intimate generation of obligation. Values are also generated as a result of engagement with all possible Others, and hence these values are of a public nature, justifying a polity that effectuates them (including being limited by them). Both private and public values can contest with one another and, for Levinas, this contestation takes place always as part and parcel of the same ethical relation itself. Values, of whatever kind, are contestable but are still creatures of a representational way of thinking and as such are linked to the ontic notion of obligation. I will attend later to the complexity of the inter-weaving of ethics and politics within the ethical challenge in more detail, but at this stage I would merely like to stress that Levinas

[6] *Ibid*, p 201.

identifies the 'valuable' and value-based thinking as primordial: 'Responsibility is what first enables one to catch sight of and conceive of value.'[7] Values are terms that are participating already in a language which presumes the ontic 'ought', which itself stems from a never-ending face-to-face encounter, proximity to, and substitution for, an 'Other'. Thinking critically with and through values is part and parcel of the representation-able nature of Levinas's thought and, as I shall argue, the primordial ethics that challenges any given ethical and political relations is already conditioned by value-based thinking.

39. In a 1954 essay 'The I and the Totality', Levinas explains the birth of politics and justice as a matter of the impossibility of absolute forgiveness. Total forgiveness is possible only where the one who did the wrong took upon himself the whole weight of the wrong. Absolute forgiveness is possible only in an intimate and transparent society, which would mean for Levinas a society of two people, between whom asymmetry can lead to moments of possibility of forgiveness. Third parties will be excluded from such a society. Any wrong committed between two people will be distorted ('objectively falsified', to use Levinas' term) through the relationship of a person with a third party. One person would remain excluded from the intimacy. Righting and forgiveness to me by you may wrong the third party. The result of the introduction of a third party is that 'my intention no longer measures the meaning of my act. In such a situation there is no forgiveness to me. I can not get forgiveness and in this sense the situation is unjust. Forgiveness needs to be collectively reasserted and hence society and its institutions are born.'[8] The order of society comes about both as a mediator and a moderator. In 'Philosophy, Justice, and Love', Levinas says it in a different way:

> If there were no order of Justice, there would be no limit to my responsibility. There is a certain measure of violence necessary in terms of justice; but if one speaks of justice, it is necessary to allow judges, it is necessary to allow institutions and the state; to live in a world of citizens, and not only in the order of the Face to Face.[9]

40. The relationship with the third party is neither first person intimacy nor the love of a neighbour. As such, this relationship is bound to compromise the particularity of the human person. But compromise need not to entail a totally objectifying discourse. In articulating the

[7] *OB*, p 123.
[8] 'The I and the Totality', in *Entre Nous: Thinking-of-The-Other* (MB Smith and B Harshav, trans) (Athlone Press, 1998) pp 13–38, at pp 19–20.
[9] 'Philosophy, Justice and Love', in *ibid*, p 105.

compromise, particularity must not be lost to universal laws and impersonal representations. In our relationship with the third party the danger is that:

> the role we play in a drama of which we are no longer the authors: characters and instruments of an order alien to the level of our intimate society – an order which is perhaps guided by an intelligence, but an intelligence which is revealed to consciousness only by its cunning. No longer can anyone find the law of his action in the depth of his heart.[10]

In 'The I and the Totality', Levinas suggests a commonality which will be based on the relationship between people rather than on impersonal reason. This commonality will be a 'third party' to the two parties of the ethical relationship. We need to grasp as 'totality of "me's", at once without conceptual unity and in relationship with one another'.[11] This third party will be grasped by negation. It is absent and present at the same time, a simultaneity of presence and absence. The third party can be approached only through injustice.[12] We can see that the structure of the third party is as open ended and infinite as the ethical relationship. The basis of the third party is ethical: 'We are *we* in that we command each other to a work through which we recognize each other.'[13] This is a theme that Levinas further develops later in *Totality and Infinity* and *Otherwise than Being*.

41. In *Totality and Infinity*, all these various explanations of the third party come together. Here, Levinas discusses the inherently turbulent relationship between ethics and politics in a short section entitled 'The Other and the Others'.[14] For Levinas, the ethical relationship with the Other does not involve the mere intimacy between two people but already includes a complex evaluation and reflection with the 'third' person [*le tiers*]. The third person conveys 'all possible Others', a universal 'we' of humanity. The third person signifies responsibility to humanity, or what Levinas referred to as 'justice'. For Levinas, responsibility to all Others implicates an infinite challenge, which, similarly to the more intimate situation with an 'Other', connotes never-ending debt and asymmetry. This asymmetry to all Others is the political dimension of the idea that one is always

---

[10] 'The I and the Totality', above n 8, p 23. See also *ibid*, pp 25–7 to the effect that impersonal, universal discourses have the tendency of suppressing both the otherness of the interlocutor and the otherness of the speaking 'I'. The particularity of people is not reducible to 'knowing'. 'Generalization is death', proclaims Levinas, as it ' inserts the *I* into, and dissolves it in, the generality of its work'.

[11] *Ibid*, p 27.

[12] *Ibid*, p 30.

[13] *Ibid*, p 36.

[14] *TI*, pp 212–14.

in a surplus of debt regardless of what these Others are doing or not doing.[15]

42. This third person, or 'the third', is not subsequent to the ethical relation but part and parcel of it. The third is part and parcel of the face-to-face encounter. The face of the third person already looks at my eyes from the face of the second person (the Other). The third person meshes in the face of the Other and brings about the inescapable tensional and conflictual relationship between ethics and justice. The tension itself, as we shall see, is a part of the overall ethical challenge that faces the first person.

43. It is just worth emphasising here that there is an internal tension that characterises the third person. Levinas speaks about the third person/party in the singular. But Levinas understands the third person to be he (or indeed she) who presses the ethical demand that comes from the infinite surplus of all possible Others. So the reduction is not only effectuated by a localised ethics, which contains its own asymmetry and infinite responsibility, but which reduces the infinite responsibility to all possible Others. Reduction also exists in the move to assimilate all ethical Others to an impersonal, objectified, third person. So the movement that we witness in Levinas is an attempt at expansion of ethical relations into the domain of justice and then a reduction again, so that it is possible to refer to 'society', 'state' and 'the third person' in the singular. The ethical asymmetry, then, is doubled up in a further asymmetry with justice, but then is reduced, as we shall see, to a 'manageable' double asymmetry between three singulars.

44. The reference to the third party, that of justice to all Others, is different from the dimension of height that characterises the face-to-face ethical relationship with the Other person. The gaze of the third person into my eyes from the face of the Other connotes that in a very important respect I am *equal* to the Other. In our service to the third person, both I and the Other (second) party are equal. The Other commands me to command and in this way we are joined as equals in service to the third. The third person is the 'we' – the collective indispensable dimension of any private ethical relations.[16] The whole of humanity looks at us and at our ethical

[15] See this idea in 'Philosophy, Justice, and Love', above n 9, pp 103–21, at 107: 'I am in reality responsible for the other even when he or she commits crimes, even when others commit crime. This is for me the essence of Jewish conscience. But I also think that it is the essence of the human conscience: All men are responsible for one another and 'I more than anyone else'.

[16] See R Bernasconi., 'The Third Party: Levinas on the Intersection between the Ethical and the Political' (1999) 30(1) *Journal of the British Society for Phenomenology* 76–87, at 77–80. Bernasconi also relies on 'The I and the Totality', above n 8. See also A Peperzak, *To the Other: An Introduction to the Philosophy of Emmanuel Levinas* (Indiana, Purdue University Press, 1993) pp 171–3.

relationship and places it in the context of all other ethical relationships, in the context of a larger quest for criticism, re-negotiation and
accommodation. The ethical relation with the Other, said Levinas,

> is not only the putting in question of my freedom, the appeal coming from
> the other to call me to responsibility, is not only the speech by which I divest
> myself of the possession that encircles me by setting forth an objective and
> common world, but is also sermon, exhortation, the prophetic word.[17]

It is part of the ethical relation, then, to engage with humanity and
not merely to allow the relationship with the Other to dominate the
whole ethical horizon. Levinas argues that exclusivity given to the
ethical relationship with another person can lead to a 'common and
objective world' whereby many Others will be excluded, unethically.
The ethical relationship, being all-comprehensive, still adheres to
alterity, but it now presses the plea for alterity between the singular
ethical perspective of two parties and the third. The disturbance, or
the limitation, posed by the third party, the antecedent political and
justice dimension, expands the range of the ethical challenge.

45. Such an infinite ethical challenge that is personalised by Levinas
through the face of the third party generates an ethical challenge in
both the 'given' of a local ethical relationship that is prone to become
selfish, *and* the uncritically accepted traditional/conventional societal
outlook. The ethical challenge, then, comprises a challenge of the
not-yet-conceptualised Other that demands justice, that is the
equality in Otherness.[18] It is in this sense of equality of Otherness
that the ethical and the political merge.

46. The open-ended nature of the relationship between ethical and the
hegemonic political order that enforces a totalised ethics is conveyed
by Levinas's conception of multiplicity. Multiplicity consists of
never-ending exteriority. Exteriority 'signifies the resistance of the
social multiplicity to the logic that totalises the multiple'.[19]

47. To sum up again, the ethical challenge that meshes ethics and politics
points to the insufficiency, and potential tyranny, of a given ethical
relationship between two people/groups, thus challenging such
relationships in the name of justice to be done to other 'Others' who
are 'Other' to that relationship. Alterity that calls in the name of
justice to be rendered to the third person challenges any localism,

---

[17] *TI*, p 213.

[18] Citizens of the state would be reciprocal not in a 'closed' way but rather in an open-ended,
asymmetrical, way: see 'Philosophy, Justice, and Love', above n 9, p 107.

[19] *TI*, p 292. See also p 295: 'The exteriority of being does not, in fact, mean that multiplicity
is without relation. However, the relation that binds this multiplicity does not fill the abyss of
separation; it confirms it.'

dogmatism, totality, *even if such a totality stems from a closure within which certain ethical relations are continually explored and confronted.*[20] The relationship between ethics and politics is itself a characteristic of a dynamic, never-ending ethical relation which challenges the 'same' in politics. This ethical challenge of bringing in new particular ethical claims pressed upon hitherto oppressed and dominated Others, demands a constant transgression of totalised boundaries and connotes relentless contestation and re-negotiation not only of the ethical perspective by the third person, but also of *the third person perspective* by the ethical.

48. Levinas called this equality of responsibility between both me and the Other, in which we are all equals in ethical responsibility towards potential Others, and the communal ethical responsibility to justice that this ethical responsibility brings in its wake, 'fraternity'. Fraternity is open-ended but can still be grasped as such. As Bernasconi puts it, fraternity connects the Other and the third party 'without reducing them to units within a totality'.[21] The notion of fraternity is arguably Levinas's invocation and articulation of the Kantian categorical imperative in which equality of beings who can be potential Others constitute a universal law, or 'Kingdom of Ends', beyond any totality, history, anthropology, beyond any periodical complacency, even beyond epochal righteousness. Fraternal community emerges as a surplus of alterity at the heart of any given rule-based and principled reasoning. A fraternal community is a diachronic community, a kingdom of ends that is characterised by infinite asymmetry and an overflow of ethical demand for justice. As Bernasconi contends, it is in politics that the ethical really bites.[22]

49. The meshing of the ethical and the political are the hallmark of Levinas. Although the ethical relationship reigns supreme as a first philosophy it is through the mediation of politics that the ethical relationship on the one hand expands its range of application but also constantly renews its powers to challenge totality. This is the way by which Levinas shows the relationship between ethics and justice, between the demand of alterity and the conventionally perceived call of justice to compare, allocate, measure, to be conflictual but also mutually reinforcing. Justice to all Others is the universal face of ethics. In this sense justice is the ethical challenge that fuels ethics and, as such, it precedes and conditions any ethical relationship which has entrenched its own limited perspective, or is

---

[20] This challenge has been described as the checks and balances between ethics and politics: see WP Simmons, 'The Third: Levinas' theoretical move from an-archical ethics to the realm of justice and politics' (1999) 25(6) *Philosophy and Social Criticism* 83–104, at 92.

[21] Bernasconi, 'The Third Party', above n 16, p 84.

[22] *Ibid*, p 80.

itself limited in an entrenched uncritically examined justification and
limitation on the reasoning of institutions within a given polity. The
primary proximity of the ethical relationship is thus made commen-
surable with fraternal open-ended community:

> Because my position as an I is *effectuated* already in fraternity the face can
> present itself to me as a face. The relation with the face in fraternity, where
> in his turn the Other appears in solidarity with all the others, constitutes the
> social order, the reference of every dialogue to the third party by which the
> We – or the party encompasses the face to face opposition, opens the erotic
> upon a social life, all signifyingness and decency, which encompasses the
> structure of the family itself.[23]

50.   But what is the conflict, the *ethical* conflict, that this reconciliation
      between ethics and politics shies away from, conceals and forgets?
      Should we at all be surprised that Levinas manages to reconcile ethics
      and politics with such apparent ease? Has he rendered justice to
      original otherness?

51.   The relationship between ethics and politics, manifested in the
      fraternal 'we' which is already prevalent in ethical relations and
      hence enhances these ethical relations is subject to double treatment
      by Levinas. On the one hand, the relationship 'aspires to a State,
      institutions, laws, which are the source of universality'. On the other
      hand, 'politics left to itself bears tyranny within itself; it deforms the I
      and the other who have given rise to it, for it judges them according
      to universal rules, and thus in absentia'.[24] Laws are needed, but the
      moment a law is uttered and applied, the more the language of law is
      being deployed, it oppresses a residual ethical meaning in it – a
      residual claim for justice by a silenced 'Other'. Levinas's phenomen-
      ological roots resonate in transcending the law and preserving the
      legal. The essence of law consists of this tension, the tension between
      necessity and impossibility, the *ethical* tension between the private
      relationship of height and public equality of Others – ethics and
      politics. The ethical relationhip anticipates law but it is constantly
      critical at being and thinking with and through law, as such thinking
      always reduces a hidden ethical significance.

52.   Perfect *aporia*, then: original in its effectuation of goodness, and
      perfect in hiding away from actuality. This *aporia* is perfect in
      forgetting that of which it is a distortion and perfect in thinking
      away the ethical call to think about this distortion. Such an *aporia* is
      the way Levinas would think 'about' law. Levinas's 'about' would see
      the thing – law – as an aporetic ethical means – something that we

[23] *TI*, p 280
[24] *Ibid*, p 300.

cannot be without but once used, is bound to be reductionist in the very language that it uses, the language of rights, obligations, rules and principles. There is a continuing tension between the right of an Other and rights of all Others, *both* of which characterise the ethical relationship. This *aporia* between ethics and politics, between ethics and justice, surrogates and protects the transcendence within ontic boundaries. But, is this *aporia* not a novel sort of ontic totality? Is this paradox not in fact a latent philosophical gesture, a self-reference of correctness which is not aware that it is ontically stuck, shunning the primordial embrace of genuine open-ended self-reference in 'ek-stasis' that hermeneutics demands from both ethical and political relations?

53. This paradox of law marks the continuity of the legal because of the representation-able ontic ethics that Levinas adheres to and antici-pates. The legal is entrenched because the very language that Levinas sees as inadequate is preserved in advance. Ontic ethical transcen-dence demands the preservation, the persistence, the continuation of attempt to re-contain not-yet-made representational instantiations in language although representations would also be indefinitely postponed. The 'not yet', the deferral in Levinas, still perpetuates being and thinking with the legal with the necessary recourse to the language of values, priority of values, rights and duties – the bedrock of the legal. The transcendence that Levinas's ethics effectuates, as well as the evident pervasive success which it enjoys among critical legal and political scholarship, is already conditioned by the need of the legal. To use his words, it 'aspires' to the legal.

54. Ethics, then, takes shape within the context of political institutions. For Levinas, the encounter with the Other must come always from alterity within the existing political context in which the ethical claim is hidden. Freedom of the heterogeneous subject, the very subjectivity that can be burdened by the Other and re-emerges in freedom, the difficult freedom of alterity, can only happen within politics:

Freedom is not realized outside of social and political institutions, which open to it the access to fresh air necessary for its expansion, its respiration, and even, perhaps, its spontaneous generation. A political freedom is to be explained as an illusion due to the fact that its partisans or its beneficiaries belong to an advanced stage of political evolution.[25]

55. Levinas continues to elaborate his complex relationship to law, which is effectuated by the constant emergence of the third party.[26]

[25] *Ibid*, p 241.
[26] *Ibid*, pp 242–6.

Institutions always reduce the ethical in their well-articulated, principled reasoning. Very much echoing Kant, Levinas argues that the very universality of law upon which institutions claim to be founded is always betrayed by the very fact of this universality being reduced to an articulatable, interpretative history. That which is universal, what Levinas referred to as 'the revolt of the apology', cannot be expelled, paraphrased or subsumed into a given history of principled interpretation and articulation: 'The invisible is the offence that inevitably results from the judgement of visible history, even if history unfolds rationally'. What is universal continues to be the submission of subjectivity to that which is absent in totalising historical interpretation – submission to the diachronic moment. In this Levinas is claiming both the necessity for, and the ethical call to overcome, dogmatic historical, impersonal interpretation of legal texts – he pleads always to consider the Other who is expelled by the act of 'interpreting' these texts. The ethical voice interrupts the false universality of judgement under seemingly universal principles. The ethical should endlessly criticise the linear, synchronised indeterminacy, historicised justice, as they interpreted in a polity of totalising fraternity. To that extent Levinas *seems* to still be within ontic confines, against the very primordiality of the craving for constructivist justification in interpretation of the text of the law:

In reality, justice does not include me in the equilibrium of its universality; justice summons me to go beyond the straight line of justice, and henceforth nothing can mark the end of this march; behind the straight line of the law the land of goodness extends infinite and unexplored, necessitating all the resources of a singular presence. I am therefore necessary for justice, as responsible beyond every limit fixed by an objective law. The I is a privilege and an election. The sole possibility in being of going beyond the straight line of the law, that is, of finding a place lying beyond the universal, is to be I.[27]

56. However, the legal, the very anticipation of re-containment and the persistence of the ontic language of values and rights, constrains this creativity within a certain, quite stagnant, conception of truth and history. To resort to Derridian terminology, the undecidability between ethics and politics as portrayed by Levinas does not yet bite into the question of the nature of complementarity between ontology and ethics. Elegantly, Levinas avoids being polemic about law. He does not renounce the need for law but he calls for overcoming the inadequate and reductionist way in which law must express itself, and in this sense he is not simply against this or that law but seems to

[27] *Ibid*, p 245.

call for ethical criticism of the very ontological language law uses. The ontic common matrix between Levinas's ethical Saying and ontological Said is now applied into a common matrix that characterises the tension between ethics and politics. There is an ontic common matrix between ethics and politics, namely between the 'legal' in the ethical that seems to call for transcending the very language that law uses, and the already prevalent anticipation of that kind of language by that ethical. To the extent of that tension, Levinas seems to present something which is 'other to law', a reasoning that is always oppressed by the way law thinks and speaks. To put it in yet another way, Levinas seems to call for overcoming thinking and being with law, but at the same time he wants to maintain the legal, the very ethical origin of the language of duties and rights towards an 'Other'. The paradox of law is nothing but the continuation between the representation-able and the representational – that complicit complementarity that perpetuates the ontic ethics of endless differentiation by radical punctuation. Levinas has his cake and eats it, in the sense that he can be against law, and hence inaugurates critical thinking about law and the legal subject. However, at the same time as calling for the continual displacement of law's content, Levinas preserves the notion of a radical subject, thereby inaugurating the ground for merely critical *legal* thinking that preserves the legal radical subject. We could almost feel as if the notion of the legal subject becomes transcendental in Levinas, in the sense of its preservation in the ontic transcendence. As this kind of radical stretching of ontic thought anticipates and perpetuates the legal, there is a continuum in language between the ethical language of values and the ethics that the language of law enforces. On the one hand, ethics does aspire to law and institutions – the maintenance of representation-ability. On the other hand:

To place oneself beyond the judgement of history, under the judgement of truth, is not to suppose behind the apparent history another history called judgement of god – but equally failing to recognise the subjectivity. To place oneself under the judgement of God is to exalt the subjectivity, called to moral overstepping beyond laws, which is henceforth in truth because it surpasses the limits of its being.[28]

57. The radicalism of Levinas, and, I think, his arrogance in going beyond history could not be more evident. In characterising the relationship between ethics and politics Levinas deflects humans from their humble and attentive essence by demanding them to be

[28] *Ibid*, p 246.

absolute Other. Is there not something detached, and thus prone to infuriate in such a call for detachment? Is it not a core of all violence which is being perturbed once human beings claim the ability to detach like that? *What superiority and holy self-imposed segregation is hidden behind preaching to humanity the craving to go beyond history and to claim that God is beyond history like that? What notion of time does Levinas' conception of history presume? Does not such detachment destroy any mystery of mutual reflection that calls for that solitary reflection 'between each human and himself' that is harboured in the mystery of the ethical? Is nourishing the most radical of punctuation not also the entrenchment of the elusive basis of alienation?*

58. Connecting to my argument in the previous chapter, in his account of the relationship between ethics and politics Levinas never ethically displaces the cycle of ontic perpetuation of the I/Other separation. His thinking critically about law does not yet think reflectively about law, does not yet think about the relationship between the essence of law and its distortion of the legal. This perpetuation of the legal causes harm by closing the gate on the very thinking about the thinking that conditions this ontic relationship.

59. Levinas's voice comes as if from an imaginary court, we can dub it an imaginary ethical court which is excluded in any principled totalising thinking through laws. He says:

Concretely to be an I presenting itself at a trial – which requires all the resources of subjectivity – means for it to be able to see, beyond the universal judgements of history, that offense of the offended which is inevitably produced in the very judgment issued from universal principles. What is above all invisible is the offense universal history inflicts on particulars. To be I and not only an incarnation of a reason is precisely to be capable of seeing the offense of the offended, or the face.[29]

60. Levinas is aware of the tension between law (which connotes a historically based *critical* morality according to which conventional morality changes) and the universally ethical that would always remain there, facing us as a trace. It is in the context of this tension that we should understand Levinas's famous dictum that 'duties become greater in the measure that they are accomplished. The better I accomplish my duty the fewer rights I have; the more I am just the more guilty I am.[30] This is Levinas's interpretation of the Hebrew dictum of 'Tzedek, Tzedek Tirdof' which means 'Justice, thou shall

[29] *Ibid*, pp 246–7.
[30] *Ibid*, p 244.

chase Justice', meaning that you can never achieve it – a radical premise of difference.

61. This tension is echoed in the relationship between three Hebrew words, all of which have the root of F, S, K: the word LIFSOK, which means to pass judgement, to decide in a adjudicative forum, including giving reasoning; the word LEHAFSIK, which means to stop; and the word LEFASEK, which means to punctuate. In a simple listening to Hebrew, this connection goes to the very heart of the Derridian ethics of exposing undecidables, for in decision, we stop something; in order to speak, we must conceal a trace of something. When we connect words so that each is dressed with meaning, we suppress that which was there and was expelled in order to make the decision possible. There is always a residue of a trace which was not taken into consideration in order to make the decision possible. But, on a deeper reading, the connection between these words can warn us about both decidability and undecidability that still see the issue of justice in punctuation and not as nearing the continuous within which both lose meaning. To chase justice, in other words, can become also the call to overcome punctuality and open up to the mystery of the continuous. According to this reading, any analogy to 'court' would be already captive of ontic and punctuating logic and hence the already derivative chase of justice. This reading which criticises punctuation thus puts both Levinas and Derrida on the same continuum of punctuation, thus not yet opening up to nearness to the continuous.

62. The tension that Levinas talks about, indeed the residue of the ethical that lurks as a trace between the punctual and continuous, is silenced by his decision to foreclose the ethical within the ontic, horizonal totality that marks the derivative tension of the representation-able and representation. The harm that Levinas causes to humanity through this foreclosure and detachment is immeasurable. The silences that he enforces, the decision that he makes, his stoppage, his punctuation, places on a common ontic matrix the tensional dynamics that persist between the ethical and the political.

63. The perpetuation of the legal in Levinas enforces the punctuable ethics of values. His account of the relationship between the ethical and the political contains the punctuable seeds of the legal. In doing so it entrenches ethics which shuns the interpretative possibility of exposing the distortion between language of an 'Other' and a more primordial continuum which prompts the subject to confront, as well as to dwell in, its groundlessness. It tries to abdicate the subject from the desire to speak about that which is his own without mediating through subjectivity. Indeed, we could say that the ethical is inescapably in the essence of law, but this is also the case with the

legal and with that ethical transcendence which perpetuates the legal. The essence of justice, to return to a theme that was explored in chapter four, resides in the 'not' between the essence of law and any of its ontic determinations, and this includes that ontic tension between ethics and politics which is critical of law and perpetuates the legal at the same time.

64.   How can a preservation of ontic-logic be free? Is the experience of freedom in ontic alterity and the constant rebirth of subjectivity out of a transcendence which anticipates and entrenches such subjectivity, a primordial experience of freedom? Would not a more primordial freedom from harm and responsibility be a one of the ontic–ontological process which does not merely predict the eternal asymptotic reduction of subjectivity but would rather be a necessary distortion in the ontic incarnation of subjectivity, one that needs to be overcome? Is not freedom experienced at a linguistic moment where ontic language, including the conception of truth as correctness that fuels it, cannot encounter what is 'there' nearest to us as a moment which is not merely unfulfilled but is inexpressible? Would not the Levinasian oscillation itself be a characterisation, coupled to harmful forgetfulness, of the possibility of a moment of primordial freedom, the freedom of letting Being be and the freedom of momentarily being nearer to the temporal stream of the unconcealament of actuality than the constrains of the ontic?

65.   The relationship between ethics and politics – that triangle of me, my Other and the third person – are refined and expanded upon in *Otherwise than Being* and other essays. In *Otherwise than Being*, using the language of complementarity between the Saying and the Said, Levinas refines and further explains the account of the tension between ethics, politics and justice given in *Totality and Infinity*. The third party is 'other than the neighbor, but also another neighbor and also a neighbor of the other, and not simply his fellow'.[31] The third party interrupts the duality of ethical relationship and Saying, and introduces a 'contradiction' into that Saying.[32] This contradiction accompanies the question of justice. On the one hand, in ethics, the Other is in his or her inviolability, which ethically demands infinite responsibility. On the other hand there is the demand of justice, which is responsibility towards my own and my Other's neighbour. Had there been only two people in the world there would have been

---

[31] *OB*, p 157. See also 'The Other, Utopia, and Justice', in *Entre Nous*, above n 8, pp 221–33, at p 229: '[the order of justice] arises from the fact of the third who, next to the one who is an other to me, is 'another other' to me'.

[32] Levinas uses the strong, not so elegant, term 'contradict', but in a subsequent 1982 interview retracted it in favour of saying that justice 'persecutes' ethics: 'Philosophy, Justice, Love', above n 9, pp 103–21, at p 104.

no need for such a contradiction.[33] This call for justice demands 'comparisons, coexistence, contemporaneousness, assembling, order, thematization, the visibility of faces, and thus intentionality and the intellect, the intelligibility of a system, and thence also a copresence on an equal footing as before a court of justice',[34] Justice is ethical in one sense but unethical in another because it demands the violation of the Other's inviolability. The moment generalisation takes place the intimacy that characterises the ethical relationship with the Other is compromised.

66. To the irreplaceability and incomparability of the Other, to the irreplaceability of the 'I', my own 'chosenness' for asymmetrical responsibility – which is referred only to 'me' confronting this irreplaceable Other – Levinas gave the term 'uniqueness'.[35] The demand of justice is impossible as it involves the obligation to compare incomparable and unique others. Justice involves the representational reduction of uniqueness.[36] Uniqueness, then, is the critical value of the polity in Levinas and it is uniqueness which is not to be lost in unity of representation. Levinas challenges us to think towards 'an ethical culture, in which the face of the other – that of the absolutely other – awakens in the identity of the I the inalienable responsibility for the other man and the dignity of the chosen'.[37] At this moment when justice commands the self there is no choice for the self but to represent and that will assume consciousness of intentionality and interpretation. As such, the demand of justice also necessarily creates injustice.

67. The third party, which demands justice, moderates or, as Levinas calls it, 'corrects' the asymmetry between me and the Other which characterises the ethical relationship. As it demands some objectification, comparison, weighing, there is, *to some extent*, a betrayal of the 'anarchic relationship with illeity',[38] because the relationship with the Other undergoes modification. My equality to the Other, to all Others, as a member of society, my alterity, is approached and respected by all Others.

68. Levinas does acknowledge that representation, objectification, calculation, neutralisation, in short, the ontological Said, is part and

---

[33] See *ibid*, p 106. See also *Ethics and Infinity: conversations with Philippe Nemo*, RA Cohen (trans.) (Duquesne University Press, 1985) pp 79–81.

[34] *OB*, p 157.

[35] 'Uniqueness', in *Entre Nous*, above n 8, pp 189–96. See also 'The Other, Utopia, and Justice', in *ibid*, p 227.

[36] *DR*, pp 166–7; 'Uniqueness', above n 35, p 196.

[37] 'The Philosophical Determination of the Idea of Culture', in *Entre Nous*, above n 8, pp 179–87, at p 187.

[38] *OB*, p 158.

parcel of taking up the ethical challenge of justice. In justice, the ethical Saying is becoming a 'book, law and science'.[39] Justice has this totalising face, but, as Levinas is quick to add, because justice also nourishes the ethical relationship, the ethical Saying itself is nourished by endless demand of justice. Being part and parcel of the ethical challenge itself, justice has ethical significance beyond a set of rules and principles, which manages a group of people *en masse*. Justice is impossible without ethics and so that very equality which reduces the anarchic nature of ethics is always challenged by the continuing asymmetry of that very equality.

69.   The following passage makes it clear how the ethical relationship with the Other relates to the relationship of justice with all others:

> Justice can be established only if I, always evaded from the concept of the ego, always desituated and divested of being, always in non-reciprocatable relationship with the other, always for the other, can become an other like the others. Is not the Infinite which enigmatically commands me, commanding and not commanding, from the other, also the turning of the I into 'like the others', for which it is important to concern oneself and take care?[40]

Levinas, then, does not 'reconcile' ethics and politics, because that would be to succumb to the reductive nature of justice. Justice does not contradict ethics but rather forms part and parcel of the ethical challenge. In *Diachrony and Representation*, Levinas characterises the ethical challenge as that of alterity which does not stem from the 'counterpart of the identity of facts and concepts, distinguishes one from another, or reciprocally opposes the notion of them, by contradiction or contrariety'. The ethical challenge that comes from the emergence of plurality of unique Others highlights the feature that the moment of justice, however propelled by ethics, proves ethically wanting.[41]

---

[39] *Ibid*, pp 158–9.

[40] *Ibid*, pp 160–61.

[41] *DR*, p 169. See also 'The Philosophical Determination of the Idea of Culture', in *Entre Nous*, above n 8, pp 184–6, where Levinas distinguishes between multiplicity under unity where distinction is derived from the whole, and multiplicity of alterity, an ethical fraternal community. Only in the latter do justice and ethics effectuate their respective paradoxes with the ontological Said and hence produce an infinite ethical challenge of justice which commands irreducible difference. 'It is precisely in this reminder of the responsibility of the *I* by the face that summons it, that demands it, that claims it, that the other is my fellow man.' See also 'Uniqueness', in *Entre Nous*, above n 8, pp 193–4.

This relationship between ethics and politics in which the very articulation of justice creates injustice and so opens the door to ethical challenge has been referred to as the democracy/politics of 'surplus'. The ethical Saying and the challenge for justice in that Saying is an undiminishing surplus – the diachrony of critical politics: see A Herzog, 'Is Liberalism "All we need"? Levinas' Politics of Surplus' (2002) 30(2) *Political Theory* 204–27.

70. Levinas refers to the 'expectation of a better justice', embodied as an ethical challenge which is conceived as 'prophetic' voice. Such a voice comes not from juridical, cold thinking but from a prophetic 'unforeseen act of kindness', a cry to defend the 'rights of man', which is in fact a cry to defend some oppressed uniqueness.[42]

71. Simmons presents a picture of a complex, mutually dependent and dynamic relationship between ethics and politics. Politics, in effectuating justice, amounts to the language of the ontological Said through institutions and laws, while ethics with its infinite anarchical intimacy demands a continuous questioning of this ontological Said.[43] Simmons' view does meet the complexity of Levinas's account in arguing that 'the third' is an extension of responsibility to all, but also a reduction of it into the Said and limitation of it in the Said. However, Simmons' account, in my view, conceives ethics and politics as distinguished realms with a dynamic relationship and hence does not emphasise enough that politics is in a sense part and parcel of the ethical relationship, a point that was emphasised in Levinas time and time again both in *Totality and Infinity* and *Otherwise than Being*. Simmons' interpretation is on the whole accurate but I feel it needs further clarification in as much as it may create the half-true impression that the realm of politics *always* reduces the ethical and so it depends on a completely distinct realm – the ethical – in order to self-criticise. In continuation of the discussion in *Totality and Infinity*, we should be very cautious in picturing two distinct realms which interact with one another so as not to cloud Levinas's crucial point that politics is part and parcel of the ethical Saying. We must not overlook the conception of two interacted realms that not only have some 'corrective' relationship with one another, but also constitute two overlapping ethical horizons.[44]

72. Despite their difference, politics and ethics come to be manifested in the gaze of the Other, alongside one another in a complex way that meshes them together.[45] It is not decidable which precedes which. In *Totality and Infinity* Levinas makes politics a part of the ethical relationship. Also in *Otherwise than Being*, as Peperzak observes, Levinas argues that politics is rooted and preceded by a more original

---

[42] 'Uniqueness', in *Entre Nous*, above n 8, p 196.

[43] See WP Simmons, 'The Third: Levinas' theoretical move from an-archical ethics to the realm of justice and politics', above n 20, pp 90–98.

[44] See R Bernasconi, 'The Third Party: Levinas on the Intersection between the Ethical and the Political', above n 16, p 85.

[45] Levinas uses the term 'alongside' in 'Philosophy, Justice, Love', in *Entre Nous*, above n 8, at p 103.

anarchic, infinity of the ethical.[46] What amounts to the ontological Said, then, thematises *both* the ethical relationship between two people, as we know, but, crucially, also a stagnant objectification of justice within a political community, namely as a fixed horizon of ethical transcendence between two parties. Both ethics and politics could thus become the ontological Said of the same. As far as Saying is concerned, ethical Saying can affect the intimacy of the personal and the generality of politics. It is also within the realm of the ethical Saying that there is an intimate connection between ethics and politics. The ethics provides the challenge, the potential injustice to an 'Other' which is left out of ethical transcendence. This challenge fuels ethical criticism and re-negotiation of the harm which is to be averted through constitutions and law in the political realm. This complex mesh between ethics and politics, which shows both their togetherness and separateness, their common matrix, is stated in Levinas's 1982 essay, 'Useless Suffering':

The interhuman perspective can subsist, but can also be lost, in the political order of the City where the Law establishes mutual obligations between citizens. The interhuman, properly speaking, lies in a non-indifference of one to another, in a responsibility of one for another, but before the reciprocity of this responsibility, which will be inscribed in impersonal laws, comes to be superimposed on the pure altruism of this responsibility inscribed in the ethical position of the *I qua I*. It is prior to any contract that would specify precisely the moment of reciprocity – a point at which altruism and disinterestedness may, to be sure, continue, but at which they may also diminish or die out. The order of politics (post-ethical or pre-ethical) that inaugurates the 'social contract' is neither the sufficient condition nor the necessary outcome of ethics. In its ethical position, the *I* is distinct both from the citizen born of the City, and from the individual who precedes all order in his natural egoism.[47]

73.   'Justice, society, the State and its institutions, exchanges and work are comprehensible out of proximity. This means that nothing is outside of the control of the responsibility of the one for the Other'.[48] The ethical relationship is the generator of both the enlargement of the ethical problem beyond two parties, and the re-particularisation of the question in the case of the political order becoming dominant and oppressive of a particular other. Thus, 'the contemporaneousness of the multiple is tied about the diachrony of two ... The equality of all is borne by my inequality, the surplus of my duties over my

---

[46] A Peperzak, *To the Other,* above n 16, pp 182–3.

[47] 'Useless Suffering' (1982), in *Entre Nous,* above n 8, pp 100–101.

[48] OB, p 159. See also 'Philosophy, Justice, and Love', in *Entre Nous,* above n 8, p 104.

rights.'[49] Justice is the need to thematise, to produce a reductionist ontological Said of some harm that causes rights and duties to reciprocate symmetrically. Such thematisation includes not only conceptualisation *per se* but also, as we saw, an all-too-restrictive horizon in which the transcendence of the ethical Saying operates. At the same time, though, justice is also the founder of the endless diachrony of ethical Saying among a community of people who are fraternally equal in that they are all 'an Other'. In some sense, the generality of the demand of justice and its source – a continuing ethical reflection stemming from equality, conflict and contestation – gives it a priority within any ethical relationship between human beings. In justice all human beings are equal in the deepest sense, and in that sense it is always already in the ethical, despite its nature, which tends to synchronise and to form the 'foundation of consciousness'.[50] Justice leads to the 'we', but can also, being embedded in ethics, critically destabilise any given 'we', thereby differentiating the Other which is oppressed and dominated in the 'we': 'The act of consciousness would thus be political simultaneousness, but also in reference to God, to a God always subject to repudiation and in permanent danger of turning into a protector of all the egoisms.'[51]

74. Levinas's account is subtle and impressive. It is difficult not to fall for it. However, are we not witnessing the unfolding of a cycle which preserves ontic thinking, one that has always been embedded in such thinking, one whose transcendence has never been attentive to, indeed thinking which has concealed, the distortion that the dynamic ontic relationship between ethics and politics gives rise to? Are we not witnessing the preservation of the cycle of representation and representation-ability? Are we not witnessing the preservation of the legal in a harmful way so that its distortion of the essence of law does not oppress and is not felt as it drowns in ontic punctuation – critical, indeed, but punctual all the same? The critical space created by the insufficiency of a given ethical reflection and its containment in the law and politics maintains the logic of still further differentiation of a not-yet-conceptualised Other that is dominated and oppressed. However radical the relationship between ethics and politics seems to be in Levinas, there is still an opening for a methodology in the Levinasian critical cycle, even if the account itself seems to be beyond methodology. And it is this methodology which endlessly nourishes, explicitly or by implication, critical legal and political scholarship. Yes, there is a constant insufficient differentiation of 'Others', that is the ethical challenge, but the method, the

[49] *Ibid.*
[50] *OB*, p 160.
[51] *Ibid*, p 161.

craving for conceptualising the otherness of the other as an Other, the crave for ontic transcendence of history, *a craving that is inbuilt in the very nature of the otherness sought*, remains unchanged. It is a craving for otherness between beings, ontic otherness.

75.   But Levinas reassures us that, despite the strife between ethics and politics, 'There is a possible harmony between ethics and the state. The just state will come from just men and women and saints rather than from propaganda and preaching.'[52] This necessary reduction gives birth to an exploration of the 'reasonable'. Such exploration gives a stable antidote to the radical impossibility of the relationship. The container becomes one of more and more 'others' but an impoverished one at that – one that cannot account for the actuality of the actual of any such 'other'. Why is this? Because, as we shall see in a little while, an 'other' is already at the furthest from his or her otherness. Indeed, the exploration of the reasonable has lurked all the time within Levinas's thought. From the very moment Levinas goes for grounding ethics in infinite responsibility for an 'Other' he imprisons ethical reflection in ontic logic. The craving to go into that logic in the ethical domain was actually twinned with, in order to be moderated by, the craving for the exploration of reasonableness in the political domain. It is in this deep sense that Levinas saw the political and the just look at you from the eye of the Other. The construction of problems as strife and the solving of problems as the exploration of reasonableness are two sides of the same craving. In fraternity the tyranny of ontic strife is matched only by the tyranny of exploring reasonable harmony. The demand for exploring the reasonable is always there, already looking at me from the eyes of the Other.

76.   The tension between the demand of alterity and reasonableness cannot be overlooked as merely a healthy tension. For all his radical character, Levinas does not go near enough to fathoming the origin of the tension between ethics and justice, between the personal and political, a tension that he himself, quite rightly, feels as that which is missing in (derivative) ontological reflection. His blind spot, his inability to go nearer to the origin of that tension, stems from nothing but the very derivative way in which he characterises not only ontology, but also alterity – such a central notion to his philosophy.

77.   Ethics that originates in otherness would see the whole Levinasian ontic strife between ethics and politics as a necessary but distorted conclusion of its own original inexpressible premise, to wit, not merely not yet expressed, but as that which can never be expressed.

---

[52] 'Philosophy, Justice, and Love', in *Entre Nous*, above n 8, p 120.

The distortion is muted, however, by the craving and demand to explore the reasonable.

78. Levinas's vision of democracy incorporates the asymmetry between the Saying and the Said and, in doing so, it embodies the asymmetry in the ethical relationship between people as mediated by the asymmetry between ethics and justice. So Levinas's account is apt for the claim that democracy does not exist meaning that a coherent structure and substance of democracy is too totality-bound to be ethical.

79. But even a democracy that sees the democratic impetus in the surplus of alterity of not-yet-conceptualised Others is ontic in being 'not-yet-fully-democratic'. Democracy, we must stress, even if understood critically and radically as a Levinasian ethical transcendence, is a most apt distortion of that which is ethical in the *demos*. We must think about the mystery that lurks in the most transcendent of democracies in order to perturb, momentarily to near, the sublime otherness of the *demos*. Democracy is unethical because even by taking democracy to its transcendent conclusion of complementarity between surplus of otherness and exploration of the reasonable, the very distortion, the confrontation of, which is an ethical confrontation, is being forgotten.

80. The 'not' of which a democracy is a distortion is not yet touched by critical legal and political scholars because their unsaid is still the anticipation of, the craving for ontic transcendence and the renegotiation of democracy. They are dominated by the ontic horizon which sanctifies democracy and the ethics of the Other behind it. Levinasian democracy is 'prophetic' and, as such, seems to see the hidden and distorted ethical in any ontological conceptualisation of the procedural and substantive democracy. But my argument has been that Levinas, with his representation-ability, foresees such conceptualisations and in fact perpetuates them to the effect of entrenching the forgetfulness of that which they are, and must be, a 'not'. The prophecy in Levinas, being ontologically derivative and hence ontically conditioned, is a derivative prophecy altogether and is itself a distortion of the prophecy of Being.

81. The necessary democratic deficit, as a result of the necessary reduction of representations in the Levinasian fraternal polity, is the ontic illusion of being critical of the totality that democracy harbours. But it still produces a critical democracy in which the strife of Otherness of an Other oscillates with the exploration of the reasonable. Such a process does not yet near the 'not' of democracy. The not-yet-conceptualised Other as the surplus of the democratic deficit, the ethical fuel of such critical democracy in which all are equal in their Otherness, is ontic. The ethical effort is towards

bringing into the language of the polity that oppressed and dominated Other. This ontic illusion of being critical *of* democracy while producing a critical democracy is unethical. Let us relate the notion of surplus of otherness, reasonableness and democracy to the origin of the legal in Levinas.

THE ORIGIN OF THE LEGAL IN LEVINAS

82. In Levinas's essay 'Freedom and Command', which was published back in 1953 – eight years before the publication of *Totality and Infinity* – we find a discussion about the justification and the origin of man-made law. This essay shows how early thinking about the legal preoccupied Levinas.

83. To recap, in *Totality and Infinity* Levinas makes a complex reference to command when he discusses the role of the third party. Both myself and my Other are equals in serving the third party, the 'we'. Levinas continues:

> [The Other] comes to *join* me. But he joins me to himself for service: he commands me as a Master. This command can concern me only inasmuch as I am master myself; consequently this command commands me to command. The *thou* is posited in front of a *we* ... The presence of the face, the infinity of the other, is a destituteness, a presence of the third party (that is, of the whole of humanity which looks at us), and a command that commands commanding. This is why the relation with the Other, discourse, is not only the putting in question of my freedom, the appeal coming from the other to call me to responsibility, is not only the speech by which I divest myself of the possession that encircles me by setting forth an objective and common world, but is also sermon, exhortation, the prophetic word.[53]

This complex use of 'command' encapsulates the relationship between ethics and politics. The infinity of the Other encapsulates equality of me and my other before the infinite otherness of all humanity. Both me and my Other are commanded to command each other in a way which will effectuate our equal responsibility before the manner of infinite Otherness that humanity challenges us with. As Peperzak observes, this formulation echoes the subsequent 'neighbour' formulation of the third party in *Otherwise than Being*. To recap, 'the third party is other than the neighbour, but also another neighbour, and also the neighbour of the other, and not simply his fellow'.[54] Peperzak also observes that if Levinas were to prolong

---

[53] *TI*, p 213.
[54] *OB*, p 157. See A Peperzak, *To the Other*, above n 16, p 181.

the'command' sentence in *Totality and Infinity* he would relate the latter command to the development of the judicial, political, economic and technological institutions that demand a world of general justice.[55] In *Freedom and Command* we find this implied extension to *Totality and Infinity.*

84. Freedom and Command considers the origin of the legal. Levinas relates the notion of commanding to that of freedom. When people are under a tyranny, however absolute, they have as a part of them unlimited force of what Levinas calls 'refusal'. This undiminishing refusal enables a person to grasp the extent of his or her own degradation, generating thoughts about how to combat that degradation: 'Freedom in its fear of tyranny, leads to institutions, to a commitment of freedom in the very name of freedom, to a State.'[56] In setting itself up against tyranny, freedom seeks to establish institutions and texts which will be 'protected from subjective degradation, sheltered from feeling. The supreme work of freedom consists in guaranteeing freedom'.[57]

85. The notion of 'protection' and 'guaranteeing' thus advocated by Levinas is to guarantee freedom by making incorruptible the condition for its flourishing against tyranny. Thus it is the act of humans to establish an order upon themselves in the form of a just state. By doing this they establish a structure which overcomes the obstacle of tyranny. Levinas continues:

> We must impose commands on ourselves in order to be free. But it must be an exterior command, not simply a rational law, not a categorical imperative, which is defenceless against tyranny; it must be an exterior law, a written law, armed with force against tyranny, such are commands as the political condition for freedom.[58]

In this passage the link to the long passage about command quoted from *Totality and Infinity* may be established. The command that protects freedom is inter-human. Both me and my Other impose commands on ourselves in order to establish an inter-human order which will protect our freedoms – protect us from tyranny. The point of view from which this order is justified is that of 'we' or 'all of us'. Importantly, this exterior law that commands us and protects our freedom comes *from* us.

86. What is at stake in this order? It is the conditions for us to maintain ethical reflection and protect our equality-as-Others. The rationale

[55] A Peperzak, *To the Other*, above n 16, p 173.
[56] FC, p 17.
[57] *Ibid.*
[58] *Ibid.*

for law is to protect ethical difference, which is in constant danger of falling into the tyranny of the Same, or more precisely, the exercise of freedom which is already conditioned by totality, by the Same. This totality, as we have seen, would include the selfish isolation of an ethical relationship. To put the justification of law in yet another way, the primordial rationale for law is not to let otherness be degraded into given conceptual relations. The freedom to be protected is that of the Other which is oppressed or marginalised by the essence effectuated by ontological tyranny.

87.   In this passage the primordiality of this justification is emphasised as being not simply a rational law, or even a categorical imperative, but a part of the ethical challenge which include the guarantees for the persistence of the open-ended nature of ethical reflection, namely institutions and laws which will secure against oppression of an 'Other'.[59] If ethics is a first philosophy for Levinas then this primordial law comes to guarantee that it retains that status in a way which can be effectuated, in the form of a continuous ethical challenge, in any given polity. We can see here a primordial understanding of the rationale for the guarantees for freedom of speech, thought and expression.

88.   We can see that the freedom to be protected by the command of this original law, to which all people are in service, is ontic freedom. What is protected is freedom to constantly re-conceptualise a new 'Other'. The origin of the law in Levinas must protect ontic rationality.

89.   But here we must ask again: where is the tyranny? Is not the prison of ontic thinking tyrannous in that it suffocates and oppresses, that is harms, othernesss – otherness in the nearness of which actuality of the actual resides? Is it not the case that the origin of law, if indeed otherness is at stake, resides in protecting otherness, that is protecting against ontic domination and the freedom that is associated with it?

90.   The feature of the primordial law that does protect otherness, and hence *from* the domination of thinking with and through a not-yet-conceptualised Other, is that it is not subjects who command it upon themselves. Rather, it is subjectivity which is commanded by this law. It is subjectivity that ought to be attentive to this law. It is not individual people but this law, whose call comes from the essence of humans, from their freedom to 'ek-sist', from the actuality of actual, thus being unshaken by the biggest commands of

---

[59] I am not sure why Levinas wants to completely distinguish the rationale for inter-human law from the categorical imperative. Perhaps he sees such imperative as the embodiment of ontological tyranny.

human-centred thought that Levinas defends. Human beings are powerless to protect themselves by exterior law against the actuality that comes from their own essence.

91. Levinas is all too aware of the tension that primordial law imposes upon ethical reflection. Ethical reflection, he acknowledges, is personal. But that 'personal' nature of ethics is what makes it so prone to degradation and tyranny. So the main characteristic of this law which guarantees freedom must be impersonal so that it can continue to guarantee the centrality of ethical challenge to the polity. The 'we', the togetherness, must be impersonal.

92. But, then, Levinas asks, does not law entail depersonalisation and tyranny? Institutions will entail the loss of the very freedom they protect: 'The freedom of the present does not recognise itself in the guarantees that it has provided itself against its own degradation.'[60] Once institutional, law would, however minimally, necessarily turn impersonal and become corrupted. The defence of personal reason ends up in impersonal reason. We witness the gradual depersonalisation by being and thinking with law even though the origin of law's establishment was to guarantee the most personal and intimate. Levinas claims that impersonal reason presumes a prior exchange and understanding between different (personal) freedoms and that this understanding occurs as a commonality but as a commonality which is not yet mediated by any impersonal reason. This indeed would amount to that primordial equality of otherness of an Other which, later, he will advocate as a part of the third party which is part of the ethical. There is, Levinas claims, an inter-human exchange which amounts to an ongoing 'command before institutions',[61] before the attempt to articulate the result of this exchange in objectified, impersonal reasoning and language.[62] The togetherness of entering into society comes out of appeal from one person to another in which beings subordinate themselves to one another. This is the first form of command, which is prior to an impersonal 'system'.[63] Levinas asks

[I]s there not already between one will and another a relationship of command without tyranny, which is not yet an obedience to an impersonal law, but is the indispensable condition for the institution of such a law? Or again, does not the institution of a rational law as a condition for freedom already presuppose a possibility of direct understanding between individuals for the institution of that law?[64]

---

[60] *FC*, p 17.
[61] *FC*, p 21
[62] *Ibid*, p 18.
[63] *Ibid*, p 21.
[64] *Ibid*, p 18.

93. Also, much later in his 1982 *Diachrony and Representation*, Levinas claims that even a discourse which is interior and representational allows association only in so far as there is a united thought that removes the distinctness of individual. However, Levinas asks, does this discourse not presume a prior sociality in which individuals are distinct and plural? Hence, the ethical diachrony is more ancient then, and is presumed by, any synchrony. The relationship between representational togetherness and the antecedent distinctness of persons as a prior genuine sociality of plurals is put by Levinas as the relationship between the Saying and the Said.[65]

94. In both *Freedom and Command* and *Diachrony and Representation*, as read together with *Totality and Infinity*, the complementary relationship between representation-able and representational is most manifest. The impersonal and representational, the necessary reduction of the law, is a result of an inter-human exchange which, however free and personal, seemingly unprejudiced, already is conducted within the anticipation of renegotiation of settlements by impersonal language. The legal is already presumed in the 'prior to law' inter-human/inter-personal exchange. The anticipation of reduction, and the anticipation of the necessary surplus of otherness in such reduction are already in-built in the free exchange between wills.

95. We can actually see how the guise of primordial inter-human ethical relations preserves the legal in latently incorporating two kinds of anticipation. The first anticipation is that of impersonal reason to establish a commonality which will claim authority over each exchanging party. The need for such commonality is in-built in the allegedly free inter-human exchange. The second anticipation is the way in which the value-based language of rights and duties will be used, in an impersonal fashion, in a way which reduces the otherness that is implicated in the inter-human exchange.

96. By declaring the basis of the impersonal institutional order to be an inter-human ethical relationship, Levinas does not 'resolve' the conflict between the two. On the one hand, he is aware that leaving people to negotiate for themselves will result in war 'where each limits the others'. So, on the other hand, people will accept that kind of tyranny by 'a rational order where the relations between separate wills are reduced to the common participation of wills in reason, which is not exterior to wills. This is the State. It is the interiorization of external relations'.[66]

---

[65] *DR*, pp 163–5.
[66] *FC*, p 23.

97. But, as we know that Levinas does not intend to resolve that conflict, the rationale of law encapsulates the continuous pressure of the personal upon that order which becomes tyrannical and impersonal. The tension is not resolved but is left at the hand of the *exploration* of the reasonable. The whole of *Freedom and Command* is written in the shadow of Plato's *The Republic*, with frequent references to it. He refers to *The Republic* to extract the reasonable. He quotes: 'Every one had better be ruled by divine wisdom dwelling within him; or, if this is impossible, then by external authority, in order that we may be all, *as far as possible*, under the same government friends and equals.'[67] The reasonable connotes both acceptance of the necessity of this impersonal order but also the need to constantly ethically challenge any tyrannical oppression that this order brings upon the personal. The continual tension between the challenge of the personal and the 'given' of the tyrannical impersonal order is the hallmark of the Levinas's polity. The perfect *aporia*: you cannot do without establishing something that you know is inadequate by its inception. What could be a better sign of that forgetfulness, that succumbing to, and with Levinas, entrenching, the ontic oscillation that brings about the constant exploration and renegotiations of the reasonable? Does the reasonable not throw dust in our eyes, in its ever ontic variations and illusions of negotiating and renegotiating togetherness-in-difference? Does it not blind by its very preoccupation with giving voice to an oppressed 'Other', attempting to find a common language and concepts instead of being attentive to the 'not', namely to the distortion of the legal? Does not the pervasive craving for the exploration of the reasonable stem from a completely ontic domination, while in fact it is, as it has always been, the hallmark of the distortion of the Being of law?

98. Drucilla Cornell sets out the case for law under the Levinasian rationale and portrays the law's aporetic relationship with ethics.[68] Cornell sees ethical relations in an entirely Levinasian manner as 'responsibility to guard the Other against the appropriation that would deny her difference and singularity'.[69] Cornell argues that the law inevitably distorts ethics but that we are 'fated to fall into it'.[70] Her argument, moreover, is that since we are in the law, that is, the third party is a part of the ethical relations, it is not desirable to overcome the legal. It would be a mistake to translate the ethical Saying into the law. The ethical Saying is that difference is not

[67] *Ibid.*
[68] D Cornell, 'Post Structuralism, The Ethical Relation and the Law' (1988) 9(6) *Cardozo Law Review* 1587–638.
[69] *Ibid*, p 1588.
[70] *Ibid*, pp 1591–2.

expellable by law and is always reduced by it. The ethical Saying is in the law as a distortion. This distortion is always violent in its remaining classificatory and bound-in representations. Any translation into the law, which we are fated to make (echoing the inevitability of the ontological Said in Levinas) would reduce the ethical Saying:

> The attempt of a direct translation of the 'ethical relation' into the sphere of law, however, misunderstands the central insight of the philosophy of alterity. The 'ethical relations' is an irremissible necessity, precisely because the other remains cannot be fully enacted in the world. The ethical relation can not be actualized because of the 'precedence' of otherness that keeps the infinite beyond the grasp of the subject and of any system of representation.[71]

Cornell's argument is a typical example of bringing in what I have called the ontic reduction between ethics on the one hand, and politics and law on the other. Although presenting the law as a reduction of ethics, and in this respect ruling out any direct translation from ethics to law, Cornell allows law to be criticised by ethics. The question is: how is it possible? How is it possible to think in terms of critical connective tissue between law and ethics if they are so different? It seems that Cornell emphasises the 'not' between ethics and law, which serves as a constant revival of open texture of the polity, but at the same time anticipates some conceptual success to account for the communication between them. She calls for the exploration of the surplus-reasonable relationship. The translation between law and ethics is not direct but indirect. It is indirect in that law takes the insight from the ethical and portrays it, reductively, in its own language. So this continuing combination of inevitable reduction and relative success of translation puts Cornell's account of the complementarity of ethics and law, as a dialect of challenge and recontainment, in the same boat with advocates of the politics of difference like IM Young. Cornell and Young do not yet attend to the common matrix between the ethics of an 'Other', values and the legal language of rights and duties. My argument is that the 'central insight of the philosophy of alterity', that which Cornell argues has been missed by any attempt of direct translation from ethics to law, does in fact still presume that ontic thinking that is the origin of the legal. Indeed, Cornell's argument anticipates the third' as part and parcel of the ethical judgement. That the law is anticipated in Levinas is evident from her interpretation of Levinas in *Otherwise than Being*

[71] *Ibid*, p 1624.

as saying that 'only a self that constantly seeks to divest itself from sovereign subjectivity will be open to relations of reciprocity.'[72]

99. The real issue at stake here is not the nature of the connection between the ethical and the relationship of reciprocity which characterises law. The issue at stake is the very ontic reciprocity/ complementarity that characterises the continuum of both Levinasian ethics and the law. Cornell overcomes the legal subject but she keeps the notion of radical-subjectivity without even making the very notion of subjectivity a characteristic of the 'falling' into the ontic Said. The heterogeneous subjectivity, as I have stressed many times in relation to reading Levinas, is still within the horizon of subjectivity. As such, heterogeneous subjectivity does not really bring forth the distortion of that logic and hence is locked in ontic reciprocity both within the law and in the ethical challenge to it. *The reduction of legal subjectivity is not the same as the primordial distortion of subjectivity itself. Again, between legal subjectivity and heterogeneous subjectivity there is a common matrix.* Cornell, in short, does not attend to the representation-able nature of Levinasian ethics and how it perpetuates the legal despite being reduced in the representational language of law. Cornell's argument is an application of the problem that exists in confining deconstruction to the punctuality of an 'Other' — to Levinasian ethics – rather than to otherness that is given to any 'Other' as its otherness. Critical legal scholarship, *à la* Cornell, embodies a Levinasian deconstruction of law and the language of law. But such deconstruction stops at the point of it being blind to the ontic nature of the otherness at its origin.[73] Cornell defends a cycle of reciprocal relations which deconstruct the Same, but it is still imprisoned within ontic logic. There is a past that Cornell does not visit by adhering to the project of aligning Levinas and Derrida. The ethical exists as the otherness to the legal which deconstructs thinking with and through an 'Other'.

100. The new form of ontic tyrannical utopia that thinks about law, does not yet think about its own aboutness. Its aboutness is not only ontic - that much would be fine as the ontic is a part of any ontological reflection, but, once ontic, thinking becomes a *transcendence* – tyrannously so. Entrenched ontic aboutness has all the 'right' overtones, that of transcendence of representation, transcendence of ego-based subjectivity, that of overcoming totality, that which responsibility seems always ready to challenge. The alarming thing is that there

---

[72] *OB*, pp 160–61, discussed by Cornell, 'Post Structuralism, The Ethical Relation and the Law', above n 67, p 1625.

[73] See D. Manderson, *Proximity, Levinas, and the Soul of Law* (Montréal, McGill-Queen's University Press, 2006).

seems to be nothing distorted by such ontic transcendence, nothing unethical. But this satisfaction is one that is brought about by the ontic complementarity between the representation-able, the legal, and the representational as the law. Ontic tyranny, in the form of complicity between the legal and the law, complicity that covers up and forgets its distortion of actuality, robs humans of the primordial way in which they can be response-able, and hence responsible, and in this sense unique, beings. The legal, once tyrannous, does not allow Being to be an ethical issue for humans because it shatters Being with the language of rights and duties, with the craving for the exploration of the reasonable. Ontic tyrannical thinking about law would see law as an unhappy necessity, a second best, although this second best is already craved for, and maintained by, the 'first best', that which is seemingly 'other to law' and which is ontic as well.

101. To recap, to think about law is not to be polemical about it. It is to regard law and the legal in complementary relationship to law's essence of which they are a distortion. Our path of exposing this ontic tyranny has shown that, from the perspective of fundamental ontology, ontic 'otherness to law' is nothing but a mature stage, perhaps the twilight, of the distortion of the essence of law.

102. But the mature distortion that the ontic tyranny effectuates harms humans, harming the path to their essence. It is a violent act of human arrogance in which the ethical is relegated. Acts of human design, that is, acts that humans think are correct, are themselves always given by Being, and so no act of human design can surpass the Saying of Being. No human law can surpass divine law or assimilate such divine law to have a representation-able human origin and centre. Indeed, such assimilation robs humans of their 'ek-sistential' essence. Any tyrannous ontic complicity is but a stage of the historicity of Being. It is a stage where Being, the Being of law, loses its audience in the forgetfulness of its distorted ontic manifestation. This may come to the decisive point that it is nearly no longer possible for human contemplation to bring humans back to their essence.

103. *It is not yet near enough, then, to simply expose that Same or totality that possesses the means of representation, oppressing and dominating an Other in the process.* The suffocating ontic process never again comes back to the elements, never faces the distortion. The reasonable supplies us with the ethical criticism and exploration, so the actuality of the actual of what is given to an 'Other' as his otherness, the actuality of the otherness of this Other, need not generate any anxiety. The entrenchment of the legal replaces anxiety with ontic responsibility. To be anxious is to be beyond the pale of reasonableness, to be nearer than the hope of the reasonable. The ambiguity of the reasonable in the following passage must not now

hide the primordial nature of the reasonable in Levinas: 'Utopia, transcendence. Inspired by love of one's fellowman, reasonable justice is bound by legal strictures and cannot equal the kindness that solicits and inspires it.'[74]

104. If reasonable relates to the ability to reason, reason-ability, then ontic exploration of reasonableness has not yet attended to reason's origin in the order of Being.

105. Levinas smothers the mystery. Ontic open-endedness is all but foretold and the legal reigns supreme and enjoys the unlimited legitimisation of its many manifestations. The complicity of surplus between ethics and politics makes it looks as if there is nothing to think about. But to recall Heidegger in *What is Called Thinking?*: what is most thought-provoking is that we are still not thinking. Still, then, this ontic hegemony contains the ethical call for thinking. It is timely, as a part of tracing the origin of the legal, to slowly embark on the origin of otherness in thinking-Being, thereby challenging the evident open arms with which Levinas's ethical transcendence has been received. This effort points out the historicity in which receivers find themselves, namely in their craving to become ethical by proceeding in a manner which is detached from historicity.

---

[74] 'The Other, Utopia, and Justice', in *Entre Nous*, above n 8, at p 230.

PART C

8

The Mystery of Otherness as Being-with

1. This chapter returns to Heidegger. In chapter four the notion that the essence of law is not legal was discussed. I argued there that a part of *Dasein*'s falling is necessarily into the legal but that the essence of law protects *Dasein* – we might say, ethically, ought to protect *Dasein* in its 'ek-sistence' – in its attentiveness to Being. Harm was conceived as the *entrenchment* of the legal – an epoch, in which calculative thinking dominates through representational norms, values and risk assessment. Such an epoch, at one level, encompasses the whole philosophical tradition, but the intensity of the harm varies as the historicity of this tradition unfolds. Another study would be required to discuss in detail the various phases within the tradition in which the legal is entrenched. I have chosen, though, to focus on what I see as a contemporaneous manner of entrenchment of the legal. In chapter seven it was argued that Levinas's transcendence, his conception of otherness and the anticipation of the Other as 'not yet conceptualised' is the most sophisticated means of entrenching the legal and calculative thought. This entrenchment of the legal, it was argued there, is effectuated by the perpetuation of the ontic in representation-ability of the 'not yet conceptualised' Other. Although Levinas overcomes representation, he stays within the grip of its horizon by the punctuating character of his ethics. The use of the notion of ontic alterity and ontic transcendence, one that consists of many Heideggerian echoes, leads to thinking critically about law. However, it does not yet think about the Being of law, as that would necessitate thinking about the legal, and this in turn necessitates thinking about that 'about' in 'thinking about law' with and through the ontically based transcendence provided by ethics of punctuable and representation-able alterity.

2. This book does not provide a theory of law. The path here is an attempt to think about law in the sense of thinking about thinking with and through law, namely thinking with and through the legal. Both the derivative 'ontology' of the legal and the ethics of it which

are based on value, rights and obligations have been revealed in their hiding place within the thought of Levinas.

3.   The task of thinking about law, then, is to think about the relationship between the ontological and ethical. Thinking about law, about the harm of the legal, is, first and foremost an ethical enquiry. Thinking about law, thinking about law's essence, its Being as distorted by the legal, requires us to reveal what lies beneath ontic thinking about law, that thinking that produces not only the practice of the legal but also theories of law and jurisprudence. We need to go into the very nature of the connection between ethics and ontology in order to respond to the Being of law and to the law of Being. The continuous mystery of otherness needs to be dwelled upon. The last two chapters of the book are devoted to that connection. The end of chapter nine will return to the issue of the legal, namely being and thinking through human law. The understanding of human law includes the human conception of Divine Law as a representational-able transcendence of any represented universal code.

4.   In order to explore the relationship between ethics and ontology, we need reflect on the ethics of the identity of *Dasein*, or the question of the 'who'. The question of the 'who' relates to the origin of alterity. The issue of I/Other is so central to thinking with and through the legal, even in a 'critical' guise. We need to slow down and dwell on the origin of the otherness of the other as other in order to near the distortion between the being that is law, and the Being of law that justly protects.

5.   I am not using capital 'O' any more in the word 'other' in order to overcome the notion of exteriority and punctuation. The otherness of the other as the mystery of identity, as the mystery of the continuous, is more ancient, and hence radical, than any 'Otherness', precisely because it does not crave for punctuation. If I quote Heidegger, I use 'O' if it appears in the translation but I should clarify that it is not the 'Other' of Levinas which is being referred to.

6.   Thinking of the otherness of the other and how it is encapsulated in the relationship between ethics and ontology is needed in order to thinking about the 'about' of the way Levinasian discourse of an 'Other' thinks 'about' law. In this chapter, then, I would like to make explicit and enhance many themes that were left undeveloped in the reading of Levinas that I have undertaken in the last three chapters.

7.   In exploring the relationship between ontology and ethics, three interrelated issues are debated. The first is the notion of Heidegger's famous silence. I should claim that silence is primordial in ethical thought of any kind. Silence is the only manner in which *Dasein* is attentive to language, that is the manner in which language is attentive to its own Saying. *Ethical reflection involves dwelling on*

the issue of silence. In so dwelling I will distinguish silence that stems from the impossibility of nearing the continuous, silence of the attentiveness to the inexpressible Saying, from the silence that stems from the radicalisation of punctuation. The second issue meditates upon the notion of 'being with' [*mitsein*] or rather 'being there with' [*mitdasein*], as a part of an overall meditation on Heideggerian ethics. The third issue relates to notion of dwelling and the relationship between mortals and the divine – it is a response to the question of what it means, *essentially*, to be a human being.

8. In distilling the connection between the notions of 'silence', 'with' and 'ethics', we need to connect Heidegger's insights in *Being and Time* with his later thought. For Heidegger uses terms in *Being and Time*, for example 'dwelling', upon which he seriously reflects only in his later work. It is very un-Heideggerian to subject Heidegger's works to some chronology – a succession of 'now-work' – which the thrust of his very writing attempts constantly to overcome. The 'now' of *Being and Time* includes the temporality of Heidegger's own possibility. My reading attempts to make Heidegger's work itself hover in temporality. The radicalisation of philosophy undertaken in *Being and Time* has its own unsaid and concealment in which its essential truth lies. The 'before' and 'after' of his thought are mingled in every articulation of a 'now' in his writing. We must not only explain the ethical *in* Heidegger, we must be ethical in reading him and, as such, we need to leap into the temporality of his own thought by continue to meditate together with him on the way. Indeed, I will argue that the ethical primarily resides in being-together 'on the way'.

9. A good text embracing Heidegger's thoughts on temporality is his 1927 lectures, now collected in the volumes of *The Basic Problems of Phenomenology*. Heidegger allows this text to be published only in 1975, a year before his death. As mentioned in the editorial preface to the volume, the text incorporates Heidegger's manuscripts of the lectures and his typewritten copy and contains many marginalia and insertions. As such, as the editor A Hofstadter tells us, the text embodies already many reflections from the so-called 'later Heidegger', in which Heidegger gives account of *Dasein* as subservient to Being. It is here that Heidegger distinguishes between, and links, the temporality that is *Dasein*'s own constitution [*Zeitlichkeit*], and Being's temporality [*Temporalität*]. The text itself constitutes much more than a fascinating summary of the thesis of *Being and Time*. It also contains many anticipations of his 'later' reflections. *The Basic Problems of Phenomenology* is fertile ground to gather many insights concerning ethics, combining *Being and Time* and his later lectures.

BEING-WITH

10. One of the chief criticisms made by Levinas of the predominance of ontology is that it conceives the relationality between subjects as that of being-with, rather than a responsible being-for-the-Other. Being-with, *including the otherness of the Other as a thinker of Being which is encapsulated in it,* has been criticised as conceiving multiplicity only within the confines of totality – an 'allergic' multi- plicity. However minimally, claims Levinas, the multiplicity of being-with, even when manifested as transcendence of simpler totality and commerce of I/Other, involves a mutually reinforcing game of representations of the other in the self and for the self. Genuine alterity is not engaged by being-with and constitutes an irreducible trace of exteriority to reflection with and through being-with. Being and thinking with law, which Levinas wants to transcend, is a manifestation of principled codes that are a result of the dominance of the ontological horizon of being-with. 'Being-for- the-Other', on the other hand, by confronting alterity, constitutes genuine thinking about law. Thinking about law, so the argument goes, involves criticising the representational nature of that totality that in turn leads to representations of harm that humans can do to one another. But we also saw that being-with and being-for, the relationship of politics/law and ethics in Levinas, is complex. I argued that although Levinas does think critically about law, he does not yet touch the primordial 'about' – Levinas's thinking still perpet- uates the legal.

11. We need to reflect upon the relationship between 'being-with' and 'being-for'. Does the most radical form of 'being-for' not already presume an antecedent 'with'?

12. Let us magnify the notion of 'with' in Heidegger's thought. This magnification will lead us to insights about the ethical and the legal. J Hodge's fascinating and comprehensive backward readings of Heidegger attempt to distil a response in his work to the question of the essence of humans. However, remarkably, there is neither a discussion of the nature of otherness in Heidegger, nor a serious discussion of 'being-with', apart from couple of pages at the very end of the book.[1] To me this is too glaring an absence from a book about the ethical dimension of Heidegger's thought. I also feel that this book seeks, however implicitly, some reconciliation with the tradi- tional notion of ethics. However, there have been some studies that do interpret the 'being-with' of Heidegger and its relationship to the ethical. For Olafson, the subject–subject relationship, that is the

---

[1] J Hodge, *Heidegger and Ethics* (London, Routledge, 1995) pp 199–200.

relationship of inter-subjectivity, captures the connection between Heidegger's notion of being-with [*mitsein*] and 'caring-for' [*fürsorge*]. Mutual disclosure for Olafson is the ground of the ethical and characterises that which is primordial in human sociality.[2] His argument is that the relationship of care between human beings occurs prior to, and in a way which is critical of, any ethical code that people are all under. Despite arguing that representation of the other reduces the otherness of the other Olafson does not make the issue of otherness a field of inquiry. Although Olafson provides an account of conscience and guilt in relationships between people[3] he still does not relate them to Heidegger's main concerns such as truth as *alētheia*, dwelling and time. Whilst Olafson gives an account of the Categorical Imperative in ontological terms of *mitsein* rather than ontic terms of various 'subjects' under some commonality of principle, he still attempts to reconcile the notion of being-with as inter-subjectivity and the notion of otherness. This reconciliation makes Olafson's account prone to all the criticisms Levinas levelled at the notion of *mitsein*, as opposed to 'being-for'. In other words, Levinas would claim that there is a 'for the other', speaking to the Other, looking at the face of an Other, before there is a 'with'. An inter-subjectivity based on 'with' would, for Levinas, disguise unethical totality and allergy.

13.   Alternatively, we could say that Olafson assimilates Heidegger into Habermas, without acknowledging it. Olafson's account falls into this tack of argument, and I feel that he 'bends Heidegger's arm' so that Heidegger's insights can be assimilated into inter-subjective ethics. Olafson tries to fill up Heideggerian silence by turning Heidegger into a Habermasian philosopher.[4] Olafson cannot bear silence, so it seems. Indeed, it is quite clear that Olafson is critical of Heidegger for not really making clear the ethical potential of his own account of *mitsein*. Heidegger, for Olafson, does not exhaust the ethical potential of his philosophy of *mitsein*. Again, I feel that Olafson did not engage in a deep analysis of Heidegger's account in his so-called 'earlier period' of *Being and Time* and *The Basic Problems of Phenomenology*. Moreover, there was no attempt to determine how Heidegger's early works relate to the later ones in terms of the way in which an interpretation of *mitsein* should be carried out and developed. I felt, in short, that Olafson did not give a charitable interpretation to Heidegger's notion of *mitsein*, with the

---

[2] FA Olafson, *Heidegger and the Ground of Ethics: A Study of Mitsein* (Cambridge, Cambridge University Press, 1998) pp 10–13.
[3] *Ibid*, pp 45–7.
[4] *Ibid*, pp 51–9.

result that he developed Heidegger's thought in a way which highly distorts many of Heidegger's chief insights. The craving to extract an ethics that is separate from ontology, rather than seeing ethics and ontology as one, is the craving which causes many people to read Heidegger apologetically. It is this craving from which I see the urgency to depart.

14. C Fynsk's interpretation of Heidegger's *mitsein* goes a long way to do justice to the account in *Being and Time*.[5] Drawing on *Being and Time* as a whole, Fynsk accounts, not without Levinasian overtones, for the problem that evidently preoccupies Heidegger, namely how '*Dasein*'s singular relation to itself is to be disclosed to the other and, of course, how *Dasein* is to encounter the other as other – that is, how *Dasein* is to discover the other's relation to itself as an instance of alterity'.[6] The problem of otherness in Heidegger was rightly identified by Fynsk as being related to understanding Heidegger's unique notion of *mitsein*. Fynsk gives a detailed analysis of *Being and Time* which includes *Dasein*'s openness to the other in anxiety. He explains how what Heidegger referred to in Part 2 of *Being and Time* as the 'voice of conscience' relates to *Dasein*'s involvement with the nothing as the experience of guilt. Guilt, in turn, precedes the resoluteness of *Dasein* to open up to its own temporality and transcend the ontic cycle of self-interpretation. Importantly, Fynsk gives an account of the 'there' which calls [*Es ruft*] to *Dasein*'s own innermost potentiality of being, a call to which *Dasein* is attentive, and the role of the other in opening up *Dasein* to that call.[7] Fynsk shows how Heidegger's notion of friendship is embodied in the relational attitude *Dasein* has towards other *Dasein*s and how friendship gives *Dasein* the impetus to repeat itself in its own innermost 'can-be'.

15. The account of this chapter is much indebted to Fynsk's account. Many of my arguments are variations on and developments of Fynsk's interpretation of *mitsein*. Further, my arguments draw the implications for ethics from the conception of otherness that is encapsulated in the interpretation of *mitsein* that Fynsk inaugurates. In my reading of Heidegger, I also comment on Fynsk's account whenever appropriate. My argument interprets Heidegger's thought by first magnifying the way the process of the 'with', within which *Dasein* is essentially involved, casts light on the issue of the 'otherness of the other' so essential to ethics. In developing the

---

[5] C Fynsk, *Heidegger: Thought and Historicity* (Ithaca, Cornell University Press, 1986) pp 28–54.
[6] *Ibid*, p 33.
[7] *Ibid*, p 41.

notion of otherness, my reading of Heidegger shares many of Fynsk's discoveries. In my own interpretation, whilst constantly bearing in mind Levinas's notion of radical otherness, I shall point to the inherent mystery, from an ontical point of view, of Heidegger's notion of *mitsein* and otherness. The mystery can be glimpsed in revealing that even absolute otherness, when neared enough, un-conceals a primordial notion of continuous otherness which is nearer to actuality, and in this sense of nearing, is other than the oppositions of same/other. Such primordial otherness neither denies nor affirms the radical distinction between self/other but it claims an irreducible mystery in which both self and other dwell together. Does being 'for' an absolute Other precede being 'with' another *Dasein*, being-with as dwelling in the otherness of the continuous? I shall argue that otherness implies neither ontic separation nor identification between two beings, arguably, options that Fynsk can sometimes still be understood as faintly echoing, although of course the thrust of his interpretation does not claim to do so.[8] My own reading of Heidegger's notion of 'with' and 'otherness' attempts to take an ontological look at the for-the-most part I/Other separation. Second, in reflecting upon *mitsein* and otherness, I also interpret the notion of the 'with', not only on the basis of *Being and Time*, but also in connection to *The Basic Problems of Phenomenology* and Heidegger's later essays.

16. Last but not least, I am highly indebted to J-L Nancy's account in *The Inoperative Community* of the experience of 'sharing' as like-being.[9] My close reading of Heidegger's early writings in this chapter, and his later writings in the next, develop his account in detail and relate it to the main argument of this book.

17. Grasping the relationship between *mitsein* and otherness in Heidegger points towards the ethical in Heidegger as involving mysterious *mirroring and identity*, other, of course, to the commerce of identification and, of course, other to radical ontic critical *justification* through values, rights and obligations.

18. I develop an interpretation of the valuable. To the extent of developing the ethical, I advance an argument about the ongoing debate about the relationship between 'is' and 'ought', between facts and values.

19. In Hebrew, there is a connection between the words YAHID (a particular, an individual; YEHIDA – a unit of something), YAHAD (together, being-with; also BEYAHAD – being-in together; and

---

[8] *Ibid*, p 36.
[9] J-L Nancy, *The Inoperative Community* (Minneapolis, University of Minnesota Press, 1991) p 33.

MEYUHAD – being special, unique) and YIHUD (some individual, innermost own, characteristics). Listening to the Hebrew language reveals something to us. Hebrew tells us that there is an intimate connection between togetherness and being special and unique. Being special and unique must involve something which is *Dasein's* innermost own. However, this 'mineness' must not be interpreted as being alone or enclosed in oneself. On the contrary, *Dasein*, being-there, *is* most originally as being together with others. Only as transcending self-enclosure can innermost particularity be instantiated.[10]

20. Hebrew, then, tells us that the relationship to the question of the 'who', of identity, already embodies a sense of 'with'. But would the question of the 'who' as related to a 'with' have to bear the totality and sameness of mere identification which results from being-with, as Levinas would like us to believe? In that case, by failing to account for the dimension of 'for the Other', Hebrew would have not disclosed to us the notion of identity that comes from a genuine relationship of alterity.

21. But do we have to rescue identity from mere identification implied by the 'with' by resorting to a surplus in terms of an 'Other'? Perhaps Hebrew tells something about the relationship of unity between identity and 'being-with', which still needs to be heeded in Heidegger? Could mere identification and identity complement one another as a part of the ontological difference? What is that in which human *Dasein*s dwell with one another in a primordial way? The argument to come reads Heidegger with particular view to connecting the themes of identity, identification, being-with and otherness.

22. If ethics is embedded in authenticity, namely in taking human *Dasein* as it essentially has to be – as both authentic and inauthentic – it ought to encompass in its essential nature that which *grounds* human choices and so-called (ontically based) autonomy. Such ethics has to relate to the distorted conception of language and truth which is used in order to enshrine and to protect this autonomy. The question of what it means to be a human being would have to have already be given to [*es gibt*]any ethical theory that explains human actions, thus rendering such a question ethical.

23. Is not being a human being, primordially, a question of 'who', that is a question of identity? In *The Principle of Identity* Heidegger recalls that in *The Sophist* Plato had reflected on identity as a 'sameness *with*' some synthesis and unity.[11] In Hebrew, the words ZEHUT (identity), HIZDAHUT (identification; also implies to state allegiance

---

[10] It is worth noting here that the word *interest* comes from Latin *intersvm*, which means both being together, being amongst as a part of a group, but also to be different, to differ.
[11] *PID*, p 25.

to some collective thought) and ZEHE (being the same, sameness, identical) have the same root. Whilst it is somewhat easier to relate *identification* to *identical* we need to ponder upon the manner in which the idea of *identity* reveals a deep sense in which all human are identical or 'same with' one another. Do humans have the same essence in which they *are* together, meaning that all have the same identity? Would such a question have an automatic tendency to destroy genuine alterity? Could plurality conditioned by sameness that nevertheless constitutes the origin of difference, that is of personal uniqueness? *We must recall that thinking the Being of beings is other than, though in complementarity to, thinking beings. The notion of identity, of the who or what of it, is not its extantness but its continuous web of relations which opens up its world. Identity is essentially in a world in which beings are related to one another. The 'in relation to one another', the 'with', is continuous and mysterious and cannot be reduced to onticl otherness as a distinction between beings. Identity is not pointing at a positive 'it' of things but as their not yet temporal unfolding relational world with the 'there' of others.*

24.   The word 'sameness' has all sorts of Levinasian echoes. In what follows we have to listen to what the word 'sameness' tells us in the simple primordial speaking of language. If identity relates originally to some sameness, does it mean that it is a non-starter in ethics in that it resorts to the 'same'? What I will argue that Heidegger is doing is deconstructing the very notion of sameness. Heidegger's argument is that humans are the same, and they dwell in their sameness with one another. But it is a peculiar kind of sameness, and a peculiar kind of 'with', both of which are not reducible to the Levinasian ontic horizon of sameness/otherness. Heidegger's account of sameness and togetherness cannot be reduced so as to point to a need for ethics that is based on absolute difference, because he argues that humans have a meeting point where they are not *different* in the ontic sense. Yet Heidegger's account cannot be reduced to an account of identity which is based on multiplicity within a totality, sameness, or even to allergy. For Heidegger, the ethical question of what it is to be a human being, which unites primordially the question of the 'how' and the 'who', is neither about being 'same' or 'other' in ontic manifestations. Sameness *or* difference? Otherness is both and neither, mysterious to its roots. The sameness of human beings, their identity, lies in their dwelling in this mystery.

25.   The infinity indicated in Hebrew between particularity and togetherness is deeply intimated in Heidegger's thought. For *Dasein* to be, to 'ek-sist', to be attentive to the Saying of Being, is not only *conditioned* by prior togetherness but it is also *a way* of being

together-with. I am not saying 'a way' to be together in order merely to signify some ontically represented way or another to be together with others, but rather, more primordially, being *on the way* with others.

26.   The notion of 'with' in Heidegger has a special sense of 'amongst', to dwell-amongst other *Dasein*s. Such dwelling is not in addition to *Dasein*, outside *Dasein*, separate from *Dasein*. To dwell-amongst is part and parcel of *Dasein*'s temporal constitution as 'care'. *Contra* the impression that Levinas conveys of Heidegger's thinking-Being and thinking-temporality, thinking-Being in transcendence, 'ek-stasis', can never be lonely. The mystery, the ontological difference, requires us to grasp the special connection between the particular and the together which is neither separation nor assimilation. To be can never be lonely. What is my innermost own way is essentially un-loneliness.

27.   To be 'amongst' means for Heidegger to be 'in the midst of'. 'Amongst' does not mean merely being present among others beings. Rather, the very character of 'in the midst of' belongs to transcendence. That which surpasses and so 'passes beyond' beings must be first situated in the midst of Being. In this 'midst' transcendence occurs, that is a world opens up for each *Dasein* who resides there.[12] Being 'in the midst' is not static and connotes 'being always already on the way with'.

28.   What is it to be on the way together with another. What way? What is a way? How is the way with others? For Heidegger, a way is an unfolding boundary of language, in the house of which the boundary of Being and time unfolds. We are on the way together and in this togetherness; indeed, this togetherness calls to my own thinking and thinging. We are all hovering in time together, and when this togetherness calls and talks to our own innermost 'how' we project our past onto the future.

29.   Ontic otherness, even when it is taken to extremes by being wrapped in seemingly Heideggerian manoeuvres, is not yet otherness. Whilst dwelling in the nothing there is no Other but 'together in the otherness of the continuous near'. The otherness that discloses itself in the face of the otherness of 'an other' is the 'with' by which *Dasein* is constituted – a 'with' that pertains to the 'how', which essentially remains concealed from *Dasein* as this 'how' discloses.

30.   We shall see shortly that the connection between the 'how' of other *Dasein*s and *Dasein*'s own entails only distortingly the notion of me and an absolute Other. The crux of the challenge to subjectivity is that in a moment of being-in-the-world there are no absolutely

---

[12] *ER*, pp 107–9.

distinct involvements, not even involvements which are inter-subjective. To be authentic and innermost own, a moment of 'mineness' does not imply any distinct subject that re-grasps itself after experiencing the caress of absolute alterity. The grasping of itself, the radicalisation of subjectivity, is already a distorted moment of the more original event of alterity that has already concealed itself. Any togetherness which implies and anticipates subjectivity is not yet a primordial 'how' but a necessary and necessarily distorted together which is 're-presented' to the subject as its innermost 'how'. We could put it differently, namely by saying that some original togeth-erness already anticipates the fall into subjectivity as a distortion, however radical this subjectivity is. Ontic togetherness is a resultant distortion of a more original togetherness and, as such, it is not yet particular in the 'together', it is not yet special and unique. 'Mine' and 'me' play hide-and-seek in the stillness of dwelling with one another. This hide-and-seek reveals the uniqueness of the 'how' and the 'who' of the particular *Dasein*.

THE ANALYSIS OF MITSEIN IN BEING AND TIME AND THE BASIC PROBLEMS OF PHENOMENOLOGY

31. In chapter IV of the first division of *Being and Time* Heidegger gives an account of being with others which, he explains, forms part and parcel of *Dasein*'s constitution. The discussion of 'being with others' relates to the question of identity of *Dasein*, or 'who is the particular *Dasein*' whose Being is an issue for it, in its everydayness. The identity of *Dasein* as a being which persists through experi-ences in a manifold of otherness has the ontic character of present-at-hand, an extant. But this conception of identity belongs only partially to the essential nature of *Dasein*. *Dasein*'s consti-tution involves temporal transcendence and, as care, it is always ahead of itself. The actuality of *Dasein* is too near, always being already temporalised. As transcendent, the world of *Dasein* is ready-to-hand, is equipmental, namely it has a characteristic of in-order-to. Being temporalised, *Dasein* is only as not yet and is constantly on the way, ahead of itself. In order to grasp the 'who' of *Dasein* as ready-to-hand, that is how it is in the world as transcendent of that self sufficient 'wholeness' of a subject, or indeed inter-subject, we need to focus on that which constitutes *Dasein* as its 'not yet'. We must ask how the 'who' as transcendent is involved in the world. How does the world of *Dasein* unfold to *Dasein*? The 'with' as a constitutive element of the world of *Dasein* comes to the fore as surplus or, Heidegger puts it: 'It could be that

the 'who' of everyday *Dasein* just is not the "I myself".'[13] What is in each case *Dasein*'s own, the 'mineness' must be understood otherwise than as the obvious understanding of merely conceiving *Dasein* ontically as a subject, although subjectivity, as we shall see, is an important *part* of *Dasein*'s temporal constitution as care. In the everyday, the notion of being-with, *as a constituent of Dasein as transcendent of subjectivity,* is prominent. Others constitute the context that is part of *Dasein*'s own understanding as transcendent, that is as a part of *Dasein*'s own innermost world.

32.   Heidegger introduces a crucial distinction that is vital for fully appreciating the depth of his notion of the 'with'. This distinction is between being with [*mitsein*] and being-there-with [*mitdasein*]. *Mitsein* is where togetherness is ontically understood as the togetherness of extant beings that are in commerce with one another in a dynamic of identity and difference. Such is the way that *Dasein* is essentially involved with others for-the-most-part, and it bears importance as to his understanding of the 'they', which I will come to shortly. This being-with [*mitsein*] is distinguished from *Dasein-with* or, as I would prefer to call it, being-there-with [*mitdasein*]. It is in this 'being-there-with' that *Dasein* is with others as a part of its own world – as a part of its own constitution as transcendent and care. It is on *mitdasein* that I would like to expand, and to corroborate my reading of the 'there' where *Dasein* is with others with Heidegger's lectures in *The Basic Problems of Phenomenology* in this chapter, and, in the next chapter, with his later reflections. It is in the proper understanding of this 'there' that the key to Heidegger's notion of otherness lies and it is central to any understanding of his ethics and, in turn, to thinking about the Being of law.

33.   For the most part we are already involved with others. Heidegger gives the example of 'that a field belongs to such and such', and there could be countless example from everyday life of that kind of relation to others as a part of *Dasein*'s own world and, importantly, a part of the world of others. The others and things associated with those others are not merely encountered as present-at-hand, but they are already ready-to-hand as worldly equipment in a way which constitutes our world too. Crucially though, Heidegger sees both present-at-hand *and* the readiness to hand at that level merely as a point of departure for deeper comportment, namely for a deeper 'with' relationship, namely the relationship between other *Dasein*s as a constitutive part of each and every *Dasein*. He says: '*Dasein*'s world frees entities which not only are quite distinct from equipment and Things, but which also – in accordance with their kind of Being

[13] *BT*, p 150.

as *Dasein* themselves – are "in" the world in which they are at the same time encountered within-the-world, and are "in" it by way of Being-in-the-world.'[14]

34. It is notable that Heidegger uses the notion of 'freeing' to characterise the deep relationship between different *Dasein*s. This is important to his ethics as something is enabled through, and by, this encounter between *Dasein*s. Something in the 'there' of each is enabled by the 'with'. The freedom of *Dasein*, its letting its own Being, as 'ek-sistence', be, is enabled by this deep encounter by *mitdasein*. We can already detect an embryonic peculiar and intriguing notion of otherness here. It is the otherness of other *Dasein*s that allows *Dasein*'s innermost own to reveal itself, to call upon the for-the-most-part ontic *Dasein* both in its present-at-hand and ready-to-hand.

35. Heidegger emphasises that 'others' in this primordial context does not mean simply other people from whom one is distinguished. 'Others' connotes a togetherness of *Dasein*s in a meeting point of each in their own innermost 'there': 'we meet them "at work", that is, primarily in their Being-in-the-world ... The Other is encountered in his *Dasein*-with in the world.'[15] Here we come across a tension. *Dasein*'s innermost 'own' is encountered only via the encounter with other '*Dasein*', in being 'amongst' other *Dasein*s in their innermost own – where their own *Dasein* transcends temporally. This 'amongst' is the particular sense in which the idea of 'with' should be understood. Heidegger called this amongst 'Being-there-too' [*auch-da-sein*]. The 'too' here connotes 'a sameness of Being as circumspectively concernful Being-in-the-world'.[16]

36. The 'with' here, then, has ontological connotations. The 'with' itself embodies a site of transcendence, again, a meeting place of two or more *Dasein*s in a moment of transcending. To emphasise, each *Dasein* at this point utilises ('utility' in the sense of readiness-to-hand, in-order-to, equipment, not in the sense of calculative instumental purpose) the meeting to hear something. This meeting point of *Mitdasein*, the 'there' of the 'amongst', is a moment where the care-structure of each *Dasein* converges. This point of 'amongst' is a point of 'mutual' care, which Heidegger refers to as solicitude [*fürsorge*]. This caring-for as a part of the 'with' understood as amongst must not be confused with the being-for-an-Other of Levinas. Ethics may well reside in this 'with' but it is a more primordial ethics than that ethics based on the notion of the 'totally

---

[14] *Ibid*, p 154.
[15] *Ibid*, p156.
[16] *Ibid*, p 154.

Other' which presumes punctuation and separation and, as such, is utmost stretch of the present-at-hand.

37. Solicitude is the special kind of concern of *Dasein*-with. *Dasein*, as care, encounters objects as equipment. In its ability to encounter beings as equipment *Dasein* transforms its own experience of the thingness of things, namely from encountering them as beings to encountering them in their Being. This transformation characterises *Dasein*'s solicitude with other *Dasein*s. At the specific meeting point under consideration here, the point of *Dasein-with*, what is encountered is not an object, a mere finite human being.

38. We now learn that a special kind of care manifests itself as *Dasein*'s own constitution. Some forms of solicitude, what Heidegger refers to as 'deficient', manifest themselves as *Dasein*s 'not mattering' to one another. As deficient, they are still very significant ontologically but they do not constitute a primordial encounter.

39. Crucially for establishing ethical relations in solicitude, Heidegger distinguishes between two types of positive (as distinguished from deficient) solicitude. It is important to contemplate these two kinds of positive solicitude because they can be easily mistaken for something similar to a Levinasian ethics of 'an Other' or as some craving for such ethics. The first kind of solicitude is where *Dasein* appropriates 'care' from another *Dasein* and puts itself in that other *Dasein*'s position. This kind of solicitude assimilates the other *Dasein*'s care-structure into some discourse whereby each *Dasein* who takes part is not attended to. This solicitude does not attend to the care-structure of the *Dasein*s. Such solicitude is characterised by reduction, and quite possibly by the domination of one *Dasein* whereby the other *Dasein*s cannot attend again to their own 'there' in the meeting. This inability would render this meeting inauthentic as one temporal structure of care dominates. In the second type of positive solicitude, one that Heidegger referred to as authentic, solicitude frees *Dasein*s. In this type of solicitude each *Dasein* mirrors back to the other *Dasein*s their own care-structure, their own 'not yet'. This solicitude attends to each and every *Dasein* who comes by. It would be a distortion to characterise this meeting as one between beings who are different, or as a representation of multiplicity under a totality or sameness. Rather, there is silence which is maintained there in the speaking, as Heidegger puts it: 'This kind of solicitude pertains essentially to authentic care – that is, to the existence of the Other, not to a '*What*' with which he is concerned; it helps the Other to become transparent to himself in his care and to become *free* for it.'[17]

---

[17] *Ibid*, p 159.

40. To be with here means to make *Dasein* free for his care. That freedom means that in the 'with' *Dasein* can 'stand before' [*vor-stehen*]. To understand in old German [*verstehen*] is to open up to the event that frees possibilities; it is the event when *Dasein* is open to the Saying of its own Being, that is to the Saying of Being – an instant of *alētheia*. In *The Basic Problems of Phenomenology* Heidegger had this to say:

> To be one's own most peculiar ability to be, to take it over and keep oneself in the possibility, to understand oneself in one's own factual freedom, that is, to *understand oneself in the being of one's own most peculiar ability-to-be, is the original existential concept of understanding*. In German we say that someone can *vorstehen* something – literally, stand in front of or ahead of it, that is stand at its head, administer, manage, preside over it.[18]

41. Let us look more closely at these two modes of positive solicitude as articulated in *Being and Time* and read them together with passages from *The Basic Problems of Phenomenology*. It is worth noting at the outset that the other is not an extant being. The other is a *Dasein*, that is essentially a 'traveller' in time whose innermost care-structure is transcendent and can be characterised by a deferral or stillness, a not-yet futural repetition, a *déjà vu* of its past. In the first, inauthentic, encounter, something in the solicitude becomes dominant and prevents the hovering in time by the various *Daseins*. Each *Dasein* who comes back to this solicitude has already confronted the possibility of its own concern. Although the authentic solicitude is given beneath the inauthentic solicitude, the latter does not yet attend to the former. An inauthentic meeting does not yet speak the nothing for each *Dasein*. The inauthentic meeting can vary along a spectrum ranging from sympathy whereby all temporalities are reduced to some common perspective. However, and more controversially, inauthentic solicitude can also occur as empathy, whereby every hovering *Dasein* stops hovering and is denied its point of concern by some meeting point with the other *Dasein* where difference is already becoming somehow managed in interpretation. I will dwell on empathy a little later.

42. In the second, authentic, type of solicitude each *Dasein* is a mirror to other participants but, as a mirror, it maintains its own care structure. It meets other *Daseins*' temporality without assimilation. They are travellers in the nothing and, as such, united in their essence as 'ek-sistents' but what is mirrored back after the togetherness in the nothing is the innermost that is particular to each *Dasein*. The

---

[18] *BPP*, p 276. Heidegger is referring here to the original German usage in which understanding was spoken of as *vorstehen*, as opposed to the contemporary *verstehen*.

peculiarity, or strangeness, of this process of understanding in mirroring – of a meeting that yields difference – can be felt. This moment where two temporalities meet precedes any empathy and is already distorted by it.

43. This meeting is characterised by mutual help, mutual letting-be. This is an encounter of the other *Dasein* as a thinker of Being *whose not-yet mirrors something that, despite its otherness, still calls for attentiveness.* The unification in this essence in the nothing and the strange and mysterious interpretation that occurs cannot be helped and cannot be assimilated into an interpretation that creates totality, that is, sympathy or empathy. The meeting is to glimpse understandingly at the 'there', where *Dasein*s hover together in time, glimpsing but always without quite grasping. This mutuality of the 'there', of the hovering, should be sharply distinguished from any allergy, reciprocity or symmetry. It should then also be, of course, distinguished from the misguided reaction to allergy or reciprocity, namely radical ontic asymmetry. The mutual mirroring-in-hovering is not reciprocal and does not diminish the abyss of the nothing for each participant or guest. A guest is OREACH in Hebrew and has the same root (A, R, CH) as OVER ORACH, which means a passer-by, one who stops for a while but is constantly on a journey. Mirroring something to other *Dasein*s, meeting them in their 'there', is helping. This helping is what makes this kind of meeting ethical. The ethical is letting and helping in 'ek-sisting'. Potent mirroring means also that *Dasein* remains open to the reception of a call from the other *Dasein*s. The meeting connotes that mirroring *Dasein* also suspends *the very anticipation of its subjectivity* thus being involved as a murmuring of its 'ek-sistence' – as an authentic moment of being there, as *Dasein*.[19]

44. *Dasein* 'ek-sists' *understandingly.* When *Dasein* is at the event of openness, of unconcealment, it projects itself as its most peculiar ability-to-be. Heidegger is careful to distinguish this from the mere projection of the ego as an object of cognition. The understanding is never 'objectified into ...' but remains both very clearly near but at the same time hint-like, furthest away from a way that can be apprehended objectively. This characterisation of the moment of understanding does not imply vagueness. On the contrary, it is a moment of clarity because it escapes objectification. The moment of possibility is not cognitive, but it is the original moment of the 'am'

---

[19] In *BPP*, p 288, Heidegger maintains that Being 'there' together means that there is an openness on the part of *Dasein* to the 'thou'. Only in a moment of individuality is there an event from *Dasein*'s resoluteness in which *Dasein* is open to the 'thou'. This event does not occur as an intrusion of the I upon the 'thou' stemmed from their common concealed helplessness. The instant is a moment of genuine individuation, where *Dasein* is free for itself.

which precedes any cognition, although it inevitably falls into some configuration or is even distorted in empathy. This moment 'unveils without making what is unveiled as such into an object of contemplation, there is present in all understanding an *insight* of the *Dasein* into itself'.[20] Heidegger emphasises that this moment does not have any character of free-floating knowledge but nevertheless has a character of truth of own-understanding – own standing-before.

45. In *The Basic Problems of Phenomenology* Heidegger again characterises the occurrence of this moment of understanding as being-with other *Dasein*s: 'along with understanding there is always already projected *a particular possible being with the others* and a *particular possible being toward intraworldly beings*. Because being-in-the-world belongs to the basic constitution of the *Dasein*, the existent *Dasein* is essentially *being-with* others *as being-among* intraworldly beings.'[21] The inter-human is most originally intra-worldly. The moment of *Dasein*'s particular understanding occurs in being-with other *Dasein*s – in *mitdasein*. But the insight here is that of being amongst together 'as one' at a moment of understanding and, as such, it is very different, Heidegger claims, from just subject-based projection or a 'solipsism of *I-thou*'. The notion of 'mineness' and otherness converge here in a way which arguably could not be reduced to any totality, either totality of the ego or ontic totality which, in deep disguise, makes possible a separation of an absolute Other. Heidegger's 'amongst' is different from, and precedes, both Buber's reciprocal I/thou, and Levinas's asymmetrical ontic account. The emphasis is that *despite* the for-the-most-part entirely different 'wanderings', *Dasein*s can nevertheless meet up: '"thou" means "you are with me in a world".'[22] This meeting-up does not reduce any difference to any kind of totality but rather produces a meeting point in temporality where 'other' and 'self' dwell together in their 'ek-sistence' — in their world as a way.

46. Ethics originates as the valuable in the authentic mode of caring-for, which momentarily successfully transcends representation. The valuable occurs as attentiveness to actuality of the actual of other *Dasein*s. The valuable originates in mutual mirroring, not in any value that can serves the basis for this or that justification through ontic distinction. Representations of goodness and badness are themselves distorting their origin in the valuable. In the valuable Being is let be as some *Dasein*s solicit in understanding. Any goodness or badness that claims to originate in justification,

[20] *BPP*, p 277.
[21] *Ibid*, p 278.
[22] *Ibid*, p 298.

including the good of the 'not yet conceptualised Other' is already a distortion of primordial authentic 'with' as being amongst in authentic solicitude. Importantly, even the distortion of goodness and badness already encapsulates a happening of positive solicitude. But with this ethics of mutually becoming near the continuous nothing as our innermost 'how', we can also see the origin of friendship.

47. In friendship, the other *Dasein* mirrors back to all guests their 'not-yet-as-having-been' while they do the same. One *Dasein* is in a part-ing of the other but is not thereby become the same as the other. Thus, while being helped in its comportment towards its finitude, *Dasein* also mirrors the unfolding boundary of its finitude to the other *Dasein*, maintaining its otherness, or being open to the other *Dasein as other Dasein*. Otherness always maintains the distinction between different paths, or ways, but it always comes by *Dasein* being already ready to hear the otherness from within. Only at the moment of attentiveness to this otherness from within which is augmented in mirroring can *Dasein* be, and because of that can also mirror to the other as other. That is why this process is not lonely. *The otherness of the other and Dasein's own otherness come from the same place but they are not the same precisely because of that.* This 'place' is a place of crossed temporal paths. Only in connecting to its own finitude, as *Dasein*'s being-towards-death is being being mirrored to it, can *Dasein* mirror back, that is can it be ethical and be mostly intimate with another *Dasein* and, because of it, other than it. *Otherness entails innermost intimacy.* It is a mystery that real difference can never come about as a result of a total and radical ontic separation. We shall come back to this in a short while.

48. Fynsk shows Heidegger to argue that the friend gives *Dasein* its possible being-towards-death – the friend, according to Fynsk, is *Dasein*'s witness, the witness that generates the feeling of *guilt* in *Dasein*. It is through a friend that *Dasein* is being held onto the nothing.[23] I would see friendship also as original kind of *utilitas*, contemplative rather than calculative. 'Help', as expounded by Heidegger, means that *Dasein* 'uses' that friendship as a hint at its 'ek-sistence'. Such is the occurrence of the 'in-order-to' spoken about in *Being and Time*.

49. Heidegger's ethics may be found in the following passage from *Being and Time*, which must be quoted in full:

In Being-with, as the existential 'for-the-sake-of' of Others, these have already been disclosed in their *Dasein*. With their Being-with, their disclosedness has been constituted beforehand; accordingly, this disclosedness

[23] Fynsk, *Heidegger: Thought and Historicity*, above n 5, pp 43–4.

also goes to make up significance – that is to say, worldhood. And, significance, as worldhood, is tied up with the existential 'for-the-sake-of-which'.
Since the worldhood of that world in which every *Dasein* essentially is
already, is thus, constituted, it accordingly lets us encounter what is environ-
mentally ready-to-hand as something with which we are circumspectively
concerned, and it does so in such a way that together with it we encounter
the *Dasein*-with of Others ... Being-with is such that the disclosedness of the
Dasein-with of Others belongs to it; this means that because *Dasein*'s Being
is Being-with, its understanding of Being already implies the understanding
of Others. This understanding, like any understanding, is not an acquaintance derived from knowledge about them, but a primordially existential
kind of Being, which, more than anything else, makes such knowledge and
acquaintance possible. Knowing oneself is grounded in Being with, which
understands primordially. It operates proximally in accordance with the kind
of Being which is closest to us – Being-in-the-world as Being-with; and it
does so by an acquaintance with that which *Dasein*, along with the Others,
comes across in its environmental circumspection and concerns itself with –
an acquaintance in which *Dasein* understands. Solicitous concern is understood in terms of what we are concerned with, and along with our
understanding of it.[24]

50. Let us untangle this passage. In solicitude *Dasein*s meet by their
    common concern. This commonality connotes a meeting place of
    *Dasein*s, each of which is in the whilst of the stillness of its own
    innermost way. But we must notice that the commonality does not
    reduce each to the 'there'. That is the gist of positive authentic solic-
    itude. The 'mineness' of each flickers with the helping happening of
    that commonality. The commonality is that of deferral, of nothing,
    of mirroring, of silence. Other *Dasein*s do something to *Dasein*'s
    own thingness, to its innermost essential temporal transcendence,
    mirroring its essential 'near-to-itself'. Thereby is established a
    common concern but such concern does not reduce the 'mineness' of
    each of us to the commonality. In the whilst of authentic solicitude
    the inexpressible for the most part murmurs in concealing itself for
    each of the participants.

51. This temporal meeting 'site', as explained in *Being and Time* makes
    Dasein and *Dasein*'s attentiveness to Being through friendship the
    focal point of reflection. But, of course, as I have described in chapter
    two, *Dasein* is authentically only in the whilst between the call of
    Being and its own belated response to this call. Only in being so
    attentive does *Dasein* prepare for its 'isness-in-ek-sistence'. So we
    need to understand the authentic solicitude in such a way that such
    solicitude, being a 'way', a clearing, is the arena for the Speaking of

[24] *BT*, pp 160–61.

Being, for-the-sake-of which each participating *Dasein* is attentive. It is in relation to Being that I interpret Heidegger's notion that *Dasein* is essentially for the sake of Others. Here is Heidegger's response to Levinasian claims about the loneliness of thinking-Being: that even if *Dasein* seems lonely, it cannot, by its constitution, be alone. *Dasein* is essentially 'with', 'amongst', other *Dasein*s.[25] The world of the 'with' is not a 'we', nor is it inter-subjective representational consensus. Solicitude is the original mode of sociality of others of which there are many derivative and distorting ontic instantiations. *Dasein* falls back into these distorting instantiations. The original mode of sociality, of commonality of *Dasein*s is a unique 'with' that connects a unique 'care-for'. It is through friendship, understood as mirroring of the inexpressible, that Being's voice becomes conspicuous and more audible for *Dasein*. Solicitude as a form of being-with is a necessary constitution of *Dasein* in its essential anxious attentiveness to Being. The artist would mirror Being through the artwork but it is each *Dasein*, even in its exposure to art, who, through its own being-with, its own 'with', opens up to its own being-in-the-world. A work of art becomes the 'friend' of many *Dasein*s, allowing them at least the gateway to a possibility of not dying inauthentically by showing them a glimmer of an opening to their own, innermost abyss. In this sense, art is allowed to speak through the work of art thereby enabling the abyss to speak *Dasein* in friendship. Thus understood, art is ethical.

52. Being speaks ethically through friendship.

53. It is in the light of authentic solicitude that we can also consider the origin of otherness. The otherness of the ontological difference means that the identity of *Dasein*, its thingness, is always already and mysteriously in the 'with' among other *Dasein*s. We must resist thinking about the otherness of the other as rooted exclusively in an extant that is 'not like me' or 'totally otherwise than me' as a matter of ontic difference. Ontic otherness leads to ethics of obligation, duties and rights that are the origin of the ethics of the legal. In ontological thought, otherness becomes mysterious because it does not involve separation between self/other in the same way that ontic otherness does. Ontic otherness as a mode of otherness that occurs in the fall of *Dasein* into the ontic, if taken to accommodate that pseudo-Heideggerian move by Levinas, contributes to the perpetuation of the legal. I have argued in chapter four that the essence of law is not legal. Now we can say that the essence of ethics, indeed in otherness, lies in mirroring so that the 'ought' is directed towards

---

[25] *Ibid*, p 160. In *BPP*, p 278, Heidegger says 'being-in-the-world is with equal originality both being-with and being-among'.

mirroring innermost mysterious 'ways' and not towards language which could either explicitly or by implicit anticipation lead to the 'ought' of value-based justification.

54. The origin of otherness is always my own innermost otherness, my own nothingness, which always mirrors back at me from the preceding 'with', that is from the way of the continuous 'there' of friends, that is other *Dasein*s. Otherness means that essentially my identity is changing by dwelling in the continuous 'there' with other *Dasein*s. It is from the 'there' which changes that my identity flickers. Strictly speaking, the otherness of other *Dasein*s that mirrors the way to me means not that there is no identity, but rather that identity is in the 'not'. My identity is essentially always already changing on the way that I travel with others who mirror my own unfolding way. *Only as a way, I am. Only in what withdraws into the continuous that is nearer than my response – into nearness in which I dwell with others – I am. In the same way as identity is a mystery, the notion of 'other as other' is also a mystery.*

55. Otherness as mirroring of the mysterious nothing and the otherness as ontic transcendence encapsulate the relationship of distortion that subsists in the ontological difference, the relationship between the ontological and the ontic – between the continuous and the punctual.

56. The origin of otherness of the other as the mysterious otherness of the nothing lays itself open. The other reveals its 'there', its own otherness, only in the encounter of authentic positive solicitude. For *Dasein* to be able to relate to another *Dasein as other* it has to traverse the manifestation of otherness which has its ground in innermost own-ness- in a form which is "mine". This own-ness is awakened by the 'there' of other Daseins – by that which is their strange nearest. Otherness shows itself only as a mirror image that also mirrors back. The meeting's mirroring exchange of innermost nearness in which both *Dasein*s dwell mysteriously together does not unite the meeting beings-in-the-world into a same.

57. Another *Dasein* can be related to as other only in preceding fateful unity. Let us listen to Heidegger: 'only because it is [for-the-sake-of-its-own-self] can [the *Dasein*] be with other *Dasein*s and only on the same condition can another *Dasein*, which in turn is occupied with its own Being, enter into essential exitentiell relations to a one that is other than itself.'[26] To be with in the 'there' grounds the ontic relations towards another being, into which *Dasein* falls. Otherness is preserved only in mutual echoing. *Dasein*'s temporal path resists any assimilation and totality as the only possible connection of it to

[26] BPP, p 296.

another path is through something mysterious that mirrors back from that other path and hence cannot be reduced to it.

58. Fynsk's writes: '*Dasein*'s resolute repetition of its own throwness is thus also a repetition of the other's resolute being toward death.'[27] The notion of 'an other' that Fynsk introduces here and in what immediately follows this quote must be understood not as an ontic other person but rather as another 'path' of another 'there' that crosses our path and allows our path to open up in its 'not'. Had there been 'an other' *simpliciter* there would be no meeting place. Where there is no self-nearing there is no perturbing, no world opens up and shows itself and there is no mirroring of alterity back to the other *Dasein*. To relate to the other *as other* is to dwell together in the otherness, the abyss, of the continuous that constitutes each *Dasein*'s essential temporal unfolding. Dwelling is the stillness of the opening up to *Dasein*'s own way, own always-too-near otherness, by listening to the call helped by mirroring from other *Daseins*. In the event of being-in-the-world, in the 'there', *Dasein* is freed for its own particular way, which is a particular 'way' in which Being temporalises itself.

59. The ground of ethics is in otherness and it hinges on grasping the mystery that involves the 'who' of *Dasein*. In this mystery *Dasein*s are particulars ontologically, but their particularity stems precisely from an absence, that is from the 'not-yet-there' of their ontic separation. Only when the mysterious notion of distinction of mirroring signifies primordially can ontic separation as a distortion become possible.

60. Our response to Levinas is: the totality of derivative ontology is indeed characterised by the idea of 'the other' in me. But once identity is grasped as 'an unfolding way' it is manifested as the mysterious togetherness of the nearness of the 'there' of *Dasein*s *manifested* as an exchange of mirroring. This murmur of the continuous near in which *Dasein*s dwell together in mirroring is neither totality nor ontic radical difference.

61. Also in responding to Levinas, we can say that the anticipation of an Other to be represented is not yet a Heideggerian anticipation that is entailed by the primordial 'with' and 'amongst'. Ontic anticipation of the representation-able is more akin to what Heidegger called 'expectation'. Heidegger saw expectation as something which characterises the for-the-most-part mode of *Dasein*, where there is no mystery in that which is being anticipated: 'The expecting of the for-which is not a contemplation of an end and much less the awaiting of a result. Expectance does not at all have the character of an ontical appre-

---

[27] Fynsk, *Heidegger: Thought and Historicity*, above n 5, p 49.

hension; nor is the retention of the wherewith a contemplative dwelling with something.'[28]

62. As an exchange of mirroring, otherness is a constitutive part of *Dasein* being essentially not yet near as 'ek-sistent', that is, always for the most part not yet as being amongst. The question of identity, or the 'who' of *Dasein*, becomes manifest only in relation to the inner 'not', inner otherness, that is mirrored mysteriously by meeting other *Dasein*s in their 'there'. The otherness of the other is accessible to *Dasein* as its own otherness, and only as its own otherness can it mirror to the other the other's own otherness. In this meeting, the *ontic* self/other become blurred, only clear as a point of departure. The issue of identity encompasses the transcendence of *Dasein* into its own 'there' rather than merely identified as a self within some web of representational totality or indeed as a radical, still ontic, heterogeneous subject.

63. *Dasein* can become free for itself in a moment of authentic being-in-the-world only when its innermost own not-yet, its own otherness, its own being as projection upon the Saying of Being, is mirrored through friendly 'there's. Only then can *Dasein* glimpse at its near, resolutely glimpse at its thingness which overflows the farness of its subjectivity. Only in mirroring does *Dasein* listen to the call that is initially opened up by the anxiety that befalls it in its for-the-most-part involvements in the world. Otherness is a process of opening up a window to own-nearness beneath the necessary for-the-most-part own furthest. The process is initiated with anxiety. Anxiety is the constant emotion that makes *Dasein* ready. *The otherness of the other Dasein is the manifestation of the for-the-sake-of-which of Dasein, namely the otherness of the continuous.* The otherness is that of the inexpressible mineness that comes from *Dasein*'s own innermost temporality and conditions the 'there' of the thrown *Dasein*. That otherness is inexpressible also in the way in which language speaks that 'not yet there' of *Dasein*. *Dasein* in its nature is a pointer to that 'there' in anxiety. Being towards *Dasein*'s own innermost death is that pointing. Pointing originates as the anxious contemplation of not-being. *Dasein* is open to, and oppressed by, the nothing – by the no-thing – and this oppression facilitates the comportment towards its own 'not yet', to the inexpressible, its innermost 'there'. Anxiety characterises *Dasein*'s openness to Being – its being spoken by Being. This *ethical* process, the process of constituting *Dasein* as care, necessitates friendship that comes to *Dasein* – the most intimate of hints. Being speaks *Dasein*, but in anxious attentiveness *Dasein* is ready to encounter that

---

[28] BPP, p 293.

mirroring of its being-in-the-world through something that calls from the 'there' of a friend. The ethical is that otherness (mystery: own/other otherness) that frees *Dasein* in its innermost for-the-sake-of-which. The friend helps *Dasein* in letting its own Being be. The other as a 'thinker of Being' is also merely a 'way' to itself and, as such, mirrors 'ways' to other *Daseins*. *Dasein* waits for clearing that will come upon to call it.

64. When *Dasein* encounters another caring *Dasein* with whom it can unite in concern for being-in-the-world (love? the mystery of love as the *purity* of the unboundedness of the continuous?), it is awakened in its own boundary or gap. *Dasein* can either look aside, pushing aside this call of Being coming from a caring other *Dasein*, by resorting to rationalisation, justifications and representation, in which case *Dasein* remains ontic, inauthentic, blocking Being from speaking. 'To be philosophical' about a situation is a typical example of such a move. Resorting to 'ethics' in the form of ontic transcendence is, as I argued, the most sophisticated way of the forgetfulness of Being. Such extreme violence of forgetting being in an ontic transcendence is the consequence of resisting being open to the mystery of otherness, reducing it to totality or allergy.

65. In positive authentic solicitude, the otherness of *Dasein* manifests itself in a way which is the occurrence that builds upon anxiety but which is still not expressible and does not yet constitute a response to the call. In the effort encapsulated in the comportment towards that moment of the inexpressible, *Dasein* is ethical. Only in this moment when the no-thing is mirrored to the attentive, ready and anxious *Dasein* can it be ethical by attentively letting the strangeness of otherness perturb itself. In mirroring something to itself, in attending to its own otherness, *Dasein* cannot help but mirror to the other *Daseins* their own otherness. The ethical effort of *Dasein* is towards sensing and seeing its own gap as it has been mirrored to it. By resorting to the term 'effort', I do not want to imply that *Dasein* makes any choice. Ethical mirroring does not represent a methodology or will. Effort of *Dasein* occurs, as explained in chapter four, in its essential erring that already establishes a meeting place of dwelling together; being amongst one another; being in the nothing with other *Daseins*.

66. From a point of view of conventional ethics what is spoken in authentic positive solicitude, the otherness of the other, must be characterised as ontic silence both because it is not paraphraseable, irreducible to values and beings, and also because it manifests a clearing that conceals itself as it reveals.

67. Otherness of the other encapsulates, then, the mysterious origin of the very relationship with the other *as other*. Otherness of the other is

already *Dasein*'s own, its own 'not yet as having been'. *Dasein* 'ek-sists' as transcendence only whilst 'other' to its fallen ontic self. Such otherness can only be mirrored to *Dasein* whilst dwelling amongst other *Dasein*s. Openness to its world involves *Dasein* facing its own innermost otherness. The meeting with other *Dasein*s, this meeting with and dwelling, is when two 'not-yet's, two 'ek-sistences', mirror to one another in murmuring.

68. Otherness, that is, the transcendence of identification with the other through ontic commerce with the other, occurs not as a Levinasian ontic transcendence of that commerce of Levinas, but rather as a mirroring by *Dasein* of something from its nearest that reinforces its own hovering along its way. *What is mirrored, it must be stressed, is nothing extant but the murmuring way.*

69. To be together in the mystery of the way is not totality. Otherness of the other and of oneself are united in the openness towards the Nothing, that is towards Being. That unification does not make them the same, but simply fellow travellers and dwellers. Each gets his or her own innermost particularity as part of this dwelling together.

70. *Dasein*'s own Being, as transcendence, is effectuated in this meeting place with other *Dasein*s. It is other *Dasein*s that call to its own thingness. The meeting place of *Dasein*s, the *mitdasein* is the 'not yet' of each, transcendence. Heidegger is then able to say that 'the world of *Dasein* is a with-world (*Mitwelt*)'.[29]

71. Being own while losing itself is part of the happening of *Dasein* being with others.[30] The characteristic of *Dasein*'s transcendence, a transcendence that *Dasein* is freed for in solicitude, is that the *extant* (thing/a being) and the *handy* (that which is given in-order-to) are met. Otherness is the transcendence. *Otherness is that strangeness that the encounter with other Daseins mirrors, both the 'not yet as having been' as my innermost own and with it, the distinct own-ness of that other Dasein that also hovers in time.* It is grasped as both an act of receiving and giving, and the otherness of own, and otherness of other thereby engulf *Dasein*.

72. Own-ness is only neared in relation to otherness but that is very different from saying that radical and heterogeneous subjectivity occurs after a proximate encounter with absolute Otherness.

73. Thus, as Levinas has claimed, ethics as alterity is a first philosophy. From an ontological perspective, Levinas's errancy is a genuine one. Otherness resides in the unsaid of Levinas. Otherness of the nothing can murmur in Levinas, showing its distorted instantiation: *otherness of the Other as exteriority originates in the otherness of the nothing.*

[29] *BT*, p 155.
[30] *BPP*, p 300.

334 Thinking about Law

Between the origin and its ontic manifestation there is a distortion. It is in that mutual hovering that the other is not really 'an Other' and yet is other all the same that the valuable originates.

74. *The hovering in the continuous means that any punctuation already originates in the mysterious together. There is no exteriority to that hovering. Any exteriority already belongs to the belated response to the call that comes from the otherness of that hovering-together,* otherness that awakens the most particular own 'way' of each *Dasein.*

75. The valuable is letting the otherness of the other show itself as a murmur of the otherness of the nothing. The valuable originates only in a relationship of solicitude. The valuable originates in that encounter with my own 'there' being attended to, a mutual concern that frees the other in its own innermost 'there'. The togetherness is not proximity or substitution. Both of these are ontic. In the poetic moment of transcendence, *Dasein* mirrors mutual concern and only because another *Dasein*s can hover, on its own innermost way. Ethics is letting oneself being claimed by Being together with other *Dasein*s. The temporality of *Dasein* [*Zeitlichkeit*], is the for-the-sake of which of the with-in-the-nothing and only as such can it be attentive to the nothing, to the moment Being temporalises itself [*Temporalität*]. The way in which *Dasein*'s own temporality is humbled before Being's temporality occurs ethically in the 'with', never in the ontic separation between same and Other. We are all on the temporal way, distinct, but never totally separate.

76. By positive solicitude Heidegger does not mean some dialectic of inter-subjective consensus and insurgency, or some continuous renegotiation of togetherness. Togetherness 'ek-sists' in the way of *Dasein*'s 'ek-sistence', attentive to the nothing. There is no practical programme, methodology or suggestion here. In dwelling together over the abyss, own unconcealment [*alētheia*] flickers in otherness.

77. *In a world of ontic dominance by thinking along the lines of 'an Other' the ontological difference, the punctuation of otherness amidst the continuous primordial dwelling-with, is itself silenced unethically by ontic transcendence.*

78. The silence that characterises the essential transcending-with towards the near must not be reduced to an exercise of self-interpretation by exposure to something different. Merely to ask myself 'is my identity as essential as I thought it was?' distorts poetic silence. These kinds of ontic contestations are for aspiring and critical 'men of affairs' and can only serve to forget the essential by assembling some reminiscences of a poetic moment. To be-with-ethically must keep its silence even at the sight of all good inspirations and derivative way of contestation.

79. Heidegger's understanding of empathy is as that of a deficient mode of being-with. Empathy occurs when other mind shows itself and is being understood as a part of being-with, in which *Dasein* proximally dwells. Empathy is based on the idea of an 'ontological bridge from one's own subject, which is given proximally as alone, to the other subject, which is proximally quite closed off'.[31] Heidegger shows how the primordial ethical meeting, being-there-with, which is part and parcel of *Dasein*'s constitution occurs and is given prior to empathy. Having said that, the *potential* of empathy, as we saw with the case of Levinas, goes beyond what Heidegger assigns to it here, but even in Levinas, the craving for the deferral, as we saw, is already embodied in, and dominated by, the ontic craving that is indeed captured by Heidegger. *As Levinas seemingly goes beyond any empathy, his detachment is nothing but the entrenchment of the ontological Said in the horizon of empathy.*

80. In reflecting on empathy, Heidegger emphasises that primordial being-there-with is not between two subjects. Being-there-with connotes a relationship between two or more *Dasein*s. Empathy is already the falling, perhaps the supreme instantiation of that falling, into error. In empathy the mystery still echoes, but *Dasein* essentially distances itself in coping, and thus in erring. The notion of otherness, or the other *as other*, has to be understood as the actuality-as-projection in a way which the notion of empathy, however sophisticatedly distinguished from the totality of sympathy, can only distort. The otherness of the other and therefore, the other as other, cannot stem from a craving for ontic separation between two different subjects. It stems from the strange togetherness which is preceded by the mysterious call to 'me' and to 'you'. The response to that particular call that is manifested in the togetherness is also particular:

> Of course it is indisputable that a lively mutual acquaintanceship on the basis of Being-with, often depends upon how far one's own *Dasein* has understood itself at the time; but this means that it depends only upon how far one's essential Being with Others has made itself transparent and has not disguised itself ... 'Emapthy' does not first constitute Being-with; only on the basis of Being-with does 'empathy' become possible.[32]

81. Hovering together and crossing each other in temporality is the unification in which every own-ness is freed for its own-event of unconcealment. Otherness of an 'own' can originate only in a

---

[31] *BT*, p 162.
[32] *Ibid.*

moment when two *Dasein*s share *every-thingness*, through their own mysterious thingness.

82. It is through this Being-with and the otherness that comes up through it that *Dasein*'s own attentiveness to Being is assisted over and above *Dasein*'s readiness in anxiety. Heidegger called this relationship of Being *Seinsverhaltnis*. Being-with shows why identity is perpetually deferred, not by the deferral of alterity of an Other, but in this play of mirroring of own-otherness, in the meeting of *Dasein*s.

83. So empathy presumes being-with, but, of course, where empathy is reflected on by *Dasein* it is already ontically distorted. The moment of the 'with' is all but gone and the positivity-in-the-deferred-there which has characterised it is replaced distortingly in some positive notion of empathy where a gulf between two 'subjects' is affirmed as an ontic meeting point. On this interpretation 'empathy' becomes part and parcel of *alētheia*, of the hermeneutic cycle or, as Heidegger calls it, 'hermeneutic of empathy'.[33] Even a relationship of otherness without assimilation is already an understanding of a positive thing, and hence ontologically derivative, namely a representation of the gap, of what cannot be understood. Empathy as the closest instantiation of error is already a taming of the continuous near and is already tainted with some representational 'correctness'; it is already a meeting that cannot bear the meeting of deferral, thus taming the deferral, making it a radical gap between 'I' and 'Other'. Empathy is the instance when the mystery speaks, namely concealing the concealment of the near.

84. We come across a striking phrase that anticipates Levinas's criticism of totality. We recall that in *Totality and Infinity* Levinas claims that in representation we represent the Other to ourselves without caring for the Other, without counting on him *as Other*. In anticipating such a statement:

> Such a number of 'subjects' gets discovered only by a definite Being-with-and-towards-one-another. This 'inconsiderate' Being-with 'reckons' with the Others without serious 'counting on them', or without even wanting to 'have anything to do' with them.[34]

85. It is only from being-there-with, where another *Dasein* is being counted upon and hence cared for, that the criticisms of not being considerate between 'subjects' distortingly derive. Ontological 'care' precedes any talk, however radical, about the ontic notion of 'not

---

[33] *Ibid*, p 163.
[34] *Ibid*.

caring'. Thus, such ontic talk is itself a deficient mode – a distortion – of being-there-with.

86. How would Heidegger reflect ethically on Levinas? We saw that ethical hovering occurs as dwelling with other *Dasein*s, establishing a place of dwelling, a common 'there', of the nothing where the continuous has already been interacted with in the face of ontic separation. This is a mystery, as togetherness and otherness are fused in their distinction. As far as Levinasian reflection is concerned, the mystery, as original otherness-in-dwelling, already conceals its own concealment before its distortion as ontic talk about a transcendence-by-separation, that is as talk of an Other. The effect of this double concealment is to establish an 'it' which is seemingly Heideggerian in its transcendence while in fact is a distorted, irresponsible response to Heideggerian dwelling.

87. *The primordial manifestation of the ethics of alterity, then, occurs as a part of thinking-Being.* Thinking otherwise than Being hinders the potential opening of the mystery to thinking as it plays to *Dasein*'s disposition to succumb to the obviousness of ethics that relates to a not-yet-conceptualised Other. Thinking otherwise than Being lures *Dasein* to stay in the pseudo-mystery of the inability to understand 'other minds', in the pseudo-mystery of empathy. Once the ontological Said as the hermeneutic of empathy is ontically confronted by thinking through alterity of an Other, thinking fails to face the mysterious origin of empathy.

88. There is a relationship between the concern that characterises solicitude, and care as the temporal structure of *Dasein*. The concern is that which *Dasein* misses. What does *Dasein* miss and what solicitude helps *Dasein* out to grasp and hence to be free to 'ek-sist'? In *The Basic Problems of Phenomenology* Heidegger accounts for the 'missing' that belongs to *Dasein*. As a reminder, one of the main moves of Heidegger is to ground Being in temporality. This means that *Dasein* transcends both its self-interpretation as subject of thought, and objects of thought that would be for that subject. *Dasein* transcends its extantness in leaping ethically into temporality. The relationship between temporality and Being that persists in the ontological difference means that everything which may be termed 'positive' is only so by privation and distortion. It is very important to distinguish privation and distortion from mere absence and negation, as we saw in chapters two and four. Care is already in the 'not yet'. Being is essentially concealed in its moment of disclosure. In attending to the near, to the Being of beings, the focus of thinking is on that 'not' of distortion or privation which just for while resists yielding any extant 'thing'. Thought attends to the unconcealing of the thingness of things. Thought is never on the

thing itself but on its thingness, not on perception but on perceivedness,[35] not on representational ideas, concepts, but on the Saying of language which lurks beneath all those representations and concepts.

89. The positivity of *Dasein*'s transcendence being grounded as 'ek-stasis' is characterised by something missing. But this something missing is not in the shape of an object or a representational idea. What is missing causes anxiety because it is inexpressible. The 'it' which is missing, which lies so near as the 'there', *cannot* be conceptualised. Nor can it be seen as ignorance. What is nearest to *Dasein*, its innermost own, is least accessible through representational ideas and concepts. In thinking about its own Being, *Dasein* cannot go nearer than that anxiety of the missing. Precisely when *Dasein* thinks about itself, the 'it' given to its 'self' becomes inaccessible. The comportment of *Dasein* towards its innermost missing, that primordial intentionality, we can refer to as *desire* (although Heidegger did not refer to it as such). In *The Basic Problems of Phenomenology*, Heidegger said: 'Missing is not a not-finding of something ... Missing is the not-finding of something we have been expecting as needed. In reference to our dealing with equipment this is the same as saying: what we need in use of the equipment itself.'[36] Missing, or desire, relates to the letting-function of the in-order-to of equipment rather than to an object or ideas. Had it related to an object it would be more of an ontic 'need'. Missing is not the craving for something – an inauthentic retention. The 'ek-statis' itself is a 'missing' of the mystery. It is in the missing that the handiness of the handy becomes conspicuous.[37]

90. The meeting place of positive solicitude as a part of the constitution of *Dasein* shows that *Dasein*, as transcendence, confronts its own 'missing' in the social. The missing murmurs itself in unconcealment through the sociality of *Dasein*s. The otherness of *Dasein* is only when the other, as other, mirrors the missing to *Dasein*.

91. It is very important to note again that in mirroring its own 'missing' *Dasein* does not assimilate its path to that of the *Dasein* that mirrors. It is only through such mirroring, when something is awakened in

---

[35] Heidegger discusses extensively Kant's position that hovers between the positive thesis that Being is an absolute position, and the negative one, namely that Being is not a real predicate. Heidegger exposes the lack in Kant of a distinction between perception and perceivedness, a distinction that, of course, is missing also in Husserl. This distinction is developed in explaining the ontological difference, as perceivedness belongs to Being which is given to beings. Heidegger argues that Kant touched on the problem, but because of his derivative ontology, he could not transform the inner tension of his thesis about Being into an insight. See *BPP*, pp 27–76, an argument returned to at pp 313–18.

[36] *Ibid*, p 310.

[37] *Ibid*, p 311.

the thingness of *Dasein* by the handiness of the handy of the other *Dasein*, that *Dasein* can open itself to the other. *Dasein* for the most part goes about an ontic self-interpretation with a past which is being retained as forgetting and a future as expecting. But in the meeting there is revisiting of the past in a strange way that awakens the most innermost familiarity with a world. In anxiety the together brings about a further leap from 'self' to 'own'. The moment of meeting, the mirroring of the missing, comes up as a thinking-back, nearer than the memory of *events* but rather a memory of something in a bygone world.

92. Openness to the other *Dasein*s can never be seen either as openness to an absolute Other, or as merely uniting different *Dasein*s under a whole. An absolute Other means that *Dasein will* not be open to it as other. Such other would not perturb the thingness of *Dasein*. Meeting at a temporal crossroads nourishes the readiness for the meeting beforehand. This meeting does not mean any kind of absolute synchrony of time, again as Levinas would have us believe. It means that temporal *déjà vu* is the very meshing of synchrony and diachrony for every *Dasein*. Levinasian absolute diachrony, a diachrony that follows from ontic separation, destroys the mystery of the authentic meeting as it attempts a binary opposition between synchrony and diachrony and hence does not touch the primordiality of *Dasein*'s hovering in time as being 'amongst'. Another *Dasein* is not another extant being that obeys an absolutely different temporality. The diachrony that constitutes *Dasein*'s transcendence creates that worldly fate, into which *Dasein* is mysteriously thrown and which brings about the meeting. The meeting, the encounter, is a moment in which *Dasein* murmurs its 'ek-stasis' as mirrored by other *Dasein*. It is a moment of openness to the other *Dasein* whose essential transcendence works to mirror the murmur of the openness to *Dasein*'s own path.

93. We can now see that the 'meeting of missings' comports *Dasein*s ethically towards the fateful togetherness which itself connotes both connectivity and otherness. Otherness of the other is the inner otherness of the nothing where two *Dasein*s essentially connect temporally. This otherness of the nothing is not anonymous but it is the particular 'there' where *Dasein* is nameless and only as nameless is it particular. Only as 'ek-sisting' in namelessness does *Dasein* respond to its own 'moment'. It is the other *Dasein* whose otherness mirrors the otherness of the own-missing, missing that is itself the manifestation of *Dasein*'s attentiveness to Being. The other *Dasein* literally *goes through Dasein*. The ethical speaks both *Dasein*s in calling them to think back their own connected missing.

94. *Dasein*'s own openness to the otherness of the other as the otherness

of its own nothing is ethical. The ethical is an authentic moment of being-in-the-world. Any otherness to that mysterious moment is not-yet-ethical. Ethics is the valuable, but is prevented by reducing the valuable into values that determine what *Dasein* ought as a matter of obligation to do. When *Dasein* pursues an obligation, its deeds and motivation are already grounded in the ethical, which is distorted by the discourse of obligations. Obligations can succeed as short-term concealments of the ethical by merely channelling behaviour. But obligations which are justified by values cannot prevent the ethical from speaking as the fate of *Dasein*. Whilst involved in an obligation-*talk*, or standard-talk, *Dasein* is the furthest from attending the other in his otherness.

95. *Obligations rooted in values must always presume another human being rather than the otherness of another Dasein. Obligations rooted in values are about ontic justification, not yet about the mirroring of the missing.*

96. As obligation-talk becomes pervasive, ethics – otherness of the other – can only speak *Dasein*, call upon *Dasein*, in a very violent way that seems to come from nowhere. This is the terrible violence of Being which engulfs the ontically tamed whether as that tamed own violent actions or as actions directed against the tamed. To put it another way, the violence which is done to the ethical through the pervasive talk that both transcends and preserves the talk of values, rights and obligations would occasion that very condition for terrible and intense violence through which the ethical speaks. Part of the fate of the ethical is to speak through intense violence precisely because human beings have developed the historicity of violence towards the ethical, silencing it by entrenching the forgetfulness of error embedded in the ethics of values. Part of the path towards the possibility of an ethical moment of positive solicitude is such violence.

97. The ethical speaks also through what are considered 'evil' actions. The valuable precedes representations of both good and evil, which are always already in an ontic process of distorting the valuable. In every so-called 'evil' action, the openness to the ethical already speaks and needs to be brought into the Said in a way which would be strange to the characterisation of good or bad actions.

98. *What has to be protected, the attentiveness of* Dasein *to the ethical, is harmed by that ethics which creates an anticipation of a discourse which protects the subject or even protects the superiority of* Dasein *over Being. The 'externality' of a 'condition for responsibility' making itself primordial to and independent from the primordial 'how' becomes the act of entrenching response-inability or irresponsibility towards the ethical.* The subject who is protected through values is being put in the name of ethics of values above that which is

ethical. The protection that is offered to the subject, *as a heterogeneous subject*, maintains the superiority of subjectivity over the ethical in the name of ethics. The protected subject is already craving to be autonomous of, to break free from, the call of the ethical. It is in a world where the ethics of value becomes pervasive that the ethical is marginalised and silenced so that *Dasein*s are free to participate in values but are, at the same time, subjugated in that forgetfulness of the ethical.

THE 'ONE' (THE 'THEY')

99.   In the essential nature of *Dasein*'s transcendence now being characterised as being-with, as being amongst other *Dasein*s, how are we to reflect upon Heidegger's notion of the neuter *das Man* – the 'they', or as Dreyfus rightly points out, the notion of the 'One'?[38] I shall adhere to Dreyfus's suggestion of using the term 'the "One"' in my commentary. For Heidegger, the 'One' is the distorted and inauthentic sociality into which *Dasein* constantly and necessarily falls.[39] In such sociality, *Dasein* is with others [*mitsein*] and this should be very carefully distinguished from the being-there-with or *Dasein*-with [*mitdasein*] upon which we have elaborated. In this distorted relationship, *Dasein* constantly reflects upon itself as a subject and its involvement in relation to others. For the most part *Dasein* commerces with others as subjects. This commerce constantly asks: How does one do this? How is one to be? This constant struggle, this inauthentic cycle of self-interpretation as subject, we may call the hermeneutic of identification. *Identification still sees identity as a commerce of the positivity of identity as extantness.* This inauthentic cycle preoccupies, dominates *Dasein* and takes it further from the near. In this cycle, *Dasein*, as 'one', is not yet ethical, although the opening for the ethical lurks in it, in anxiety. Identity lurks in identification. The innermost 'there' of *Dasein*, its attentiveness to Being, through dwelling-in-the-continuous-with, is covered up in substitutes, and chief among them is the forgetfulness fostered by an ethics of ontic radical alterity. *Dasein* loses itself in the One precisely because it 'finds' itself in the big 'yeses' and 'nos' that the One offers. *Dasein* is anxious because being immersed in the One takes thinking away even from its own's being-towards-death. Even

---

[38] HL Dreyfus, *Being-in-the-world: A Commentary on Heidegger's Being and Time, Division 1* (Cambridge, MA, MIT Press, 1991) pp 141–62, at p 143.
[39] Contemporary Lacanian commentators would call the 'One' symbolic order. Although these notions overlap, I am not sure that they are identical. As shown with Levinas, the One can go beyond symbolic *order*, and still preserve and perpetuate the 'One'.

death becomes the One's death. The language of the One is structured, craving to create further and further differentiation within that
structure. *Dasein* falls into the symbolic world of the One-language,
into its preconditioned diversity, and is thereby levelled down. In the
everyday world of the One, *Dasein* is always an 'other' that
self-describes as other to others. No interaction reaches that ethical
meeting place which matters most to *Dasein*, this point of mirroring
of distortion. Mirroring takes place but always within the domain of
the One. The One's essential nature is that it dominates mirroring
but is rather preoccupied with the ontic commerce of differentiation.
Any thinking which matters is levelled down to this game of representations and representation-ability. Levinasian ethics of ontic
otherness, for all its Heideggerian pretensions to transcend the One
as a totality and sameness, can establish an allegedly 'for an Other'
which precedes that *mitsein*. From a Heideggerian perspective
however, Levinas is the most sophisticated anticipation of the One,
within the hegemony of the ontic horizon of the One. Ontic
difference can be taken to extremes and even becomes 'Heideggerian'
in a way which, as I argued in my reading of Levinas, echoes *alētheia*
and, moreover, which preserves the legal so the very distortion of the
essence of law in the legal remains hidden. The ethical in its essence is
hidden and distorted by the One.

100. To the going further away from its innermost own, in average
everydayness of *mitsein* where *Dasein* is preoccupied with others
(and Others) and as such finds itself more and more under the dicta-
torship of the One, Heidegger calls 'distantiality' [*Abständigkeit*].[40] I
interpret distantiality as the necessary distortion, or disturbance (as
well as the concealment of that distortion) of *mitdasein*. The
distortion is in terms of distance from the near. The inauthentic solicitude in the One, in the everyday, is part and parcel of the
constitution of *Dasein* as its innermost 'not', as its very own
distortion. As Heidegger maintains, the more *Dasein* engages with
others under the dominance of the One, the less conspicuous the
'there' of engagement becomes to *Dasein*. *Mitsein* with its levelling
down hints at the origin and the potentiality of the way towards
Being, the way towards the near. Even the unethical has its own
for-the-sake-of-which, namely the ethical, although it is perfectly
possible that *Dasein* will remain closed off from its innermost
'can-be' and will die without traversing authenticity. It is the characteristic of the One that it eliminates uniqueness and particularity by
preventing being-with from opening its occurrence to *Dasein*s. The
uniqueness of both the 'who' and the 'how' are assimilated into the

[40] *BT*, p 164.

consensus of the impersonal One and, I may add, into the Levinasian ethical attempt of the One to re-represent itself, in representation-ability. As Heidegger puts it, *Dasein* in its everydayness is *disburdened* by the One. When *Dasein* is comfortably in the One, it is 'amongst' otherness inauthentically, so that both it and the others lose any particularity. Proximally and for the most part *Dasein is* the One.

101. Again, it is helpful to reflect back on Levinas's criticism of the impersonal nature of thinking-Being because it is at this point that the extent to which he either misunderstands or caricaturises Heidegger's notion of *mitsein* is most poignant. *Levinas uses the notion of totality to purport to overcome thinking-Being.* Levinas's understanding of 'being-for', which maintains subjectivity, seemingly surpasses the totality of the One, but does actually still remain in the One's ambit and grip. The One in Heidegger does not connote merely a hegemonic totality which levels down, but the whole part of *Dasein*'s constitution, namely the ontic and the essential falling of *Dasein* back into this average everydayness of the ontic. The One connotes the necessary ontic involvement of *Dasein*.[41] All ontic involvements of *Dasein* occur within the One's world and, including Levinas in such a horizon, unfold as the world of the One.

PUBLICNESS

102. Heidegger reserves the term *publicness* for averageness, levelling down and distantiality, all characteristics of *Dasein* losing itself in the One. But this must not lead to a contrast between public and private. The sense of unification between private and public, namely private which is always already public, varies in the *mitsein* of the One and *mitdasein* of the togetherness-in-the-mystery. As we have seen with the event of *mitdasein*, the public nature of otherness is that which enables *Dasein* to listen to the call of Being. The public and the private do not distinguish themselves so clearly. As *Dasein* is essentially further on the way, it is always in others that its innermost possibilities lie. It is a characteristic of the dominance of the One that *Dasein* is lost in the public and egoistically establishes for itself an inauthentic private enclosure within that public sphere. Public sphere, *in its original sense*, is not the public sphere of commerce between extant beings and existence. Public sphere is the 'there' where *Dasein*s meet fatefully. Essentially, then, *Dasein* is public. Ethics occurs as public fate, namely as a public temporal crossroads.

---

[41] See also *BPP*, pp 279–80.

Fynsk reads *Being and Time* to the effect that the very notion of the relation between *Dasein*s is a fate of a community, of a people.[42]

103. In *The Basic Problems of Phenomenology*, Heidegger sets out further reflections on publicness in the authentic sense of positive, authentic solicitude. The discussion takes place in the context of the main theme of this series of lectures: time and temporality. Heidegger assigns publicness a central importance in his meditation upon time, or more specifically, upon the nature of the 'now'. Heidegger criticises Aristotle's punctual notion of time as a succession of 'nows' and shows that any 'now' is already on an ongoing temporal horizon of past, present and future – that of retaining (something happened 'at the time', earlier), empresencing and expecting (something happening 'then').[43] This temporal horizon has the characteristics of significance, namely, it opens a space and directionality of a world for *Dasein*. It also has the character of datability and spanedness which signifies the 'when' which is implicitly attached to any statement of 'now a such and such event occurs'. The 'when' again connects past, future and present on a temporal horizon which constantly temporalises itself. But the public character of time – time's publicness – is important for our preoccupation at the moment. Heidegger writes: 'As we express the dated and spanned now in our *being with one another,* each one of us understands the others.'[44] The 'now' that we all meet in publicly occurs despite our coming from different paths and pasts. Publicness in this primordial sense is the 'now' where we all arrived together in time, each with our own comportment towards, or readiness to, a *déjà vu.* Mirroring is first and foremost temporal. Time and Being are revealed in the public event of the 'with'. Crucially, we do not have to agree on the dating in order to meet up. 'The expressed now is intelligible to everyone in our being with one another.'[45]

104. In the public meeting of positive solicitude we have seen that otherness is not being assimilated into totality and sameness. We may also say that only in that publicness what is innermost private becomes possible. The publicness of 'they', including the preservation of the 'they' through the inter-humanity of ontic radical alterity, is not yet public.

105. Being-with characterises the 'present' phase of temporality, which 'ek-sists' futurally as it has been. The 'with' is the moment of meeting of past and future.[46] Over such forces, as manifested in its innermost

---

[42] Fynsk, *Heidegger: Thought and Historicity,* above n 5, pp 45–6.
[43] BPP, pp 256–64.
[44] *Ibid,* p 264.
[45] *Ibid.*
[46] *Ibid,* pp 266–7.

own-ness, *Dasein* has no control. Combining this temporal characterisation with the argument of authentic positive solicitude
advanced in *Being and Time* we can say that at the meeting place of
*Dasein*s, the dwelling-with is temporal. It is that temporality which
fuses 'own' and 'public' time in this meeting. *Dasein* is connected to
others in its essence and its essence as *Dasein* can only essence if its
temporality meets with that of others in an event when mirroring
occurs for its innermost 'own'. Temporality as *stepping outside itself*
– *ekstatikon* – is traversed by each and every *Dasein* that participates
in this community of Being-in-the-world. Temporality pertains to the
publicly accessible world. What is given to commonality is what is
understood by *Dasein*, by mirroring *Dasein* back to the future. Each
ek-stasis of time is open to everyone as their own.[47]

106. The effort towards letting-dwell together in temporality, in attentiveness, is ethics. Ethics occurs only when *Dasein* clears the centre
stage to the Saying of Being by dwelling temporally amongst other
*Dasein*s. Any enslavement to the time of the One, to the impersonal
time in which one is lost in the inauthentic publicness of the
succession of nows, which 'uses' and 'stores' time, is looking away
from the ethical. That looking away from the ethical would include
not only the entrenchment of subjectivity in transcendental phenomenology and ontic radical alterity. Any thinking which is closed off
from the dwelling-with in-temporality is a perversion of ethics. But
even such a perversion of ethics is 'on the way' to the ethical, the
near, and it is out of the hands of this or that inauthentic *Dasein* to
hinder the fatefulness of the ethical.

107. That ethical reflection which takes away and imprisons *Dasein*s in
clock-time and inauthentic *mitsein*, we will call the act of
'time-*stealing*'. Stealing involves paraphrasing any moment of
dwelling-with together in temporality, any authentic present, into a
chronology of events, of facts, of values (or even values as objective
facts), into a calculative assessment of risk. Stealing involves
transcendence by radical punctuation and exteriority. Value-based
ethics, rights and obligations according to justification, the legal, are
all instances of stealing and the inauthentic prisoners of the One. The
One's secret agents, namely the detached punctuating moralist, the
politician, the lawyer, are all *time thieves*.

108. Ethical *Dasein*s hold up mirrors in constant struggle to be with other
*Dasein*s and in constant efforts to transcend either the averageness of
the One and crucially the absolute punctuation of the detached.
Ethical *Dasein*s, it may be said, are not *Dasein*s who choose to do
anything the One regards as 'good'. Ethical *Dasein*s let their 'own'

---

[47] *Ibid*, p 270.

'ek-sist', be claimed by Being. Further, those who commit crimes against the One are closer to awakening the original place of dwelling-with than those who try to steal time and abstract justification into values, rights and duties. Crime, transgression, is a work of art itself, a mode of letting *Dasein* dwell-with on the boundary of the nothing.

109. An instance in which we can hear temporality call upon *Dasein*, a call to which *Dasein* is entrenched to distortingly respond, is indeed the origin of crime. In themselves, both the definition of crime and the commission of it are ontic instances, but, mysteriously, it is in crime that the Saying of Being lurks. Any occurrence that comes from otherness of the nothing is a hint of an ethical opening, and crime is one such occurrence. Criminals and artists, crime and artwork, *in their essence*, are not as different as it seems. But, of course, any attempt to express such a hint of an echo between a work of art and a crime in moral terms of 'good' and 'evil' will have already been undertaken by a *Dasein*, rendering the happening of crime unethical within the horizon of the One.

110. In reflecting upon temporality, Heidegger mentions the problem of finitude and infinitude. The notion of the infinite, he argues, is made possible only because of the punctual conception of time, namely as a succession of 'nows'. Only by viewing the 'now' in isolation can the idea of the infinite as 'infinite differentiation' become possible. We have seen how that applied itself to Levinas's conception of time that led to a 'not yet now' and with it, a not-yet-conceptualised encounter with an absolute Other. Heidegger claims that in falling, temporality forgets its actual finitude through which its unboundedness calls upon *Dasein* as a contemplation of its own death. It is such forgetfulness of the intimate murmur of finitude, of a wave in the infinite, of the call from the continuously unbounded essence of manifestation, that *Dasein* arrogantly retains as an inauthentic past that is projected into an infinite future, thereby forgetting its innermost own death.[48]

111. Let me explain. Fynsk relates finitude of *Dasein* to the hermeneutic cycle of repetition: 'The factical possibility that comes down to *Dasein* is, of course, a possibility that has been defined historically – and thus we encounter again a mode of being-with insofar as the possibility of existence that has been is that of *Dasein* that "has been there".'[49] Fynsk cites Heidegger as saying that repetition is a reply 'to the possibilities of the existence that has-been-there'.[50] But should we understand finitude as the opposite of infinitude?

[48] *Ibid*, pp 272–4.
[49] Fynsk, *Heidegger: Thought and Historicity*, above n 5, p 46.
[50] *Ibid*, p 47.

112. Finitude can indeed be understood not ontically, but rather as a necessary *déjà vu* which characterises the very moment when openness murmurs in closing up/withdrawal. We can talk about the infinite ontically as the eternally punctu-able notion. But we can also see the infinite as a more wondrous 'unbounded', or 'unlimited', or 'impermanent', notions which evoke reminiscences of the continuous which is always nearest to me, inside me, transcends me as my nearest. The continuous harbours finitude, although the finitude does not necessarily represent a *datum*, an end. *Dasein*'s transcendence means that it only gains ground as 'ek-sistent', as a 'not', as the 'not' of 'not near enough to its innermost own', rather than as the not of negation which relates to the hegemony of clock-time. *Dasein is* only as outside itself, as already erring, and only as an intimation of the moment of finitude can *Dasein* transcend itself and leap into its own innermost 'there'. For Heidegger, the transcendence of subjectivity into the temporally unbounded can happen only in an instance of finitude. Thus finitude is the instance that is already disappearing into the unbounded.

113. The 'now' can only be neared in finitude. Ethics originates in finitude in a moment of nearing the nothing, nearing own-death. The challenge of ethics is how to reach a possibility which is grounded on slowing down into the event of finitude. Only as *Dasein* contemplates its own death can it unconceal an event during the whilst of which Being has spoken. It is the duration of such a finite event which is nearer than the duration of clock-time, leaping into the temporal infinitude of Being. *Dasein*'s own temporality [*Zeitlichkeit*] is attentive to the 'ek-stasis' unboundedness of temporality [*Temporalität*] only in being towards death as being essentially finite. We can say, then, that in positive solicitude *Dasein* understands, that is standing before [*vor-stehen*], the call to its innermost own way to open up to its finitude.

114. The inexpressible is vividly grasped as the *unconditioned earlier* whose otherness as strangeness is ontically obscured and distorted as the 'other-to'. Otherness as strangeness is confronted in *mitdasein*, in the encounter between intra-worldly beings, which frees *Dasein*s toward the otherness of their own innermost world. The temporality encapsulated in this otherness, which is *Dasein*'s innermost projection of its own finitude, is furthest from ontic as the near. Heidegger terms the inexpressible *pre-ontological*.[51] Pre-ontological is presupposed as the understanding which is *strange to* ontic understanding. The pre-ontological already lurks as the strange in the 'there' of the ontic. The resolute comportment towards pre-ontological understanding is *ethical*. It is in the dwelling-together, *Dasein*'s being amongst intra-worldly beings as being-with, that helps

Dasein to understand, that is to stand before, the pre-ontological. Dwelling together is ethical in that it frees *Dasein* into its own innermost world.

115. From ontic perspective, such primordial innermost 'ek-sistential' freeing is no-thing. Ontic thinking, when entrenched, is blinded, drowned in denial. Ontic thinking cannot conceptualise freeing. The nothing amounts neither to an ontic interpretation of a concept nor to ignorance of something in the rich manifold of human experiences. The nothing is always already understood, already interpreted as a reference to *Dasein*'s innermost own, before it is further articulated and expressed distortingly. An already withdrawing self-reference is already and fatefully flickering in the place of dwelling-with. In the ontic encounter with extant beings the authentic expression of dwelling is silence, that is not surrendering, speaking differently, to the ontic demand to speak, to distinguish, to fit together. In silence *Dasein* lets language to impose its Saying on itself – 'itself' refers to both language and *Dasein* – and the impetus to such letting can occur only in the mirroring of the dwelling-together. But dwelling is silent because it is in silence that it speaks the mystery. The Saying of dwelling remains concealed as it reveals. *Dasein*'s essential falling makes the event already passing as it occurs. A free event in the dwelling-with – ethics – occurs only for-the-sake of reinstating the abyss of the mystery.

116. The reading of Heidegger offered here should not be confused with ontic claim that ethical unconcealment amounts to a general reflection about the groundlessness of *Dasein*. As the essence of *Dasein* is 'ek-sistence', *Dasein* is essentially transcendent and dwelling-with helps *Dasein* to comport nearer and to leap ethically. The ground of *Dasein* is in transcendence towards the near, towards the futurity of the earlier. The ground of *Dasein* is temporal. This is mirrored again in the Hebrew connection between KADIMA (to move forward to the future) and KEDEM and KADUM (which connote the earlier).[52]

117. Grasping that *Dasein* has already been in the continuous before reducing its own thingness into punctualisation of this thingness – the realisation that the continuous is *given* to the punctual as its world – is very important to ethics. The tension between the continuous as given to the punctual, while, as a part of the same event, the continuous is the very furthest from the punctual, not as ignorance, but as a concealed nearer, is again important for grasping the ethical as the valuable. Fundamental ontology is a precondition

---

[51] *BPP*, p 281.
[52] See Heidegger's discussion of the earlier in *ibid*, p 324.

for any ethics of an Other, because not only is the caress of the face of the absolute Other not near to the origin of otherness – it grabs *Dasein* in the far and holds it in there.

118. Ethics is a call – a call for *Dasein* to wake up from being totally immersed in any dealing with others as extants. This call comes from a place which is more *Dasein*'s than both the totality of the One and any account of a 'not-yet-conceptualised Other'. Otherness of a not-yet-conceptualised Other is a sophisticated historical instance of concealing that it is merely a mode of falling from the otherness of the Nothing.

119. Ethical involvement relates to things and other *Dasein*s as the world of what Heidegger referred to as the *handy*. To be handy is to keep open the transcendence as the in-order-to. In making shoes, shoe-making is the handy and as such, the ethical. But we can conceive how, with the contemporary technological way of the making of shoes, the depth and unboundedness of shoemaking is being destroyed unethically. Shoemaking, which is more primordial than the making of shoes in that it opens up a world, has no more relevance in the technological design and manufacture of shoes. The fitting of the leather, the texture of the leather, the preparation of the glue, the bringing the world of the shoe to that of the person who wears it, all these are part of shoemaking. The world of shoemaking is an instance of the handy. In learning to make a shoe, an apprentice gets involved in a world and there is a way for him in this world. If we relate this example to the interpretation of the ethical we can see that ethical theory, or ethical philosophy of values, distorts, and, if entrenched, buries the world of the ethical. The world of the ethical is not the world of extant things but a world of handiness towards the thingness of the things and other *Dasein*s. Letting *Dasein* into a handy moment of being-in-the-world as being amongst is ethical.

120. When the handy is buried by the hegemony of present-at-hand-in-order-to, that is an entrenched usefulness which coalesces representational and calculative thinking, the process of transcendence is silenced by violence of extant-ness. Burial means that the inherent vulnerability of attentiveness towards the handy is punctuated, and hence legalised, away. In burial, ontic *entrenchment*, entrenchment of legal thought by the ethics of the Other, suffocates the handiness of the ethical and imposes silence on it.

121. The character of the freedom to which *Dasein* is being helped in mirroring in the meeting place with other *Dasein*s has the character of *letting function*. The ethical lets function the equipmental character of *Dasein*. In letting-function relations, we do not deal with things as objects but we rather move in the worldliness of function-ality relations as such. Functionality relations characterise dwelling in

the equipmental context.[53] Now, because *Dasein* is preoccupied with his own ability to be, the equipmental context of letting function is made possible only as *Dasein* is involved *for-the-sake-of that which can be.* If there is a notion of 'use' here, it should be understood not in the notion of calculative ontic commerce but as a contemplative equipmental context. It is in this context that *mitdasein*, being 'there' with other *Dasein*s, is conceived. *Dasein*'s essential being with other *Dasein*s is for-the-sake-of letting itself be claimed by Being.[54] This last sentence does not imply any 'purpose'. This mode of for-the-sake-of-which is the equipmental context in which friendship and the ethical moment of being amongst other *Dasein*s helps *Dasein* to hear the flicker and to dwell awhile in the near. The *in-order-to* of the meeting place between *Dasein*s is not to be understood as purposive, value-based, or virtue-based. It is to be understood as an 'in-order-to', to help *Dasein* in its *in-order-to,* that is, in letting *Dasein* being attentive to the Saying of Being. Again, the original in-order-to does not signify some purpose, but it is just conveys the 'meeting' of in-order-to(s), meeting of functionality, a meeting which is for the sake of mirroring the transcendence, a meeting that is convened as the comportment of the constant struggle of language to say the inexpressible. Heidegger is careful to note that being-with in functionality does not entail the 'exploitation' of one *Dasein* by another. Such exploitation would be ontic, factual and instrumental: '[*Dasein* is not] merely a dwelling among things so as then occasionally to discover among these things beings with its own kind of [B]eing; instead, as the being which is occupied with itself, the *Dasein* is with equal originality being-with others *and* being-among intraworldly beings.'[55] *Dasein* in its own 'thingness' cannot avoid being perturbed by intra-worldly beings. To meet intra-worldly is to attend a temporal 'gap', a gap between the ontic 'clock-time' and the deeper temporality in which *Dasein* is grounded that constitutes its functionality. This intra-worldly meeting awakens *Dasein* understandingly.

122. The ethical Saying precedes the meeting of *Dasein*s. It is the anxious waiting for that is the precursor for such a meeting understandingly. The ears are ready for the 'there' before the meeting but the meeting amplifies the murmurs of the 'there' and makes them audible through the whilst of dwelling-together. The meeting of friends helps attentiveness, hearing and responding.

---

[53] *Ibid*, p 293.
[54] *Ibid*, p 296.
[55] *Ibid*, p 297.

123. To be together with intra-worldly beings, then, could not be more different than the notion of inter-subjectivity. The former is dwelling in the nothing, while the latter is a process of negotiation and commerce, including the contestation of subjectivity. Inter-subjectivity is still within the grip of the utility of representations and with it in the grip of common-sensical dialectics of problem construction and solving. Inter-subjectivity is not even yet the intra-human ontic transcendence of Levinas. Both inter-subjectivity and the inter-human are possible only because of prior understanding in which *Dasein* already 'ek-sists'.[56] The world of *Dasein as its innermost own in transcendence is intra-worldly.* Otherness and particularity coalesce in the dwelling-together. Own world and intra-world unite in the in-order-to, for-the-sake-of the Saying of Being.

[56] *Ibid.*

9

Ethical Dwelling: the Origin of the Ethical and Law

> You dwell, and hear how within,
> From silver vessels of sacrifice
> The source murmurs, pours out
> By pure hands, when touched.
>
> Hölderlin, 'The Journey', in *Eludications of Hölderlin's Poetry*, p 41.

A thing that is not temporal, whose being is not determined by means of temporality, but merely occurs within time, can never have been, because it does not exist.

> *The Basic Problems of Phenomenology*, p. 290

This strange state of affairs indicates that it is not the immediately given facts – the singular actual, tangible visible and that which in each case is meant and argued – which has the definite nearness to our 'life'. Closer to life – to use the current term – 'closer to life' than the so-called 'actuality' is the Essence of things which [Essence] we know and do not know. The near and distant is not that which the so-called man of facts (*Tatsachenmentsch*) thinks he grasps but the nearest in Essence, which indeed remains for the most the most hidden.

> *Grandfragen der Philosophie*, A Griedder (trans), *Gesamtausgabe*, vol 45
> (Frankfurt, Vittorio Klostermann, 1975), p 82

1. The term 'dwelling' has been mentioned a lot. Indeed, Heidegger mentioned it repeatedly in both *Being and Time* and *The Basic Problems of Phenomenology*. 'Dwelling-with' is to be there with, in this meeting place that characterises the relationship of authentic positive solicitude. The notion of dwelling is important for the development of Heidegger's understanding of being-there-with (*mitdasein*). It has an important implication for the ethical in Heidegger. In the account which follows, I contemplate the notion of dwelling. In doing so, I connect themes of last chapter to a reading of Heidegger's later lectures 'Building, Dwelling, Thinking'; 'Poetically Man Dwells ...'; 'Principle of Identity'; 'The Way to Language'; 'The Thing' and 'Letter on Humanism'. As in all his later essays,

Heidegger lets language speaks. Language speaks, and Heidegger listens to the unsaid. The murmur of the simple unsaid is traced to ancient etymological connections which, as history unfolds, have been lost. He listens to that simple, hidden voice of language.[1]

2.   The listening to language that emerges from these lectures – the etymological excavation that these lectures bring-forth – can bring further insight into the account of *mitdasein* and in turn, otherness and the ethical in Heidegger. The silence that characterises this ethics, as well as the manner in which it is silenced by ontical hegemony, can show itself. I will also bring forth a lot of Hebrew connections that will be made in supplementing my interpretation of Heidegger's various etymological paths. In contemplating the notion of dwelling the Hebrew language lends itself very readily to Heideggerian listening.

3.   In the most immediate way, to dwell in Hebrew is LISHCHON (*wohnen*, to live in a place as a dweller), which has the root of SH, CH, N. A Atzmon points out the relation to the word SHACHEN (neighbour) – a connection that Heidegger elaborates upon in 'Building, Dwelling, Thinking' and which I will further explore.[2] LISHCHON (to dwell, to be a dweller in a place) also relates to the notion of the divine SHCHINA, and this connection will also feature in the interpretation to follow.

4.   But I would like to start with a different emphasis of the word 'dwell'. In Hebrew, the word 'dwell' also means SHEHIYA (staying, to spend time in a place, usually while travelling, but in temporary fashion, not really to live there permanently). SHEHIYA is etymologically very intimately connected to another word HASHHAYA (delaying, deferring) and its verb LEHASHOT (to defer, to delay, to suspend). I say 'intimately', because both SHEHIYA and HASHHAYA imply one another. To stay somewhere while travelling means to attempt to open up to that place rather than merely being an occasional visitor. While staying in a place (SHOHEH), the person is attentive to, absorbs, the place he or she is in. SHEHIYA – dwelling – is more than merely visiting but it is still more dynamic than living there. SHEHIYA still has this wanderer's quality to it –being on the way. However, SHEHIYA, as slowing down and delaying, occurs while on the move. It is the 'being on the move' that gives sense to the dwelling. So in dwelling there is a slowing down while still being on the move. Dwelling involves slowing down, to delay the next move, to try to contemplate more deeply. As

---

[1] *BDT*, p 350.

[2] A Atzmon, 'Homeland as a gift of Destiny: Homecoming, between Dwelling and Settling', (2006) *Lo Straniero*, *(Journal of the International Movement for Interdisciplinary Study of Estrangement)* 4320–22.

suspending (HASHHAYA) that occurs in dwelling, there is an element of *waiting* in expectation of what the place of dwelling is about to bring. Quite often in Hebrew to say HASHHAYA is to ask people to wait just a little longer just until something happen, not to rush – 'stay for a while and let's wait' – to dwell and contemplate.

5.   These senses of dwelling, the sense of staying while on the way, and that of a stay in which there occurs some delaying, deferring, suspending and waiting that is conditioned by deep and intimate anticipation, are all touched upon in 'Building, Dwelling, Thinking'. Heidegger establishes an essential etymological connection between *dwelling* and *building*. Let us follow his steps in listening to language.

6.   In old German, 'to build' [*bauen*] relates to staying in a place, 'to dwell'. Heidegger traces that building/dwelling – *bauen* –from an old German understanding of the verb 'to be', or '*bin*'/'*bist*'. I am [*ich bin*], you are [*du bist*], etc, then, relates to dwelling. To say 'I am' means *essentially* 'I dwell'. 'To be' in an essential sense is to dwell. But, as Heidegger points out, the old use for 'to build/dwell' [*bauen*] also includes taking care of, preserving.[3]

7.   The essence of Man is to be, that is to be a dweller in language. All Heidegger's essays dwell in language. To dwell is to let language appropriate during what Heidegger referred to as the showing of the Saying of language. Language's speaking is the the unsaid Saying which always calls from near to the actuality of the actual rather than the 'said of that Saying' of the linguistic response. Man's essence is to dwell in language, to let himself be appropriated by the Saying of language. Listening to the unsaid is to dwell on the actuality of the actual, which is nearest to *Dasein*. *Dasein* dwells when it does not say anything, does not express, resisting the temptation to merely move on in entrenching the realm of the said. Delaying involves attentiveness, contemplation, listening to the simple Saying that language murmurs. The showing of the Saying of language is not an exposure of a thing.

8.   'World' means the unfolding significance of the near in language rather any representational totality. Language transgresses itself and constantly struggles to impose silence on itself, reinvents itself as unsaid as it speaks its 'not-yet' through *Dasein*'s moment of being-in-the-world. *Alētheia* involves that moment where the unsaid flickers before the eye and speaks to the ear. At that moment, at that occurrence, language speaks its own unsaid, and while in the stillness of the whilst of dwelling, *Dasein* listens. *Dasein* is free only when it let itself be overflowed by language. *Dasein* is free only in contem-

---

[3] *BDT*, p 349.

plative silence that is both overcome and preserved in poetic language. Silence is, doubly, both not resorting to representations/re-representations and also successfully dwelling in the Saying of language, that is when language manages, momentarily, to shake itself of its representations and expressions – when it thinks the unsaid by itself. Heidegger elaborates on Hölderlin's phrase 'poetically Man dwells ...' to make the point that the dwelling is not a mere activity, a verb like any other. To connect this to his 'Letter on Humanism', we can say that to dwell refers to the essence of humans to be the guardians and the preservers of language as the house of Being.

9. It is in the house of Being that humans dwell and of which Heidegger claims they are the guardians. But humans are also builders of this house. What is the house of Being? What kind of house it is? It is a special house because it has no outside. There is no exteriority. At the same time the 'houseness' of the house can never be reduced to a 'house'. This house as 'house' is not near its houseness. All dwellers go about this house, having their own path within it. Each dweller, for the most part, makes their own 'house' in this boundless house with no outside. They do not realise that it is not 'the path' which is really theirs but that it is the shape and curvature of the concealed boundary of that path that makes up this path as theirs. They are aware of the boundary by their habitual marching along the path but they are not attentive to the boundary as such. The boundary is given to their path. It is *their* path 'as such' only because of the boundary. What these dwellers repeat as their path is the boundary. They dwell in their path but they can 'feel' the boundary which is close to them, alongside them, all the time as they going along their paths. The boundary is what belongs most intimately to the path. It is that 'pathness' of the path which makes the path by being both felt and hidden from the walker in the perceived 'path'. The combination of being aware of the boundary which is theirs and the inability to be attentive to it causes anxiety, which creates comportment towards attending to the boundary, to fathom it, to dwell in it.

10. The 'no outside' is a boundary. What does it mean that the house that humans dwell has no outside? It means that whenever the boundary is confronted, the path is felt as a part of the house. The 'pathness' of the path, its unfolding as a path, as a boundary, is always antecedently in the house. There a mystery here as the dweller both builds that 'pathness' that constitutes the 'houseness' of the house, 'houseness' whose intimate familiarity to the builder/dweller is always antecedent. We could also say that the house has no outside because the house *is* a web of boundaries and as such it is made of repetitions of these boundaries that keep concealing themselves. The

dwellers are always inside the house and it is always *their* house. The house is not a structure that contains but rather the boundless containing of the unfolding of a web of boundaries.

11. The house is a house of boundaries. As the 'is' of the house consists of boundaries, the 'houseness' of the house is characterised by emptiness. In 'The Thing', Heidegger ponders what constitutes the 'jugness' of a jug. Heidegger contemplates that emptiness that does the containing of the jug and that makes the jug what it is. It is not, Heidegger contends, the physical material walls of the jug and certainly not the material that fills the jug as this material can be replaced. The 'jugness' is the containing itself. The jug does not contain because it was built. Rather, it had to be made because it does the containing.[4] The walls of the jug that holds the material inside are not yet containing. Only in the outpouring does that which the jug gathers and contains as a jug come to light. It is not the representation of the jug and its physical dimensions and structure, sides and bottom, that constitute the 'jugness' of the jug. The 'jugness' of the jug is the boundary that opens up a world of the jug that manifests itself in the outpouring. It is the void that contains that makes the 'jugness' of the jug. The 'jugness' of the jug, as the nearest of the jug, cannot be captured as a representation but only momentarily as an outpouring. Also, as complementary to the outpouring, the void of the jug that does the containing can be seen only in its taking in and keeping. What the jug contains, that which is taken in and kept is gathered as the 'jugness' of the jug only when there is an outpouring. What is given to the jug as a jug unfolds only in an outpouring.[5] The boundary of a world unfolds as the unity of taking and keeping. Outpouring becomes the world in the space of which the jug faces us in its jugness. The outpouring can be many things and can become a part of a world, of drinking, reviving, washing, singing. There is a merging of the void of the jug with the unfolding world in which it takes a part as being handy. But *that* world which is given to the jug as its 'jugness' is gathered as a boundary, it is endless movement that opens up rather than a representational definition which closes (in Hebrew, HAGDARA (definition) has the same root as GADER (fence, like a border). The 'jugness' of the jug is an unfolded boundary. To dwell on this boundary is to see that the jug is as divine as any 'thingness' of things. Its own 'jugness' has a special unfolded way which merges in a world that is far beyond its characteristics as extant, as jug. The 'out' in the term 'outpouring' signifies that ever-moving boundary. But the word 'pouring' is also

---

[4] *TT*, p 166.
[5] *Ibid*, pp 169–70.

significant here. Hebrew speaks to us in showing that the vulgarity of HAGDARA does not yet near the dynamic boundary of outpouring. In Hebrew LIMZOG/MEZIGA (outpouring) and LEHITMAZEG (to merge with) have the same root. 'Thinging' the jug, as a gathering of an unfolded boundary, outpours. 'Thingness' merges into an unfolding world and, as such, outstrips any extantness, representation, definition. There is no 'thing' and no 'outside' which is outside the thing.

12.   But dwellers are seemingly alone in this house with no outside. Their path is their own particular path, and the boundary is their own particular boundary. They do not, however, delay, dwell, on the boundary which is given to their own path. In this house they do not go alone in this path, they see many other people who walk the same paths. Each person marches along with the others, sometimes like the others, sometimes unlike them. We can say that they go along the 'pathness', too. In this house with no outside there is a path of 'all'. The path of 'all' is seen as the 'path' that conditions all individual paths. *But even this path of 'all' has its own pathness.* Each individual expression within this community of the 'all' does not yet dwell on, attentive to, its own 'pathness' as an aspect of the 'pathness' of all. For the most part, people do not dwell on that 'pathness of all' because they concentrate on their path as 'a path' which is somehow conditioned by the 'path of all' rather than on both their 'pathness' and the 'pathness' of all that unfolds as a boundary. To wit, they do not yet dwell in the house even when their path is conceived as absolutely distinct from others' paths. As long as they think in terms of *a path* rather than 'pathness' as a boundary they do not dwell. It is the boundary within which their 'isness' dwells. The boundary is given to their paths, it is constantly alongside, in the near, but they do not for the most part as 'selves' go near it, slowing down, that is transforming their thinking in order to appreciate the nearness. A terrifying, indeed tragic and debilitating experience – for the most part not to dwell, to bathe, in that which is their innermost own. Yet, their essence as guardians of this house keeps them hanging back at a distance from the boundary, drawn to look nearly blindfolded into their 'there'. It is for the most part blindness that turns them into anxious dwellers and it is their essence as dwellers which calls upon them. *The near-blindness is what makes them guardians of the house.* Their essence as dwellers-of-the-boundary *preserves* and *protects* them from just becoming aimless and sceptical path-wanderers. The anxiety generated by their blindness is that which opens their thinking up to the truthfulness of the boundary. Indeed, they are comported towards the boundary. Nothing can completely obliterate their essence as dwellers in the

boundary. It is their innermost actuality of the actual which is in the boundary. Their essence manifests as the guardian, the preserver, the protector, of the space that opens up as a boundary, although for the most part they remain closed, falling back into the path grasped as a thing-path.

13. The essential nature of boundary of the house is that it is *unbounded*. Because the boundary is in the unbounded it is a boundary. The boundary is the 'missing' of *Dasein*, that is comportment towards the 'missing' of Being. A boundary (in Greek, *peras*), Heidegger clarifies, 'is not at which something stops but, as the Greeks recognized, the boundary is that from which something *begins its essential unfolding*'. Boundary has a spatial character.[6] This is the sense in which I would interpret the notion of 'world' in *Being and Time* as having a space and directionality. The notion of de-severance which connotes nearness means that the boundary is a characteristic of the ontological difference, where the 'not' that lies beneath the present-at-hand extantness of things is the point of departure towards the near.[7]

14. The word for 'world' in Hebrew – OLAM – is connected to the words NEELAM and ALUM that connote the hidden, the mysterious and secretive yet near, that which remains perturbing while vanishing. The boundary is the site of that which hides and releases its positivity only as that inner world of language which speaks from a hidden world that constitutes the 'thingness' of things. The poetic world is a world which vanishes at the moment it shows itself – a boundary. The house is built in the boundary between the positivity of things, of beings, and the unbounded, the openness to which is their innermost own. The house with no outside is not a very big building, a very big container of things. The space, the site, the 'there', where the act of building takes place is in the opening boundary between the punctual positive 'isness' and the unbounded. The essence of human being as the builder and the guardian of the house, who nears, and dwells in, the boundary. The essence of humans is that they are the builders of the boundary. They are in essence builders/dwellers of the house of Being which has no outside.

15. The boundary is language – in Hebrew, SAFA, meaning boundary as well as a lip. In 'lipping', in the moving of the lips, significance remains in the boundary. Language speaks only as boundary. Building/dwelling is letting language speak the boundary. The house is nothing but language which speaks *from the boundary* whilst the

---

[6] *BDT*, p 356.
[7] *BT*, pp 138–48.

guardian of the boundary, the dweller, listens to the unsaid of that boundary.

16. Borders are not boundaries and therefore conceive the unsaid as a 'gap' that is not yet there. Borders are there to be demarcated, separating beings. Boundaries are more alive and changing. A boundary does not eliminate distinctions but disturbs separation. Between the sea and the shore there is a boundary, not border. Boundaries give us only a clue to the unbounded as the unbounded can never be fully open before us. We cannot dwell in the sun but only in the boundary between dark and light. The boundary from which the light shines [*Lichtung*] reveals itself only as a flicker, a hint of brightness. The boundary flickers as language unfolds poetically. Language as comported towards its unsaid is poetic language. Only as words gain their significance from the 'not', that is whilst wrinkling, or inflecting their signification, when their sound also hints at the saying of the inexpressible, can the boundary be neared and dwelled in. What is significant in signification is not the correctness of the sign, its correspondence between word and thing, but its shifting boundary that nears the thingness of things.

17. Silence is not 'not speaking'. Actuality can only be spoken in silence. Silence is rather dwelling on the boundary, that is, not merely confronting the boundary in passing, but rather, staying, dwelling in it, lingering awhile, slowing down, transcending the inevitable fall into the ontic domain where Man speaks language and through language of the extantness of the world around him. Silence as dwelling on the boundary is listening before articulating, barely but accurately, to that mystery of the temporally fleeting spatial moment of dwelling. Authentic talk is merely an attempt by a dweller at unmediated reflection upon the experience of dwelling in silence. It is not a moment where the person 'describes an entity' but articulates the unconcealment of the Saying as such.

18. Building is referred to by Heidegger as *letting-dwell*[8]. I interpret this as explaining that mortals have the capacity to dwell. However, mortals' building, as letting-dwell, manifests itself before the dwelling. Building also refers to preparing, making-ready for the dwelling. Building, as the letting-dwell, can be done only *with* one's neighbour, that is also *for* the neighbour and *through* the neighbour.

19. Letting-dwell together, in the boundary, involves helping, that is nourishing the protecting voice of Being, thereby protecting that voice which calls for, and thus as, the essence of humans as dwellers. The inter-*Dasein*, intra-worldly waiting for the divinities, for that

[8] BDT, p 360.

divine in them, involves dwelling-in-common, as neighbours, in the boundary, waiting for the ethical moment.

20. The building site, the space where the boundary opens up, a site in which what Heidegger calls 'the fourfold' is being gathered: a place where earth, sky, mortals and divinities meet in simple unfolding unity. It is the site for that oneness which is preserved by the building for the house of Being to unfold as a boundary. The fourfold consists of: earth – from which everything grows; the heavens – the movement of that which signals periodic change for the earth; the divinities – a word which conveys the mystery; and mortals – who dwell together in the boundary of the word.[9] The fourfold is unfolding constantly as a boundary, and humans guard that space of unfolding by attending to its unfolding. Language is the unfolding of the boundary – the temporal unfolding of the *simple* unity of the fourfold. Language speaks simply, as itself, that is, as constantly out-saying its said. Language is language, not a game, as Levinas might say, not a philosophy. 'Simple' means here not only the opposite of complicated, but also a primordial mysterious voice. Heidegger does not want to resort to a language that 'maps' but to language that speaks. Philosophy of language that maps is not yet attendant to the unfolding boundary. Philosophy of language still tries to map language as a 'thing' rather simply listening to, dwelling on, the boundary of the fourfold that is unfolded in language. This is why Heidegger warns that contemplation about language is simply language and not about the 'nature' of language.[10] The simple voice of language is the simple unfolding of the unity of the fourfold in which Man dwells and preserves, guards.

21. Let us now go back to Heidegger's essay, 'The Thing'. The jug is used by Heidegger not only as an example of a thing whose 'thingness' is being investigated, but also as a metaphor for emptiness. The emptiness of the gathering of the outpouring is a characteristic of the 'thingness' of things. Nearer than the 'thing-jug', Heidegger contemplates the ontological difference as featuring the emptiness of the jug as its 'jugness'. The emptiness of the jug, its 'thingness', is built into a world. The building is carried out by overcoming the language of extantness, thereby keeping and saving the ontological difference as the emptiness which does the containing of the jug.

22. Dwelling and 'thinging' is outpouring, dwelling in the way the 'thinging' gathers the simple unity of the fourfold. To dwell is to be

---

[9] *Ibid*, pp 351–2.
[10] Heidegger, 'Language', in A Hofstadter (ed and trans), *Poetry Language, Thought* (New York, Perennial (Harper Collins), 1971) pp 187–208, at p 188.

attentive to the 'thingness' of the thing – to the way 'thingness' itself dwells on the boundary:

The spring stays on in the water of the gift. In the spring the rock dwells, and in the rock dwells the dark slumber of the earth, which receives the rain and dew of the sky. In the water of the spring dwells the marriage of the sky and earth ... In the gift of water, in the gift of wine, sky and earth dwell. But the gift of the outpouring is what makes the jug a jug. In the jugness of the jug, sky and earth dwell.[11]

23.   The simple unity of the fourfold unfolds as language speaks and humans listen in dwelling. *Mortals* are contemplative of their death. They *save* the earth, *receive* the sky and *await* the divinities.[12] The site, or as Heidegger calls it the *locale*, of the preservation of the fourfold in its essence occurs in the 'thingness' of things. The 'thingness' of things is unconcealed whilst dwelling in the site together. The 'thingness' of things, their essence as unconcealment, *alētheia*, occurs in building the site, the house with no outside. The 'thingness' of things occurs in language. Heidegger speaks about the 'thingness' of the old bridge in Heidelberg, to illustrate how its world is gathered the simple unity of the fourfold.[13]

24.   'Thing', DAVAR in Hebrew, has the same root as LEDABER, DIBUR, which means to talk, to speak. But the same word, LEDABER, could also be a translation of the word 'thinging' (although, strictly speaking, 'thinging' would be LEDAVRER). LEDABER has therefore this double meaning of speaking/'thinging'. Only in authentic speech [*Rede*], only when *Dasein listens first* and brings into the Saying what language has already hinted at, does the 'thingness' of the thing flicker in unconcealement. Interestingly, in listening to language Heidegger picked up a similarity with the Latin word for a thing, *res*, as the word which for the Romans denoted 'what pertains to man, concerns him and his interest in any way or manner ...accordingly which concern man as a manner of dis-course'.[14] But *res* comes from the ancient Greek word *eiro*, which forms the basis of the words *rhetos*, *rhetra* and *rhema*, and denotes to speak about something, to deliberate on it.[15] 'To thing', then, is to speak in opening up a world on the way of saying. It is in 'worlding' that man dwells poetically. We can say that Man 'things' and

---

[11] *TT*, p 170.
[12] *BDT*, pp 352–3.
[13] *Ibid.* pp 353–9.
[14] *TT*, pp 173, 175.
[15] *Ibid*, p 172.

'worlds'.[16] Mortals dwell together in the boundary as thinkers/ 'thingers'/'worlders'.[17]

25. To speak, also to speak to one another, to communicate, is not essentially a transferring of information so that everybody knows what is being talked about. It is not about contract, definition and epistemology. It is not looking together at a map, playing a game in which everybody antecedently somehow knows the rules and other representational devices. Communication is equally not some process of arriving at inter-subjective consensus. Communicating is, first and foremost, dwelling in 'thinging'. In Hebrew, LETAKSHER (to communicate) has the same root as KESHER (a knot, but also a bond between people): to communicate 'thinging' in the sense of being tied together, to be in a bond both with one another and within the world that the simple unity of the fourfold keeps opening up. *Together: to communicate is to-gather.* It is to dwell in the boundary of the unity of the fourfold gathered as the 'thingness' of things.

26. In dwelling together, Mortals *save* the Earth. That which is human in being-there appropriates towards the earth, the ground. Being-there grounds. To dwell is to comport towards the near. ADAM (Man) is related to ADAMA (earth). But mortals also receive the sky. To receive, LEKABEL, and the noun, KABALA, also means to be humble, attentive, anxious, full of awe. In Hebrew there is an expression to be YERE SHAMAYIM, or to be full of awe before the skies, in receiving them. But in Hebrew it is also said that to go up, to grow in the sense of transcending – LEHAAMIR – is to be AMIR – to be on high. But AMIR means also 'capable of bearing the saying'. AMIR has the same root as AMIRA, Saying. In being full of awe and receiving the sky, in dwelling, mortals receive the sky, thereby grow into their world, towards the earth that grounds. That

---

[16] *Ibid*, p 178.
[17] Silvia Benso attempts to combine Levinas and Heidegger in order to give a proper account of the 'thingness' of things. Benso exposes the anthropocentrism of Levinas's account whereby only humans, but not things, acquire an ethical face. This is the case despite the imperative of Levinasian alterity to transcend anthropocentrism. Things have face in Levinas only through the mediation of human reflection, and hence Levinas does not yet face their otherness. Benso claims that Heidegger does account for the otherness of things, especially in *BDT*, but does not give them an 'ethical face' as 'Others'. Her effort is to bring together Heidegger and Levinas by both explaining the otherness of things and giving them an ethical face: *The Face of Things: A Different Side of Ethics* (Albany, State University of New York, 2000). But any attempt to make Levinas and Heidegger supplementary in that way is arguably suspect, as it does not discuss the *problem* of the link between the origin of 'thingness' and otherness. By making Levinas and Heidegger supplementary, Benso does not yet near the complementarity between things' extantness and their mysterious 'thingness', the very complementarity the distance within which constitutes otherness and indeed gives them an ethical face. In short, I ask: does the complementarity between Levinasian and Heideggerian transcendence establish a common denominator between them as far as the 'thingness' of things is concerned?

grounding and receiving mortals do in listening to the Saying of language. Only as a part of the simple unity of the fourfold do humans transcend ontic-based humanism and attend to their essential finitude as mortals. But this can be done with awe before the Saying of language – an awe that makes mortals listen to the Saying of language. We can hear language: to dwell nearer is to go into the earth, into the essence of things as the unfolding world of their 'thingness' in a moment of un-concealment, whereby the skies are received. Mortals receive the sky in dwelling in the holding of the earth. But in awaiting the divinities from whom the word flows, mortals relinquish control over their thought and wait for thoughts to come to them, to call them, to speak to them: 'For the poet's care there is only one possibility: without fear of appearing godless, he must remain near to the god's absence, and wait long enough in this prepared nearness to the absence till out of the nearness to the absent god there is granted an originative word to name the high one.'[18] In the simple unity of the fourfold, thinking and 'thinging' undergo an ongoing events of unity. *The divine in the mortal unites with the divine of the word that transcends towards the sky in a moment of grounding.*

27.   Dwelling poetically is essentially what Heidegger, in interpreting Hölderlin, calls *measuring*: 'The taking of measure is what is poetic in dwelling.'[19] In poetry the Unknown One speaks and this unknown *is* the measure of the poet. The unknown mysteriously becomes that which is to be measured, I would say – a measuring of distance – measuring of nearness and farness. The divine is measured as a distance to the mysterious nearness. We can also say that poetry is measured by how it says the unknown without reducing it to a said, without losing the flickering of nearness. 'Unknown' does not mean 'privation of knowledge' *stricto senso*, but unknown in the sense of 'speaking always from a place which is already too near'. Poetry measures the distance from the boundary, that is the measure to the unsaid, to the inexpressible. The unfolded boundary is the mystery of nearness that conceals its own concealment as it reveals. The poetic word is on the way to nearness:

This bringing-near is nearing. Nearing is the presencing of nearness. Nearness brings near – draws nigh to one another – the far and, indeed, *as* the far. Nearness preserves farness. Preserving farness, nearness presences nearness in nearing that farness. Bringing near in this way, nearness conceals its own self and remains, in its own way, nearest of all.[20]

---

[18] 'Homecoming/To Kindred Ones', in *EHP*, pp 46–7.
[19] *PMD*, pp 218–22.
[20] *TT.*, p. 175.

The Unknown One, the divine, for which mortals essentially wait, is the guardian of the mystery – the mystery of the simple unity of the fourfold, the mystery of the sSaying of language.

28. In his reading of Hölderlin's poem 'Homecoming', Heidegger had a reflection about poetic dwelling as witnessing the guardianship of the mystery. Going near has the character of remaining far in exile. To near the essence of things, in their 'thingness', the *conatus essendi* the mystery of which Levinas reduces so much to totality/game/allergy, is the preservation of the unfolding of the boundary, preservation of the mystery of the near and as such, homelessness. The origin of joy lies in this concealed *conatus essendi* of homelessness. Coming home is not simply to describe the characteristic of the place. Both the longing for home and coming home involve poetic dwelling whereby the attentive exile can receive call of the near. No representational ideas can really articulate the experience of dwelling in the near. *Conatus essendi* means to preserve and also to reproduce – *poesis* of the near.[21] Hebrew speaks to us again: 'to preserve' – LESHAMER – is related to 'to guard' – LISHMOR. Man is the guardian – SHOMER – of the mystery of the near. To maintain the distance by drawing nearer is poetic dwelling. Man dwells poetically in the fourfold as a listener to the mystery. Mortals' own guardianship consists essentially of being guardians of listening and speaking the boundary. Poetically, Man dwells – a 'gathered taking-in, that remains a listening'.[22]

29. But, as being involved as a part of the unfolding unity of the fourfold, of the boundary, mortals dwell *together* with one another. I must clarify: this does not only mean being together in a place. It is the togetherness that enables the essential dwelling in the mystery of the near. Human beings are essentially in a boundary, and they are essentially in the boundary together as dwellers. The boundary calls from the togetherness. Dwelling on the boundary is never alone. Dwelling consists of mirroring the boundary to one another. Dwelling on the boundary is essentially dwelling-together on the boundary in the mirroring of the unity of the fourfold. Dwelling is building the 'houseness' of the boundary, the house where all *Daseins* are together in Being. Dwelling together is an act of common guardianship of the house of Being.

30. People dwell in language together. They can only listen to language when together in the 'there' that mysteriously speaks them both. Man is a social animal – human beings desire one another as their own nearest of the near. This is the deepest meaning of the word

---

[21] 'Homecoming/To Kindred Ones', above n 18, pp 39–46.
[22] *PMD*, p 221.

'neighbour'. Heidegger shows a connection between the old sense of 'building' and the word 'neighbour', *Nachbar*, namely *Nachgebur*, *Nachgebauer*, the near-builder/dweller.[23] The question 'Who is my neighbour?' is one to which Levinas gives a lot of thought and responds with an ontic stretch of a totally Other, a notion of caressing border and separation. I have tried to stress the distortion, indeed historical and epochal distortion, between the notion of caressing a not-yet-conceptualised border and what is given to it, an already antecedent unfolding boundary.

31.   Is otherness a border? Is it a boundary? Heidegger responds to the question 'Who is my neighbour?' as a question of a boundary which precedes the grasping of neighbour as an other-dweller-together-in-the-boundary of the mystery of the near. The relationship between *Dasein* and its neighbour is the relationship of friendship understood as freeing one another to each's particular comportment towards the unfolded boundary. Freedom, then, is attained as dwelling. We recall that in positive authentic solicitude *Dasein*s free one another for their own particular boundary. But in the moment of dwelling, they stand together as a part of the unity of the fourfold that witnesses them. They witness one another but they are both being witnessed by the nothing, by that speaking of the unfolding boundary.

32.   Love: the *mystery* of being together and apart, apart and together.

33.   Humans walks along distinct paths but not separate ones and it is in the boundary they meet as have-beens in their most peculiar ability to be. Only in their unity of the way the fourfold speaks their respective 'thinging' can they remain distinct. The distinction that is maintained in mirroring is like the poetic exile of nearness and farness. Ontologically, there is only a distorted way in which *Dasein*s can be 'separate', be considered simply as 'other minds'. Each *Dasein* is the homecomer into exile. In the same way the dwelling-together on the boundary is not fixed, in that the ontological difference presents an unfolding boundary, there is a boundary between *Dasein*s which is not between two other 'minds', two other wholes, that can be affirmed in their wholeness by a genuine separation.

34.   The boundary of the ontological difference is, then, as the speaking of Being, the unfolding site preserved for the fourfold. *Dasein* stands before the boundary, understandingly, opening up to the 'there' of its neighbour. The otherness of Being, the otherness of the boundary, opens up *Dasein* to the other, as a fellow dweller/traveller. Dwelling together is not sameness, as each person is between themself and their own 'not yet' in front of the fourfold. But *Dasein*s coincide in mirroring to one another that murmur of their own respective

[23] *BDT*, p 349.

boundary. Dwelling together, then, is 'how' the otherness of the other comes to the 'there' of *Dasein* from the otherness of the nothing. To relate to the other as other must retain the mystery of otherness and sameness, the boundary between the two. To dwell-together in the boundary is to be near one another.

35. Building and thinking is Heidegger's reference of how humans dwell together in the boundary. Both building and thinking involve silence and contemplation. Ethics resides in building and thinking. Both the 'aboutness' of thinking and the 'site' of building are the ways mortals meet and dwell, guarding the 'thingness' of things as the simple unity of the fourfold. In 'The Principle of Identity', Heidegger recalls Parmenides, who said that that Being and Thinking were identified in 'the Same'. They, as he says, *belong* together. Also, Man, in essence, belongs with them. We can see how this sameness connects Being-with, building-with, thinking-with, 'thinging'-with. It is the belonging together in building that makes Being and Thinking united. Such belonging together in building is what brings together the question of Being and that of human *Dasein*.[24] It is, as we saw, this togetherness of Being and *Dasein* as essentially being-*there*, that encapsulates the 'with' and the 'otherness' as a question of ethics, as a question of dwelling together in the unfolded boundary.

36. The peculiar idea of dwelling with another human *Dasein* is the mirroring of the nothing. Only in mirroring the nothing can *Dasein* think/'thing' and be attentive to Being, face Being's way as its own mortality. Only in so dwelling in mortality can *Dasein* face the 'thingness' of things, that is, transcending representational ideas about their 'thingness'. Listening to the essence of things involves being ready and listening to the otherness of the nothing. Thinking/'thinging' relates to the way things call mortals to guard the fourfold as it unfolds and can happen only when *Dasein* has already listened to otherness, the otherness of the nothing. To be able to see things 'as they are', when a thing is particularised in its 'thingness' can only occur after the moment of being-with. Only after *Dasein* has faced its identity as *Dasein* by opening to other *Daseins* as other *Daseins*, by dwelling on the boundary with them, can *Dasein* face the identity of things by 'thinging'. In short, only whilst dwelling-with can *Dasein* be awake to 'thinging'.

37. What is mirrored in the authentic solicitude between *Daseins*? The exchange of mirroring between *Daseins* – their 'there' – is itself a manifestation of a more primordial mirroring within the fourfold. The nothing is itself the most original mirroring and it is this mirroring that calls upon *Daseins* as their own in the solicitude.

[24] *PID*, p 28.

Ethics, as grounded in the otherness of the nothing occurs in mirroring. Mortals are ethical only in a moment of Saying during which mirroring between the various aspect of the fourfold occurs. Such mirroring is the occurrence of the unfolding of the fourfold. Gathering is mirroring and 'worlding' occurs in mirroring:

> The Mirroring that binds into freedom is the play that betrothes each of the four to each through the enfolding clasp of their mutual appropriation. None of the four insists on its own separate particularity. Rather, each is expropriated, within their mutual appropriation, into its own being. This expropriative appropriating is the mirror-play of the fourfold. Out of the fourfold, the simple onefold of the four is ventured.[25]

> Worlding occur as a constant mirroring in which the riddle of the unity of the fourfold is repeated. The hermeneutic cycle of attentiveness to language – thinking and thinging – occurs as worlding and mirroring within the fourfold.[26]

38. The openness to such mirroring occurs as that which enhances essential anxiety, namely otherness of the other. Otherness of the other that mirrors own otherness of the nothing – positive solicitude – brings forth the circling of the riddle of the fourfold into onefold.

39. Otherness of the nothing as the origin of the otherness of the other conditions the 'worlding'/'thinging'. Ethics is grounded in otherness. Only in mirroring the nothing to one another, *Dasein*'s innermost nothing, are we ethical, valuable. 'Valuable' means here only to speak by letting be spoken by the otherness of the nothing – the riddle that makes up the simple enfolding of the onefold of Being. Valuable, in the sense of letting, has only the sense of preserving the essence of Being as *conatus essendi*, namely that of a riddle.

40. Ethics, for Heidegger, the valuable, occurs as identity of *Dasein* transcends extantness including the most radical extantness in relation to 'an Other'. Ethics is the opening up of *Dasein*'s *identity* to the continuous world of the nothing while dwelling together with other *Dasein*s. The 'thingness' of *Dasein* keeps dwelling in the mystery of otherness, in the nearest of the near, as its world unfolds together with the world of other *Dasein*s. In so dwelling together, *Dasein* also attends to, thinks, the identity of things as they really are, not as extants but as unfolding worlds which are their 'thingness'. To be ethical is to contemplate the essence of a human being as that which is constantly and dynamically bringing the innermost world of *Dasein* to mesh in the world of things. These

---

[25] *TT*, p 177.
[26] *Ibid*, p 178.

meshed 'worlds' are the way, are the otherness of the nothing in which identity resides. To be ethical is to listen and respond to the Saying of language which comes as these unfolding worlds. To be ethical is to poetically dwell in the otherness of these worlds – dwelling in the Origin, thereby coming nearer to actuality than the horizon of extantness. This Origin is hinted at as the mystery of otherness mirrored to *Dasein*, in the whilst of the togetherness of the dwelling in worlds. Grasping that identity remains 'mine' only in that all-too-near place of the merging of worlds in which it is already 'not' identical to an extant 'self' is ethical.

41. The ethical as otherness concerns dwelling in the mystery of identity and difference. Identity as that nearing deference that points towards the continuous near is given to any identity and difference that persists between beings. Difference as nearness occurs not between beings but as dwelling intra-worldly.

42. It is time to prepare for heading back to the essence of law. Freedom happens as the dwelling with the otherness of the other. Freedom occurs as the being-together in the fourfold. Heidegger relates the old Saxon word *wuon* and the Gothic word *wunian*, which both mean 'to remain' and specifically 'to be brought to peace, to remain in peace'. In this connection he says:

> The word for peace, *Friede*, means the free, *das Frye*; and *fry* means pre-served from harm and danger, preserved *from* something, safeguarded. To free actually means to spare. The sparing itself consists not only in the fact that we do not harm the one whom we spare. Real sparing is something *pos-itive* and takes place when we leave something beforehand in its own essence, when we return it specifically to its essential being, when we 'free' it in the proper sense of the word into a preserve of peace. To dwell, to set at peace, means to remain at peace within the free, the preserve, the free sphere that safeguards each thing in its essence.[27]

43. To think about law is to think about the boundary between the legal and the essence of law. It is to look at the mystery of protection, that mystery that preserves itself as the divine law that lurks within the legal. We need to 'thing' the 'thingness' of law. We need to look at the language of the legal and to listen to the essence of law that is unsaid amidst the inauthentic temporality that the hegemony of the legal fastens in its grip. The essence of law, lurking beneath the legal, is the law that preserves *Dasein* in its dwelling-together with its neighbour. The essence of law, *dikē*, the law of Being, is the divine law within which human beings preserve their essence as dwellers in the boundary of the fourfold by dwelling together as neighbours,

---

[27] *BDT*, p 351.

that is, by being attentive as Being unfolds as the simple oneness of the fourfold. *Dikē* connotes the protection offered to the guardian of Being against the harm done to it by the entrenched legal. The divine law in this sense *is* human law, the law according to which we can protect Man as he is, as Man's essence, rather than construct representations as to how Man ought to be. *Dikē* protects against the violent entrenchment of the language of representation-ability of values, rights and obligations. It protects against the aversion of violence by violence. Value-talk constitutes the legal, the law that human being fall into as merely commercing with one another, differentiating themselves from one another rather than dwelling together as neighbours.

44.   In listening to the Being of law as an aspect of the law of Being and in understanding the human *Dasein* as essentially ethical, we can grasp the ethical moment of transcending the legal, the moment of encountering the divine, or Divine Law.

ETHICS AND ONTOLOGY

45.   It is Levinas who is inspired by Plato's notion of 'good beyond Being' to defend his notion of the origin of goodness, or ethics as 'otherwise than Being'. In his attempt to articulate the 'beyond' of Being and in locating ethics as that Beyond, Levinas is absolutely right. Ethics is located beyond Being – beyond ontology. The only thing that Levinas misses is that this very insight – that ethics is located beyond ontology – *is* the insight of fundamental ontology.

46.   Heidegger devoted a section of 'The Basic Problems of Phenomenology' to the claim precisely that fundamental ontology is beyond Being. How can that be? In explaining how ethics is indeed beyond Being we are interpreting Plato so as to develop the ethical space that constantly opens up as the 'not' that constitutes the distortion between essences and their ontic determination. The whole point of fundamental ontology is to go beyond 'Being' as a thing – that is thinking-beings – and into the unfolding of the being of Being and the Being of beings. In his *Republic* Plato tells the myth of the cave. Heidegger interprets the myth as having the sole point of bringing forth the primordiality of going beyond Being. How to go beyond Being *was* Plato's problem, claims Heidegger. For beings which are visible to the eye, Plato argued that there has to be *phos*, light, which illuminates all beings before the eye can see them. Beings are first bathed in light, in which they can be seen. As the origin of ethics, Plato likens the necessity of light for seeing beings to the necessity of

good, of knowing things. This is Plato's key statement, which Heidegger quotes in full:

You will, I believe, also say the sun furnishes to the seen not only the possibility of being seen, but gives to the seen, as beings, also becoming, growth, and nurture, without itself [the sun] being a becoming ... So then you must also say that the known not only receives its being known from a good, but also it has from thence *that* it is and *what* it is, in such a way indeed that the good is not itself the being-how and being-what, but even outstrips being in dignity and power.[28]

The good is good beyond being-how and being-what. As light, it is given to perception. As such, the good is given to beings and makes it possible for them to be known. Good precedes knowledge and is given in any knowledge. Beings are immersed in the good in a way which makes the knowledge of them possible. Light and good are given together to beings so that beings can unveil themselves to us. Thus, Heidegger interprets, only if we stand in the light can beings unveil themselves. What outstrips Being is the light of understanding Being itself. Being has the character of outstripping itself as light. Heidegger connects the standing in the light and goodness. Light and goodness outstrip a derivative, ontically based, notion of 'Being', that is a derivative ontology. What makes ontology fundamental is the outstripping of Being as light and goodness. 'Fundamental' does not mean a unique being but rather essential outstripping. Being is not a thing, however unique this thing may be. *Conventional ontology must derive from primordial understanding which has its origin as the goodness of standing in the light.* Plato saw the need to go beyond ontology in touching primordial light and goodness in order to explain the actuality of the actual. But such a move was a problem for Plato because he did not turn ontology itself into a question, and the 'outstripping', as it were, could not be made itself into philosophical issue, although Plato had the insight of the need to go beyond (beyond what Heidegger would later show to be derivative or ontic) ontology. Heidegger claims that the understanding of this continuous light was for Plato beyond philosophical inquiry, so much so that Plato had to resort to simile – the simile of the cave.

47. The people in the cave are sitting with their backs to the entrance of the cave. They are tied in such a way that they cannot turn around towards a narrow passage behind them from which light is coming. So all they can see is the shadowy images of themselves on the wall in front of them. Behind them there is a path with a partition between

---

[28] Quoted in *BPP* at pp 283–4; the editorial translation is from Plato, 'Republic, Politeia', in J Burnet (ed), *Platonis Opera* (Oxford, Oxford University Press, 1899).

them and the light through which other people bring over and take out everyday objects. All the people can see are the shadowy images on the wall before them. The shadowy images constitute the 'things' they talk about. The light is thus given to the things they see but the light itself is never glimpsed. These shadowy images are their world. Now, what would happen if one person were released so he could step out into the light? He would look, or rather glimpse, into the light and then come and converse about it with his fellow inmates.

The inmates would think he was mad because he would talk about how things looked, not as shadows but directly as a result of the light bestowed on them – their 'thingness' as such. This insight would enable him to see the distortion of his inmates' conception of 'things'. Crucially, though, this distortion does not stem merely from a different way things actually are which is appreciated after seeing the light. Heidegger says: 'the condition for the possibility of recognizing something as a shadow in distinction from the real does not consist in my seeing an enormous quantity of given things'.[29] The distortion between light and shadow occurs at the level of the conception of the 'thing', the light being a condition for the actuality of the actual in things. The distortion occurs between seeing things in 'shadows' and glimpsing at the light which is given to them. It is the impoverished nature of 'shadows' and as a result, *the impoverished notion of light that is presumed on the basis of the shadows of things*, in short an impoverished ontology, which leads to conceptualisation of things as grounded in the derivative ontology of extants. An ontology of shadows, that of extant things, is itself impoverished and extant. This impoverished ontology is why the person who looks at the light, would transform his conception of 'thingness' to such an extent that his fellows would see him as mad. He would say to them that the actual light preceded their own conception of light – their 'ontology' which is based on 'how that being in the shadow would look like in the light'. He would tell them how the light would look as essence. The attempt to understand the light as a boundary rather than a positive essence would be regarded as madness. In this sense, the myth of the cave tries to illustrate the need to go beyond the ontology of things into the light of ontology of 'thingness'.

48.   The person who sees the light is not constantly in the light but must go back to his fellow inmates and try to express what he saw as the origin of the actuality of their 'shadows'. But any words with which he tries to express this mystery of the light, if amounting to new grasp of the 'thingness' of things, will not reflect the depth of his insight. His language must conceal itself as it speaks if he wants to

[29] *BPP*, p 285.

convey to them the *very insight of light* that is bestowed and is given to the things they actually see, *the light which is given to their philosophical horizon of derivative ontology*. Most crucially, he cannot fully explain that game of hide-and-seek between lights and shadows that pertains to his fellow men's derivative conditioning. The light is that continuous which is given to the actuality of the actual. For human *Dasein*, unconcealing the light, glimpsing into it, at a moment of being-in-the-world, can only involve flickers – the constant battle that poetic language fights, in murmuring for-the-sake-of nearing silence. Unconcealment occurs only when the shadows are seen for what they are: things that are shadows of their 'thingness'. In this unconcealment, the saying of language, as light, as the place from which the word emanates, abandons any shelter of representation thereby touching actuality. Shadows, then, are an ambivalent metaphor. On the one hand, as the simile goes, we can only see shadows as the light is in the shadow. But, on the other hand, shadows lead to that coherence manifested in the language of representations, concepts and definition. We cannot, then, see the light without looking at that light which is the shadowiness in the shadows. The light only shows itself as the shadowiness in the shadows. The metaphor of the cave is so strong because the people who are confined to definitions, concepts, representation, shadows, either are imprisoned in idealising/making 'realistic' claims about the shadows or they are imprisoned in the ultimate escape route that their inability to turn into the light inflicts on them – scepticism and nihilism. It is plausible to see how a sceptic can deduce from the argument about 'shadows' the claim that there is no way in which these shadows can represent the true nature of things. But it is also clear to see in this simile why the sceptics have not yet looked at the shadowiness that lurks in the shadows as light. It can be seen how the sceptic's thesis depends on the ontic logic of shadows of 'things', despite his proclamation of dissatisfaction with any vantage point from which to think about them. It is also clear how metaphysics, including transcendental phenomenology, is born in such a cave, namely seeing the shadows as prejudices that lead to the construction of transcendental 'things', that is in the light as *eidetic* essences. To look into the light, or, having looked at the light, being 'enlightened', is to understand that shadows are the necessary situations that humans are in for the most part. The positivity of things, their thingness, their actuality, can only be neared by looking at 'thingness' as a temporal *possibility* that belongs to beings rather than at the craving for continuing to looking at 'shadows' as extant beings. *Dasein* always already understands the workings of the simile of the cave, as anxiety, in a way which perturbs but is not reducible to expression. *Dasein* always is in part in the shadowiness of the shadow. *Dasein* as essentially 'ek-sistent', as erring, is in language, tragically, in the sense that what is its own is too near to it. In that sense *Dasein* has always already looked at the light, *Dasein* under-stands that there is truth which is nearer to actuality than the 'shadows' of the truth of correctness. Being enlightened is to let the light shows itself. Being in the light is to outstrip being and with it the craving for philosophy. It is almost like saying that in the simile of the cave Plato had the insight and the urge, inexpressible in philo-sophical terms, to raise a big question mark over the whole of his philosophy – over the whole philosophical tradition that he felt he was inaugurating. It is this outstripping that involves letting the light shine upon beings that is the valuable. It is in this way that the good converges with how things are in a way of which Plato had an intuition.

49. Just a brief remark. One thing in the myth of the cave which is slightly misleading is the very need for a person to 'to turn around' towards the light. For the actuality of the actual, that which is given to the shadow is distorted in ontic representation as shadows of extant things. To look into the light, *Dasein* needs to be attentive to what extantness, or shadows, does not say – again, into the shadow-iness in the shadows. The light, then, in a sense comes from behind, and is given to the shadows but it is *from the shadows* that light of thingness flickers. So, the metaphor of 'turning around and walking towards the light', so to speak, actually bites by looking even more contemplatively at the shadows themselves. The 'turning around' itself is metaphorical. To understand the turning around literally would involve the danger of theory, of a supreme being which is the light – the danger of metaphysics.

50. The point I wanted to convey is that Heidegger wants to interpret the simile of the cave as the need to look at the light. In looking at the light we are going beyond any thinking-Being which is the culmi-nation of derivative ontology. My main point here, *contra* Levinas, is that Heidegger did not merely radicalise ontology in the account of the ontological difference as embodied in the myth of the cave. Heidegger went beyond Being, beyond making ontology the centre of philosophy, into the grasping of Being as such, outstripping itself as a light that is always concealed as a shadow, or trace, of itself. This essential 'ek-stasis' of Being and not only of *Dasein* which is 'ek-sistent' in attentiveness to it, the mystery that it encapsulates, is something that derivative ontology, including that which Levinas presumes, does not grasp. That is the basis of the claim that Levinas has not yet done justice to the radicalisation of the ontological Saying by Heidegger, does not do justice to the mystery.

51. If philosophy has been, first and foremost, about Being, Heidegger uses the simile of the cave to argue that philosophy goes beyond any 'philosophy of Being'. Heidegger thereby shows the grounding of Being in poetic language, and with poetic language, in the ethical. The simile of the cave identifies the ethical, the origin of goodness and the valuable, and fundamental ontology.

52. Values are distortions of the valuable. Values themselves are similar to other shadows on the cave wall. Values are representational entities that lead to prescriptive language used by humans who capture themselves as subjects and who can make representations, through values and prioritisation of values, to govern the actuality of the relationship between them that the legal enforces. The good beyond Being, 'the valuable', would involve the very goodness of good that is embedded in the actuality of things, in 'thinging', the actuality towards which *all Dasein*s are being helped to be free in letting their own being be in thinking.

53. The idea of the valuable as related to knowledge is precisely in overcoming epistemology.[30] Any epistemology, including epistemology of the good, thinking with and through value, is not yet valuable. For goodness we need to look at the light of what is given to thinking itself, light, not to any theory that explains intelligibility in general or ethical intelligibility in particular. Even undeniable intuitions that are still grounded in values, echoing the craving for values or the futurity of conceptualising values, do not yet face the mystery which grounds that intuition. The question of how I feel whether my action is good or bad must be understood as a question of *distance from the light* and must be measured by the nearness to actuality rather than through the mediation of values, and representation of actions.

54. The gist of Levinas's notion of the ethical is the humble offer and announcement 'here I am', HINENI in Hebrew. This notion can now be read as a humble offer of dwelling before Being, that is dwelling in unbounded light. We can now see how the 'am',[31] the 'is' and the 'here' and 'there' all relate to otherness as the unfolding boundary of the nothing, a boundary which unfolds in the mirroring of being 'there' with, dwelling-with our neighbouring *Dasein*s. HINENI. To be 'there' as *Dasein*'s innermost own, to let own-ness linger in the

---

[30] *Ibid*, p 304: 'We must keep in mind the point that the usual approach in theory of knowledge, according to which a manifold of arbitrarily occurring things or objects is supposed to be homogeneously given to us, does not do justice to the primary facts and consequently makes the investigative approach of theory of knowledge artificial from the very start.'

[31] *BDT*, p 349.

'there', to outstrip Being in attentiveness to Being, is the most unmediated sense of HINENI and indeed represents a divine *invitation*, an invitation that always comes from within me, to gather the fourfold in thinking and 'thinging'. To return to Hebrew again: LEHAZMIN – to invite – is connected to ZIMUN – to call upon, to summon; also, ZAMIN – to be available; 'here I am'. But this availability connotes 'being available in time'. The word for time is ZMAN. But the word ZMAN is related to the word ZMANIYUT. ZMANIYUT has a double meaning: it is to be in time – to be temporal; but it also connotes the state of being fleeting. Reading these two meanings together means to be in time, always on the way. It means to be summoned to the fleeing moment of the 'am' when Being has already withdrawn. To say HINENI, here I am, then, is to offer my innermost own, to invite and to be invited, to be called upon – to be summoned by Being, to leap ethically into temporality and to dwell together as fleetingly connected 'am[s]' in the open, on the way.

55. It is no accident that people who cannot hover above the discourse of ethical philosophy do not see the ethical in Heidegger and deduce a lack of ethics in his thought because of his silence regarding the atrocities of his generation. Some, like Levinas, say that his thought did not accommodate ethics in that it starts from Being, not from goodness towards other people. Some try to bend his hand to show that his theory could accommodate ethics in the traditional sense. Some, apologetically, push him into the defence of naivety about 'practical matters'. But Heidegger is first and foremost an ethical philosopher in that he uncovers the origin of the ethical. *His complete oeuvre is about the ethical, about the Valuable.* Thinking-Being big atrocities, grasping their temporality, their move in the order of Being, must not assimilated into conventional ethics and morality. Has anybody yet thought the Being of actions that are represented as 'the Holocaust'? Thinking-Being the 'Holocaust' is to understand it, although in the ontic mind this will be conceived as 'denying' it or 'revising' the 'facts' about it. Heidegger would be silenced in advance and he knew that. But there is more to his silence than mere omission. In being silent, refusing to compromise the ethical position that he 'shouts' prophetically in his essays, he remained ethical and kept genuine the ethical dimension that permeates the whole of his efforts. His was the ethics of understanding the actuality of the actual and the ethics of struggling amidst the impossibility to bringing actuality into language. His ethical horizon was grasping that that this impossibility is the edge of the unbounded – the boundary of the light.

56. No doubt many ethical philosophers would see my argument as an attempt either to idealise Heidegger's thought or, worse still, to condone the atrocities that are coming upon on us so frequently. No doubt those ethical and legal philosophers, the agents of the legal, prove that it is easy to tranquillise humans with value-talk. Traditional ethics bursts into an open door – that much cannot be helped as it is the human condition. But in doing that they continue to shy away from thinking ethically, thinking actuality. Their thinking attempts to constantly exhaust actuality by representational ideas and actions. Thinking and 'thinging' do not pass their 'common sense' filters. Their actuality is that of harming a value – thus harming people – justification of an adequate representation-able response to that harm. But thinking about harm has not yet been reached. Harm is intensified by such common-sense thinking, which is oblivious to the light, and human capacity to ethically listen to the harm is being muted. In the big, original mirror of the ethical moment of thinking about harm all those ethical philosophers will see things that are not pleasant for them, things about their own innermost un-readiness as *Daseins*. In this mirror they would see that forgetfulness on behalf of which they construct their cathedrals.

57. Human beings, to whom the simile of the cave is addressed, to whom it applies, are essentially beings who can be open to the light – to the inexpressible valuable distorted in representation of good and evil. In going beyond Being, then, in going beyond any representation of Being, in not making ontology the centre of 'philosophy', in outstripping Being, philosophy touches its own birth and decay by glimpsing nearer than the shadows, near than *Richtigkeit*, thereby ethically nearing actuality. Ethics is, as Levinas says, without yet grasping the full sense, a first philosophy, precisely in outstripping any first 'philosophy'.

58. It is important to emphasise the connection between the valuable and light, between the ethical and poetic language which nears the silent and mysterious continuous nature of the light. The relationship between the 'said' of language and its 'Saying' is to glimpse at the light, not just locating or anticipating, to use the cave allegory, a big shadow which is an 'Other', namely 'not yet expressed' or 'oppressed' from view. To be ethical is to grasp the light, to outstrip Being, and to deploy poetic language to bring outthe light from the Saying or language into its said as the Saying conceals itself, and hence in *maintaining the silence*. Ethics is the struggle to let *silence be maintained in the speaking of the word*. This silence of the speaking continuous precedes the silence of a gap. However radical a gap is, it is still preceded by the inexpressible continuous.

THE ORIGIN OF THE 'OUGHT' AS THE 'IS' OF THE BOUNDARY

59.   How are we to understand the ethical question, 'What does it mean to be a human being?'. What is *ethical* about that question? What is the 'how' that can generate *confidence* that we are asking the primordial question of ethics? Is not the primordial question of ethics the question of good and bad, good and bad actions, that is, a question of value? On a simple reading, we can say that certain values are representations of what is valuable because the way human beings are, and as a result of what they are, they can harm one another in a way which offends a value. But does this reading, which is conditioned upon the notion of truth as representational ideas and things, connect in an original manner the valuable with what it means to be a human being?

60.   What is the origin of 'ought'? The 'ought' is comported towards the deepest and most original 'isness' of humans – their essence as 'ek-sistent' – the 'isness' of transcendence, of the boundary. Such comportment of the *ought* relates to the *ground* of *Dasein* being a thinker of Being – a rational animal. In being preoccupied with Being, through being-there-with, *Dasein* has gained ground.[32]

61.   To let *Dasein* gain ground, to let *Dasein* ground as one with the simple unity of the fourfold, is to be ethical. To let *Dasein* be open towards its unfolding world as the grounding of its nearest is ethical. To protect and enforce such ground is the essence of law.

62.   *Alētheia*, the unconcealment of Being, cannot be deceived by the ethics of the legal. Grasping this is one of the deepest grounds for *Dasein*'s ethical insight.

63.   The origin of 'ought' is in responsibility, that is in the ability to respond to the mystery of Being that always already speaks to them from the near. The origin of 'ought' is too near and is essentially distorted by value-based ethics.

64.   By developing a value-based 'ought' to protect humans from the manifestation of their essence and by justifying the separation of ethics from attentiveness to actuality, humans essentially err. Error distances humans from their essence. But if entrenched, when error is entrenched, such distancing results in deafening them to their essence, thereby silencing their essence, their essence of responding to the call of Being. The 'ought' of value-based ethics, as separated from the 'is', is either a characteristic of erringly falling into the ontic or, if entrenched, an oppressive practice, oppressive of what is essential in human beings. It is tragic that the more humans are inattentive to their essence in the name of protecting themselves, the more they

[32] *ER*, p 113

produce ethical frameworks that enslave them. The more they distance themselves from their nature, and fortify this protection, the more unprotected their essence becomes and the more intensely anxiety will bite. Anxiety intensifies the more elaborate the false protection of the being-in-error.

65. The essential 'ought' comes from the abyss, and it is the abyss that must remain unresolved in facing that 'ought'. To listen to the ground of 'ought' means to face the moment that resists thinking with and through values. It also means not to succumb to the all-too-easy unethical shrugging of the shoulders in the face of the indeterminacy of value-based thought. If ethics has *conatus essendi*, the entrenchment of the ethics of values and the internalisation of 'oughtness' of values takes humans away from their essence. Ethics of values badly harms humans' ethical contemplation of their essence and, with it, harms their *dealing* with the boundary-like unfolding way along which thinking about 'aboutness' is manifested.

66. Once we identify the manner in which Being and thinking are connected as a boundary, we can grasp the ethical. The ground of the ethical is not in the falling into the representation of things that includes a representation-able Other, although such falling is necessary for primordial ethical engagement. The ground of the ethical, its 'ought', lies in the depth of the 'is' in the way that humans essentially are, namely as dwellers in the mysterious continuous otherness of the nothing. The 'ought' in this sense means 'letting be'. The ground of the ethical is letting the 'thingness' of things, their identity, literally ground *Dasein*, in resisting philosophical correctness, and looking to the ground in the nearest. In short, for *Dasein* to wrestle the impossibility of letting identity that lurks as the boundary, as language, appropriate it is the 'oughtness' that precedes any ontic 'ought' of value. We dwell in the boundary of language, and the comportment towards the boundary as the essential human characteristic: 'We dwell in the appropriation inasmuch as our active nature is given over to language.'[33]

67. Taking Man as he is, then, is an *ethical*, not a factual, statement. The ethical in it is precisely the grasping that neither 'facts' nor 'values' can capture the way Man *is*, as *Dasein*. The 'isness' of Man has depth, a ethico-temporal depth. The relationship between the 'is' and 'ought' needs to be revisited. Can it be that an 'ought', ethics, grasped as a response to the call for thinking-Being, is the origin of goodness?

68. What is the relationship between the 'is' and the 'ought' in Heidegger's account of the ethical as has just been interpreted,

[33] PID, p 38.

namely as dwelling together in the mystery of the otherness of the nothing? Can we describe *factually* how *Dasein is* in relation to other *Dasein*s so that this relationship can be assessed by a separate value-based *ought*? Can we capture the relationality which can be ascertained and verified, so that it could be then evaluated (and to that extent evaluatively described) according to some set of values and prioritisation of values? Of course we can, but only in erring and in entrenching the error, thus becoming unethical.

69. Both the 'is' and the 'ought' are radicalised in ethical thinking-Being. It would be merely ontic, whether through representation or representation-ability, to admit either that there are, in terms of actuality of the actual, either 'facts' or 'values'. The craving for both facts and values is an ontic craving, and the facilitation and entrenchment of such a craving is unethical – a forgetfulness of a distortion, albeit a necessary distortion, a distortion that is always already part and parcel of the ethical. Both facts and values are distortions of the way in which *Dasein* is ethically attentive to Being through its being 'there' with other *Dasein*s. I am not merely advocating an ontic hermeneutic by saying that facts are inherently always already interpretative of values. It is a manifestation of ontic hegemony to claim that any fact is already based on some value judgement, and with it evaluative interpretation.

70. Heidegger, but not Levinas, as this book has argued, incorporates the discussion of facts and values into the very historicity in which Being shows itself to *Dasein*, including the distorted epochal way in which *Dasein thinks* and understands itself ethically – its 'actions' and their 'effect' on not-yet-conceptualised 'Others'. Both the 'factuality' of events and the 'factuality' that lies in the interpretation of values, namely representation of some facts about humans because of which humans cause a represented harm to others, are radicalised by Heidegger. The way in which the ontic notion of truth, of correctness [*Richtigkeit*], is incorporated into the discussion of both 'facts' and 'values' is itself a part of the ethical process of *alētheia* which is a part of the relationship of positive solicitude between *Dasein*s. The perpetuation of the very debate on the distinction between 'facts' and 'values' is itself based on the assumption that 'facts' and 'values' are somehow extant beings, however contested these beings might be, and thus however critically they might be approached by critical thinking. Such a debate is itself an ontic manifestation, an error, and, as such, it is a part of the ontological difference, the grasping of which, again in an ethical encounter by *Dasein* of its innermost world, un-conceals the murmur of the continuous. It is within the continuous that both 'is' and 'ought' distortingly perpetuate themselves as beings. In the continuous, no real distinction, or

separation, is possible. *As the Saying of the continuous the 'ought' is derived from the 'is'.*

71. No real distinction between facts and values – including epistemology that leads to the understanding of actuality through both facts and values – is primordial to actuality. The ethical insight of Heidegger, an insight with which he had to persist in adhering to in silence in an ontically dominated world, is that there *are* 'not' facts nor values. Beneath the 'not' of the distortion of the discourse of facts and values lies the simple, near saying of actuality, and with it, that of the valuable. Both facts and values take our eyes away from the actuality of the valuable. The tale of Thales who fell into a well because he was constantly looking at the stars is first and foremost a tale about not looking at the nearest, that is at the valuable.

72. In the deconstruction of the ground of ethics – otherness – we must insist that the 'ought' and the 'is' are not normative and factual. The way in which the 'ought' and the 'is' are for the most part is the necessary distortion between the actuality of the actual and representation of the actual. This representation occurs through assimilation of what is primordially rational – the essence of reason in thinking-Being – into representations of the rational. Even worse, as a response to the necessary scepticism that arises from the indeterminacy of ontic rationality, representation-ability surpasses both ontic representation and scepticism by the vulgarity of radical transcendence that complements the inter-subjectively reasonable.

73. The origin of 'ought' lies in the innermost ground of *Dasein*. The 'ought' stems from the essential comportment towards the near and so its call will lurk distortingly within any value-talk. Nearing does involve an 'ought' that comes from a still nearer 'is'. As such, this 'ought' is directed towards the world of *Dasein* and not towards the subjectivisation of *Dasein* and the objectification of this subject's 'acts'. The radicalisation of 'is' and 'ought' stem from the radicalisation of the subject of ethical thought with a more primordial 'being-there' and the object of ethical thought – the value, the act – with the valuable.

74. The persistence and entrenchment of the fact/value ontic distinction, conceals itself most harmfully in Levinasian transcendence, which keeps insisting on the 'otherwise' of ethics to ontology. In Levinas, the 'is' which is to be evaluated by the transcending 'ought' embodies a whole philosophical tradition which has ontology at its heart while the 'ought' which is the origin of value and the good is embodied in the ethical departure, the ethical Saying of alterity. Jewish thought (ethical Saying of a not-yet-conceptualised Other) is the origin of 'ought'. Greek thinking, including the valuable as dwelling together in the mystery of essence, becomes the original 'is' (ontological Said –

thinking-Being). With Levinas, we witness the paragon of the distinction between 'is' and 'ought', namely the most radical of punctuation and ontic alterity.

75. *The origin of the legal is as the enforcer of this paragon of separation between 'is' and 'ought'. The legal is encapsulated in an ethics that effectuates the Levinasian transcendence not only of Greek thinking but also of the pre-Socratics (as well as their Eastern origin?) by Jewish thinking. This ethics legalises the mystery.*

76. It has been said that an 'ought' cannot be derived from the 'is', namely that the evaluative cannot be derived from a fact of human nature – the naturalistic fallacy. This argument is based on the notion that the valuable, and with it, goodness, is simple and indefinable and as such cannot be reducible to facts. But such an argument *could* still be based on the idea that there are things-facts, which are separate from simple and indefinable things-values, both of which are out *there* to conceptualise, to define, to represent and to method-ologically investigate. We could say, for example, that values arise out of a factual way in which humans can cause harm to one another.

77. When the claim is made, then, that the valuable is indefinable, inexpressible and therefore not reducible to facts, what characteristic of the valuable does such a claim indicate at? How should we re-read the naturalistic fallacy in the light of what has been said so far in this chapter?

78. GE Moore's so-called 'naturalistic fallacy', namely that goodness is simple and indefinable, resonates intensively with the valuable as thinking-Being. The deepest intuition that propels the naturalistic fallacy involves a deconstruction of 'nature'. This intuition originates by challenging the whole grasp of 'nature' as an extant from which facts about human nature, harm and therefore values and goodness derive. The fallacy challenges the 'ontic fallacy' of nature. The deepest and most profound insight of this fallacy criticises any under-standing of goodness and the valuable as related to the ontic understanding of nature. Thus understood, it would be a mistake, I would claim, to understand the insight of naturalistic fallacy as separating the 'is' and the 'ought'. *The origin of the naturalistic fallacy distinguishes rather both extant-based and ontically separated 'is' and 'ought' from a simple and indefinable grasp of the valuable in which the 'ought' is derived from the 'isness' of nature understood as a mystery.* The insight of this fallacy criticises both representational 'is' and 'ought' as based upon forgetful ontic conception of nature as present-at-hand. The mystery of goodness that the argument about the natural fallacy brings forth is connected to the mystery, rather than the fact, of what it is to be a human being, a mystery that is not

reduced to any definable characteristics. The moment there is craving for 'natural' reality that establishes both facts and norms about these facts there is externalisation and distancing from the naturally ethical. Goodness as a call for thinking, as the 'oughtness' of letting thinking/'thinging' occur, is in nature as a mystery. The 'is' calls upon *Dasein* as the 'ought'. The 'ought' *primordially* derives from the 'is' – an ethical 'is-ought'. 'Facts' and 'values' are ontic points of departure, which are in complementarity of distortion with the 'ought-as-derived-from-the-is', or the 'is–ought'. The naturalistic fallacy means that the 'is–ought', then, is *evident* and is arrived at by intuition and not by definition. I shall dwell on *evidence* shortly. The naturalistic fallacy helps us to shake off the ontic fallacy of nature understood by the separation of 'is' and 'ought' in the Levinasian transcendence.

79. The conventional understanding of this fallacy does not yet see that the derivation of the 'ought' from the 'is', of values from facts, can become a problem only in an ontically dominated horizon. As an opening of a world as a boundary, the 'ought' *must*, as explained, be derived from the 'is', going deeper into the 'is' in a relationship of near/far. Understanding the naturalistic fallacy as the ontic 'is'/'ought' distinction looks away from the 'is–ought' of the near/far.

80. Of course, nature as an unfolding mystery harbours the historicity of *Dasein* which necessarily embodies *Dasein*'s inauthentic involvement. *Dasein*'s involvement as the perpetuation of the ontic cycle of forgetfulness through the establishment, and separation, of 'facts' and 'values' is itself an act of waiting for the natural ethical is-ought to speak. *To recap, there is no ontological without the ontic – nature as extant is itself a necessary error of grasping nature as unfolding.* The 'ought' of the call of nature belongs to *Dasein*'s fate whatever *Dasein* represents to itself as either fact or value. This is the sense, the distorted ontic sense, in which facts, values and with them, the legal are *in* nature. Nature includes inauthentic involvements because it *is*, in essence, complementarity between the ontic and the ontological.

81. Goodness, as far as representation by the human *Dasein* is concerned, has little to do with the manner by which the ethical will come about. The valuable involves, perhaps must involve, what would be considered in ethical discourse of values as 'evil' occurrences. Violence is originary, both in terms of the necessary silencing that is manifested by *Dasein*'s ek-sistence, that is, error, and even more so when error becomes entrenched and hence more intensively violent in the way in which it becomes part of the unfolding of the ethical. Violence is also originary in that to be attentive to the ethical involves violence to the word and, as such, silence must consist of an event which overcomes ontic silencing.

82. The valuable is a part of essential constitution of *Dasein*. As such it is

manifested in ontic language in which *Dasein* has to immerse itself attentively, thus standing at the door of the chamber from which language speaks, that is the door of the holiness of the holy. Such a chamber, in Hebrew, KODESH HKODASHIM, is not accessible to one person alone – the Grand Cohen of Jewish mythology – but to every human *Dasein* as its essence. This chamber from which the 'is–ought' emanates as the word of the mystery is the only chamber where there *is silence*. *Silence is the chamber from which the word flows*. *Silence* is what Man must learn to speak, thus to speak the valuable, to be the valuable. Ethics – being on the boundary of the open – being open to a world – with others – involves a constant unlearning of philosophy, chiefly ethical 'philosophy'. Ethics calls upon us to think/'thing', to *be* ethically.

83. As Heidegger says many times, inspired by Hölderlin, when danger lurks, saving power shows itself too. Levinasian ontic transcendence is on the way to the ethical. The ethical, the listening to the language of the near, can be learnt only by unlearning Levinas. We must leave it an open question whether Man can do anything to reduce the inevitable fateful violence that awaits as the manifestation of such unlearning. As violence is originary, Man, in an essential sense, cannot do a lot. But can Man be educated to be more readily violent towards the word, that is to be more contemplative of the unsaid and in that way channel violence differently? *Dasein* is in anxiety. *Dasein* by its nature must be aware of its essence in originary violence. *Dasein* attempts to respond to that originary violence by resorting to representation of values – we have seen much of this recently. In this way, *Dasein* neither listens to the ethical nor creates the conditions for doing so. Such conditions are not created because representation becomes *Dasein*'s essential self-understanding. Indeed, Levinas first and foremost answers the question 'What is Man?', not 'What ought Man to be?'. The response of responsibility *ought* not to be a distancing one to originary violence but rather a response that nears originary violence by contemplating the unsaid that such violence harbours. Heidegger, with his silence, never gives us methodology, remedy or false hope. We can just heed his prophetic warning to the effect that if Man does not quickly learn to listen to language it will be catastrophic. The discourse of hope he left to ethical philosophers, politicians and lawyers. Let us just grasp that the question of the origin of the 'ought' has not been asked yet.

84. Indeed, Heidegger does not have an 'ethical theory' as he does not seek to make humanity better according to some account of goodness and badness. Levinas is absolutely right on that point. The 'climate' of fundamental ontology, as Levinas calls it, is not necessarily

pleasant. For an ontic world, the silence that shrouds Heidegger is intolerable at best, criminal at worst. But we can now appreciate that it would be unethical for Heidegger to reduce his ethics to an ethical discourse of representation-able values. Yet it is Heidegger, and not Levinas, who is ethical in absorbing the full implication of the tragic essence of the human *Dasein*. The complexities advanced by ethical philosophy nevertheless preserve *Dasein*'s world as ontologically superficial and, by taming the mystery, simplistic.

85. Heidegger speaks to us ethically after Levinas as that which is antecedent to Levinas. The ethical voice that both speaks *Dasein* and calls upon *Dasein*, to which *Dasein* is responsible and response-able, is one that *Dasein* can least listen to especially in times of ontic Levinasian hegemonious transcendence. The craving to protect the 'individual' does leave unprotected the particular *Dasein*. *Dasein ought* to be comported toward re-personalisation in letting itself be spoken by the Saying of Being rather than in conceptualising Being through either value or fact – a conceptualisation under which subjectivity will be both radicalised as heterogeneous and preserved.

86. The 'ought' of this book requires us to be attentive to the language of the subject and value-based ethics, as well as to any trace of the legal. It calls upon us to expose not merely the dominated and oppressed 'not-yet-represented Other', but rather the distortion of otherness effectuated by the language that craves the capturing of the valuable in values and facts.

87. The 'ought' always involves the never-ending/never-beginning showing of how the language of law and the language of ethical 'philosophy' prevents language from speaking. Again, this is not merely finding a gap or inconsistencies in the web of the language of values, rights and duties. The ethical is also not about how the current, ideological content of values and duties is ignorant about as yet unknowable future human experiences. The ethical exposes the legal in whatever critical form it reinvents itself. 'Ought' involves a call for thinking about those ethical and legal pursuits rather than perpetuating them with the pretence of being 'critical'.

88. The ethical hermeneutic cycle does not condition language in some anticipation of conceptualisation through values, rights and duties. To recap, the falling into those conceptualisations is a necessary of the part of the ontological difference, but this is different from critical thinking which perpetuate an inauthentic cycle by anticipating value-talk.

89. The 'ought' is the hermeneutic of 'isness', whereby the ontological 'isness', the nearest of the near, dwells in the ontic 'is' (an 'is' which would include the error of the onticallly based perpetuation of

separated 'is' and 'ought'). The originary 'ought' traverses the ontological difference that is the 'not', and does not just pretend to provide a critical, yet representation-able, realm of transcendence. The primordial 'ought' is inexpressible within the oscillation of the ontic value-based transcendence. Silence.

90.   If *Dasein* loves or oppresses it is because that person is not ontically other to you but rather mysteriously so. The oppressed always already mirrors to the innermost otherness of *Dasein*. To be an Other does not yet face, cannot yet explain facing. Each and every *Dasein* faces its mysterious *déjà vu*, common 'oughtness' that frees *Dasein* to think and to 'thing'. The origin of evil, that to which the ethical responds, it is not letting Being speak through mirroring of the mystery of otherness. The absolute Other resists being-there-with. It resists the impetus of the boundary. It resists the divine and simple connection that language calls upon *Dasein* to listen to between togetherness and particularity. Further, the absolute Other relies on the legal to enforce that resistance and unethically claims that the legal protects against the oppression of totality.

91.   The origin of the 'ought' speaks as transcendence of an ethical theory of values, morality of representation-able harm, and the legal which enforces it. The 'ought'is the constant looking and dwelling on the unsaid of the language of rights and duties of the legal. This origin of 'ought'as a letting-Being-be brings forth the boundary of the valuable.

92.   We must conceive Kant's categorical imperative as treating *Dasein* as end in itself. That means approaching humans in their essence as distorted in every view of them as Others. Being an 'end' means being always already in the mystery and not as a gap of an Other. To 'be-there', in freedom, is an end in itself. This end means not assimilating *Dasein* into being an *individual* but rather sharpening the attentiveness to the call/response that characterises the dwelling together in the unfolded boundary. The Categorical Imperative, morality, is not the mutual ontic radicalisation of negative and positive freedom, but connotes the humbleness before the mysterious end of 'ek-static' freedom. What is anticipated is not an 'ontology' to which some dialectic is evolving but a mystery that reveals and conceals itself as the nearest to *Dasein*. The comfort of dialectics is not yet ethical. The Categorical Imperative is first and foremost the ethical duty to language and, as such, a constant deconstructive challenge to any ethical theory, however critical. The Categorical Imperative demands attentiveness to Being rather than distancing and generalising a master value-based obligation. This imperative is what is nearest to humans and it is this imperative that makes them the only creatures that are infinite by grasping

their finitude. Standing before – understanding – this imperative, can only occur in the midst of its necessary distortion that externalises the 'ought' to the 'is'.

ETHICS, RESPONSIBILITY AND THE LEGAL

93. The overlap between ethics and morality is that between goodness and harm. In morality some values need to be protected from encroachment, as encroaching on them harms people in a way that is reflected upon as fundamental. The participation of a human being in a value becomes protected in a discourse of rights and duties calculations. The 'howness' of this, however, is just an ontic façade and does not yet near, indeed essentially distorts, the primordial 'how'. The ethical lurks beneath every involvement, and the switch to an act of externalisation through values, harm and the legal does not listen to the ethical. *The ethical demands not only a change of content of values but a transformation of thinking.*

94. The ethical is indeed about indicating the essential ability of people to respond to the mystery. This is the original relationship between freedom and responsibility. The ethical is not about the representation-able conditions of making people ontically responsible 'individuals'. This ethical is not about making subjectivity radical and heterogeneous. The talk about conditions of responsibility is violent in that it tames the violence of that calls for responsibility. There are such conditions only as a distortion of thinking. *To think about the ethical, to think about the harmful, thereby making people responsible, is not the same as the act of separating ethics and ontology so that ethics can be sorted out in the realm of values and ontology in the realm of Being.* The thought that we can sort out the ethical first and only then can we internally and freely be personally responsible is understandable as a response to the oppression of the mystery, but it is distorting and misleading all the same. Both the representational value-based façade and the representational personal accountability to one's 'self' that this façade enables are merely a house of serfdom that tranquillises humans, and robs them of their sublime and divine essence. As personal responsibility to Being is essential mirroring, mirroring of the fourfold in which humans dwell together, we can see the notion of harming as a part of the temporality of mirroring, not of representational justification. The primordial voice from mirroring will haunt and unleash its powers underneath any façade of moral representations. The unpleasent path that involves the call of the ethical cannot be avoided and holding it at bay by external representation only serves

to make it speak more violently. In a place which is nearest to them, people do not comport towards, do not originally desire (although of course they do 'want') value based ethics, morality and the legal. Although people have the desire to protect themselves they cannot be protected from a desire which is mostly and essentially 'theirs'. The desire to protect through representations of values is essentially their error, on the way to the ethical.

SILENCE AS THE ESSENCE OF ETHICS AND LAW

95. Our reflections on being-with the otherness of the other, dwelling together in the boundary, the origin of 'ought', allow us to glimpse at the essence of ethics and law. The ethical as the attentiveness, as thinking/'thinging'/'worlding', comes nearer to *Dasein*, and the essence of law protects and enforces that unfolding of the coming. What is protected is the togetherness in the place of mutual gathering of *Dasein*s in positive solicitude which is the locale of mutual dwelling in the boundary. As it has been argued, this meeting place of thinking/'thinging' is characterised by the gathering of the simple unity of the fourfold. The Being of beings is this gathering, and the ethical is letting this gathering happen.

96. It is in 'thinging' that the deepest interest of Man lies. The Latin word *intersvm* means 'being together' as being amongst. It connotes being to-gather, face to face, and it is primordial togetherness as dwellers that the essence of law guards, protects and enforces. In the protected togetherness of the fourfold, allowing otherness to speak, the essence of law guides *Dasein* to the humble path –intimately to himself or as it is said in Hebrew 'between himself and himself" – before the Saying of Being. Dwelling together in the boundary in positive authentic solicitude is mutual 'thinging'.

97. The 'thingness' of law, law's Being, preserves the togetherness, the interest, the unity, of mortals as dwellers on the boundary anxiously comported in mirroring towards the divinities, earth and skies. Let us look closely at this. As we saw, Heidegger relates the word 'thing' to the Roman words *res* and *causa*. These words both denote a 'case', in the sense of that which is the case, that which 'comes to pass and becomes due.'[34] The relationship between what is the case and the surplus of the 'due' is the primordial sense of justice. Justice is what is due, and any attempt to reach the depth of this 'due' is for-the-most-part reduced to distributions and allocations, risk assessment, calculations, all of which depend on the representations

[34] *TT*, p 173.

and definitions (including representation-ability) of facts and values. The primordial due is the 'that' of the *res*, that of 'thinging', that which is the case. A case in law, a *cause of action*, before any case which is already colonised by the legal, is the case that has as its essence to give back the due – nearing the thing.

98. Give *back*? What is a just giving back? Giving back justly is not merely restoring stability, or returning something to an *individual* owner. Original ownership is related to thinking-back, that is the giving back that which has already been given as the case of howness-which-is-mine – as the boundary.

99. The legal characterises the fall of thinking and 'thinging' into a thing-law, into a discourse in which *evidence* of facts is given this or that importance in an ethics of values, rights and duties. In thinking the Being of law, in 'thinging' law, the 'aboutness' relates to the ethical effort of the ongoing struggle to confront the language of this discourse, the language of the legal. This struggle is most desperate when, as we saw in Part 2, the legal appears and preserves itself in the guise of ethical transcendence of a not-yet-conceptualised-Other. The reality of the legal is a perpetuation, through enforcement, of the entrenched ontic notion of evidence of reality whereby the essence of thinking and 'thinging' – the distortion of the ontic – is violently screened out by common sense, representation and logic or, most violently, by detached punctuation of an 'Other'. The legal distorts, and at worst, nearly destroys the mystery of Otherness. What is logic without the centrality of punctuation, definitions and representations? The entrenchment of the legal and the scientific, facts, norms, risk assessment, sanctifies thinking as the human arrogance of making representations about values, about facts, about the prediction of the probability of a represented 'happening', of an event. The entrenchment of the legal brings together the forgetfulness of thinking and 'thinging' in making technological thinking, calculative thinking seemingly the objective arbiter of actuality including the actuality of human beings and of things. Ontic hegemony of the legal screens out non-representational thought as illogical, poetic, irrational 'noise'. The distortion of the notion of reason by this hegemony itself becomes a supreme religion. The pervasive proliferation and sanctification of legal and the scientific conditions of prudence, efficiency, measurability, predictability, are all signs not merely of the current ontic conception Reason, but of the deep forgetfulness of the distortion of the essence of reason. As we saw in chapter seven, making the Other the centre of thought acknowledges the implicit need for calculations, allocation, mediation, representations as constituting the inevitable part of the relationship between justice and ethics. Although actual representa-

tions and risk assessment seem vulgar and can be criticised as such by the ethics of the Other, at heart, such ethics of the Other and calculative thought are mutually reinforcing.

100. The legal presumes representation-able *evidence*. The notion of facts, including facts that ground things-values, can legitimate a structure of 'if facts occur, then this occurrence can be criticised by this or that that priority of values/norms'. The belief in the reality of facts, evidence and the epistemology of evidence-as-facts, the supremacy of nourishing the obsession for factual evidence through risk assessment, all become pervasive under the ontic hegemony of the legal. The punctuation of facts is the bedrock of the legal. The sancti-fication of risk assessment is achieved by ontic recognition of complexity and indeterminacy which leads to the scaling down of truth into probability, moderating truth, into the artistry of calcu-lation and prediction of risk. Risk assessment and norm-based thinking supplement one another – both constitute the pursuance of representation by other means. Both depend on the religion of repre-sentation. To be risky can only be understood when already assimilated into the ontic. The only reflection which is absolutely free of risk is the belief in the epistemology of norms and facts.

101. Everybody assesses risk according to the evidence. Everybody ponders whether to justify a risk according to some representational norms. And yet nobody is being risky, nobody risks the inexpressible but only the probable. The only thing that is thought about is the calculative, prediction-able, probable. In Hebrew, the word for danger, SAKANA, has the same root as that for risk, SIKUN. Primordial risk lies in the contemplative resoluteness to face the dominance of calculative/metaphysical thought. Such a risk cannot be assessed and calls upon us to be silent, to be attentive amidst the barrage of representations and calculations. We have to listen to the relationship between danger and risk and ask where the danger lies.

102. Can the word 'evidence' give us a clue as to that which is primor-dially 'risky'? Let us dwell on the term 'evidence'. In his essay *The End of Philosophy and the Task of Thinking*, Heidegger listens to this word. What is evidence? What is the evident and, furthermore, what can be said to be *self-evident*? In that essay, Heidegger saw the historicity of the completion of metaphysics manifested as technical relations as an *end* of philosophy as we know it. But he also conceived a philosophical moment which connects to the utmost *end* of philosophy, namely to the question of 'how is philosophy?'. The end of philosophy, then, is also conceived as the moment of completion of philosophy, where philosophy thinks itself back to the moment of its own unconcealment of its basic question – the question of Being. The historicity of philosophy brings us fatefully

back to the moment of unconcealment of the 'there' of philosophy. The title of the essay creates both a feeling of an end of something, in the sense of finishing, but at the same time transcends any question of ends and beginnings, preoccupying itself with the hermeneutic cycle of philosophy itself.

103. The completion of philosophy, as we saw, manifests itself in the everyday call for thinking and 'thinging'. Unconcealment – *alētheia* – has concealment [*lethe*] as a part of its historicity. *Alētheia* occurs only in luminosity – in the lightening [*Lichtung*]. Heidegger used the term 'lightening' in three related senses: the first sense as light as opposed to darkness – brightness, luminosity. The second sense is light, as in making light, being weightless. The third sense is that of clearing – as freedom and openness. This last sense stems from a translation which arrives from the French word *clairière* as the light which occasions a *clearing*, as in an opening in the middle of the forest where there are no trees. Heidegger claims that key to these three senses is the third, that of 'clearing'. For something to be in the luminosity and to make light, there must already be a clearing of something in the sense of an open space which the light lightens. The 'clearing' is a moment of openness of a world of thinking and 'thinging', a place of dwelling.[35]

104. That which is evident is that which, in the moment of clearing, in the moment of openness, shows itself understandingly to the intuition which comports to think and to 'thing'. The word *evidentia* is the way Cicero translated the Greek word *energia*, which in turn comes from the word *argentum* (silver), namely that which radiates and brings itself to light.[36] In Hebrew, the word REAYA, REAYOT, evidence, is connected by root to the verb LIROT, to see. The moment of evidence is the moment of clearing, a moment of vision of the flickering inexpressible. Unconcealment of the evident in the whilst, the stillness, of a clearing – in dwelling. What is evident in clearing occurs in thinking which is always already ready to see, to hear, to make light, to free up.

105. Heidegger used the term 'clearing' to connote the boundary that opens up but remains a boundary all the same in its opening. But the very moment of clearing conceals itself as it clears, and conceals its own concealment whilst it clears. *The evident is essentially re-concealed in the evidence.*

106. *Such is the mystery of the evident: it gets further in the whilst of its nearing; it involves listening only to the audibility of silence; it*

[35] *EPTT*, pp 441–2.
[36] *Ibid*, p 443.

involves seeing only in flickering light; it makes light – alleviates weight – only under the heaviness of anxiety (in Hebrew, MUAKA).

107. What is self-evident, then, that which is beyond not only the need for, but also the craving for, representational proof? Self-evidence is the evident. Self-evidence is never a thing extant but only the unconcealment of the 'thingness' of things. The only moment of self-evidence is a moment of dwelling nearer than facts, a moment of a boundary that stands on its own as an event of clearing. The evident, that which is self-evident, is a trace of 'isness'. The evident stands on its own, the only source of speaking the authentic way of being spoken by Being. Being speaks the evident, and *Dasein* listens in dwelling in the evident amongst other *Dasein*s. The evident shows itself in a way which is not craving for any facts but which is dependent on facts as its point of departure towards nearing the Saying that is distanced in those facts. The moment of the distortion of the craving for facts is a poetic moment. *The Nothing evidences the evident.*

108. We have dwelled a lot in this work on the question of how the completion of philosophy signifies in the boundary between the essence of law and the legal. This distortion that makes up the boundary between the essence of law and the legal has been shown to be related to the manifestation of that boundary of the ethical as being the otherwise to the transcendence of that thinking that conditions the work of Levinas. Thinking about law calls upon us to think about the ethical as that which is cleared in the evident. Such thinking and 'thinging' of law involves the constant ethical attendance to the distortion by ethics that pretends to be otherwise than ontology, an ethics which the legal enforces. To think about law is to think about, to dwell on, the boundary between law's essence – its 'thinging' – and the distortion of law's ontic manifestation – the legal. The legal as encapsulated in the ontic perpetuation and entrenchment – the perpetuation of the derivative ontology of facts/norm/risk assessment – is the sanctification of evidence whilst forgetting the evident. But that forgetting is all the more evident as it represses the evident. The entrenchment of the legal is unethical in that in it *Dasein* is coaxed, lured, into the belief that there is no ethical reflection apart from that kind of ethics which can be protected and enforced by the legal. This entrenchment occurs in the grip of calculative and representational reasoning which stipulates that there is no evidence beyond an evidence that can be verified in a court of reason, a court of representation, a court of law. Sanctifying the legal is to forget the essence of reason as the self-evident grounding of the evident.

109. But the legal does belong to the essence of law which protects and enforces the evident. The inauthentic dwelling and forgetfulness of

Being is itself the ground of the evident. Drowning in the anticipation of justice of representations of the factual, norms, risk assessments, is itself a necessity for the showing of the evident.

110. The essence of law – *dikē* – is in protecting. In protecting it enforces that which is morally right and just, that which is valuable and due. The 'thingness' of law is to protect but in protecting, dwelling together in the boundary, it also protects mortals in their essence. Law, indeed divine law which is distorted in human law – the legal, preserves mortals in their thinking and 'thinging'. The *conatus* of human law, most intense with Levinas, deludes mortals so that they think themselves beyond the divine.

111. Again, one of the main arguments of this book is to stress that the legal *belongs* to the essence of law – is complementary to it. That which the legal expels through distortion and burial is part of the occurrence of the essence of law. The ontic belongs to the onto-logical, and there is no ontological without dwelling in the ontic. It is in the legal that we should look for the distortion of the essence. It is in the language of the legal that the evident hides in calling us. We need the legal in order to be ethical. To think about the how which is to be protected is to look for that which is left unprotected in the 'whatness' of the legal. To think about law is to look for that which is left unprotected in the ontic ethics of a not-yet-conceptualised, and thus oppressed and dominated, Other. The legal, including Levinas's legal, is needed in order to immerse in that which is left unprotected within it.

112. However, that which is to be protected is mysterious and can never be captured as an object of protection. It is the mystery which is protected *as* mystery, and it is the particular mystery of *Dasein*, the dweller, which is protected. The mystery is always evident beneath the legal. To near that which has to be protected we have to see how any object of protection distorts the protecting. Such a distortion is the emptiness of law, and the Saying of that which ought, first and foremost, to be protected is to listen to the stillness of the boundary of the legal. To think about law is to listen to the boundary of the legal, and such listening is not merely criticising the content of law, or even seemingly going deeper by criticising the positivism and objectivity and thus, totalisation, of the 'legal subject'.

113. The legal belongs to the essence of law in an epoch in which the essence of law is more readily neared by mortals, that is when mortals are more readily disposed to think about that which is not yet protected by the legal. Such epochs can be seen as 'primitive' or unenlightened. Such arrogance can be manifested only by tyrannising thinking in which humans conceive themselves as subjects. But, crucially, the legal belongs to the essence of law also in the epoch of

entrenching the legal in a manner that coerces thinking away from
that which needs protection by the sanctification of science and
risk assessment as well as by the enforcement of ethics of values,
rights and duties. It is only the manner of protection by *dikē*
which changes between such epochs. Man in his essence as a dweller
in the boundary does not change. As a dweller in the boundary, the
boundary dwells within him. As a dweller in erring, Man already
dwells essentially in the emptiness of the legal and thus essentially
necessitates the saving power. The call of the saving power may be
responded to by mortals in different ways. Their thinking/'thinging',
in responding, may take very unpredictable tacks, certainly not ones
which can always be controlled by them. Both the legal and the
essence of law which is antecedent/futural as the distortion that
creates the boundary, the temporal locus of protection, fugally unite
the essence of Man, the essence of ethics and the essence of law.
Man's essence is to fall back to the legal, in 'ek-stasis' and error. The
'about' in thinking about law is generated as Man's dwelling in the
boundary of the legal. To think about law is to instantiate the
boundary of the legal, the boundary that opens up beneath either the
idle chatter of the legal or the transcendence of the legal that
preserves it. Critical scholarship within the legal can challenge the
representational content but not the very thinking that effectuates the
fall.

114. Philosophers of subjectivity, inter-subjectivity, ethical philosophers,
critical legal scholars, do their utmost to interpret the practice of law
from the point of view of that *Dasein* which simply participates in
the practice of philosophy, ethics, politics, law. Ironically, quite often
theorising a practice is called '*verstehen* method', as if the practice in
which they participate has an ontology which makes sense to their
consciousness. By subjecting the participant's involvement to *method,*
to *correctness,* to *consciousness* that craves the expression of the
essence of a practice, these theorists focus thinking on what participants think and not on their very thinking that conditions the very
notion of 'practice'. This focus on practice of a 'thing-law'/'thing-
ethics'/'thing-philosophy' forgets any thinking about distortion of the
ontological difference. This focus on practice perpetuates the ontic
way in which people describe both themselves and the practice they
participate in. No *method* can think about aboutness. All it does is
attempt to articulate a fresh aspect of the legal – to construct a grand
phenomenology of the essence of the legal and of the subjects who
experience that essence. What I have tried to show in this book is
that we need to invoke a much more radical notion of thinking and
participating. To understand is to stand before. Thinking back about
law needs to reach the 'before' that 'stands' nearest to the ontic

participant who knows, who has common sense of the practice. That which is standing-before in participation is always evident as the boundary of the practice, of that which relates in some way to the practice but is nevertheless fundamentally distorted (rather than simply reduced) in any representation of it. The essence of law resides nearer to any construction of purpose, or ground, that can justify 'truth-claim' in the practice. Even presented this purpose as interpretative already craves for a construction of this practice because it is already dominated by ontic thinking. Ontic interpretation, constructive at heart, does not yet interpret that which is evident in practice. The ontic understanding of *verstehen*, the craving for the articulation of the 'thing-law' rather than the 'thinging' of law, keeps the human *Dasein* far from the authentic moment by preserving the entrenchment of the legal as a part of a prudent universe.

115. *Ethics occurs as Being thinks valuably for Dasein as Dasein's essence in 'ek-sistence'. Dikē enforces that ethics. If ethics is the conatus of Being, the essence of law is a conatus of the ethical. Dikē preserves the 'oughtness' of the ethical.* Even in the entrenched inauthenticity of *Dasein*, even in its deafness, Being speaks ethically. The essence of law, *dikē*, enforces the ethical, the dwelling together as neighbours.

116. It may asked whether a value-based ethics of rights and duty is not necessary to protect *Dasein* against the possibly horrible consequences of Being speaking as the ethical? To put this observation another way, there are two kinds of equally primordial ethics. The first preserves attentiveness to the unfolding of actuality. The second is external to the way actuality unfolds, and is representational, an ethics of values that can anticipate representations of actions, distributions, allocations, to protect humans from their own essential, irreducible, unenlightened and harmful nature. Crucially, this representation-based ethics protects people from the violence that is unleashed by the tormented, essentially 'ek-static' Being of humans. Here we have it than, no one ethics has supremacy, they are both irreducibly essential and 'balance' one another as in any doctrine of separation of powers. The ethics of Being and the ethics of the legal are, according to this dualism, in constant strife and reconciliation.

117. I have not denied the persistence of these two kinds of ethics in this book. What I wanted to give was an account of the relationship between them, an account of the rift between them. I have argued that these two kinds of ethics are complementary, complemented by an irreducible distortion that is part of the ontological difference. It is part of the ontological difference, and the tragic characteristic of humans, that the Saying of Being makes the water boil in the pot and the error of protection through the ethics of representation and

representation-ability puts the lid on that pot. Only by lifting the lid a little can it be realised that the water is boiling. What I contest is that representation ethics, by externalising the realm of ethics to the realm of Being, provides any protection. The essence of *Dasein* is that it is helpless against the forces that shape its manifestation. *Dasein* can never see near enough but it can feel the near in anxiety of the nearest. No representation-ability can protect from the order of Being. *Dasein*'s tragic essence stems from its essential grasp of its always inexpressible Being. This grasp is so powerful that no representation can tranquillise it or protect from what it brings in its wake. But that is not to say that *Dasein* is not protected. *Dasein* is always already protected from the *forgetfulness* of its own essential erring, that is from the entrenchment of itself in the ontic. The forgetfulness of erring is itself an instantiation of erring. This well-embedded epochal erring generates a call upon *Dasein* to which *Dasein* must respond. It has been a central claim of the book that the generation of an ethics that offers protection for humans by cutting them away from their essence – that is from traversing the onto-logical difference – is itself a manifestation of erring. So I attempted to articulate the relationship of protection to *Dasein* as the main-tenance of the opening towards the complementarity, that is the distortion, that prevails between these two kinds of ethics. So instead of being content with some cosmic *modus vivendi* as the mutuality of protection between the two kinds of ethics, I have defended the persistence of the ethics of representation-ability as the tragic and essential error from which *Dasein* is preserved by the ethical, by the ethics of Being. It is precisely the interpretation of the comple-mentarity between the two kinds of ethics as mutual protection, namely that one ethics protects from the other, that constitutes the origin of the error, the origin of the ontic separation from which the mystery of *Dasein* needs to be protected.

118. The two ethics indeed exist alongside one another but they belong in the ontic–ontological ethico-temporal unfolding. Any attempt to separate them does not yet grasp their distortion-bound comple-mentarity. Talk of protecting humans from the voice of Being is itself part of the historicity of Being.

119. Thus, to accept the complementarity of the ethics of values and the ethical is to remain ethical. This is not the same as saying that the ethics of value has some irreducible and separate purpose. We must ask the ethical question of what it is that has brought us to believe that the representational has that independent purpose. What has taken us away from ethical complementarity between the ontic and the ontological? What is that which silences the 'aboutness' of this

complementarity so successfully? Perhaps the overcoming of such success is already under way.

120. When the legal dominates, Man does not listen to actuality. Man creates a discourse of right and duties, to be generalised, defined and refined. The house, the cathedral, of the legal is made so refined that the inhabitants are looking up to admire it rather than looking at what is just in front ofthem, near to them. The inhabitants of the house of the legal become guardians of that house rather than guardians of the house of Being. The ontic slaves and their ethical philosophers of value believe that their cathedral offers them protection.

121. To contemplate the ethical as letting the evident show itself is the law that protects mortals in their essence regardless of how entrenched the legal has become.

122. Thinking about law is to be silent with Heidegger. It is to be attentive to the mystery of otherness and that which protects and enforces it. It is to be with him in silence, listening to the evident that lurks in the language of legal materials, case law, theories of law – even the most critical legal accounts – and the Levinasian otherness that they develop.

123. To think about law is to think about the ambit of the legal. Thinking about the ambit of the legal involves *Dasein* ethically letting Being be as the evident that is rewriting the notion of otherness of the Other, thereby overcoming otherness that the ontic authors. The otherness of the other person as embodied in the otherness of the nothing is fugally connected to the ethical imperative that demands attentiveness to the otherness of the essence of law within the legal.

124. In the last two chapters I have tried to destabilise the ethical/ontological distinction by showing the ontological difference as both the primordial and ethical. The ontological difference of law – the ethical thinking of distance – clears and conceals the relationship between law and its Being – between law as a thing - the legal – and the thinking/'thinging' of law. The legal is not yet near its world.

125. In their essence humans dwell ethically together in the law, thereby outstripping the separation that grounds their togetherness in the legal and the ethics that the legal enforces. To respond through language to the silence of the inexpressible in the midst of those responses by which the inexpressible is legally tamed by punctuation and separation, including the transcendence of alterity that criminally conceals such taming, is to ethically dwell in the law. To dwell ethically in the law is to think about law in silence and to say this silence.

Coda

In Silence with Heidegger

Language withdraws from man its simple and high speech. But its primal call does not thereby become incapable of speech; it merely falls silent.

Heidegger, *BDT*, p 350

'*Es lasst sich nicht lesen*' – it does not permit itself to be read – quotes Edgar Allan Poe at the beginning and end of his short story 'The Man of the Crowd'. What is that which is secretive and extraordinary in everydayness? What is that which every person – the man of the crowd – hides – something that can grip us to the point of obsession when encountering that person? What is that self-preserving mystery that is assimilated into misleading ordinariness the more persistent the attempts to unravel it? What is that human secret – that intimacy that draws us to one another whilst simultaneously protecting itself against disclosure, thus also sublimely protecting *us* in our essence?

Humans are essentially, and thus fatefully, drawn to the law. They have to obey the law in the same way an eel has to obey a call to the sea of Saragossa. It is some self-preserving secret of our humanity that draws us into the law. To be free as human is to let the law draw us.

The saving power of the law is violent. Thinking about law involves thinking about violence – originary violence. As Derrida points out, the word *Gewalt*, while it connotes the notion of violence, also rings of legitimacy, justification and authority.[1] The legitimacy of the law, I would say, has nothing to do with this or that expedient justification of authority but involves the very necessity of the divine.

The violence of the law is silent. To think about law *in silence* involves the primordial 'not' in relation to the mere deconstructive deferral of a decision – a deferral which still lingers within the realm of the mystical foundation of the authority (*Gewalt*) of the legal.[2]

This book points towards originary violence that manifests itself between the essences of law, ethics, language, humans, truth and the ontic manifestations of these essences. The authority of law consists in the very

---

[1] J Derrida, 'Force of Law: The Mystical Foundation of Authority', in D Cornell, M Rosenfeld and DG Carlson (eds), *Deconstruction and the Possibilities of Justice* (London, Routledge, year?) pp 3–67 at p 6.

[2] Montaigne, quoted in *ibid*, p 12.

Gewalt of Being. The force of law, of divine law, is the originary violence of Being. At the same time, this book has brought forth the extent to which the *Gewalt* of the legal is violent towards Being. This violence-towards Being is already on the way to the violence of Being. It is in this violent unfolding that humans dwell. Law protects this dwelling, which is manifested by humans as the nearing of their strange essence.

Human dwelling connotes an essential error. The ethics of values, rights and duties that is enforced by the legal is itself violent towards the mystery of the divine law. Humans either open up to this violence towards the mystery or they do not. Originary violence of Being is preserved – as a call for humans – as the violent strangeness and uncanniness that characterises the relationship between divine law and human law. Humans are summoned for violence towards their ontic violence towards Being in their attentiveness to the originary violence of Being.

Humans ought ethically to attend to the violence of Being rather than hiding away from this attentiveness through the violence that is trapped in the legal, violence that takes thinking away from Being. Humans ought to let language speak in a much more immediate fashion. The ethical effort consists in resisting that deconstruction that transcends the law and preserves the legal. Humans ought to open themselves to, and let themselves be claimed by, Being.

In the complementarity between essences and ontic manifestations we can see the origin of the strife in which humans dwell *together*. This strife conditions the violence which is anticipated by the divine intervention that directs humans to prudently preserve the legal.

Within the horizon of the legal, justice can self-preserve, mystically, by keeping alive the various *aporia*s of undecidability that Derrida hints at, *aporias* that are prevalent between the deconstruction of law and the impossibility of such deconstruction.[3] To conceive the force of law as the preservation of deconstruction in the light of impossibility is the hallmark of the deep-seated amnesia that preserves the legal. The very hesitation is already legal.

The violence of preservation of the legal through deconstruction tames originary violence. It assimilates it to transcendence that in actuality increases the distance from the event of violent clearing. This distancing conceals by distortingly reproducing a gap that persists within the horizon of correctness (*Richtigkeit*) rather within that of *distance*. A gap, however, does not yet near the mystery. Distancing holds sway by merely contesting the deconstruction of any conceptual coherence. Thinking itself is not transformed by such contestation. On the contrary, an idle form of thinking is preserved by such deconstructive acrobatics. The alluring scent of the philosophical tradition is not yet overcome in terms of thinking.

[3] *Ibid*, pp 14–15 and 22–9.

When the legal is entrenched as harbouring an *aporia* the possibility of violence towards, and thus of, Being, is foreclosed, and with it any ethical possibility.

Being is always itself. Taming originary violence is by no means eliminating it. Indeed, the impossibility of elimination is that which makes such violence originary. Humans, without noticing, are already on the ethical way of reinstating the violence of Being, that is reinstating the error that, through the legal, is to come (*à venir*) nearer to them.

On the one hand, preservation of the origin of the legal in error is becoming less conspicuous and less obvious by deconstructing the law within the horizon of the legal. On the other hand, such preservation is precisely what makes audible the intense coming back of ethical violence. The violence of law is already harboured in the process of thinking violently and silently transforming itself.

The legal reigns supreme within the deconstruction that constantly explores the space between justice and justice according to law, between the undecidability of justice and what Derrida refers to as the necessary 'madness' of decidability in law.[4] Justice, as Derrida rightly observes, is the question of moment of origin.[5] But does Derrida, with his constant reference to Levinas in seeking that surplus between justice and law, tackle that primordial event, that origin, the nearing of which is justice?[6] Does justice as responding to that moment of origin involve the mystical preservation of the law amidst its destruction or suspension?[7] Ought justice, as the ethics of deconstruction, improve the law? Derrida's explanation of that which cannot be decided but has to be traversed in order to bring about a decision 'worthy of the name' still preserves the horizon of decidability despite the continual lurking of the undecidable as a ghost in every such worthy decision.[8] Derrida mystifies correctness without transcending the very thinking that conditions correctness. There is much scope, then, to meditate about the legal origin of such deconstruction.

Let us listen to the origin of silence. Let us, for a moment, be in silence with this silence. Let us listen to the uncanny manner which already pervades, as legality, that apparent transcendence of legality by deconstruction. The seemingly authentic echoes of the origin of justice in Derrida's characterisation of the surplus between justice and law serve precisely to conceal the origin that involves a leap nearer than any deconstructive move within the legal.

Critical legal scholarship already harbours the secret that it does its best

---

[4] *Ibid*, p 26.
[5] *Ibid*, p 20.
[6] *Ibid*, pp 17, 19. See p 25, where Derrida refers to infinite responsibility towards the other. See also p 27 where he says 'the other coming as the singularity that is always other'.
[7] *Ibid*, p 23.
[8] *Ibid*, p 24.

not to touch. In such scholarship, the foundation of authority remains mystical but not mysterious. The legal self-preserves by self-mystification. The legal self-preserves within the hegemonious horizon of thinking that silences the mystery. The mystical deferral that deconstruction of law brings about takes thinking away from the mystery of law.

Deconstruction transcends the law but at the same time disguises that the very *thinking* about law that is being deconstructed remains unchallenged. What lingers in silent poetic speech is this otherness of *thinking* that lurks beneath the overwhelming nature of the still-legal transcendence of the legal carried out by deconstruction.

Resisting positivism, constructivism and objectification does in fact increase the distance for thinking from what calls for thinking about law. Critical lawyers share a common matrix with the positivists and the constructivist legal theorists in a horizon of thinking and the notion of truth that grounds such thinking. Critical theorists are lawyers who are still captives of the legal. It is the legal that they desire to return to.

To be human is to open up to the violent way to the mystery. Walter Benjamin's distinction between the two kinds of violence – the divine violence and that violence which preserves the law – ought to be understood as the mystery that persists between the law of Being as the Being of law and the legal.

Silence is manifested as the inexpressible and always already understanding wonder at the legal. This book wonders how the legal is still able to possess a surplus that distorts actuality into the deconstruction of legalism. It is in this sense that the Saying of this book is in silence with Heidegger.

Originary violence is the violence that comes from the mystery. The possibility of justice is the possibility of attending to the error in responding to the mystery.

In its essence, the ethical is the *conatus essendi* of the mystery that law in its essence protects and enforces.

Law, morality and ethics essentially dwell together in the Order of Being. This book has attempted to clarify that statement. Heidegger famously claimed that art is essentially poetry in a broad sense. Poetic saying, the saying of the mystery, is divine in that it connects both infinite temporality and the eternal stillness of no outside. The house of Being rages with ubiquitous violence. Law, morality and ethics are essentially art, and as art, they belong to the order of Being. They all constitute different aspect of the unfolding fugal order of Being. Humans essentially poetically dwell in the mystery of Being. Being open to the mystery is our humanity.

This book, rather than being about human rights, is about the right to be human amidst the pervasive domination of human rights and the ethical ground of these rights. The 'right' to be human could not be further away from the legal notion of human rights.

The very language of human rights makes it seems unnecessary for the language of Being to speak out. Again, amidst the sanctification of the idle chatter of human rights lurks, in silence, the ethical imperative that preserves the Being of humans. In this violent lurking, the essence of law, ethics and humans are fugally connected.

This silence of the mystery, of the near, is the very self-preservation of Being. The silence of the mystery cannot be legalised. However, humans have entrenched such legalisation to such an extent that they see such legalisation as a paragon of their ethical life. In doing that that, all humans are *essentially guilty*. This guilt is the very manifestation of human dwelling in freedom. No one can ever be presumed to be innocent.

The legalisation of ethics and morality, as entrenched by Levinasian transcendence, seem to successfully take humans away from their essence, the essence of poetically dwelling together in the mystery. The divine becomes arrested in ontic deferral. Humans entrench the legal as that thinking that paraphrases into punctuation both the question of goodness – ethics – and the question of harm – morality. By legalising the valuable, by approaching morality and ethics critically through radical separation, the legal still confines moral and ethical transcendence to the horizon of representation and calculation. The legal smothering of ethics and morality punctuates also what it is that unbearable silence to legalism – that mysterious silence of primordial otherness.

Being human, being attentive to the mystery, is *the difficulty* – the *problem* of problems that ought to persist necessarily as essential part of human poetic dwelling. This problem involves the very characterisation of thinking. The paraphrase of this difficulty into Levinasian transcendence and deconstruction is violent without yet travelling on the ethical way to originary violence. Originary violence anticipates itself by keeping the problem manifest as the double concealment of the mystery.

Entrenching the legalisation of ethics and morality is, for all its radicality, still the easy way out for humans. Such entrenchment stops them from being attentive to that positivity of the problem that ought necessarily to pervade their essence.

Humans have to learn their place in the order of Being, as its guardians.

Complementarity of distortion between ontic thinking and ontological attentiveness to the mystery is itself the unfolding way of the mystery. Being ethical is hovering in the mystery, nearing and getting further away from the continuous temporal order. Error, then, characterises this hovering of distance. The comportment towards constant response to that error is human and, as such, ethical. Opening up to error characterises the ethical moment. Any punctuation, as error, is already necessary on the way to the nearest of the near, to the continuous.

Degrees of error vary. But the more error is entrenched, the more the desire to respond to error is repressed. The more repressed is this desire to respond to the mystery, the louder should be the voice of Being as the voice which always summons us back to the mystery, to the essence.

The origin of legalism is not in representations and calculations but in that seemingly ethical thinking that punctuates otherness. The mystery of otherness that characterises the Categorical Imperative – as letting Being be in freedom – is distorted by approaching radical alterity through punctuation. Radical alterity seemingly puts the seal of ethical critical thinking by which this imperative's subsequent interpretations are imprisoned..

This origin of legalism has been argued to have the face of Levinasian transcendence. Levinas's thought constitutes the most radical ontic transcendence but it takes us back to the deepest origins of error. At the same time, Levinas takes thinking away from being on the mysterious way *to* error as that which is ethical in our Being. Levinas exploits humans' essential vulnerability – that of being unable to be left hanging over the abyss of the mystery. The complementarity he advocates purports to take us to a moment *beyond* Being, beyond the mystery of otherness that is encapsulated in thinking-Being. Indeed, so deep is his denial of the origins of error. His notions of radical separation, exteriority, and 'Other' give rise to punctuating the mystery, reducing the mysterious to totality and allergy. Levinasian transcendence as the ground of entrenched legalism makes legalism the *a priori* nature of all ethics and morality. This punctuation and legalism, echoing the mystery, transcends any ethics of values and legal representation. But, because its essence is in punctuation, it anticipates the preservation of the legal and value-based ethics. The so-called post-modern transcendence defended by Levinas is the most sophisticated entrenchment of the legal.

Thinking-Being is to be silent. Being silent is to heed the inexpressible and to respond to it. To maintain that silence in a Saying is to respond to, rather than to ignore the mystery of otherness through legalism of values, rights and duties. Law in its essence protects the ethical engagement with the mystery and protects our ability to respond to the mystery. That is how law makes us responsible. It is the law that comes from our essence, law which we have no choice but to obey, no matter how strong the denial mounted by the legal.

The authority of law stems originally from the distortion entailed by the manifestation of its authority through the legal.

Levinas's caricaturisation of the secret of Being – the secret which does not permit itself to be told – into mere totality of interpretation of essence is nothing but a crime against humanity. *It is literally that.* The criminality of this caricature – a caricature which seems to win Derrida over – plays to the Achilles' heel of humans, namely their tragic essential nature to distance themselves from their humanity. The manner in which Levinas exploits this tragic human nature, that is *qua* transcendence of an 'Other', is grossly inhuman. No human crime, though, however cleverly and cruelly concealed, can diminish that call of Being that perturbs our own 'thingness'.

The entrenchment of the legal is a crime against humanity, and Being sends us constant reminders of that. It is callous to take humans away from being open to the way they are necessarily in the mystery, making them believe that punctuation of the Other is the paragon of ethics – beyond Being, otherwise than Being. There is no court of law in which this crime against humanity can be evidenced and judged. The manifestation of the force of law that this crime brings in its wake must grasped and manifested as divine judgement and intervention.

What are we to make of Levinas's claim that his thought characterises the essence of Jewish thinking?

The insight that every interpretation involves a totality does not hold sway once interpretation is understood as that of the mystery of nearness. Being in the order of Being involves being always already interpreted by that continuous whilst of this order. Letting Being be as a response to that order involves letting the law of Being protect us. The utmost clarity of interpretation sharpens the mystery but that does not mean that any totality is involved in such response. Once actuality is approached as temporal *world*, interpretation of distance is the directionality towards which thinking is comported. The legal nature of Levinas is that he pretends, inhumanely, to go beyond interpretation, beyond intentionality, beyond desiring the mystery. *Levinas legalises that very desire.* That there is no 'is' of a beyond – that a beyond is itself already thrown on the way to error which is 'in' the world – is something that he takes humans away from.

The legalisation of poetic language of the Other finds itself in scholarly reflections. On this occasion, I can point to an ethical trend of the all-too-arrogant human tendency to uproot humans from their essence. In the last chapter of her *Heidegger and the Poets*, V Fôti offers an analysis of Heidegger's poetic reading which portrays Heidegger's reading of poetry as over-interpretative.[9] Heidegger, she argues, does not allow primordial otherness to speak through the poems that he reads, those of Hölderlin and Trakl. Fôti also offers a reading of P Celan's speech 'The Meridian'. The theme of the Other and the yearning for poetic language that faces the otherness of the Other is indeed central to Celan's speech and verse. Celan could be read as being a Levinasian, thus being other to Heidegger's thought. The Levinasian tone of Fôti's impressive and intensive book is dominant, although Levinas himself is mentioned very briefly.

However, Celan, despite speaking about the 'other' in his speech, does

[9] VM Fôti, *Heidegger and the Poets: Poiesis, Sophia, Techne* (New Jersey, Humanities Press, 1992).

not really dwell on the origin of otherness. It would be a mistake to legalise Celan by grafting Levinas onto him. The true greatness of Heidegger's writings is that those *ethical* insights that embody the radicality of the impossibility of discourse (like that which characterises Celan's poetry and prose, for example) are always already in that mystery of language. Radical otherness is only possible as a mystery and not as a separation. Thus, even stuttering and gaps are necessary in that place where language is torn between a call and a response – that very place where humans dwell together. Heidegger grasps that the original otherness, although it seems like yearning for an Other, is in actuality, a continuous unfolding of the only possible moment of authentic speech.

This book attempts to articulate an epoch of radical forgetfulness of Being that is brought about by radical legalism, namely that critical legalism of thinking about the Other.

Humans ought to beware. Critical legal studies already evidence the sanctification of calculation and representation. *The very possibility of legalism constituting the opening towards the ethical is becoming more and more remote as legalism is entrenched. The divine must intervene in order to protect itself against its own legalisation. As humans we are already conceived as messengers of the divine.*

Like the all too important sound of a triangle in an overwhelming orchestra, we must hear a different thing in Shelley's saying that poets are the unacknowledged legislators of the world. The world legislates for poets. Poets, then, as the messengers of 'worlding' are thus always comported to retain Man in his essential abode. That is their silent and violent obedience to the law.

In this epoch of entrenched legalisation of the divine we must end this book by heeding Heidegger's prophecy that only God can save us.

Bibiliography

WORKS BY HEIDEGGER (IN CHRONOLOGICAL ORDER)

Being and Time [1926], J Macquarrie and E Robinson (trans) (Oxford, Blackwell, 1962).

The Basic Problems of Phenomenology [1927], A Hofstadter (trans), revised edn (Bloomington/Indianapolis, Indiana University Press, 1982).

'What is Metaphysics?' [1929], DF Krell (trans), in DF Krell (ed), *Basic Writings: Martin Heidegger* (London, Routledge, 1993), pp 93–110.

The Essence of Reasons [1929], T Malick (trans) (Evanston, Northwestern University Press, 1969).

'On the Essence of Truth' [1930], J Sallis (trans), in DF Krell (ed), *Basic Writings: Martin Heidegger* (London, Routledge, 1993), pp 115-38.

'The Self-Assertion of the German University' and 'Political Texts' [1933–34], in R Wolin (ed), *The Heidegger Controversy* (Cambridge, MA, MIT Press, 1991), pp 29–60.

An Introduction to Metaphysics [1935], R Manheim (trans) (New Haven/London, Yale University Press, 1961).

'The Origin of The Work of Art' [1935], in A Hofstadter (ed and trans), *Poetry Language, Thought* (New York, Perennial (Harper Collins), 1971), pp 17–79.

What is a Thing? [1935–36], WB Barton Jr and V Deutsch (trans) (Indiana, Regnery/Gateway Inc, 1967).

'The Scope and Context of Plato's Meditation on the Relationship of Art and Truth' [1936–37], in DF Krell (ed and trans), *Nietzsche (Vol 1: The Will to Power as Art)*, (New York, Harper Collins, 1991), pp 162–70.

'Letter on Humanism' [1947], FA Capuzzi and J Glenn Gray (trans), in DF Krell (ed), *Basic Writings: Martin Heidegger*, (London, Routledge, 1993), pp 217–65.

'Homecoming/To Kindred Ones', in *Elucidations of Hölderlin's Poetry*, K Hoeller (trans) (New York, Humanity Books, 2000), pp 24–49.

Holtzwege (Frankfurt Am Mine, Vittorio Klostermann, 1950).

'The Thing' [1950], in A Hofstadter (trans and ed), *Poetry, Language, Thought* (New York, Perennial (Harper Collins), 1971, pp 163-80.

'Language' [1950], in A Hofstadter (ed and trans), *Poetry Language, Thought* (Perennial (Harper Collins), New York, 1971), pp 187–208.

'A Letter to a Young Student' [1950], in A Hofstadter (ed and trans), *Poetry, Language, Thought* (New York, Perennial (Harper Collins), 1975 and 2001), pp 181-4.

'The Anaximander Fragment' [1946], in *Early Greek Thinking*, DF Krell and FA Capuzzi (trans) (London, Harper and Row, 1975).

'Poetically Man Dwells ...' [1951], in A Hofstadter (ed and trans), *Poetry Language, Thought* (New York, Harper and Row, 1971), pp 211–27.

What is Called Thinking? [1951–52], J Glenn Gray (trans) (London, Harper and Row, 1968).

'Building, Dwelling, Thinking' [1951], in DF Krell, *Basic Writings: Martin Heidegger* (London, Routledge, 1993), pp 347–63.

'The Question Concerning Technology' [1954], W Lovitt (trans), in DF Krell (ed), *Basic Writings: Martin Heidegger* (London, Routledge, 1993), pp 311–41.

The Principle of Reason [1957], R Lilly (trans) (Bloomington, Indiana University Press 1991).

'Only God can Save Us', *Der Spiegel's* interview with Martin Heidegger, reprinted in R Wolin (ed), *The Heidegger Controversy: A Critical Reader* (Cambridge, MA, MIT Press, 1991), pp 91–116.

'The Way to Language' [1959], DF Krell (trans), in DF Krell (ed), *Basic Writings: Martin Heidegger*, 2nd edn (London, Routledge, 1993), pp 397–426.

'The Principle of Identity', in *Identity and Difference*, J. Stambaugh (trans) (New York and London, Harper and Row, 1969), pp 23–41.

'The End of Philosophy and the Task of Thinking' [1964], J Stambaugh (trans), in DF Krell (ed), *Basic Writings: Martin Heidegger* (London, Routledge, 1993), pp 431–49.

'Time and Being', in *On Time and Being*, J Stambaugh (trans) (New York, Harper and Row, 1976), pp 1–54.

WORKS BY LEVINAS (IN CHRONOLOGICAL ORDER)

Existence and Existents [1947], A Lingis (trans) (Pittsburgh, Duquesne University Press, 2001).

Time and the Other [1947], RA Cohen (trans) (Pittsburgh, Duquesne University Press, 1987).

'Is Ontology Fundamental?' [1951], in *Entre Nous: On Thinking-of-the-Other*, MB Smith and B Harshav (trans) (London, The Athlone Press, 1998), pp 1–11.

'Freedom and Command' [1953], in *Collected Philosophical Papers*, A. Lingis (trans), (Pittsburgh, Duquesne University Press, 1998), pp 15–23.

'The I and the Totality' [1954], in *Entre Nous: On Thinking-of-the-Other*, MB Smith and B Harshav (trans) (London, The Athlone Press, 1998), pp 13–38.

'Language and Proximity' [1967], in *Collected Philosophical Papers*, A Lingis (trans), Pittsburgh, Duquesne University Press, 1998, pp 109–26.

Totality and Infinity: An Essay on Exteriority, A. Lingis (trans) (Pittsburgh, Duquesne University Press, 1969).

'*La Pensée de l'être et la queston de l'autre*', (1978) 369 *Critique*, pp 187–97.

Otherwise than Being or Beyond Essence, A Lingis (trans) (Pittsburgh, Duquesne University Press, 1981).

'Useless Suffering' [1982], in *Entre Nous: On Thinking-of-the-Other*, MB Smith and B Harshav (trans) (London, The Athlone Press, 1998), pp 91-101.

'Peace and Proximity' [1984] in A Peperzak, S Critchley and R. Bernasconi (eds), *Basic Philosophical Writings* (Bloomington, Indiana University Press, 1996), pp 161–9.

'Philosophy, Justice, and Love' [1984] in *Entre Nous: On Thinking-of-the-Other*, MB Smith and B Harshav (trans) (London, The Athlone Press, 1998), pp 103–21.

Ethics and Infinity: Conversations with Philippe Nemo, RA Cohen (trans) (Pittsburgh, Duquesne University Press, 1985).

'Emmanuel Levinas and Richard Kearney: A Dialogue with Emmanuel Levinas', in RA Cohen (ed), *Face to Face with Levinas* (Albany, State University of New York Press, 1986), pp 13–33.

'Wholly Otherwise' [1973], S Critchley (trans) in R Bernasconi and S Critchley (eds), *Re-Reading Levinas* (Bloomington, Indiana University Press, 1991), pp 3–10.

'Diachrony and Representation' [1982], in *Entre Nous: On Thinking-of-the-Other*, MB Smith and B Harshav (trans) (London, The Athlone Press, 1998), pp 159–77.

'The Philosophical Determination of the Idea of Culture' [1983] in *Entre Nous: On Thinking-of-the-Other*, MB Smith and B Harshav (trans) (London, The Athlone Press, 1998), pp 179–87.

'Uniqueness' [1986], in *Entre Nous: On Thinking-of-the-Other*, MB Smith and B Harshav (trans) (London, The Athlone Press, 1998), pp 189–96.

'The Other, Utopia, and Justice' [1988], in *Entre Nous: On Thinking-of-the-Other*, MB Smith and B Harshav (trans) (London, The Athlone Press, 1998), pp 223–33.

OTHER WORKS

ATZMON, A (2006) 'Homeland as a gift of Destiny: Homecoming, between Dwelling and Settling', *Lo Straniero* (*Journal of The International Movement for Interdisciplinary Study of Estrangement*) 4320-22.

AWERKAMP D (1977) *Emmanuel Levinas: Ethics and Politics* (New York, Revisionist Press).

BAUMAN, Z (1993) *Postmodern Ethics* (Oxford, Blackwell).

BENABIB, S (1986) *Critique, Norm and Utopia: A Study of the Foundation of Critical Theory* (New York, Columbia University Press).

BEN-DOR, O (2000) *Constitutional Limits and the Public Sphere: A Critical Reconstruction of Bentham's Constitutionalism* (Oxford, Hart Publishing).

de BEISTEGUI, M (1998) *Heidegger and the Political: Dystopias* (London, Routledge).

BENSO, S (2000) *The Face of Things: A Different Side of Ethics* (Albany, State University of New York Press).

BERLIN, I (1969) 'Two Concepts of Liberty', *Four Essays on Liberty* (London, Oxford University Press), pp 118-72 (and 'Introduction', pp xxxviii–xl and xliii–l).

BERNASCONI, R (1991) 'Skepticism in the Face of Philosophy', in R Bernasconi and S Critchley (eds), *Re-Reading Levinas* (Indianapolis, Indiana University Press), pp 149–61.

— (1993) 'Deconstruction and the Possibility of Ethics: Reiterating the "Letter on Humanism"', in R. Bernasconi (ed), *Heidegger in Question*, (New Jersey, Humanity Press, 1993), pp 211–24.

— 'The Third Party: Levinas on the Intersection between the Ethical and the Political' 30 (1) *Journal of the British Society for Phenomenology* 76–87.

BORGMAN, A (2000) 'Heidegger and Ethics: Beyond the Call of Duty', in M Wrathall and J Faulconer (eds), *Appropriating Heidegger* (Cambridge, Cambridge University Press), pp 68–82.

CARR, D (1999) *The Paradox of Subjectivity: The Self in the Transcendental Tradition* (Oxford, Oxford University Press).

CELAN, P (1995) *Poems of Paul Celan*, M Hamburger (trans) (London, Anvil Press Poetry).

CORNELL, D (1988) 'Post Structuralism, The Ethical Relation, and the Law' 9 (6) *Cardozo Law Review* 1587–628.

CLARK, T (2002) *Martin Heidegger* (Manchester, Manchester University Press, 2002).

CRITCHLEY, S (1991) '"Bois": Derrida's Final Word on Levinas', in R Bernasconi and S Critchley (eds), *Re-Reading Levinas* (Indianapolis, Indiana University Press), pp 162–89.

— (1992) *The Ethics of Deconstruction: Derrida and Levinas* (Oxford, Blackwell).

DERRIDA, J (1973) 'Speech and Phenomena', in *Speech and Phenomena and other essays on Husserl's Theory of Signs*, DB Alison (trans) (Evanston, Northwestern University Press), pp 1–104.

— (1978) 'Violence and Metaphysics: An Essay on the Thought of Emmanuel Levinas', in *Writing and Difference* (London, Routledge), pp 97–192.

— (1989) *Of Spirit: Heidegger and the Question*, G Bennington and R Bowlby (trans) (Chicago, The University of Chicago Press).
— (1991) 'At This Very Moment in This Work Here I Am', in R Bernasconi and S Critchley (eds), *Re-Reading Levinas* (Bloomington, Indiana University Press), pp 11–48.
— (1992) 'Force of Law: The Mystical Foundation of Authority', in D Cornell, M Rosenfeld and DG Carlson (eds), *Deconstruction and the Possibility of Justice* (New York and London, Routledge), pp 3–67.
DICKSON, J (2001) *Evaluation and Legal Theory* (Oxford, Hart Publishing).
DOUZINAS, C (2000) *The End of Human Rights* (Oxford, Hart Publishing).
DREYFUS HL (1991) *Being-in-the-world: A Commentary on Heidegger's Being and Time, Division 1*, (Cambridge, MA, MIT Press).
DWORKIN, R (1986) *Law's Empire* (Cambridge, MA, Fontana Press).
d'ENTREVES, AP (1970) *Natural Law*, 2nd edn (London, Hutchinson).
FARÍAS, V (1989) *Heidegger and Nazism*, J Margolis and T Rockmore (eds), P Burrell and D di Bernardi (French materials trans), GR Ricci (German materials trans), (Philadelphia, Temple University Press).
FERRY, L (and A Renault) (1990) *Heidegger and Modernity*, F Philip (trans) (Chicago and London, The University of Chicago Press).
FÔTI, VM (1992) *Heidegger and the Poets: Poiesis, Sophia, Techne* (New Jersey, Humanities Press).
FOUCAULT, M (1977) *Discipline and Punish: The Birth of the Prison*, A Sheridan (trans) (London, Penguin).
FRANK, J (1966) *Courts on Trial: Myth and Reality in American Justice* (New York, Atheneum Press).
FULLER, L (1965) *The Morality of Law* (New Haven and London, Yale University Press).
FYNSK, C (1986) *Heidegger: Thought and Historicity* (Ithaca, Cornell University Press).
GALIPEAU, CJ (1994) *Isaiah Berlin's Liberalism* (Oxford, Clarendon Press).
GEAREY, A (2001) *Law and Aesthetics* (Oxford, Hart Publishing).
GRAY, J (1995) *Isaiah Berlin* (London, HarperCollins).
GREEF, de J (1986) 'Skepticism and Reason', in RA Cohen (ed), *Face to Face with Levinas* (Albany, State University of New York Press), pp 159–79.
GRIEDER, A (1992) 'What did Heidegger Mean by "Essence"?', reprinted in C Macann (ed), *Martin Heidegger: Critical Assessments* (London, Routledge), pp 183–212.
HALPIN, A (2001) *Reasoning with Law* (Oxford, Hart Publishing).
HAMMOND, M, HOWARTH, J and KEAT, R (1991) *Understanding Phenomenology* (Oxford, Blackwell).

HAMPSHIRE, S (1977) *Two Theories of Morality* (Oxford, Oxford University Press).

HART, HLA (1961) *The Concept of Law* (Oxford, Clarendon Press).

HERZOG, A (2002) 'Is Liberalism "All we need"? Levinas's Politics of Surplus', 30(2) *Political Theory* 204–27.

HODGE, J (1995) *Heidegger and Ethics* (London, Routledge).

— (1994) 'Heidegger, early and later: the vanishing of the Subject', 25(3) *Journal of British Society for Phenomenology* 288–301.

INWOOD, M (1999) *A Heidegger Dictionary* (London, Blackwell).

KEYES, CD (1972) 'An Evaluation of Levinas' Critique of Heidegger', 2 *Research in Phenomenology* 121–42.

KRELL, DF (1992) *Daimon Life: Heidegger and Life Philosophy* (Bloomington, Indiana University Press).

LACOUE-LABARTH, P (1990) *Heidegger, Art and Politics* (London, Blackwell).

LANG, B (1996) *Heidegger's Silence* (London, Athlone Press).

LISSKA, A (1996) *Aquinas's Theory of Natural Law: An Analytic Reconstruction* (Oxford, Clarendon Press).

LLEWELYN, J (1995) *Emmanuel Levinas: The Genealogy of Ethics* (London, Routledge).

— (2002) 'Levinas and Language', in S Critchley and R Bernasconi (eds), *The Cambridge Companion to Levinas* (Cambridge, Cambridge University Press), pp 119–38.

LUHMANN, N (1985) *A Sociological Theory of Law* (London, Routledge).

MAINE, H (1931) *Ancient Law: Its Connection with The Early History of Society and Its Relation to Modern Ideas* (Oxford, Oxford University Press).

MANDERSON, D. (2005) 'Proximity: The Law of Ethics and the Ethics of Law', 28(3) *University of New South Wales Law Journal* 696–719.

— (2006) *Proximity, Levinas, and the Soul of Law: Tort, Ethics and the Soul* (Montréal, McGill-Queen's University Press).

MANNING RJS (1993) *Interpreting Otherwise than Heidegger: Emmanuel Levinas's Ethics as First Philosophy* (Pittsburgh, Duquesne University Press).

— (1996) 'The Cries of Others and Heidegger's Ear: Remarks on the Agriculture Remark', in A Milchman and A Rosenberg (eds), *Martin Heidegger and the Holocaust* (New Jersey, Humanity Press), pp 19–38.

MAY, R (1996) *Heidegger's Hidden Sources: East Asian Influence on His Work* (London Routledge).

MILCHMAN, A and ROSENBERG, A (eds) (1996) *Martin Heidegger and the Holocaust* (New Jersey, Humanities Press).

MINKKINEN, P (1999) *Thinking Without Desire: A First Philosophy of Law* (Oxford, Hart Publishing).

MOORE, GE (1993) *Principia Ethica* [1903] (Cambridge, Cambridge University Press).

NANCY J-L (1991), *The Inoperative Community* (Minneapolis, University of Minnesota Press).

OLAFSON, FA (1998) *Heidegger and the Ground of Ethics: A Study of Mitsein* (Cambridge, Cambridge University Press).

OTT, H (1993) *Martin Heidegger: A Political Life*, A. Blunden (trans) (London, Basic Books (HarperCollins)).

PEPERZAK, A (1983) 'Phenomenology-Ontology-Metaphysics: Levinas' Perspective on Husserl and Heidegger', 16 *Man and World* 113–27.

— (1993) *To the Other: An Introduction to the Philosophy of Emmanuel Levinas* (Indiana, Purdue University Press).

— (1997) *Beyond: The Philosophy of Emmanuel Levinas* (Evanston, Northwestern University Press).

PEROTTI, JL (1974) *Heidegger and the Divine: The Thinker, The Poet and God* (Ohio, Ohio University Press).

RAWLS, J (1993), *Political Liberalism* (New York, Columbia University Press).

RAZ, J (1986) *The Morality of Freedom* (Oxford, Clarendon Press).

REED, CW (1986) 'Levinas' Question', in RA Cohen (ed), *Face to Face with Levinas*, (Albany, State University of New York Press), pp 73–82.

RICHARDSON, WJ (1963) *Heidegger: Through Phenomenology to Thought* (The Hague, Martinus Nijhoff).

ROCKMORE, T (1992) *On Heidegger's Nazism and Philosophy* (London, Harvester Wheatsheaf Press).

ROCKMORE, T and MARGOLIS, J (eds) (1992) *The Heidegger Case: on Philosophy and Politics* (Philadelphia, Temple University Press).

ROTH, M (1996) *The Poetics of Resistance: Heidegger's Line* (Illinois, Northwestern University Press).

SAFRANSKI, R (1999) *Martin Heidegger: Between Good and Evil*, E Osers (trans) (Cambridge, MA, Harvard University Press).

SALLIS, J (1993) *Reading Heidegger: Commemorations* (Bloomington, Indiana University Press).

SCHEURMAN, R (1987) *Heidegger: From Principles to Anarchy*, C Marie-Gros (trans) (Bloomington, Indiana University Press).

SIMMONS, WP (1999) 'The Third: Levinas' theoretical move from an-archical ethics to the realm of justice and politics', 25(6) *Philosophy and Social Criticism* 83–104.

SMITH, SG (1986) 'Reason as One for Another', in RA Cohen (ed), *Face to Face with Levinas* (Albany, State University of New York Press), pp 53–71.

SPINOZA, B (1985) 'Ethics', in *The Collected Works of Spinoza*, E Curley (ed and trans) (Princeton, Princeton University Press), pp 408–617.

— (1985) 'Treatise on the Emendation of the Intellect', in *The Collected*

Works of Spinoza, E Curley (ed and trans) (Princeton, Princeton University Press), pp 3–45.

STAMBAUGH, J (1991) *Thoughts on Heidegger* (Washington, DC, Centre for Advanced Research in Phenomenology and University Press of America).

STEINER, G (1992) *Heidegger* (London, Fontana).

TONTTI, J (2004) *Right and Prejudice: Prolegomena to a Hermeneutical Philosophy of Law* (Aldershot, Ashgate).

WOLIN, R (1989) *The Politics of Being* (New York, Columbia University Press).

— (1993) *The Heidegger Controversy: A Critical Reader* (New York, Columbia University Press/Cambridge, MA, MIT Press).

— (2001) *Heidegger's Children: Hannah Arendt, Karl Löwith, Hans Jonas, Herbert Marcuse* (Princeton and Oxford, Princeton University Press).

WYSCHOGROD, E (1993) 'From Ethics to Language: The Imperative of the Other', 97 *Semiotica* 163–76.

YOUNG, IM (1990) *Justice and the Politics of Difference* (Princeton, Princeton University Press).

YOUNG, J (1997) *Heidegger, Philosophy, Nazism* (Cambridge, Cambridge University Press).

ZIAREK, K (1994) *Inflected Language: Toward A Hermeneutics of Nearness: Heidegger, Levinas, Stevens, Celan* (Albany, State University of New York Press).

ZIMMERMAN, ME (1986), *Eclipse of the Self: The Development of Heidegger's Concept of Authenticity* (Athens, Ohio University Press).

— (1991) *Heidegger, Modernity, Technology* (Bloomington, Indiana University Press).